PRAXIS MAKES PERFECT

Distributed Ethnography in Theory and Practice

The Cynefin Company

Edited by Emma Jones & Rhiannon Davies
Contributions by:

Anna Panagiotou
Dave Camlin
Dave Harris
Dave Snowden
Eleanor Snowden
Jackie Counts
John Van Breda
Jules Yim
Kai Mausch
Keil Eggers
Ken McHugh
Linda Doyle
Marianne Yim
Nina Abrahams
Paul Ader
Rebecca Gillam
Rosanna Hunt
Wendy Elford

SenseMaker®: Praxis makes Perfect
Distributed Ethnography in Theory and Practice

Edition 1 |

Building on Weaving Sense-Making into the Fabric of Our World, the second book by The Cynefin Company takes a deep dive into SenseMaker®, shifting the focus from the broader Cynefin Framework to an in-depth exploration of its theory, application and real-world impact.

SenseMaker® is a pioneering research and decision-making tool that blends data with human insight. It captures observations from diverse organisations and communities to provide a real-time understanding of dynamics.

The Cynefin Company is a pioneering research and strategy business that helps industry, government, and society navigate complexity to create positive change. SenseMaker® is part of a suite of theory-informed tools and methods tested with clients for 20 years.

The Cynefin Company collaborates with our global network of innovators, changemakers and leaders who have contributed their expertise to this book, sharing firsthand insights into working with SenseMaker®. Their generous contributions to this book offer firsthand insights into the power of SenseMaker® in action.

By The Cynefin Company

Editors & Curators: Emma Jones & Rhiannon Davies

Production Editor: Gustav Rischmüller

Published by Cognitive Edge Ltd

THE CYNEFIN CO
MAKING SENSE OF COMPLEXITY

Plas Eirias Business Centre, Abergele Road, Colwyn Bay, Conwy LL29 8BF
www.thecynefin.co

ISBN 978-1-7353799-4-4

This collection represents the hard work, contributions and reflections of our valued global community of SenseMaker practitioners, users and developers, each of whom has left their fingerprints on this tool in many ways, both great and small.

Without the care, curation and dedication of our editors, Emma Jones and Rhiannon Davies, as well as Donna Glanvill and Natalie Smith, this book would not exist and we give then our gratitude and appreciation. Our thanks and appreciation also to the broader Cynefin Co team and particularly our software team, who turn the visions into reality.

We dedicate this book to all the users and partners who have shaped, stretched and contributed to the growth of SenseMaker since 2003.

TABLE OF CONTENTS

EDITOR'S INTRODUCTION

JOURNEY OF THEORY AND PRACTICE - HOW IT CAME TO BE WHAT IT IS NOW

Building on *Weaving Sense-Making into the Fabric of Our World*, the second book by The Cynefin Company takes a deep dive into SenseMaker, shifting the focus from the broader Cynefin Framework to an in-depth exploration of its theory, application and real-world impact.

SenseMaker is a pioneering research and decision-making tool that blends data with human insight. It captures observations from diverse organisations and communities to provide a real-time understanding of dynamics.

The Cynefin Company is a pioneering research and strategy business that helps industry, government, and society navigate complexity to create positive change. SenseMaker is part of a suite of theory-informed tools and methods tested with clients for 20 years.

The Cynefin Company collaborates with our global network of innovators, changemakers and leaders who have contributed their expertise to this book, sharing firsthand insights into working with SenseMaker. Their generous contributions to this book offer firsthand insights into the power of SenseMaker in action.

This book is split into three sections: SenseMaker theory, SenseMaker application, and SenseMaker cases. This work is very dear to our hearts, so we hope you enjoy diving into the world of SenseMaker. Hopefully, this book is one of many to come as we venture further into complexity.

We have decided to honour each contributing author's own voice and narrative, following the same philosophy we take with SenseMaker. Therefore, you will notice a mixture of Anglicized or Americanized English due to the international authors. However, all references will be APA formatted for consistency.

From all the team at The Cynefin Co, we thank all the authors for sharing their experiences, insights, and knowledge. We hope this book inspires new applications of SenseMaker and new projects.

Emma Jones
Bristol, UK

ABOUT SENSEMAKER®

WHAT IS SENSEMAKER®

SenseMaker is a pioneering way to gather qualitative and quantitative data about people's observations and experiences. What's remarkable is that the people taking part analyse their own responses. So, we get authentic analyses of real experiences, rather than external interpretations of them. Results are demonstrated using simple graphics that make it easy to spot patterns and themes. This perspective can reveal things we might, ordinarily, have missed. Or perhaps not even looked for. The result? We can make sense of what's really happening and determine the next steps or actions.

SenseMaker is really powerful in the following areas:

- Strategy & Innovation
- Leadership
- Organisational Development and Design
- Decision Support
- Knowledge Management
- Monitoring, Evaluation and Impact
- Wellbeing and Staff Retention
- Narrative Research Methods
- Complex Facilitation

WHO ARE THE CYNEFIN CO

SenseMaker is a product of The Cynefin Company, a pioneering research and strategy business. We help leaders in society, government and industry make sense of a complex world, so that they can act and create positive change. SenseMaker is one of a whole body of tools, methods and approaches, that have been theory-informed and tried tested with our clients over 20 years.

Besides SenseMaker, The Cynefin Co does:

- Commercial engagements
- Software applications
- Methods and research
- R&D
- Consulting
- Training
- Hexi kits
- And much more…

This plays out in various spaces and industries:

- Design and Agile
- Education
- Environment & Sustainability
- Government & Citizens
- Healthcare and Pharmacology
- International Development & Human Rights
- Religious and Spiritual Institutions
- Defence and Military
- Safety & Risk
- Organisational Design and Development

GLOSSARY OF TERMS

A

Abduction

Abduction is a type of logical connection. Other types of logical connection create connections from a general rule to a specific example, or from specific examples to a general rule. Abduction, instead, creates connections that are plausible based on what we know about a situation. It cannot give us certain knowledge, but it can give us new knowledge, especially in situations where there is a lot we don't know. We use abductive reasoning because we have no choice. Going from a general rule to a specific example is safe, but limits us to only what we already know for sure. Going from specific examples to general rules is risky, and we need to repeat it many, many times to be even close to sure. When we need to know something new, and we don't have a long history of collecting observations that we repeat again and again and again, or if we are in an area where this will never happen, our only option is to make connections between things that are likely, but not certain. This is abduction.

Abductive Research

Abductive Research is where one considers a series of apparently unrelated events on the suspicion they may be connected. It involves creating a pre-hypothesis, hypothesis generation leading to other methods and objectivity based on numbers & distributed cognition.

"The Problem of" Abduction

Abduction is making a probable conclusion from what you know. The problem of abduction refers to how to determine which abductive hunches are coherent to the facts.

Anthropocene

A widely used term for the geological epoch that would follow the Holocene, dating from when humans began to have significant environmental impact on Earth up to the present day. It is not an officially recognised defined geologic period having been rejected by the International Commission on Stratigraphy in 2024 and by the International Union of Geological Sciences. The term was created and proposed to acknowledge the impact of human activity on Earth's oceans, geology, geomorphology, landscape, limnology, hydrology, ecosystems and climate, in particular biodiversity loss and climate change. Proposed start dates for the Anthropocene vary widely from the beginning of the Neolithic Revolution (12,000–15,000 years ago) to the 1960s. The biologist Eugene F. Stoermer is credited with creating the term anthropocene informally in the 1980s and Paul J. Crutzen re-invented and popularized the term.

Antenarrative

Antenarrative theory is concerned with exploring the gaps and excesses not considered in traditional narratology (study of stories). An antenarrative is a gambler's bet that a pre-story (i.e. something that does not have a plot) can disrupt and change narrative practice and become a fully fledged narrative itself. Antenarratives derive their organising force through emergent storytelling where plots are either impossible or contested and/or speculative. Antenarrative stories do not have a beginning, middle or an end. Antenarrative stories are many voiced, open to multiple interpretations and operate as pre-narrations that can disperse into and penetrate wider social contexts.

Assemblage Theory

Assemblage theory, especially associated with Gilles Deleuze and Felix Guattari, explores the way things come together in diverse, dynamic, and changing combinations. This allows us to understand phenomena that have many causes and effects, or that are always changing by giving us theoretical tools to break things down into different parts, without making the mistake of ignoring the relationships between the parts.

B

Bounded Applicability

The concept that different and contradictory things work in different bounded spaces.

C

Cluster Points

Cluster points are attractors, or the patterns which form from the interactions of many connected entities." In complexity, attractors are the results, not the cause.

Coherence

One of the features of Emergence. Coherence or correlation meaning integrated wholes that maintain themselves over some period of time.

Complexity

A complex system is a system composed of interconnected parts that as a whole exhibit one or more properties (behavior among the possible properties) not obvious from the properties of the individual parts. A system's complexity may be of one of two forms: disorganized complexity and organized complexity. In essence, disorganized complexity is a matter of a very large number of parts, and organized complexity is a matter of the subject system (quite possibly with only a limited number of parts) exhibiting emergent properties.

Complex Adaptive System

Deeply entangled, highly uncertain spaces that do not operate on simple causality models.

Context

Traditionally, in sociolinguistics, social contexts were defined in terms of objective social variables, such as those of class, gender or race. More recently, social contexts tend to be defined in terms of the social identity being construed and displayed in text and talk by language users.

Culture and Complexity

Culture is the patterning of our interactions with our environment and it is not susceptible to design principles appropriate to the creation of bridges or software programs. In organizations, we want the most efficient systems, on in which each component of the organization is optimized in order that the system as a whole can be optimized. However, human systems are not ordered systems and the path to their optimization is to allow sub-optimal behaviour in parts.

(The) Cynefin Framework

The Cynefin framework has five domains. The first four domains are:

- **Clear**, in which the relationship between cause and effect is obvious to all, the approach is to Sense – Categorise – Respond and we can apply best practice.

- **Complicated**, in which the relationship between cause and effect requires analysis or some other form of investigation and/or the application of expert knowledge, the approach is to Sense – Analyze – Respond and we can apply good practice.

- **Complex**, in which the relationship between cause and effect can only be perceived in retrospect, but not in advance, the approach is to Probe – Sense – Respond and we can sense emergent practice.

- **Chaotic**, in which there is no relationship between cause and effect at systems level, the approach is to Act – Sense – Respond and we can discover novel practice.

- The fifth domain is **Aporetic**, which is the state of not knowing what type of causality exists, in which state people will revert to their own comfort zone in making a decision. In full use, the Cynefin framework has sub-domains, and the boundary between simple and chaotic is seen as a catastrophic one: complacency leads to failure. In conclusion, chaos is always transitionary and dynamics are a key aspect.

See Chapter 3 or 5 for a graphic of the Cynefin framework.

D

Disintermediation

Removal of intermediaries in a supply chain (in this context, an information supply chain from the ground to senior management)

Distributed Cognition

Move away from attempting failsafe design towards setting up safe-fail experimentation'. Because you cannot analyse the problem space fully in advance, and you have to be prepared to adjust systems interactively until you find that they work. Distributed cognition is a branch of cognitive science that proposes that human knowledge and cognition are not confined to the individual. Instead, it is distributed by placing memories, facts, or knowledge on the objects, individuals, and tools in our environment. Distributed cognition is a useful approach for (re)designing social aspects of cognition by putting emphasis on the individual and his/her environment. Distributed cognition views a system as a set of representations, and models the interchange of information between these representations. These representations can be either in the mental space of the participants or external representations available in the environment.

Distributed Ethnography

Concern about time-saving shortcuts being taken led to the creation of distributed ethnography using SenseMaker. The key point is that SenseMaker allows people in the subject communities to act as ethnographers to those communities. SenseMaker acts as a quantitative interpretative framework for ethnographers. When people interpret their own material they add layers of meaning, they don't just interpret the material. High abstraction signifiers that can't be gamed and for which there is no "right" answer, and use of metaphor/abstract language empower respondents and ethnographers to use their descriptive capability which has always been the goal of ethnography. This is called distributed ethnography because the sense-making is done by participants and community members who collect the stories rather than an outsider who emerges themselves in the community.

E

Edges

A term borrowed from yogic practices to mean one's growth zone. Edges are used to mean the place where one is working at maximum ability without risking damage.

Emergence

In a complex system, you don't have linear relationships between cause and effect which means you have inherent uncertainty. The only thing we know with any certainty is that any intervention will have both intended and unintended consequences i.e. emergent patterns and experiences. That means we need lots of small interventions where we can afford multiple small failures. Emergence will happen anyway, but it can also be given a helping hand. Sensor networks are put in place to detect the early signs of emergence so that you can push more energy in the direction of patterns that appear to be beneficial and shift it away from others. In some cases you may know in advance what you would like, but you know you can't achieve it until the eco-system indicates it can support it.

Epistemic Justice

Epistemic justice refers to justice in processing and sharing knowledge. It relates to the sharing of knowledge or knowing something and is not about abusing this or "epistemic power". The concept of Epistemic justice is relevant in the field of Naturalising Sense-making because in order to navigate complexity in general, but particularly in a crisis, detecting and monitoring weak signals is essential, in both situational assessment and scenario planning.

Exaptation/ Exaptive

Also known as radical repurposing, exaptation is the taking of an idea, concept, tool, method, framework, etc., intended to address one thing, and using it to address a different thing, often in another domain.

Ethnographer

Ethnographers systematically study and describe a society from the perspective of that society. To do that would normally require deep immersion in that culture not only as observer but as participant with continuous examination of your own influence and biases. There are multiple approaches to ethnography including feminist ethnography, confessional ethnography and critical ethnography which seeks to liberate marginalised groups. Concern about time-saving shortcuts being taken led to the creation of distributed ethnography using SenseMaker. See glossary entry on distributed ethnography above for further details.

L

Liberation Theology

Liberation theology is a Christian socialist theological approach with roots in 1960s Latin American Catholicism emphasizing the liberation of oppressed people. It emphasises socio-economic analyses of the conditions of the poor in order to advocate for political liberation for oppressed peoples. It is also concerned with other forms of inequality.

M

MassSense

MassSense is an assessment tool that rapidly gathers perspectives on situations, events, and/or decisions. It can be used to inform decision-making and scenario planning. MassSense is an application of SenseMaker and it is based on the same core principles. The core difference is that something is selected and presented to a network for interpretation and response whereas SenseMaker collects micro-narratives.

Messy Coherence

A key aspect of living with complexity; The point is that you can the structure which was there, depending on the degree of disintegration it may or may not still fulfil its original purpose. It's sticky, you can be woven into its pattern or you can fly through the gaps. It has beauty even as it disintegrates, it cannot be rebuilt but has to be replaced with something that will in its turn fade. The metaphor carries with it the concepts of transience, but is also of purpose and for a time solidity. Depending on the context they can last for days, months or even years before they have to be rebuilt. It's not the best metaphor for an organisation, but it is a good metaphor for thinking about degrees of coherence.

N

Narrative Theory

Narrative theorists study what is distinctive about narrative (how it is different from other kinds of discourse, such as poems, lists, conflicts, descriptive accounts, mathematical analyses, and so on), and how narratives can be collective and powerful. A key consideration is how narrative helps people make sense of the world, while also studying how people make sense of stories. Narrative health refers to a healthy diversity of narratives within a community.

R

Rhizome/ Rhizomatic

A rhizome is a concept in post-structuralism describing a nonlinear network. The term is used by French theorists Deleuze and Guattari to describe networks that establish connections with no apparent order or coherency. A rhizome is purely a network of multiplicities that are not hierarchical and do not work with dualist/ binary categories and choices. By contrast rhizomatic networks have properties similar to lattices. As a mode of knowledge and model for society, Deleuze and Guattari use the terms "rhizome" and "rhizomatic" (from Ancient Greek ῥίζωμα, rhízōma, "mass of roots") to describe a network that connects any point to any other point. Rhizomatic understandings of history and culture do not apply a clean narrative, but rather presents history and culture as a map or wide array of attractions and influences with no specific origin or genesis.

Ritual Dissent

Ritual Dissent is a workshop method designed to test and enhance proposals, stories, ideas or anything else by subjecting them to ritualised dissent (challenge) or assent (positive alternatives). One of the points of ritual dissent is not to be reasonable. To make it more of a game, less personal. In all cases it is a forced listening technique, not a dialogue or discourse. The basic approach involves a spokesperson presenting a series of ideas to a group who receives them in silence. The spokesperson then dons a mask, or turns their chair, so that their back is to the audience and listens in silence while the group either attack (dissent) or provide alternative proposals (assent). The ritual of donning the mask or turning the chair de-personalizes the process and the group setting (others will be subject to the same process) means that the attack or alternative is not personal, but supportive. Listening in silence without eye contact increases listening quality. Overall plans that emerge from the process are more resilient than consensus-based techniques, while conflict increases the amount of information taken into account at the same time as it is being constrained by the ritual character of the technique.

With thanks to Anna Panagiotou and Natalie Smith for their contributions.

USING SENSEMAKER®

DIFFERENT WAYS TO USE SENSEMAKER

Different SenseMaker entry points are depending on the situation:

- QuickSense applications represent the culmination of over two decades of client collaboration, offering ready-to-use SenseMaker applications that are academically rigorous and battle-tested, designed for commonly found client requirements.

- QuickStart training for building a bespoke SenseMaker engagement while you learn, either on your own or with a team, with background theory and design supporting materials.

- FastLaunches are for when you are short on time and want one of our SenseMaker experts to co-create a bespoke engagement with you to get insights for your team fast.

- Narrative BaseCamps focus on the background of SenseMaker. The mastery of sense-making through storytelling and working with narrative data, from practical applications in organisations to ethnographic practices in community-based work.

The workbench's visual layout allows you to see both the exact location of individual stories and a heatmap showing the spread of stories.

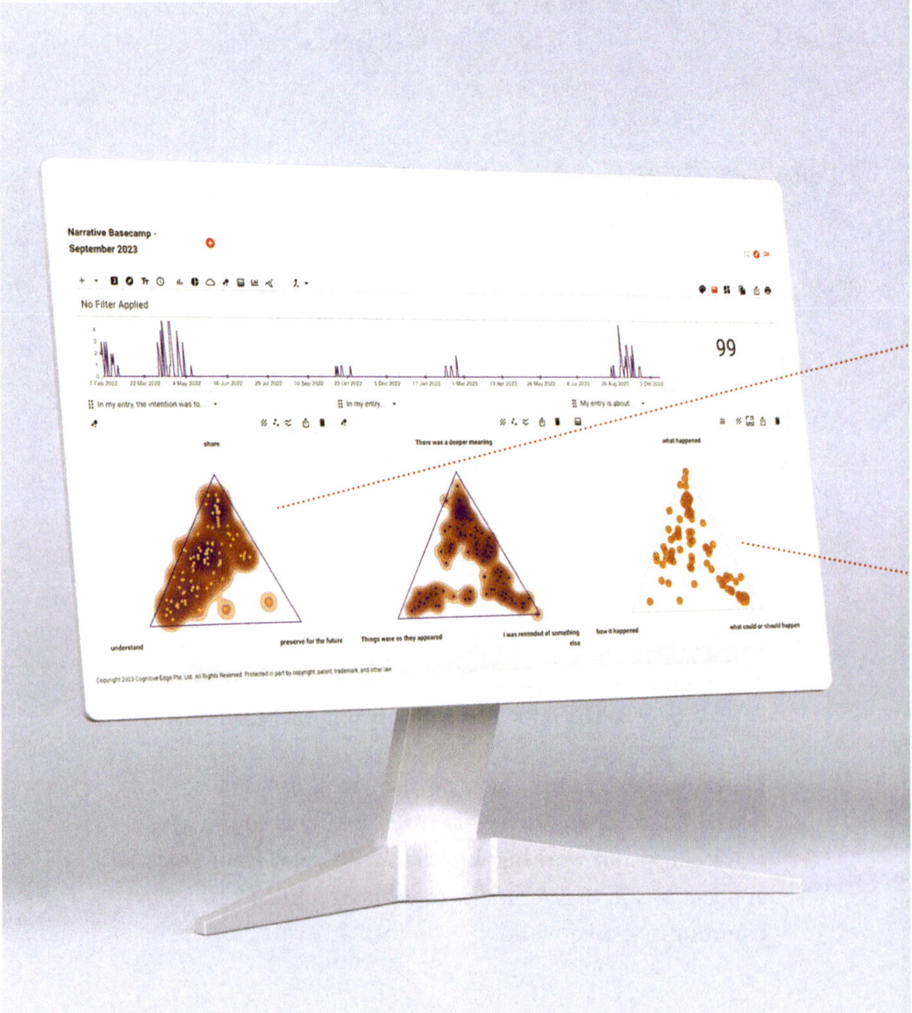

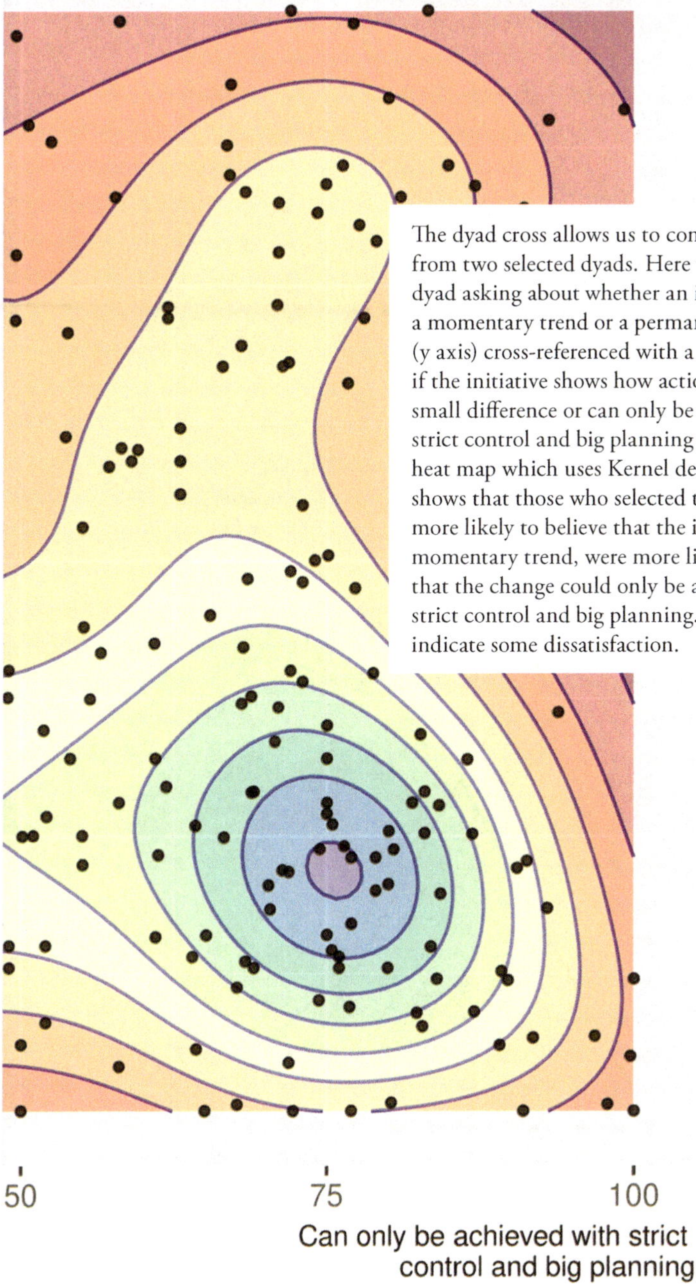

The dyad cross allows us to compare responses from two selected dyads. Here we have a dyad asking about whether an initiative was a momentary trend or a permanent change (y axis) cross-referenced with a dyad asking if the initiative shows how actions make a small difference or can only be achieved with strict control and big planning (x axis). This heat map which uses Kernel density formula shows that those who selected that they were more likely to believe that the initiative was a momentary trend, were more likely to believe that the change could only be achieved with strict control and big planning. This would indicate some dissatisfaction.

N=310

n=280

N/A=3

filter n=288

%age=100%

filter N/A=3

skipped=19

MEAN AND CONFIDENCE INTERVALS

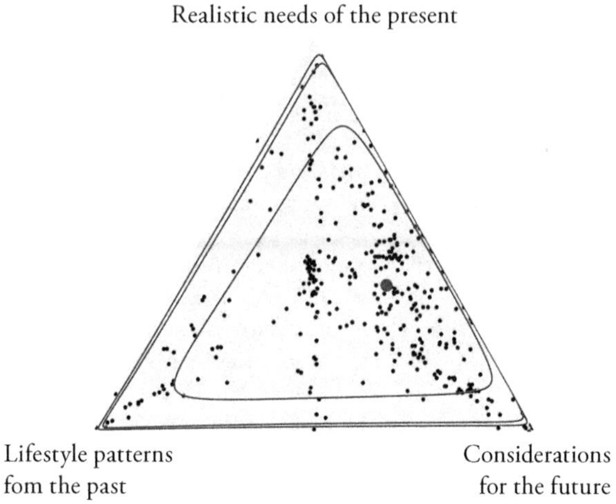

PERCENTAGE OVERLAYS ON PATTERNS

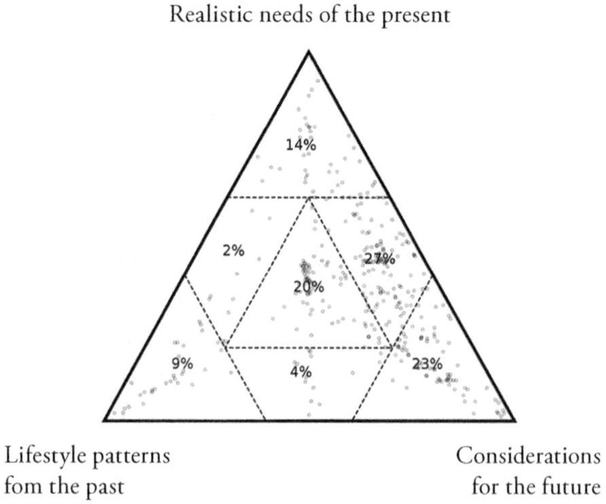

LANDSCAPE CONTOURS

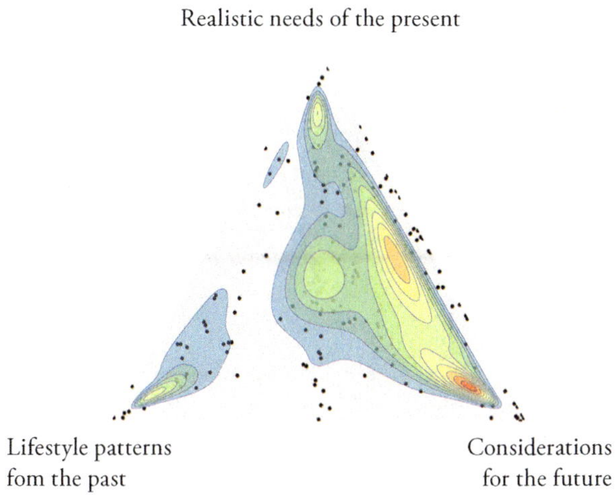

USING "STONES" QUESTIONS TO COMPARE FACTORS AND META-PERSPECTIVES

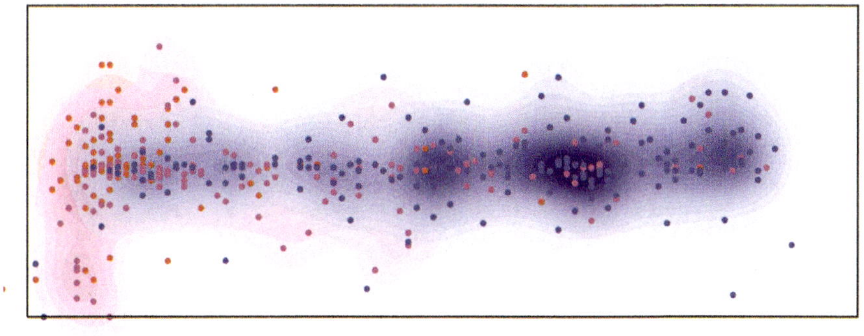

THE SENSEMAKER® ORIGIN STORY

PROFESSOR SNOWDEN INTERVIEWED BY LINDA DOYLE AND NINA ABRAHAMS

ABOUT THE AUTHORS

While at The Cynefin Co, **Linda Doyle** supported communities and citizens to have their voices heard by decision-makers. With a penchant for deliberative democracy, she has put her learnings from her Research Masters in social psychology and decision-making to use as a freelance facilitator. Linda is currently working on a project that aims to bring the firm grounding in complexity science she gained with The Cynefin Co. to the realm of social movements and changing society.

Nina Abrahams completed an internship with The Cynefin Co in mid-2021 and afterwards, officially joined the team as a researcher and SenseMaker® practitioner and part of the Centre's Health Programme. Nina holds an MPH in health systems and a cotutelle PhD in Exercise, Nutrition, and Health Sciences between the University of Cape Town and the University of Bristol. Her PhD explores the role of social network analysis in scaling up and sustaining community-based health programmes in low-resource settings. Her research interests include health promotion, non-communicable diseases, urban health, and disability studies.

Discretionary Note: This chapter contains a detailed discussion of suicide. If needed, you can skip this chapter and rejoin us later.

As the newest members of The Cynefin Co team, we've been using SenseMaker to help clients understand more about the context they're working in and what their next steps could be. We've been enthralled by how many fascinating concepts are interwoven into the fabric of SenseMaker, from epistemic justice to the psychology of how people game evaluation.

We were curious about how SenseMaker evolved and what that journey looked like. So we decided to drink our own champagne, as they say! And use the idea of intergenerational pairing to interview Dave about the origins of SenseMaker. Here is the interview (edited for clarity and conciseness).

So, Dave, what were the questions that were being asked that inspired SenseMaker and its related concepts and approaches?

The origins of virtually everything in both SenseMaker and the methods go back to knowledge management. I moved out of a strategy role in Data Sciences, following the IBM takeover of the company I was working in at the time, to a creative role in method development and what IBM deemed 'thought leadership'. At that time, knowledge management was taking off, and my background was designing and building decision support systems. So, from my point of view, knowledge management was just a new variant—I didn't really see any difference. One of the strengths of knowledge management is that it didn't originate from a single source; it was more a coming together of several different strands of thinking, like complexity theory today. Early on in that period, I created three basic rules of knowledge management, which later expanded into seven (Snowden, 2008). One was an adaptation of Michael Polanyi's: "We always know more than we can say," to which I added "and we will always say more than we can write down". Namely, when I take something from my head to my mouth to my hands, I lose content; I lose context. That made it easy to talk about things that require time and experience to know at a more or less instinctive or intuitive level, the stories and anecdotes I use to explain and communicate and the more limited range of material that can be codified into structured text and taxonomies.

Later, Max Boisot and I produced a matrix which plots abstraction against codification, which helps situate these narratives. Low abstraction and low codification are well illustrated by the London taxi driver who takes two years (or more) to acquire 'the knowledge'. Their hippocampus is enlarged through the training period. At the other extreme, we have a map which is high abstraction and high codification and thus, the knowledge embodied in it can be diffused widely at a low cost compared with training taxi drivers. I often asked, "Is this a job for a taxi driver or a map?" which is an example of using a metaphor in narrative work. Both have utility; the map may appear attractive, but the assumptions made to get to high abstraction often mean that critical context is omitted. I found that to my detriment when I ended up in a dangerous area of New York late one night simply by following a map—it didn't say, 'here be muggers and other strange beasts'. A taxi driver would never make that mistake. What Max and I then realised that narrative is a halfway house between the two; it is abstract enough to defuse (and entertainment and curiosity are a part of that) but also ambiguous enough to adapt quickly to different contexts. The parables of the bible continue to speak to a modern situation because they are narratives, they carry essential ambiguity and can adapt easily to different contexts. This is exemplified by the oral tradition.

So narrative work was increasingly important and it started to be a critical proxy to capture 'meaning' in organisations and in workshops. And again, as we scaled into the very early versions of SenseMaker.

How did you go about doing this?

Well, we had most of the basics worked out. In addition to anecdote circles and story construction, I pioneered a participative ethnography approach in the context of organisations. I didn't go into organisations to study people as an expert ethnographer but instead went in as an apprentice to do the job for a week in a junior role. No use of notebooks or recording devices without explicit permission. This meant I heard authentic stories and gained insights into how the organisations worked. The first time we did this at scale, we got students to act as assistants to New Zealand lorry drivers, and they recorded stories from lorry drivers in the act of helping them to do their jobs. The students came from the local culture, and the act of working together built trust and a willingness to share stories. This process formed an early development of the idea of epistemic justice (which John van Breda will talk more about in his chapter), which became a core design feature of SenseMaker. We knew we needed to do ethnography because it gets closest to people's lives. But we also needed to do it at scale, and the students represented an early example. However, we were still transcribing and interpreting the material as experts, with only the occasional token presence of some of our subjects.

Then we had a bright idea one day: "Why don't we make people their own ethnographers?" So that was when the first software was designed by myself, Sharon Darwent, Fiona Incledon, Nick Pow, Nick Hines and Cynthia Kurtz, who we met as a part of the IBM story group. Because Cynthia and I wrote the third of the significant Cynefin paper, people tend to forget the contributions of the UK team, so I'm correcting that here. At that time, we asked people fairly conventional questions, they'd write it out, and we'd put things on Likert scales. The Likert scales were generally descriptive, for example, about emotional intensity and power. It is also important to remember that my work on narrative and complexity had brought us to the attention of the intelligence community in Washington, and by this time, we were starting work on using both in counter-terrorism. So that also drove the need to understand micro-narratives at scale and, consequently, the quantitative as well as qualitative data.

So, what kind of projects did you apply this new method to?

One of the first big projects we used SenseMaker software for was the one on an agrochemical product that Australian farmers were using to commit suicide. There was a political movement to ban the agrochemical to reduce suicides. If you swallow it, there's nothing we can do about it. It's a slow, painful, agonising death. Now, there are plenty of reasons to ban such chemicals, but what we found is that banning would have little or no effect on suicide. We captured stories across Australia, allowing people to interpret their own stories and that was when we discovered the power of self-interpretive stories to find something that nobody expected: people were deliberately choosing this product, knowing how horrible it would be. There was a whole subclass of suicidal people who actually wanted to pass away painfully and have people witness it.

That must have been quite a shocking finding?

I can't say I enjoyed reading the material or working with it. But we made people aware that they needed to do something about depression, not simply ban the chemical. If we did that, then people would use neurotoxins or something worse. The finding was quite valuable as it allowed us to support the people who really needed it. It also was a lesson in removing experts from the primary interpretation of data – the narrative method broke the assumed causality that the experts had, which opened up space for new interpretations to emerge.

What other projects were happening at this time?

As previously mentioned, we had a DARPA contract on counterterrorism. The thing we were looking at there was the sort of conditions in which the populations decide they will tolerate terrorism, because when they do that, all of a sudden things flip. We knew we needed to gather street narratives and stories in the field. We couldn't rely on how people respond to interviewers or focus groups because that's a performance; they know what's expected of them. What we want are the street stories.

From that, we also got one of the first big projects with the UK Foreign Office in Pakistan. That was the first time we got children in schools to gather stories from adults. So, at that time, we were using tablets to record the stories with manual indexing. That pulled in 50,000 stories. We found some fascinating stuff. We'd given people a set of images to choose from and then tell the story about it. We put in a Vogue cover with an emaciated white model on it. And everybody expected "filthy white women" responses, but most of them were "Oh, she's beautiful. Maybe if I'm beautiful, I can leave my village." And then we had an imperial picture of three white Sahibs on an elephant, which everybody said was violently racist and imperialist. Except for the kids who responded with, "Three men have gone for a ride on an elephant, and I'd like to go on one too". So it showed that there were many different perspectives. The narratives also showed that attitudes to women hadn't changed, when more conventional hypothesis research said it had. We also showed that a significant level of radicalisation was from people from the UK moving to Pakistan and not the other way around. Again, we got novel and unexpected insights by allowing people to interpret their own experiences at scale.

So when did the idea of signifiers like triads come in?

After I left IBM 18 years ago, we had to go back to basics. And that was when I brought in triads. The principle being that balancing three positive concepts will force people to think differently. I didn't know about the cognitive neuroscience of it then. But I knew that we didn't want people to know what the right answer was; that became a massive differentiator. It wasn't popular with some of my colleagues, so I snuck it in on the back of a series of projects for the Welsh Audit Office, one of our earliest customers. And it's still in active use – that was when we first started working with Chris Bolton.

So what other projects did you do after leaving IBM?

The first major project after IBM was working for Paul Khan, who became a good friend. The project was engaging school children with museums in Liverpool. In the International Slavery Museum, the children went around the museum, told stories about their visit, and interpreted their own stories. That gave us insights into the children's experience and the nature of the exhibits, which nobody had ever gotten before. Other early pioneering projects were with the health sector in Northern Ireland and with Milica Begovic and her team in UNDP – these are clients who we continue to work with to this day. I still remember the bereavement stories in Northern Ireland to this day, along with the Roma 2017 project and other projects with the UNDP: we were getting to people and insights that no one else had ever done.

It was also at this time that Irene Guijt, then an independent consultant and now a research director at Oxfam, started to use SenseMaker. That resulted in much wider development sector work, and as a result of a quick side trip to Baltimore on one Washington trip, Catholic Relief Services picked it up. In fact, this year Oxfam and Catholic Relief Services teamed up to produce a book on over ten years of SenseMaker experience.

We also did pioneering projects for the Singapore Government on connections and disconnections between the civil service and future studies projects with young people. The post-DARPA contract with the Singapore Government to design and build the complex aspects of the risk assessment and horizon scanning system was vital here as it provided the funding to build the first real version of the software and set up the company in 2005. Peter Ho, who I first knew as Permanent Secretary of the Ministry of Defence and later as head of the Civil Service, was a key and insightful champion along with Patrick Nathan and Lock Pin. Angelina Seah, Jules Yim, Zhen Goh and Steve Bealing formed the core consultancy team in Singapore at that time and their various projects, along with those that Michael Cheveldave led in Canada, were important. I remember working with Michael on one crazy project for which we were paid but never executed because someone very senior decided they might learn something they didn't want to know.

I've almost certainly missed some key projects here – but all of the projects and some very tolerant clients effectively allowed us to build SenseMaker as a product without investment or debt.

So the concepts that are now integral to SenseMaker were emerging from each of the different projects you were using it for?

That's correct. To give another example, we did a project in a country where there is low literacy. This was before smartphones became prevalent. So, we would record a story from people on a very basic mobile device. Then, we put a canvas on the ground with drawings on it and stones with symbols, which are easier to explain. People then placed stones on the canvas and we took pictures of the canvas. That became what is now stones (a type of signifier). So that was how it developed. Gradually, we got more and more of the theory. We understood more and more why we'd done things. For example, self-interpretation: people should interpret their own story so that we know what they mean. We can now justify that concept in academic terms, but at the time, it just felt right, it felt authentic and morally correct – my Liberation Theology background was more influential than I thought! Then we started to shift from surveys to MassSense and then from MassSense to GENBA, which is about continuous capture. SenseMaker seems to fit quite well with indigenous research methods, something we've been exploring in our Complexity Yarn discussions with indigenous thinkers.

What moments surprised you or are highlighted for you along the journey?

Well, I've already mentioned risk assessment and horizon scanning. Back in 2006, Peter Stanbridge and I, over two days, produced a complete bid for $ 1.3 million that funded SenseMaker. It meant we could build proper teams; Steve came on board to manage the company and Ken McHugh also got involved at that time. IBM in Singapore, especially Jimmy Kwang and Janet Ong (Country General Manager), were supportive in getting us to that point.

I don't think there's been a narrative project where we didn't discover something that wasn't self-evident with the benefit of hindsight, but nobody realised it upfront. I think that shows the power of the approach. The other thing that keeps surprising me, but I haven't done the research to make it anything other than anecdotal, is that the lessons learned seem similar independently of sample size. I think it's probably because human narrative structures are fractal: Our individual stories reflect society's larger trends and tropes and vice versa.

I hadn't realised the impact until Cat Swetel jumped on stage at a Wardley Mapping conference to tell Simon Wardley and I that we were the first people to take epistemic justice seriously. And she's a heavyweight feminist in the Agile movement! I hadn't really thought about it until she said that. That was quite powerful. We're making a huge difference for people and we don't always recognise it. That was also when Cat, Simon and I formed the Epistemic Justice League, but that is another story!

We're almost unique as a software company; nobody's ever invested in us. We funded everything from client projects; we've never even had a loan. So it's always been on the back of client development that we've done things. That's been good and bad. It means that we've had to sell it. If we couldn't sell it, we couldn't develop it, and that's actually quite a good test. From the beginning, we made sure to get the architecture right so that we could do things we hadn't anticipated.

Are there any specific theories that are vital to the development of SenseMaker?

I think assemblage theory has been vital. I think my recognition that an assemblage was a strange attractor and a trope was important. This brought together three bodies of knowledge: assemblage theory, the mathematics of attractors, and narrative studies. I haven't properly proved this, but nobody's disputed it and it's been endorsed by several deep experts. To me, it's self-evident, but that's the dyslexic in me speaking. This is linked to the realisation that what we were doing with SenseMaker was to produce a way of mapping assemblages, in the sense of DeLanda's (2013) interpretation of Deleuze. We were into neo-materialism before the neo-materialists, and we were building tools to represent that. New materialism or neo-materialism argues for a real and active material reality that nonetheless is evolving and historical, and doesn't have unchanging essential identities. For example, the whole concept of scaffolding from Andy Clarke (1998) helped us to design SenseMaker upfront as a form of extended consciousness. Used with peer-to-peer flow of knowledge ideas, SenseMaker actually acts as a scaffolding for collective consciousness and for distributed memory. So I think that whole assembly/strange attractor principle was a key one on that.

Did other disciplines influence or inspire SenseMaker?

There was a whole bunch of anthropology. So Mary Douglas' *Purity and Danger* was fundamental. Before she died, I spent a bit of time with her, which had a profound influence on SenseMaker design, particularly in the concept of removing power from the interpretation framework. I also followed the controversy between anthropologists Margaret Mead and Derek Freeman which is summarised in *The Trashing of Margaret Mead* (2009). To briefly explain Freeman stated that Mead had been "hoaxed" by Samoans whose stories about their sex lives he alleged she took at face value. There's since been arguments both for and against Mead's research. I followed that controversy and I thought we've got to avoid this.

We can't afford to have a limited number of actors gathering and reviewing that sort of material.

From the wider narrative side, Yiannis Gabriel, Barbara Czarniawska and David Boje come to mind. Boje's antenarrative concept (see Boje (2011) for a summary) was and remains important. I, and the IBM story group were heavily engaged in narrative theory back then, and I started to develop the idea of the anti-story. These are not the same thing as Boje's antenarrative. Anti-stories undermine specific narratives by pointing out the inherent hypocrisy in the original story. For example, a politician who advocates for social distancing but attends a party. Anti-stories pointing to hypocrisy tend to spread faster than the original message, and early detection is key, as is not triggering them by the wrong messaging. Ritual Dissent emerged as a method to help there with its focus on finding gaps and contradictions to ultimately strengthen an intervention or proposal. A lot of people said we can't study people's narratives as independent observers. The answer is you can't. So, some of them went down the full immersion route. They wanted to become part of the environment, to tell a story and recognise their bias. And I was thinking, "Well, there's got to be a better way!" That was when we thought if we make people their own ethnographers, and we give them highly abstract signifiers structures, then we can actually study it, but we'll study it through the metadata, and not through anything else.

There's a body of narrative theory there, which is key. Max Boisot was absolutely fundamental. He and Alicia Juarrero were the main mentors on this. Boisot coined the phrase micro-narratives (James, 2011). And he also said that with this tool, you can solve the problem of abduction, and that drove MassSense.

What are your hopes for the future of SenseMaker?

For SenseMaker to be in every member of staff's hands, doing multiple functions and creating a human sensor network. That's the big ambition I've got. So, moving away from the individual as the unit into the Cynefin concept: different threads or pathways in people's timelines and entangling them. Imagine you could entangle a British Prime Minister's timeline with timelines of people suffering from austerity measures so that they can see the real impact of their decisions. That way, SenseMaker can be used to build empathy.

SenseMaker has been born out of a fair amount of struggle. There's still a tendency in the social sciences to gather stories, interpret them and write a report, which I've been trying to move away from for 15 years now. But there are still a lot of constraints that hinder progress. So moving into continuous scanning and continuous profiling, that's where we need to go. I'd really like to create tools by which people without a university background can use SenseMaker to generate an analytical evidence-based approach to make a case, for example, for funding, so they're not reliant on external mediation from an educated, liberal middle-class person or other gatekeepers.

References

1. Boje, D. M. (2011) *Storytelling and the Future of Organizations An Antenarrative Handbook.* Routledge Taylor & Francis Group.
2. Clark, A. (1998). *Being there: Putting brain, body, and world together again.* MIT Press.
3. DeLanda, M. (2013). *Intensive science and virtual philosophy.* Bloomsbury Publishing.
4. James, R. (2011). Out of the box–A life with rubbish information. *Business information review*, 28(3), 179-183.
5. Snowden, D. (2008). *Rendering knowledge.* The Cynefin Co. https://thecynefin.co/rendering-knowledge/ (retrieved October 7, 2022).
6. Shankman, P. (2009) *The Trashing of Margaret Mead.* University of Wisconscin Press.

BUILDING SENSEMAKER®: THE TWO BIRDS PRINCIPLE

KEN MCHUGH

ABOUT THE AUTHOR

Ken McHugh has carved a niche for himself in the world of technology, underpinned by a deep-seated passion for harnessing data to unlock actionable knowledge. With over two decades of experience, Ken's prowess lies not just in tech but in connecting technological solutions with human processes, ensuring optimal outcomes across the board. His leadership journey is both varied and impactful: from co-founding YouCommentate, providing a mobile streaming technology that emphasised scalable, high-transaction volume solutions, to initiating ICatalyst Pte. Ltd. to deliver tailored tech solutions for industry leaders, as well as pivotal roles at Tigerspike and Cognitive Edge Pte. Ltd.

A graduate of the University of Oxford and Sheridan College, Ken's foundational expertise in software engineering and computer programming amplifies his holistic approach to problem-solving. Beyond his corporate roles, he has been associated with the e-Challenges European ICT Conference and co-holds a US Patent centred on Computer-aided methods and systems for pattern-based cognition from fragmented material. Ken is driven by using technology to enhance human potential, championing innovation and data-driven decisions for organisational success.

Software has a bad rap. Beyond those directly involved, it is seen to be a closed, constrained system with strict rules, borders, and requirements. The problem with this belief is that it leads to thinking that creating requirements and specification documents is all that is needed. A bit of time-boxing, a few iterations, track velocity, and don't forget boards, the more the merrier. Simple, easy, anyone can do it, now off you go and sprint.

Almost a decade ago, I started to give a talk about why IT projects fail, creatively titled "Why IT Projects Fail". Since then, I would have frequently delivered the talk to business leaders, IT executives, development managers, and development teams from various industries, backgrounds and perspectives. Over the years, as that talk evolved, I realised that really, the only content changing was the percentage of failure, and it wasn't changing by much. I don't need to quote the numbers here, as they are easily Googleable. Also, enough people reading this will have dealt with or experienced a failed project to get a general feeling that the numbers are much higher than they should be and regardless of the methodology, the numbers are not coming down. Importantly, the reasons for failure are basically the same.

Each year new software development methodologies are presented as the silver bullet, new ribbons are awarded and new belts achieved, mostly with little overall impact.

It was through the evolution of these talks that I started to believe that there are two fundamental omissions from most methodologies being used.

Before discussing those omissions, I will set up:

CORE CONCEPTS

Following are some of the base terminology and beliefs that are essential in understanding the omissions.

Time

As individuals' time is our most precious resource. Given enough time, anything can be achieved. However, once a minute ticks past, that minute is gone forever. Staying up a minute later in the evening doesn't recover it. Time can't be saved, restored, and most certainly cannot be refunded when misused and misspent. This implies that it is our prerogative to waste our own time, but our responsibility to ensure we do not waste the time of others. Moreso, to create efficiencies, we have the responsibility to enable others to leverage time. Looking for opportunities to share information and make connections that help to complete multiple related tasks in the time it would normally take to complete a single task. Two birds with one stone.

Business

A business has a primary goal, mission, vision, or intent. This is the answer to the question of why does the business exist. Usually, it comes in the form of a brief but powerful future-focused statement that is easy to consume and easily understood. It includes what the business does and why it does it.

- Tesla - To accelerate the world's transition to sustainable energy.
- Microsoft (at its founding) - A computer on every desk and in every home.
- Invision - Question Assumptions. Think Deeply. Iterate as a Lifestyle. Details, Details. Design is Everywhere. Integrity.

Naturally, a business also has secondary goals. These secondary goals help to achieve the primary goal either directly or by enabling individuals to spend their time focused on the primary goal instead of getting lost in the secondaries. Some examples of secondary goals may be::

- Be a healthier, happier workplace
- Hire top talent to accelerate the mission
- Be an agile thinking organisation

These secondary goals are enablers. Their intent is to optimise process and flow to achieve the primary goals. Oftentimes, entire teams and departments are built around the secondary goals – such is their importance. Secondary goals should be defined with regards to the impact on the primary. Ensuring that success in a secondary goal contributes measurably to success in the primary.

Two birds with one stone.

SOFTWARE

Software, for the most part, sits in the complex domain and in some cases it is downright chaotic, insufferable, and messy.

Software should essentially be designed to give time back to its users so that they can focus on what actually matters.

Software, whether purchased or created, should have the explicit goal of either helping to drive and enable the mission, or help to remove the inefficiencies in the organisation to allow teams to focus on the mission. The impact of software should be measurable: if there is no intended or perceived impact, then there is no point.

Software is also a (very) fine balance between giving the users what they think they need and giving them what they actually need. As Henry Ford may have said, "If I had asked people what they wanted, they would have said faster horses." When done correctly, software becomes a window into the very heart of a problem space, allowing a business to navigate not just the current needs but to map out, plan, and prepare for the future and all of its potential.

Software is a tool for creating efficiencies as well as a conduit to the users. Treating software as such enables you to understand if you are doing well on the path you have chosen and if that was the right path to go down.

Two birds with one stone.

FAILURE

Failure, put quite simply, is not achieving the desired impact within the designated time frame. Failure is something we do not value as much as we should.

Failure is often hidden away, pushed aside, and rarely analysed. In reality, failure is a tool for learning, experimenting, and pushing boundaries. Success on a first attempt may be lucky, success after a number of failures allows a deeper understanding of the problem and confirmation that the problem has been understood.

Creating opportunities for failure is an often-unused aspect of software development. Identifying safe-to-fail experiments, each with its own metrics for what is considered a success and what indicates that the experiment has failed. Metrics can be as simple as showing that something is possible, or may be more detailed, such as achieving a detailed impact within a specific timeframe. Increasing user retention by 17% in 3 months. Reducing the time it takes to complete a task by 10%. Enhancing the perceived value of data flowing through the software validated by positive feedback from 10% of users within 60 days. These are all examples of impact based metrics that allow you to identify if an experiment was a success or not. Planning features and updates as safe-to-fail experiments helps to ensure that every failure is a success.

Two birds with one stone.

THE OMISSIONS

Here are the omissions as I see them. I call them omissions because they are not often explicitly called out in most methodologies. If they are even mentioned, they are not assigned the importance with which I generally view them.

Don't deliver software, deliver impact

Software shouldn't exist just because it can be done. Software is also not the only answer. When embarking on the creation or implementation of a software-focused initiative, start with answering the most basic question: What is the impact we are looking to create within our problem space? Without an understanding of what we are trying to change, it becomes easy to get caught up in the methodology and forget about the true purpose and the true impact. It is easy to create software for the sake of creating software.

I often see "ivory tower" solutions within software, where the code is absolutely perfect and the delivery mechanisms are automated. Every variable is perfectly named, the Agile Manifesto followed religiously, and every member of the team is a black-belt, purple-ribbon-certified enthusiast of one methodology or another. Most often, when talking with the teams that developed these solutions, they are immensely proud (and rightly) of what they have achieved. They can link every decision point back to a clause, phrase, core tenet, of <insert methodology here>. Usually, however, what they are unable to do as developers is directly link those decisions back to how they made a difference to the impact created by the software. The developers are closer to the methodology than they are to the users or process they are trying to impact. Any decisions made are coincidentally linked to the end users and impact created. They have been given their specification and built that out perfectly. It is the equivalent of building the perfect house but not putting in a front door because it wasn't explicitly in the requirements.

A frequent term used within my teams is value. The teams commonly raise questions such as:

- How does that decision provide value?
- How does that change the value proposition?
- Will that decision remove value from the system?"

These questions are used to challenge on another at decision points. Impact and value are synonyms in this case. This type of questioning keeps the intent top of mind for the developers and the value of such thinking becomes apparent when you see the shift in the team to presenting concepts and ideas in terms of value and impact. When the features, ideas, and suggestions are coming from the team in a way that improves the lives for those using the software, not for those building the software. In particular, the conversation moves away from concepts such as story points, velocity, and burndown and instead shifts to a strange loop of testing assumptions against user needs and expectations, amplifying positive impact, and dampening negative impact. Repeat in the new state of being.

Ensuring each and every member of the team understands the value (read impact) of what they are building ensures that each and every member of the team is capable of and, importantly, responsible for making the "right" decisions, or at least aligning the decisions made along the way with the intended impact. Note the use of quotes around the word right. In each iteration of the strange loop, knowledge and understanding are expanded. This implies that what was correct for today may not be correct in the future when the environment has evolved.

The benefits to approaching a problem in this way are many. The entire team not only understands what they are actually trying to achieve, they also engage with each other and challenge each other based on the intended impact. The entire team is capable of making decisions quickly, creating tight loops and fast feedback cycles. This allows the team to assess themselves and their decisions in order to understand their impact, learning fast what works and what doesn't. This automatically reinforces positive behaviours and dampens detrimental ones, and helps to show each member of the team their own value and impact, helping to keep them motivated. This in itself has the result of reducing the management overhead on a team and creating a team that is more engaged with the end users and process they are impacting.

There is a wonderful story that I always tell at this point, which even after years of telling, still gives me goosebumps when I say it out loud. I am paraphrasing it here. It is not my story, but I will say that I have been telling it a lot longer than Mark Zuckerberg.

John F. Kennedy was touring the NASA facility and had just turned down a long hallway. As he walked down the hallway, surrounded by his secret service agents, he saw a janitor at the other end. The janitor was walking up the hallway with his mops and buckets on his cart and stopped midway to slop out soapy water on the floor. As JFK got closer to the janitor, he casually asked the janitor what he was doing. The janitor responded: "Well, Mr President, I'm sending people to the moon."

Apparently, it gives me goosebumps when I write it too.

That understanding on the part of the janitor of their own role and contribution to the larger goals is something that many organisations, as well as the people within them, often ignore. People wonder why they are not happy in their workplace and, at the same time, are unable to draw a direct link from their own role to how they are contributing to the mission of the organisation. When you think back through your life and focus on the times that were difficult, the times you got through were when you understood the reasons for your struggle. You understood what would be better by just getting through to the other side. The times when you gave up were those times where there was no reason, or at least you were unaware of the reason, for the struggle. There is no better feeling than to look back and say "Wow, look what we achieved".

The only way to create these opportunities within a team is to ensure that at all times the team is fully aware of why they are doing what they are doing. Ensure that a team has bought in by giving them the space to make the decisions (and mistakes) they need to, so that they recognise their individual contribution to the whole and how, by being part of the team, they make things a little better for everybody. Every single member of the team, from the most senior to the most junior, should feel that they are part of the initiative and they are making a difference. Every member of the team brings a unique perspective and insights to the initiative that should be harnessed rather than nudged away. Most importantly, through this way of working, every member of the team is thinking about the chain of work. How work passes from one hand to the next, with each hand adding value to the output. With that awareness, individuals have an understanding of how their outputs will be used by the next person in the chain. They are able to cater to the needs of the next person in line and make the job easier for the next person. If everyone in the chain is operating the same way, then the output at each stage in the work chain is more than a single individual could produce. Each individual becomes aware of the value provided by others on the team as their own outputs are more than they could contribute without those before them. This also creates a mechanism within which the team is able to monitor the contributions of other members of the team without the need for management oversight.

Software is grown not built

Planning a software initiative, whether it is a full scale solution or a small feature, should always begin with understanding the problem space. In what domain does the problem currently sit? Is it a simple problem? Complex? Do we even know, or do we need to probe the problem space to get a better understanding? What does tackling the problem do overall? Does it shift the problem to a different domain, or does it start to move it closer to a domain boundary where it is easier to manage and deal with?

Answering these questions informs the initial approach. For example, a simple problem most likely has an off-the-shelf solution. There is no need to build if something already exists that is fit for purpose, provides exactly the value you need, and costs less than is generated by solving the problem yourself.

Understanding where the problem sits allows you to understand the impact that needs to be created to shift the problem to another domain. It guides the conversation of the initial intent of the software and helps to create that initial focus. It allows you to map the intended impacts and understand the interplay between different types of impact. Essentially, it enables you to derive a hierarchy of desired impacts, where knowing that the required impacts lower in the hierarchy will help to drive impact in the higher levels of the hierarchy as well. Prioritising the lower levels in order to achieve the greatest impact up the hierarchy. Rather than "tackling low-hanging fruit" this takes into account the entire environment and creates a focus on the smaller tasks which will have the largest impact in the environment.

Of course measuring actual impact is important and often forgotten. I have seen many teams creating a plan that is defined based on impact, and celebrating on completing the plan rather than celebrating when the impacts have been achieved. The job is not done until the results have come in. Don't count your chickens as they say. Having very clear definitions around the success and failure of the desired impacts is essential. Meaning visibility of the heuristics or metrics that will help to measure actual impact in relation to desired impact. This also becomes important by creating a framework for teams and individuals within which to make decisions they will need to make during the execution of the plan and to assess the effectiveness of decisions and changes made. It is counterproductive to plan an impact that cannot be measured either qualitatively or quantitatively as this lack of measurement prevents a fast feedback cycle and results in guesses rather than decisions.

Then comes education. Rather than jumping right in and making decisions, which is a fatal mistake at this point in the process, step back and educate the team. The entire team, not just key stakeholders, or key decision makers, or senior management, etc. If you want every individual on the team to be effective, then every individual on the team must have a clear understanding of the intended impact. If you have never had a conversation with your team that started with "This is the impact we are trying to achieve, and this is the difference we expect it to make", then you cannot challenge the team's decisions with regards to impact. You also cannot hold a team accountable or responsible for achieving an impact that they not only knew nothing about, but never got the opportunity to understand and map their own roles and strengths to its achievement.

This disseminates the framework around which teams and individuals can then create their own impact hierarchies to make decisions that feed back into the whole. Teams are then able to autonomously define many smaller initiatives from which to learn and explore the problem space. They can understand the impacts they intend to create and if needed, particularly with complex problems, carve out smaller pieces of the problem for resolution.

From here on let evolution take place. With the constraints and boundaries set, the trellis around which the teams are then able to grow and create their own safe-fail experiments is defined. Teams can focus on amplifying successful initiatives, refining initiatives that did not quite have the desired impact, and importantly analysing and exploring initiatives that either detracted from the desired impact or failed to achieve success within the defined bounds. Safe-fail experiments are executed in quick succession and trimmed as required based on the results. Failed experiments may be discarded or spliced with other experiments, while successful experiments are amplified, fed, and nurtured on their path to growth. Many experiments may be started with the intent to kill off the majority as they start to interfere with the growth or diminish the intent. This prevents over-defining the end goals as most likely what was needed today will be different from what is required tomorrow, which may be poles apart from what will be needed in six months as the environment shifts. Make decisions when they need to be made. Ensure those decisions are informed by the potential impact. Do not get attached to decisions made today as they may hinder the growth needed for tomorrow.

This also has the advantage of allowing teams to introduce new features and initiatives quickly in a basic form through the Chaotic domain and then respond to need, use, and results to drive that feature into the Complex space. A value proposition has been identified and tested, and can now be used to continue the feature's journey through to the Complicated and on to the Obvious, while the teams that are closest to the initiative define the path taken.

The benefit of teams that form in this manner, around impact rather than KPIs, is that they tend to work together using their strengths. They understand the reasoning behind the decisions of other departments and groups. They have everything they need to make decisions that not only help themselves but also positively impact each other, both inside the team and outside. They recognise the common goals across the business and are able to identify the value that others provide as it directly enables their own work.
It creates a self aware gestalt. A team that recognises the value contribution of each of its parts and that without the whole it would be unable to achieve as much as it did. It generates trust within the teams and organisation. It creates a common language to talk about success across teams internal and external. It allows the team to think about and assess itself as a team. It creates a true team, not just groups of people who happen to be working on the same things.

TWO BIRDS

Whenever approaching new software, or even when taking over existing software, it is with this approach that I have seen the most success from the teams I have worked with, and not just software teams. Through introducing this approach I have seen individuals go from lost and despondent to being motivated and engaged.

The approach itself tries to take the path of most impact, ensuring that for every action there are multiple benefits extracted. Hence the name "Two Birds".

The meta-cognitive gestalt described above is really the crux of the two birds principle. A colony of ants is often described as a gestalt due to how they communicate and what they achieve. One of the most amazing functions of an ant is to change their role based on the needs of the colony. In highly functional teams individuals will temporarily change their role in order to take advantage of strengths and weaknesses of themselves and other members of the team as the situation changes.

A highly functional team always knows what tasks can be taken on today that will have an impact well beyond the initial investment of time or resources. Or, in terms of the impact hierarchy: Which impact can be achieved that will also help to achieve a small percentage of other related impacts simultaneously? How do I pay forward my efforts to make the next person in line more effective?

This implies that every individual has all of the information they require to make the right decisions at the right time. Every team member can answer the question "how do we hit two birds with one stone?".

After applying an initiative, every individual can see the impact of that action fast enough to be able to correct, kill, or amplify the initiative. The success and failure of the initiative is not emotional but rather an expected part of the process. A failure is an opportunity to gain focused learning.

Implications here are that the constraints and bounds are clear and understood by all individuals. Current positioning of the system is known and evidence of change is tracked and communicated to all. An individual is able to define the expected impact of a change to the system. Make the change. Monitor and see the impact in an appropriate timeframe for the change. Understand the success or failure of that change and then optimise, refine, or remove that change. After every day, week, month, every team and individual must be able to answer the question "Did we hit two birds?".

Did you hit two birds today?

References

1. Hofstadter, Douglas (2007). *I Am A Strange Loop*. ISBN 978-0-465-03078-1.

CYNEFIN AND COMPLEXITY: REFLECTIONS ON ETHICS AND AESTHETICS

JULES YIM AND MARIANNE YIM

ABOUT THE AUTHORS

Jules Yim is a multi-hyphenate dabbler with interests ranging from computational linguistics to the role of the rising Global South in the next century. She relishes her occasional forays from corporate life into the weird, maddening, but ultimately rewarding world of writing for an audience. Jules has worked with the Cynefin Company since 2009, when she was brought on board to participate in the delivery of government projects in Singapore. Since then, she has worked with public, private and third sector clients in Asia-Pacific, Europe, the Americas, and Africa.

Marianne Yim is most familiar with the Western canons of knowledge, but her heart truly lies in Chinese history and the role of modern China in global affairs, so much so that it has led her to currently work for a Chinese tech start-up. When she is not busy bingeing on current affairs, she can be found nursing a fledgling interest in technology, frantically chasing down writerly inspiration for her novel-in-progress, and burying her face in her collection of Chinese classics. Marianne first learned of Cognitive Edge as a teenager, through her elder sister Jules who would come home from work and occasionally share insights into the field of knowledge management. She has grown into young adulthood hearing much of Cynefin's framework and its relation to other knowledge frameworks in the field: writing this short essay was as natural a step as she could imagine.

The authors labour under the belief that a saturated industry of tech commentary does not preclude yet another critique, given that technological inventions seem to outpace due ethical consideration. This is relevant particularly in the realm of ethics and aesthetics, seen through the lens of anthro-complexity.

In this chapter we discuss the role that axiology – under which ethics and aesthetics sit – plays in the discussion of value. We discuss how axiology can and does influence the way decisions are made and the way technological products are developed and designed. The unintended consequences that are part and parcel of agents interacting in a Complex Adaptive System (CAS) are also highlighted as a cautionary tale, with the Cynefin framework and SenseMaker offered as a potential framework for thinking about such issues and taking action.

In laying the foundation for this chapter, we first revisit anthro-complexity. It is distinct from computational complexity, which as a point of comparison uses ants as agents in simulation models of complex systems. In anthro-complexity, the networks of interaction between humans (agents) are thought to comprise complex systems in and of themselves. One can say that to study anthro-complexity is to study those networks of agent interactions, and SenseMaker was architected to capture large amounts of those interactions in the form of micro-narrative, because "narratives express the cultural, institutional, and social embeddedness of our human decision-making", and "decisions reflect the value systems of the people concerned; they are shaped in the interaction networks of these people" (Van der Leeuw, 2019: 515).

AXIOLOGY : VALUE JUDGEMENTS AND WHY THEY MATTER

Axiology is a relatively recent coinage but its roots stretch back all the way to classical antiquity; humans have been discussing the value of things for a very long time. Where the question of value arises, axiology is there as the philosophical glue. Whenever we discuss ethics and aesthetics, we implicitly understand that we are talking about value: why do we hold one judgement over the other, and what is our justification for doing so? It is a largely two-pronged discipline with aesthetics and ethics underpinning it, and it is this focus that the authors would like to urge readers to turn to.

Aesthetics matter as it is the basis for the creator bias in technological products that increasingly fill our digital spaces, such as photo editing software, image sharing services, social media algorithms that rely heavily on visual media (Instagram's Explore feature), selfie-improving apps (the ubiquitous Meitu app), and music recommendations on music streaming services like Spotify and iTunes (Manovich, 2019). All of these apps, unsurprisingly, lean on Artificial Intelligence (AI) technologies to produce the services they do. A list of aesthetic adjustments made possible by Tencent (a leading Chinese IT company) includes "dermabrasion, skin whitening, and eye enlargement" just to name a few (Manovich 2019, Chap. 1, para. 14). This will be wearingly familiar to Asians. It may not be immediately obvious to the Western reader, but the list provided by Tencent shows a long cultural tradition of beauty that is common to many Asian cultures, in particular the cult of skin-whitening, which in some Asian countries like India, Thailand, and Philippines, has led to an alarming trend where people in pursuit of a fairer complexion bleach their skin with products of dubious chemical formulation. It is a good time for tech creators to question what kind of internal cultural biases they are perpetuating, or what unconscious biases they are incorporating that in turn will be used by potentially millions worldwide.

Ethics, the twin concern of the AI debate looms large; it is safe to say that most people are concerned with potential misuses. Most AI policies are currently concerned with what should be done and what precise courses of action can be taken (Coeckelbergh, 2020). However, Coeckelbergh shares that it is important to take into account that not all artificial intelligence is constructed the same way. The most common form of AI (known as symbolic AI) is relatively straightforward, drawing data from given inputs and making decisions using a decision tree. Such AI is called an expert system. (Coeckelbergh, Chap. 5, para. 12). What is potentially rife with possibilities for unintended consequences – which we will discuss later in the chapter – is the deep machine learning technology which combines several layers of neural networks.

What is potentially rife with possibilities for unintended consequences – which we will discuss later in the chapter – is the deep learning application in machine learning which combines several layers of neural networks – networks connected together by basic processing units called neurons, so named because these networks are meant to mimic the workings of the human brain. When such an algorithm is used in machine learning, it then becomes what is called deep learning. It is this form of machine learning that Coeckelbergh thinks to be a potential "black box" as the interaction between multiple layers of neural networks are not easily analysed by human agents and are not readily understood by most except its programmers (Coeckelbergh, Chap. 5, para. 13). Initial programmers of the algorithm cannot foresee how their creation might be used in the future, or who might modify it to fit their own needs, or how its applications may be further developed in different spheres. All this, "let alone all the unintended effects of the future use of their algorithm." (Coeckleberg, Chap. 8, para. 10) It is with this context that we discuss our CAS approach to the AI debate later on in this chapter.

THE ETHICS OF UNINTENDED CONSEQUENCES

"So managing complexity is about a reflective awareness of, and acceptance of, the unintended consequences of our acts both individually and collectively." - *Dave Snowden*

In contrast to even a mere ten years ago, laypeople today view a lot of technological advances through the wary lenses of consumers of digital services and products; we worry about our data being misused, our digital footprints tracked by governments, our personal devices hacked into, our identities being stolen. For the creators of these ground-breaking technologies, however, should they even be cognisant of it, they have a much bigger burden to grapple with: one which brings to mind the famous horror of Frankenstein when he has realised what came of his fascination with scientific experimentation.

Harking back to the celebrated classic in which Victor Frankenstein has to contend with the monster, we can see how apt Shelley's critique still is, of the dark twists and turns a creator's work may very well take. An Aeon article brilliantly encapsulates the pertinence of this 200-year old science fiction novel in today's age of technological innovation. The Intelligencer captures Mark Zuckerberg's Frankenstein moment during his testimony before the U.S. Congress in 2018, in which the journalist describes the apology Zuckerberg made in acknowledgement of Facebook's mismanagement of its affairs. The journalist then goes on to give a laundry list of names, people who had been there from the beginning and who all had a part to play in pushing some of the most life-changing and disruptive technologies onto the world stage. In interviews, they admit, in no uncertain terms, that humans have created a real monster of their own: the Internet.

It has nothing to do with robots gaining sentience one day and massacring the humans who created them, of course. The truth is that human design and agency will always be the cause of some of the worst technological breaches in time to come. Unchecked and unexamined, technological advancement will only serve to expose the soft underbelly of human fallibility/ambition.

It is inherently frightening to think of things beyond our human foresight and knowledge, to know that we may never be able to anticipate what we don't know. That very thought, if considered deeply, could well cause analysis paralysis, something undesirable in most cases of decision making. But this is the exact key to managing complexity, maintains Cognitive Edge's very own Dave Snowden in a 2015 blog post, entitled "The ethics of unintended consequences".

In a June 2021 article by The Pew Research Center in conjunction with Elon University's Imagining the Internet Center, various experts who were interviewed expressed personal doubts as to how ethical future AI frameworks would be. It would appear that there are a number of factors that stand in the way of a truly cohesive framework to regulate the way AI operates. Leaving aside discussions of positive AI policies, we look instead at what they have to say. A theme emerges. It was never truly about the AI itself, but the myriad forces and actors that converge upon it from all sides. In other words, if one were to look past the technological bluster and hype, the common denominator has always been the same -- humans, bringing uncertainty in their wake. Such is a fertile ground for application of the Cynefin framework and SenseMaker.

We examine two current examples of ethical issues in AI, and how one might go about making sense of such situations.

The ethics of automating workforces - putting the "human" back in "humane" work

The modern workforce of late has been bracing itself for disruptive tech to hit their industries, no doubt due in part to hearing politicians and industry leaders parrot each other about the need to upskill and retrain in the face of increasing automation.

After the election of Donald Trump into office in 2016, public leaders and news outlets began a period of soul-searching, wondering how populist sentiment was enough to elect such a controversial candidate into the White House. There were many factors at play, but one that could not be ignored was that job security, or rather, the lack of it, was one of the political tactics which Mr Trump wielded with considerable aplomb. The Financial Times ran a 2019 article which takes a closer look at the state of jobs in the states that voted overwhelmingly red in the 2016 Presidential elections. Economist Carl Frey found social patterns leading up to the elections that matched those of the Industrial Revolution in the late 18th century. Both industrial revolutions had one thing in common: political unrest followed in the wake of disruptive technology, where deep-reaching social changes were not accounted for when such technology was implemented. What lies ahead when automation edges workers out of their jobs? History does not give us happy indicators.

Fans of the Brontë sisters and of English literature in general might recall the iconic scene in the novel *Shirley*, where a group of dissidents wreck the new textile machinery ordered by local mill owner Robert Moore, machinery that was slated to destroy the livelihoods of many of his employees. Lest this be mistaken for mere fictional occurrence, that inciting incident in the novel was in fact based on a famous real-life clash between rioting Luddites and mill owner William Cartwright in 1812, thereafter known as the Battle of Rawfolds Mill. The real incident was not resolved as neatly as in the novel. Seismic aftershocks would follow: mill owners lynched, Luddite men sent to the gallows, families ruined.

Destruction of machines by the Luddists (the movement against the mechanisation of the textile industry) in the United Kingdom, in 1811. (Photo by API / Gamma-Rapho via Getty Images)

Happily, employers today are more receptive to more humane ways of laying off employees when costs need to be cut. MIT's Sloan School of Management released an article (Mayor 2019) outlining plans for ethical layoffs of employees (despite best efforts layoffs will be inevitable in some way or form with the inexorable forward march of automation), citing Harvard Kennedy fellow Susan Winterberg and Sandra J. Sucher's case study on Nokia (Sucher & Winterberg, 2015), which compares two separate layoffs in the company's history, one in 2008 and another in 2011.

The contrast between these two incidents bring to life the Chinese idiom "as different as sky and earth (天壤之别)". The way the 2008 layoff was handled cost Nokia goodwill from local communities and her brand reputation, while the 2011 layoff was better handled and can be viewed as putting the "human" back in "humane" work. What changed was that Nokia took steps to " accept its responsibility as a driver of local economies". Humans were the fore of their priorities as they worked to set up support programs, career fairs, bridging programs which would allow existing employees to transfer to other roles within Nokia, and went the extra mile to stabilise the local communities who would be affected by their withdrawal.

The realist would not be amiss to observe that this approach gained the best of both outcomes for Nokia, that of the goodwill of the local communities and minimal losses for the company, all which Winterberg points out in her presentation. The authors cannot help but draw on their Chinese heritage to say that Nokia demonstrated that they understood what it meant to have 两全其美, which roughly translates to "having the best of both worlds" in English, but the literal translation sheds more light onto an attitude that might very well prove beneficial for companies to adopt. 两 (Pinyin reading: liang) is the numeral "two", ie. two (or more) rival sides, and 全 (Pinyin reading: quan) means "all, whole, encompassing", while 其美 (Pinyin reading: qi mei) means "the good of it". The key lies in the 全 character, because it indicates that 其美, the good, refers to the benefits that both or all sides gain as a result of a more inclusive approach, whereas the English equivalent focuses on benefits for one side only.

It is not so much altruism as it is practicality that drives this mindset, as pacifying each opposing side naturally leads to a satisfactory outcome for all, and less undesirable future consequences.

There will be more and more of such "unintended consequences" surrounding the automation of work and its impact on human activity. Such is the nature of a Complex Adaptive System, that leaders and creators are ethically responsible for the unintended consequences of their actions. As the Nokia 2011 layoff shows, ethical actions are not mutually exclusive with positive business outcomes.

The Repercussions - when use of facial recognition technology backfires

Many people recognise that facial recognition has its many commendable uses, and most do not think that scientists set out deliberately to create technology of Frakensteinian proportions. It is wise for creators, researchers, executives, and even consumers like ourselves to stop and question ourselves about all the things that could possibly go wrong.

Van Norden (2020) delves into the ethical issues that come with the research material that goes into training facial recognition algorithms. "For facial-recognition algorithms to work well, they must be trained and tested on large data sets of images, ideally captured many times under different lighting conditions and at different angles." He highlights that these days scientists typically no longer use volunteers and collect facial images without asking permission. No further elaboration is needed when one considers the dangers of private data being taken without consent from internet platforms. This is compounded by the fact that much of "what goes on the Internet, stays on the Internet."

This is not the worst of it. We are reminded of the one sector for which facial recognition seems to be eerily suited. Kate Crawford calls for a freezing of the use of facial recognition technology as legal and regulatory frameworks simply cannot keep up the rapid pace at which facial recognition technology is being commercialised and contracts are being brokered between law-enforcement agencies and merchants of such technologies.

Yet again, we cannot escape the role of aesthetics when it comes to facial recognition, especially in relation to CAS. Aesthetic judgement concerns itself with values and value judgement (not to be confused with artistic judgement which has more to do with the recognition and appreciation of art). IIt seeks to understand what makes something beautiful? Inspiring Unsettling? It asks how should we approach the appreciation of art? What makes an aesthetic judgement objective or subjective? It is a close companion of Ethics, and together these two form a powerful hybrid tool with which we judge and evaluate the responses to any form of art or, indeed, technological developments.

That the SenseMaker approach affords unpredictable humans epistemological and phenomenological dignity is no accident; it was crafted that way. A Kantian perspective on aesthetics is not merely unfashionably out of date, it is also fundamentally incompatible with an anthro-complexity view of human systems and potentially unethical.

A description of our "philosophical DNA" would go as follows: [Our] approach gives phenomenology (experience) priority over ontology (categories of being), through an epistemology (theory of knowledge) which relies not on analysis, but on hermeneutics (interpretation). Narratives (fragmented stories) are signified (given meaning) by the storytellers to create an attractor landscape (map of important issues) which decision makers can use to intervene (act).*

There are a lot of big-sounding philosophical terms to unpack, but one that is especially relevant in this milieu is that of the epistemic justice mentioned earlier, a concept expounded by contemporary British philosopher Fricker (2007) – who gets to know? To interpret? Whose knowing is listened to and even lauded? Whose are sidelined or ignored?

* Editor's note: With thanks to Tom Klein whose sadly now deleted blog post helped us put this so succinctly.

Vintiadis (2021) asserts that objectivity is neither impartial nor universal, and that contextualised enquiry as advocated by feminist theories might instead be "the only way to bring to light important truths and expand our understanding of the world by exposing biases that are so firmly rooted in patriarchal societies that they have become imperceptible.

We shall avoid a diversion into feminist theory, saving it for exposition in future chapters, and instead focus on the potentially knotty issue that Vintiadis presents above – that whilst contextualising inquiry is indeed a moral imperative in anthro-complexity, it has to be balanced by the objectivity of cold, hard numbers to be useful in policy making as much as product design.

There is not in fact a dichotomy here if you blend qualitative and quantitative research techniques, the foundation upon which SenseMaker is built, because it overcomes the inherent biases and pitfalls in conventional frames of research developed from very culturally specific times by allowing each individual to have their story (the qualitative bit) heard and self-interpreted (which action provides quantitative meta-data), but aggregated with the masses to provide objectivity in numbers that decision makers can better rely on.

This blended approach, then, allows us to parse aesthetic judgement and straddle the three-part Venn diagram between ethics, aesthetics, and epistemic justice especially in the rapidly evolving world of technology. This is because, as Klein summarised elegantly, the approach puts phenomenology at its heart and places an epistemological analytical layer on that phenomenology so that sense can be made collectively. This is not to say that ontology does not matter, but that it should take second place in relation to phenomenology. The approach allows people to start to see the world for what it is, through multiple perspectives, instead of how they wish it to be, an apparently common desire amongst tech creators.

CONCLUSION

Having come to the end of our chapter, we hope that some of the points we have raised will give readers something to think about. We made points about current AI and tech innovation as being the sometimes monsters to their Frankenstein creators, and how some have the potential to become monsters. Of course, not all are quite so dramatic as Cambridge Analytica's case, but all are equally important in the impact they bring to our world. All have significant impact on us, but most disproportionately on the less-fortunate and disenfranchised amongst us.

So what then, of us non-creators of technology, who might possess a modicum of privilege?

Our role, the authors believe, lies in active input of ethical objections. We must start from the ground-up with grassroots and community participation, where more consideration is given to the concerned public: to ethicists and scholars, to employees of companies which would adopt new disruptive technologies, and even to the people working these very technologies. Technology and everything else under its umbrella, and the myriad networks which intertwine with them from all directions, can be considered in the context of CAS.

It is our hope that we can inspire you to adopt the calm attitude of a CAS approach, coupled with the consideration of what values make our communities tick (by mapping those values into a narrative landscape, of course), in which you become comfortable with knowing that you can never fully know, and prepare yourself to respond swiftly and appropriately to unforeseen circumstances that lie ahead.

The authors acknowledge the unintended consequences this chapter might have on the reader, and abjure themselves of any responsibility surrounding dives into rabbit holes on this topic.

References

1. Botting, E. H. (3 October 2018), *Godmother of Intelligences*, Capx.co https://capx.co/external/godmother-of-intelligences/ (retrieved 13 Dec 2024).

2. Brontë, C. (2006) *Shirley* (Jessica Cox, Ed.) Penguin Classics.

3. Coeckelbergh, M. (2020), *AI Ethics*. The MIT Press essential knowledge series, The MIT Press. Ebook.https://direct.mit.edu/books/book/4612/AI-Ethics.

4. Cooper, David E. (2019) *Aesthetics: The Classic Readings* (2nd ed.) John Wiley & Sons Inc.: Blackwell Publishing Ltd.

5. Crawford, K. (2019). Halt the use of facial-recognition technology until it is regulated. *Nature*, 572(7771), 565. https://doi.org/10.1038/d41586-019-02514-7.

6. Fleming, S. (23 Jan 2019), US states that voted for Trump most vulnerable to job automation. *Financial Times*. https://www.ft.com/content/cbf2a01e-1f41-11e9-b126-46fc3ad87c65 (retrieved 13 Dec 2024).

7. Fricker, M. (2007) *Epistemic Injustice: Power and the Ethics of Knowing* (online edn) https://doi.org/10.1093/acprof:oso/9780198237907.001.0001 *Axiology*, Routledge Encyclopedia of Philosophy https://www.rep.routledge.com/articles/thematic/axiology/v-1.

8. Kulwin, N. (13 Apr 2018), An Apology for the Internet, from the people who built it, *New York Intelligencer*, https://nymag.com/intelligencer/2018/04/an-apology-for-the-internet-from-the-people-who-built-it.html (retrieved 13 Dec 2021).

9. Lee, Kai-Fu. (2018) *AI Superpowers: China, Silicon Valley, and the new world order*. Boston: Houghton Mifflin Harcourt.

10. LeVine, S. (8 Jul 2018), *Robots may have given Trump an edge in 2016*, Axios. https://www.axios.com/robots-automation-populist-uprising-2016-presidential-election-45400a64-9ee3-4a46-b473-ab822429631b.html (retrieved 20 Aug 2021).

11. Magrani, E. (3 Sep 2019) *New perspectives on ethics and the laws of artificial intelligence*. https://policyreview.info/articles/analysis/new-perspectives-ethics-and-laws-artificial-intelligence (retrieved August 11, 2021).

12. Manovich, L. (2019), *AI Aesthetics*. Moscow: Strelka Press.

13. Mayor, T. (8 Jul 2019) *Ethics and automation: What to do when workers are displaced*. MIT Management Sloan School. https://mitsloan.mit.edu/ideas-made-to-matter/ethics-and-automation-what-to-do-when-workers-are-displaced (accessed 13 Dec 2024).

14. McCormick, P. (2015) *In The Moment Of Your Passage, Essays in Ethics: the Aesthetic, the Metaphysical, and the Interpretive*. Ukrainian Catholic University Press, published in association with the Eastern European

Ethics Network (EEEN) and the International Institute for Ethics and Contemporary Issues (IIECI).

15. Mizzoni, J. (2017) *Ethics: The Basics*, (2nd Edition.) John Wiley & Sons Ltd.

16. Noble, A. (9 Aug 2019). *Skin lightening is fraught with risk, but it still thrives in the Asian beauty Market—Here's why*. Vogue. https://www.vogue.com/article/skin-lightening-risks-asian-beauty-market.

17. Perez, Caroline C. (2019) *Invisible Women: Data Bias in a World Designed for Men*. Abrams Press, Harry N. Abrams, Inc.

18. Raine, L. Anderson, J. and Vogels, E.A. (16 Jun 2021) E*xperts Doubt Ethical AI Design Will Be Broadly Adopted as the Norm Within the Next Decade*. Pew Research Centre https://www.pewresearch.org/internet/2021/06/16/experts-doubt-ethical-ai-design-will-be-broadly-adopted-as-the-norm-within-the-next-decade/ (retrieved 12 Dec 2024).

19. Simanowski, R. (2018) *The Death Algorithm and Other Digital Dilemmas. Untimely Meditations Series*. (Chase, J. Trans) Cambridge, MA: MIT Press.

20. Snowden, D. (27 Jan 2015), *The ethics of unintended consequences* https://thecynefin.co/the-ethics-of-unintended-consequences/ (retrieved 13 Dec 2021).

21. Sucher, Sandra J. and Susan J. Winterberg. Nokia's Bridge Program: Redesigning Layoffs (A). Harvard Business School Case 315-002, February 2015. (Revised August 2016.) https://www.hbs.edu/faculty/Pages/item.aspx?num=48539 (retrieved 12 Dec 2024).

22. Taliaferro, C. (2011), *Aesthetics: A Beginner's Guide*. Oneworld Publications.

23. Trump, D. (2016), *Full Transcript: Donald Trump's jobs plans speech*. Politico, https://www.politico.com/story/2016/06/full-transcript-trump-job-plan-speech-224891 (retrieved Aug 21, 2021).

24. Van der Leeuw, S. (2019). The role of narratives in human-environmental relations: an essay on elaborating win-win solutions to climate change and sustainability. Climatic Change, 160, https://doi.org/10.1007/s10584-019-02403-y.

25. Van Noorden, R. (2020). The ethical questions that haunt facial-recognition research. Nature, 587(7834), 354–358. https://doi.org/10.1038/d41586-020-03187-3.

26. Vannatta, S. (Aug 2016) Problems at the Intersection of Aesthetics and Ethics, Response The journal of popular American Culture. https://responsejournal.net/issue/2016-08/article/problems-intersection-aesthetics (retrieved 13 Dec 2024).

27. Vintiadis, E. (Aug 16 2021). Is there something special about the way women do philosophy?. Aeon. https://aeon.co/essays/is-there-something-special-about-the-way-women-do-philosophy (retrieved 13 Dec 2024).

'LOOKING FOR THE MAP IN THE UNDERGROWTH': ASSEMBLAGE THEORY, THE CYNEFIN FRAMEWORK AND COMPLEXITY

DR ANNA PANAGIOTOU
AND ELEANOR SNOWDEN

ABOUT THE AUTHORS

Dr Anna Panagiotou was born in Greece and studied history, archaeology, and anthropology, initially in her home country. She has an MA in Egyptian Archaeology and a PhD in Mediterranean Archaeology from UCL. She first encountered Deleuze and assemblages when archaeological theory started picking them up in the 2010s. Eventually, the complexities of human material culture turned out to be a perfect preparation for anthro-complexity. Through a roundabout path that passed through copy editing, post-doc funding applications, and Agile training companies, Anna became a part of the Cynefin Centre at the start of 2020. She manages the Centre programmes on climate change and sustainability as well as education and helps members use SenseMaker® and other complexity-appropriate methods to make sense of their complex challenges.

Eleanor Snowden is a research consultant at the Cynefin Company, currently leading the health and care programme of work. Her role is focused on supporting organisations and healthcare professionals to work with narrative at the intersections of human sense-making and technology, with the objective of prioritising lived experience in informing policy and culture change. Holding an MA in the anthropology of social development and transformation, with a specialism in medical anthropology, Ellie is curious about how individuals navigate knowledge networks in their quests to understand health and healing and the power of bringing new perspectives to challenge our taken for granted assumptions in the workplace and beyond.

Authors note: This chapter was originally written in 2021, and so thinking , ideas and contexts will have changed since this time. We have chosen to keep the chapter intact, as a reminder of the particular time, space and feeling from which we were writing our experiences of the world. The core ideas and concepts, however, remain unchanged.

"Interest in... assemblage [is] a critical response to a growing awareness... of a social and cultural problem which John Law aptly named 'messy'." – Buchanan, 2020: 9

This chapter was written at the late stages of the COVID-19 pandemic, informed by the particularly heightened awareness of transformation that it provoked. Despite closing things down for us on a social level, the COVID-19 pandemic opened us up to noticing the aliveness of our worlds in terms of the very real interdependencies we share across time and space. It also brought to the fore that if we are going to adequately respond to "systemic issues" such as a global pandemic, or the climate emergency, we need to have the courage to step away from our reductionist need for order, and find ways to sit within the messiness and vitality of life.

The Cynefin Framework and principles of Complex Adaptive Systems (CAS) have long provided heuristics and tools for stepping outside of the "known knowns" and into a comfortable level of uncertainty, as well as situating people in the messiness of complexity in ways that allow for contextually-relevant action. In order to explore this in more depth, the authors of this chapter have long held a desire to bring the elements of Cynefin and CAS together with the Deleuzian-Guattarian Assemblage Theory in order to experiment with the affordances that such a linking might entail – the new ways of thinking it makes possible.

Ellie found herself in assemblage theory whilst getting lost in her anthropology dissertation and working in public policy research. She found the notion of an assemblage an intriguing and mysterious antidote to the more linear approaches to doing research, but also felt as though it just made sense in a way that could not be explained or written away by words. Anna encountered it when it started becoming the new hot thing in archaeological theory circa 2013. Her archaeological background had its own perspective of what an assemblage is and its own appreciation of our world's often-invisible material entanglements. This background primed her in approaching this theory, which felt like it drew from understandings that had previously been sidestepped or ignored.

This chapter has emerged as the first of (what we hope to eventually be) a series on various relationships between the two bodies of work. In this first part, the authors focus not on the practical implications of assemblage theory for SenseMaker design (a space where the authors dedicate most of their working practice at the Cynefin Centre) but on positioning the tool in relation to CAS and assemblage theory. Having laid out the theoretical foundations here, we plan to move to their implications for SenseMaker in future instalments.

In the spirit of the generative intent behind the theory, we will explore the relationship between CAS and assemblages by exploring some core concepts that stand out to us as being at the heart of both modalities. As such, we might see this chapter and those thereafter as a sort of roadmap, whereby we do not seek to enclose the space but rather acknowledge our position relative to it. In the words of Deleuze and Guattari: "The map does not reproduce an unconscious closed in upon itself; it constructs the unconscious". As opposed to restricting ourselves only to the more defined logic of tree-like structures (Bazzul & Kayumova, 2015) with distinct trunks and branches leading neatly from one to the next, we wish to draw attention to something more rhizomatic in structure: mycelia, symbiotic fungal threads spreading under the ground, with entangled tendrils, connecting one tree to another and making a forest out of them all, until we cannot say where fungus ends and plant begins. What we present will, therefore, only ever be incomplete and unfinished. Indeed for anyone familiar with both bodies of work, we are certain that there is much more that could be said and so we add in an invitation to the reader to add their perspectives and their "edges" and dig deep with their own roots to map out this Complex domain from various vantage points, so that together we can paint a broader and messier picture.

WHAT IS "ASSEMBLAGE THEORY"?

Assemblage theory itself has been given multiple interpretations and has been put to use in a myriad of different ways. Not least from the scores of philosophy and social science academics who have turned to the Deleuzio-Guattarian approach to life especially in more recent years, but even from the original sources, who themselves (much like their admirer, Franz Kafka) did not live long enough to "complete the task" of "'working out'" their theory (Buchanan, 2020: 10; 14).

Ever an evolving concept, the idea of "an assemblage" is somewhat of a misnomer, as it cannot be understood to be a mere collection of things (noun), or even the machinic process of assembling things (verb) (Buchanan, 2020: 10). Both of these definitions would in any case be far too individual-centred, ordered, and reductionist for such a complex array of events remembered, stories told, and contexts overlapping. The very fact that assemblage theory has proved generative across such a variety of disciplines shows both its versatility, but also betrays something about the biases and edges of these spaces.

Assemblage actually translates to *agencement*; meaning "to arrange, to play out, or to piece together" rather than gathering or bringing things together in a bounded sense of completion (Buchanan, 2020: 26; Nail 2007). The immediate implication, which also permeates the previous section, is that an assemblage in this sense is not a unified whole, but a more heterogeneous co-existence. This aspect of the assemblage also resonates with one of the key properties of complex systems: they are different from the sum of their parts. As a conceptualisation, it brings us straight into the complex space of the Cynefin framework and away from the temptation that an assemblage can be dis-assembled into its constituent parts so that we can learn how it works.

So how exactly is assemblage theory put to use in theory and in practice and what is the backdrop of the increased attention? Let us take the example of how chronic disease is framed in public health in the UK and the changes in research practice and focus around it. In the last two decades we have seen a research emphasis on social determinants along with biological markers (Guel, 2012; Lupton, 2013). Alongside this shift we have also observed an increased interest in preventative care as well as self-management, from which originates the health identity of an "expert patient". On the one hand, this move is situated within an attempt to recontextualise care and move away from more paternalistic ideas of control and one-way information flow. On the other hand, we see critiques of "soft-paternalism" and what anthropologist Nickolas Rose has dubbed a "politics of life itself" (Rose, 2007) . Here, control is moving away from institutions as the boundaries become more blurred and more densely enmeshed in networks: "social control is now achieved in fluid and unnoticeable manner because the instruments of control have begun to operate beyond their original containments" (O'Byrne & Holmes, 2009: 58).

Within this context, there has been an interest in using complex adaptive systems as a lens for approaching some of the more intractable issues (Health Foundation, 2010) that emerge as biomedicine no longer monopolises "somatic expertise" (Rose, 2007: 28-29). At the same time, some health researchers have begun to use assemblage theory as a lens through which to explore complex relational spaces in a non-reductionist way. Nikolas Rose (2007: 10) has spoken of "new medical assemblages" or "networks of expertise"; Marcus and Saka (2006: 102-104) use the term "assemblage thinking", and Nick Fox shows how the assemblage approach to embodiment as embedded opens up the body as a site of analysis, extending bodies into networks through relations of constraint and potential (Fox & Ward, 2008; Stirling, 2005). Within this comes the acknowledgement that a more "substantive account of health" is required, beyond solid boundaries of health and illness that also take on moral associations (Duff, 2014: 6) and instead focuses on the journey of *becoming* (ibid.; Fox, 2011: 434-440).

To continue our exploration of assemblages, we will next discuss agency, before moving into principles of generative structure, "difference" and constraints, and then social change and transformation.

AGENCY, OR HOW THINGS HAPPEN

"Men believe themselves to be free, simply because they are conscious of their actions, and unconscious of the causes whereby those actions are determined." – Baruch Spinoza, 1981. Part III, Prop II

Agency is frequently conflated with individual power or initiative. In this section, we will take a closer look at the concept of agency in the context of assemblage theory. We want to arrive at an understanding that allows us to consider the individual actor and their choices while understanding the more subtle role that a more relational, or contingent agency has to play in systems, assemblages, and their dynamic evolution.

"Agency" as an idea almost embodies a specific tension. On the one hand, Deleuze and Guattari wanted to move away from Freudian models of behaviour as determined (Buchanan, 2020: 21); alongside them, we want to recognise the impact and power of the individual agent and avoid the impression of a generic, lifeless, faceless system. On the other hand, as most assemblage-based approaches argue, agency goes much further than personal power. It can almost be identified as the "ghost in the machine" (with a reminder that there is no distinction between ghost and machine), the animation in the assemblage.

A good starting point is "personae" in the assemblage (Nail 2007). Personae can be read as agents within the assemblage that connect its concepts, the same element that manifests as the linked agents of CAS. For Deleuze and Guattari, personae are not the self-aware, independent actors that the word "agency" often brings to mind (Deleuze and Guattari 1994). Instead, they are part of the larger assemblage and act only as such. This more Spinozian focus on agency that does not rely on intention (Roberts 2012) also allows us to build connections to another critical property of complex adaptive systems: unintended (but genuine and material) consequences. In other words, agents are not just humans that choose to do something and then carry that action out – agents are anything that interacts within and across assemblages. In turn, agency is not located within but is rather an emergent property "distributed across the assemblage" (Bennett, 2010, cited in McLeod, 2017: 17).

In addition to helping us better understand change and the parts agents play in bringing it about, this approach to agency also allows us to highlight non-human agents' roles. This helps us pay serious attention to our world's materiality and capacities (see also the section on difference and constraints below), as Jane Bennett (2010) amongst others have argued. The practical implications of this attention to the non-human and material world will become apparent in the following instalments of this series that focus more explicitly on SenseMaker.

It is important here to not fall once again into the binary trap. We argued that not all agency is articulated action driven by intention. This, however, does not mean that there is no intentional action and that purpose-driven action does not have an effect or that embodied humans are not also agents. Human actors and agents working consciously can change the assemblage, make new connections, and create new possibilities to achieve their purposes. To return to the map metaphor, the agent's desires can act as a compass that orients them, and their course changes the territory in ways that are intended and unintended. Agents can have strategic goals and aims, and so can assemblages themselves.

At the same time, agents are constantly reproducing and changing the assemblage even if they have no intention of doing anything of the sort. In the assemblage, agency is a constant, not a characteristic that some have and others do not, or one that can be given or taken away. One implication is that we cannot always define the outcome of intentional activity in a linear way. This also has to do with the nature of causality in CAS, where small actions can have large-scale unintentional consequences.

A common distinction in anthropology, geography, and other fields that draw from the same theoretical well is that between agency and structure. Getting into the details of those concepts would require a lot more space than we have here. Still, it is worth knowing that Gidden's (1986) theory of structuration was primary in developing that agency/structure framework. Structures, just like constraints in complexity, both constrain and enable agents' behaviour, and they are also reproduced and changed by them. Vital as that theory was (and is) for the conceptualisation of alive, peopled social structures, it does run the risk of reinforcing the idea of an "agent vs structure" duality in some of its applications. Another benefit of an assemblage-based perspective is that it makes challenging a binary conception of agency and structure easier (Savage 2020) as the structure becomes less rigid and the agent becomes more complex and relational. By decoupling agency from being strictly an interior human endeavour, Deleuze and Guattari opened up agency as an *emergent property* (Bennett, 2021, cited in McLeod 2017: 17), which brings us onto our next section.

GENERATIVE STRUCTURING, "DIFFERENCE" AND CONSTRAINTS

"The young man will smile on the canvas for as long as the canvas lasts... In a novel or film, the young man will stop smiling, but he will start to smile again when we turn to this page." – Deleuze & Guattari, (1994: 163)

Continuing with the idea that assemblage theory opens up the embodied subject to a network or "collocation of interacting associations" (Latour, 2004: 206-214, cited in Duff, 2014: 62) it can be acknowledged that the approach allows us to see and work with structure differently (McLeod, 2017). By moving away from more reductionist views of the body as a bounded whole which is somehow "stable" in identity as in opposition to external "structure", our focus turns to the relational as a means to situate diverse lived experiences in context: paths are made by walking. Here, bodies, signs or abstractions, technologies, the physical landscape together create assemblages, through a flow of "processes, events, affects and relations" (Duff, 2014: 61). This is about understanding "what a body can do" by exploring the constraints on "its capacity to be affected by other bodies" (Deleuze, 1992: 217, cited in McLeod, 2017: 16) as much as any intentional capacity to affect others in a unidirectional way.

In this regard, as has been argued above, in Deleuzio-Guattarian language, power is about relational capacity to affect and be affected, and importantly both human and non-human actors have intrinsic capacities for agency (Edensor 2011). In this "collaborative connective labour" (McLeod, 2017: 19), as we enter into new assemblages, new types of interdependent agencies are made apparent when we bind things together. We cannot reduce any of these emergent capacities to any one of the individual components alone, nor should the relations themselves be fetishised in any way (Escobar and Osterweil, 2010: 193). Instead the ethnographic approach is to ask about the conditions that lead to its existence (Whyte, 2009).

"The mixing of many orders of relational processes made the possibilities for what could emerge. Relationships build relationships build relationships build relationships...and then after a good deal of responses to responses in multi-directional oscillation, there is emergence. – Nora Bateson, 2021

In order to avoid falling into the trap of reifying relationships themselves (see Friend, 2014) the generative structuring of assemblages and the liminal phase shifts in Cynefin help us to see that this is as much about dynamic or adaptive movement as it is situational or contextual awareness.

This is not to say that difference is not still important, as it is through differential relations that both "systemic orderings" and "open-ended events" occur (Escobar and Osterweil, 2010: 194). There is an inherent tension between the desire to change motivated by a desire for difference and modulating, and a desire for coherence. Cameron Duff (2015) refers to this throughout his piece as an "affective atmosphere": the things that prime and enable actions in certain directions, and the related ways these potential actions are used, resisted, embraced, or changed. We can see our environments as invitations to enter into a relationship with some of their aspects. Some of those invitations are never taken up, while others are almost impossible to refuse. For example, we will almost always drink from a tall thin glass by tipping it backwards towards our mouths, or using a straw (unless perhaps we have a case of the hiccups). But to an animal such as a cat, this mode of drinking is almost entirely inaccessible (until that time where evolution enables opposable thumbs in our feline companions).

Deleuze and Guattari often speak of the relationship between the *virtual* and the *actual*; the virtual is a *generative* space for all *potentiality*; where this generative potential interacts with what is possible becomes fulfilled in the actual. The tension between the two can be explained in a brief manner by "risk" - the danger of something happening, which has yet to be actualised. Here, Deleuze turns our attention to the collective: "life is conceived as what can be actualised, or made present, from all the virtual differences or possibilities" (Colebrook, 2009; Esposito, 207: 80, cited in McLeod, 2017: 15). In a similar way, the different domains of the Cynefin framework give different possibilities for both seeing a situation, as well as for assessing how best to act in it. These pathways of possibility allow practitioners to move between the virtual and the actual, through the noticing of there being different types of constraints afforded to each of the domains.

Chaos in Cynefin might be seen to be "the essential ground zero of desire" in Assemblage-speak (Buchanan, 2020: 21). When we are in this type of a context, having no effective constraints can be both confusing and messy - a particularly non-ideal space to reside in - but they also have a transformative power to change up the way things were before. Think the phoenix from the ashes type metaphors now present in many guises but especially in a lot of healthcare discourse since the Covid-19 pandemic hit. Chaos, however, in the Cynefin sense, can also be destructive, especially for those who ended up in it by over-constraining a situation they assumed to be Clear. This quote from *A Thousand Plateaus* (1987: 161) is actually an excellent description of going over the cliff into the Chaotic domain from an agential perspective: "Staying stratified...is not the worst thing that can happen...[the worst case is that you] throw the strata into demented or suicidal collapse." According to the authors, these causes the strata to collapse back on us "heavier than ever."

In line with the generative becoming in assemblage theory, we understand that constraints in the Complex Adaptive domain are more *enabling* in nature. Here, a sense of coherence emerges over time through the interdependencies and interactions between agents. In simple or ordered systems in Cynefin the nature of the constraints is such that behaviour can be said to be predictable: *governing* or *rigid*. In the ordered domain, repeating cause and effect relationships are observable empirically and once we understand these, we can use them to predict what might happen in the future. This resonates with Deleuze and Guattari's "abstract machine":

the assemblage is not random and unconnected, but neither is it defined and united: it is complex. The abstract machine that makes an assemblage out of elements is the (contingent and ever-changing) relationships (Deleuze and Guattari 1987: Nail 2007). Here, as with CAS, we strive for coherence over uniformity. Deleuze uses the example of symbiosis in the sense of things that form an alliance and work together.

Importantly in CAS, constraints are not necessarily pejorative or only restrictive. Engaging various heuristics for action is an exercise in noticing differences between domains. The mistake people often make is to apply principles from an ordered domain when in reality they are operating in a very different context, or indeed to see one situation from the perspective of only one domain and to ignore the others. The world of social research can be a prime example here; often the research questions posed and objectives claimed betray all sorts of assumptions and biases about perceptions of what is possible, which creates an artificially-imposed governing constraint through which all formal or rather, noticeable action is funneled. The related phenomena that David Mosse (2005) uncovers in the world of international development is that of "predefining criteria for success and failure", whereby policy can often become more about legitimating development activities than about changing or influencing practice (ibid.: 2005: 14). This is not to say that there are not positive effects, more so that by using tight constraints, we are in danger of rendering ourselves "inattentionally blind" to the potential for unintended consequences (both good and bad). Mosse advocates for taking a liminal perspective; the process of becoming an anthropologist "in and of" allowed him to breach any imposition of one boundary condition over another, and so open up the space for a different way of seeing by surfing the edges (Mosse ibid).

Figure 1: Liminal Cynefin Framework diagram

Thinking reflexively, much as assemblage theory has emerged in academia through multiple epistemological and ontological ways of being and knowing, the Cynefin framework itself has evolved and transformed over time in its own sort of assembling, both through addition of theory, but also importantly through praxis, i.e. lived experience and context. The stories weave rhizomatically from the framework as they are told and enacted by practitioners across the world. Each geographic context offers new pathways to travel and a diversification of understanding and application. The technology of blogging has informally led to the Cynefin framework's updating not only by its original author, but also to variants emerging across the world wide web (some approved of, some not so much!) As it spreads across physical, technological, and material boundaries, "my place of multiple belongings" becomes visible in previously untold ways*.

* This paraphrases of the meaning of Cynefin by drawing on the work of the Welsh poet Kyffin Williams (1918-2006)

In many ways, Cynefin gives a pragmatic and contextualised lens through which to explore assemblages. These values are after all part of its high value to practitioners as well as those more academically inclined. By offering a space for the certainty of cause and effect where it is due and an understanding of the porous boundaries between domains, the framework itself offers a sense of dynamic vitality, whilst also acknowledging the realities of the processes we carve out and their relative affordances that they give. Layering layers on layers.

The approaches of both assemblage theory and the Cynefin framework open us up to the act (and indeed art) of noticing. Much like the cultural turn in the 1970s, both the Cynefin framework and assemblage theories demand of us a certain professional reflexivity to both uncover where we are, but also make visible more realistic and less direct ways to act which target the relations between things, rather than individual behaviour itself. As in the concepts underpinning Nora Bateson's (2017) "warm data" approach, when we open ourselves up to the relational or ecological world, we have a certain sense of cultural responsibility to tend to these relations in ways that continue to give life. Part of this requires us to take note of "observing the observer", both in ourselves, but also to recognise this process in the so-called "other"; both within and across the paths we tread together. This is all the more important when we consider the generation of change and transformation, which will be discussed in the section below.

APPROACHING CHANGE AND TRANSFORMATION

"You do not know beforehand what a body or mind can do." – Deleuze, 1988: 125

Today's issues did not begin last week, or in 2016, they were possibilities fermenting through time. – Nora Bateson, 2021

Deleuze says that "'a theory is exactly like a box of tools… It must be useful. It must function.'" (cited in Buchanan, 2020: 14) One way assemblage theory functions is in dealing with the problem of change and creating it. But what exactly is the problem with change? To sum it up, in a world of equilibrium, change is impossible: a perfectly balanced, homogeneous system will only alter if change is somehow imported from the outside. Conversely, a heterogeneous, dynamic assemblage with connections beyond itself is like a complex system: it can change in multiple ways, both from the interaction of its parts and through the effect of changes that are external to it, its connection with other assemblages.

In Deleuze and Guattari (1987), lines of flight are both points and drivers of change. Lines of flight allow one thing to become another. More than just change, lines of flight imply the possibility of escape, referring to the potentially restrictive properties of assemblages. The French original "fuite" also summons associations of flowing and leaking, moving in a liquid way instead of from point A to point B. Change is a part of the emergent and dis-united nature of an assemblage (Nail 2007:23): assemblages can recombine in new ways, enabling unexpected processes and discoveries. This is adjacent to what Dave Snowden, drawing from Stephen Jay Gould (Gould and Vrba 1982), calls exaptive discovery, in other words, the radical repurposing of something that already exists in a different context, creating novelty. The Cynefin framework places this practice at the centre of the Complex domain.

Let us stay with change as discovery, in addition to change as evolution. Assemblages allow us to conceptualise discovery not as the work of the lone, dogged genius but as the outcome of multiple relationships. This does not exclude the role and importance of the individual change agents in the assemblage (some of which are human actors, as the section on agency discussed), but it places those agents in the context of their interactions and draws attention to their impact beyond conscious choice. No matter what we do, or do not do, or want to do, the assemblage will change, with our action or inaction playing an active role in it. The whole is constantly in motion, always in some dynamic tension. An assemblage always contains the seeds of change which does not mean that it is chaotic and unknowable.

We cannot talk about change without talking about the dynamics of continuity. Maintenance and continuity are assumed to happen on autopilot. However, a glance at the anthropological literature, not to mention Cynefin, shows us that the reality is otherwise. Keeping things as they are, and especially keeping them behaving orderly, requires energy investment and continuous maintenance. This is reflected in Cynefin's 3D renderings that illustrate the energy cost in transitioning things to the ordered domains and keeping them there. In assemblage terms, reproducing the assemblage and absorbing change within it is also an important process (in Deleuzian terms, such processes are "relative negative"). What we perceive as stability is actually dynamic. That dynamism carries within it the seeds of change and simultaneously draws our attention to the mechanisms and components of maintenance, putting problematisation in the place of naturalisation.

That brings us right back to deliberate change, big change, the kind of change we dream about, bringing about a better world (or at least a better bit of the world). The point is that we do not need to work with assemblage theory with any notion of it being some kind of bounded whole. Still, we can use its collection of concepts and ideas and formulate it in different ways to help orient ourselves both to what is there and to a direction of travel we may wish to go towards, creating our own lines of flight. Consistently with both assemblage and complexity theory, we can drive conscious and real change without directly aiming for a specific goal. Instead of tackling a problem head on, we might nudge more obliquely, changing things around it and watching for shifts in the system. We do that, for example, when we use SenseMaker to approach intractable problems obliquely and set a course for a direction of change without knowing what the actual outcome is going to be.

SOMETHING LIKE A CONCLUSION

Given the nature of this chapter as an exploration, this is not the place to make definitive statements. We would like to close it by emphasising some of the key connections we have made here and that we are planning to pick up on in the future. Not quite a plan, but more like a path up the slope that we can see from the distance, and a description of the landmarks that we expect to encounter along the way. This chapter contains many hints of interesting directions that we hope you will go off and follow, but if there is one sensation we would like to leave you with it would be the sense of the assemblage as a variable arrangement of things, buzzing and shifting, where attention is drawn from things to relationships, and the whole is open and connected.

Here we described some important aspects of the connections between the Cynefin framework, CAS, and assemblage theory – next we will try to move to practice. From the virtual, the infinite field of possibilities, to some of the actual: we will follow those collections as they lead us to the form they take in SenseMaker design and projects. We will continue drawing from the theoretical well of assemblage theory as we explore the implications of mystical-sounding words like "territorialisation" and "deterritorialisation". We will also seek different ways of prodding the spaces of affordances and dispositional states - understanding "what a body can do" by exploring the constraints on "its capacity to be affected by other bodies" (Deleuze, 1992: 217, cited in McLeod, 2017: 16).

References

1. Bateson, N., (2017), *Warm Data: Contextual research and the evolution of science.*
2. Bazzul, Jesse & Kayumova, Shakhnoza (2015). Toward a Social Ontology for Science Education: Introducing Deleuze and Guattari's assemblages. In *Educational Philosophy and Theory: Incorporating ACCESS.*
3. Bennett, J. (2010) *Vibrant Matter: A Political Life of Things.* Duke University Press: Durham.
4. Bennett, M. (2012) Emergence and Assemblage Theory: The Challenge of

'Mechanism-Independence', PhD seminar, text available online: https://www.academia.edu/1313153/Emergence_and_Assemblage_Theory (accessed 9 Apr 2021).

5. Buchanan, I. (2020). Assemblage theory and method: An introduction and guide. Bloomsbury Academic.

6. Deleuze G, (1988) Spinoza: Practical Philosophy (City Lights Books, San Francisco, CA).

7. Deleuze, G., and F. Guattari. (1987). *A Thousand Plateaus: Capitalism and Schizophrenia*. Minneapolis: University of Minnesota Press.

8. Deleuze, G., and F. Guattari. (1994). *What Is Philosophy?* Translated by Hugh Tomlinson and Graham Burchell, Columbia University Press.

9. Deleuze, G. (1986). *Kafka: Toward a minor literature (Vol. 30)*. U of Minnesota Press.

10. Duff, C. (2014). *Assemblages of health: Deleuze's empiricism and the ethology of life*. Springer.

11. Duff, C. (2015). Atmospheres of recovery: Assemblages of health. In *Environment and Planning A*, 48(1), 58–74.

12. Edensor, T. (2011). Entangled agencies, material networks and repair in a building assemblage: The mutable stone of St Ann's Church, Manchester. *Transactions of the Institute of British Geographers*, 36(2), 238-252.

13. Escobar and Osterweil, (2010), Chapter 9. Social Movements and the Politics of the Virtual: Deleuzian Strategies, in *Deleuzian Intersections: Science, technology, anthropology*. Berghahn Books. Chicago.

14. Fox, N.J., (2011), 'The ill-health assemblage: beyond the body-with-organs', *Health Sociology Review*, 20(4): 359-371.

15. Fox, N.J, & Ward, K.J., (2008), 'What are health identities and how may we study them?' *Sociology of Health & Illness*, 30(7): 1007-1021.

16. Friend, J., (2014), 'The Biopolitics of Policy-Making: Medical Activism in the Century of the Brain', *New Political Science*, 36(1): 32-51.

17. Giddens, A. (1986). *The constitution of society*. Polity Press.

18. Gould, S., & Vrba, E. (1982). Exaptation-A Missing Term in the Science of Form. *Paleobiology*, 8(1): 4-15.

19. Guel, C., (2012), 'Self-Care at the Margins: Meals and Meters in Migrants' Diabetes Tactics', *Medical Anthropology Quarterly*, 26(4): 518-533.

20. Health Foundation, (2010). *Evidence Scan: Complex adaptive systems.* Article available online: https://www.health.org.uk/sites/default/files/ComplexAdaptiveSystems.pdf (accessed 15 Apr 2021).

21. Juarrero, A. (1999). *Dynamics in Action: Intentional Behavior as a Complex System.* Cambridge, MA: MIT Press.

22. Lupton, D., (2013), 'Digitised health promotion: personal responsibility for health in the Web 2.0 era', Sydney Health & Society Group, Working Paper, 5, Sydney: Sydney Health & Society Group: 1-19.

23. McLeod, K. (2017). *Wellbeing machine: How health emerges from the assemblages of everyday life.* Carolina Academic Press.

24. Mosse, D. (2005). *Cultivating Development: An Ethnography of Aid Policy and Practice* (Anthropology, Culture and Society Series).

25. Nail, Thomas (2017). "What is an Assemblage?" SubStance, vol. 46 no. 1, p. 21-37. Project MUSE.

26. O'Byrne, P., & Holmes, D. (2009). Public health STI/HIV surveillance: Exploring the society of control. *Surveillance & Society*, 7(1), 58-70.

27. Roberts, T. (2012) 'From 'New Materialism' to 'Machinic Assemblage': Agency and Affect in IKEA', *Environment and Planning A: Economy and Space*, 44(10), pp. 2512–2529. doi: 10.1068/a44692.

28. Rose, N., (2007), 'Introduction' and 'Biopolitics in the Twenty-First Century' in The Politics of Life Itself: Biomedicine, Power, and Subjectivity in the Twenty-First Century, ed. Rose, N., Princeton University Press, Princeton and Oxford: 1-40.

29. Savage, Glenn C. (2020) What is policy assemblage? In *Territory, Politics, Governance,* 8:3, 319-335, DOI: 10.1080/21622671.2018.1559760.

30. Spinoza, B (1981) "Ethics", Commodius Vicus.

31. Stirling, A., (2005), 'Opening up or closing down? Analysis, participation and power in the social appraisal of technology', chap 15 in *Science and Citizens*, ed Leach, M., Scoones, I., 7 Wynne, B., Zed Books Ltd, London".

32. Whyte, S.R., (2009), 'Health Identities and Subjectivities: The Ethnographic Challenge', *Medical Anthropology Quarterly*, 23(1): 6-15.

NARRATIVE ACTION RESEARCH (NAR) FOR DOING TRANSFORMATIVE TRANSDISCIPLINARY RESEARCH (TTDR)

DR JOHN VAN BREDA

ABOUT THE AUTHOR

Dr. John van Breda is a research associate with the Centre for Sustainability Transitions (CST) at Stellenbosch University (SU). Prior to the CST, John was actively involved in building and managing an inter-faculty Hub for Transdisciplinarity, Sustainability, Modelling and Assessment – known as TsamaHub – for working on a wide range of sustainability challenges across disciplines and departments at SU. This TsamaHub work also included developing a transdisciplinary doctoral programme – known as TRECCAfrica – and leveraging the necessary international funding for conducting this intra-Africa doctoral programme.

John holds several post-graduate degrees in philosophy, theology and sociology. In his PhD he developed the notion of methodological agility as a broad approach for tackling sustainability transitions in and under radically different contextual conditions. At the methods level, John has translated this broad approach into an innovative Narrative Action Research (NAR) method for doing transformative transdisciplinary research (TTDR), particularly when facing complex socio-ecological systems challenges in the context of the anthropocene.

The main goal with this chapter is to develop some of the main concepts, principles and practices of narrative action research (NAR) as an appropriate research approach for doing transformative transdisciplinary research (TTDR) for tackling the double planetary crisis we are facing in the Anthropocene (Crutzen and others, 2002). On the one hand, we are facing a set of interconnected, non-reducible challenges such as: climate change, poverty, public health, security, energy futures, and sustainability – which has been described in the literature as a *polycrisis* (Morin and Kern, 1999). What these different problems of the polycrisis have in common is their anthropogenic character – i.e. they are human-induced and can no longer be approached as purely "natural" phenomena. Facing the unintended planetary consequences of our own actions in the world today, this, in turn, means that the planetary Anthropocene is just a mere set of interconnected "external" problems "out there", as it were, with nature or the environment. We are also, at the same time, facing a very different kind of crisis of our inner world of lived experiences – what has been described in the literature as a *meta-crisis* (Bhaskar, 2019).

It is from this perspective of a double poly/meta-crisis that the complexity of the Anthropocene becomes transparent – something which transcends any single science, discipline or agency. However, the disciplinarisation of scientific knowledge production into single disciplines and their sub-disciplines (specialisations) have made them rather ill-equipped for tackling the complexity of this coupled poly/meta-crisis. Although both the natural and social sciences have contributed immensely to the better *understanding (Verstehen)* and *explaining (Erklärung)* of the world (nature and society), they have also, at the same time, developed some severe shortcomings for figuring out how to *change (Verändern)* the world we are facing today. Therefore, in short, the coupled poly/meta-crisis cannot be tackled from within the single disciplines only; it warrants both inter- and trans-disciplinary approaches capable of working across, between and beyond disciplinary boundaries.

However, not all the challenges we are facing in the world today are necessarily complex problems. Some are indeed complex; others complicated; others chaotic. Their differences are not merely superficial differences in kind, but rather ontological in nature in that they are being brought about by radically different kinds of causal dynamics. So, for example, complicated problem situations are characterised by linear causal relationships and complex problem situations by non-linear causal relations. This, then, means that we cannot approach each and every problem situation in the Anthropocene with exactly the same approaches, but rather with different context-sensitive approaches.

THE CYNEFIN FRAMEWORK: FOR MULTI-ONTOLOGY DECISION-MAKING AND ACTION-TAKING

Making sense of these many kinds of problem situations can indeed become quite confusing. The multi-ontology decision-making framework – known as the Cynefin framework – has been expressly developed as a useful heuristic for both sense-making and action-taking purposes when facing these radically different kinds of contexts – or domains. "Cynefin" (pronounced phonetically kunev-in) is a Welsh word denoting a place of multiple belongings, in the sense of a cultural holding space where people continuously negotiate their different identities. This definition is also close in meaning to two other important concepts, namely: (a) Bourdieu's use of the notion 'habitus' (Bourdieu, 2008; Costa and Murphy, 2015; Goh, 2012), and (b) the notion of dynamic formative contexts (Bateson, 1972; Ciborra and Lanzara, 1994; Crawford and Mills, 2009; Garfinkel, 1991; Unger, 2014, 1998). When all these concepts are taken together, Cynefin signifies the social places and spaces where people are continuously assembling and re-assembling the 'social' (Latour, 2007)– whilst, in the process of doing so, adopting different roles and identities as social actors.

However, and more importantly for our purposes, the Cynefin framework goes beyond the phenomenological level of lived experience, by positing the notion of the *ontology of context* for exploring different contexts in terms of their fundamentally different kinds of causal dynamics or cause–effect relationships. To better understand the latter, the Cynefin framework distinguishes conceptually among four distinct contexts – also referred to as *domains* – at the following two levels: practical (Clear, Complicated, Complex and Chaotic domains) and abstract (meta-theoretical Ordered and Unordered) systems. Taken together, this framework facilitates performing research within the Clear and Complicated domains as concrete examples / manifestations of Ordered systems and the Complex and Chaotic domains as examples / manifestations of Unordered systems. Figure 1 is a graphic illustration of the framework.

Figure 1: The Clear and Complicated domains are illustrated in this graphic as examples of the more meta-level Ordered domain and the Complex and Chaotic domains as examples of the Unordered domain. The acronym "A/C" signifies the double meaning of this domain in the sense that it deals with the tensions caused by unclear matters. "C"

indicates the state of being confused caused by apparent conflicting or contradicting perspectives and "A" the aporetic approach seeking to work with the tensions caused by the latter, rather than trying to absolve them.

The epistemological and methodological implications of dealing with these ontologically different kinds of problem situations (contexts) are indeed far-reaching – which will now be discussed in some more detail under two separate headings below.

EPISTEMOLOGICAL CHALLENGE: EPISTEMOLOGICAL AGILITY

The four above-mentioned domains are not only ontologically different, but also epistemologically different in that each of the said domains have their own epistemic / knowledge objects. For example, in the clear domain we are dealing with *known knowns*; in the complicated domain with *known unknowns*; in the complex domain with *unknown unknowns*; and in the chaotic domain *unknowable unknowns* (Snowden, 2005; Snowden and Boone, 2007). How these are being translated into dynamic problem statements and research questions (Cetina, 2009; Cetina et al., 2005; Knorr Cetina, 2001; Knorr-Cetina, 2013) is a matter of research strategy, which can only be figured out contextually.

From a trans-disciplinary perspective in the complex domain, of particular significance is the question of how we go about using said unknown unknowns for *co-producing* (Hadorn and Pohl, 2008; Pohl and Hadorn, 2007):

- *Systems knowledge* – descriptive knowledge of why the current situation 'is' the way it is
- *Target knowledge* – normative knowledge of what is more desirable or 'ought to be'
- *Transformation knowledge* – practical-strategic knowledge of transitioning from the current to a more desirable situation

To be sure, there are no methodical short cuts for doing this but can only be figured out in the context of the actual emergent / non-linear real-world dynamics at hand. However, this does not translate into a position of *against methods* per se (Feyerabend, 1993). On the contrary, what methods we use and how we use them is indeed of critical importance and will be discussed in more detail in section 5, 6 and 7 below.

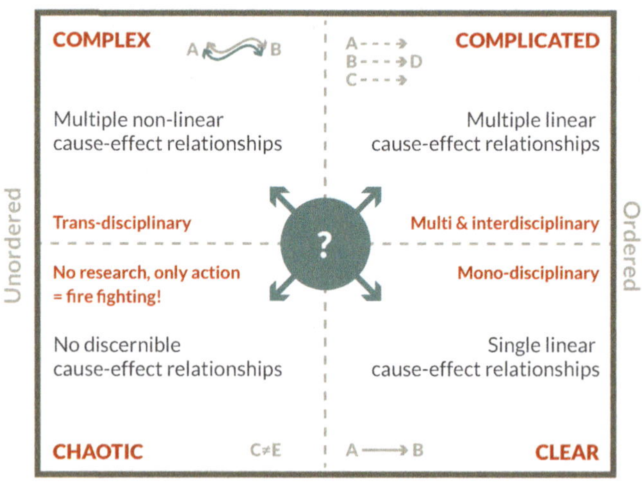

Figure 2: The arrow signifies the process of adopting and adapting the Cynefin framework for the purposes of situating / contextualising mono-, multi-, inter- and trans-disciplinarity as four equally valid domain-relevant research methodologies. The question mark in the figure on the right signifies the methodological state of being confused by the apparent different and differing (conflicting) methodological approaches, seeking to work with the tensions caused by the latter, rather than trying to absolve them.

MONO-DISCIPLINARITY FOR PROBLEMATICS IN THE CLEAR DOMAIN

In the Cynefin framework, the Clear Domain is characterised by self-evident systems where linear causality is straightforward. In this domain, there are clear-cut epistemic objects (Cetina et al., 2005; Knorr Cetina, 2001; Knorr-Cetina, 2013) which can be described as 'known knowns' (Snowden and Boone, 2007), presenting high levels of certainty and predictability. In other words, there is very little doubt that an effect (the manifest problem) has a very particular cause – i.e. the nature of things can only be explained in this particular way and in no other way(s). In such cases an appropriate epistemological strategy is through categorisation of the different types of knowledge(s) produced by the individual disciplines, by classifying them according to well-established disciplinary concepts, theories, principles, practices and methods; such as the consistent application of the principle of parsimony, also known as Occam's Razor (LLC and LLC, 2010; Sober, 2015), dictating that 'entities should not be multiplied unnecessarily', or put differently: 'when there are two competing theories that make exactly the same predictions, the simpler one (with the least assumptions) is the better one.'

Problematics in the Clear Domain are normally characterised by linear causality, or linearity for short. This means that events / occurrences that are caused by single, clear-cut and repeatable cause–effect relationships, in which, if conditions are held consistent, action / interaction A will cause B, and the same action or combination in A will always cause B. This causality is repeatable, and self-evident through simple measurement and observation.

In this domain, mono-disciplinarity is a domain-relevant methodological and institutional approach. The nature of the problem might lend itself well to disaggregation and categorisation into parts of the whole problem. This allows different disciplines to work on each part separately and to arrive at suitable insights through a single disciplinary lens. It also helps if the challenges are seen as unconnected problems, and where there are not existing complex interrelationships around, and between, the phenomena. In this mono-disciplinary mode of doing research, the individual disciplines therefore do not see any need for knowledge co-production – by crossing disciplinary boundaries to come up with integrated perspectives for the explaining (Erklärung) and understanding (Verstehen) of the clear-cut issues at hand. See Figures 3 and 4 below for a more detailed graphic illustration hereof:

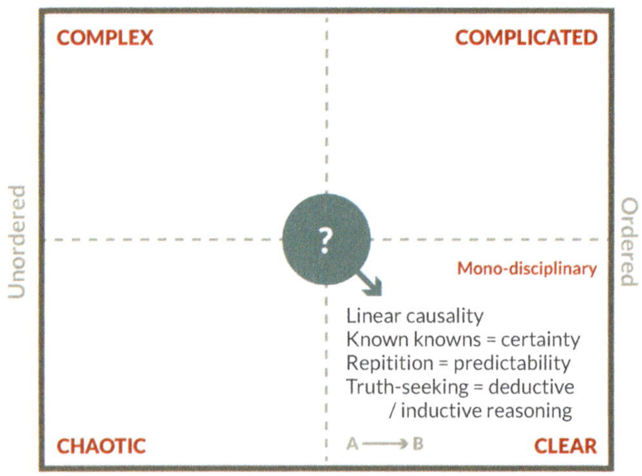

Figure 3: Focusing only on the Clear Domain, characterised in the main by single, repeatable linear cause–effect relationships (A causes B) which can be successfully theorised by the individual disciplines concerned by using the well-established deductive / inductive logics and principles for developing discipline-specific epistemic objects – i.e. problem statements, research questions, hypotheses etc. – without any interaction and collaboration between the individual disciplines or any relevant social actors.

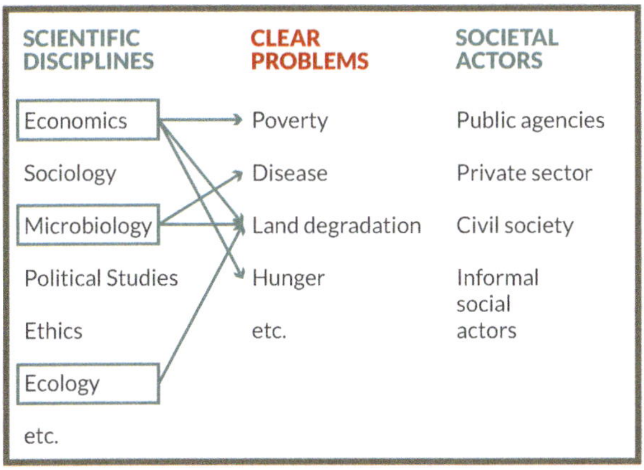

Figure 4: The teal arrows linking the three disciplines concerned (highlighted in teal boxes) with the different problems / issues here, signify the gist of the mono-disciplinary approach in the Clear Domain, where the individual disciplines are not only working on separate issues, but also working separately from each other – without any form of interaction and collaboration between them or with any of the relevant societal actors.

When problems are identified as situated in the Clear Domain, we will experience single-discipline experts, with very limited, or no interaction with other disciplines, and/or any societal stakeholders outside of academia. Bringing the perspectives of social actors / stakeholders into the research process is generally considered amongst the disciplinary experts as redundant or counter-productive to the research process. For doing so can only lead to "contaminating" the "objectivity" of the knowledge (Popper, 1979, 2005) produced in the research process – thereby making the problem situations at hand unnecessarily "complicated" or "complex".

MULTI- AND INTER-DISCIPLINARITY FOR PROBLEMATICS IN THE COMPLICATED DOMAIN

The difference between the Clear and Complicated domains is one of degree, and not of kind. Linear causality is applicable in both. However, where the Clear Domain is characterised by single linear cause–effect relationships, the Complicated Domain is characterised by multiple linear cause–effect relations, and strong assumptions about the conditions around those causal relationships. For example, that water boils at 100 degrees Celsius is an accepted truth; however, there is also an assumption of the atmospheric conditions being held consistent at sea-level. This "truth" changes in lower atmospheric pressures as the environmental conditions alter the causal relationship. These linear causal relationships are illustrated in Figure 5 below, indicating that any one cause or combination of A, B or C can be the cause of effect D. In other words, there is a shift from one-to-one linear causal relationships in the Clear Domain, to many-to-one or even one-to-many linear causal relationships in the Complicated Domain – the linear relationships of causality are traceable, and repeatable.

Given the multivariate nature (Bai et al., 2010) of the Complicated Domain, it is not always immediately clear which of the many different causal relationships are actually the most significant in any given situation. This gives rise to epistemic objects which can be described as known unknowns (Snowden and Boone, 2007) – with less certainty and predictability than in the case of 'known knowns' in the Clear Domain, but certainly not as unpredictable and uncertain as in the case of the Complex and Chaotic domains. Experts, therefore, undertake an epistemological strategy of analysis to test and identify which of the multiple linear causal relationships are more significant ones, and to understand how these are significant. In practice, this means that the complicated nature of the problem situation at hand can be thoroughly revealed through sufficient, in-depth analysis of the multiple linear causal relationships at work. This can be done through hypothesis testing, and hypothesis elimination or validation.

Where in the Clear Domain, single-discipline expertise would be the appropriate methodological approach, in the Complicated Domain there is a need for either multi- and inter-disciplinary expertise, or both. If taking a multi-disciplinary approach (see Figure 6 below), individual disciplines are no longer working on separate issues as in the Clear Domain, but on the same issues. However, they are not working together / collaborating (as in inter-disciplinarity), but rather still working independently from each other with each discipline still using its own stock of ideas, concepts, frameworks and methods etc. with which to develop hypotheses for unravelling the complicated nature of the problem situation at hand. This mode of working independently on the same issues, without the need for collaboration, is made possible by the linearity of the causal relationships – enabling individual disciplines to theorise and hypothesise on the predominance of multiple causal relations in this domain – but always as determined by the disciplinary perspectives of independent disciplines. In this mode, the expert analysis of the complicated situation at hand will be provided by the principal investigator of the research project, charged with the responsibility of coming up with some or other integrated perspective and explanation of the multiple causal dynamics at work – normally at the end of the research, when all the participating disciplines have had a fair chance to complete and submit their own discrete research findings.

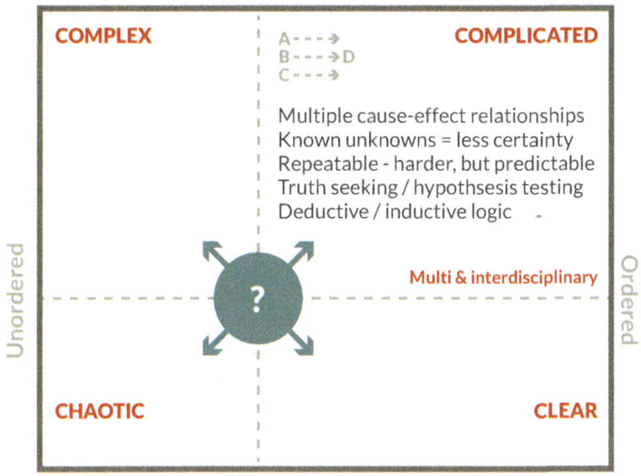

Figure 5 Focuses only on the salient dynamics of the Complicated Domain, characterised mainly by the multiple, repeatable linear cause–effect relationships (A, B, C causes D). Of these different causal relationships, it is not immediately clear what the degree of significance is of each. This is something which can be successfully theorised by the individual disciplines if allowed to work separately, using the well-established deductive / inductive logics and principles for developing discipline-specific problem statements, research questions, hypotheses etc., without any interaction and collaboration between the individual disciplines or any relevant social actors.

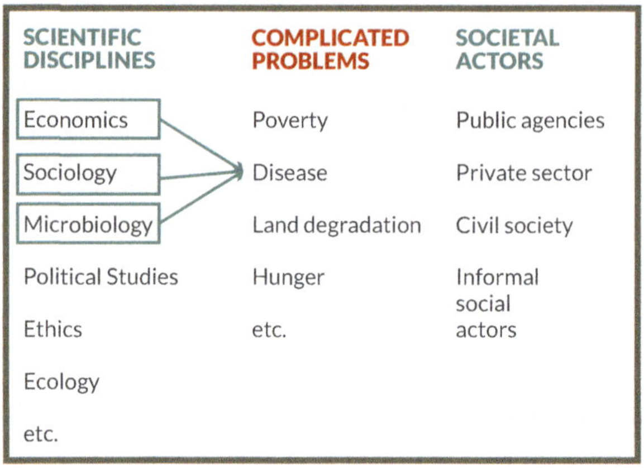

Figure 6: The teal arrows in this figure denote two important aspects of multi-disciplinarity: (a) the different disciplines now focusing their efforts on the same issues in the complicated problem situation at hand, and (b) the disciplinary certainty that comes with this, assuming that through sufficient analysis of the repeatability in the same problems at hand will produce sufficient understanding / insight into the predominant causal relations to be focused on. The listed disciplines, highlighted in the teal-coloured boxes, signify the fact that they are still working separately from each other, with no interaction / cooperation between them or any of the relevant social actors listed here.

However, where inter-disciplinarity (see Figure 8 below) is adopted, individual disciplinarians start to realise that working strictly within their own disciplinary boundaries presents limitations for dealing with the multivariate dynamics at play in the Complicated Domain. Collaboration with each other provides more opportunity for developing integrated hypotheses at different stages during the research process, allowing them to better investigate these multivariate dynamics. This collaboration can take many different forms, but normally entails some form of exchange of information and methods amongst the relevant disciplines – i.e. borrowing concepts, perspectives and practices etc. from another discipline in order to come up with a more enriched, multifaceted, integrated interdisciplinary understanding (Verstehen) and explanation (Erklärung) of the complicated causal dynamics of the problem situation at hand – something which cannot be achieved by the individual disciplines working in isolation from each other. However, in both approaches, there is limited, or no, engagement and inputs sought from social actors or stakeholders. The subject matter at hand is seen as being separable from the environment and context.

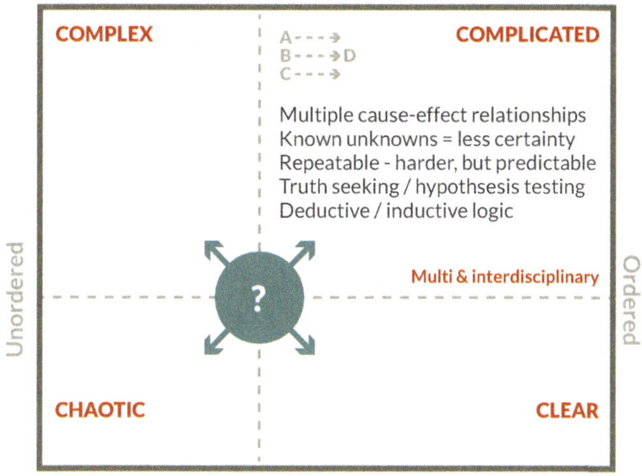

Figure 7: Focuses only on the salient dynamics of the complicated domain, characterised mainly by the multiple, repeatable linear cause–effect relationships (A, B, C causes D). Of these different causal relationships, it is not immediately clear what the degree of significance is of each. This is something which can be successfully theorized by the disciplines working together and cross-pollinating ideas, theories, concepts, data and frameworks. There is a process of collaborative hypothesis development, and testing. This is, however, done without any interaction with social actors who might be a part of the problem.

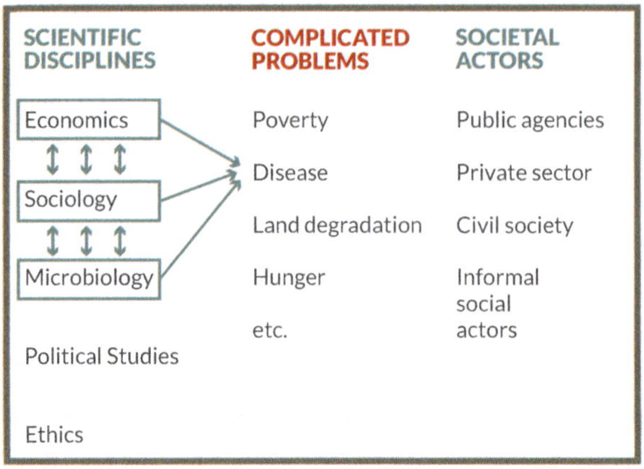

Figure 8: The teal arrows in this figure denote the shift taking place in the inter-disciplinary methodology in which the different disciplines are now focusing their efforts on the same problems / issues at hand. The smaller teal arrows (between the highlighted disciplines) signify the second important feature of this approach, the fact there is now some form of interaction / collaboration between the different disciplines mentioned – exchanging some information, insights, practices and methods. However, the absence of any lines or arrows to and from the listed social actors signifies the fact there is still no engagement with them in an attempt to bring their embodied understanding of the issues at hand into the research process.

TRANS-DISCIPLINARITY FOR PROBLEMATICS IN THE COMPLEX DOMAIN

In the complex domain we encounter a shift from linear to non-linear causality – meaning that events / occurrences in this domain are no longer caused by direct cause–effect relationships between A (cause) and B (effect), but rather by bi-directional or circular feedback loops occurring between A to B and back from B to A again (Colchester, 2016).

It is also important to be mindful that the nature of A and B are not static, and that A or B might become something completely different as it becomes embedded in this, as well as multiple other feedback loops. The nature of the connectedness of things in the Complex Domain means that there are multiplicities of ongoing relationships between unknown variables that account for the emergence that is typical of complex systems. As mentioned above, the differences between the Complex (Unordered), and Clear and Complicated (Ordered) domains are ontological in nature – and, thus, display differences in system type (Ordered vs. Unordered), and not just in degree. See Figures 9 and 10 below for some simple graphic depictions of this:

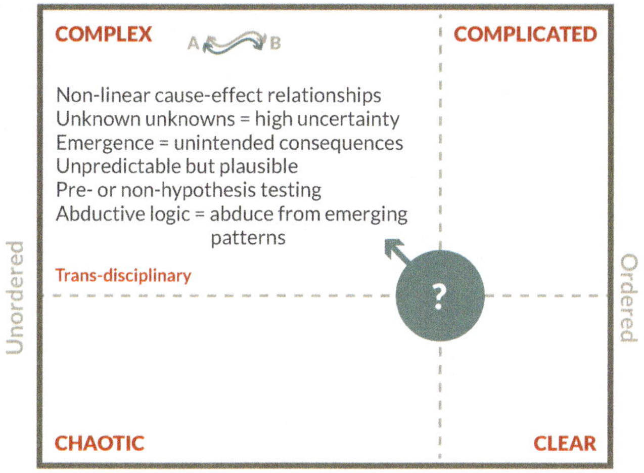

Figure 9: The wave-like arrows between A and B here signify bi-directional non-linear cause–effect relationships producing emergent events in the Complex Domain, which, in turn, are non-repeatable and unpredictable, the limits of which (enabling boundaries) are both driving and guiding our epistemological endeavours in this domain.

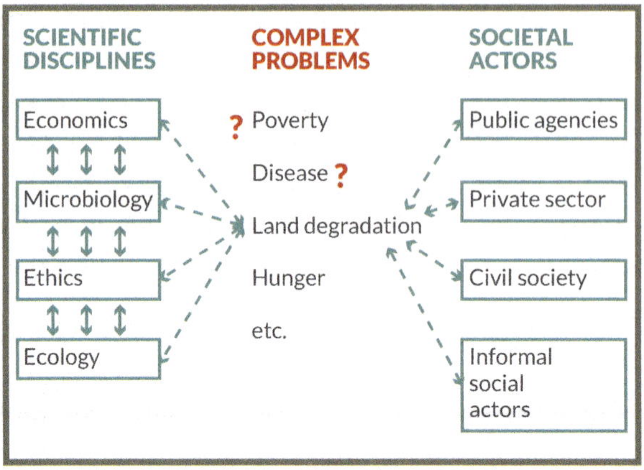

Figure 10: The two red question marks next to the issues in this visualisation signify the uncertainty / of the complex problems (referred to as unknown unknowns in Figure 9) in the Complex Domain. The teal dotted lines to the left and right of the complex problems denote the fact that it is not immediately clear which disciplines and social actors should be brought into the research process. This may only become clearer during the unfolding research process, which, in turn, means that the stakeholders may enter and exit at various stages of the dynamic research process.

In complex systems everything is seen as irreducibly connected (Boulton et al., 2015; Cilliers, 2008; Cohen and Axelrod, 2000) making it more useful to think about the nature of things relationally rather than focus on the things themselves. In the Complex Domain, causality can never be reduced to some or other ultimate cause (Funtowicz and Ravetz, 1994), because in complex systems there are no centralised power nodes responsible, as it were, for the ultimate / final causality of things. Instead, it is because of their fundamental interconnectivity in emergent complex systems that things always happen through a multiplicity of intense local and external interactions. This, as said, rules out the possibility of reducing causality to just a limited number of sources or locales (nodes) with more concentrated or stronger causal relations and powers than others in the system. In fact, the very notion of causality – i.e. what causes what in space and time – needs to be seen and understood more as a *distributed* phenomenon, something which is part and parcel of the dynamic, emergent property of complex adaptive systems (Juarrero, 1998, 2010, 2002). Or, put differently: the system itself is characterised by non-linear causality (Rosen, 2005); seeking causality might become futile, as the system can better be described as one of dynamic correlation (Beck, 2015; Chandler, 2018; Latour, 2017, 2012).

Non-linearity gives rise to epistemic objects which can be described as unknown unknowns (Snowden and Boone, 2007) – with far less certainty and predictability, when compared to known knowns in the Clear Domain and unknown knowns in the Complicated Domain. However, non-linear causal relations are not completely random / ad hoc events as in the Chaotic Domain. They certainly do produce some patterns which can only be detected after the event, and therefore not predicted in advance. This means that the task of sensing or sense-making of such emerging patterns cannot be conducted by disciplinary experts, with their theoretical knowledge systems, only. It requires epistemic engagement with various publics (stakeholders) to incorporate their practical / embodied / tacit / experiential knowledge of the complex problem situation at hand as the knowledge developed would be incomplete without it.

Working strictly in mono-, multi- and inter-disciplinary ways in the Complex Domain is, therefore, ontologically inappropriate. Since we can no longer make sense of the complex nature of emerging problem situations within the epistemic boundaries of theoretical knowledge only, we are compelled to go beyond (the 'trans' in trans-disciplinarity) and engage with non-academic actors and *their* everyday ways and means of knowing / understanding things in the Complex Domain. This means working collaboratively in the trans-disciplinary mode by bringing such pre-theoretical knowledge into the research process – from the very outset of defining / developing the problem statements and research questions (epistemic objects).

However, working collaboratively does not ipso facto imply trying to assemble all the relevant "legitimised" stakeholders (Scholz, 2011; Scholz et al., 2006) into the same room, as it were. The reason for this may be very practical in that such representatives, with a mandate to speak and make decisions on behalf of others, may not always be ready and available for engagement in collaborative research processes – in which case, different and more appropriate approaches are warranted, capable of working with individuals in many different places and spaces – at the same and/or different times. Such approaches are known in the literature as distributed cognition / ethnography (Enfield and Kockelman, 2017; Hutchins, 1991; Snowden, 2016a, 2016b). When adopted and adapted for the purposes of dealing with complex problem situations in the Complex Domain, this would certainly signal a radical departure from the well-established mono-, multi- and inter-disciplinary practices of developing epistemic objects (including hypothesis-testing and -integration) by certain disciplinary experts, located in academia, *only*.

CHAOTIC DOMAIN – NO RESEARCH, ONLY ACTION

The Chaotic Domain (see Figure 11 below) is, ontologically speaking, radically different from the other three domains in the sense that things happen in a completely ad hoc manner with no discernible causal relationships. The domain of Chaos can be seen as the extreme end of the spectrum between the Ordered and Unordered systems, with it representing complete *un*-ordered and randomness. It is in the absence of any causal relations that things manifest themselves in a completely random manner.

In this domain, we are facing epistemic objects known as unknowable unknowns (Snowden and Boone, 2007), basically rendering any form of systematic/substantive research in this domain impossible – at least in terms of the said four methodologies. Chaos is also, ontologically speaking, a very temporary state, as complete randomness requires massive energy to create, and is impossible to maintain (Prigogine and Stengers, 2018). In the Chaotic Domain, the main focus is on strategic action-taking, specifically aimed at bringing the chaotic events under beneficial control. When such strategic action-taking proves to be effective, parts of the system will likely transition into the other domains. Systems that undergo chaos become fundamentally different, and there is an irreversibility to the system-level disruption. All research is therefore likely conducted in retrospect, and the appropriate approaches can be determined by using the framework as a meta-methodological frame.

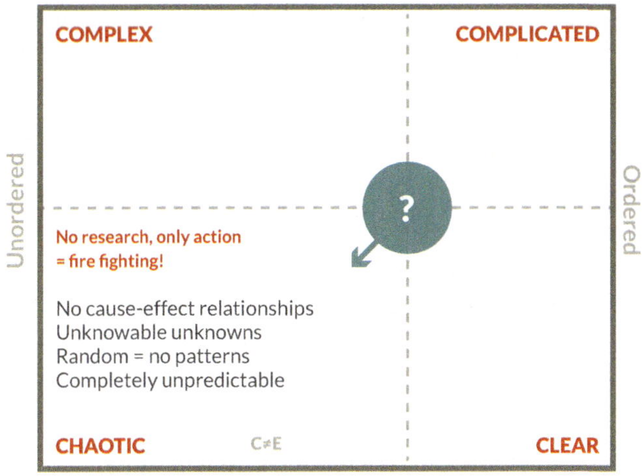

Figure: 11 The 'C ≠ E' symbol signifies that in this domain there are no discernible cause–effect relationships – meaning that things happen / occur in a completely random / ad hoc manner in the Chaotic Domain. This, in turn, makes it basically impossible to conduct systematic research of any kind in this domain. Instead, facing the very urgent consequences of random / ad hoc events, the strategic focus in this domain is squarely focused on taking appropriate real-time action(s) to bring the situation under control as quickly and effectively as is practicably possible.

THE CONFUSED / APORETIC DOMAIN - AWARENESS OF METHODOLOGICAL TENSIONS

Our discussions above have provided a typological discussion of how research in the Clear, Complicated, Complex and Chaotic domains present different methodological considerations. The "causal dynamics" discussed in the sections above, however, are often not always obvious; there are always nested causal dynamics (that is, research often takes place in systems which are nested, and which will display elements across all domains), and domain recognition is not always straightforward. The methodological tensions that arise will come from different and differing perspectives, backgrounds and epistemological politics.

For these tensions, the final domain in Cynefin provides us with a holding space which encourages a state of aporetic contemplation. Creating an aporia allows for researchers to contemplate research methodology in its philosophical underpinnings. It encourages epistemological politics and paradoxes, and in so doing, encourages us to consider the intra- and extra-disciplinary needs and limitations of knowledge production. Trans-disciplinary research intersects and impacts upon social and human worlds, and by that very nature needs to factor the practical overlaps which present themselves as social knowledge in the making.

The aporetic domain allows us to contend with the fact that heterogeneous social knowledge practices will occur "in tandem, layered upon one another, looping around and through each other, interweaving and branching, sometimes pulling in the same direction, sometimes in contrary directions." (Camic et al, 2012). We are reminded that these practices cannot be contained within traditional disciplinary enclosures but rather are an intricate spider's web (Camic ibid). In Strathern's (Strathern, 2020) contemplation of how relations and relationality is an innate part of all social knowledge production, she remarks that the belief that we can unravel or untie the essential knottiness of the self-consciously interventionist act of trans-disciplinary work is nothing more than an epistemological lure. The domain of the aporetic therefore aptly allows us to contend with the tensions that are necessary for engaging with trans-disciplinarity in the face of complexity.

The aporetic domain highlights the importance of reflexivity and awareness of one's state of confusion. Aporia was originally introduced by Aristotle to describe a state of impasse in our thinking. Translating from the Greek root of the word," '*a*' not + '*poros*', path or passage, aporia means no way through." (Goh, 2020). In the Aporetic domain, we are well aware that we are confused, and we know that we need to adopt different ways of learning, perceiving, interpreting, and exploring to work our way out.

"The aporia of our thinking points to a knot in the object; for in so far as our thoughts are in aporia... it is impossible to go forward" (Madigan, 1999). Aristotle also emphasised that the undoing of this "knot" can only be done by those who are aware of this impasse. In the Aporetic/Confused Domain, we place importance on our awareness of being in a new type of confusion. This awareness is what shifts the Aporetic from domain to methodology.

Derrida has employed Aporia or an Aporetic ethic to his deconstructive approach (Zlomislic and Zlomislić, 2007). Derrida subscribed to a very purist definition of what qualifies as a decision. He believed that for something to qualify as a "decision", it is defined by the fact that it was "undecidable". That is, where things had worked before, and we did not have to ponder the decision, then they are not in essence "decisions", but part of programming. Derrida, (1995, 147–8) asks us to '(t)hink here of Kierkegaard: the only decision possible is the impossible decision. It is when it is not possible to know must be done when knowledge is not and cannot be determining that a decision is possible as such.' He highlights that the alternative is the decision where it is clear what is to be done, in other words there is no other possible decision and thus it is more akin to "an effect, an application, a programming" than a decision.

In summary, this final domain in Cynefin can be seen as the learning space(s) opening during emergent research processes, where mono-, multi-, inter- and trans-disciplinary scholars can interact with each other and seek to work with the tensions to create truly transformative work. Methodological tensions are part and parcel then of the learning of be/coming methodologically agile as we seek to work with them, rather than to absolve them. As trans-disciplinary research continues to develop, these emerging and contradictory perspectives need critically to be considered. Beginning first with this aporetic contemplation will contribute to more effective methodological agility.

Figure 12: The acronym "A/C" signifies the double meaning of this domain in the sense that it deals with the tensions caused by unclear matters. "C" indicates the state of being confused caused by apparent conflicting or contradicting perspectives and "A" the aporetic approach seeking to work with the tensions caused by the latter, rather than trying to absolve them.

SYNERGIC METHODS:

However, methodological agility is not only about the understanding of switching between said four methodologies, but it is also about figuring out how to work with different methods within each of the four methodologies. Becoming methodologically agile also implies working with flexible / dynamic methods, capable not only of working in different real-world settings *within* the complex domain, but also, very importantly, performing the role and function of co-producing said systems, target and transformation knowledge in the complex domain.

A useful concept with which to describe such flexible / dynamic methods is that of 'synergic methods', deduced from the key concept 'synergic satisfiers' in Human Scale Development (Van Breda and Jones, In press). An example of synergic satisfiers is of a mother breastfeeding her baby; thereby satisfying the baby's needs of subsistence, affection and identity – in short, one action (breastfeeding) satisfying more than one human need at the same time. Similarly, following this logic of one-to-many relations, synergic methods are research approaches capable of co-producing said systems, target and transformative knowledge during transdisciplinary research processes.

With its strong focus on using quantitative and qualitative methods in complementary ways, the 'mixed methods' approach (see figure 13 below) is a good example of synergic methods. However, its strong point is also its weak point because it tends to omit transformative methods from its repertoire of methods. For example, (participatory) action research approaches are either completely absent from mixed methods, or if mentioned, relegated into the background by said quant-qual methods. This results in yielding valuable insights into the understanding and explaining of problem situations, but not necessarily into changing them.

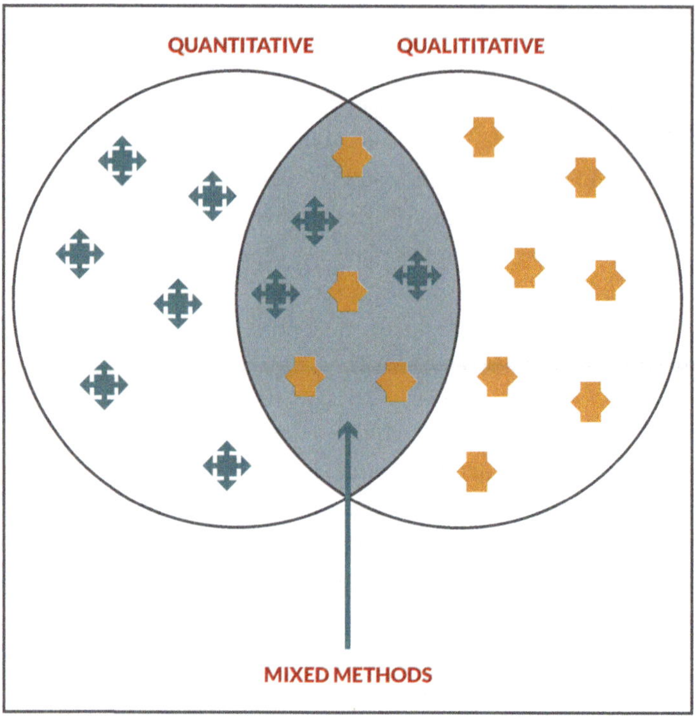

Figure 13: Depicting the 'Mixed Methods' approach, basically amounting to using quantitative and qualitative methods in complementary ways, but, importantly, excluding transformative approaches from its repertoire of methods.

Narrative Action Research (NAR) is another good example of synergic methods because it wants to fill this gap created by mixed methods by bringing transformative approaches into its repertoire of methods – thereby, not only setting out to developing better insights and understandings of peoples' lived realities – in short, sensemaking – but also figuring out how to change things.

SENSEMAKER® AS NAR:

Over the last couple of years (since 2014), SenseMaker (SM) has been at the core of developing NAR for conducting Transformative Transdisciplinary Research (TTDR processes). The latter may not have been part of the (original) design intentions of SenseMaker, but via adopting and adapting some of its core ideas, principles and practices, SenseMaker has certainly been "exapted" for TTDR purposes. the extent that it is possible to speak NAR and SenseMaker interchangeably. To this end, when compared to the mixed methods approach, NAR / SM can therefore be visualized as follows:

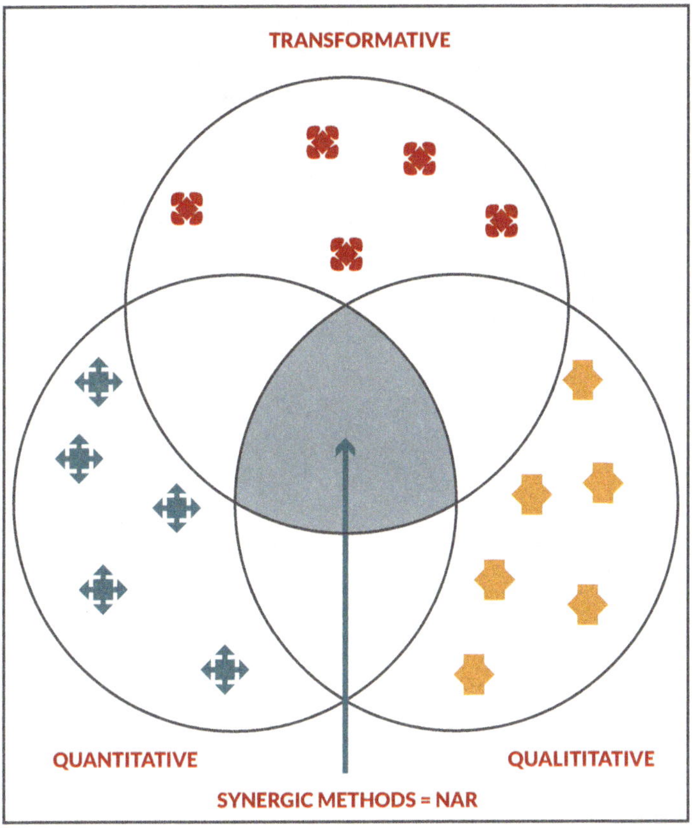

Figure 14: Depicting the methodological space (signified by the light teal triangular area) left vacant, as it were, by the Mixed Methods approach, to be filled by NAR / SM method.

NAR / SM PROCESSES

NAR / SM research processes are essentially iterative processes but can also be depicted as multi-phased linear processes (see figures 15 and 16 below):

1. **Iterative Process**

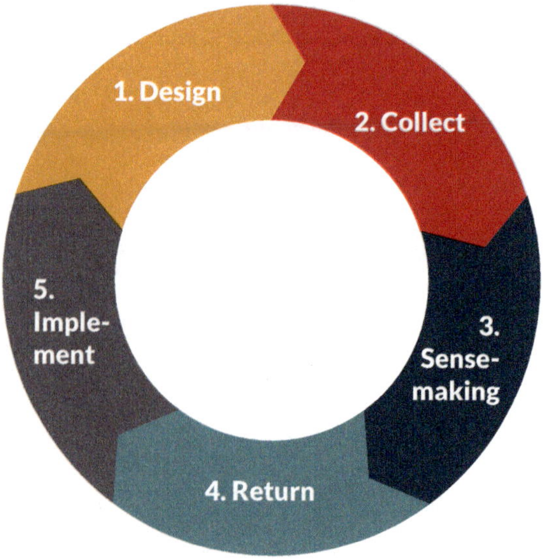

Figure 15: The iterative NAR/SM process, consisting of five phases: I.Designing, II.Collecting, III. Sense-making & Analysis, IV.Returning, and V.Implementing

2. **Linear Process**

When depicted as a multi-phased linear version, the above iterative process can be presented as follows with some more detailed steps (signified by the bullet points below):

1. **Preparation**
   - Context description
   - Stakeholder analysis
   - Developing some guiding problem statements + research questions (epistemic objects)

- Research mapping tools

2. **Design**
   - Co-designing the signification framework with enumerators (co-researchers) from the community
   - Make co-designed framework available online as SenseMaker Collector tool
   - Decide on narrative capturing strategies (formal/ informal social networks; gatekeepers)

3. **Narrative / Data Collection**
   - Decide on capturing methods (audio, paper, online, interviews, iPads, Smartphones)
   - Decide on ways of collection (indirect questions, text, anecdote circles, journaling, naïve interviewing etc.)
   - Doing field work (story collections)

4. **Analysis & Sense-Making**
   - Read and discuss individual stories
   - Training enumerators (co-researchers) in using relevant SenseMaker software for detecting and visualising emerging narrative patterns
   - Do necessary logistical / practical planning for returning stories to original story-tellers; who, when, where and how?

5. **Returning Stories**
   - Returning stories to storytellers and doing joint sense-making
   - Discuss what needs to change to have fewer negative stories and more positive stories
   - Develop context-relevant strategies for implementing small, safe-to-fail social change experiments

6. **Implementation**
   - Implement small safe-to-fail social change experiments
   - Amplify what works, dampen what does not work
   - Conducting ongoing vector monitoring & evaluation

If embedded into the Jahn TDR framework (Jahn, 2008), this linear version of the iterative NAR / SM process can be visualised as follows:

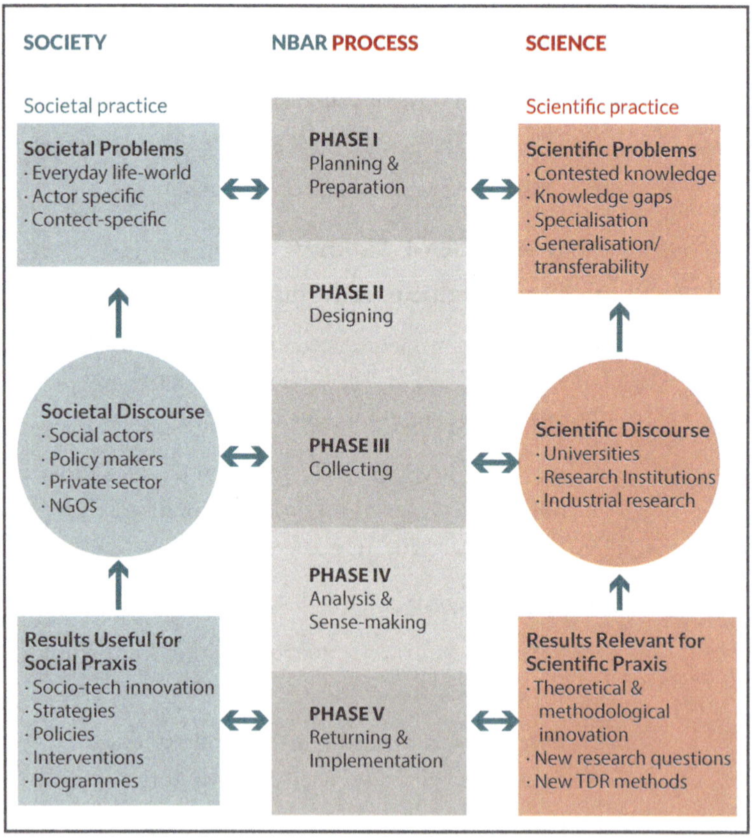

Figure 16: The linear version of the iterative process incorporated into the Jahn TDR framework.

GUIDING PRINCIPLES

NAR / SM processes are guided by the following guiding principles.

- **Co-design:** Rather than assuming atomism, NAR / SM takes a communitarian approach. This is akin to, metaphorically speaking, a dynamic interaction between actors and the stage with emergent connections between social agents and their social contexts – in which people – both individuals and groups – are constantly shaping and being shaped by each other. In other words, co-designing key aspects of the research process – starting with the signification framework – is part and parcel of the dynamic interactions involved in formative contexts (Bateson, 1972; Ciborra and Lanzara, 1994; Crawford and Mills, 2009; Garfinkel, 1991; Unger, 2014, 1998), making the NAR / SM process a thoroughly collaborative, co-creative process. In so doing – taking into consideration the richness of social actors' different and differing experiences and voices – helps to ensure participant engagement throughout the entire research process as they feel like active agents, rather than passive onlookers, in and to the change process.
- **Self-signification:** The idea behind self-signification is that people self-interpret their stories into their own structure; they give further meaning to their experiences by placing their story onto signifiers. As SM allows for written narratives, audio dictations, or the uploading of pictures, it comes with the advantage that the story always stays in its original form rather than relying on a transcription or algorithm to interpret it later. Epistemological power remains at the subject level, encouraging epistemic justice. (Snowden, 2010, n.d; Snowden, 2011).
- **Distributed cognition:** A famous study by Simons and Chabris (1999) introduced inattentional blindness: the cognitive bias we have where we do not see what we do not expect to see. Scholars often point to the "wisdom of crowds"

(Surowiecki, 2004) to overcome these innate biases, where the aggregate of stories coalesce into a more representative collective judgement. This distributed cognition of a wide, diverse group allows wisdom to emerge through voices of real people, living their own unique lives and contexts.

- **Distributed ethnography:** Traditional ethnography is an anthropological method that consists of long-term participant observation, often in people's day to day environments (Geertz, 1994). It is a deeply contextual, inductive method that is often used to avoid essentialism and scientific reductionism. However, one of the difficulties of this method, as well as others which place contextuality at the centre, is their notorious lack of scalability. Snowden (2010) positions SM as a way "respondents can contribute stories in their own contexts, in their own time and place" therefore overcoming the hurdle of scalability whilst benefiting from the advantages of ethnography in practice. Snowden (2010) calls this distributed ethnography.
- **Epistemic justice:** Epistemic justice refers to a fairness of knowing, including the need for inclusion in the "knowing process." If there is a lack of representation from one group or an overabundance from another, or if people are excluded based on their socio-cultural-economic status, demographic, or geographical context, then this can be seen as an epistemic injustice as there is an unjust power dynamic (Byskov, 2020). It is not enough to collect more perspectives about an experience or event or situation. To attend to shifting knowledge, and seeing differently, people have to create new knowledge about a system by identifying what their experiences mean and how they are making sense of, and finding meaning, in the world.

However, epistemic justice is not only a moral concept, seeking fairness in co-producing knowledge in unequal knowledge / power relations. It is also a way of ensuring that we avoid falling into the reductionist trap of peddling "single stories" (Adichie,

2009). There is a direct link between epistemic justice and ensuring variation in, and diversity of, stories, which, in turn, plays a critical role in the sensemaking of both positive / synergic and negative / destructive satisfiers; the (contextual) understanding of the many different ways and means people are expressing and communicating satisfying their fundamental human needs (see section 3 above).

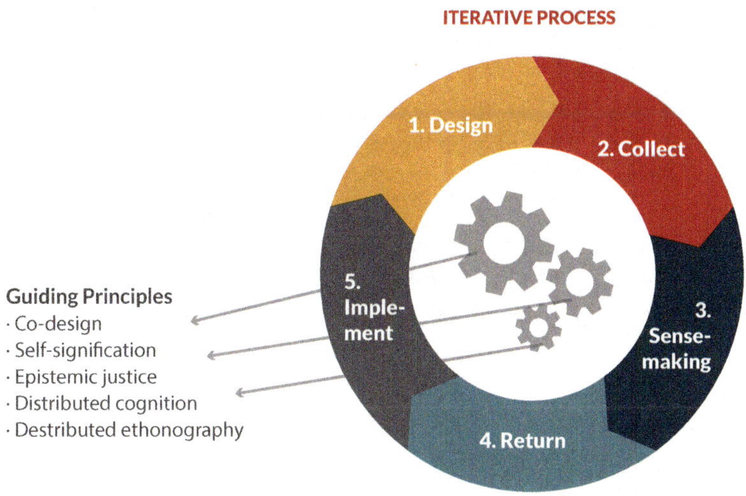

Figure 17: Signifies the guiding principles as being at the core of NAR / SM processes.

CONCLUSION

This chapter introduced the novel concept of synergic methods capable of co-producing systems, target and transformative knowledge during TTDR processes. The Cynefin multi-ontology framework was introduced as a useful heuristic for agile methodological decision-making (methodological agility) – including the strategic decision-making over when and how to use methods synergically during continuously changing contexts encountered in real-life problem situations.

References

1. Adichie, C. N., (2009We). The Danger of a Single Story [video]. TED Conferences. https://www.youtube.com/watch?v=D9Ihs241zeg&ab_channel=TED.

2. Althusser, L., (2005). *For Marx*. Verso, London.

3. Bai, Z., Wong, W.-K., Zhang, B., (2010). Multivariate linear and nonlinear causality tests. *Mathematics and Computers in Simulation* 81, 5–17. https://doi.org/10.1016/j.matcom.2010.06.008.

4. Bateson, G., (1972). Steps to an Ecology of Mind: Collected Essays in *Anthropology, Psychiatry, Evolution, and Epistemology*. University of Chicago Press, Chicago.

5. Beck, U., (2015). Emancipatory catastrophism: What does it mean to climate change and risk society? *Current Sociology* 63, 75–88. https://doi.org/10.1177/0011392114559951.

6. Bhaskar, R., (2019). *Metatheory for the Anthropocene: Emancipatory Praxis for Planetary Flourishing*. Routledge.

7. Boulton, J.G., Allen, P.M., Bowman, C., (2015). *Embracing Complexity: Strategic Perspectives for an Age of Turbulence*. Oxford University Press, Oxford.

8. Bourdieu, P., (2008). *Structures, Habitus*, Practices.

9. Braidotti, R., (2005). Rhizomes: Issue 11/12: [WWW Document]. URL http://www.rhizomes.net/issue11/braidotti.html (accessed 10.19.16).

10. Byskov, M.F., (2020). What Makes Epistemic Injustice an "Injustice"? *Journal of Social Philosophy*.

11. Camic, C., Gross, N., Lamont, M., (2012). *Social Knowledge in the Making*. University of Chicago Press.

12. Cetina, K.K., (2009). *Epistemic Cultures: How the Sciences Make Knowledge*. Harvard University Press.

13. Cetina, K.K., Schatzki, T.R., Savigny, E. von, (2005). *The Practice Turn in Contemporary Theory*. Routledge.

14. Chandler, D., (2018). *Ontopolitics in the Anthropocene: An Introduction to Mapping, Sensing and Hacking*. Routledge.

15. Ciborra, C.U., Lanzara, G.F., (1994). Formative contexts and information technology: *Understanding the dynamics of innovation in organizations. Accounting, management and information technologies 4*, 61–86.

16. Cilliers, P., (2008). 3.1 *Knowing Complex Systems: The Limits of Understanding. A Vision of Transdisciplinarity: Laying Foundations for a World Knowledge Dialogue 43*.

17. Cohen, M.D., Axelrod, R., (2000). *Harnessing Complexity: Organizational Implications of a Scientific Frontier.* Simon and Schuster, New York City.

18. Costa, C., Murphy, M., (2015). *Bourdieu, Habitus and Social Research: The Art of Application.* Springer, New York City.

19. Crawford, J.B., Mills, A.J., (2009). The Formative Context of Organizational Hierarchies and Discourse: Implications for Organizational Change and Gender Relations. *Gender, Work & Organization.* https://doi.org/10.1111/j.1468-0432.2009.00470.x.

20. Crutzen, P.J., others, (2002). Geology of mankind. *Nature 415*, 23–23.

21. Deleuze, G., (2004). *Difference and Repetition.* A&C Black.

22. Derrida, (1995) *Points: Interviews*, 1974–1994, Stanford University Press.

23. Descartes, R., (2008). *Discourse on the Method and the Meditations.* Cosimo, Inc.

24. Descartes, R., (1961). *Rules for the direction of the mind.* Liberal Arts Press.

25. Enfield, N.J., Kockelman, P., (2017). *Distributed Agency.* Oxford University Press.

26. Feyerabend, P., (1993). *Against Method.* Verso.

27. Freire, P., (2014). *Pedagogy of the Oppressed: 30th Anniversary Edition.* Bloomsbury Publishing USA.

28. Funtowicz, S.O., Ravetz, J.R., (1994). Uncertainty, complexity and post-normal science. *Environmental Toxicology and Chemistry: An International Journal 13*, 1881–1885.

29. Garfinkel, H., (1991). *Studies in Ethnomethodology.* Wiley, New Jersey.

30. Genosko, G., (2001). *Deleuze and Guattari: Deleuze and Guattari.* Taylor & Francis, Oxfordshire.

31. Goh, Z., (2012). *Understanding Cynefin through Social Theory.* Cognitive-Edge Vol.10.

32. Hadorn, G.H., Pohl, C., (2008). *Handbook of transdisciplinary research.* Springer, Dordrecht.

33. Horton, M., Freire, P., (1990). *We Make the Road by Walking: Conversations on Education and Social Change.* Temple University Press.

34. Hutchins, E., (1991). The social organization of distributed cognition. *American Psychological Association* 283–307.

35. Jahn, T., (2008). Transdisciplinarity in the Practice of Research. In: Matthias Bergmann/Engelbert Schramm (Hg.): *Transdisziplinäre Forschung. Integrative Forschungsprozesse verstehen und bewerten.*, German (No English translation yet) 21–37.

36. Juarrero, (1998). *Causality as Constraint, in: Evolutionary Systems.* Kluwer Academic Publishers, pp. 233–242.

37. Juarrero, A., (2010). *Complex dynamical systems theory.* Cognitive Edge Network.

38. Juarrero, A., (2002). *Dynamics in Action: Intentional Behavior as a Complex System.* MIT Press.

39. Knorr Cetina, (2001). *Objectual practice.* Routledge.

40. Knorr-Cetina, K.D., (2013). *The Manufacture of Knowledge: An Essay on the Constructivist and Contextual Nature of Science.* Elsevier.

41. Kurtz, C.F., Snowden, D., (2007). *Bramble bushes in a thicket: Narrative and the intangibles of learning networks.* Strategic networks: Learning to compete 121.

42. Latour, B., (2017). *Facing Gaia: Eight Lectures on the New Climatic Regime.* John Wiley & Sons.

43. Latour, B., (2012). *We Have Never Been Modern.* Harvard University Press.

44. Latour, B., (2007). Reassembling the Social: An Introduction to Actor-Network-Theory. OUP Oxford. LLC, B., LLC, G.B., 2010. Reductionism: Occam's Razor, Reductionism, Monism, Reduction, Type Physicalism, Dialectical Monism, Separation of Concerns. General Books.

45. Lovelock, J., Lovelock, J.E., (1991). *Gaia: The Practical Science of Planetary Medicine.* Oxford University Press.

46. Madigan, A., (1999). *Metaphysics: Book B and Book K 1-2.* Clarendon Press.

47. Morin, E., Kern, A.B., (1999). *Homeland Earth: A Manifesto for the New Millennium.* Hampton Press, Incorporated.

48. Pohl, C., Hadorn, G.H., (2007). *Principles for Designing Transdisciplinary Research.* Oekom.

49. Prigogine, I., Stengers, I., (2018). *Order Out of Chaos.* Verso Books.

50. Rosen, R., (2005). *Life Itself: A Comprehensive Inquiry Into the Nature, Origin, and Fabrication of Life.* Columbia University Press.

51. Scholz, R.W., (2011). *Environmental Literacy in Science and Society: From Knowledge to Decisions.* Cambridge University Press.

52. Scholz, R.W., Lang, D.J., Wiek, A., Walter, A.I., Stauffacher, M., (2006). Transdisciplinary case studies as a means of sustainability learning: Historical framework and theory. *International Journal of Sustainability in Higher Education 7,* 226–251.

53. Simons, D.J., Chabris, C.F., (1999). *Gorillas in our midst: Sustained inattentional blindness for dynamic events. perception 28,* 1059–1074.

54. Snowden, (2016a). Ethnography Part I [WWW Document]. Cognitive Edge. URL /blog/ethnography-part-i/ (accessed 6 Nov 2018).

55. Snowden, (2016b). Ethnography Part II [WWW Document]. Cognitive Edge. URL /blog/ethnography-part-ii/ (accessed 6 Nov 2018).

56. Snowden, (2010). Snowden narrative research - Google Search [WWW Document]. URL https://www.google.com/search?q=snowden+narrative+resaearch&ie=utf-8&oe=utf-8&client=firefox-b (accessed 4 Nov 2018).

57. Snowden, D., (2010). *Naturalizing sensemaking. Informed by knowledge: Expert performance in complex situations* 223–234.

58. Snowden, D., (2005). *Multi-ontology sense making: a new simplicity in decision making. Journal of Innovation in Health Informatics* 13, 45–53. https://doi.org/10.14236/jhi.v13i1.578

59. Snowden, D., n.d. Signification [WWW Document]. Cognitive Edge. URL /resources/glossary/ (accessed 2 Jul 2019).

60. Snowden, D., Blignaut, S., Goh, Z., (2021). Cynefin. Cognitive Edge Pte Ltd, Singapore.

61. Snowden, D.J., Boone, M.E., (2007). A leader's framework for decision making. *Harvard business review* 85, 68.

62. Sober, E., (2015). *Ockham's Razors*. Cambridge University Press.

63. Strathern, M., (2020). *Relations: An Anthropological Account.* Duke University Press.

64. Unger, R.M., (2014). *The Religion of the Future.* Harvard University Press.

65. Unger, R.M., (1998). *Democracy Realized: The Progressive Alternative.* Verso.

66. Van Breda, J., Jones, E., In press. *Narrative-based Human Scale Development.* IJSD.

67. Van Breda, J., Snowden, D., Goh, Z., In press. Methodological agility for sustainability transitions in the Anthropocene. ISDRS, Transdisciplinary research approaches for sustainable development Special Edition.

68. Van Breda, Swilling, (2018). *The guiding logics and principles for designing emergent transdisciplinary research processes: Learning experiences and reflections from a transdisciplinary urban case study in Enkanini informal settlement*, South Africa. Sustainability Science.

69. Zlomislic, M., Zlomislić, M., (2007). Jacques Derrida's *Aporetic Ethics.* Lexington Books.

APPLICATIONS OF SENSEMAKER® TO SYSTEM CHANGE IN HEALTH AND CARE

DR ROSANNA HUNT

ABOUT THE AUTHOR

Rosanna has been helping teams, leaders, organisations and systems achieve complex change in the NHS and wider public sector as part of NHS Horizons since 2014. Prior to this, she co-developed the Energy for Change model at the NHS Institute for Innovation and Improvement and used it to support many teams to develop skills for leading emergent change.

She brings her Ph.D. research in Psychology and Learning Theory together with co-design principles to convene stakeholders to build shared purpose and create effective organisational learning environments across many programmes of work. For example, her skills as a SenseMaker practitioner have been combined with her strategic facilitation skills on several high-priority policy areas of work in NHS England to accelerate large scale change, such as the creation of the staff Wellbeing Guardian role on Trust Boards and the retention and recruitment of international nurses in the "Stay and Thrive" programme. These are two examples where SenseMaker has been extremely effective for gathering intelligence on a large scale, distilling the insights and mobilising action for change through stories.

SenseMaker is now a major tool in the suite of methods for rapid insight generation currently in use by NHS Horizons and offers a unique contribution to its work by providing impact evidence through longitudinal application. Rosanna also shares her perspectives on leading change through community management of the School for Change Agents, a Massive Online Open Course hosted on the FutureLearn platform and attended by thousands of front-line staff in the NHS each year.

Health and care systems are typically characterised by hierarchical structures between and within their component organisations. This kind of structure is beneficial in high-risk environments where staff need to quickly respond to tasks to secure the best possible outcomes. However, health and care systems are also faced with increasing demand within a resource-constrained environment, which creates the need for innovative ways of meeting the healthcare needs of patients and communities (Crisp, N. cited in Leedham-Green et al., 2021). As David Marquet observed in his book *Turn the ship around*, the pace of innovation and change is negatively affected by hierarchies: "Those who take orders usually run at half speed, underutilizing their imagination and initiative" (Marquet, 2020).

Collaboration and co-production across the system are key activities for enabling large scale change at pace (NHS England, 2018) and a major focus of our work. SenseMaker is a complementary tool for this work because it enables more voices to be heard and provides a mechanism for those voices to also signal what is important to attend to for enabling change and improvement. We work in a system in which evaluation is often done by others and people are rarely empowered to promote their own view of what is of value. SenseMaker is not just a measurement tool but is a change intervention in itself. It is probably our most efficient outlet for making change whilst also gathering evidence about the change.

In the context of facilitating system change in health and care, we define a successful SenseMaker project as one that enables system-level behaviour change in alignment with a collectively agreed direction of travel. Since 2019, NHS Horizons has been applying the tool to support change programmes that reside in the complex domain of the Cynefin framework (Snowden, 1999). This chapter describes three recent projects to which we have applied SenseMaker and reflects on the contribution the tool has made to our work on system change in health and care.

Each section below provides an explanation of the national context associated with each project, why it is important and why it needs a complexity approach. I then describe how we designed SenseMaker to facilitate the attainment of the agendas alongside our reflections on the process and challenges of implementing a successful SenseMaker project. Each section also includes a summary of the insights gained from the projects as well as the signifiers and workshopping activities that have supported participants in the process of eliciting these insights.

A concluding section reflects on the contribution the tool has made to our work to influence system change in Health and Care. This also takes a look at where SenseMaker sits in the wider context of our work to create adaptive spaces for innovation and change and build change agency across the NHS.

All projects described here used SenseMaker to collect narratives from staff working on system change in health and care in England.

PROJECT 1: STAFF EXPERIENCES OF LEADING SYSTEM INTEGRATION IN THE NORFOLK & WAVENEY AREA OF ENGLAND

Teams that are tasked with the job of removing the barriers that impede the provision of quality of care in all its interlocking parts are struggling to lead and make sense of situations. How can we help them unravel the complexities they encounter in their work? One approach is to do that via storytelling and analysis. After asking participants to share their experiences on the SenseMaker platform, we then ask them to interpret their own experiences. This section provides an overview of the method and results from a project investigating staff experiences of leading system integration in 2020.

The respondents in this project were participating in a system leadership training programme between January and September 2020. The design of this SenseMaker project was longitudinal; deliberately tracking alongside the course in order to capture and reflect on change throughout the learning process. We began by codesigning the narrative data capture survey with key stakeholders (including some participants). We then engaged that group in a testing phase, to refine the survey further. Three data collection rounds were conducted: a pre-training baseline, mid-way through the training, and three months after its completion to see if any changes had been sustained beyond completion of the training programme.

Our question for this project was: How can system leaders best facilitate progress towards system integration? System integration involves integrating existing, often disparate, systems to increase value to the patient. System integration is becoming an increasingly important and growing area of the UK's national agenda and involves enabling systems to communicate with each other and share information and resources effectively. NHS England's intent is to achieve integrated care: "Integrated care is about giving people the support they need, joined up across local councils, the NHS, and other partners. It removes traditional divisions between hospitals and family doctors, between physical and mental health, and between NHS and council services." (NHS England, 2021). A complexity approach to this question was needed, because the process of leading system integration requires responding to dynamic and contextual factors in day-to-day work.

This was demonstrated profoundly in March 2020, when the NHS began to face unprecedented levels of pressure from the COVID-19 pandemic. The need to support staff to free up management capacity and resources to focus on the challenges created a new environment for system leaders and integrated care. We developed a SenseMaker survey that was completed by participants at two points in time: the first set of data was captured in January 2020 when the participants embarked on a System

Leadership training programme. A second set of data was captured in June, which permitted the respondents to now engage in a process with real experience in the rapid need for integration.

The question we asked to elicit experiences was: "Please tell us about an experience you've had at work in the last month that reflects what it feels like for you at the moment, bringing together different parts of the health and social care system". Some profound shifts occurred between January and June 2020. Before the training programme and the Covid-19 pandemic, (in January) there was a cluster of negative stories where the focus was on building trust whereas at the later date (June) there were no negative stories where the focus was on building trust. In June, we observed a cluster of positive stories where the focus was on both building system connection and trust (Figure 1).

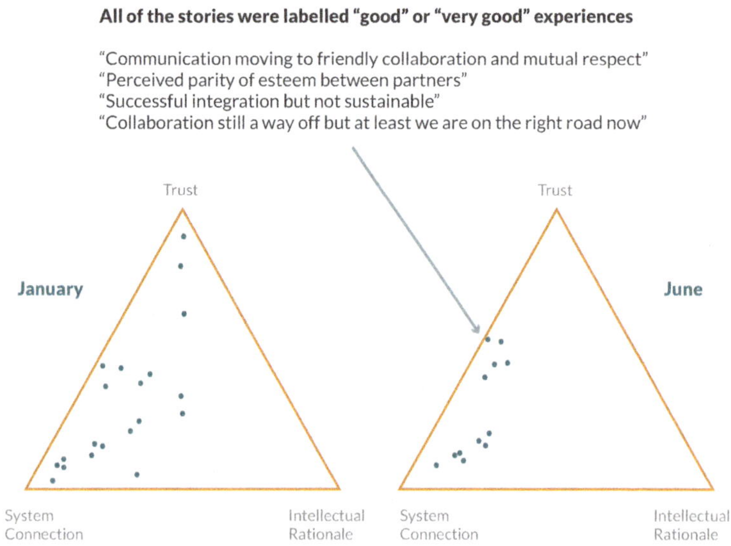

Figure 1 Comparing narratives in January and June revealed a shift from negative to positive experiences of trust

In this story, the focus was on building......

Figure 2 below shows a shift in participant's experiences of what was valued between January and June. In January, the triad indicates that Power was given some weight. By June, the stories had moved as a result of the respondents' experience in dealing with the Covid-19 crisis. There were no longer any dots located in the Power corner, indicating a downgrading of the importance of Power. The stories also reinforce this.

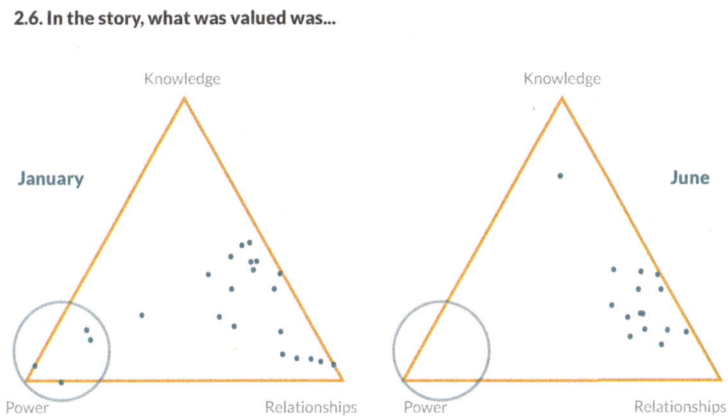

Figure 2 Negative experiences of power in January were replaced with a complete absence of stories associated with power in June 2020

The patterns observed were initially treated with caution, because there were fewer participants in June, compared to January. To build a collective understanding of the data captured, a workshop was designed and delivered in August 2020. The aim was to identify what is needed to enable effective system integration. The approach was to divide the group into smaller breakouts and ask each group to sort the narratives into two piles: experiences they want "more of" and experiences they want "less of", to enable system integration. Four stories were identified across both breakout groups as examples of experiences participants wanted "more of".

One triad distinguishing stories we want "more of" is shown below in Figure 3. It indicated that all four stories were associated with attention on the "needs of the present" rather than the "values of the past" or the "opportunities for the future".

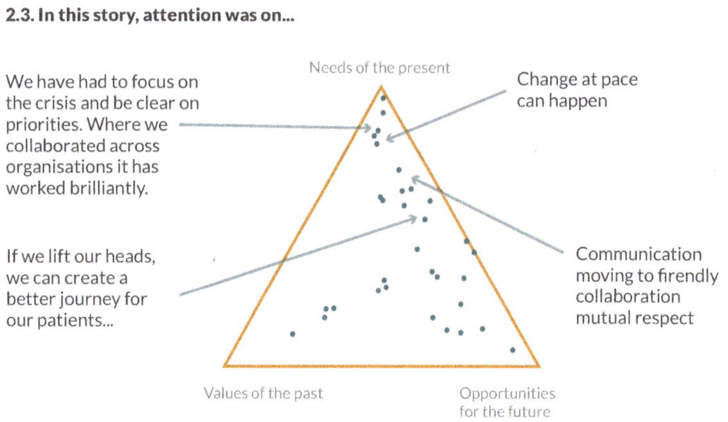

Figure 3 Triad showing the importance of attending to the "needs of the present" for enabling stories system leaders want "more of" to enable effective system integration

The workshop provided an essential opportunity for participants to ratify the data, make sense of it and use it to collectively decide what they could individually do to facilitate integrated care in the current and evolving context. The data shows that changes that occurred during the 2020 phase of the pandemic removed previously limiting factors such as power, trust, and organisation-centric views of the world. The facilitation of dialogue centred on the data, enabled collective agreement that certain leadership behaviours, such as the decision to start sharing PPE (Personal Protective Equipment) across organisations to meet the immediate need and the focus on a common purpose were worth retaining. System leaders could, in their positions, continue to influence the system, to retain the beneficial experiences emerging.

Kate, a participant in the project and General Practitioner and Clinical Director for a Primary Care Network in the region, was interviewed for a podcast. In this interview, she reflected on the opportunities she took to take an active role in enabling collaboration and building trust. This is one example of how sensemaking experiential data in a collaborative space enabled an agent of change to define their role in facilitating change in the desired (co-designed and agreed) direction.

This project showcases an example of a planned longitudinal SenseMaker project that identified key points in the leadership training programme for narrative data to be captured. We have found this to be particularly effective in supporting the evaluation of training programmes. Perhaps the real value of SenseMaker though, is preparing people to accept positive change as a sustainable effort, which goes beyond the end of a training intervention.

This was apparent following another longitudinal application of SenseMaker the evaluation of the 2019 School for Change Agents. A key finding from that study was that participants reported more positive stories when they encountered resistance to change, as their mind-sets about the value of resistance shifted. However, three months after the training programme was complete, negative stories about resistance began to re-emerge. A SenseMaker workshop conducted with participants suggested that the continual support of the community is needed to maintain motivation to deal with this resistance to change beyond the end of the programme.

A key challenge we have experienced with the longitudinal application of SenseMaker is persuading participants to complete the survey a second or third time – especially if we ask them to complete it a few months after the intervention has ended. This is a challenge we continue to grapple with, but it is worthy of continued pursuit as SenseMaker provides us with a robust way of demonstrating sustainable change.

The next section provides an example of how we applied SenseMaker at a live online event with system leaders to support a collaborative effort across 14 systems to enhance occupational health services and create a wellbeing culture at work.

PROJECT 2: STAFF EXPERIENCES OF LEADING SYSTEM CHANGE IN OCCUPATIONAL HEALTH SERVICE PROVISION

As an employer of 1.6 million people in the UK, the NHS has an opportunity and a responsibility to prevent ill health by influencing and improving the wellbeing of its own workforce. Ten years ago, the UK Government launched 'Healthy staff, better care for patients' (DHSC, 2011) which set out the Government's proposals for the practical realignment of occupational health services in the NHS. The aim was to help NHS organisations to be exemplary in occupational health provision and staff health and wellbeing.

Covid-19 presented a new context and opportunity to accelerate and shape change on this agenda. Towards the end of 2020, as the NHS entered what was anticipated to be its toughest winter yet, the government launched a programme across 14 health systems to enable piloting of new approaches to enhance occupational health and wellbeing (OHW). The ambition was to create a 'wellbeing culture' that empowers the workforce to maintain and improve their health and wellbeing, to feel cared for by the NHS, and to be empowered to pass that care onto patients. One of the goals of this programme was to "test and refine what it will take to develop and embed a proactive culture of wellbeing, rather than H&WB [health and wellbeing] being seen as a specialist activity" (NHSE&I, 2020).

The leadership challenge presented by this project is positioned in the complex domain of the Cynefin framework as system leaders were working in ambiguous spaces, without a defined set of cause-effect variables. In this case, vector measures (descriptions of the current reality and the ongoing journey) provide the best opportunity for leaders to identify where they could take action in this emerging space to facilitate change towards desirable results.

It was the job of the national team to convene the 14 systems and provide supportive spaces for these transitions from ambiguity to meaning-making. Shortt (2015) named these liminal spaces "transitory dwelling spaces". Furthermore, by providing opportunities for experiences to be shared and collective meaning to be derived from them, the national team could build awareness of the effective mind-sets, perspectives, and approaches of system leaders, thus energising collective action across the group. By extracting and workshopping experiences of system leaders on the programme, the national team was able to provide the space for systems to collaborate on change as the dynamic situation imposed by the pandemic unfolded. An adaptive space is defined by Mary Uhl-Bien (2016) as an interface between innovations and business as usual (Figure 4).

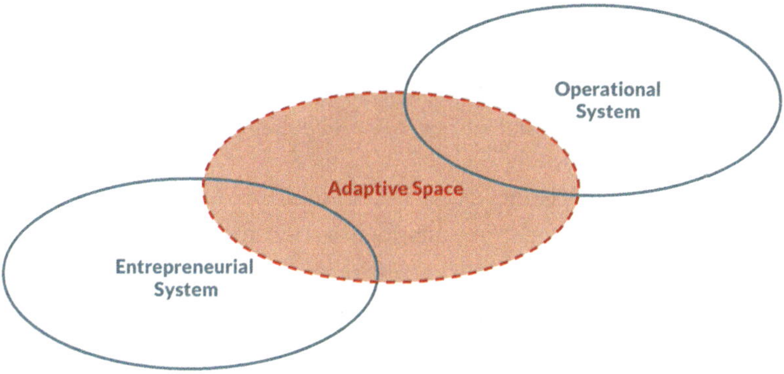

Figure 4: Adaptive Space – an interface between innovations and "business as usual" - Source: Mary Uhl-Bien (2016)

Following a rapid co-design process involving a SenseMaker practitioner, two national leads, and two system leads, the survey was tested and refined in time for a 2-hour virtual collaborative event with system leaders. At the beginning of the event, participants were given 10 minutes to complete the survey. Then the results were analysed behind the scenes while participants shared their progress on the change agenda with the group.

A short presentation of the findings followed. This focussed on highlighting any differences between the patterns of positive versus negative stories on each of the six triads. Participants were offered the option to attend one of six breakout rooms, each corresponding to one triad. They were asked to share, in the breakout group, where they had located their story on the triad and whether this was the optimal position for creating change, using the results as evidence to inform their decisions.

This model for event design, which is used routinely by NHS Horizons supporting system change, is known as an "unconference". It is participant-driven, in that participants choose the themes that are important to them. By asking participants to choose which triad they wanted a further discussion about, we were also able to find out which triads provided the best opportunities for meaning-making for participants. This approach, which facilitates participants to execute meaning-making in a public forum and make explicit how they interpreted their personal stories, helps to avoid gaming behaviours.

All the participants chose to attend virtual breakout rooms 2 and 5 indicating that the two signifiers asking about the focus of the programme ("delivery", "culture", "diversity" and "equitable access", "barriers" and "perceptions") were particularly meaningful.

Figures 5 and 6 show how we presented their data back to them – attempting to highlight the patterns of positive vs. negative stories on the triads (although in future this could be made clearer by presenting only positive stories on one triad and only negative stories on another).

Figure 5 below shows that the triad under discussion in breakout 2 revealed two clusters of positive stories – one focussing on culture and one focussing on delivery. However, a focus on culture seemed to be more important for eliciting a positive experience on the programme.

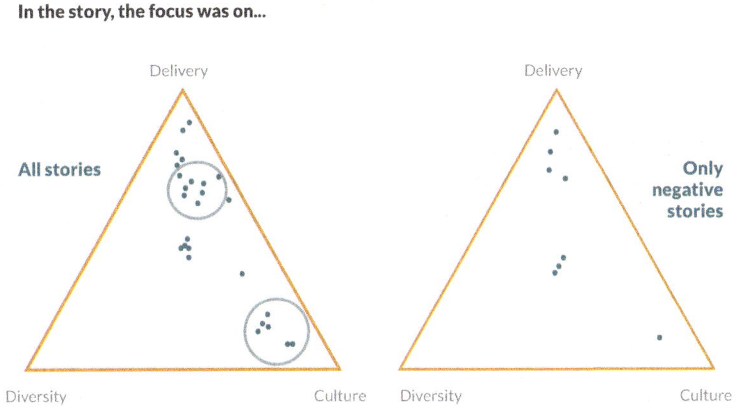

Figure 5 Triad showing two clusters of positive stories around "culture" and "delivery"

Figure 6 below shows that the second triad participants chose to discuss demonstrated a cluster of positive stories focussing on "equitable access".

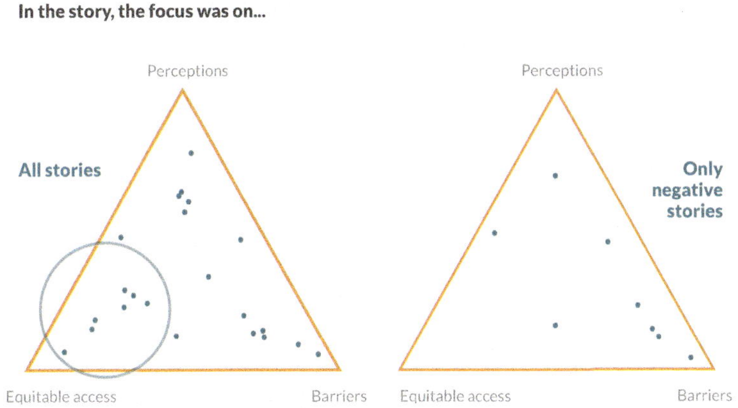

Figure 6 Triad showing a cluster of positive stories around "equitable access"

Collaborative events, facilitated online, provide an opportunity for participants from widespread geographical locations to convene quickly, with minimal costs to collectively agree what they want "more of" and what they "want less of" using evidence in the form of stories. We use a number of different collaborative platforms to enable participants to work with the stories and signifiers to make sense of experiences on the programme.

The aim of this project was to monitor experience over time and also provide a platform for programme leads to reflect on their experiences and explore how they can shift their programmes in a positive direction. Rather than looking directly at programme outcomes such as reduction in sickness absence, the reflective discussions use obliquity – the principle that complex goals are best achieved indirectly. Thus, sickness absence reductions are perhaps more likely to be achieved through a focus on organisational agility, culture improvement and improving equitable access to staff health and wellbeing services in NHS Trusts. Currently, the evidence-based NHS Health and Wellbeing Framework helps Trusts to identify gaps in provision, not whether staff have equal access to the services provided.

SenseMaker provided the evidence of current experience for workshopping, and the workshops enabled collective use of stories to determine action. This is really where the value of SenseMaker lies and it is where we have begun to prioritise our resources and efforts, sharing results quickly (within 2 hours of acquiring it in this case!) and facilitating dialogue.

PROJECT 3: STAFF EXPERIENCES OF LEADING EQUALITY DIVERSITY AND INCLUSION (EDI) IN THE NORTH EAST AND YORKSHIRE REGION (NEY) OF THE UK'S NHS

NHS England's Equality and Diversity Council aims to bring together people and organisations to realise a vision for a personal, fair and diverse health system, where everyone counts. The North East and Yorkshire region of NHS England asked NHS Horizons to facilitate a launch event for a new EDI programme that would re-invigorate action on this important agenda. The aim of the online event, delivered in April 2021, was to generate a "qualitative mandate" which gives the NEY EDI team the "authority" granted by the people (NHS staff) and framed by their lived experience to act as its representative through the implementation of the new NEY EDI programme.

SenseMaker was used to collect the experiences of people leading Equality Diversity and Inclusion in the North East and Yorkshire Region of the UK's NHS. These staff members were also invited to the event and the event itself was then used to generate the themes for the programme to take forward. A review workshop ratified the themes and launched a reference group to formulate the recommendations.

The ambition is for the reference group to shape up the recommendations and assist with the design of a second event one year on, in 2022. By comparing the 2021 SenseMaker data with the results of a second 2022 data collection round, it is anticipated that SenseMaker will provide the evidence of what has changed and that this data can also be used to facilitate further dialogue about "what next". Evidencing change is very important to this programme, as a key message from stakeholders is that evidence of change is currently lacking.

The flow chart below shows how we aligned the SenseMaker project into the design and delivery of a programme launch event aiming to facilitate virtual collaboration between EDI leaders and National programme leads working on this important change agenda in the North East and Yorkshire region of the NHS.

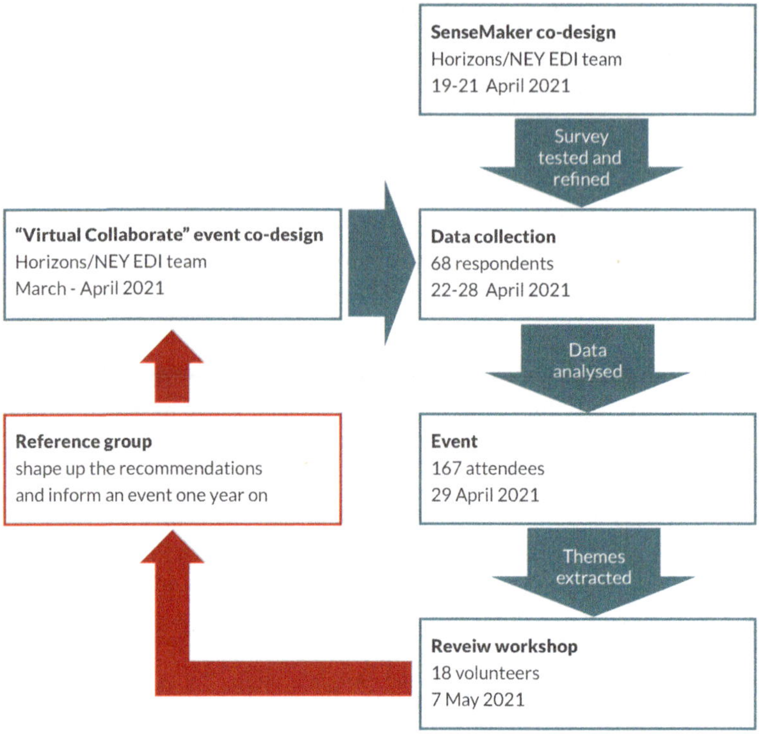

Figure 7: Flow chart showing the process of integrating and aligning a SenseMaker project to the co-design of a virtual collaboration event for NHS staff

Participants were contacted a week prior to the launch event and asked to share an experience in the NHS where either they or those around them felt that they did or did not belong. 68 people responded and 36 gave permission for their stories to be shared at the EDI event. We used online break-out groups and Google Docs collaborative platforms to create the space for participants to discuss the stories and categorise them into two groups: "those we want more of" and "those we want less of".

Prior to the event, we also compared the positive and negative stories and presented the findings prior to the break-out sessions taking place. Figure 8 shows a key insight from the data; positive stories were overwhelmingly about inclusion exclusively (48%) OR equally about Diversity, Equality and Inclusion (31%) whereas negative stories were less likely to be about inclusion (21%) exclusively and more likely to be about equality (12%) or both inclusion and equality (21%). This led the programme leads to consider the question: if we focus our programme on inclusion, will equality and diversity follow?

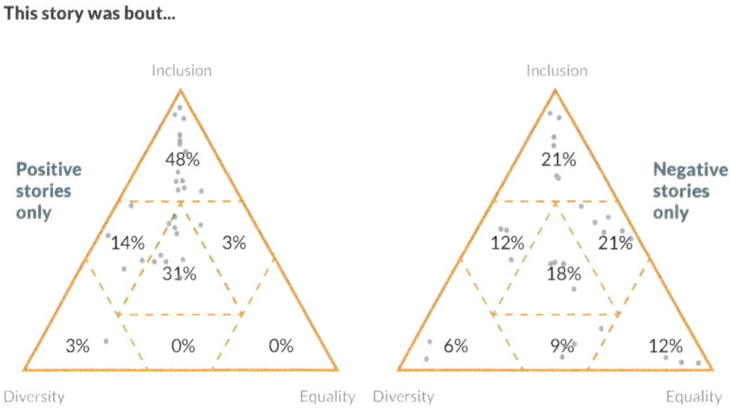

Figure 8 Triad showing a dominance of positive stories associated with "inclusion"

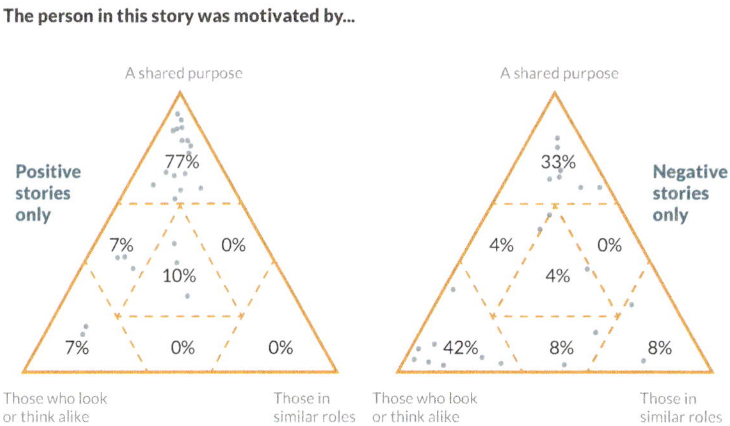

Figure 9 Triad showing the importance of motivating people around "a shared purpose"

Figure 9 shows that most (42%) of the negative stories were about people who are motivated by those "who look or think alike", whereas positive stories were overwhelmingly about people who are motivated by "a shared purpose" 77%. This led programme leads to consider the question: How do we create more environments that are about positive shared purpose?

Following the event, the themes identified by participants were analysed for commonalities. These four meta-themes, listed below, were then reviewed at a smaller online workshop a week later by a reference group assigned to shape up the recommendations and assist with the design of the overall programme. The four meta-themes were:

1. Trust/fear of speaking up

The most commonly-identified meta-theme across the breakout groups related to building trust and creating the conditions for people to be able to speak up without fear of retribution.

2. Communication, co-production and active listening

This meta-theme captures a desire for more co-creation of innovative solutions, which captures other themes around appreciative inquiry, active listening, and the need to identify and work towards a common purpose.

3. Culture - structure interplay

Many groups identified structural barriers to culture change in the NHS such as "gradism" - where staff are referred to by their NHS pay band, rather than by their role. They also identified some structural initiatives that could shift the culture away from inequality and exclusion, such as role-modelling from the top. Setting an inclusive tone was seen to be an important role for senior leaders in the NHS.

4. Allyship & networks

This theme is about creating opportunities for cross-team and cross-organisation conversations in safe spaces that focus on providing opportunities to share lived experience. These spaces currently do not exist, but are important to facilitate the honesty that is needed to progress change. It was thought that these activities could be more effective than training as they are context- and situation-specific. Development of networks and allyship should be supported by the Board.

CONCLUSIONS

The projects outlined here describe how we have used SenseMaker in adaptive spaces, where the voices of multiple key stakeholders involved in change are at the centre. Using the data, stories, and facilitated dialogue in online, collaborative spaces, national programmes have had the opportunity to explore new insights that reinvigorate action and provide new perspectives (often oblique) to accelerate innovation and change agency. So much of our system change work at a national level requires the participation of multiple stakeholders with competing agendas on issues with emotional content and therefore, "soft complexity" (Singfield, A. cited in Ketley, 2021). We are finding that the demand for access to experiential data from a diverse range of voices is on the rise and shows no signs of stopping here.

NHS HORIZONS

NHS Horizons provides support for health and care related networks and programmes that are seeking to achieve large-scale change at local, regional and national levels. The team is part of NHS England and Improvement. We work across government and internationally. More information about our work can be found on our website: http://horizonsnhs.com/

References

1. Arena, M.J. & Uhl-Bien, M. (2016). "Complexity Leadership Theory: Shifting from Human Capital to Social Capital" People + Strategy 39(2) https://www.sagewaysconsulting.com/wp-content/uploads/2017/03/ComplexityLeadershipTheory_HRPS_39.2_Arena_Uhl_Bien.pdf (accessed Apr 2021).

2. DHSC: Department of Health and Social Care (2011) "Healthy Staff, Better Care for Patients: Realignment of Occupational Health Services to the NHS in England" Policy Paper July 2011 Healthy Staff, Better Care for Patients: Realignment of Occupational Health Services to the NHS in England - GOV.UK (www.gov.uk) (accessed Apr 2021).

3. Ketley, D. (2021) *Understanding and Working with Complexity*, Diane Ketley (passle.net).

4. Leedham-Green K, Knight A, Reedy GB. (2021) "Success and limiting factors in health service innovation: a theory-generating mixed methods evaluation of UK projects" *BMJ Open.*

5. Marquet, D (2019) *Turn the Ship Around!: A True Story of Turning Followers into Leaders* Penguin books, London.

6. NHS England (2021) What are Integrated Care Systems? https://www.england.nhs.uk/integratedcare/what-is-integrated-care/ (accessed Apr 2021).

7. NHS England. (2018). Leading Large Scale Change – A practical guide https://www.england.nhs.uk/wp-content/uploads/2017/09/practical-guide-large-scale-change-april-2018-smll.pdf (accessed Apr 2021).

8. NHS E&I (2020) Staff Health and Wellbeing https://www.england.nhs.uk/wp-content/uploads/2020/11/261120-item-6-staff-health-and-wellbeing-offer.pdf (england.nhs.uk) (accessed Apr 2021).

9. NHS Institute for Innovation and Improvement. (2011). *Building and Aligning Energy for Change*

10. http://ihpme.webservices.utoronto.ca/Assets/IHPME+Digital+Assets/IHPME/hpme/events/bevan/bevan-bldg-align-lit-review.pdf (accessed Apr 2021).

11. Shortt, H. (2015). "Liminality, space and the importance of 'transitory dwelling places' at work". Human Relations 68(4), 633-658. https://doi.org/10.1177/0018726714536938 (accessed Apr 2021).

12. Snowden, D. (1999). "Liberating Knowledge", in Liberating Knowledge. *CBI Business Guide.* London: Caspian Publishing.

13. Acknowledgements: Thanks for comments on earlier drafts of this chapter to Sasha Karakusevic, Ron Bloom, Ruth Germaine, Tom Underwood.

SENSEMAKER® IN PEACE AND CONFLICT RESOLUTION

KEIL EGGERS

ABOUT THE AUTHOR

Keil Eggers is a PhD Candidate and Peace Engineering Fellow at the Jimmy and Rosalynn Carter School for Peace and Conflict Resolution. He holds an M.A. of International Peace Studies from the UN-Mandated University for Peace. His mission is to develop a complexity-informed conflict resolution methodology that helps people understand conflict through their own stories so they can take action and make better-informed decisions. In his dissertation research titled "Us Against When: The Futures of Complexity-Informed Conflict Transformation in the United States" he has adapted SenseMaker methodology to explore interpretations of future artifacts generated by prominent US-based peacebuilding organizations in order to make interventions more meaningful, scalable, and successful. The work contributes to growing streams of research on US-based conflict transformation and de-polarization. As the Peace Engineering Lab manager, he has fostered connections between the Cynefin Centre for Applied Complexity, a leading institution in complexity and narrative methods, and the Carter School. He also co-taught the first Carter School course on peace engineering with Dr. Solon Simmons titled, Peace Engineering and Participatory Approaches to Narrative.

He began his complexity journey at the University of Kansas Center for Public Partnerships (CPPR) and Research where he led the Our Tomorrows project to establish a state-wide SenseMaker Story Bank to inform decisions about the early childhood system. He has ongoing SenseMaker projects in Basque Country, Southern Thailand and has previously worked with the Organization for Economic Cooperation and Development's Observatory of Public Sector Innovation, Cognitive Edge, the Cynefin Centre for Applied Complexity, ThinkClarity, and Davidson College as a SenseMaker consultant.

A common refrain in conflict resolution textbooks is that conflict is both complex and dynamic. This is based on the argument that the boundaries of a conflict system are open and fluid and with many factors (identity, attitudes, trauma from violence, political economy, structures) acting as constraints on an ever-evolving dynamic system. The goal of peace studies as a trilateral science is to empirically understand conflict dynamics, critique violent systems and structures that deprive people of their needs, and to combine theory and practice to construct a more peaceful future. In other words, the peacebuilder must understand the disposition of a conflict system, identify what should be changed, and lead others toward a vision of a better future. All three aspects are essential to the mission of the field: reducing and eliminating violence and building peace.

With these elements in mind, this chapter will introduce how SenseMaker can be used as a tool for *naturalized sensemaking* that powers a participatory narrative inquiry process for peacebuilders. The chapter will outline the important theoretical concepts that should drive SenseMaker work for conflict resolution and peacebuilding. The concepts introduced here will be further elaborated by experimental work being completed by the Carter School Peace Engineering Lab at George Mason University. I will focus on the implications for SenseMaker practice in dealing with social conflict in contexts where there is not yet direct violence. SenseMaker practice in a warzone or active conflict would likely require different framework design, story collection strategies, domains for sensemaking, and more focused action steps related to achieving a ceasefire. However, I believe that the concepts I describe below would contribute to violence prevention efforts or improve resilience should violence occur.

The chapter is split into three sections: The need for new tools in peacebuilding, conditions for success, and implications for practice/future directions.

Throughout the years, the relatively young field of conflict resolution has changed in name and form to reflect its role in responding to the relevant challenges of the day. This chapter seeks to define the problem space of "complexity-informed conflict resolution" by building on the works of past advocates who have grappled with the challenges of complex systems and propose new participatory conflict resolution approaches powered by SenseMaker. Ideally, SenseMaker practitioners will see how they can be peacebuilders and vice versa as the theoretical foundations of the tool point to theories of change that support novel peacebuilding practice.

THE NEED FOR NEW TOOLS IN PEACEBUILDING

The challenges listed below are well-established issues within the field of peace studies and conflict resolution. While peacebuilders tend to share a similar analysis of what is going wrong, to date, the field has lacked tools adequate for the task.

The field hasn't fully shifted to a complex adaptive systems orientation: Authors like Ricigliano, Coleman, Vallacher, and de Coning have contributed to a turn to complexity within the field by adapting learnings from the complexity sciences and developing new tools and methods for analysis (Coleman, 2018, 2011; Coning, 2020; Ricigliano, 2012; Vallacher et al., 2013). However, many of the methods that have emerged are rooted in Dynamical Systems theory and seek to create conflict maps with feedback loop diagrams that require intensive resource investment but quickly become out-of-date (*Dynamical Systems Theory in Practice - Advanced Consortium on Cooperation, Conflict, and Complexity (AC4), n.d.*). These methods are both not practical and inadequate for capturing the rapidly changing landscapes of complex conflicts.

Dealing with Complex, Structural, and Intractable Conflicts: The field has struggled to develop approaches to analyze and intervene in three types of conflict: complex conflict, structural conflict, and intractable conflict. While the full definitions of these types of conflict are beyond the scope of this paper, a basic introduction is necessary to situate the domain of SenseMaker practice. Complex conflict has been defined by Galtung as constituted by a conflict formation with a minimum of two actors and two incompatible goals. These 'conflict molecules' become an entangled web of actors, goals, and relationships between them (Galtung, 2010). This complexity is further complicated by structural conflicts, where an underlying contradiction reproduces similar manifestations of conflict over time (Rubenstein, 2017). In their work on structural conflict resolution and critical conflict resolution, Rubenstein and Sweetman & English have outlined the many challenges associated with defining a conflict by its latent structures (English & Sweetman, 2017; Rubenstein, 2017). Complexity and structural conflict contribute to intractable conflict, where a conflict continues to draw in more actors and issues and sustain itself beyond the original cause of the conflict (Crocker et al., 2005). This 'wicked problem' of conflict requires peacebuilders to continually monitor for emergent properties of the conflict formation and separate complex problems from simple or complicated problems (Hauss, 2015).The field needs tools that are better suited to monitoring the rapidly changing environment and that can be used to establish a baseline analysis and shared understanding for all parties to the conflict that is beyond political dispute. This tall order is difficult to achieve by a single practitioner or small team writing a report based on their views.

The indicators of peace constantly shift: People experience conflict differently and therefore define peace differently. If you walk down the street and ask people in conflict, "What does peace mean to you?" you will receive a different answer every time. The understanding of these terms is culturally bound and highly contextual. Recent methodological innovations like the Everyday Peace Indicator Project have utilized participatory approaches to monitor and evaluate peacebuilding interventions (Firchow, 2018). The Everyday Peace Indicator Project harvested peace indicators by asking people what peace looks like in their local community in facilitated workshops. These indicators are then translated into a longitudinal survey that is collected periodically in the community of interest. Unfortunately, the methodological limitations of survey research strip the narrative richness of the peace indicators and lump sets of local indicators into broad categories defined by the focus of funders and organizations that commission the research. Peace research methods have also not been effectively applied at scale because methods are too slow to provide useful information. For example, conducting 30 interviews in a community affected by conflict and analyzing them for common themes could take six months. By the time results are produced, the conflict has already shifted (at least at a very local level) for any of the knowledge to be useful for intervention. For these reasons, peacebuilders should continue to build on the participatory trend in monitoring and evaluation, but need tools that help navigate the multiple meanings of the core concepts at hand without sacrificing complexity for the sake of measurement.

People have different experiences of the same conflict: The purpose of conflict analysis is to understand the underlying dynamics of a system and identify root causes of a conflict. However, an expert analysis can only get us so far. In terms of the Cynefin framework, analysis as practice is best left to elements in the complicated domain where relationships of cause and effect can be uncovered through analysis. Experts familiar with the system can then provide equally plausible forms of practice to achieve the desired outcome (in this case peace). In the case of structural conflicts, parties tend to not agree on what the conflict actually is in the first place (Rubenstein, 2017). Many theoretical lenses are appropriate, but none of them provide a unified theory that can consistently provide guidance for practice. In the case of partisan conflict in the United States, the conservative might experience the conflict as an attack on "American values" by leftist anarchists; an African American would experience it in the context of racism, police violence, and continual disregard for black life. A liberal might experience it through events like the Jan 6th invasion of the capital and see a threat to liberal democratic norms. Aspects of the same conflict affect and matter to different groups differently. While it might be attractive for conflict analysts to simplify things to a select group of factors, the conflict is everything at once. As a transdisciplinary field (Lappin, 2009), analysts can have trouble finding footing in a sea of possibilities – both theoretical and practical – and risk missing important emerging possibilities due to the application of theoretical blinders. Peacebuilders find footing with a methodology that can consistently provide forward momentum and direction within rapidly changing conflict contexts.

Getting the Right Information to the Right People: The final challenge that peacebuilders must overcome is that actors within a conflict system need different types of information to support decision-making. For example, international donors want metrics to determine if their money is supporting meaningful impact, while local peacebuilders might want more practical information about an emerging extremist narrative that can immediately inform their action. Due to the time required to produce evaluation reports for funding, peacebuilders are forced to decide between spending time on research to support their livelihoods and doing the work necessary to build peace. Peacebuilders need tools that support the necessary work of peacebuilding while simultaneously providing evaluation metrics that can support financing.

CONTRIBUTIONS OF SENSEMAKER AND SENSEMAKING VIA PARTICIPATORY NARRATIVE INQUIRY

SenseMaker is a complexity-informed narrative research method that shows promise for helping peacebuilders 'come to grips' with complex conflicts through distributed ethnography (Bartels et al., 2018; Eggers, 2020; *SenseMaker® for Monitoring and Evaluation of SGBV Programs,* n.d.). The method is a form of participatory narrative inquiry (Kurtz, 2014) and a naturalized sensemaking approach (Snowden, 2010). The process consists of several stages: project planning, story collection, catalysis, sensemaking, intervention, and data return (Kurtz, 2014). The process begins by working with local community partners (peacebuilders, community leaders, local governments, NGOs, etc.) to establish the goals of the project, identify upcoming actions or decision points that could be supported with SenseMaker data, and defining a story collection strategy. The SenseMaker practitioner (used as a synonym for peacebuilder in this context) then facilitates the design of the SenseMaker framework and adapts it to the local context through emergent design workshops with partners, stress testing against relevant literature, and 'paper testing' with potential respondents in the field. During the story collection phase, partners collect stories from their own communities or constituencies with the goal of capturing a minimum of 80-100 stories. This is the minimum number to be able to detect patterns. In the catalysis phase, the SenseMaker practitioner conducts an initial scan of the data for any patterns that might be relevant to the peacebuilding project. These 'emergent patterns' are then prepared for the next phase of sensemaking through the creation of mini-reports, story packs – a collection of stories as defined by a 'cluster' within the SenseMaker data, or any variety of data visualizations. During sensemaking, partners that helped collect stories and respondents themselves interpret patterns in the stories and search for surprises, unmet expectations, or any insight that can be used to plan actions in the intervention phase. Generally, complexity-informed interventions would comprise a portfolio of 'safe-to-fail' probes that could be implemented simultaneously. This portfolio rapidly tests hypotheses about the conflict and the reaction of the conflict system to these experiments determines which might be eligible for wider effort. Additionally, sensemaking participants might take action by asking themselves the question, "what can I do tomorrow to create more stories like the ones I want to see?" The combination of managed experimentation and 'fractal engagement' (people taking coherent action toward the same end goal with actions appropriate to their level of skill and authority within the system) provides a powerful coherence to peacebuilding interventions powered by SenseMaker (AcademiWales, 2016). At the end of the sensemaking cycle, all data should be made available or returned to participants as a resource for decision-making.

The products of the process briefly outlined above includes: a stable 'human sensor network' of local partners gathering stories from their communities, data dashboards that visualize patterns in self-signified micro narratives in real-time, and highly local interventions derived from insights from local stories.

CONDITIONS FOR EFFECTIVE USE OF SENSEMAKER IN PEACEBUILDING

At this early stage in this pioneering work for SenseMaker in the field of conflict resolution, there are three basic factors for practitioners to keep in mind.

Expanding the human sensor network: Stories must be collected from a wide range of actors within a conflict formation. Because the boundaries of a complex conflict are porous, the SenseMaker data set must find footing by grounding collection by either social group/network or geography. Within a particular setting, minority groups that are underrepresented should be oversampled so that story data reflects a coherent 'viewpoint' of a group. Additionally, the story collection network should be inclusive and open to any group that hopes to participate to provide a full picture of perceptions of the conflict.

Participatory Design: The SenseMaker design lightly constrains the meaning that respondents are able to provide to the experience that they share. Therefore, the framework design process is an opportunity to find agreement between local partners, scholars, practitioners, and respondents themselves on what is important and meaningful to include. Because conflict can potentially be about everything, peacebuilders might lean on a particular theoretical focus to bring clarity to the work. However, SenseMaker practitioners should reduce this urge and utilize participatory processes to gather input and find balance between theoretical interest and practical application that is relevant to local peacebuilding partners. The design phase is an opportunity to build trust in the story collection process and ensure buy-in to the results that will emerge after story collection.

Sustaining Massive Engagement: A successful intervention in a complex, structural, or intractable conflict must be built on a foundation in citizen engagement. The nature of the problem cannot be solved by one expert's 'genius' plan or by planning activities out in advance.

Successfully intervening in a complex, structural, or intractable conflict requires a large number of people to take action wherever they can. Achieving large scale transformation requires practitioners to reach a broad audience and create affordances within the conflict environment for people to recognize how their actions can make positive change. If these actions are in a coherent direction, the conflict formation can ultimately move toward a more peaceful dispositional state. At the start, it will always be unclear what causes transformation; the action that creates the 'spark' for change is only revealed in retrospect. The SenseMaker practitioner helps others become part of a movement by utilizing the data set to break down complex problems that seem to be beyond the agency of potential peacebuilders (this could be anyone!) into meaningful opportunities for action. Although people in conflict will universally recognize that 'something needs to be done,' it takes an additional push for desire for change to translate into action. Thus, the sensemaking process provides feeling of hope and meaning that supports ongoing engagement.*

* The term 'hope' is used here as defined by Lopez to mean a sense of agency and of having a pathway (2013).

IMPLICATIONS FOR RESEARCH AND PRACTICE

The following section builds on the theoretical and methodological foundation described above with reflections from the author's overall experience with SenseMaker and a recent informal experiment testing narrative prompts for the Carter School's Peace Engineering Lab framework for conflict resolution work in the United States. Findings from testing the prompt, "What is a recent experience that made you feel hopeful or worried about the future of the country or your community?" indicate potential directions for future research and practice.

Conflict Narratives aren't necessarily helpful for identifying opportunities for action: From the small sample of respondents, experiences that made people feel more hopeful were ones in which the storyteller had agency to take action. Negative conflict narratives tended to reflect deeper psychodramas with no apparent solution that were also amplified by an anxiety-inducing social media environment. For example, several hopeful stories dealt with mutual aid and community work. Respondents took matters into their own hands to make change in spite of structural factors. Negative experiences on the other hand, were beyond the control of the respondents and focused on problems like "the Trump presidency" or "decline of the country." A SenseMaker design that focuses too much on an evaluation of what is going wrong in a conflict might do more to reinforce feelings of helplessness rather than a sense of agency necessary for massive engagement in peacebuilding.

Abandoning Analysis: In the past, conflict analysis has been seen as a precursor to resolution. After all, people must have better information in order to act. SenseMaker shifts the burden of analysis, creating a decisive picture of the true reality, from the conflict resolution practitioner to the people in conflict. The method of gathering information about the conflict context becomes an intervention in itself; people are forced to reflect on their experience in a different way and a network of people is participating in conflict resolution work. As SenseMaker practitioner Graham Day has put it, the SenseMaker data set forms a 'virtual peace table' that parties have bought into by collecting stories from their own people. The assemblage of stories then constitutes a version of reality that forces action. People might disagree on what should be done but cannot disagree that the experiences are real. While a conflict analysis report could easily be dismissed as one person's view, a bank of thousands of stories developed through shared commitment and responsibility cannot be shucked off so easily. Facilitating the SenseMaker process increases the interactions that people have with the stories and allows large numbers of people to come to their own situated understanding.

Abstraction as friend and enemy: Abstraction is an important part of the sensemaking process, both grounding practice through theory and through visualizations of SenseMaker data that represent patterns in and between the signification elements of the SenseMaker framework. Due to the philosophical and theoretical foundations that ground SenseMaker research, it can be easy for peacebuilders to accuse the approach as being too theoretical. This would be an issue if theory of change was to resolve conflicts by ensuring that conflict parties reached consensus on the structural drivers of conflict and the peace theory behind the intervention. While theory grounds practice and should be mastered by a competent SenseMaker practitioner, the sensemaking process relies on using an understanding of complex systems to provide sensible "on-ramps" for any person regardless of their level of knowledge. Although the data visualizations of a SenseMaker triad might seem unduly abstract to an observer, respondents are able to quickly grasp patterns and contextualize them within their own experience. SenseMaker practitioners, especially in conflict settings, must maintain a level of abstraction that 'breaks sense' of the conflict and triggers sensemaking while avoiding abstractions that make the conflict too big to solve. This can be achieved by searching for patterns that represent abstractions like 'capitalism' or 'racism' and reading raw narrative material for context. Thus, the practitioner helps people navigate through different levels of granularity in a comprehensive way without becoming too distant from what is really going on. Dervin's approach to sensemaking from the field of communication can be a helpful lens. A "basic premise of the sensemaking approach: people seek external input (i.e., information) to help them fill the gaps they see in their understanding of their worlds. Based on this thinking, a core element of the sensemaking approach is to ask respondents what questions they had about situations, what understandings they saw themselves as needing, what they needed "to make sense out of, find out, learn, or unconfuse" (Dervin et al, 2003: 204) In other words, by grounding discussions of conflict in specific situations, the practitioner can better identify how an abstract conflict formation affects an individual and localize strategies for change.

Baking in Advocacy: People are more likely to change their minds if they come to a conclusion on their own. Through the process of self-signification and community sensemaking, the SenseMaker practitioner introduces novelty and surprise that disrupts the conflict narratives of participants. An individual's story about the conflict must either adapt to accommodate the meaning of the experiences that are shared or change completely. Although a person might momentarily reject the veracity of a single story, the resulting cognitive dissonance must ultimately be reconciled either through a change of attitude or through action. While the peacebuilder might not know which conclusions a person could come to after interacting with the SenseMaker data, the process makes it more likely that a person will take action on 'reality' as represented in the story data and grapple with truly shared problems. Peacebuilders using SenseMaker must vigorously advocate for integrity of the SenseMaker process while remain agnostic about emergent intervention strategies.

Focusing on the Basics: As Dr. Marc Gopin frequently states in his work on religious conflict resolution, much of the work of peacebuilders is building relationships, making friends, and listening. Gopin says that peacebuilders are often expected to come up with a brilliant solution or multi-faceted intervention strategy, while their true genius lies in basic community building. Therefore, there is often a fundamental misalignment between peacebuilding projects and the peacebuilding work that needs to be done by many actors over a sustained period of time and analysis. For example, peacebuilding activities might be as simple as hosting a dinner with groups from different religious traditions, bringing food to a community under fire, or building a friendship and providing emotional support to an 'enemy' (Gopin, 2009). To reap the benefits of a 'human sensor network' and a large SenseMaker story set, the SenseMaker practitioner must focus on these basics of peacebuilding by building relationships with local communities slowly over time. The practitioner must establish shared values and a 'superordinate goal' with story collection partners that would be the building blocks for any successful and sustainable peacebuilding intervention.

CONCLUSION

This chapter has introduced the theoretical building blocks for utilizing SenseMaker for peacebuilding practice, outlined the overall sensemaking process, and several insights for practice that can be further explored in future research. The field of conflict resolution desperately needs methodological innovations that empower local peacebuilders while also meeting the needs for conflict analysis and evaluation. SenseMaker can potentially be a useful tool in the quest to engage large numbers of people in peacebuilding and expanding the impact projects and programs doing the important work of reducing violence.

References

1. AcademiWales (Director). (2016, July 26). *Dave Snowden—How leaders change culture through small actions* [Video recording]. https://www.youtube.com/watch?v=MsLmjoAp_Dg.

2. Bartels, S. A., Michael, S., Roupetz, S., Garbern, S., Kilzar, L., Bergquist, H., Bakhache, N., Davison, C., & Bunting, A. (2018). Making sense of child, early and forced marriage among Syrian refugee girls: A mixed methods study in Lebanon. *BMJ Global Health,* 3(1), e000509. https://doi.org/10.1136/bmjgh-2017-000509.

3. Coleman, P. T. (2018). Conflict Intelligence and Systemic Wisdom: Meta-Competencies for Engaging Conflict in a Complex, Dynamic World. *Negotiation Journal*, 34(1), 7–35. https://doi.org/10.1111/nejo.12211.

4. Coleman, P. T., 1959-. (2011). *The five percent: Finding solutions to seemingly impossible conflicts (1st ed..).* New York : PublicAffairs.

5. Coning, C. de. (2020, July 25). Insights from Complexity Theory for Peace and Conflict Studies. *Complexity 4 Peace Operations.* https://cedricdeconing.net/2020/07/25/insights-from-complexity-theory-for-peace-and-conflict-studies/.

6. Crocker, C. A., Hampson, F. O., & Aall, P. (2005). Introduction: Mapping the nettle field. *Grasping the Nettle: Analyzing Cases of Intractable Conflict*, 3–30.

7. Dervin, B., Foreman-Wernet, L., & Lauterbach, E. (Eds.). (2003). *Sense-Making Methodology Reader: Selected Writings of Brenda Dervin.* Hampton Pr.

8. *Dynamical Systems Theory in Practice—Advanced Consortium on Cooperation, Conflict, and Complexity (AC4).* (n.d.). Retrieved March 10, 2017, from http://ac4.ei.columbia.edu/research-themes/dst/dynamical-systems-theory-and-practice/.

9. Eggers, K. (2020). *SenseMaker in the Deep South of Thailand SenseMaker Pilot Report.* UNDP.

10. English, M. D., & Sweetman, D. (2017). Critical Conflict Resolution, Systemic Consciousness and Systemic Contractions. *Journal of Mediation & Applied Conflict Analysis*, 4(1), 56–79.

11. Firchow, P. (2018). *Reclaiming Everyday Peace: Local Voices in Measurement and Evaluation After War.* Cambridge University Press.

12. Galtung, J. (2010). *A Theory of Conflict: Overcoming Direct Violence (Vol. 7).* Kolofon Press.

13. Gopin, M. (2009). *To make the earth whole: The art of citizen diplomacy in an age of religious militancy.* Rowman & Littlefield Publishers.

14. Hauss, C. (2015). *Security 2.0: Dealing with Global Wicked Problems.* Rowman & Littlefield Publishers. http://ebookcentral.proquest.com/lib/gmu/detail.action?docID=4085875.

15. Kurtz, C. F. (2014). *Working with Stories in Your Community Or Organization: Participatory Narrative Inquiry* (3rd edition). Kurtz-Fernhout Publishing.

16. Lappin, R. (2009). Peacebuilding and the promise of transdisciplinarity. *International Journal on World Peace*, 69–76.

17. Lopez, S. J. (2013). *Making hope happen: Create the future you want for yourself and others* (1st Atria Books hardcover ed). Atria Books.

18. Ricigliano, R. (2012). *Making Peace Last: A Toolbox for Sustainable Peacebuilding* (1st edition). Routledge.

19. Rubenstein, R. E. (2017). *Resolving Structural Conflict.* New York, NY : Routledge.

20. *SenseMaker® for Monitoring and Evaluation of SGBV Programs.* (n.d.). Elrha. Retrieved October 15, 2017, from http://www.elrha.org/map-location/sensemaker-monitoring-evaluation-sgbv-programs/.

21. Snowden, D. (2010). Naturalizing sensemaking. *Informed by Knowledge: Expert Performance in Complex Situations*, 223–234.

22. Vallacher, R. R., Coleman, P. T., Nowak, A., Bui-Wrzosinska, L., Liebovitch, L., Kugler, K., & (auth.), A. B. (2013). *Attracted to Conflict: Dynamic Foundations of Destructive Social Relations: Dynamic Foundations of Destructive Social Relations* (1st ed.). Springer-Verlag Berlin Heidelberg.

USING MACHINE LEARNING TO SUPPORT SENSE-MAKING AND SENSEMAKER® PRACTICE

DR WENDY ELFORD, PAUL ADER, KEIL EGGERS

ABOUT THE AUTHORS

Dr Wendy Elford is a narratologist passionate about embedding inclusion and lived experience within data-informed design. She brings coherence to design practice blending clean language, machine learning and AI with expertise in SenseMaker. Clients learn how to find broad and deep patterns in text and the stories people tell. Her 2010 PhD study explored 'tomorrow's work' using SenseMaker, introducing human factors professionals to the Cynefin Framework. Wendy partners with leaders, technologists and designers determined to weave values into their thinking and strategy. She aims for collective intelligence and real time data to inform co-design and for decisions to deliver measurable results.

Paul Ader is a principal consultant and director at ThinkClarity – a consultancy he established in 2003. ThinkClarity works with communities, organisations and institutions to inform, nudge and navigate adaptive change in complex situations. This work is based on the use of SenseMaker® and application of the widely cited Cynefin Leaders Framework for Decision Making. Paul is a leading practitioner in the emergent design and use of SenseMaker® to: collect, map and explore the aggregate hopes and fears of different groups of stakeholders; enable the discovery of insights and, in particular, those that are counter-intuitive; co-design small 'safe-to-fail' initiatives to facilitate emergent change; and monitor the impact of these initiatives to allow adaptive management.

See previous chapter for short biography of **Keil Eggers**

Where there is an intention to shift the lived experience of smaller or larger groups of humans to improve life outcomes, it's useful to have quick and practical access to metadata about their story worlds. Why are stories and their shared forms of micronarrative so important? Victor Frankl once wrote that humans are driven to make meaning from their experiences (Frankl, 2004). Humans seem drawn to sharing these life experiences as micronarratives or small 's' stories, what Brene Brown calls "data with a soul" (Brown, 2010). These stories appear to carry potentially valuable detail of sensory aspects of experience, perceptions on the context or setting of the interactions of the story teller within a single story world, interwoven with evidence of the story teller's "voice" (Mellman, 2010). Dave Snowden's belief in the value of micronarrative to support change is part of what inspired the creation of SenseMaker software (Snowden, 2009).

SenseMaker practitioners are constantly refining their methods for capturing, curating and sense-making in collections of micronarrative as the software itself evolves (Van der Merwe et al., 2019). This growing community of practitioners around micronarrative and the use of SenseMaker software might see themselves as learning alongside other practitioners changing how distributed ethnography and rapid qualitative research are carried out. Methods kits or assemblages of methods are now openly promoted in systems science forums (Delia Pembrey-Macnamara, personal communication, 2021). More and more, modelling of complex dynamic systems appears to benefit from new and emerging approaches to multi dimensional scaling (MDS) (Saeed et al., 2018, Blumstein and Kvinge, 2018, Page, 2021) and specifically, machine learning.

The challenge for SenseMaker practitioners may be to utilize emergent machine learning methods in conjunction with SenseMaker data. The aim is to model the system of text to support sense-making, not to displace human sense-making with natural language understanding. Even a small selection of earlier literature on text analytics, machine learning and scaling qualitative data reveals the promise of modelling to support practitioners to make sense of large volumes of text (Weber, 1990, Podolefsky and McCarty, 1983, Papadimitriou et al., 2000, Park, 2008). The field is now vast; highly technical papers reveal recent approaches and applications to experiment with (Crowston et al., 2012, Lynam, 2016, Chakrabarti and Frye, 2017, Stoyanova and Wallace, 2019). We suggest that machine learning can be added to SenseMaker projects without sacrificing what is special about naturalistic sense-making.

Features in suitably configured text modelling software will support three key principles in working with anthrocomplexity (1) focussing on fine-grained text data in nature; (2) leverage through distributed cognition: and (3) disintermediation. We also believe that this application of artificial intelligence will become increasingly important with large and varied data sets where practitioners or their clients/partners want to track changes in stories and how people make sense of their world over time. It will also assist when practitioners have configured their enquiry to compare and contrast data collected through SenseMaker with contextual data from other sources – for example, demographics, topography, political discourse, options appraisal, risk management and performance metrics.

SenseMaker practitioners might expect that narrative capture will support improved dynamics within complex systems and help to track what is changing and how. As the situation and people's behaviour coevolve in potentially unexpected ways, the capacity of the SenseMaker framework to understand and keep pace with the system can be challenged.

In our view, a repository of stories where meaning is interpreted at source through the addition of signified layers of meaning is still not enough to support sense-making that integrates the full variety of possible contexts into intervention design and evaluation at scale and over time (Rogers et al., 2019, Datta and Petticrew, 2013). We see this gap as currently being filled by individual members of the community of practice working with SenseMaker projects as they use a variety of processes including sense-making workshops, bespoke approaches to pattern recognition, and sophisticated statistical analysis (Deprez et al., 2012, Omoding et al., 2020, Mager et al., 2018, Carvalhaes et al., 2021).

As each participant's unique story worlds take in new and changing sensory and perceptual experiences of an often-changing context, the potential for variety within the story repository should build. This challenge is starting to be addressed in an area of enquiry called 'big qual' (Brower et al., 2019). Coping with greater volumes and more variety in the story-set is an expectation of the SenseMaker practitioner's role. They must also support the bid for the project and ensure that SenseMaker is framed correctly, manage co-design of the framework, support formal and ad hoc sense-making, apply analytics, and often report on the projects (Van der Merwe et al., 2019). Successful projects rely on individuals and small teams of practitioners to weave together many disparate strands of activity and sustain energy in what is, itself, a complex undertaking; these practitioners also rely on a deep understanding of what the project is intending to accomplish. However, there are foreseeable limits to practitioner performance because, when individuals and groups are sense-making with large data sets, it can become cognitively and emotionally taxing to move from open exploration of patterns to more focused interpretation of what these patterns might mean. This is the case even when interpretation, referred to by some practitioners as second or third order sense-making, is distributed through participatory activities. Combining SenseMaker with new technology such as machine learning, sometimes known as artificial intelligence, can help designers, sense-makers and analysts as it can provide a flexible, efficient and effective means to view and model the lexical concepts within hundreds or thousands of signified micronarratives while retaining the power of self-signification.

We suggest that text modelling - made possible by recent advances in machine learning - can make the detail in the increasing volumes and variety held within a SenseMaker project more accessible. Selecting fit-for-purpose text modelling software does require some knowledge of computational linguistics and within that field, we believe not all approaches are appropriate for this application. There are several starting points from which to explore early work contributing to today's text modelling (Weber, 1990, Manning and Schütze, 1999) with serial authors and innovators Jurafsky and Martin synthesising over 20 years of work in this field in An Introduction to Natural Language Processing, Computational Linguistics, and Speech Recognition (Jurafsky and Martin, 2020). To follow trends the reader might explore topics like word embeddings (Schnabel et al., 2015, Karlgren and Kanerva, 2018, Österlund et al., 2015, Mikolov et al., 2013, Goldberg and Levy, 2014) and more recent work on natural language understanding (Devlin et al., 2018); for a thorough review of the field of distributional semantics see Boleda (Boleda, 2020). Researchers are even discussing the potential of quantum NLP (Meichanetzidis, 2020). What we rely on in selecting a single software package to illustrate the potential of machine learning of SenseMaker data is the already established body of literature on the use of Leximancer for systematic reviews and cross validation of qualitative data (Haynes et al., 2019, Lemon and Hayes, 2020, Harwood et al., 2015). Open source software for text modelling based on R and Python programming languages are also options for practitioners willing to learn, apply and refine the necessary skills.

Curating hundreds or thousands of interpreted stories creates powerful metadata. The signification of each story at source provides a measure of face validity and structure not present in expert signification making the raw text in such story sets potentially more valuable. Interpretation of patterns in this data can support decision makers designing what Dave Snowden calls 'safe to fail' experiments based on the key axiom that those involved want 'more stories like these and fewer stories like those' (Snowden, 2016). To act on Snowden's axiom requires at least some of the stories to be brought into focus. We propose that currently within a SenseMaker project, the rich detail found in the corpus of text is largely untapped as a resource.

Once an individual micronarrative is signified, there might be a sense that the interpreter would rely on the signified meaning rather than still attempt to interpret the words that comprise the text. The actual text may, in many, or perhaps most micronarratives, involve deletions, distortions and generalisations. We believe that with signified micronarrative we can still use words in the 'utterance' as a source of meaning, that the words within an instance of micronarrative still carry a sense of the individual and unique context in which the text was created. Multiple micronarratives can then scale the number and variety of word concepts available in the larger narrative 'system' of say, a cohort within SenseMaker. Text modelling using machine learning is a means to create and monitor lexical patterns in these word concepts – elements of micronarrative across a larger corpus of micronarratives. We propose that these text models can then give an alternative perspective on multiple micronarratives which can provide input to the design and implementation of initiatives, to assess impact and for reviewing and adapting the SenseMaker framework over time.

We have used Leximancer software (Smith and Humphreys, 2006) to carry out text modelling for the Our Tomorrows project led by the Centre for Public and Partnership Research (CPPR) based at the University of Kansas (University of Kansas Center for Public Partnerships & Research); see Elford and Eggers (2021). The Our Tomorrows project aims to improve life outcomes for Kansans over time by focusing on support for families with children under five. The intent is that this work will enable these families to move from surviving to thriving largely through reducing the number of adverse childhood experiences that have such a debilitating effect on life chances (Metzler, 2017). The project has been collecting SenseMaker data since 2019 and now has over 5,000 narratives from across Kansas. This data is being used by communities and groups across Kansas to identify, implement and monitor the impact of small 'safe to fail' projects referred to as 'actionables'.

Leximancer allows bespoke processing of large volumes of unstructured and structured text in multiple languages and formats including the types of .csv files exported from SenseMaker. This software returns statistical outputs and metadata centred on visual concept maps (Erwin and Pollari, 2013, Tufte et al., 1998, Knaflic, 2015) derived from the underlying frequency and co-occurrence matrices of concepts based on groups of related words. The key feature of the software for the use described here is that it includes signification values in the way it clusters concepts and, by doing so, builds on the aggregate patterns provided by SenseMaker. By providing easy to use functionality to zoom in and zoom out of the concept maps – and to see these at different levels of granularity – Leximancer provides further support for disintermediation. Evidence from initial training of practitioners at CPPR and elsewhere shows that the ability to see specific areas of the concept map in the context of a greater whole helps avoid premature convergence, retrospective coherence and pattern entrainment.

Early results also show how this additional form of metadata can support sense-making workshops by decreasing the level of abstraction that comes from relying on clusters of dots placed on signifiers coupled with the explanatory power of selected stories. It has been noted that participants in the workshops experimented with using concepts on the maps to write new meta-narratives as part of their sense-making process. In short, we suggest that text modelling might facilitate and strengthen exaptation by allowing word concepts and themes within the current story set to be repurposed in a new context, and by keeping the audience engaged and curious about the outcomes of their own experiments.

The initial work we carried out for CPPR is illustrated below. This is one of many visuals and is provided only as an exemplar. In this example, the whole corpus of stories is processed as an abridged .csv file to develop a text model in Leximancer. This model was developed using the results from two triads (one is shown), two sets of stones data (childcare assistance and cash assistance, either government or self-acquired), and eight other MCQs including sentiment, income earned and region. To get a best fit for the count and co-occurrence concepts, Leximancer applies a stochastic learning process to develop the concept map.

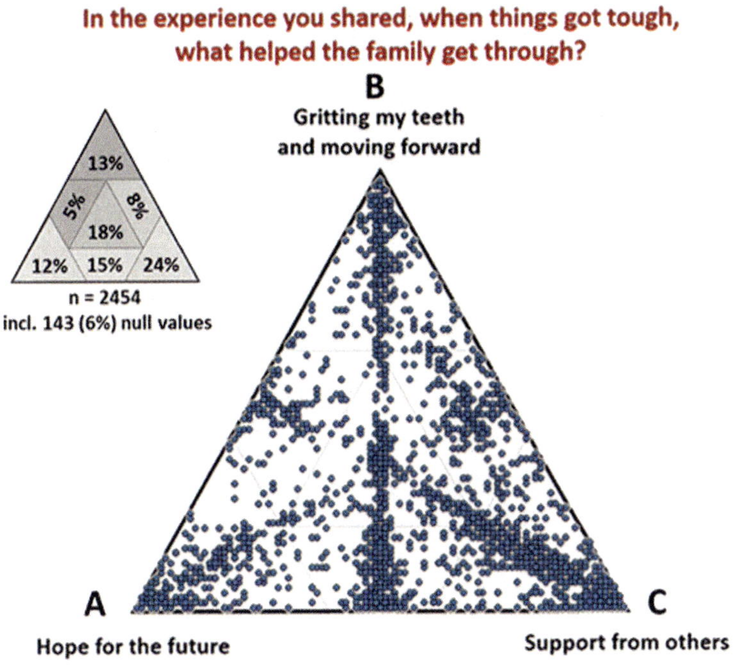

Figure 1a shows the triad "when things got tough"

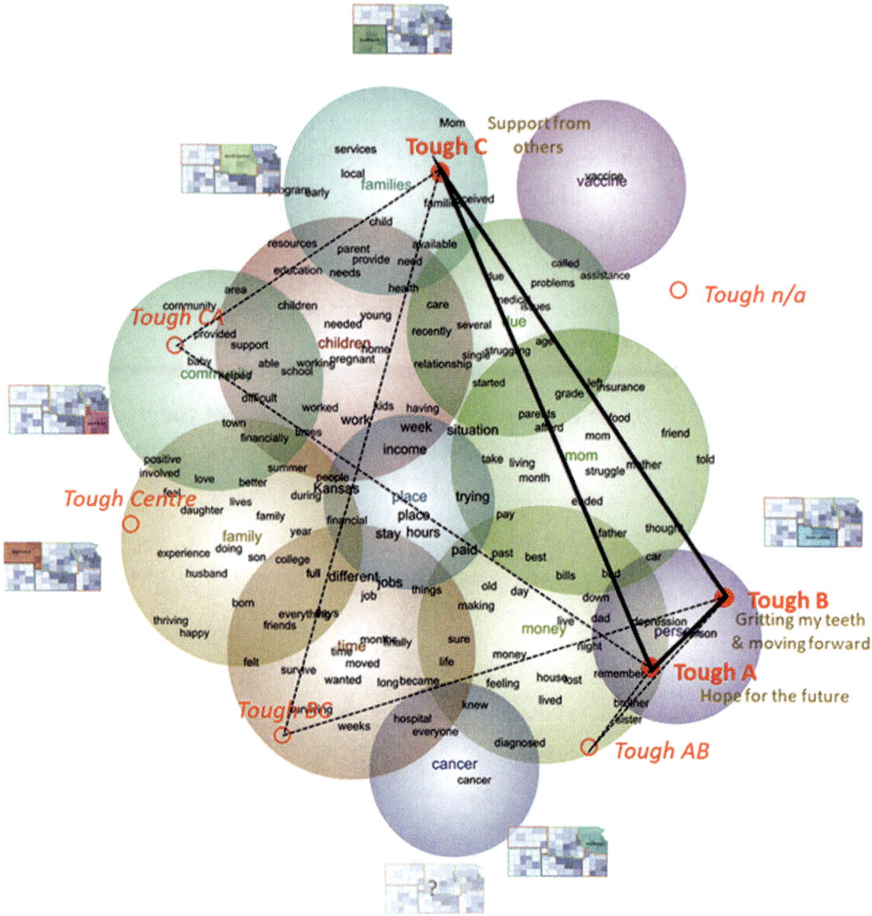

1

Figure 1b shows a text model of the entire corpus with 12 question types including 2 triads. The bubbles show themes, small black text concepts and the red lables the points of the "tough" triad. Solid black lines mark out the apices of the triad and light black lines mark the relative positions of the halfway points on this triad. Concepts on the right of this map are more associated with negative sentiment, and those on the left with positive sentiment. Small maps show where the model places the content of stories from 6 regions, a seventh show where the region of the story was not shared.

The 'tough' triad (Figure 1a) shows that people found support and a mix of support and hope to help them get through the situation. The less often signified midpoint between gritting teeth/support was potentially more relevant as a transition towards thriving on the left hand side of the map than was midway between hope/gritting teeth. On viewing a triad, discerning the influence of multiple factors represented by multichoice questions on region, sentiment or income in this triad is challenging. Practitioners may use colour variations, small multiples or statistics. The concept map on the right supports the conclusion from the triad that the signifier 'support' is indeed relevant as a concept. One insight that the triad does not show but text modelling does reveal is that there is a clear overlap in the word concepts present in the text the signifiers hope and gritting teeth and that the halfway point between them, AB, also has similar content. This region would be a powerful place to look for stories to dampen this part of the larger system.

What stands out is that on the left side of the concept map there are two points – CA and BC on the more positive side of the map. We find these are two useful potential locations on the concept map which link to stories that could be amplified. We also note that at the top of the map the tag for the signifier support is equidistant from positive and negative sentiment. This could be explored as a transition point to more positive stories on the left side of the concept map. We also note that the centre of the triad is located on the left-hand side of the concept map, close to where positive stories are centred.

Alternative narratives, not described here, can be created around the position of midpoint BC close to the theme of time and related concept job and perhaps importantly jobs as a plural. Might having more than one job be related to time and what could that imply for nudges towards "more stories like these, fewer stories like those?". The distribution of word concepts on a concept map appear to provide the elements for participants to reimagine story data, to socialise and stress test their thinking on different options.

APPLICATION AREAS

The example described above relates to the first of four application areas that we are continuing to explore in collaboration with CPPR. The first three of these areas are outlined below and the last one signposted for further development.

1: Supporting a foraging and sensemaking process.

Interviews with several highly experienced SenseMaker practitioners suggest that the individual and participatory work they carry out to analyse, explore and interpret SenseMaker data includes a recursive process of opening and closing learning loops. This is like a double/triple diamond design process that 'works through' different representations of the metadata and finely grained data in a similar way to that described in the framework put forward in Pirolli and Card's paper on using technology to leverage tasks involving significant components of sense-making by an analyst (Pirolli and Card, 2005). This process both broadens and deepens the practitioners' exposure to outputs from the SenseMaker project.

Extending SenseMaker to include text modelling follows the same recursive approach and can help practitioners and their partners and clients find coherent patterns in larger groups of micronarratives than those that can be accessed through story packs. This is discussed further in Elford and Eggers (Elford and Eggers, 2021) which describes the interplay of work with micro, meso and macro levels of the system.

2: Knowledge design and support for ongoing SenseMaker codesign

There are a number of activities in this application area that are of interest. These include the use of text modelling to:

- design or refine the signification framework for a SenseMaker project. Text modelling can act as both a trigger and guide for change. The different levels and detail in the text models can provide new materials to adjust anchors/labels for important signifiers so that these are relevant and remain viable for the evolving context.

- use the nascent lexical patterns identified within visualisations of the full corpus of stories from SenseMaker.
- note a gradual change in language use or identify the need for polymorphic signifiers as evident based on the text models for different cohorts of respondents.
- carry out AB testing of responses captured with different frameworks to help decide which is providing more useful patterns and insights.
- navigate the larger system of narrative to explore at a more abstract level, looking for enabling constraints within the system which may not be evident in smaller cohorts of stories.

3: Adding insight to responses to time critical questions on specific themes in the narrative data.

In the Our Tomorrows project, SenseMaker practitioners reported that project partners frequently ask for specific data, say on the number of respondents that mentioned a particular topic in their narratives. While this is not the primary purpose of SenseMaker, it is one way to make sense of qualitative data and a response needs to be provided quickly and without demur. However, the response should ideally be accompanied by nuanced interpretation and insight to provide additional context and trigger different thinking. Concept-maps based on the text modelling described earlier can provide this context by enabling rapid construction of relevant meta-narratives based on the location of, and connections between, concepts related to the requested topic. Since these concept maps include the scaffolding provided by signification they can also bridge back to the 'more like this' function provided by the new Analytic Workbench available with SenseMaker. Taken together these methods can give decision-makers the data they require while at the same time nudging them towards a more complex appreciation of the system.

4: Developing a system of systems approach to designing solutions and tracking outcomes.

One of the key areas of development in the SenseMaker community is to enable continuous rather than periodic capture of signified narratives and to encourage the use of patterns in the data to inform and monitor the impact of safe to fail initiatives. This endeavour requires SenseMaker, extended as proposed here by the use of text modelling, to be part of a whole system or system of systems approach that encompasses the work and priorities of many different actors over potentially quite extended time frames (Indulska et al., 2012, Van Hemelrijck and Goh, 2015). This approach supports monitoring for emergence in larger systems. It may be most effective where the overall design connects narrative experience-based data with more structured data on decisions and activities to also allow successful safe-to-fail initiatives to be scaled, institutionalised and open to further exploration without loss of flexibility.

CONCLUSION

There appears to be increasing willingness, even a sense of urgency, to deal with complex issues at multiple levels of systems; the awareness of and applications for SenseMaker software appear to be increasing. Sense-making and analytics are key activities in working with outputs from this software in collaborative efforts to nudge and navigate change. We have highlighted the opportunity to use machine learning and specifically text modelling in an assembly of methods as a means of leveraging the many minds available, not just the practitioner's, to make finding 'more stories like these, fewer like those' feasible and more successful in the long term. The affordances and value of this assembly of methods will become clearer as decision-makers continue to move from seeking to avoid or minimise complexity to recognising the need for continuous and deliberate engagement with complexity. This move will lead to a significant increase in the scope and scale of sense-making and the workload of and challenges faced by sense-making practitioners. In continuing to explore the application of this assembly of methods, we are mindful of the need to focus on demonstrating its clear and practical value for decision-makers. At the same time, there is further work to do to test and confirm the underpinning theory, streamline interoperability between the different software tools and ensure that SenseMaker practitioners are able to add this skillset to their practice. We encourage readers who are experienced SenseMaker practitioners and who are interested in learning how they can use this new approach to join our work.

References

1. Blumstein, M. & Kvinge, H. (2018). Letting symmetry guide visualization: Multidimensional scaling on groups. *arXiv preprint arXiv:1812.03362.*

2. Boleda, G. (2020)We . *Distributional semantics and linguistic theory. Annual Review of Linguistics*, 6, 213-234.

3. Brower, R. L., Jones, T. B., Osborne-Lampkin, L. T., Hu, S. & Park-Gaghan, T. J. (2019). Big Qual: Defining and Debating Qualitative Inquiry for Large Data Sets. *International Journal of Qualitative Methods,* 18, 1609406919880692.

4. BROWN, B. (2010). *The power of vulnerability* [Online]. Available: https://www.ted.com/talks/brene_brown_on_vulnerability#t-3442 (accessed 5 May 2021).

5. Carvalhaes, T., Rinaldi, V., Goh, Z., Azad, S., Uribe, J., Chester, A. & Ghandehari, M. (2021). Integrating Spatial and Ethnographic Methods for Resilience Research: A Thick Mapping Approach for Hurricane Maria in Puerto Rico. *Available at SSRN 3863657.*

6. Chakrabarti, P. & Frye, M. (2017). A mixed-methods framework for analyzing text data. Integrating computational techniques with qualitative methods in demography. *Demographic Research*, 37, 1351-1382.

7. Crowston, K., Allen, E. E. & Heckman, R. (2012). Using natural language processing technology for qualitative data analysis. *International Journal of Social Research Methodology*, 15, 523-543.

8. Datta, J. & Petticrew, M. (2013). *Challenges to evaluating complex interventions: a content analysis of published papers.* BMC Public Health, 13, 568.

9. Deprez, S., Huyghe, C. & Van Gool Maldonado, C. (2012). *Using sensemaker to measure, learn and communicate about smallholder farmer inclusion* [Online]. Available: https://ttdr.net/wp-content/uploads/2020/09/VECO-2012-Small-farmer-case-study.pdf (accessed 5 May 2021).

10. Devlin, J., Chang, M.-W., Lee, K. & Toutanova, K. (2018). Bert: Pre-training of deep bidirectional transformers for language understanding. *arXiv preprint arXiv:1810.04805.*

11. Elford, W., & Eggers, K. (2021). Scaling micronarrative with machine learning to model human and environmental wellbeing in macro, meso and micro systems. In N. Black, W. P. Neumann, & I. Noy (Eds.), *Proceedings of the 21st Congress of the International Ergonomics Association* (IEA 2021). Springer, Cham.

12. Erwin, K. I. M. & Pollari, T. (2013). Small packages for Big (qualitative) Data. *Ethnographic Praxis in Industry Conference Proceedings*, 2013, 44-61.

13. Frankl, V. E. (2004). *Man's search for meaning: The classic tribute to hope from the Holocaust*, New York, Random House.

14. Goldberg, Y. & Levy, O. (2014). word2vec Explained: deriving Mikolov et al.'s negative-sampling word-embedding method. *arXiv preprint arXiv:1402.3722.*

15. Harwood, I. A., Gapp, R. & Stewart, H. (2015). Cross-check for completeness: exploring a novel use of Leximancer in a Grounded Theory study. *The Qualitative Report*, 20, 1029-1045.

16. Haynes, E., Garside, R., Green, J., Kelly, M. P., Thomas, J. & Guell, C. (2019). Semiautomated text analytics for qualitative data synthesis. *Research Synthesis Methods*, 10, 452-464.

17. Indulska, M., Hovorka, D. S. & Recker, J. (2012). Quantitative approaches to content analysis: identifying conceptual drift across publication outlets. *European Journal of Information Systems*, 21, 49-69.

18. Jurafsky, D. & Martin, J. H. (2020). *An Introduction to Natural Language Processing, Computational Linguistics, and Speech Recognition,* Uttar Pradesh, Pearson.

19. Karlgren, J., & Kanerva, P. (2018). Hyperdimensional utterance spaces. In O. Alonso & G. Silvello (Eds.), *DESIRES 2018* (pp. 29-35). CEUR-WS.

20. Knaflic, C. N. (2015). *Storytelling with data: A data visualization guide for business professionals*, Hoboken, John Wiley & Sons.

21. Lemon, L. L. & Hayes, J. (2020). Enhancing Trustworthiness of Qualitative Findings: Using Leximancer for Qualitative Data Analysis Triangulation. *The Qualitative Report*, 25, 604-614.

22. Lynam, T. (2016). Exploring social representations of adapting to climate change using topic modeling and Bayesian networks. *Ecology and Society*, 21.

23. Mager, F., Smith, B. & Guijt, I. (2018). *How Decent is Decent Work? Using SenseMaker to understand workers' experiences* [Online]. Oxfam. Available: http://hdl.handle.net/10546/620476 (accessed 5 May 2021).

24. Manning, C. & Schütze, H. (1999). *Foundations of statistical natural language processing,* Cambridge, Massachusetts, MIT Press.

25. Meichanetzidis, K. (2020). *Quantum natural language processing* [Online]. Medium. Available: https://medium.com/cambridge-quantum-computing/quantum-natural-language-processing-748d6f27b31d (accessed 7 Jul 2021).

26. Mellman, K. (2010). Voice and perception: An evolutionary approach to the basic functions of narrative. In: Aldama, F. L., Aldama, A. J. & Hogan, P. C. (eds.) *Towards a cognitive theory of narrative acts* Austin: University of Texas.

27. Mikolov, T., Yih, W.-T., & Zweig, G. (2013). Linguistic regularities in continuous space word representations. In *Proceedings of the 2013 Conference of the North American Chapter of the Association for Computational Linguistics: Human Language Technologies* (pp. 746-751).

28. Omoding, J., Walters, G., Andama, E., Carvalho, S., Colomer, J., Cracco, M., Eilu, G., Kiyingi, G., Kumar, C., Langoya, C. D., Nakangu Bugembe, B., Reinhard, F. & Schelle, C. (2020). Analysing and Applying Stakeholder Perceptions to Improve Protected Area Governance in Ugandan Conservation Landscapes. *Land,* 9, 207.

29. Österlund, A., Ödling, D., & Sahlgren, M. (2015). Factorization of latent variables in distributional semantic models. In *Proceedings of the 2015 Conference on Empirical Methods in Natural Language Processing* (pp. 227-231).

30. Page, S. E. (2021). *The model thinker: What you need to know to make data work for you,* New York, Basic Books.

31. Papadimitriou, C. H., Raghavan, P., Tamaki, H. & Vempala, S. (2000). Latent Semantic Indexing: A Probabilistic Analysis. *Journal of Computer and System Sciences,* 61, 217-235.

32. Park, J. (2008). Topic maps, dashboards and sensemaking. In: Maicher, L. & Garshol, L. (eds.) *Fourth International Conference on Topic Maps Research and Applications,* TMRA 2008. Leipzig, Germany.

33. Pirolli, P. & Card, S. (2005). The sensemaking process and leverage points for analyst technology as identified through cognitive task analysis. Available: http://vadl.cc.gatech.edu/documents/2__card-sensemaking.pdf (accessed 5 May 2021).

34. Podolefsky, A. & Mccarty, C. (1983). Topical sorting: A technique for computer assisted qualitative data analysis. *American Anthropologist,* 85, 886-890.

35. Rogers, L., De Brún, A. & Mcauliffe, E. (2019). Assessing the impact of context during the implementation of a codesigned, collective leadership intervention. *International Journal of Integrated Care* (IJIC), 19, 1-2.

36. Saeed, N., Nam, H., Haq, M. I. U. & Saqib, D. B. M. (2018). A Survey on Multidimensional Scaling. *ACM Comput. Surv., 51,* Article 47.

37. Schnabel, T., Labutov, I., Mimno, D., & Joachims, T. (2015). Evaluation methods for unsupervised word embeddings. In *Proceedings of the 2015 Conference on Empirical Methods in Natural Language Processing* (pp. 298-307)

38. Smith, A. E., & Humphreys, M. S. (2006). *Evaluation of unsupervised semantic mapping of natural language with Leximancer concept mapping. Behavior Research Methods*, 38(2), 262-279. https://doi.org/10.3758/BF03192712

39. Snowden, D. (2009). *Introducing SenseMaker* [Video]. YouTube. https://www.youtube.com/watch?v=SkRe7Xg7pk4 (accessed 5 May 2021).

40. Snowden, D. (2016). *How leaders change culture through small actions. In Proceedings of the Summer School* (pp. 21–26). AcademiWales. Cardiff, UK.

41. Stoyanova, L., & Wallace, W. (2019). *Topic modelling, sentiment analysis and classification of short-form text: Purchases, customer journey of Insurance.* Master of Science Thesis, University of Strathclyde.

42. Tufte, E. R., McKay, S. R., Christian, W., & Matey, J. R. (1998). *Visual explanations: Images and quantities, evidence and narrative.* American Institute of Physics.

43. University of Kansas Center for Public Partnerships & Research. (2021). *Our Tomorrows* [Online]. https://ourtomorrows.kucppr.org/ (accessed 12 May 2021).

44. Van der Merwe, S. E., Biggs, R., Preiser, R., Cunningham, C., Snowden, D. J., O'Brien, K., Jenal, M., Vosloo, M., Blignaut, S., & Goh, Z. (2019). Making sense of complexity: *Using SenseMaker as a research tool.* Systems, 7(1), 25. https://doi.org/10.3390/systems7010025

45. Van Hemelrijck, A., & Goh, Z. (2015). *Methodological reflections on the use of SenseMaker® for impact M&E of adaptation in the Mekong Delta (AMD)* [Online]. https://static1.squarespace.com/static/5be90a21e7494039a4941b51/t/5bfbcb7903ce64e76c3463cb/1543228283446/Methodological+Reflections+on+SenseMaker+for+IM%26E+in+AMD-18May2016+copy.pdf (accessed 22 Jul 2021).

46. Weber, R. P. (1990). *Basic content analysis.* Sage.1

OUR TOMORROWS - A CASE STUDY TO EXPLORE FAMILY THRIVING AND SURVIVING

DR JACQUELINE COUNTS AND DR REBECCA GILLAM
ILLUSTRATED BY: SARA O'KEEFE

ABOUT THE AUTHORS

Jacqueline Counts, MSW, PhD, is the director of the University of Kansas Center for Public Partnerships & Research, a nonprofit research institution that provides research and evaluation and other program assistance to organizations working to optimize the well-being of children, youth, families, and communities. As co-founder of KU-CPPR's Our Tomorrows and as a recognized leader in the field of social services,she applies her expertise in systems evaluation with strategic foresight and the Cynefin framework to advance community-based research into action. Counts is a partner to local communities, state agencies, and other sector leaders, and brings together a collective agenda to re-envision social services to strengthen families and secure their futures. She is the founder of Kansas Future Fellows, which aims to spread civic foresight and foster imagination and decision making for future generations. She believes that complexity research and narrative plays a huge role in this work and giving communities the tools they need to take action.

Rebecca Gillam, MSW, PhD, has over 20 years of experience working in the often complex spaces of social service and public health. She has worked at the national, state, and local levels to build community, improve public health, and increase well-being. Her social work background includes direct service, program administration, evaluation, and leadership. Dr. Gillam has designed and conducted qualitative, quantitative, and mixed methods evaluations to support ongoing quality improvements in systems, program design, and service delivery. She spent five years using SenseMaker® as an approach to inform decision making and promote collaborative change by engaging unique perspective across communities. Dr. Gillam currently serves as the Associate Director of the Home and Community-Based Services Portfolio at the West Virginia University Health Affairs Institute, and is the co-founder of Hopeward Consulting, LLC.

This case study is a retrospective look at the ups and downs of a project, and the typical challenges that are faced when rolling out an ongoing capture framework at the state-wide scale. Through three reflection sessions, our internal graphic recorder documented the collective experiences of thirteen staff members who worked on Our Tomorrows during various stages. The sessions consisted of open-ended discussions with minimal facilitation, and the conversations were visually captured to create an illustrated overview of Our Tomorrows to date. Reflection is a key and often under-utilised element of our work; the opportunity to pause and reflect was useful in recognising progress, identifying lessons learned about the process, and celebrating the successes of an idea that was sparked by a Google search years ago. Here, we share three takeaways from the reflection sessions that inform and shape our overall approach: 1) embracing complexity; 2) maintaining momentum; and, 3) getting to impact.

As is often the case with complexity, our journey with Our Tomorrows – a sensemaking initiative – has been a circuitous one. We learned about SenseMaker and the Cynefin Framework in 2015 through some choice Googling by one of our staff members. We were attracted to the transformative potential of the method and the tool for going deeper than traditional evaluations and including diverse voices to inform policy decisions.

The 'we' in this case study is the Center for Public Partnerships and Research at the University of Kansas. With over 70 staff and a cadre of consulting partners, we have been working towards finding solutions to complex problems since 2013. To optimise the wellbeing of children, youth, and families, the Center partners with communities and organisations to create a happy and healthy world where families thrive. The Center's multidisciplinary team bridges research and practice with a social justice lens, advancing policy and practice agendas to meet the needs of children and families.

After a few pilot programs with SenseMaker, we launched Our Tomorrows 1.0 in 2018 to explore how families understand and experience thriving and surviving. In response to the pandemic, we launched a revised framework in 2020 to capture how COVID was affecting Kansans. By April 2021, and over the two frameworks, we had collected over five thousand stories, facilitated 25 sensemaking sessions and supported over 70 safe-to-fail experiments.

Over 15 Center staff were trained by Cognitive Edge in 2015 and the team was highly engaged in learning. Yet, we struggled to translate the theory into practice, continuously defaulting to known methodologies. We spent considerable time convincing staff and partners that the approach, despite being different, had value. We created a visual to help explain the steps of the work (Figure 1), but over time realised that the linear process does not capture the ups and downs that staff experienced trying to implement a new approach, understand what it meant, share findings, and honour the narratives that individuals in Kansas shared with us.

Figure 1: The hypothetical process for Our Tomorrows

EMBRACING COMPLEXITY

Building buy-in from stakeholders is critical at all stages. It takes time for the community to engage, own, and invest in the work. We spent the first couple of years convincing people that the method had promise and distinguishing how the method was a value-add, not a replacement for traditional strategies.

Once the stories started to come in, staff began to feel a new weight of responsibility for the work. Now that we had these experiences and insights, there was a sense of urgency to act. The stories were powerful, and there was an impetus to move into sense-making and safe-to-fail interventions (action labs) in response. Staff at times struggled with this heavy lift, but ultimately learned that the best place to start is somewhere. There are no "right" choices or absolutes in this process. The Our Tomorrows' team found success in leveraging strong partnerships to just get started.

Figure 2. Embracing the Complexity (Reflection Session 1) Lessons learned: Slow down, take time to build trust, and establish relationships with partners.

MAINTAINING MOMENTUM

Collecting stories requires a dedicated strategy. Posting a link and waiting for stories did not work. Recruitment takes focused and ongoing effort. We needed story collectors on the ground making personal invitations; a coordinated social media approach; and, program partners who could champion the work and capture stories from both family and provider perspectives. We created a process for onboarding citizen journalists and community partners. As a part of a university, we had to navigate options for offering incentives while maintaining the integrity of the process and accumulating enough stories in specific regions to have the volume needed for meaningful sense-making.

Momentum was maintained through a combination of story collection and workshop engagement strategies. Stakeholders could not commit eight hours to reviewing stories and making sense of the data. We had to reduce the cognitive load and shortcut the process for participants to review and sort stories and give data back in a way that breadcrumbed a different way of receiving, understanding, and using narratives. There were ongoing demands to provide stories as testimony to prove a point, not to understand patterns. Advocacy organisations have requested stories that back their positions; state agencies have asked for positive stories that show successes and what is working well. We were in constant continuous quality improvement mode and had to view and shape our work as a series of safe-to-fail actions rather than developing checklists or roadmaps. We had to continuously affirm that the process was as easy as it sounded - they could try out ideas without a lengthy application process and justification of the evidence base.

Our Tomorrows had to add value on multiple levels, while also maintaining integrity of the method. We were often asked for stories about a specific topic to demonstrate that a particular intervention worked. We stressed the patterns, but emergent pattern reports were cumbersome to prepare and not digestible in the short amount of time stakeholders had. Stakeholders also wanted to see the outputs of the work, not just the stories and patterns, so we mapped story counts by county and launched a "Zero Zeroes" campaign as a friendly competition to have your county represented.

Our Tomorrows 2.0 was implemented with a COVID module in April 2020, and the stories became more reflective of the present - more personal, more specific. The race protests after the killing of George Floyd heightened ethical concerns to ensure that individuals of historically underserved communities were both heard and protected. We employed double-authentication of stories, removed personally identifiable information, and explored additional ways to gather stories from poorly engaged communities and build agency.

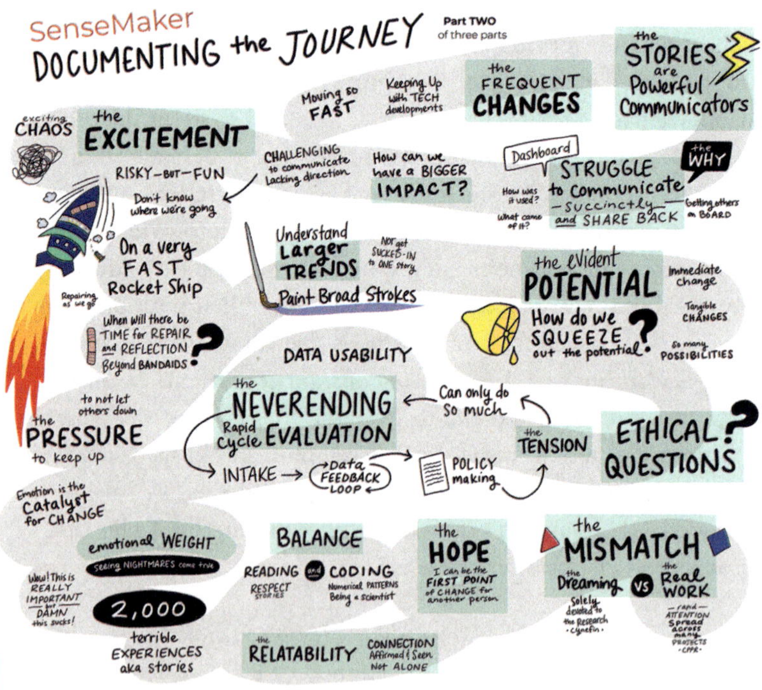

Figure 3: Maintaining Momentum (Reflection Session 2) – Lesson Learned: Commit to an iterative cycle, let go of your ego, and be prepared to improvise in the moment.

GETTING TO IMPACT

Our team reflected that Our Tomorrows is like bamboo. It was carefully planted in one area and then began to pop up and grow fast in other areas. There is a need to harness a diverse team of talents – relationship builders, project coordinators, data engineers, complexity practitioners, communicators, and researchers – to expand the networks and partnerships in coordinated and sustainable ways.

Years into the work, Our Tomorrow is still evolving. We still struggle with ethical issues, providing sensemaking experiences that are engaging and patterns and stories that are meaningful and promote thinking and conversation. The process has required a high level of adaptability and challenged the team to grow along with it.

It takes a lot of smart, committed staff to contain the growth and manage emergence. To date, we have relied on a network of internal staff (both part and full time) and consultants to deliver. There is a need to continuously build capacity to keep up with the pace of the work.

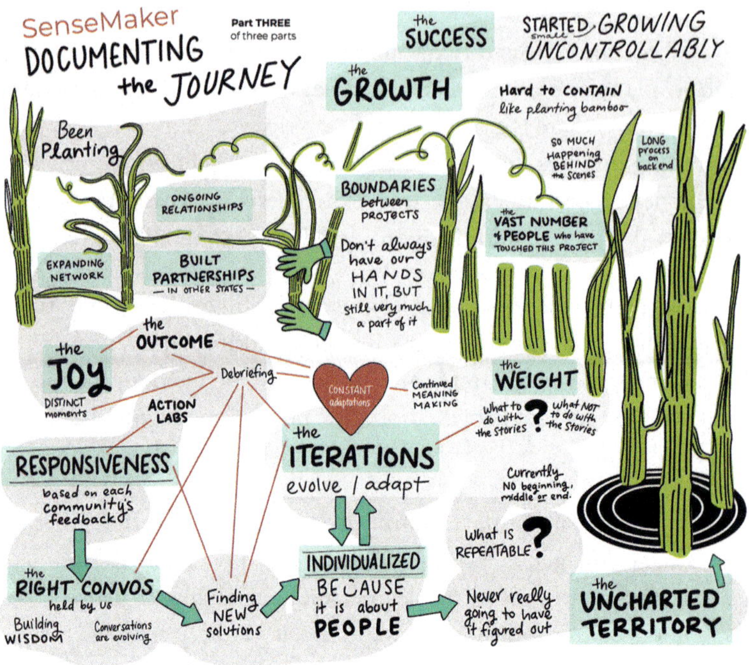

Figure 4: Getting to Impact (Reflection Session 3) – Lessons Learned: Plan for a long-term investment of resources in staff to build capacity and support the emotional rollercoaster of running a large-scale complexity project.

SenseMaker is not software that is plug and play and is not for those who want immediate results or a linear process to follow. It takes time, financial resources, emotional investment, and strong leaders who see the vision and can maintain constraints for the project and staff to flourish.

Despite the tremendous growth, buy in, and investments in Our Tomorrows, we are still working toward long-lasting impact. The ongoing story bank of lived experience has unlimited potential to shape decision-making. We feel the responsibility to get data back to the communities in timely and meaningful ways and to provide support to those who typically lack the agency and authority to inform decisions. This is no easy task and requires constant assessment of practices and tools to determine what needs to be continued and what needs further evolution and adaptation.

While complexity is not a new concept, the adoption of tools and practices that harness the power of complexity is just getting started. Recognition of the Cynefin framework in the Equitable Evaluation Framework™ and the Observatory of Public Sector Innovation's case study of Our Tomorrows suggest that the work is gaining momentum. Particularly now, governments, communities, and individuals across the globe are determining who they want to be post-pandemic. Now is the time to embrace the complexity, build and maintain momentum, and grow impact using tools like SenseMaker and Our Tomorrows to imagine and shape systems where children and families can flourish.

GROUP SINGING AS HEALTHY PUBLIC

DR DAVE CAMLIN

ABOUT THE AUTHOR

Dr Dave Camlin's musical practice spans performance, composition, teaching, socially-engaged music practice and research. A singer / song-writer by trade, his practice is motivated by the idea of music making as a creative resource for fostering kinship and living more sustainably, as a potent form of civic imagination. His research explores the relationship between aesthetic and participatory traditions of music making, and highlights how the implicit tensions within these contrasting perspectives can be resolved through a foregrounding of their 'paramusical' benefits and effects. His research focuses on group singing, music health and wellbeing, musician education, music and virtuality and Community Music (CM). He has pioneered the use of SenseMaker® as a method for research into cultural phenomena.

I came to Cynefin through some chance encounters made with Dr Petia Sice at Northumbria University when I was working at Sage Gateshead. We developed a methodology using SenseMaker® for use on an AHRC-funded project with the University of York in 2018, and I've more recently used it as the key method on research led by the International Centre for Community Music into the motivations of the organisers of Ethno music camps - an international musical residential opportunity for young people from all over the globe.

In summer 2018, I and a group of musician / researcher / outdoor professional colleagues took choirs of 50-60 singers at a time to sing on mountain summits in the Lake District, UK, recording their performances using virtual reality (VR) technology to make the experience more accessible to those unable to climb mountains. We used SenseMaker to collect the experiences of those involved and compared them with the experiences of singers involved in regular weekly singing. We published the findings of our research as an article in the Springer Nature journal *Humanities and Social Sciences Communications* in 2020 (Camlin, Daffern and Zeserson, 2020). SenseMaker enabled us to derive much clearer insights into people's experiences than we feel we would have achieved through more traditional research methods, highlighting subtleties of experience which proved to be very important in developing a more sophisticated understanding of the cultural phenomenon of group singing. Our approach was broadly phenomenological, in the sense of trying to understand the complexity of experience of group singing "in terms of the meaning it has for the subject" (Gallagher and Zahavi, 2012: 7), and to use SenseMaker to read across those multiple individual narratives to draw out any essential or invariant characteristics of the experience.

A significant body of evidence points to the positive health and wellbeing benefits associated with group singing (Skingley and Bungay, 2010; Clift, 2013; Fancourt et al., 2016; Dingle et al., 2019) which have broad appeal to a wide public (Eno, 2008; Burkeman, 2015), with associated benefits especially in relation to mental health recovery (Clift and Morrison, 2011; Coulton et al., 2015; Clift, Manship and Stephens, 2017; Dingle et al., 2017; Shakespeare and Whieldon, 2017; Williams, Dingle and Clift, 2018). In this study, we were looking to understand the meaning that people attach to their experience of group singing, especially as it relates to supporting or maintaining positive mental and physical health and wellbeing, drawing on notions of 'healthy public' found in the emerging literature around Health Humanities (Crawford et al., 2015; Hinchliffe et al., 2018). To do this we chose to compare the experiences of singers involved in an innovative outdoor singing project with the experiences of those involved in regular weekly singing, expecting to find that the experience of singing outdoors would strengthen participants' connection to a sense of place through the communal act of singing together. The Fellowship of Hill and Wind and Sunshine was a partnership with the National Trust and University of York, supported by funding from Arts Council England and the UK's Arts and Humanities Research Council (AHRC). (National Trust, no date) The project won the National Trust's Outstanding Achievement award 2019, and also Cumbria Culture's Best Partnership project 2019.

As a practitioner-researcher and the musician leading the project, SenseMaker was a clear choice to help mediate some of the bias that is inevitably present in "close-to-practice" (BERA, no date) research, collecting the stories of participants and their interpretation of meaning that it would have been hard for me to do in person without compromising the resulting data. We used SenseMaker to collect (n=78) stories from singers in the Fellowship project as soon after each event as possible. Similarly, over a period of about six months we collected (n=89) stories from singers in regular weekly singing, especially after a public performance or other significant singing event.

What we found was unexpected, in particular that the "communitas" (Turner, 2012) effect of group singing prevails even where we had expected it to be overshadowed by the experience of surrounding natural beauty. In the stories that participants shared of their experiences it appeared to be more the other way round, with the outdoor surroundings amplifying the profound interpersonal experience of group singing, with one commenting, "somehow it was the mountains that were reverberating with us, if you see what I mean, rather than an audience". If we had used other methods e.g. interviews, questionnaires to test our assumption that singing outdoors would help people connect more to a sense of place, we suspect that we would probably have confirmed that assumption, because we would have been analysing unidimensional concepts. What SenseMaker enabled respondents to do was to attach relative significance to their experiences, developing a more nuanced understanding of the meaning of those experiences. In this instance, in the polymorphic triad of [me; my people; my place] respondents in both populations attached more significance to the dimension of [my people]. It is this feature of SenseMaker as a method that we feel has particular significance for cultural research, directly countering more instrumentalised or reductionist approaches.

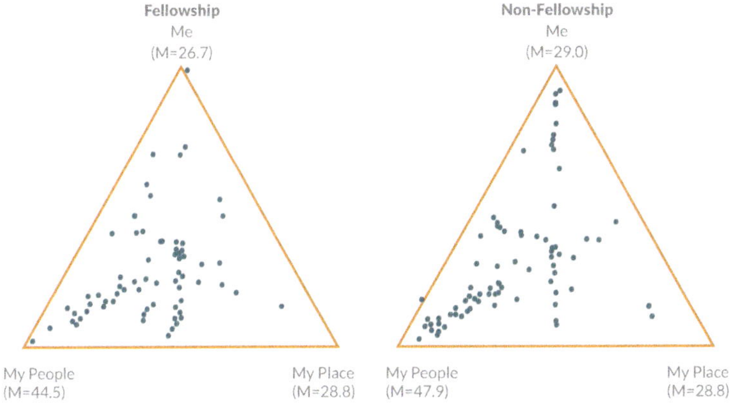

Fig. 1 – Belonging Triad

Similarly, while we expected that the Fellowship singers would attribute greater significance to the considerable physical exertion required to participate in the mountain singing project, their self-signification against complementary physical, spiritual and emotional dimensions of the activity pointed strongly toward the spiritual (e.g. "I felt my precious sense of self drifting away on a wave of harmony") and the emotional (e.g. "As I struggle to find meaning to my life following the death of my [spouse] the chance to sing with the Fellowship has given me purpose."). There was little difference in the geometric data between the Fellowship participants and the regular weekly singers in this regard. While the physical demands of participation were considerable, these were played down in respondents' minds as "the price that's been paid forward for the experience" (SenseMaker fragment).

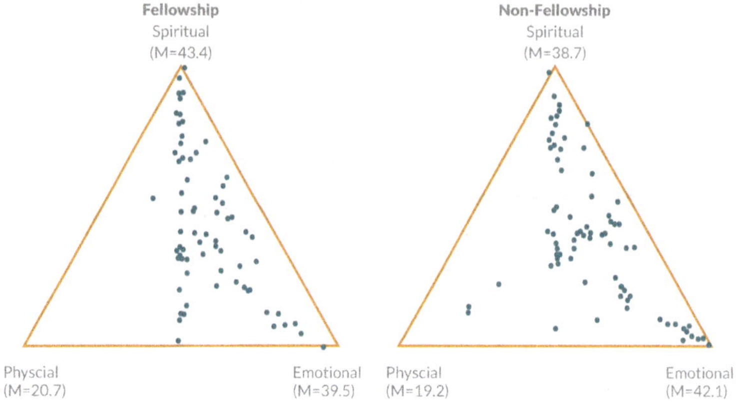

Fig. 2 – Experience Triad

The geometric data around a third triad considering the relative significance of aesthetic, participatory and paramusical dimensions of the experience further validated the notion that the paramusical dimension of music making i.e. the wellbeing effects which go along with group singing (and music making more generally) arise from an activation of complementary dimensions of musical experience - the performance of musical works (aesthetic dimension) on the one hand balanced with the performance of human relationships (participatory dimension) through the act of making music on the other (Elliott, 1995; Small, 1998).

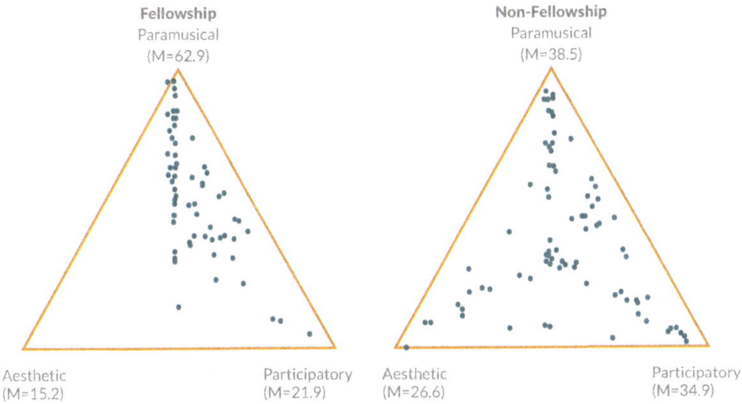

Fig. 3 – Value Triad

The findings also enabled us to suggest that music is an *adaptive complex* underpinned by multiple psychological, social, neurobiological, neurohormonal and musical mechanisms which are inter-dependent, challenging more reductionist notions of how music achieves its affect. Further investigation of the findings through focus group interviews with participants also enabled us to suggest that music making might provide the conditions of "safe danger" for people to negotiate the intimacy of human relationship in a more controlled way through the experience of music making. Being faced with complex visual and written SenseMaker data relating to their experiences in a 'theming' workshop, the focus group participants were required to reflect more deeply on those experiences, leading to more sophisticated insights into those experiences.

Interestingly, in order to get the article into the journal Nature, we had to remove all references to both phenomenology and ethnography, as different peer reviewers found the kind of qualiquant approach represented by SenseMaker problematic. Claims to be an emic approach when using pre-determined categories for data analysis in the self-signification phase were perceived to compromise both a phenomenological and an ethnographic methodology. While this surprised us, it also highlighted the epistemological challenges of having heterodox research methods accepted within more orthodox academic discourse; there is certainly more work to do to position SenseMaker as a valid method for phenomenological ethnographic research.

Preserving the integrity of people's individual accounts of their experiences, while facilitating their subsequent interpretation of those experiences through conceptual frameworks derived from the literature remains a thorny and contested epistemological process. However, as an approach, SenseMaker holds considerable promise for wider research into cultural experience, effectively addressing the call to look at "the actual experience of culture and the arts rather than the ancillary effects of this experience" (Crossick and Kaszynska, 2016, p. 21). As a 'qualiquant' method it facilitates an understanding which is grounded in participant experience yet able to identify trends and patterns of experience beyond that of the individual, potentially leading to a more general understanding. While this approach may face some epistemological challenges in terms of how it positions itself within more established traditions of phenomenological and ethnographic research, its potential is considerable, highlighting the complex and interdependent ways in which cultural experiences are meaningful for participants.

References

1. BERA (no date) *BERA Statement on Close-to-Practice Research.* Available at: https://www.bera.ac.uk/publication/bera-statement-on-close-to-practice-research (accessed 22 Feb 2020).
2. Burkeman, O. (2015) 'Want to be happy? Join a choir', *The Guardian,* 18 December. Available at: http://www.theguardian.com/lifeandstyle/2015/dec/18/why-singing-makes-people-happy-oliver-burkeman?CMP=share_btn_fb (accessed 20 Dec 2015).
3. Camlin, D. A., Daffern, H. and Zeserson, K. (2020) 'Group singing as a resource for the development of a healthy public: a study of adult group singing', *Humanities and Social Sciences Communications*, 7(1), pp. 1–15. doi: 10.1057/s41599-020-00549-0.
4. Clift, S. (2013) 'Singing, Wellbeing and Health', in *Music, Health and Wellbeing.* Oxford, UK: Oxford University Press.

5. Clift, S., Manship, S. and Stephens, L. (2017) 'Further evidence that singing fosters mental health and wellbeing: Findings from the West Kent and Medway project', *Social Inclusion and Mental Health*, 21(1), pp. 53–62.

6. Clift, S. and Morrison, I. (2011) 'Group Singing fosters mental health and wellbeing: findings from the East Kent "singing for health" network project', *Mental Health and Social Inclusion*, 15(2), pp. 88–97. doi: 10.1108/20428301111140930.

7. Coulton, S. et al. (2015) 'Effectiveness and cost-effectiveness of community singing on mental health-related quality of life of older people: randomised controlled trial', *British Journal of Psychiatry*, 207(3), pp. 250–255. doi: 10.1192/bjp.bp.113.129908.

8. Crawford, P. et al. (2015) *Health Humanities. 2015* ed. edition. London ; New York: Palgrave Macmillan.

9. Crossick, G. and Kaszynska, P. (2016) *Understanding the Value of Arts and Culture: The AHRC Cultural Value Report*. Swindon, UK: Arts & Humanities Research Council. Available at: http://www.ahrc.ac.uk/documents/publications/cultural-value-project-final-report/.

10. Dingle, G. et al. (2017) 'Choir singing and creative writing enhance emotion regulation in adults with chronic mental health conditions', *British Journal of Clinical Psychology*, 56(4), pp. 443–457. doi: https://doi.org/10.1111/bjc.12149.

11. Dingle, G. et al. (2019) 'An Agenda for Best Practice Research on Group Singing, Health, and Well-Being', *Music and Science*, 2, pp. 1–15. doi: 10.1177/2059204319861719.

12. Elliott, D. J. (1995) *Music Matters: A New Philosophy of Music Education*. New York / Oxford: OUP USA.

13. Eno, B. (2008) *Singing: The Key To A Long Life*, NPR.org. Available at: http://www.npr.org/templates/story/story.php?storyId=97320958 (accessed 10 Apr 2014).

14. Fancourt, D. et al. (2016) *'Singing modulates mood, stress, cortisol, cytokine and neuropeptide activity in cancer patients and carers'*, ecancer, 10(631). doi: 10.3332/ecancer.2016.631.

15. Gallagher, S. and Zahavi, D. (2012) *The Phenomenological Mind*. 2nd edition. London ; New York: Routledge.

16. Hinchliffe, S. et al. (2018) *'Healthy publics: enabling cultures and environments for health'*, Palgrave Communications, 4(1), p. 57. doi: 10.1057/s41599-018-0113-9.

17. National Trust (no date) *Songs on the Summits 1918-2018*, National Trust. Available at: https://www.nationaltrust.org.uk/borrowdale-and-derwent-water/features/songs-on-the-summits-1918-2018 (accessed 14 Mar 2018).

18. Shakespeare, T. and Whieldon, A. (2017) *Sing Your Heart Out: community singing as part of mental health recovery*. Norfolk: University of East Anglia. Available at: https://ueaeprints.uea.ac.uk/65446/1/Accepted_manuscript.pdf.

19. Skingley, A. and Bungay, H. (2010) 'The Silver Song Club Project: singing to promote the health of older people', *British Journal of Community Nursing*, 15(3), pp. 135–140. doi: 10.12968/bjcn.2010.15.3.46902.

20. Small, C. (1998) Musicking: *The Meanings of Performing and Listening*. Middletown, CT: Wesleyan University Press.

21. Turner, E. (2012) Communitas: *The Anthropology of Collective Joy*. New York: Palgrave Macmillan.

22. Williams, E., Dingle, G. A. and Clift, S. (2018) 'A systematic review of mental health and wellbeing outcomes of group singing for adults with a mental health condition', *European Journal of Public Health*, 28(6), pp. 1035–1042. doi: 10.1093/eurpub/cky115.

ASPIRATIONS AS COMPLEMENTARY ENTRY POINTS FOR RURAL DEVELOPMENT

DR KAI MAUSCH AND
DR DAVE HARRIS

ABOUT THE AUTHORS

Kai Mausch is Senior Economist at the Center for International Forestry Research - World Agroforestry (CIFOR-ICRAF). He joined in 2018 after having worked for more than 8 years at ICRISAT in Malawi and Kenya. Kai has over 15 years of experience in working on rural development from the agricultural and the non-agricultural perspective. Currently focusing on household aspirations to improve the understanding of how these can be better supported through projects. His extensive work on the understanding of technology adoption and barriers along the process is feeding valuable insights into the broader aspirational perspective. While the majority of his work is located in Eastern Africa, his projects also cover other African regions as well as Asia, Latin America and Europe.

Dave Harris has spent more than 40 years working to improve the livelihoods of resource-poor farmers in developing countries, initially for DFID in India, Botswana and Saint Lucia, then at Bangor University, UK, and most recently for the International Crops Research Institute for the Semi-Arid Tropics in Kenya and the World Agroforestry Centre. He is currently an Honorary Lecturer at Bangor University and a Senior Research Associate with CIFOR-ICRAF. Originally a developer of improved farming technologies, since 2012 Dave has been trying to better understand the limitations on making a decent living from a small farm and the drivers of rural smallholder households' attempts to increase their incomes and wellbeing. Recent work has highlighted the complex ways in which society interacts with individuals and groups to form aspirations and expectations. This interaction has important consequences for sustainable development as smallholder rural households juggle on-farm and off-farm opportunities and their aspirations influence the relative degree of enthusiasm and commitment to each.

INTRODUCTION – THE CHALLENGE IN AGRICULTURE FOR DEVELOPMENT

Despite decades of rural development programs, rural poverty is still one of the biggest challenges throughout Africa. With most rural households being involved with farming, agricultural technology development and promotion have been the most common entry points for raising rural incomes. More recently, increased concern about the production of sufficient amounts of food for the growing populations in countries facing food security challenges has further increased the focus on enhancing agricultural production. Advances in technology development have been made and a recent study found that investments by the CGIAR (a global agricultural research partnership) have generated a 10:1 return (Alston et al, 2020).

However, these investments and benefits have not been sufficient to meet the challenges as improved technologies tend not to reach the poorest households. Similarly, Nature (2020) in their editorial on CERES 2030 emphasize that food system investments in general do not address smallholder issues. One likely reason is that the livelihoods of rural smallholder households in developing countries are diverse and rarely rely solely on farming (see Figure 1).

With increasing reliance on income sources other than from farming, particularly for small farms (Harris, 2019), investment decisions are complex and involve trade-offs between multiple livelihood activities. Earlier research found that not all those who farm may want to be farmers (Verkaart et al. 2018). It has been argued that peoples' aspirations are likely to play an important role in decisions to invest time, money and effort (Mausch et al. 2018). Standard methods do not facilitate understanding of these complex, intangible concepts.

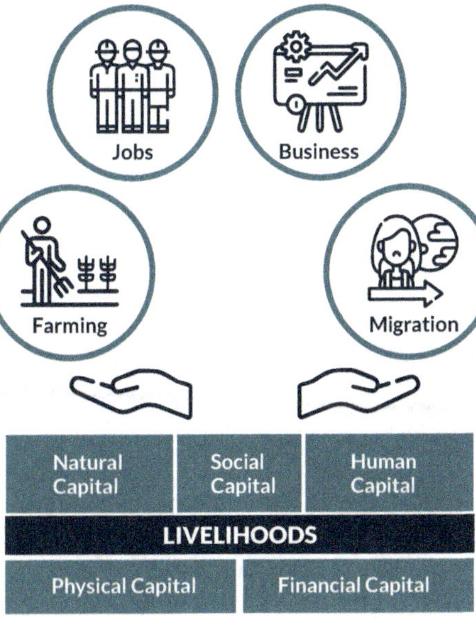

Figure 1: Rural Households tend to juggle mixed livelihoods

WHAT WE WERE TRYING TO UNDERSTAND USING SENSEMAKER

The income composition of rural smallholder households is highly complex and changes over time. Often, which of the multiple income sources is the main driver of behaviour and which, if any, are supplemental is unclear. With agriculture as our main interest, this begs the question: what types of technology are people looking for to fulfil their farming needs? If they aspire to make a living from agriculture but have to supplement this with other businesses or wage income, they are more likely to look for high-value, profitable options that would allow them to upgrade their farming and perhaps phase out supplementary incomes - Dorward et al. (2009) dubbed this 'stepping up'. Other households may see farming as a safety net while they are trying to establish their futures outside agriculture –in Dorward et al's (2009) concept "stepping out" of agriculture. These people would more likely be looking for technologies that require little investment and effort so that they can focus on their aspirations outside farming. These dynamics and the trade-offs involved are complex. Triads were an interesting tool to ask directly about underlying trade-offs between different influences and drivers of future visions. Aspirations are shaped by preferences, but people's "opportunity window" further influences them and moderates their decisions. The opportunity window is a combination of physical realities that affect farming potential and market access and social dynamics such as gender, age or norms that frame desirable lifestyles (see figure 2).

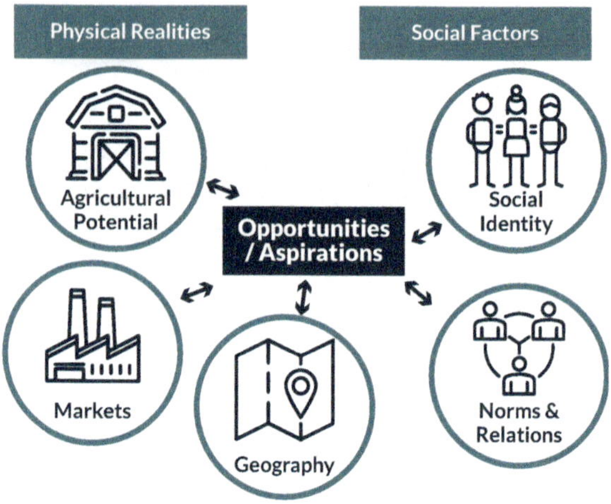

Figure 2: Opportunities and aspirations moderated by the opportunity window

Both aspirations and the opportunity window will implicitly affect life choices. However, these concepts are not normally directly verbalised or explicitly considered when making decisions. This adds further complexity when researchers attempt to understand them.

Direct questioning often biases results when respondents, consciously or unconsciously, try to 'game' the situation, perhaps hoping for benefits such as free fertilizer or seed if they provide answers that they believe the researchers desire. Attempts to use choice experiments have also highlighted that concepts such as aspirations or livelihood strategies are too abstract and can't be specified concretely enough to allow their application (Mangham et al. 2009). Stories or short narratives, in response to a neutral, open prompting question, appeared to be more appropriate for identifying underlying sentiments without biasing the results towards researcher interest, in this case agriculture.

WHAT WE FOUND

The results of this work with SenseMaker were published in a Special Issue of the European Journal of Development Research (*Rural aspirations in Africa – livelihood decisions and rural development trajectories*). The papers in that Special Issue used a variety of methods and tools, representing different disciplinary approaches. The overview (Mausch, Harris and Revilla Diez, 2021) highlights the different potential entry points for eliciting aspirations that can take a "bottom up" or "top down" form. It is not only target groups who have aspirations; other development actors (including governments and civil society institutions) also have visions for change in their target regions and aspirations for their futures.

Mausch et al. (2021), using the SenseMaker approach, focused specifically on aspirations and their influence on income portfolios across three sites differing in their agricultural potential and in the range of available off-farm opportunities in rural Kenya. Their analysis highlights the importance of the perceived opportunity space in the formation of aspirations. Here, the pursuit of aspirations is often hindered by immediate needs. When, for example, school fees have to be paid or the family has to be fed, the pursuit of new endeavours can be restricted by inherent risks. Yet within regions with apparently similar opportunities and personal preconditions, great heterogeneity of aspirations exists and highlights that aspirations are affected by more than just current realities. In particular, the notion that rural households that are engaged in farming are, by default, receptive to new agricultural technologies is being challenged here. In response to the prompt "Imagine your life in 10 years' time, tell a story about how you got to that point from this present day", only 65% of the respondents shared narratives involving agriculture.

Within the same population, La Rue et al. (2021) shed light on the sub-group of young people and their general interest in farming futures. Their work emphasises that standard approaches often fail to capture the prevalence, and importance, of mixed livelihoods. Using open prompts revealed that the tendency of the young to look for opportunities outside agriculture does not imply their complete abandonment of farming. Their rural roots appear relatively strong and urban migration is less attractive than has often been argued. Offering young people diverse options within rural areas would, in many cases, support their aspirations.

Urban migration currently implies an imbalance as there are social restrictions on who can pursue this opportunity. As Crossland et al. (2021) show using focus group discussions to deepen SenseMaker generated insights for a sample from Makueni county in Kenya, women face social norms that tie them to the rural areas whereas many men migrate to urban areas to supplement household incomes. This, however, results in women increasingly becoming *de facto* farm managers with greater freedom to make their own farming decisions and pursue their own aspirations within that (externally restricted) opportunity space. This increased agency of women also translates into greater confidence in reaching their aspired futures. Their views and ideas are, therefore, becoming more important for the design and roll out of agricultural support systems.

The implications of actors' aspirations for the effectiveness of extension services are the focus of Dilley et al. (2021). After analysing the farming aspirations of residents of Meru county in Kenya, extension workers and private sector technology providers were interviewed to understand if, and how, aspirations feature in their approaches. Extension agents appear cognisant of externally-designed development programs that do not account for local aspirations. Their daily work in turn is made more difficult as farmers' requirements are not met. The more explicit incorporation of these local voices in future project design and focus could significantly improve extension outcomes. Tools such as SenseMaker could support this design process to ensure stakeholder representation and a more explicit focus on heterogeneity.

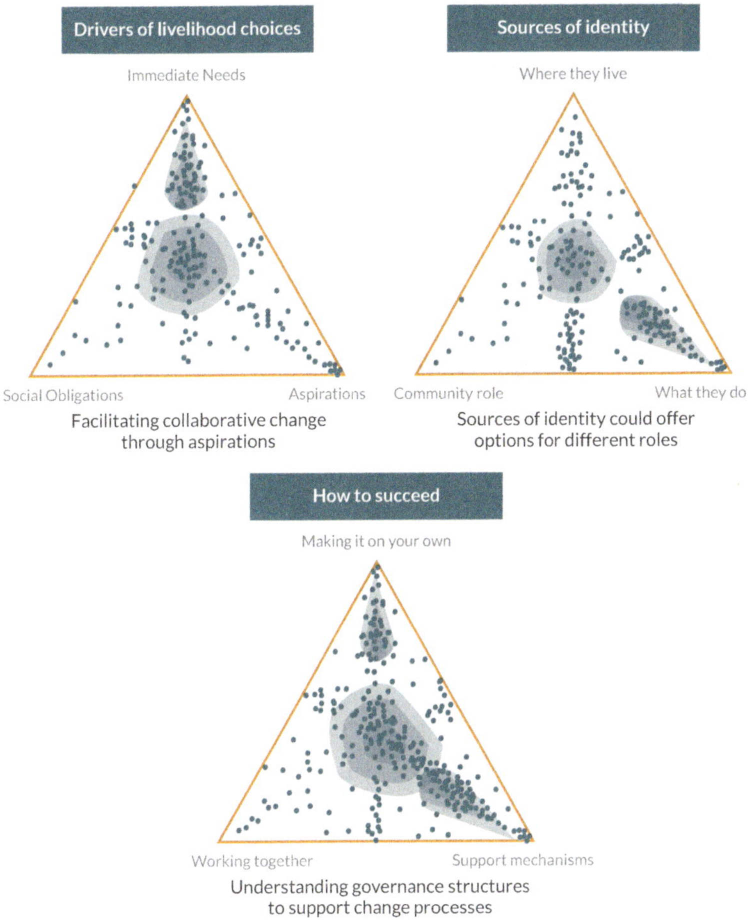

Figure 3: Entry points for development planning.

For this to be successful, projects may need to rethink their definition of success and acknowledge that any agricultural solutions will only serve some rural people while others demand different products. Furthermore, there is a need to investigate the dynamics of aspirations as they are deeply embedded in local realities and may well also vary across different times of the year (e.g., pre- and post- harvest) and between years. Identifying and engaging with aspirations could provide a better understanding of the drivers that matter to those who farm. Wider development planning could benefit from the incorporation of aspiration-based considerations (see Figure 3 for examples).

SENSEMAKER AS A TOOL IN THIS CASE

The publication of our results alongside other studies using different approaches offers insights on the niche SenseMaker occupies and how its combination with other methods provides an even richer picture. New approaches to targeting interventions could emerge and any inhibiting factors identified could be addressed to broaden opportunities and aspirations and support their achievement.

SenseMaker is one tool for using narratives as a diagnostic option and it has the advantage that it can be implemented regularly at large scale and with relatively low cost per interview. In the context of our interest in rural development, we think that its emphasis on probing an individual's motives and behaviours is well suited to the study of intra-household dynamics. Previous studies, including our own, have made the standard assumption that the household is the decision-making unit, something that we no longer believe to be the case. Properly designed and implemented it is able to reduce researcher bias, minimise gaming and provide new viewpoints on topics. On their own, however, SenseMaker results do not appear to be sufficiently actionable for most people and should be combined with other survey methods to provide the broad data required for planning.

References

1. Alston, J.M., Pardey, P.G and Rao, X (2020), *The payoff to investing in CGIAR research*, Report commissioned by the Supporters of Agricultural Research (SoAR) Foundation. https://supportagresearch.org/assets/pdf/Payoff_to_Investing_in_CGIAR_Research_final_October_2020.pdf

2. Nature (2020), *To end hunger, science must change its focus*. Nature, 586, 336 https://doi.org/10.1038/d41586-020-02849-6.

3. Crossland, M., Paez Valencia, A.M., Pagella, T., Mausch, K., Harris, D, and Winoweicki, L. (2021), Women's Changing Aspirations Amid Male Outmigration. Insights from Rural Kenya, *European Journal of Development Research*, 33-4, 910-932. https://doi.org/ 10.1057/s41287-021-00362-8.

4. Dilley, L., Mausch, K., Crossland, M. and Harris, D. (2021), What's the story on agriculture? Using narratives to understand farming households' aspirations in Meru, Kenya, *European Journal of Development Research*, 33-5, 1091-1114. https://doi.org/10.1057/s41287-021-00361-9.

5. Dorward, A., S. Anderson, Y.N. Bernal, E.S. Vera, J. Rushton, J. Pattison, and R. Paz. (2009), Hanging in, stepping up and stepping out: Livelihood aspirations and strategies of the poor. *Development in Practice* 19 (2): 240–247.

6. Harris, D. (2019), Intensification Benefit Index: How Much Can Rural Households Benefit From Agricultural Intensification? *Experimental Agriculture* 55: 273–287.

7. LaRue, K., Mausch, K., Daum, T. and Harris, D. (2021), Making Sense of Intergenerational Aspirations in Agrarian Households and their Implications for Technology Adoption: Evidence from Kenya, *European Journal of Development Research*, 33-4, 885-909. https://doi.org/10.1057/s41287-020-00352-2.

8. Mangham, L.J., Hanson, K. and McPake, B. (2009), How to do (or not to do) … *Designing a discrete choice experiment for application in a low-income country, Health Policy and Planning*, Volume 24, Issue 2, March 2009, Pages 151–158, https://doi.org/10.1093/heapol/czn047.

9. Mausch, K., Harris, D., Dilley, L., Crossland, M., Pagella, T., Yim, J. and Jones, E. (2021), Not all about farming: capturing aspirations is a challenge to assumptions about rural development, *European Journal of Development Research*, 33-4, 861-884. https://doi.org/10.1057/s41287-021-00398-w.

10. Mausch, K., Harris, D. and Revilla Diez, J. (2021), Rural aspiration in Africa – Reflections for development planning and design. *European Journal of Development Research*, 33-4, 795-808. https://doi.org/10.1057/s41287-021-00407-y.

11. Mausch, K., Harris, D., Heather, E., Jones, E., Yim, J. and Hauser, M. (2018), Households' aspirations for rural development through agriculture. *Outlook on Agriculture,* 47(2), pp108-115. https://doi.org/10.1177/0030727018766940.

12. Verkaart, S., Mausch, K. and Harris, D. (2018), Who are those people we call farmers? Aspirations and realities in Kenya, *Development in Practice* 28(4), pp. 468-479. https://doi.org/10.1080/09614524.2018.1446909.

Printed in Great Britain
by Amazon

62007422R00117

THE GOD WHO SEES YOU

A JOURNEY THROUGH BIBLICAL STORIES OF HOPE AND UNDERSTANDING

GEORGIE TENNANT

To Rachael!
God bless you in your
walk with Him!
Love
Georgie
x

kevin
mayhew

First Published in 2023 by Kevin Mayhew Ltd,
Fengate Farm,
Rattlesden,
Bury St Edmunds,
Suffolk, IP30 0SZ

ISBN (paperback): 9781838581572
ISBN (eBook): 9781838581589
Paperback product code: 1501730
eBook product code: 1501731

ENDORSEMENTS

This is a beautifully written devotional which fed me, heart, mind and soul. With a range of reflections, biblical examples and key questions, Georgie Tennant gently challenges the overlooked and unnoticed, to trust in the God who sees. And who doesn't feel like this at times?

There are thirty readings, prayer prompts and song suggestions, but these can be used flexibly without the need to read daily for one month. The writing style is informal, lyrical and totally chimes with the theme, as Georgie's wise words bring clarity and insight. She uses the stories of both well and lesser-known bible characters such as Hagar, Joseph, Asaph and Bezalel to show how God lifts the lonely, surprises the sad and comforts the careworn, making us feel loved and seen.

With testimonies from the author's own life and

examples of her exquisite poetry, this devotional, while appealing to the well versed, is emotionally as well as intellectually satisfying. Georgie's devotional writing is that rare thing, a comfort and a challenge, emotional and thoughtful. It satisfies on so many different levels.

I would heartily recommend this wise and lovely book. It will inspire you to know that you are loved, you are seen. It will remind you that '...each seed of goodness that we sow, in our jobs, our caring roles, our experiences of poetry and art, our family lives, the grace-filled, ordinary conversations we have, is seen and valued by God.'
I will be reading this devotional again and cannot commend it to you more highly.

- Deborah Jenkins - author of "Braver"

Join Georgie Tennant as she gracefully digs into Scripture and reveals the God who sees us and loves us. Bringing to life stories and key passages from the Old Testament and the New, she leads us in a thirty-day journey to the heart of God. With her as a guide we find ourselves encouraged and strengthened in our faith in God.

- Amy Boucher Pye - author of "Transforming Love" and "7 Ways to Pray"

"In 'The God Who Sees You' Georgie Tennant leads us through a gentle and assuring journey into the way God sees every part of us; not only the parts we present to the world, but all that we are, all we hide behind our daily masks and all those parts of us we yearn so much to be really seen.

With 30 reflections on people and situations in Scripture - from Old Testament giants of faith with all their flaws through to impetuous Peter and the broken woman at the well - we are reminded of how God actually saw them in their very depths, and then worked in their hearts.

These reflections give us great hope and encouragement, knowing that God sees us in all our situations and doesn't expect perfection.

Georgie writes with clarity and beauty, sharing snippets of profound poetry, thoughts for further reflection and ideas for prayer, but she also writes with the authority and empathy of one who has suffered, and one who is not afraid to explore struggles with matters of faith. Upbuilding, refreshing, sustaining and real, I will come back to these reflections again and again, and I warmly recommend them."

- Liz Carter - poet and author of "Catching Contentment" and "Valuable"

"For any Christian who isn't constantly riding on the crest of a faith-wave (hint: that's all of us), Georgie's devotional is balm to the soul. Tracing the stories of well-known and lesser-known characters from the start of the Bible to the end, she reminds us at every turn that we have a God who sees us - in all our weakness, fears and failures. Scarcely a page went by without me gaining some fresh insight into a familiar Bible story from Georgie's beautiful, faithful writing. A spiritual gem to return to whenever we're feeling invisible or insignificant: for this is the God who sees."

- Lucy Rycroft

I love The God Who Sees You - it takes the reader through 30 reflections, providing background information to the passages chosen, as well as personal reflection questions to ponder. I particularly enjoyed the unique addition of suggested songs to listen to, which provided another dimension I hadn't experienced before with a devotional. For anyone who has felt unseen or unloved, this book reveals the heart of God for us all and gently encourages us to look at how he interacted with a variety of biblical characters. I appreciated the inclusion of lesser known figures, as well as the honesty about the messiness of life in Georgie's writing.

- Claire Musters - writer, editor, speaker and host of the Woman Alive book club.

CONTENTS

INTRODUCTION

God refers to Himself (and is referred to) by many titles in the Bible, each one encapsulating something of His character. One title that speaks to me the most is in Genesis 16 – the story of Hagar. In the story, things have gone horribly wrong for Hagar and she flees to the desert, feeling hopeless and alone. There, the angel of the Lord speaks to her, giving her a promise and hope for her future. Hagar, *"…named the Lord who spoke to her, 'You are El-roi,'"* – the God Who Sees.

For the first time in her life, Hagar felt seen. Not just looked at, but noticed and deeply understood. When we see someone – really see them – we offer them a place to be themselves, to be real about their struggles and to receive companionship for the journey.

Too often, we feel unseen and that can make us feel alone, unloved, isolated, misunderstood. At the beginning of the Covid pandemic in 2020, I felt just like that. Lockdown had removed all social contact. Roles I held in my job, church and friendships were ripped away like a plaster, leaving a smarting wound.

A few months in to lockdown, I sat in the garden and read the story of Hagar. Afterwards, I wrote in my journal that I felt seen, understood, heard – not by the people I felt so cut off from, but by God, who saw into my heart and understood. A peace settled that I hadn't felt for a while.

I wrote a reflection on Hagar and then a second and circulated them to my church. They were well received – a needed message. From there, the idea for this book grew. I began to read stories that were so familiar to me, but with fresh eyes. All through the Bible, there are people who needed that reassurance from God – that He saw them, understood them and could give them hope, whatever their situation.

In the book there are 30 daily sections which I have deliberately called 'Reflections' rather than 'Days.' Whenever I start a Bible study book or reading plan, I start with great gusto, determined to make it a regular, daily habit. By Day 4 or 5, I'm already behind and already feel like a complete failure. But I believe God sees my feeble efforts too, and smiles about them, instead of condemning me. Every bit of truth I read, however sporadic, combats the lies that so easily fill my mind. He understands my tiredness and busyness and reaches out through the pages of Scripture to refresh and restore my soul, however and whenever I come to them.

So make this book work for you and use it in whatever way is helpful. Each "Reflection," is broken into several parts; a whole passage to read, a key scripture to focus on, my reflection on the passage, a song to listen to and some questions to help you to respond. You might want to do a whole "Reflection," each day, for thirty days. Or you might want to break up each "Reflection," doing part of it each day, for as long as it takes to get through it. The book can last you a month, a year or even longer – work through it at the pace that is right for you.

I have included, in the "Follow-Up Ideas," for each section, a suggestion of a song to listen to, that fits with the theme of the section. For copyright reasons, song lyrics or links can't be printed. However, all the songs are easy to locate online by putting the song title into a search engine. Most music platforms – Spotify, Amazon Music, YouTube – will carry the songs I have suggested. I hope they add a fresh dimension to your exploration of the themes.

From Hagar, Moses and Joshua in the Old Testament, to Zacchaeus, Thomas, Peter and the women at the resurrection in the New, I hope this book will help you to reflect on the God who sees our suffering, our grief, our fears, our failure – our innate "human-ness," in all its messy glory – but still loves us, accepts us and calls us higher.

REFLECTION 1

THE GOD WHO SEES US WHEN OTHERS DON'T (HAGAR - GENESIS 16:1-14)

Focus Scripture: Genesis 16:1-14

Focus verse: "So she named the Lord who spoke to her, "You are El Roi," for she said, "Have I really seen God and remained alive after seeing him?" v13

REFLECTION

Let's be honest for a moment - how often do you feel completely unseen – by others and even by God? When weeks go by and no-one calls to see how we are doing, we feel unseen. When we are passed over and someone else is called on for a job we would love to do, we feel unseen. When we aren't included by friends or family, we feel unseen. When we pray desperately for an answer and everyone's prayers seem answered but our own, we feel unseen.

Perhaps we feel unseen more than we would care to admit. Feeling unseen is synonymous with feeling unloved, unnoticed. It can provoke in us feelings of shame and unworthiness and lead to negative thought patterns and destructive behaviour. Counselling can be so effective because it provides a place for people to feel "seen," for their deepest hurts to be acknowledged and talked through. Only then can we see a way out of our pain and begin to glimpse ourselves as God does – broken yes, but precious, loved, His.

I have always loved the story of Hagar. Her revelation is something we all need. I feel for her plight. Her mistress, Sarai, had run out of patience with God's timing to give her a son. Sarai decided to "help God out," by commanding Hagar to sleep with Abram, so he would get his desired heir.

As Sarai's maidservant, she would have had no choice but to be complicit in her mistress' attempts to "help" God out; but once she delivered what Sarai had wanted, she found herself out of favour with her mistress, who jealously mistreated her. When things reached breaking point, she fled into the desert, lost, alone and ready to face inevitable death.

But God had other plans. His angel spoke to her, declaring her destiny and sending her back, better equipped to cope, however her life looked, with His help.

I love Hagar's words in this encounter – "*You are the God who sees me*." El Roi. The God Who Sees Me.

How different would we feel, how much better equipped would we be to handle disappointments and disasters if we truly grasped what Hagar did that day: that God sees us. Really sees us. Sees us with a seeing that no human relationship can give us. Sees our plight, our hurts, our pains, our disappointments, our fears and our joys and meets us in them, loves us anyway, draws us forward to live with them, better, in His strength.

I wrote a poem to capture a fresh sense of the God Hagar encountered. I pray that, as you read it, you will have a fresh revelation of the God who sees you - that you will sense the loving eyes of God on you and that it will be enough.

THE GOD WHO SEES:

When I'm totally spent and overcome
You are the God who sees.
When all I can feel is exhausted and numb
You are the God who sees.

Wherever I am, wherever I run,
Soaring or on my knees,
El Roi gently calls my name –
He is the God who sees.

When my day has left me uninspired,
You are the God who sees.
When I wake up, already feeling tired,
You are the God who sees.

Wherever I am, wherever I run,
Soaring or on my knees,
El Roi gently calls my name –
He is the God who sees.

When I make the right choice, though there's no-one around,
You are the God who sees.
When the stresses of life bring my face to the ground,
You are the God who sees.

Wherever I am, wherever I run,
Soaring or on my knees,
El Roi gently calls my name –
He is the God who sees.
When I give it my best, though I'm desperate to quit,
You are the God who sees.
When I grow and change, even the tiniest bit,
You are the God who sees.

Wherever I am, wherever I run,
Soaring or on my knees,
El Roi gently calls my name –
Always the God who sees.

When my heart knows you love me, in smooth times and rough,
You are the God who sees
When I trust that your love is more than enough,
You are the God Who sees.

Wherever I am, wherever I run,
Soaring or on my knees,
El Roi gently calls my name –
Always the God who sees.

FOLLOW-UP IDEAS

1. READ

Read the whole passage: Genesis 16:1-14.

Are there any parts of the story that really strike you? Which and why?

2. LISTEN

Listen to the song "*Unashamed*," by Starfield.

I love how the song describes us as whole, despite our brokenness.

Which lines speak to you?

3. THINK AND PRAY

Are there times that come to you as you pray, where you've felt unseen, unnoticed, unloved, ashamed? *Spend some time taking these to God. Ask for His healing in these areas.*

Can you think of times where you felt "seen," "loved," by God – that is, understanding that God loves us just as much in our worst times, as our best? Spend some time celebrating and thanking Him for these. *Ask for His help placing your worth in His hands only.*

REFLECTION 2

THE GOD WHO SEES US EVEN WHEN WE DON'T SEE HIM (HAGAR PART 2 - GENESIS 21:8-20)

Focus Scripture: Genesis 21:8-20

Focus verse: "Then God opened her eyes, and she saw a well of water. She went and filled the skin with water and gave the boy a drink." v19

REFLECTION

As the book of Genesis unfolds and the story of Hagar develops, her plight continues to fascinate me.

In Genesis 16, Hagar was feeling unseen and her revelation that God "saw" her got her life back on track, enabling her to live out the next part of her story more confidently. Contained within the essence of God's "seeing" was the sense that he understood her – really grasped her deepest fears, and helped her to carry them well into the next part of her destiny.

• • •

Here we see her, a number of years after the Genesis 16 encounter, this time being sent off into the desert by Abraham, after an incident where Sarah could no longer tolerate the sight of Ishmael playing with Isaac, her promised son.

You may have come across the practice of Lectio Divina – a spiritual discipline where you mentally put yourself *in* a bible passage, imagining in technicolour detail what the people you are reading about might have seen...heard...felt...experienced. In today's reading, I wonder how Hagar had felt, approaching this crunch point, watching Sarah's pregnant belly swell. What was it like to look on from the outside, at the joy and jubilation of the miracle of her master and mistress' promised son arriving? What doubts and fears did she have about her place in their family? Did she feel the precariousness of her position? Did she anticipate that, one day, she would be alone in the desert once more?

As she headed out into the desert again, she must have felt that her life was over. How would she survive with her son's needs to care for, as well as her own? This passage resonates with me so much: I face a difficult situation; God somehow provides and brings me through. Life carries on. I face a difficult situation again – and forget, completely how God provided for me in the last one! It's so easy to find ourselves there.

The same Hagar who had a life-changing revelation of the "God who sees," forgot that He saw her now, too. She sat down and cried, putting her son a distance away, so she didn't have to watch him die. Yet again God steps in. This time, it is Hagar who does the seeing. The angel of the Lord delivers his mighty promise to make Ishmael into a great nation. Then we are told *"God opened [Hagar's] eyes and she saw a well of water."* This was the difference, for her, between life and death. She saw the life-giving water where before, she had only seen the desert and a near-certain death.

When we are in tough situations, we don't always remember what God has done before and we don't always see His provision, right before our very eyes. It is so easy to sink into discouragement and gloom. Don't feel condemned if that is you today – it happens to us all – bible characters and twenty-first century humans alike. Use the story of Hagar today to remind yourself to ask God to open your eyes afresh to all he has done and all he is continuing to do in your life, whatever situation you are in today.

FOLLOW-UP IDEAS

1. READ

Read the whole passage: **Genesis 21:8-20.**

Are there any parts of the story that really strike you? Which and why?

2. LISTEN

Listen to the song *"Do It Again,"* by Elevation Worship.

I love the continued refrain that God's promise remains and he is faithful, whatever our circumstances.

Which lines speak to you?

3. THINK AND PRAY

Are there times that come to you as you pray, where you know God has brought you through a really difficult situation? *Spend some time remembering these times before God. Thank Him for them and notice His encouragement and His hand at work.*

Are you facing a situation today that makes you feel abandoned and is causing you to forget that God has brought you through before? *Ask for His help to place your situation into His capable hands. Pray for Him to open your eyes to see what He is ALREADY doing in the situation and in your life.*

REFLECTION 3

THE GOD WHO SEES OUR SUFFERING AND PATIENT ENDURANCE (JOSEPH - GENESIS 45:1-8, GENESIS 50:15-21)

Focus Scriptures: Genesis 45:1-8, Genesis 50:15-21

Focus verses: "So it was not you who sent me here, but God," v8.

"Even though you intended to do harm to me, God intended it for good, in order to preserve a numerous people, as he is doing today," v20

REFLECTION

The story of Joseph spans thirteen of the final fourteen chapters of the book of Genesis and is a rags-to-riches tale of epic proportions. His story reminds us that God does not abandon us in the difficult trials of life and, more than that, he brings good from even the hardest things we face: "*... all things work together for good for those who love God, who are called according to his purpose,*" Romans 8:28.

In Genesis 37, the seventeen-year-old Joseph didn't endear himself to his older relatives – he was the favourite son of his ageing father, frequently reporting his brothers' misdemeanours. Things didn't improve when he was gifted a special robe. Then the dreams started - sheaves bowing down to Joseph's sheaf, then the sun, moon and stars bowing to him too, interpreted by his father in a way the brothers didn't appreciate.

We know the story. The eleven brothers had gone ahead to Shechem to pasture sheep then onto Dothan, where they sold Joseph into slavery and faked his death, ten of them caring nothing for the crippling grief they caused their father.

From there, the Midianite traders sold Joseph to Potiphar, a high-ranking officer of Pharaoh, King of Egypt, where he served so well that he was made Potiphar's personal attendant. He excelled at this too, so much so that he soon found himself with complete administrative responsibility over Potiphar's affairs.

We love to see the rise of Joseph and assume this is going to be the point of the story. If *we* were writing this "redemption" story, the injustice would be repaid at this point and Joseph would live happily ever after. But God has an even bigger plan.

From Genesis 39, it goes quickly downhill for Joseph. Potiphar's wife hounds him to sleep with her but, being a man of godly integrity, Joseph repeatedly resists. She persists until she becomes so frustrated with his rebuttals that she frames him – so convincingly that Potiphar believes her and throws Joseph into prison.

. . .

Joseph could be wholeheartedly forgiven here for becoming disillusioned with God. Anyone, in these circumstances, might begin to believe that God had forgotten or abandoned them to rot, unseen, in a gloomy jail cell. But Joseph seems never to waver in his belief that the God of his ancestors sees his heart and his situation. He serves wholeheartedly, even in prison, still looking for opportunities to use the gifts God has given him: *"the Lord was with Joseph and showed him steadfast love; he gave him favour in the sight of the chief jailer,"* Genesis 39:21.

When the next twist of the story finds Pharaoh's chief cup bearer and baker out of favour and thrown into prison (Genesis 40), again we might hope that their presence would be key to Joseph's circumstances improving. They both have dreams, which Joseph interprets: the cup bearer loved his dream interpretation, but the baker wished he hadn't asked. Both dreams lead to the situations Joseph had prophesied. But, upon his release, the cup bearer forgets all about Joseph and he continues to languish in prison – for yet two more years. There must surely have been long days and difficult nights when Joseph wondered whether God still saw him, still had a plan for him.

Finally, Pharaoh himself has a dream and the cup bearer remembers the one who can interpret it. At last, in God's perfect timing, Joseph's moment arrives. Pharaoh gives Joseph a new name and promotes him to a rank answerable only to himself. Joseph handles preparation for a drought and famine in the land so competently, that people from miles around come to him to ask for sustenance (Genesis 41). Eventually, this includes his betraying brothers too (Genesis 42).

Joseph initially hides who he is and doesn't make the brothers' experience of purchasing supplies easy. A lengthy drama plays out, before he finally reveals his true identity (Genesis 45:3). As his brothers reel at this revelation, instead of hurling bitter accusations, Joseph tells them not to *"...be distressed, or angry with yourselves, because you sold me here; for God sent me before you to preserve life,"* Genesis 45:5, going on to add, *"So it was not you who sent me here, but God,"* v8. Here was a man, who had had more time than most to ponder and observe God's hand at work in his life. Far from feeling forgotten, unseen, bitter, he chose to see beyond relentlessly difficult circumstances, to the ultimate purpose God had for his life – the saving of many lives.

Ultimately, Joseph has an emotional reunion with his father, who has never stopped grieving his son's apparent death. Even after his father dies, the brothers are still concerned, concocting a story to prevent Joseph from punishing them. Luckily for them, Joseph's thoughts far transcend theirs. He makes the final, faith-filled declaration of his story and one that we can hold onto too: *"Even though you intended to do harm to me, God intended it for good, in order to preserve a numerous people,"* Genesis 50:20.

When we are going through times of trial and events we don't understand, it will help us to remember Joseph's faith-filled declarations. Sometimes, we cry out to God desperately and things get worse instead of better. Even in those times, we can trust that God still sees us, that He has not forsaken us and that He is, somehow, working all things together for our good.

When my sister was diagnosed with terminal cancer, to which she lost her life six months later, it felt impossible to trust that God would work out any "good," from it. Five years on, I would still do anything for the outcome to have been different – but I *can* see God shaping my life because of it and bringing some good out of it, somehow. I pray that you will find the same encouragement from God today, however bleak your circumstances might look.

During my sister's illness, I wrote this short haiku. May God speak through it, into your difficult and challenging circumstances today.

Are you with me, God,
Even in this? My child,
Especially this.

FOLLOW-UP IDEAS

1. READ

Read the whole of both passages:

Are there any parts of the story that really strike you? Which and why?

2. LISTEN

Listen to the song *"Sovereign Over Us,"* by Aaron Keyes.

I love the thought that God is always working for our good, even when our circumstances don't look promising.

Which lines speak to you?

3. THINK AND PRAY

Are there times that come to you as you pray, when you've been through some awful circumstances, but, looking back, you can see God's hand of protection and provision? *Spend some time thanking God for giving you those opportunities.*

Is there something you are going through today that doesn't make sense to you? Are you questioning God about why He is allowing this? *Ask God to reassure your heart today that He is with you, even in this. Express your trust that you know He can use anything that happens in your life for good.*

REFLECTION 4

THE GOD WHO SEES OUR INADEQUACIES AND LIMITATIONS AND STILL HAS PLANS FOR US (MOSES - EXODUS 4:1-17)

Focus Scripture: Exodus 4:1-17

Focus verse: "But Moses said to the Lord, 'O my Lord, I have never been eloquent, neither in the past nor even now that you have spoken to your servant; but I am slow of speech and slow of tongue,'" v10

REFLECTION

We tend to think of Moses as one of the "spiritual greats," of the Bible – rescued as he was from certain death as a boy born under Pharaoh's decree to kill all the Israelite boy babies, and rising up to lead the entire Israelite nation out from centuries of oppression and enslavement to the Egyptians. But do we ever stop to observe the limitations and inadequacies he battled, as he gradually accepted his place in God's great plan for His chosen people?

Despite his privileged upbringing by Pharaoh's daughter, Moses holds on to his roots and retains an interest in his people. After he fled to Midian and married Zipporah, the Egyptian king dies and the Israelites, sensing the winds of change, begin to cry out to God afresh, for their deliverance.

Throughout Exodus 3, God prepares Moses to be his chosen spokesperson, getting him ready for this intimidating role through dramatic revelations of His person and His presence. God reveals Himself to Moses through the burning bush, as the *"God of your father, the God of Abraham, the God of Isaac, and the God of Jacob,"* (v6). In doing so, He reminds Moses of the chosen genealogy of which he is a part. God then reveals Himself as, *"I am who I am,"* v14. God foresees the struggles going on in Moses' heart and Exodus 3 records how He prepares Moses to face them, by revealing to him exactly who it is who will give him the strength to go. God's declaration carries with it all the reassurances Moses would need – that God is eternal, ever-present, constant – not a powerless idol, like the Egyptian gods that would have surrounded him, growing up.

Just before our passage for today, Moses has been commissioned by God to go and present a plan to the elders of the Israelites, who will then go with him to the king. In Exodus 4, Moses is filled with doubts and expresses them, honestly, to God: *'Then Moses answered, 'But suppose they do not believe me or listen to me, but say, "The Lord did not appear to you?"'* v1. God sees Moses' need for reassurance and provides it, spectacularly.

First, the staff in Moses' hand becomes a snake, as he throws it on the ground. When God tells him to grasp it by the tail, he obeys and it becomes a staff again. Moses wouldn't have missed the symbolism in this miracle; snakes were revered in Egyptian culture, and were a symbol, worn on the headdress of Pharaoh, of the right to rule. If this weren't enough to convince Moses of God's power and authority, God performs another instant miracle. Moses' hand becomes leprous and is then restored, as he puts his hand in and out of his cloak. He even promises a third sign (river water turning to blood), in the presence of the elders of Israel, if the first two won't suffice.

Even after this persuasive display of God's miracle-working power, and a promise that it will be repeated when he goes to the elders, Moses still isn't convinced. He informs God, *"O my Lord, I have never been eloquent, neither in the past nor even now that you have spoken to your servant; but I am slow of speech and slow of tongue,"* v10. God isn't deterred, reminding Moses that he made all tongues and ears and He will personally give Moses the words to say. Either because Moses puts his assessment of his own limitations before God's mighty power, or because he doesn't want his inadequacies to mess up God's plan, Moses blurts out, *'O my Lord, please send someone else,'* v13.

It is impossible not to feel empathy for Moses here and resonate with his doubts. The commission he has been given feels too big. He sees only his own limitations and inadequacies and chooses to let them stand in the way of God's call on his life. God understandably becomes frustrated with Moses' refusal to accept His reassurances. But God does not revoke the call, instead bringing Aaron, Moses older brother and a Levite high priest, to fill the skill gap Moses feels is there. Aaron will do the talking on Moses' behalf and, in turn, on God's behalf.

. . .

Ultimately, Moses faces his fears, goes with Aaron. The elders of the Israelites see the signs and believe God is with them. This starts in motion the incredible chain of events that culminate in the Israelites being set free and walking through the Red Sea on dry ground, to their freedom from Egyptian enslavement.

Where Moses only saw his own limitations and inadequacy, God saw a man who could lead the Israelites to freedom. God did whatever it would take to get Moses to fulfil his destiny. Moses doesn't start out as a "spiritual great." He starts as a man with doubts who almost misses God's call for his life because he can't see in himself what God sees.

I am grateful that, *"God chose what is foolish in the world to shame the wise; God chose what is weak in the world to shame the strong; God chose what is low and despised in the world, things that are not, to reduce to nothing things that are, so that no one might boast in the presence of God,"* 1 Corinthians 1:27-29. Moses' insecurities might look "foolish," to us, but don't we feel and act similarly to Moses sometimes, too? However inadequate or unprepared we feel, God sees us differently and will empower us to do whatever it is He is calling us to do.

FOLLOW-UP IDEAS

1. READ

Read the whole passage: **Exodus 4: 1-17**

Are there any parts of the story that really strike you? Which and why?

2. LISTEN

Listen to the song *"Who Am I?"* by Casting Crowns.

I love the idea that our lives are not about what we are or what we have or haven't done, but are all about who God is and what He has done.

Which lines speak to you?

3. THINK AND PRAY

Are there times that come to you as you pray where you can remember feeling completely inadequate for a task you needed to complete or a situation you needed to face and God gave you His strength and motivation? *Spend some time thanking Him for those occasions today.*

Are you facing something at the moment, where you could do with a reminder that God sees your inadequacies and limitations and wants to partner with you anyway? *Ask for God to speak His reassurance into your heart today.*

REFLECTION 5

THE GOD WHO SEES OUR FEARS AND SPEAKS REASSURANCE (JOSHUA - JOSHUA 1:1-18)

Focus Scripture: Joshua 1:1-18

Focus verse: "I hereby command you: Be strong and courageous; do not be frightened or dismayed, for the Lord your God is with you wherever you go.'" v9

REFLECTION

Just before today's passage of Scripture, Moses, Israel's great leader and Joshua's irreplaceable mentor has died and Israel has just completed thirty days of official mourning. Joshua is a man carrying a very heavy burden, as he is to be the one who will finally lead the Israelites out of their interminable wandering in the wilderness.

Joshua had been Moses' faithful assistant. Moses had changed Joshua's name from Hoshea (salvation) to Joshua (Jehovah is salvation), reflecting the call of God on his life and reminding him who to look to for its fulfilment (Numbers 13:16). Earlier in Joshua's life as Moses' assistant, Moses had commissioned him to be the one who would succeed him as leader because God saw, in Joshua, a spirit of leadership (Numbers 27:18).

I imagine Joshua was feeling under-prepared and under-qualified for the mission entrusted to him. The writer of Deuteronomy closes the book with quite an epitaph for Moses, describing him as *"unequalled,"* in the *"signs and wonders,"* and *"mighty deeds and...terrifying displays of power,"* that he had performed, anointed by the Almighty. What a hard act to follow. How could he, Joshua, take the place of such a significant, anointed person?

God, of course, in His great mercy, sees Joshua's trembling heart and provides what he needs to fortify it. Previously, in Deuteronomy 31:7-8, when Moses summoned Joshua to prophecy his future, Moses used the words, *"Be strong and bold, for you are the one who will go with this people into the land that the Lord has sworn to their ancestors to give them; and you will put them in possession of it. It is the Lord who goes before you. He will be with you; he will not fail you or forsake you. Do not fear or be dismayed."* In verse 23 of that chapter, God himself commissions Joshua, saying, *"Be strong and bold, for you shall bring the Israelites into the land that I promised them; I will be with you."*

Here, we read significant echoes of these words. God speaks directly to Joshua, reminding him of his commission to lead His people into the Promised Land, reiterating that he would not be alone and, most significantly, commanding him, again, to, *"Be strong and courageous; do not be frightened or dismayed, for the Lord your God is with you wherever you go."* v9. The words he uses are not lightly chosen, or coincidental. They are heavily laden with significance, echoes of the ones Joshua had heard, earlier, both from Moses and from God. They would have reminded him of the times he walked beside his mentor, gaining wisdom and encouragement. They would have reminded him that the God who anointed Moses was the one anointing him too.

If these encouragements weren't enough, God confirms his word one more time. When Joshua takes God's command to the Reubenites, Gadites and the half tribe of Manasseh, they recognise his authority, agree to obey his commands and remind him: "Be strong and courageous!" v18. Isn't it great when we need a boost of courage from God and He speaks through others to confirm what we believe God is saying?

Over the next few chapters, Joshua proves that he had taken to heart the words God had spoken in three different ways – directly Himself, through Moses and through the people Joshua was leading. They had imparted the courage he needed. He was encouraged (the literal meaning of this is to "put heart into") by a God who saw exactly what he needed to take bold and brave steps when he wasn't feeling bold or brave. Over the following chapters, the Jordan parts, just like the Red Sea before it, and the walls of Jericho fall. Joshua is raised to the status of a great leader in the eyes of the people, because he takes God's promises to heart and they embolden him for the terrifying task ahead.

This story resonates with us because all of us have situations where our courage fails and we need a fresh word from God to jump start it again. I pray that this passage will remind you, today, that we serve a God who can give us just that. We can walk forward from where we are, secure in the knowledge that we can *"be strong and courageous,"* not in our own strength, but because *"the Lord [our] God is with us, wherever [we] go."* That is a promise to "put heart into," us today.

FOLLOW-UP IDEAS

1. READ

Read the whole passage: **Joshua 1: 1-18**

Are there any parts of the story that really strike you? Which and why?

2. LISTEN

Listen to the song *"No Longer Slaves,"* by Bethel Music.

I love the idea of God's perfect love drowning all our anxieties and fears.

Which lines speak to you?

3. THINK AND PRAY

Are there times that come to you as you pray where you can remember feeling God's comforting hand in your life and knowing that God was helping you to face your fears? *Spend some time thanking him for those occasions today.*

Are you facing something at the moment, for which you need a huge dose of God's courage, to stop you from being frightened and dismayed? *Ask for God to en-courage or "put heart into" you today, so that you can go forward in His strength, whatever you are facing.*

REFLECTION 6

THE GOD WHO SEES OUR NEED FOR REASSURANCE (GIDEON - JUDGES 6:36-40, JUDGES 7:1-21)

Focus Scripture: Judges 6:36-40
Judges 7:1-21

Focus verse: "I am going to lay a fleece of wool on the threshing-floor; if there is dew on the fleece alone, and it is dry on all the ground, then I shall know that you will deliver Israel by my hand, as you have said.' 38And it was so. When he rose early next morning and squeezed the fleece, he wrung enough dew from the fleece to fill a bowl with water," Judges 6:37-8.

REFLECTION

The story of Gideon is so famous that his attempts at sign-seeking left their mark on the English language; the meaning of the idiom "putting out a fleece," is well-known to most as testing something before committing to it. For Gideon, in our passage for today, it meant far more than that and was the reassurance he needed from God to lead a small band of men to victory over huge armies that had oppressed the land for years.

At the beginning of Judges 6, things are looking bleak. The Midianites had been plundering the land for seven years, leaving the Israelites cowering in mountains, caves and strongholds. The Midianites didn't even steal the crops and livestock to feed themselves, they were simply out to destroy anything that fell into their hands. When the unrepentant Israelites cry out to God in dismay about their desperate situation, He reminds them, through a prophet, that these are the consequences of them turning their backs on Him and not listening to His voice.

In verse 11, Gideon cuts a lonely figure, threshing wheat inside a winepress, in the hope that the Midianites won't find it and destroy it before it can provide sustenance for his people. To his great surprise, the angel of the Lord appears, declaring, *"The Lord is with you, you mighty warrior,"* v12. Albeit politely, Gideon begins to question the angel of the Lord, pointing out that it frankly doesn't feel as if God really *is* with them, with all the death and destruction they are experiencing all around them. God then delivers a surprising commission to Gideon – he is to save Israel out of Midian's hand. Gideon's response clearly articulates his doubts: *"He responded, 'But sir, how can I deliver Israel? My clan is the weakest in Manasseh, and I am the least in my family,'"* v15.

Despite God's reassurance that Gideon's success will come from God, much of the rest of the chapter is given over to Gideon asking for, and God providing, signs that this really is true. Gideon begins by making an offering to the Lord and the fire that falls and consumes it gives Gideon temporary peace that he hasn't just dreamed up the recent commission. Gideon then finds the courage to build an altar that declares just that (The Lord is Peace) then, in the dead of night, tears down the altars his people had built to false Gods.

After death threats from his own people and the news that a huge Midianite and Amalekite army were advancing, Gideon's peace evaporates and he needs further reassurance. This time, he asks God to reassure him in two distinctive ways. He lays a fleece on the ground and asks God to make the fleece wet whilst the surrounding floor is dry. And that is exactly the situation Gideon finds the next day (v38). Twenty-four hours later, Gideon asks God to provide the same miracle in reverse: wet ground and dry fleece. He does (v40).

As Gideon prepares his army to fight, his faith is tested still further. He assembles 32 000 men, but God allows the 22 000 who are too scared to fight to head back home. If the remaining 10 000 are beginning to feel a little thin-on-the-ground to Gideon, God depletes them further still; all who kneel to drink from the stream are sent away, whilst those who lap like dogs remain. 31 700 men had gone home, leaving 300 to fight, so God could demonstrate to Gideon that victory would come from Him alone, not from human supremacy.

As the enemy troops begin to assemble, *"as thick as locusts; and their camels were without number, countless as the sand on the seashore,"* v12, God provides one final reassurance for Gideon, tipping him off that eavesdropping on the conversation in the enemy camp will give him the final push he needs to lead his army to victory. Overwhelmed by God's goodness, Gideon bows down and worships Him, before he and his army charge at the countless Midianites, causing them to flee in fear before 300 men. God indeed granted them victory, as He had so firmly promised.

One of the most striking things about the story of Gideon, is that God never belittles or berates Gideon for needing a bit more reassurance. When we read the story, we might be shocked by Gideon's cheek – surely one fleece test would be enough? But God isn't fazed by his request, and gently provides Gideon with reassurance after reassurance, until he is ready to do what God had ordained for him to do.

Whilst physical signs of reassurance like this are quite rare, the song included in today's reflection offers some useful insights into other ways God might give us the reassurance we need when we are doubting, upset, confused or needing guidance. Sometimes these "signs," come through words of scripture or lines from songs. Sometimes they come from words others speak into our lives, or simply from feeling the presence of God afresh in our lives. Whatever reassurance you need from God today, may He draw close to you in a tangible way to give you the courage you need to carry on.

Sign

Insisting on a
wet fleece, wall-writing, fire, we
miss the still, small voice.

FOLLOW-UP IDEAS

1. READ

Read the whole passage: **Judges 6:36-40 and Judges 7: 1-21**

Are there any parts of the story that really strike you? Which and why?

2. LISTEN

Listen to the song *"Small Enough,"* by Nichole Nordeman.

I love the idea the song expresses that the infinite, omniscient God of the universe would take time to be "small enough" to be present with and personal to each one of us.

Which lines speak to you?

3. THINK AND PRAY

Are there times that come to you as you pray where you can remember needing a little extra comfort and reassurance from God and He provided it, either directly or through others? *Spend some time thanking Him for those occasions today.*

Are you facing something at the moment, where you could do with a little clarity or a nudge to walk forward and be brave? *Ask for God to speak His reassurance into your heart today.*

REFLECTION 7

THE GOD WHO SEES OUR CHOICES AND SACRIFICES (RUTH - RUTH 1, RUTH 4)

Focus Scripture: Ruth 1, Ruth 4

Focus verses: "Where you go, I will go; where you lodge, I will lodge; your people shall be my people, and your God my God," Ruth 1v16

"So Boaz took Ruth and she became his wife. When they came together, the Lord made her conceive, and she bore a son. Then the women said to Naomi, 'Blessed be the Lord, who has not left you this day without next-of-kin; and may his name be renowned in Israel!" Ruth 4:13-14

REFLECTION

The story of Ruth only spans four short chapters of the Bible, but the loyalty, humility and sacrificial love she demonstrates within them leads to a union with Boaz, which produces Obed, whose grandson would be David. A stranger, an outsider in her mother-in-law's culture, Ruth could not have had the faintest idea that her selfless actions would lead to lasting fame as a key player in the genealogy of Jesus.

• • •

At the beginning of our passage for today, there is a famine in the land, so a man from Bethlehem named Elimelek, his wife Naomi and their two sons, Mahlon and Kilion, flee to a new country – Moab. Elimelek dies and Mahlon and Kilion marry Moabite women and they settle in Moab for ten years. Then disaster strikes: the sons die too.

Now, Naomi is a widow without sons to take care of her in her old age, and hearing that the famine is over, she sets off back to her homeland, taking her daughters-in-law with her. On the way, she has a change of heart and realises it would be kinder to allow them the freedom to stay with their own people, rather than follow her to a land that would be foreign and unfamiliar to them (Ruth 1v11-13). Orpah takes her up on her suggestion and leaves after an emotional goodbye. Ruth, though, says, *"Where you go, I will go; where you lodge, I will lodge; your people shall be my people, and your God my God,"* Ruth 1v16. She seals her declaration with an oath and sets off with Naomi for Bethlehem, both of them unsure of the future they would find there - Naomi after such a long absence and Ruth, having never been there before.

At the end of Ruth 1, they arrive in Bethlehem, causing quite a stir. Upon being recognised by locals, Naomi joins the ranks of many people, biblical characters and otherwise, who express honest disappointment in the God they used to trust: She tells them, *"Call me no longer Naomi, call me Mara, for the Almighty has dealt bitterly with me. I went away full, but the Lord has brought me back empty; why call me Naomi when the Lord has dealt harshly with me, and the Almighty has brought calamity upon me?"* (Ruth 1 v 21-22). Her self-inflicted name change, from "pleasant / beautiful," to "bitter," reflects the honest fear of her heart: that

God has abandoned her and no longer "sees" her as He used to. Events that are about to unfold, of course, prove otherwise. God sees her, and her loyal, faithful daughter-in-law. He has a plan to provide for them both – it will just take a little time to work out.

Over the course of Ruth 2-3, the story of Ruth and Boaz is told. Ruth gleans on the margins of the fields of Boaz, whom, we are told, is *"a kinsman on [Naomi's] husband's side,"* Ruth 2 v 1. Instead of leaving her to collect from the edges, Boaz notices Ruth, asks after her and, upon discovering who she is, prays a prayer of blessing over her and shows her favour by providing her with grain and water. When Ruth returns to Naomi, Naomi declares: *"Blessed be he by the Lord, whose kindness has not forsaken the living or the dead…the man is a relative of ours, one of our nearest kin,"* Ruth 2v20. Other versions of the bible call Boaz a "kinsman redeemer," a position, in those days, that carried with it a weight of responsibility. Being a "kinsman redeemer," was a role of protector and provider, which included saving (redeeming) family members from loss. In Naomi's declaration, she begins to recognise that God does see her plight after all and hasn't turned His back or forgotten her. God, through Boaz, is accomplishing His provision and giving her hope.

In Ruth 3, Naomi helps Ruth to present herself to Boaz as a potential bride: as kinsman redeemer, he would be obliged to take her as his wife. Being a man of godly integrity, Boaz explains that he will have to go through a process to make sure he really is the closest kinsman redeemer willing to marry Ruth. The next day (Ruth 4 v 1-8), Boaz holds an official meeting with the next closest kinsman-redeemer, who isn't interested.

Ruth 4v13 is the pinnacle of the story of God's provision and redemption: Ruth and Boaz marry and Ruth bears a son – Obed. Look at what the women of the neighbourhood declare over Naomi: *"Blessed be the Lord, who has not left you this day without next-of-kin; and may his name be renowned in Israel! He shall be to you a restorer of life and a nourisher of your old age,"* v14-15. Look at the difference between the sense of blessing she feels here and the sense of abandonment she expressed in Ruth 1. Naomi had felt empty, that the Lord had treated her *"bitterly," "harshly,"* and *"brought calamity upon her,"* (Ruth 1 v 21-22). Life has, at last, swung back round to a place of blessing, for her and for Ruth, and she can see God's hand of blessing on her once more.

The story of Naomi in the book of Ruth follows a pattern many of us will be familiar with: life is going well and we can see God's hand of blessing. Life takes a difficult turn and we feel God no longer sees or loves us. Naomi is a good lesson in handling such times: she expresses her pain and grief honestly before God. She does what she can to get through the tough times. And she is able to hold fast to God, even in her pain, and recognise and praise Him when He brings her through to a place of blessing again.

Life will take us to tough places, as it did for Naomi and Ruth. But God still sees us and He still loves us. Hang on in there, if you are in one of the tougher seasons today. He hasn't abandoned you and He will carry you through.

FOLLOW-UP IDEAS

1. READ

Read the whole passage: **Ruth 1 and Ruth 4 (or the whole book if you have time)**

Are there any parts of the story that really strike you? Which and why?

2. LISTEN

Listen to the song *"Goodness of God,"* by Bethel Music.

I love the idea the song expresses that God is faithful through every season of life and, not only that but his goodness chases us.

Which lines speak to you?

3. THINK AND PRAY

Are there times that come to you as you pray where you can remember having to sacrifice your own needs or comfort for the comfort of someone else? Did you find that God somehow blessed you for your surrender and sacrifice? *Spend some time thanking Him for those occasions today.*

Are you in a situation, at the moment, where you feel as though you are having to put your own needs last to serve others? *Ask for God to speak His reassurance into your heart today that His goodness is still pursuing you and that He sees your sacrifice and surrender.*

REFLECTION 8

THE GOD WHO SEES THE DESIRES OF OUR HEART (HANNAH - 1 SAMUEL 1:1 – 1 SAMUEL 2:10)

Focus Scripture: 1 Samuel 1:1 – 1 Samuel 2:10

Focus verses: "Elkanah knew his wife Hannah, and the Lord remembered her. In due time Hannah conceived and bore a son. She named him Samuel, for she said, 'I have asked him of the Lord.'" 1 Samuel 1:19-20

REFLECTION

The story of Hannah and Samuel is a tricky one. Too often it is used to illustrate that God sees our heart's desires and, if we pray enough and are desperate enough, He will grant them. Yet anyone who has been a Christian any length of time will be able to testify that it isn't always as simple as that. There is much to celebrate, learn and take hope from, in Hannah's story – but it must be stated from the outset, that prayer isn't a simple slot machine: desire in, desired outcome out.

• • •

The story, however, is a great encouragement that God hears the painful, desperate prayers of our hearts and listens to them even when we don't see them answered as quickly or as specifically as we would like at times.

The book of 1 Samuel begins with a portrait of unhappiness. Elkanah is married to both Hannah and Peninnah, such was the culture then, that allowed this. The simple statement, *"Peninnah had children, but Hannah had no children,"* v2, communicates a heavy weight of pain and shame. In a culture where a woman's value was measured by her child-bearing (particularly son-bearing) abilities, one can only imagine how Hannah felt, daily comparing herself to her husband's other wife and coming up short. To make matters worse, Peninnah constantly niggled and gloated, bullied and jibed. Elkanah is kind to Hannah but lacks real understanding of her plight, suggesting that their relationship should be enough. It isn't though, and Hannah is pushed to the brink and desperate for divine intervention.

Each year they would all go to Shiloh to make sacrifice to the Lord. On this occasion, after they finish the sacrificial meal, Hannah stays behind to deliver her own plea to the Almighty. She intercedes for a son, promising to deliver him into God's service at the temple, as soon as he is old enough (v11). To add to her pain, Eli, the priest, thinks she is drunk, mouthing as she was, the words of a silent, anguished prayer. She explains, though, that she had simply been pouring her soul out to God, out of pain and frustration, so Eli blesses her prayer, saying *"Go in peace; the God of Israel grant the petition you have made to him,"* v17. Hannah goes away more peace-filled and less burdened, just from feeling that she had been seen and heard by God and by His representative on Earth.

I imagine the time between the prayer and its fulfilment wasn't easy. Did Hannah wait, expectantly and hopefully, feeling that this time it was going to be different? Or did old doubts and disappointments, creep in, stealing her peace and hope? Ultimately Samuel is born, named to reflect her joy that God had heard her desperate cries (v20).

Three years passes (v21-24), which was the culturally expected time for a child to be weaned. As is so often the case, Scripture is silent on the intricate details: how much joy did this tiny blessing bring Hannah, as he grew? Was the long-awaited role of motherhood tainted by the knowledge that she would soon have to relinquish it once more, or was it made sweeter by knowing that the Almighty was working out His plan in both of their lives, mother and son?

Either way, verse 24 depicts her arriving at the temple with an offering costlier than any bull, ephah of flour or skin of wine could ever be. Hannah explains to Eli who she is and leaves Samuel with him. She tells Eli, *"For this child I prayed; and the Lord has granted me the petition that I made to him. Therefore, I have lent him to the Lord; as long as he lives, he is given to the Lord,"* v27-28. God has granted her desperate prayer and she has returned to fulfil her vow to Him.

Whilst I imagine painful and tearful goodbyes, Hannah's prayer at the beginning of 1 Samuel 2 suggests otherwise. The words she speaks are triumphant and celebratory and the lesson they contain is valuable. She praises God's character and actions – His steadfast trustworthiness and His bringing down of the "*mighty,*" and lifting up of the "*feeble,*" (v4). She seems to have an awareness of God's "bigger picture," and her anointed words express an unwavering trust in God that many of us long for. In the New Testament, Mary's Magnificat, when she hears the news that she is pregnant with Jesus, echoes Hannah's words, expressing a similar, sacrificial trust.

The very child she had to surrender went on to be a significant prophet in Israel. The boy would become the man who would call Israel to corporate, public repentance and who would anoint two influential future kings (Saul and David). His death would be mourned by the whole nation. Hannah couldn't have known this, as she surrendered her son and her heart to God. But here was a woman who felt seen by the Almighty, who knew He had heard her desperate prayer and answered and who could trust Him with her next steps.

Of course, although this is the only time we get to hear Hannah praying for her miracle, it wouldn't be a stretch to assume she had prayed similar prayers throughout her life, without seeing fruit. Like Hannah, we will be able to point to times in our lives when our prayers have been suddenly and dramatically answered. And, like Hannah, we may have lived or even be living through seasons when we feel they go unheard and we feel unseen. Her story is a reminder that it is perfectly acceptable to lament and be honest with God in our prayers, but also that we should never give up expressing our heart's desires to a God who sees our prayers within a much bigger picture, sometimes incomprehensible to us.

FOLLOW-UP IDEAS

1. READ

Read the whole passage: **1 Samuel 1:1 – 1 Samuel 2:10**

Are there any parts of the story that really strike you? Which and why?

2. LISTEN

Listen to the song *"Trust in You,"* by Lauren Daigle.

I love the idea the song expresses that we can trust in God's character and good plans for our lives, even when immediate circumstances don't seem to be changing.

Which lines speak to you?

3. THINK AND PRAY

Are there times that come to you as you pray when you have prayed for something your heart has longed for and God has answered as you hoped and dreamed? *Spend some time thanking Him for those occasions today.*

Have you been praying for something on your heart for a long time, but it feels as though your heart's desire isn't being granted? *Ask for God for wisdom and insight today, to try to trust Him for the bigger picture of your life. Ask Him, too, for faith to keep trusting Him with the thing you're praying for.*

REFLECTION 9

THE GOD WHO SEES OUR HEARTS (DAVID - 1 SAMUEL 16:1-24)

Focus Scripture: 1 Samuel 16:1-24

Focus verse: "But the LORD said to Samuel, 'Do not look on his appearance or on the height of his stature, because I have rejected him; for the LORD does not see as mortals see; they look on the outward appearance, but the LORD looks on the heart.'" v7

REFLECTION

The story of David, which plays out dramatically through the books of 1 and 2 Samuel, shows us another life that began unnoticed and in obscurity.

It would take more than a few words to sum up the finer details of David's epic story; his rise from the obscurity of shepherding his Father's flock of sheep, to his going back and forth from his Father's fields to play the lyre to sooth a Saul increasingly troubled-of-mind. His many dramatic flights to take shelter in other places, to save himself from the spear of

Saul, jealously intent on destroying him. And the absolute integrity he showed, in sparing the life of the very same pursuer on more than one occasion.

There is so much to learn from the life of David, but I want to highlight one of the things that struck me, relevant to our theme – **the God who sees** into the depths of our hearts: "for the Lord does not see as mortals see; they look on the outward appearance, but the Lord looks on the heart.'" *v7.*

I wish that we knew more about David at this moment in his life - his feelings, his situation, his position within his family. What we *are* told is that, when Jesse got the message that Samuel was on his way to anoint one of his eight sons as a future king, he only presented seven of them, leaving the eighth, David, in the field with his sheep. I long to know how David felt that day – was he feeling left out, frustrated, wondering why he didn't deserve an audience with the great prophet who was sizing up his brothers, as he continued to tend the sheep? Or was he content, doing what he knew best, happy to leave future kingship to those more suited?

I suspect it was the latter. Those are the people God tends to use the most: the ones who faithfully do what is in front of them - dreaming, of course, praying for the things God has placed in their hearts - but faithfully doing what they need to do now, well and with integrity, until God steps in. *"The Lord does not look at the things people look at. People look at the outward appearance but the Lord looks at the heart." v7.*

• • •

Even the prophet Samuel had come with a set of preconceptions, but God stepped in. I suspect no-one was as surprised as David was, when he was called in from the fields at last to find his bigger, finer brothers rejected and himself anointed before their astounded eyes. From the stories that follow, we begin to see what people hadn't yet seen - David's bravery, passion, integrity, determination and faithfulness. But *God* had seen.

We can be sure that God sees us too. We can be sure that He sees all the unseen things that we do, all the heart-matters we face, all the struggles we are working through. It matters when we have integrity, where we could have glossed over the facts. It matters that we put in 100% in the moments when others might put in less. It matters that we are the best we can be in the parts of our relationships that no-one will ever see but us and those closest to us. It matters that we bring things before God when we might be tempted to take them all into our own hands.

I don't know about you, but I long for the day when I will hear God say, "Well done, good and faithful servant." And I want Him to see me, now, doing the best I can, repenting and repairing when it all goes wrong and glorifying Him in the unseen moments, as much as the seen. Only then can He use me, promote me and anoint me for the purposes for which He has chosen me.

FOLLOW-UP IDEAS

1. READ

Read the whole passage: **1 Samuel 16:1-24.**

Are there any parts of the story that really strike you? Which and why?

2. LISTEN

Listen to the song *"Where Were You?"* by Francesca Battistelli.

I love the iconic footprints-in-the-sand imagery in this song. Which lines speak to you?

3. THINK AND PRAY

Are there times that come to you as you pray, where you've felt as if you can't understand why your life is working out in the way it is, while others' lives seem to "go to plan?" (This is a myth, by the way – none of us find life exactly as we imagined it!) *Spend some time taking these to God. Ask for His perspective and guidance in these areas.*

Can you think of times where you have felt strongly that God is leading, guiding, providing, bringing the right people and opportunities across your path? Spend some time celebrating and thanking Him for these. *Ask for His help, placing your life's path back into His hands today.*

REFLECTION 10

THE GOD WHO SEES OUR SKILLS (DAVID PART 2 - 1 SAMUEL 17:1-50)

Focus Scripture: 1 Samuel 17:1-50

Focus verses: "His eldest brother Eliab heard him talking to the men; and Eliab's anger was kindled against David. He said, 'Why have you come down? With whom have you left those few sheep in the wilderness? I know your presumption and the evil of your heart; for you have come down just to see the battle.'" v28

"Saul said to David, 'You are not able to go against this Philistine to fight with him; for you are just a boy, and he has been a warrior from his youth.'" v33

REFLECTION

The story of David contains many fascinating interactions between David and others. Each one gives us an insight into how David had to cope with criticism and opposition while not wavering in his single-minded determination to use his gifts to serve the God he knew had great plans for him. His skills and gifts were not seen by others, but he trusted that they *were* seen by God.

. . .

There must have been some pretty hard feelings between David and his older brothers, after they had been rejected as future kings and David had been anointed for the position that some of them had perhaps assumed was rightfully theirs. When David turns up on the battlefield, carrying provisions of roasted grain, loaves of bread and cheeses for them and their commanders, and starts asking questions, Eliab's welcome is less than warm. *"Why have you come down here? And with whom did you leave those few sheep in the wilderness? I know how conceited you are and how wicked your heart is; you came down only to watch the battle."* v28

Eliab calls into question David's integrity (deserting his job), his worth ("those *few* sheep, which belittles his job) and the condition of his heart. The David we have seen so far in 1 Samuel is anything BUT conceited and lazy, so Eliab's remark seems unfair. David, though, does little more than mutter under his breath and turn away. He continues to pursue his line of questioning amongst the other men and doesn't take long to confidently declare, *"Let no-one lose heart on account of this Philistine; your servant will go and fight him."* v32. Even then, Saul, too, discourages David: *"You are not able to go out against this Philistine and fight him; you are only a young man, and he has been a warrior from his youth."*

The crux of the issue was this: Saul, Eliab and the other men saw only David's limitations. David knew that God saw Him differently – as someone to whom He had given skills and abilities to be used to advance His kingdom and topple evil. David had great confidence in the God who he knew had given him these skills and abilities. It was confidence honed from many weeks, months, years alone with the sheep and his Maker, enabling him to declare, without a doubt, "'*Your servant has killed both lions and bears; and this uncircumcised Philistine shall be like one of them, since he has defied the armies of the living God.' David said, 'The Lord, who saved me from the paw of the lion and from the paw of the bear, will save me from the hand of this Philistine.' So Saul said to David, 'Go, and may the Lord be with you!'*" v36-37

David had such a close relationship with the God he served that he knew without a doubt that, when he stepped forward to fight in His name, He would be with him and deliver him. He knew God would use the skills He had placed within him to bring about His plan for David's life and peace for those around him. Whatever others said about him, however others discouraged him, however unlikely victory looked, David clung to all He knew about God and trusted God to fulfil His will for him.

The New Testament tells us, too, that "*he who began a good work in you will carry it on to completion until the day of Christ Jesus,*" (Philippians 1:6). We need to take a firm hold of that promise in our lives. Are there gifts and abilities that He has placed in you that you are yet to see bearing fruit in your life? Hold onto them, thank him for them, pray them into fruition in your life. Are there desires He has put into your heart that you haven't yet had an opportunity to fulfil yet? Don't lose hope – if the discouragement of circumstances or the discouragement of others has caused you to push them down and feel unseen, ask for God's courage to get them re-ignited, to give you fresh vision and purpose for them in your life today. What He has begun, He *will* complete in us.

FOLLOW-UP IDEAS

1. READ

Read the whole passage: **1 Samuel 17:1-50.**

Are there any parts of the story that really strike you? Which and why?

2. LISTEN

Listen to the song "*Bigger than I Thought,*" by Sean Curran.

I love the idea, expressed in the song, that our fears and doubts don't frighten God.

Which lines speak to you?

3. THINK AND PRAY

Are there times that come to you as you pray, where you've felt discouragement that your circumstances or comments from others have stopped you from stepping into God's plans for your life? *Spend some time taking these to God. Ask for His help to forgive, if that's needed, and for His strength to pick you up and move you forward.*

Can you think of times where you have seen God at work in your life and seen Him using your gifts for His glory? Spend some time celebrating and thanking Him for these opportunities and giftings. *Ask for His help with trusting Him to outwork the next part of His plan for your life.*

REFLECTION 11

THE GOD WHO SEES OUR SIN (DAVID PART 3 - 2 SAMUEL 12:1-25)

Focus Scripture: 2 Samuel 12:1-25

Focus verses: "David said to Nathan, "I have sinned against the LORD."" v13

"Then David rose from the ground, washed, anointed himself, and changed his clothes. He went into the house of the Lord, and worshipped; he then went to his own house; and when he asked, they set food before him and he ate." v20

REFLECTION

David's story continues to unfold through 1 and 2 Samuel. We follow his progress through a dramatic series of battles, both against armies and with Saul, whose jealousy of David never fades away.

In all that David faces and battles, he never ceases to follow God, trust Him for his next steps and walk with integrity before Him. His life is anointed and blessed by God, who provides for him in countless ways throughout the books of 1 and 2 Samuel. This is a man who understands that he serves a God who sees him, in public and in private, and this spurs him on.

Until.

With all that we have learnt about David up to this point, together with his track record of righteousness and integrity, we would be forgiven for feeling shocked and perplexed by what happens next. David, walking on his roof, late one afternoon, *"saw from the roof a woman bathing,"* and *"sent someone to inquire about the woman." (2 Samuel 11:2-3)*. However many times we read the story and *will* him to do the right thing and look away – we know the unstoppable force with which this story hurtles David to the depths. He learns she (Bathsheba) is another man's wife, summons her and sleeps with her, finds out she is pregnant, tries to cover it by summoning her husband back from battle and, when that doesn't work, ultimately has him killed. What a downfall for such a spiritual giant.

But perhaps that is the point. If the Bible contained only stories of the great successes of spiritual giants, there would be no hope for us ordinary people, limping along in our doubts, sin and shame. David had a moment of temptation. Instead of walking away, he gave in to it, setting into motion a stream of other sins and consequences he couldn't have begun to imagine. Does that sound familiar? In the New Testament, Paul writes, *"Since all have sinned and fall short of the glory of God," (Romans 3:23)* so if it does sound familiar, you're not alone!

. . .

Even in the middle of the bleakness of this section of David's story, there is hope for us to find – hope for us who, like David, slip and fall and sin and feel the burn of shame and need forgiveness and redemption. When Nathan the prophet comes to David, using a parable to hold up a mirror to David's behaviour, David immediately repents, declaring, *"I have sinned against the Lord," 2 Samuel 12:13*. As he prays and fasts, the consequences of his sin still hit hard, and the son born to him tragically dies. I am in awe of David's response after he has lost his son, for how hard it is to do this when tragedy strikes us: *"Then David rose from the ground, washed, anointed himself, and changed his clothes. He went into the house of the Lord, and worshipped; he then went to his own house; and when he asked, they set food before him and he ate," v20.*

David's story reminds us we are still seen and loved by God, even in the midst of our sin. Like a small child, who hides, knowing that his parents have uncovered a misdemeanour, isn't it our instinct to hide when we have sinned, avoiding God and others because our sin feels too great? Hasn't that been how mankind has dealt with sin, since the beginning? (*"[Adam and Eve] hid themselves from the presence of the Lord God among the trees of the garden," Genesis 3:8*). But David, here, shows us a better way. When he is confronted with his sin, he confesses and repents. When he has to face the consequences of his sin, instead of excusing and justifying himself, he faces the hard reality, stands up tall and worships God afresh. This is a man who knows he has sinned, but knows God looks upon his repentance with eyes of grace. David worships the God who sees his sin, but is gracious to forgive, as soon as he turns back to Him. We should all be encouraged by this.

. . .

The verse I mentioned above (*"Since all have sinned and fall short of the glory of God,"*) feels all too true most days. The great news comes in the verse that follows: *"...they are now justified by his grace as a gift, through the redemption that is in Christ Jesus" Romans 3:24*. Instead of writing ourselves off when our choices cause us to "fall short", let's be people who turn back to God, each time we sin. Let's repent and worship Him, restored and replenished by His loving gaze and gracious forgiveness.

FOLLOW-UP IDEAS

1. READ

Read the whole passage: **2 Samuel 12:1-25.**

Are there any parts of the story that really strike you? Which and why?

2. LISTEN

Listen to the song *"Coming Back,"* by Ben Cantelon.

I love how he expresses a sense of God's grace overwhelming and purifying our hearts.

Which lines speak to you?

3. THINK AND PRAY

Are there times that come to you as you pray, where you are painfully aware that you have *"…sinned and fall short of the glory of God?" Spend some time taking these to God, today. Ask for His forgiveness and for His assurance that you are forgiven and set free.*

Can you think of times where you know God has helped you not to go down a negative road, not to give in to the temptation to sin in a certain area? Spend some time celebrating and thanking Him for these times. *Ask for His help resisting temptations in areas that you know are trickier for you and trust Him to help you walk with integrity.*

REFLECTION 12

THE GOD WHO SEES US IN OUR LOWEST MOMENTS (ELIJAH - 1 KINGS 19)

Focus Scripture: 1 Kings 19

Focus verse: "But he himself went a day's journey into the wilderness, and came and sat down under a solitary broom tree. He asked that he might die: 'It is enough; now, O LORD, take away my life, for I am no better than my ancestors.'" v4

REFLECTION

The part of Elijah's story in 1 Kings 19 will always rank highly in my personal list of all-time-greatest-Bible-stories. It is a story that gives us permission to have off days and crushing lows, just like this great prophet. *His* story wasn't over when he thought it was and this reminds me that *my* story isn't over when I think it is either.

A chapter earlier, in 1 Kings 18, God has anointed Elijah to see off the prophets of Baal in huge numbers, proving to them beyond doubt that *his* God was the only true God. Such was his trust that God would prove faithful, he ordered the onlookers to pour twelve huge jars of water on the offering and around it – an extra flourish to prove there was no cheating or human-intervention.

After the fire of God had fallen (conclusive proof of His power and might), Elijah prophesied that there would be rain and sent his servant to look for signs of its coming. Repeatedly, the servant returned to report there was nothing. Elijah persevered and on the seventh occasion, the servant reported a small rain cloud and soon there was a great storm. In addition, after sending King Ahab ahead in his chariot to beat the impending downpour, God supernaturally enabled Elijah to run ahead of the chariot, to Jezreel.

We might be forgiven for assuming Elijah had seen enough signs, wonders and miracles for him to ride a wave of faith for months. He hadn't. In 1 Kings 19, we find a different Elijah – broken, exhausted, hopeless. He sits down under a broom tree and declares that he has had enough, and feels burnt out, exhausted and alone (verses 4 and 10). I love how God nurtures Elijah back to health first and faith second. He eats and drinks the supplies God sends via an angel, to replenish his waning strength. This gives him the energy to make the long trek to Mount Horeb (believed to be synonymous with Mount Sinai), where he can encounter God in a way that sets him back on his feet and breathes new life into his purpose and destiny.

In this sacred place of faith to which the Israelites had been led after their escape from Egypt and where Moses had received the Ten Commandments, God speaks to Elijah. He does not speak in ways that reiterates his power and might but in a gentle, still small voice. The wind, earthquake and fire pass, but, when silence is all that is left, Elijah is still enough and at peace enough to hear God's voice afresh (v12-13). He is re-commissioned to anoint kings and a prophet to follow in his footsteps. He learns that the fears that led him into the wilderness are unfounded. In verses 1-3 we are told that it was Jezebel that had threatened his life and in fear he had fled to Beersheba. He was also afraid that he was the last of God's followers (verse 10). God reassures Elijah and he learns that in fact there are the 7000 other followers of God who are still alive. Our fears are most often as a result of other's people's actions rather than God's. So it was with Elijah.

Elijah's story in these books of 1 Kings, is a riches-rags-riches story that should encourage us all. God didn't give up on Elijah in his darkest of times. Elijah could rant and be honest with God about how he was feeling. God used practical resources to restore him to strength, as well as giving him an encounter with Himself that breathed fresh life and hope into him. This story reminds us that crushing doubts and lows can happen to anyone – even those we consider the great heroes of faith. If Elijah can be walking in great power and anointing for God, experience doubt, exhaustion, and burn out, then be restored, gently, by a loving God, then so can I and so can you.

God sees and loves us as much in our bad days and lowest moments as he does in our good ones and mountain-top experiences. I pray that whichever end of the spectrum you are living today, you will hear God's still, small voice and allow you Him to meet you there.

FOLLOW-UP IDEAS

1. READ

Read the whole passage: **1 Kings 19**

Are there any parts of the story that really strike you? Which and why?

2. LISTEN

Listen to the song *"In the Hands of the Potter,"* by Casting Crowns.

I particularly like the idea of being shaped by God's love, instead of broken by our circumstances.

Which lines speak to you?

3. THINK AND PRAY

Are there times that come to you as you pray, where you felt like life as you knew it was over? How did God encourage you and help you to get up and go forward again? *Spend some time remembering these times before God. Thank Him for them and remind yourself of these times, "building an altar," to remember his faithfulness for when you face such times again.*

Are you facing a situation today that makes you feel like giving up or as if there is no-one else who is facing what you are facing? *Ask for His help to place your situation into His capable hands. Pray for Him to open your eyes to see how he is providing for you and encouraging you, even in the midst of your difficult situation.*

REFLECTION 13

THE GOD WHO SEES VALUE IN THE SMALL THINGS WE OFFER HIM (THE WIDOWS AND THE OIL - 1 KINGS 17:8-16 AND 2 KINGS 4:1-7)

Focus Scripture: 1 Kings 17:8-16 and 2 Kings 4:1-7

Focus verses: "But she said, 'As the Lord your God lives, I have nothing baked, only a handful of meal in a jar, and a little oil in a jug.'" 1 Kings 17:12

"She answered, 'Your servant has nothing in the house, except a jar of oil.'" 2 Kings 4:2

REFLECTION

There are two short passages to read for today's reflection, rather than one, as they both offer us similar insights into the same theme: that God sees and values everything we offer him, however small our offerings might feel to us.

In 1 Kings 17, we follow the life of Elijah during a drought which he prophesied, following an apparently endless succession of wicked kings who *"did what was evil in the sight of the Lord,"* – a continued refrain throughout the book of 1 Kings. He had been living beside a brook, drinking from it and being miraculously fed by a troop of ravens. But now the brook, like the other water sources in the land, had dried up and he needed help.

In our passage for today, God prepares a meeting between Elijah and a widow that will be life-preserving for them both. Elijah arrives in Zarephath and asks a widow, who is gathering sticks by the city gate, to bring him a little water to drink (v10). When she consents to this request, he adds, *"Bring me a morsel of bread in your hand,"* (v11). Whilst sharing her water would have been costly, the extra request was a step too far. She stands up to him this time, telling him that she has nothing but a little oil and a handful of flour: she and her son are about to eat their last meal and prepare to die.

Elijah then delivers the mind-blowing prophecy that, if she bakes and brings him a cake first, then prepares something for herself and her son, the flour and oil will keep replenishing, supernaturally, until the land sees rain again. We may be so familiar with this passage that we fail to appreciate just what a sacrifice and offering this was for the widow. What trust in the God of Elijah she must have had, to carry out his instruction. What doubts might have crept into her mind as she used what appeared to be the very last of her resources, to give sustenance to this man of God? The ingredients she offers are not just store-cupboard staples, but the final lifeline of a dying family. What an amazing trust she showed, as her small offering was transformed by God into something huge.

Something that seemed so small and worthless, carried worth into future generations. If the widow hadn't offered what little she had, neither Elijah nor her family would have been saved from an imminent demise. If Elijah hadn't lived, Elisha wouldn't have inherited a double-anointing that would shape the course of future generations for good. God multiplies the widow's offering and it goes further than she could ever have dreamed.

Similarly, in 2 Kings 4, we see another widow, this time in need because her husband is dead and her children are about to be taken by her debtors as slaves. God has just begun to establish Elisha as his anointed prophet, now Elijah has gone, and the miracle in this passage exemplifies the double anointing he has just received.

Once again, oil takes centre stage – an ordinary offering from an ordinary woman in great need. This time, the widow's part in the miracle is to borrow jars of all shapes and sizes, from far and wide. All she must do is keep pouring the oil until all the jars are full. Like the oil in 1 Kings 17, it keeps replenishing and keeps replenishing until all the jars are full and the widow's financial future is secure. God, again, takes a jar of oil and a lot of trust and turns it into something much bigger.

Isn't it easy to downgrade the things we can offer to God and assume they are too small, too insignificant, for Him to notice, bless or use? Whether it's our time and energy, our talents or our money, we compare ourselves to others and judge ourselves lacking. Like both widows, we find ourselves saying, "I have nothing, except..." Perhaps today is the day to realise that "nothing, except," is not nothing. God sees the small things we offer Him, today and every day, and, as we trust them to Him, with obedience and faith, He can use them to bring about transformation in our lives and the lives of others.

FOLLOW-UP IDEAS

1. READ

Read the whole of both passages: **1 Kings 17:8-16 and 2 Kings 4:1-7**

Are there any parts of the story that really strike you? Which and why?

2. LISTEN

Listen to the song *"I Surrender,"* by Kim Walker.

I love the idea of surrendering everything to God – our time, talents, money for example – and not holding anything back for ourselves.

Which lines speak to you?

3. THINK AND PRAY

Are there times that come to you as you pray, when you've given some of your time, resources, talents to serve God and others, even when you felt they were inadequate, but God used them more than you could have dreamed? *Spend some time thanking God for giving you those opportunities.*

Is there something you need to bring to God as an offering today? Is there anything you are holding back from Him because it feels too small to offer? *Ask God to show you if there is anything He would like you to offer Him today. Express your trust that you know He can use anything you surrender to Him, more than you can begin to imagine.*

REFLECTION 14

THE GOD WHO SEES OUR EMPTINESS AND DRYNESS AND BREATHES LIFE INTO IT (EZEKIEL - EZEKIEL 37:1-14)

Focus Scripture: Ezekiel 37:1-14

Focus verses: "I will put my spirit within you, and you shall live," Ezekiel 37:14

REFLECTION

In my (not exceptionally theological opinion), parts of Ezekiel equal only parts of Isaiah and Revelation in their levels of metaphor, imagery – and ability to bemuse! I'm grateful for theologians that break these inspiring-yet-puzzling books down so that us "ordinary people," can access them. The Bible Project is one of these and I would highly recommend you watch their videos on any snippet of scripture whose interpretation eludes you, this one especially.

That said, Ezekiel's vision of the Valley of Dry Bones in our scripture for today is extremely well known and, as well as being given for the encouragement and hope of the people of Judah, can still give us encouragement and hope today.

. . .

Ezekiel lived in a turbulent time for the people of Judah. Large numbers of Judeans had been carried off into exile by the Babylonian armies, as they moved in and wreaked havoc and destruction on God's people. The young Ezekiel is thought to have been in the first wave of exiles, carried off around 597BC and it was in exile that God called him to be a prophet.

Throughout the Bible, prophets were known both for their messages of judgement and their messages of hope and Ezekiel was no different. Throughout the early books of Ezekiel, he engages in a multiplicity of prophetic acts to depict God's heartbreak at Judah's rebellious acts and attitudes. In Ezekiel 8-11, he has a vision of the destruction of the temple and God's spirit leaving it. Shortly afterwards, in Ezekiel 33, a fresh wave of captives arrives in exile, confirming that this is exactly what has just happened, as the temple has been destroyed.

For the Judean exiles, the future must have looked bleak. Because of the culture of the time, they might have been consumed with the belief that their God had simply been defeated by a stronger, Babylonian god. Although they needed an honest assessment of why things had unfolded as they had, they also needed fresh faith and fresh hope.

Ezekiel's vision in today's passage provides just that. In his vision, Ezekiel sees a valley of dry bones – people without life or breath, stretching as far as the eye can see. Ezekiel is unsure how to answer when God asks him, *"Mortal, can these bones live?"* v3. God then instructs Ezekiel to prophesy life over the bones, repeating the word *"breath,"* several times to remind him that it is only through God breathing His life into these dry bones that they can live.

Ezekiel reports that he, *"prophesied as he commanded me, and the breath came into them, and they lived, and stood on their feet, a vast multitude,"* v10. The vision continues, with God acknowledging that He has heard the hopelessness of His people (v11), and is reassuring them that, *"I will put my spirit within you, and you shall live, and I will place you on your own soil; then you shall know that I, the Lord, have spoken and will act,"* v14. He will breathe His life back into their dry, empty hearts and restore them to hope and stability.

There have been times in my life when I have felt dry and empty for good reason – catastrophic loss and overwhelming grief. There have also been times when I haven't been able to put a finger on exactly why I am feeling empty and dry. Sometimes, life simply wearies us and grinds us down. In both of these situations, I can point to times when I have prayed, or asked others to do so if I haven't felt able to pray myself, and the life and breath of God has lifted me in ways that nothing else could. The situation I was facing might not have changed – but filled with a fresh sense of God's presence and involvement in my life, I could get up and live with hope, feeling less broken and less alone.

Even when things are good, we must remember to call on God to breathe His Holy-Spirit-inspiration into our comings and goings. If we don't, it is so easy to quickly find ourselves empty and dry, as we carry out our lives' callings in our own strength.

Wherever you are at today, be inspired by Ezekiel's vision. It may have been intended for a specific time and place in Biblical history, but we can take hope and courage from it today and use it as a prayer for God to breathe fresh life into all we do and all we are.

FOLLOW-UP IDEAS

1. READ

Read the whole passage: **Ezekiel 37:1-14**

Are there any parts of the story that really strike you? Which and why?

2. LISTEN

Listen to the song *"I Lift My Hands,"* by Chris Tomlin.

I love the sense the song gives of turning back to God and trusting him afresh, after struggling and doubting.

Which lines speak to you?

3. THINK AND PRAY

Are there times that come to you as you pray when you have felt dry and empty, but the Holy Spirit has filled you with fresh hope? *Spend some time thanking Him for those occasions today.*

Are you feeling dry and empty today? *Ask for God to fill you afresh with his spirit, and breathe fresh life and hope into your weary soul.*

REFLECTION 15

THE GOD WHO SEES OUR INTEGRITY (SHADRACH, MESHACH AND ABEDNEGO - DANIEL 3)

Focus Scripture: Daniel 3

Focus verses: "If our God whom we serve is able to deliver us from the furnace of blazing fire and out of your hand, O king, let him deliver us. 18But if not, be it known to you, O king, that we will not serve your gods and we will not worship the golden statue that you have set up," Daniel 3:17-18

REFLECTION

Like Ezekiel in our previous reading, Daniel and his friends Hananiah, Mishael and Azariah (later renamed Shadrach, Meshach and Abednego) were amongst those living in the turbulent times of the Babylonian exile. They had been part of the royal household, serving Jehoiakim, king of Judah and now the Babylonian king, Nebuchadnezzar, wanted them in his service (Daniel 1v3).

• • •

By the end of Daniel 1, the four young men have already made quite a name for themselves. In training for the king's service for three years, they are supposed to eat the royal food and wine – which they knew had been offered to other gods. They refuse to do this, instead existing on a diet of vegetables and water. God and the royal official have favour on them all and they remain healthier than any of the other young men in training. God has not abandoned them in a strange land and they are confident that He sees the integrity they display and will reward them.

If we define integrity as living out in our actions and attitudes the values we claim to hold, the whole book of Daniel is a lesson that this quality is very much seen and prized by God. He sees whether our hearts are arrogant and power-hungry or humble and filled with integrity, even under pressure. Working on being the latter, not the former should be a life goal, with God's help.

The three kings in the book of Daniel whose hearts are filled with evil (Nebuchadnezzar, Belshazzar and Darius) have ample opportunity to make things right with God but don't and things don't go well for them. The four young men whose hearts are set on serving God with integrity and humility continually experience His grace and favour, even in the hardest of situations.

In Daniel 2, God gives Daniel the gift of interpreting Nebuchadnezzar's dream – something the top magicians and astrologers in the land can't even do. The arrogant king briefly recognises Daniel's God as the *"revealer of mysteries,"* (Daniel

2v47), before reverting to his usual, self-idolising behaviour, setting up a gigantic statue of himself made from pure gold, for his people to bow down and worship, as we read in our chapter for today (Daniel 3).

At over twenty-five metres tall and two and a half metres wide in modern measurements, the statue would have looked imposing and intimidating. To Shadrach, Meshach and Abednego, who were among the officials ordered to bow down and worship it, the threat for not doing so was more intimidating still: comply or, *"...immediately be thrown into a furnace of blazing fire,"* v6. Imagine the courage it took to stand tall as others bowed and the fear that might have taken hold when news of their defiance got back to the terrifying king.

Shadrach, Meshach and Abednego have such a strong conviction that God is with them and will deliver them when they won't comply with the king's order – but their faith goes as far as trusting God, even if He doesn't deliver them. They famously declare, *"If our God whom we serve is able to deliver us from the furnace of blazing fire and out of your hand, O king, let him deliver us. 18But if not, be it known to you, O king, that we will not serve your gods and we will not worship the golden statue that you have set up,"* Daniel 3v17-18. They will not budge from their conviction that their God is the only god they should worship, whatever the cost.

And God does deliver the three young men - from a furnace so hot that it devours the soldiers on duty, but not them. The story contains such a powerful image of God with them in the furnace – a fourth man *"with the appearance of a god,"* v25, standing with them, protecting them – a God who saw their integrity, humility and trust of their hearts and delivered them from certain death.

God sees our integrity too – the occasions when we are tempted to "go along with the crowd," but choose to hold fast to our values – His values. The big sacrifices that we secretly question. The small, unseen decisions we make every day that honour Him.

It's worth noting that acting with integrity isn't solely reserved for big crises in our lives or more "spiritual" activities. Mark Greene's book, "Fruitfulness on the Front Line," (which you can find out more about on the *London Institute for Contemporary Christianity* website) is a great encouragement to live with integrity in every area of our lives, whatever it is we spend them doing.

We can model integrity as we volunteer in our local communities, work hard at menial or high-powered jobs, full or part time, or care in our homes for small children or aging relatives. The character we model, the love and grace we show, the people we stand up for are all ways that God sees us working tirelessly, with an integrity that pleases Him so.

Be encouraged today that you are seen. Be encouraged that He values the integrity of your faith in a world that doesn't. Be encouraged that, one day, your reward and recognition will be complete. In the meantime, keep trusting Him and keep walking with integrity, inspired by the example of the four young men in this book.

FOLLOW-UP IDEAS

1. READ

Read the whole passage: **Daniel 3**

Are there any parts of the story that really strike you? Which and why?

2. LISTEN

Listen to the song *"Even If,"* by Mercy Me.

I love the idea in the song that, even when things don't turn out as we have hoped and prayed, we can still trust God and have hope for the future.

Which lines speak to you?

3. THINK AND PRAY

Are there times that come to you as you pray when you have shown integrity and made the hard choice to hold fast to your beliefs when it would have been easier to let them slide? *Spend some time thanking God for those occasions today.*

Are you recalling times in your life when you feel you haven't lived with the integrity you should have done? *Ask for God to forgive you for those times and ask Him for strength and conviction to walk with integrity, whatever the situation or the outcome.*

REFLECTION 16

THE GOD WHO SEES A BETTER WAY FOR US (THE WOMAN AT THE WELL - JOHN 4:1-30, 39-42)

Focus Scripture: John 4:1-30, 39-42

Focus verses: "Jesus said to her, 'Everyone who drinks of this water will be thirsty again, but those who drink of the water that I will give them will never be thirsty. The water that I will give will become in them a spring of water gushing up to eternal life,'" v13-14

REFLECTION

Our reading for today contains in it so much hope and joy. A shunned woman finds herself in the direct gaze of Jesus, who sees and knows everything about her yet offers her kindness, acceptance and a better future.

Just before today's reading, Jesus delivers (in conversation with Nicodemus) the declaration of ultimate truth that would be so central to his ministry and to the Christian gospel: *"For God so loved the world that he gave his only Son, so that everyone who believes in him may not perish but may have eternal life,"* John

3v16. As always, the Pharisees were lurking in the background, keeping a close eye on Jesus' words and actions, waiting to catch him out. Feeling it was time to continue his ministry elsewhere, Jesus headed back to Galilee, via the region of Samaria (John 4 :1-4).

In a town called Sychar, Jesus reaches a well (Jacob's well). Tired from the journey, he sits down (v6). A Samaritan woman comes to draw water and Jesus asks her for a drink. This is not as straightforward a request as it sounds. A centuries-long enmity between Samaritans and Jews meant that they would not, ordinarily, associate. Jews considered Samaritans to be heretics. So ethnically and in religious terms, she was someone to avoid.

Additionally, here was a woman, drawing water in the heat of the noon-day sun. Drawing water, for women in these times, would have been a social experience – they would have come in groups, in the cooler part of the day, chatting and sharing lives as they lowered their receptacles. Drawing water on her own, at this time of day would have pointed clearly to this woman being a social outcast. So, both her gender and her ethnicity placed her very low on the social ladder of the time – someone no-one would have noticed or cared about. Except Jesus.

It is hard to tell, from verse 9, what tone the woman uses to respond to Jesus' unusual request. She replies, *"How is it that you, a Jew, ask a drink of me, a woman of Samaria?"* Aside from the incongruous conversation, Jesus' drinking from her water vessel would have made him ceremonially unclean –

something no-one would willingly choose. Jesus rather cryptically answers her, *"If you knew the gift of God, and who it is that is saying to you, "Give me a drink", you would have asked him, and he would have given you living water,"* (v10).

This whets her curiosity for further conversation and she continues to try to draw him out, bringing Jacob and his sons, the original providers of the well, into the conversation. Again, Jesus hints that he is talking about more than physical water, when he tells her, *"Everyone who drinks of this water will be thirsty again, but those who drink of the water that I will give them will never be thirsty. The water that I will give will become in them a spring of water gushing up to eternal life,"* (v13-14).

The Samaritan woman expresses her desire for such water. Jesus pushes a little harder and tells her to, *"Go, call your husband, and come back,"* v16, a bold, prophetic move that gets to the root of why the woman is here, at this time – a social outcast. The woman's answer as to why she won't call her husband is vague and evasive, but Jesus delivers the insight that convinces her he is more than just a man beside a well: *"You are right in saying, "I have no husband"; for you have had five husbands, and the one you have now is not your husband. What you have said is true!"* (v17-18). In one sentence, he conveys to the woman that he sees her – her sinful past and her troubled present – and yet, still wants to speak to her, still wants to offer her hope and help.

Even then, she tries to draw him into a theological conversation about where people should be worshipping. He brings the matter back to the crucial issue of the heart, though:

"...true worshippers will worship the Father in spirit and truth, for the Father seeks such as these to worship him," (v23). She continues to demonstrate her knowledge of religion, telling him that, one day, the promised Messiah will come and make it all clear to everyone. Did she already suspect that Jesus might be the very Messiah she spoke of? It is impossible to tell, but I imagine she was still pretty stunned when he spelt it out: *"I am he, the one who is speaking to you,"* (v26). The promised saviour, the Messiah about whom she had been taught, was standing here, seeing into the depths of her soul and, instead of judging and condemning her, offering her living water that would end the thirsting and yearning that had got her into such a desperate situation.

Abandoning her water jar, even at this hot hour, the woman went back to the city and began to talk to many others, telling them of what Jesus had done. His insightful, prophetic words, gentle handling of her difficult life and offer of living water was one she couldn't keep to herself (v28-9). Because of *her* testimony that, *"He told me everything I have ever done,"* (v39), more Samaritans come to see Jesus for themselves, and come to believe in him because they hear his message for themselves and believe, as she has, that he is the Saviour of the world (v42).

Jesus saw into the woman's past and present and deep into the issues of her heart. He sees into ours too. Where we can be extremely self-critical and self-condemning, writing ourselves off as unworthy of support from others, or help from on high, Jesus sees, forgives and calls us higher. He still offers us living water today. If we will drink of it, our dry, life-weary thirst will be satiated by the refreshing, cool waters he offers.

FOLLOW-UP IDEAS

1. READ

Read the whole passage: **John 4:1-30, 39-42**

Are there any parts of the story that really strike you? Which and why?

2. LISTEN

Listen to the song *"Living Waters (As the Deer),"* by Shane and Shane (acoustic version).

I love the way the writer of the song combines the inspiring words of the old and well-known hymn, with his own, fresh thoughts about the living water freely available from God.

Which lines speak to you?

3. THINK AND PRAY

Are there times that come to you as you pray when you remember feeling dry, empty or hopeless and God offered you His living water to drink? This might have been through an encouraging song or bible verse, being in nature or through the kindness of others. *Spend some time thanking God for those occasions today.*

Are you feeling dry, empty, thirsty or life-weary today? *Ask God to fill you afresh with his living waters, repeatedly, through the day. Watch for how he answers and praise Him when He does.*

REFLECTION 17

THE GOD WHO SEES OUR PAST AND GIVES US A FUTURE (ZACCHAEUS - LUKE 19:1-10)

Focus Scripture: Luke 19:1-10

Focus verse: "When Jesus came to the place, he looked up and said to him, "Zacchaeus, hurry and come down; for I must stay at your house today."" v5

REFLECTION

Zacchaeus was not just a tax collector but an important one – perhaps a superintendent above many others in his field. Far from being an esteemed position in biblical culture, this would have made him a hated outcast. He would have been a Jew collecting taxes for the Romans, which, in the eyes of the people of the time would have made him a traitor. And additionally, he would have used every means possible to extort extra taxes from them to line his own pockets.

So when he joined the crowd, hoping to catch a glimpse of Jesus, who was passing through their town, Jericho, on his journey to Bethany, he wouldn't have passed the time chatting happily to the expectant throng. It was more likely that they would have given him a wide berth, shunning him in case he found yet more impromptu ways to part them from their already-stretched earnings.

Luke's account tells us that Zacchaeus "*...was trying to see who Jesus was, but on account of the crowd he could not, because he was short in stature*" v3. Desperate to catch any glimpse he could of this extraordinary man whose fame would have, by now, spread far and wide, he departed from his professional image and, childlike and expectant, climbed into the branches of a nearby sycamore tree.

Perhaps he had even caught echoes of Jesus' teaching that Luke records just a chapter earlier (Luke 18:9-14). Anecdotes involving tax collectors in those days would not have painted them favourably. Jesus' Parable of the Pharisee and the Tax Collector was different. If news of that parable had reached Zacchaeus' ears, it might have intrigued and excited him. Perhaps he saw himself painted in the word-picture Jesus had delivered to the stunned crowds and wanted to know if such redemption was possible, even for him.

In his wildest dreams, he couldn't have predicted what was going to happen next. He wanted to see Jesus but could not have foreseen that it would be Jesus who saw him – and not just saw him but saw into his heart and mind and wanted to change it for the better.

. . .

In verse 5, Jesus stops at the base of the tree and calls out, "*Zacchaeus, hurry and come down; for I must stay at your house today*." Zacchaeus must have been stunned, but we are told that he "hurries," down, delighted to welcome Jesus. The stories he'd heard and his experience of being an outcast had left his heart wide open to wanting a better way to live – one that he knew, instinctively, Jesus could offer. Somehow, this incredible teacher knew his name and saw into the depths of his sinful heart, yet wanted to come and dine with him.

As he hurried happily away with Jesus, the crowd "began to grumble," (v7) that Jesus had gone to the home of such a notorious sinner. Knowing he was experiencing Jesus' grace and favour, Zacchaeus announced an immediate change he would make: "Look, half of my possessions, Lord, I will give to the poor; and if I have defrauded anyone of anything, I will pay back four times as much," v8. Zacchaeus' heart and mind were instantly changed when he came into Jesus' line of vision. He knew that Jesus saw his heart, his motives and his deeds and he wanted to make sure that he would see something different from now on. He changed because Jesus saw him and, instead of shunning him, brought him out into the light and hope of salvation.

Jesus declares, at the end of this story, ""Today salvation has come to this house...For the Son of Man came to seek out and to save the lost."" v9-10. Zacchaeus' story was an example to all who would hear it that Jesus' message was for everyone, not just the "religious" and those of good standing in society. He was a living example of all the "lost," things parables that feature earlier in Luke's gospel – the coin, the son, and the sheep.

. . .

It can be all too easy to write ourselves (and others) off as being too peripheral, too marginalised for Jesus to see us, to notice us, to be able to enter our hearts and change us. But, as this story illustrates, if even a notorious tax collector could invite Jesus into his home and his heart, so too can we.

I close with a poem I wrote, from Zacchaeus' perspective, to summarise today's story.

ZACCHAEUS

On hearing that the teacher good and wise,
was travelling through Jericho today,
I yearned to see but, hindered by my size,
knew I would have to find another way.
Extorted taxes heavy on my mind,
I sensed this teacher had the power to free
me from a life I longed to leave behind;
with pounding heart, I struggled up a tree.
And, as he neared, instead of going past,
he called, "Come down! Dear Zach, at yours I'll dine!"
The grumbling crowd were looking on, aghast.
My heart rejoiced, eternal peace now mine.
What lasting joy to hear Lord Jesus say,
"Salvation has come to this house today!"

FOLLOW-UP IDEAS

1. READ

Read the whole passage: **Luke 19: 1-10**

Are there any parts of the story that really strike you? Which and why?

2. LISTEN

Listen to the song *"O, Come to the Altar"* by Elevation Worship.

I love the idea that, even whilst we are broken, hurting and weighed down by sin, Jesus sees us and calls us. Which lines speak to you?

3. THINK AND PRAY

As you pray, bring to mind a time that you became aware of Jesus' love and forgiveness for you, personally, for the first time. *Spend some time thanking Jesus for coming into your life and for the on-going impact he has on your heart and mind.*

Are there any actions you might need to implement today, as an expression of the outworking of God's love and grace in your life? *Ask God to help you to see others as he sees you and to help you to practically demonstrate the grace and mercy He has shown you, to everyone around you.*

REFLECTION 18

THE GOD WHO SEES THE MOTIVATIONS OF OUR HEARTS AND CALLS US HIGHER (THE WOMAN CAUGHT IN ADULTERY - JOHN 7:53 – 8:12)

Focus Scripture: John 7:53 – 8:12

Focus verse: "Jesus straightened up and said to her, 'Woman, where are they? Has no one condemned you?' [11]She said, 'No one, sir.' And Jesus said, 'Neither do I condemn you. Go your way, and from now on do not sin again,'" John 8:10-11

REFLECTION

Our scripture for today is one that has been the subject of much puzzlement over the years. Some versions of the Bible omit it altogether, believing it to have been added into the canon of scripture later than the rest of John's Gospel. But it is generally accepted, now that it is in keeping with both the style of John's Gospel and the character of Jesus and therefore a valid text. It makes for fascinating and challenging reading, as Jesus sees and speaks directly into the hearts of both the accusers and the victim in this unpleasant scene.

. . .

In the build up to this scripture, it had been a significant and dramatic week. Jesus had been speaking openly at the Festival of the Tabernacles, puzzling and intriguing the crowds and enraging the religious leaders with his dramatic statements about who he was. His timing was no coincidence. Jews from all over would have travelled to Jerusalem for this great feast, which commemorated God's provision for them in the past (in the Wilderness) and looked forward to his provision of a Messiah in the future. Some were beginning to catch on that they might just be living in that future now.

The Pharisees and religious leaders were becoming more and more upset and unsettled and had already, in John 7, sent temple guards to arrest Jesus. Instead, the guards were captivated by Jesus' words, returning to the Pharisees, having made no arrest. The Pharisees had begun to devise ever more elaborate traps to try to catch Jesus and have a reason to arrest him.

On the morning of today's scripture, the Feast of the Tabernacles had ended, but Jerusalem would have still been bustling with visitors. Eager to continue to learn from a "rabbi," whose fame was spreading, *"All the people came to him and he sat down and began to teach them,"* v2. It was into this peaceful moment that the Pharisees marched a woman, *"caught in the very act of committing adultery,"* v4. This was about as far from discreet as they could be and the confrontation was deliberately designed to make noise, draw attention and trap Jesus, as publicly as possible, to discredit him.

The Pharisees draw on the law of Moses to goad Jesus into condemning her for her act of adultery. Biblical law demanded that she is deserving of death by stoning, conveniently passing over the fact that there must have been a man involved as well. No-one brings him out for a public showdown. Jesus is backed into a corner. On the one hand Jewish law demanded her death as punishment for her sin, while on the other Roman law forbade execution without permission of the government. Whichever way Jesus turned, he could be accused of not following one law or not following the other. The Pharisees wait eagerly to see which one he will choose.

Jesus, of course, sees right through them and sees exactly what they are up to. He sees the scheming hearts of the Pharisees and the sinful (and probably now terrified) heart of the accused woman and takes a path out of the situation that none of them could have predicted. His first action is to bend down and, *"[write] with his finger on the ground,"* v6. Wouldn't it be wonderful to know what he wrote? Some imagine he was writing the ten commandments, reflecting the idea in Exodus 31v18, that the commandments were, *"written with the finger of God,"* hinting again at his divinity, hidden in his humanity. Others ponder whether him drawing in the dust was symbolic of humans being created from dust and therefore vulnerable to weakness and sin. Perhaps he was simply buying time to think.

Either way, his next sentence is radical and controversial: *"Let anyone among you who is without sin be the first to throw a stone at her,"* v7. One by one, they slope away, leaving Jesus and the woman in the middle of the astonished crowd. Next, he turns to her and asks whether any of her accusers have condemned her. When she replies, *"No one, sir,"* Jesus adds, *"Neither do I condemn you. Go your way, and from now on do not sin again,"* v11.

Jesus saw into many hearts that day – the heart of the woman, the hearts of her accusers and those of the listening crowd. He saw the hypocrisy of the Pharisees, who were clearly out to make a public example of the woman and trap him in the process. He wasn't going to give them the satisfaction and sent them packing with their "tails between their legs." He saw the sin of the woman and neither condemned nor condoned her sin, forgiving her but, at the same time encouraging her to turn from it. He gave the listening crowd a lesson they wouldn't forget – that true fulfilment of the law was about heart-righteousness, not an external show.

I imagine the grateful woman, probably not dressed for a public appearance, leaving the scene, redeemed, thankful for a second chance and determined to live differently, in gratitude for the life-changing words of the man who didn't condemn her, but called her higher.

Are any of the characters in this story any different from any of us? The Bible says *"the heart is devious above all else,"* (Jeremiah 17:9) and Hebrews 4 talks of the word of God *"judging the thoughts and intentions of the heart,"* (v12). We can sometimes be as judgmental and hypocritical as the Pharisees, or as wrong-doing as the woman caught in adultery. When we find ourselves, like them, caught up in external shows of righteousness or called out for our wrong-doing, we too can find forgiveness and grace in Jesus, who sees into the depths of our wrong-doing, yet forgives us and calls us higher.

Psalm 139 is a prayer we can all benefit from praying, regularly: *"Search me, O God and know my heart; test me and know my thoughts. See if there is any wicked way in me and lead me in the way everlasting,"* (v23-24). We can be sure God will answer with gentleness and grace.

FOLLOW-UP IDEAS

1. READ

Read the whole passage: **John 7:53 – 8:12**

Are there any parts of the story that really strike you? Which and why?

2. LISTEN

Listen to the song *"Forgiven,"* by David Crowder.

I love the idea that the weight of our sin is lifted from us and God holds His arms wide open to welcome us, as soon as we come to Him.

Which lines speak to you?

3. THINK AND PRAY

Are there times that come to you as you pray, when you've found it hard to make the right choices and gone down wrong paths, but have come back to God, asked for His forgiveness and felt forgiven and free? *Spend some time thanking God for the tangible moments of His forgiveness and His grace.*

Are you stuck in a particular pattern of wrong-doing today? Are you feeling defeated and unable to beat it? *Ask God to remind you that He can give you a way out, the strength to defeat the pattern and the forgiveness for you to start afresh.*

REFLECTION 19

THE GOD WHO SEES OUR SIN AND OFFERS US LOVE AND GRACE (THE WOMAN WHO ANOINTS JESUS - LUKE 7:36-50)

Focus Scripture: Luke 7:36-50

Focus verse: "Therefore, I tell you, her sins, which were many, have been forgiven; hence she has shown great love. But the one to whom little is forgiven, loves little," Luke 7:47

REFLECTION

This passage of Scripture starts with the intriguing revelation that Simon, a Pharisee, had invited Jesus to his home to eat with him – intriguing, because, in the two chapters before this one, members of the Pharisee party had begun to mutter and speak against Jesus. When he forgave a paralysed man for his sins, they had accused him of blasphemy. When he healed a man with a shrivelled hand on the Sabbath, they were incensed and looked for a reason to bring Jesus down. So, when Luke 7 begins with Jesus dining at Simon's home, we are alert to the fact that this might well be a trap, rather than an act of hospitality.

. . .

We are confident that Simon will be watching and waiting to trip Jesus up and his opportunity to do so arises quickly. A woman, whom we are told *"was a sinner,"* arrives with an alabaster jar of ointment, this descriptive detail added by Luke to reinforce what unsavoury company the Pharisees would have considered her to be – way below their religious image of outward perfection.

Jesus would have been reclining at a low table, as was the custom of the time, his head in the middle of a circle of feasting company and his feet stretching outwards. The woman stands behind him, *"weeping,"* then begins to, *"bathe his feet with her tears and to dry them with her hair."* Then she continues, *"kissing his feet and anointing them with the ointment,"* (v38). The act would have taken great courage and abandon from the woman. As a known sinner in the community, it is likely that she may have been a prostitute, so she would have been very clear about the reception she would receive upon entering the home of someone as influential and important as Simon. She gambles on the fact that Jesus might look at her differently – perhaps she had even met him and experienced his grace before.

The spectacle could not have been more intrusive or more awkward and the Pharisees watch, waiting to see how Jesus would react. Simon clearly felt that Jesus should have recoiled in horror, as he thinks to himself, *"If this man were a prophet, he would have known who and what kind of woman this is who is touching him—that she is a sinner,"* (v39). At the very moment Simon was dismissing Jesus' prophetic abilities, Jesus demonstrates that he sees Simon's very thoughts and stands up to answer them (v40).

. . .

Jesus tells a story of two debtors, one who owed five hundred denarii and the other fifty (one denarius was about a day's wage for a labourer at that time). Jesus questions Simon about which debtor will love the creditor more, if he cancels their debts. Simon's response reveals his reluctance to answer the question as he can already see where this conversation is going: he replies, *"I suppose the one for whom he cancelled the greater debt,'* (v43). This, Jesus tells him, is the correct answer.

Jesus turns to look directly at the woman, asking Simon if he sees her and understands the enormity of her gesture. At the same time, he criticises Simon for his lack of hospitality (of huge cultural importance at that time), reminding Simon that he hadn't given him any water for his feet, yet the woman, *"has bathed my feet with her tears and dried them with her hair,"* (v44). Jesus points out that Simon didn't even greet him with a kiss, *"yet but from the time I came in she has not stopped kissing my feet,"* (v45). Finally, Simon didn't even anoint Jesus' head with oil, but the woman, *"has anointed my feet with ointment,"* (v46) – feet, in those times, perpetually dirty and dusty from the roads. Jesus' criticism would have infuriated Simon all the more and simultaneously let the brave and humble woman know that Jesus had seen and appreciated every gesture she had made and saw the heart of worship and repentance behind her gestures.

Jesus then turns and speaks gently to the woman, as he does to so many women during his ministry. He tells her that her sins have been forgiven then concludes the encounter with the words, *"Your faith has saved you; go in peace,"* (v50). Where the

Pharisees would have dismissed the woman and sent her away, ashamed, Jesus shows her he sees deeply into her heart and values the gratitude she demonstrates for his forgiveness and love. Her lavish adoration demonstrates her deep love for Jesus, who had given her the grace she needed to turn from the sinful lifestyle she had been trapped in.

Jesus' stories of debt and debtors, as well as his response to the woman who anoints him, leaves the Pharisees even more puzzled and perplexed about who Jesus is and what he has come to do. The woman demonstrates an understanding and response that the Pharisees would do well to emulate. In the encounter with the woman, Jesus sends them a clear message – that he sees into their hearts and minds too and won't be cowed by their tactics of intimidation and entrapment.

The story should encourage all of us that, whoever we are and wherever our past has led us, however unsavoury, Jesus sees, forgives and loves. None are too far from his grace and mercy. Let's approach him today, with the spirit of the anointing woman, not that of the Pharisees who couldn't see their need for him, as she did.

FOLLOW-UP IDEAS

1. READ

Read the whole passage: **Luke 7:36-50**

Are there any parts of the story that really strike you? Which and why?

2. LISTEN

Listen to the song *"Seas of Crimson,"* by Shane and Shane.

I love the idea that God's love and grace rushes in, in place of our sin.

Which lines speak to you?

3. THINK AND PRAY

Are there times that come to you as you pray, when you know you have "sinned and fallen short," of God's standards, but you came back to Him and knew you had received His forgiveness? *Spend some time thanking God for His forgiveness and grace.*

Do you need to come back to God today and pray for His forgiveness and grace? *Come to Him with a simple prayer and have faith that your relationship with Him is instantly restored.*

REFLECTION 20

THE GOD WHO SEES OUR FAITH AND LIFTS US WHEN IT FAILS (PETER - MATTHEW 14:22-33)

Focus Scripture: Matthew 14:22-33

Focus verse: "Peter answered him, 'Lord, if it is you, command me to come to you on the water.' He said, 'Come.' So Peter got out of the boat, started walking on the water, and came towards Jesus." v28-29

REFLECTION

When you think of Peter in the Bible, what stories spring to mind? Perhaps his passionate refusal to accept Jesus' impending death and resurrection in Matthew 16:22-23, earning him a rebuke he would never forget? Or maybe his powerful declaration of who he believed Jesus to be, a few verses earlier in the same book?

John records that it was Peter who struck out in the Garden of Gethsemane (John 18:10-11), cutting off the ear of the slave of the High Priest. Luke and Matthew, recording the same event, spare the detail of the name of the disciple committing this act.

Matthew charts Peter's declaration that he will never deny Jesus (Matthew 26:33-35), as well as (in verse 75) the anguish of the very same man, as he wept bitterly because the very thing he was sure would never happen, now had.

Peter was a passionate and impetuous character. He didn't hide in the shadows, or do things by halves. This is why I am not surprised that it was he, rather than any of the other disciples, who got out of the boat and walked towards Jesus in our reading for today.

The story of Peter walking on water comes half way through Matthew 14. It had been an emotional day: Jesus had heard news of the execution of his beloved cousin, John the Baptist, and had been heading off for some time alone with his Father, when a crowd desperate for his ministry pressed in. He had stayed, healing them and providing sustenance for them, feeding 5000 men, plus women and children (around 15000 people by the estimates of some Bible scholars), before trying again to withdraw to a quiet place for some time on his own.

Verse 24 tells us, *"by this time the boat, battered by the waves, was far from the land, for the wind was against them."* Jesus saw them. He had not abandoned them to the storm. He was far off, up a mountain, but he saw their peril and *"early in the morning he came walking towards them on the lake,"* v25. Far from being merely an opportunity to still the storm, something even more miraculous was about to happen.

• • •

Whilst the other disciples cried out in fear, believing Jesus to be a ghost, Peter responded: "'Lord, if it is you, command me to come to you on the water.' [Jesus] said, 'Come,'" v28-29. I often wish I knew more about these iconic moments in the Bible: what made Peter respond in this way? What motivated him? Why did Jesus allow him this miracle that defied the laws of nature?

I believe Jesus saw in Peter a raw, impetuous faith. Peter exhibited it again and again, in the stories I mentioned earlier. Jesus saw Peter's willingness to step out in faith and rewarded him with a miracle. I don't know about you, but any time I have felt the power of God at work in my life, I have ridden the wave of it for some time afterwards. I can only imagine how Peter felt after walking on water towards Jesus.

We know how the story ends – Peter takes his eyes off Jesus, notices the wind whipping up the waves, and begins to sink. Jesus catches him by the hand, saving him from sinking beneath the tumult of the waves, addressing him, as he does so, as "you of little faith." I like to believe that, far from being a chastisement from Jesus, it's a gentle rebuke, a loving sigh of longing that Peter would have trusted him that little bit more for that little bit longer. Jesus sees the tiny bit of faith that Peter had summoned, and this is enough for him to experience a miracle he would remember for the rest of his life, and one we would read about centuries later.

Peter took his eyes off Jesus and fixed them on the threatening surroundings and began to sink, but the fact remains – he was the only one who had the faith to step out of the boat in the first place. I imagine Jesus smiling, even as he delivers his "rebuke," seeing with pleasure the faith Peter had in him, even as he yearned for it to have lasted longer. The word used by Jesus for "little faith," has caused debate over its meaning. It was not the same Greek word used to chastise the hard-hearted people of Nazareth for their complete lack of faith. Some argue, from its later appearance in other books, that the word Jesus used meant "brief" faith – he saw Peter's faith, granted him a show-stopping miracle, but wished he could have sustained his faith a little longer, before it was snuffed out by the wind and waves.

Is there something today that you need a "little" faith for? It is so easy to berate ourselves for not having "enough" faith, especially when we think of it in terms of the "size" of our faith. But Jesus sees your faith today, however small. He sees your attempts to pray and trust him, to step out and fix your eyes on him. He calls you not to "more" faith but to "longer" faith. Keep looking to him. Keep praying for that thing you're losing hope over. Keep your eyes on him, not on the waves that will inevitably come. He has his eyes on you and will give you all the courage and resilience you need.

FOLLOW-UP IDEAS

1. READ

Read the whole passage: **Matthew 14:22-23**

Are there any parts of the story that really strike you? Which and why?

2. LISTEN

Listen to the song *"Walk on the Water,"* by Britt Nichole.

I love the questions she asks and her encouragement to take just one step.

Which lines speak to you?

3. THINK AND PRAY

Are there times that come to you as you pray, where you can remember having faith for a difficult situation, that God brought you through, as you and others prayed? *Spend some time thanking God for these memories of his faithfulness and use them to help you trust Him in the current situations you are facing.*

What metaphorical boat do you need to step out of today? Is there something God is asking you to do that you are not sure you have the faith to step out and do? *Ask for His help to keep your eyes fixed on him; ask him for the long, slow-burning faith that leads, however slowly, to a breakthrough in your situation.*

REFLECTION 21

THE GOD WHO SEES OUR GRIEF AND CALLS US TO HOPE (MARY MAGDALENE - JOHN 20:11-18)

Focus Scripture: John 20:11-18

Focus verse: "Jesus said to her, 'Mary!' She turned and said to him in Hebrew, 'Rabbouni!' (which means Teacher)." v16

REFLECTION

Every Easter, I love to ponder the undocumented space between Good Friday and Easter Sunday. I like to imagine what Jesus' disciples were doing in that time (both the twelve and the wider group that followed him, including many women). I often wonder whether they waited with hope, or with a devastating grief for a hope unravelled, an imagined future mourned, since Jesus had taken his last breath.

They had waited out Easter Saturday – the only detail we are told are that the disciples had *"locked the doors, for fear of the Jews."* Now it was Easter Sunday and Mary Magdalene was about to play a part in the resurrection story she could never have foreseen.

Other gospel writers have other women in their accounts, bringing spices to anoint Jesus' body for burial, but John chooses to portray Mary Magdalene alone at the tomb. She had already run to tell John and Simon Peter that Jesus' body was not there, perhaps assuming, in the drama of the weekend's events, that it had been stolen. They had come and gone and now here she was again, weeping outside the empty tomb, her heart not yet grasping the full picture emerging.

Why do any of the gospel writers position the women as the first witnesses at all? In the ancient world their testimonies carried little, if any weight, and they were not admitted as witnesses in courts of law. Even the disciples (other than Peter), dismissed their report that perhaps Jesus had risen, just as he foretold, as an "*idle tale*," (Luke 24v11).

The stories of the women being first to see the risen Jesus exemplify the great value and respect he had for them, contrary to the cultural norms of the time. Jesus saw and valued the women, at a time when others would have looked past them and considered them inferior. He had been kind, not judgmental to the woman at the well (John 4) and compassionate to the woman with the issue of blood (Luke 8). He had praised, not chastised, the woman who poured expensive perfume on his feet at Bethany. On each of these occasions, he had seen into the women's hearts and sent them on their way healed, restored, redeemed.

. . .

What did he see in Mary Magdalene on the morning of the resurrection? I imagine he saw her faithfulness and dedication. He had delivered her from seven demons, early in his ministry (Luke 8:2). Since then, she had been a loyal follower, even supporting him financially. She had stayed to the last, as he died a cruel death on the cross, not turning away, when it might have been dangerous for her to be associated with him, political prisoner that he had become. Now here she was again at the tomb, to embalm him, to mourn him.

As she wept, perhaps he saw her grief and vulnerability, her crushed hopes for all that she felt she had lost. The scene that follows is tender and loving. He asks her, *"Woman, why are you weeping? For whom are you looking?"* v15. Believing he is the gardener, she begins to question him about Jesus' body. Then he calls her by name. *"Jesus said to her, 'Mary!' She turned and said to him in Hebrew, 'Rabbouni!' (which means Teacher),"* v16. In calling her name, he spoke to the deepest part of her and she responded instantly. In that moment she moved from mourning to rejoicing, deep grief to delighted hope. "Rabbouni!" she responded, showing that she saw him too, not as the gardener, but as her risen Lord.

"The Resurrection," a famous painting by Heinrich Hoffman depicts this scene movingly. In it, Jesus stands just behind the weeping Mary Magdalene. He is right there, seeing her, ready to give her strength and hope. With eyes blinded by tears in the dim light of the dawning day, she doesn't see him yet. When she does, her world changes, instantly, for the better.

• • •

He sees you too. He sees the times you weep and grieve and despair. Even amidst those hard emotions and difficult days when all hope seems lost, he is right there, behind you. When you open your ears and heed his voice calling your name, he can raise you up to a better place of joy and hope. As Mary's story powerfully illustrates, "*Weeping may linger for the night, but joy comes with the morning,*" Psalm 30:5.

FOLLOW-UP IDEAS

1. READ

Read the whole passage: **John 20: 11-18**

Are there any parts of the story that really strike you? Which and why?

2. LISTEN

Listen to the song "*I Will Rise,*" by Chris Tomlin.

I love the idea that God touches and heals our grief and sadness, as He calls our name and we respond.

Which lines speak to you?

3. THINK AND PRAY

Are there times that come to you as you pray, when you've felt sadness, grief and pain, but God has stepped in and breathed life into your broken heart afresh? *Spend some time thanking God for the hope He gives you in your life, even in the darkest of times.*

Are you grieving today? Are you feeling defeated and broken? *Ask God to breathe life and hope into you afresh today, to enable you to rise up and keep going, fortified by the hope He brings.*

REFLECTION 22

THE GOD WHO SEES OUR DOUBTS AND MEETS US IN THEM (THOMAS - JOHN 20:24-31)

Focus Scripture: John 20:24-31

Focus verse: "Then [Jesus] said to Thomas, 'Put your finger here and see my hands. Reach out your hand and put it in my side. Do not doubt but believe.'"

REFLECTION

Am I the only one who feels that poor Thomas has had bad press for a couple of centuries? Ask anyone what comes to mind at the mention of Thomas' name, and the adjective "doubting," will spring from their lips without a moment's hesitation.

How easily we have forgotten some of Thomas' finer moments in the Bible. In John's gospel, as Jesus' ministry gathered pace, the Jews were becoming more and more disgruntled and outraged at his claims. In some places, they were seeking ways to kill him and, in the region of Judea, some had threatened to stone him. Being Jesus' disciple was a risky business. So when

Jesus informed the disciples that they would be heading back to Bethany, in the Judea region, because of the news of the unwell Lazarus, John reports that the disciples tried to persuade him otherwise. It is only Thomas who says, *'Let us also go, that we may die with him,'* John 11:16.

Additionally, whilst Thomas doesn't get as much 'airtime' in the gospels as some of the other disciples, we later find him setting up one of Jesus' most famous declarations of all. We know the declaration – probably from Sunday School upwards – but few could name Thomas as the one who gave Jesus the opportunity to articulate it. *'I am the way, and the truth, and the life. No one comes to the Father except through me,'* (John 14;6) is foundational to our faith. But less well-known is the verse before it: *"Thomas said to him, 'Lord, we do not know where you are going. How can we know the way?'"* It was Thomas' inquiring and loyal nature that led Jesus to declare one of the most central tenets of the Christian faith.

Why does any of this matter? I think it contextualises the exchange that happens between Jesus and Thomas after Jesus' resurrection and gives us a fresh perspective. Far from being a doubter with little faith to speak of, Thomas is instead a loyal disciple, who is struggling with the death of his Lord and needs something more concrete to hold onto, to move him from doubt to faith. Doesn't that make him just like most of us? And Jesus, who sees his doubts and disillusionment, gives him just what he needs to dispel them.

I can hardly bear to imagine the anguish contained in the short verses that open our scripture for today: *"But Thomas (who was called the Twin), one of the twelve, was not with them when Jesus came. So, the other disciples told him, 'We have seen the Lord,'"* v24-5. If you've ever missed out on something spectacular, whilst others have experienced it in full, you might be able to understand a small fraction of what Thomas went through here.

We are not told where he was or why he wasn't with the other disciples. But imagine the bitter anguish of returning to where the disciples were gathered, to find that he was the only one who had missed out on seeing the risen Lord. Thomas found himself entirely unable to take their word for it, making his famous declaration that *"Unless I see the mark of the nails in his hands, and put my finger in the mark of the nails and my hand in his side, I will not believe,"* v25.

Imagine then, the whole week of emotional conflict that followed. The rest of the disciples, going about their business with a peace and joy in their hearts and hope for the future. Thomas – gloomy, despondent – wondering whether he would ever get to experience that same peace, hope and joy, or whether he had missed his opportunity forever. What an eternity that week must have felt for him.

But Jesus doesn't leave him languishing in his gloom and his doubts. He sees Thomas' need for irrefutable proof and once again visits the house where he and the disciples were gathered. He declares, as in the previous visit, *"Peace be with you,"* v26, then turns to Thomas, offering him the opportunity to *"'Put your finger here and see my hands. Reach out your hand and put it in my side. Do not doubt but believe,'"* v27. It is not recorded whether Thomas takes him up on this offer, or whether the risen Jesus standing in front of him was enough for his doubts to flee. Either way, *"Thomas answered him, 'My Lord and my God!'"* v28

I love how the story concludes: *"Jesus said to him, 'Have you believed because you have seen me? Blessed are those who have not seen and yet have come to believe,'"* v29. Jesus encourages us to grow to a faith that doesn't require constant proof – yet at the same time, shows, through his response to Thomas, that he is still willing to step in and give us what we need to strengthen our faith when it wavers, as it so often does.

Jesus saw Thomas' scepticism and doubts and challenged them with evidence. I believe he does this in our lives too. Far from rejecting Thomas or pushing him away because of his doubts, he provides reassurance that grows Thomas' faith and trust. When we are wavering, hesitating or uncertain, I believe God can give us the same reassurance, if, like Thomas, we are willing to step out and seek it. Sometimes just experiencing the presence of Jesus is all the proof we need.

FOLLOW-UP IDEAS

1. READ

Read the whole passage: **John 20: 24-29**

Are there any parts of the story that really strike you? Which and why?

2. LISTEN

Listen to the song *"Praise you in the Storm,"* by Casting Crowns.

I love the way the songwriter expresses the idea that God is still God and we can still trust Him, even amidst doubts, fears and "storms."

Which lines speak to you?

3. THINK AND PRAY

Are there times that come to you as you pray, when you were doubting any aspect of God's character or care for you but you remember how He stepped in and alleviated your doubts and helped restore your trust in Him? *Spend some time thanking God for the hope He gives you in your life, even when doubts arise.*

Are you doubting God in any way today? *Ask God to meet you in your doubts and to encourage you in some way today that helps to lift you out of them and trust Him afresh.*

REFLECTION 23

THE GOD WHO SEES OUR REGRETS AND GIVES US A SECOND CHANCE (PETER PART 2 - JOHN 21:1-19)

Focus Scripture: John 21:1-19

Focus verse: "When they had finished breakfast, Jesus said to Simon Peter, "Simon son of John, do you love me more than these?" He said to him, "Yes, Lord; you know that I love you." Jesus said to him, "Feed my lambs."" v15

REFLECTION

This passage depicts the reunion between Peter and the master and saviour he had so recently denied. How do you imagine Peter behaving here? Running towards Jesus, eager to make reparation for his desperate denials? Or head down, defeated, wondering whether any of this was redeemable, forgivable?

We have to remember that Peter, here, is a man with a heavy burden weighing on his heart. He has lost his friend, his Lord and all his hopes for the future. Not only that, but he had not stepped in, following Jesus to the death as he said he would, instead denying he knew Jesus, even to someone as uninfluential as a servant girl. The gospel accounts of Jesus' appearances to his disciples after the resurrection are scant in details. We know that Jesus had a conversation with the women and with "doubting" Thomas and that Peter had probably already seen the risen Jesus by the time today's incident occurs. However, there is no record of any conversation with Peter that had yet put things right or lifted his burden of guilt.

John tells us that, *"Simon Peter said to them, "I am going fishing." They said to him, "We will go with you." They went out and got into the boat, but that night they caught nothing,"* v3. Here we perhaps see a heavy-hearted Peter, trying to find solace in fishing - the only other thing he was trained for, aside from being Jesus' disciple. In his declaration that he is "going fishing," I wonder if it was a hint to the others that he wanted to be alone – he doesn't invite them, merely tells them he is going. Perhaps the disciples glanced at each other, intuitively knowing lonely introspection wouldn't be good for Peter that day, and jumped into the boat too.

In an atmosphere potentially laden with grief, imagine their disillusionment when even fishing brings them no solace or reward. Then the risen Jesus, appearing on the shore close by, tells them to cast their nets to the right. The result was a catch of such a huge number of fish that they were unable to haul it in. The parallel to the beginning of their life as Jesus' followers wouldn't have escaped Peter or the other disciples here. In Luke 5, Jesus had commissioned Peter, James and John to be "fishers of men," following a catch of fish very similar to this one.

. . .

I have always imagined joy and delight in what Peter does next: *"When Simon Peter heard that it was the Lord, he put on [his outer] clothes...and jumped into the sea,"* v7. But was it? Some theologians note that, since they were so close to the shore and the huge catch of fish could not be pulled aboard, it would have been dragged behind them in the nets. Instead of eagerness to be the first to get to Jesus, could Peter's leaping into the sea have been a distraction tactic – one where he busied himself pulling and adjusting the net dragging behind the boat, hoping to avoid, rather than face the reckoning he knew must come?

Whether he was the eager first or the reluctant last to arrive, Peter joins the other disciples to have breakfast with Jesus, who had been cooking fish for them on the beach. It is here that their relationship is restored. Jesus addresses Peter 3 times, once to make up for each denial, in another parallel that Peter couldn't have missed. Jesus repeatedly asks Peter if he loves him, and Peter repeatedly affirms that he does. With each affirmation comes the instruction to tend and feed Jesus' future followers. This must have been so gloriously redemptive for Peter. He had fallen so spectacularly and failed so miserably. Now he was restored and commissioned to carry the gospel message to those around him, his own experience of failure and redemption, perfectly placing him to do so.

It is so easy to berate ourselves when we, like Peter, fail and go our own way. But we, like Peter are human and frail too. Jesus made the first move to bring about restoration for Peter, and will for us, too. If we can respond positively and turn our hearts back to Jesus, instead of hiding our burden of shame and regret and trying to carry it ourselves, he can speak the same redemption into our hearts and minds. And we, in turn, can speak it to others who need it just as much.

FOLLOW-UP IDEAS

1. READ

Read the whole passage: **John 21: 1-19**

Are there any parts of the story that really strike you? Which and why?

2. LISTEN

Listen to the song "*Second Chance*," by Rend Collective.

I love the idea that second chances are at the heart of the Christian faith.

Which lines speak to you?

3. THINK AND PRAY

Are there times that come to you as you pray, when you came back to God, brought him your regrets and felt that He gave you a second chance...or a third or fourth? *Spend some time thanking God for His continual grace and mercy in your life, with all its imperfections and regrets.*

Are you carrying a burden of regret today? *Ask for a fresh touch from God today, to enable you to move past your regret and step into a new season, with a new sense of purpose, guided by Him.*

REFLECTION 24

THE GOD WHO SEES OUR PAST AND TRANSFORMS US (PAUL - ACTS 9:1-22)

Focus Scripture: Acts 9:1-22

Focus verse: "At once he began to preach in the synagogues that Jesus is the Son of God. All those who heard him were astonished and asked, "Isn't he the man who raised havoc in Jerusalem among those who call on this name?" Acts 9:20-21

REFLECTION

We first meet the cruel, zealous character of Saul two chapters before today's reflection, in Acts 7. Stephen has been threatened with severe consequences if he doesn't stop spreading the message of Christ's resurrection throughout Jerusalem. He explains that he simply can't comply with the commands of the authorities as he is answerable only to God and this results in his brutal, public stoning. The witnesses to the stoning, we are told, *"laid their coats at the feet of a young man named Saul,"* (Acts 7:58) implying an approval which is confirmed in the next chapter.

• • •

Things go from bad to worse when a, *"severe persecution breaks out against the church in Jerusalem,"* (Acts 8:1) with Saul as a key perpetrator, *"ravaging the church by entering house after house; dragging off both men and women,"* (Acts 8:3) and imprisoning them. God causes even these horrors to work for good, as the scattered disciples speak of the Messiah wherever they go, resulting in the conversions of some influential people: Simon the Sorcerer and the Ethiopian Eunuch (Acts 8).

In Acts 9, things take a dramatic turn. Saul is still, *"breathing threats and murder against the disciples of the Lord,"* (v1) and even asks for written permission from the high priest to validate his capture and imprisonment of those who, *"belonged to the Way,"* (v2). He doesn't get very far on the road to Damascus before he is halted in his tracks by a blinding light from heaven and the voice of Jesus himself asking him, *"Saul, Saul why do you persecute me?"* (v4). Even in his confusion, as he falls, blinded, to the ground, he addresses the voice as, *"Lord,"* (v5), as if his soul already recognises what his mind has not yet admitted.

I wonder what Saul and the men travelling with him thought and felt for the three days Saul was without sight, powerless and vulnerable, after the dramatic encounter on the road (his companions had heard the voice but not seen the light). Even more extraordinarily, what might have gone through the mind of Ananias, when Jesus appeared to him in a vision, telling him to go to *"the house of Judas [and] look for a man of Tarsus named Saul,"* (v11)? Saul's terrifying reputation had very much spread, causing Ananias to double check that the Lord meant the very man who had authority to make Ananias' life very unpleasant indeed. What a level of faith and trust in God it must have taken from Ananias to believe God's message that

Saul was to be, *"an instrument whom I have chosen to bring my name before Gentiles and kings and before the people of Israel,"* (v15) to set out to knock on that door with a deep breath and Holy Spirit-inspired courage, and to pray for Saul?

Upon Ananias' staggering act of obedience, *"something like scales,"* (v18) fall from Saul's eyes, his sight is restored and he gets up and is baptised. The heart-transformation that takes place so suddenly and finally is astonishing to us, reading the sequence of events as it unfolds, but not to God who saw Saul's heart and knew He could transform it into something for His glory and honour.

We might read of Saul's actions and liken his persecution of the early Christians to other persecutions of God's people in the Bible – at the hands of Pharaohs or wicked, idolatrous kings. But Saul's was subtly different: belonging to the Synagogue of Freed Men, as he did, he was zealous for his Jewish heritage and for the preservation of the Mosaic Law. He truly believed that his persecution of "the Way," was protecting his fellow men from a dangerous sect peddling false teaching. Whilst Saul was unwittingly using his zealous nature for evil, God saw that zealousness and transformed it for good and His glory. We are told that, after a few days with the disciples in Damascus, *"immediately he began to proclaim Jesus in the synagogues, saying, 'He is the Son of God,"* (v21). Whilst people were initially suspicious, Saul's words and his dramatic conversion proclaimed the truth of Jesus' transforming power – a message he would go on to give his whole life to spread in all circumstances, at all costs, his name changed to Paul to reflect his new identity.

. . .

Sometimes, we can feel the force of our past, pulling us back, bringing us down. We feel the pull of guilt and shame for things we have done and experienced, and might write ourselves off, disqualifying ourselves from God's blessings and plans for our futures. God doesn't disqualify us. He sees into our hearts and can use the character, personality and skills He has given us, for His good and His glory, even if they were used otherwise, in the past. If God can transform someone like Saul – who went onto preach, plant churches and write letters that still inspire readers today – He can transform our hearts too, if we respond to His call.

FOLLOW-UP IDEAS

1. READ

Read the whole passage: **Acts 9:1-22**

Are there any parts of the story that really strike you? Which and why?

2. LISTEN

Listen to the song *"The God Who Stays,"* by Matthew West.

I love the idea the song expresses, that there is literally nothing that has the power to separate us from God's love, and that God stays with us, despite everything we might think can send Him running.

Which lines speak to you?

3. THINK AND PRAY

As you pray, are their times in your life that come to mind, when you know God has turned around an event or difficult situation to use for His glory? *Spend some time thanking God for His transforming power today.*

Are there still "unredeemed" parts of your character and personality that you need to surrender to God today? Are there aspects of your past that still burden you with guilt and shame? *Come to Him today, and ask Him to continue the work of transformation in your life, to complete the "good work," He has started in you.*

REFLECTION 25

THE GOD WHO SEES OUR ORDINARY LIVES AND CAN STILL WORK THROUGH THEM FOR HIS GLORY (ONESIPHORUS, SHIPHRAH AND PUAH - 2 TIMOTHY 1:16-18, EXODUS 1:15-20)

Focus Scriptures: 2 Timothy 1:16-18
Exodus 1:15-20

Focus verse: *"So God dealt well with the midwives; and the people multiplied and became very strong. And because the midwives feared God, he gave them families,"* **Exodus 1: 20-21"**

REFLECTION

If we have been Christians any length of time, the names listed in the "faith roll of honour," in Hebrews 11 will be very familiar to us. Some of them are the stuff of Sunday school legend – Abraham, Noah. Others, like Rahab, appear in the less 'sanitised' stories of faith we encounter as adults.

Most of us could retell the story of Moses, Joseph and David... But let's play, for a moment, a slightly harder round of the "Bible Knowledge Bumper Quiz." Ready?

. . .

What was Onesiphorus known for? How did Shiphrah and Puah help save a nation? What did Asaph write? What was created by Bezalel and Oholiab? What laws did Zelophehad's daughters get changed?

How many of these less well-known Bible characters had you heard of? Possibly none or very few. Yet they all played obscure but important roles in the unfolding history of God's chosen people and their presence in the Bible should be an encouragement to us all. Their contributions and roles were not as heralded or celebrated as the "greats," of faith we are so familiar with – and yet God saw their talents and the contributions they made and they had value in the midst of their ordinary, uncelebrated lives.

Onesiphorus is such a great example of this. 2 Timothy 1 is written against a backdrop of dissension and disloyalty. Timothy had been helping Paul to challenge some renegade leaders in Ephesus, who were causing divisions and confusion amongst the Christians there. Paul writes 2 Timothy from his final imprisonment in Rome to encourage Timothy not to lose heart.

In the letter, he asks God to, *"grant mercy to the household of Onesiphorus, because he often refreshed me and was not ashamed of my chain; when he arrived in Rome, he eagerly searched for me and found me —may the Lord grant that he will find mercy from the Lord on that day! And you know very well how much service he rendered in Ephesus,"* 2 Timothy 1:16-18. The NIV translates *"service he rendered,"* as *"how many times he helped me,"* v18. In such a brief mention, in three short verses, Onesiphorus is immortalised for his servant heart. Whilst others deserted Paul, Onesiphorus sought him out and refreshed him – time and time again. I love that what we might consider unworthy of notice or mention is mentioned here. God sees Paul's need and Onesiphorus' servant heart and brings the two together.

Another pair of people whose deeds cover just six verses, but who had a lasting impact on God's people, were Shiphrah and Puah, two Hebrew midwives, who had the courage to stand up to the cruel, Egyptian king. They were ordered to instantly kill any Hebrew boys that were born but, *"The midwives feared God; they did not do as the king of Egypt commanded them, but they let the boys live,"* v17. When summoned to explain themselves to the king, the midwives came up with an excuse, explaining that the Hebrews were stronger and more vigorous that the Egyptians which meant the midwives did not get there in time.

God sees and blesses the actions of these fearless women: *"So God dealt well with the midwives; and the people multiplied and became very strong. And because the midwives feared God, he gave them families,"* v20-21. They only appear in six short verses, but their legacy was the strengthening of the numbers of the Israelites, God's chosen people. It might not be stretching it too far to imagine that their noble actions might even have saved someone like Moses. In doing their ordinary jobs, in difficult circumstances, God sees their loyalty and faithfulness and they unknowingly end up being a vital part of God's great plan for the freedom for His people.

In the next reflection (on a similar theme) I will reveal all about how Asaph, Zelophehad's daughters and Bezalel and Oholiab feature in the Bible, but for now, let us be encouraged by the stories we have read today. Not everyone preaches from a platform or rises through the ranks to become a notable and influential leader. But, as "one body and many parts," God knows and sees each one of us in our ordinary, "unnoticeable," lives. When others do not notice the positive things that we bring to the world around us, God *does* see and He celebrates them.

FOLLOW-UP IDEAS

1. READ

Read the whole of both passages: **2 Timothy 1:16-18, Exodus 1: 15-20**

Are there any parts of the story that really strike you? Which and why?

2. LISTEN

Listen to the song *"We Seek Your Kingdom,"* by Noel Robinson, Andy Flannagan and Graham Hunter.

I love the idea the song expresses, that God can use everything we do in our ordinary lives, to bring revival, transformation and healing to our world.

Which lines speak to you?

3. THINK AND PRAY

As you pray, are their times in your life that come to mind, when you know God has furthered His kingdom and influence in the world, through something ordinary you have been involved with? *Spend some time thanking God for those occasions today.*

Do you ever feel that your life is too "ordinary," and unremarkable for God to work through? *Come to Him today, and ask Him to help you to see your life and actions the way He sees them.*

REFLECTION 26

THE GOD WHO SEES OUR SMALL ACTS AND CAN STILL USE THEM FOR HIS GLORY (ASAPH, ZELOPHEHAD'S DAUGHTERS, BEZALEL AND OHOLIAB - LUKE 13:18-22, PSALM 73, EXODUS 31:1-11, NUMBERS 27:1-11)

Focus Scriptures: Luke 13:18-22
Psalm 73
Exodus 31:1-11
Numbers 27:1-11

Focus verse: ***"What is the kingdom of God like? And to what should I compare it? It is like a mustard seed that someone took and sowed in the garden; it grew and became a tree, and the birds of the air made nests in its branches,"*** **Luke 13:18-19**

REFLECTION

The parable of the mustard seed appears in three of the four gospels (only John leaves it out) and the parable of the yeast appears in two (Matthew and Luke). Both reiterate the idea from our previous reflection that God sees infinite value in the smallest of things. He sees the long-lasting impact of the smallest acts of our lives and watches them echo into eternity, while we catch only a brief, temporary glimpse.

. . .

Firstly, the mustard seed. Both Matthew and Mark call it the "*smallest*," of all seeds, and all three gospel writers point out that it grows to such proportions that the birds can make nests in its branches, or its "*shade*," according to Mark. On average a mustard seed is only 2mm in diameter yet, depending on the variety, the tree, with its distinctive shaped branches, can grow up to twenty or thirty feet tall.

It is clear why Jesus used this parable to illustrate the nature of the kingdom he had brought to earth. As they went around, Jesus and his first followers carried out small, daily acts of healing, forgiveness, grace and kindness that might not have looked much to the ruling powers of the day. They were scattering 'seed', like the mustard seed which over time grew with far-reaching effects, not necessarily visible at first

Similarly, the yeast. As Luke and Matthew point out, it only takes a little yeast, mixed in with lot of flour, for the whole batch to be leavened.

This is again a great encouragement. I wrote in the previous reflection about the small acts (seeds sown) of Onesiphorus, Shiphrah and Puah – not known leaders of any celebrity, but whose act shaped the future of God's people. In this reflection we will recall some other people in the Bible, faithfully going about the small tasks set in front of them, with big repercussions – mustard seeds, growing into huge trees, seen by God, even if not by themselves.

. . .

Asaph is one of these. Whilst we might unwittingly consider the Psalms to have been written by David, because many of them are, there are other writers who contributed to this incredible canon of prayers, poetry and lament. Psalm 73 is one penned by this little-known writer. Most of us can probably quote its stirring, encouraging conclusion: "*Whom have I in heaven but you? And there is nothing on earth that I desire other than you. My flesh and my heart may fail, but God is the strength of my heart and my portion for ever,*" Psalm 73: 25-6. The words of a largely unknown writer, echo down the generations, providing encouragement and reassurance for those going through difficult times, even today.

Behind-the-scenes craftsmen also get a mention in the Bible. In Exodus 31, we are told that God has filled Bezalel with, "*divine spirit, with ability, intelligence, and knowledge in every kind of craft, to devise artistic designs, to work in gold, silver, and bronze, in cutting stones for setting, and in carving wood, in every kind of craft,*" Exodus 31:2-5. We also learn of Oholiab, working with Bezalel to craft the many fine, intricate details of the Temple, that God has revealed to Moses. We remember Moses' name, not theirs, but without their patient skill and craftmanship, the Israelites wouldn't have had such an awe-inspiring place in which to meet God and pass on their faith to the next generation worshipping there. God sees and values their unseen efforts.

Finally, Zelophehad's daughters get a mention in Numbers 27, driving an unprecedented policy-change that would have improved the lives of generations of women yet to come. Mahlah, Noah, Hoglah, Milcah, and Tirzah stand before Moses and all the other influential people in their community and pluck up the courage to explain their plight: their father had died, leaving no sons and, as women, they were not legally allowed to receive his inheritance. This isn't fair. As a result of their courage, Moses takes the situation before God and come back with a complete statute change for the whole of Israel: daughters, brothers, uncles, and distant kin would henceforth be able to inherit, in the absence of a son, Numbers 27:9-11. Imagine how many people through the generations were impacted by their actions, provided for rather than in poverty, due to this change.

These small, unknown-to-most-of-us acts are recorded in the Bible because God sees them an values them. Each of these treasured people took the tiny mustard seeds they had, planted them and probably had no idea of the vastness of the spread of the branches that provided shelter and hope for others, generations later.

God sees all of our small acts too. Our acts might be still different to those we've looked at today, and feel still smaller, even more unseen. But each seed of goodness that we sow, in our jobs, our caring roles, our expressions of poetry and art, our family lives, the grace-filled, ordinary conversations we have, is seen and valued by God. Only He can see the full impact they have on our world and its future.

FOLLOW-UP IDEAS

1. READ

Read each of the passages: **Luke 13:18-22, Psalm 73, Exodus 31:1-11, Numbers 27:1-11**

Are there any parts of the stories that really strike you? Which and why?

2. LISTEN

Listen to the song "*Stand in Faith,*" by Danny Gokey.

I love the idea the song expresses, that it's by walking in faith that even the smallest things grow and change.

Which lines speak to you?

3. THINK AND PRAY

As you pray, are their times in your life that come to mind, when something ordinary that you did felt God-ordained and God-inspired? *Spend some time thanking God for those occasions today.*

Do you ever feel that your "ordinary," acts are unseen and unvalued? *Come to Him today, and ask Him to help you to understand that He sees and values every part of your life as you seek to live it for Him.*

REFLECTION 27

THE GOD WHO SEES THE STRUGGLES IN OUR MINDS AND CAN STILL THEM (ROMANS 12:1-18, PHILIPPIANS 4:4-9, 2 TIMOTHY 1:3-7)

Focus Scriptures: Romans 12:1-18

Philippians 4:4-9

2 Timothy 1:3-7

Focus verse: "Do not be conformed to this world, but be transformed by the renewing of your minds," Romans 12:2.

REFLECTION

So many Christian books have been written about the struggles we face, mentally and emotionally, as we seek to live our lives as Christians. Such struggles are often couched in military terms – winning a war, fighting a battle. And it truly is a battle. Every day, we face a multitude of issues, vying for our time and attention. Global events feel like they are unravelling, out of control. In our personal lives issues around such things as health, finance and family life compete to brings us down and destroy our peace and joy.

• • •

The Bible doesn't shy away from these issues. It contains honest admissions of the struggles faced by all of humankind throughout the centuries and encourages us not to give up and lie down, defeated, but to stand up and fight the battle for our minds, equipped with truth, in place of the lies that can so easily creep in. God sees the battles that rage for our minds and wants to speak truth and light into the most distorted thought patterns we have, and free us from them.

Romans 12 issues the daunting exhortation not to be, *"conformed to this world, but [to] be transformed by the renewing of your minds,"* Romans 12:2. This imperative is central to stilling the thoughts raging through our minds and living with a greater sense of hope and peace. It is a life long and on-going work – the Greek verb for being transformed is in the present continuous tense. It might be translated as *"be being transformed,"* in other words, keep being transformed, over and over, as we fight each fresh thing that comes along to assault our racing thoughts.

Philippians 4 gives us some extra insight into how we might go about this daunting task. Firstly, Paul writes that we are to give everything up to God in prayer, however big or small, instead of worrying about it all (v6). Additionally, we are to dwell on and think about, *"whatever is true, whatever is honourable, whatever is just, whatever is pure, whatever is pleasing, whatever is commendable…excellent…worthy of praise,"* v8. God didn't design us to carry our burdens and stresses on our own, but longs for us to pour everything out to Him and allow Him to assist, guide and empower us. How easy it is to forget that in the chaos and busyness of life, and what a negative impact it has on our peace of mind when we do forget. God understands, too, how automatically our thoughts career off down a negative path and reminds us, through Paul's letter here, to actively pursue a different course by meditating and dwelling on the good things Paul lists. This takes time and effort and doesn't happen automatically.

Romans 12, too, gives us some practical steps to overcome the anxiety, fear and doubt that can creep into our minds. The actions suggested by Paul here are counter-cultural, against the grain, but are ones that will bring peace, joy and hope in place of the swirl of negative thoughts that can take us captive. Paul asserts, *"not all the members have the same function,"* (Romans 12:4) – a reminder not to compare ourselves, which comes at a huge cost to our peace, but instead to serve with the gifts we have been given. He reminds us, too, that loving and serving others and living at peace with them, is vital, if we are seeking for our minds to be transformed (v10,13,18).

Having key scriptures to read and reflect on when our minds become overwhelmed is a great strategy in our battle to renew our minds. 2 Timothy 1:7 is one of those key scriptures: *"God did not give us a spirit of cowardice, but rather a spirit of power and of love and of self-discipline."* Several versions of the Bible translate *"self-discipline,"* as *"a sound mind."* This is something we all long for. It is good to remind ourselves, when we are feeling anxious and overwhelmed, that God has equipped us with a *"sound mind,"* and He can help us feel more confident that this scripture actually describes *us*, as we allow Him to impart his peace in place of our fears.

. . .

It is all too easy to condemn ourselves for our mental and emotional struggles and write ourselves off, give up hope. Yet the Bible is full of encouragement and exhortation to be honest about our struggles and lean on the support of God and other Christians to lift us out of anxiety, fear and stress and find the *"peace that transcends all understanding,"* that Paul describes. It is important to note that we will sometimes also need professional and medical support to lift us when our minds are troubled – there is strength, not shame, in admitting that we need help and support and seeking it out.

Whatever battles we face in our minds today, God sees, has compassion and empathy and walks with us on our journey to hope and peace.

FOLLOW-UP IDEAS

1. READ

Read the whole of each passage: **Romans 12:1-18, Philippians 4:4-9 and 2 Timothy 1:3-7**

Are there any parts of the passages that really strike you? Which and why?

2. LISTEN

Listen to the song "*You Already Know*," by J.J. Heller.

I love the idea the song expresses, that God holds all our hopes and fears and walks through both, with us.

Which lines speak to you?

3. THINK AND PRAY

As you pray, bring to mind times in your life when you have battled something in your mind and God has helped you to overcome it and set you free? *Spend some time thanking God for those times today.*

Can you identify thought patterns that you find yourself sliding into, still, that you need help overcoming? *Come to God today, and ask Him to fill your mind with His truths, to help drown out any lies you might be believing.*

REFLECTION 28

THE GOD WHO SEES OUR FRAGILE SELF-IMAGE AND CALLS US LOVED (EPHESIANS 2:1-10)

Focus Scriptures: Ephesians 2:1-10

Focus verse: "For we are what he has made us, created in Christ Jesus for good works, which God prepared beforehand to be our way of life," Ephesians 2:10.

REFLECTION

This reflection is a natural follow-on from the previous one. Our minds and our self-image are intrinsically linked and God wants to redeem them both and enable us to live free of the negative thought patterns that lead to a fragile self-image. Strengthening our image of ourselves as God sees us goes a long way to a greater sense of security and joy, even in the midst of trials and challenges.

Many of us find it easy to be naturally self-critical. We look at a photograph and home in automatically on the flaws we can see, even while others are telling us what a great picture it is. We replay conversations in our heads and judge the way we expressed ourselves to be sorely lacking. We look at others' lives and consider ours to be inferior in a multitude of ways.

Our focus verse for this reflection is an important antidote to these thoughts that are so common to so many of us. *"For we are what he has made us, created in Christ Jesus for good works, which God prepared beforehand to be our way of life,"* Ephesians 2:10. Let that sink in for a moment. The God of the universe has created us to be just as He wants us to be. We, of course, have the lifelong responsibility of working with Him to allow Him to bring out the full potential He has placed in us, as we grow and develop. But even in our imperfect, flawed, human state, He has things in mind for which our unique set of gifts, characteristics and skills are going to be a perfect fit.

On one occasion, in a particular season in my life, I was lamenting to God how inadequate and useless I felt. Mixing a career with early motherhood left me feeling wrung out and not much good at either. Arriving at a church toddler group one day, I stopped dead in my tracks and laughed out loud: the new poster, dominating the entrance to the church, declared this very verse – even better that, in the New Living Translation, it called me a *"masterpiece,"* rendering the verse, *"For we are God's masterpiece. He has created us anew in Christ Jesus, so we can do the good things he planned for us long ago."* I felt seen by God that day, and felt a heart-deep reassurance that He had not forgotten me, still delighted in me and still had good purposes for me, even in this complicated season.

The Greek word Paul uses for the phrase, *"what he has made us,"* in verse 10 is poiema, from which we get our modern word, "poem." Different Bible translations render *"what he has made,"* as *"masterpiece,"* (NLT), *"handiwork,"* (NIV) and *"workmanship,"* (AMP), all of which are powerful truths to meditate on when we find ourselves in a whirl of self-criticism and inadequacy. God is not unrealistic about our flawed humanity and doesn't expect us to be perfect. But where we see a mess, God sees a potential masterpiece, as we grow under his expert care. We bemoan our lack of abilities: God admires the flawed beauty of His handiwork.

The "faith roll of honour" I mentioned in Reflection 25 (Hebrews 11) should be a comfort to us too, as we seek to see ourselves as God sees us, not as our fragile self-image sometimes causes us to see ourselves. The author's great list reminds us of those whose faith God saw and was pleased with – a faith we too should emulate. We assume that means perfection, but, on closer examination, this couldn't be further from the truth. When Sarah was told she would have a baby in her old age, she laughed. Jacob had favourites, which led to some of his sons' jealousy of Joseph. Moses initially suggested he wasn't up to the job and implored God to send someone else. David made great errors of judgement. And Gideon needed multiple points of reassurance before he was willing to act. And those are just the headlines. Whilst we might look at the stories behind these names and judge them wanting (in the same way we judge ourselves wanting), God saw them differently. He calls us to higher levels of faith and better ways of living, but knows that we will never be perfect and that we need His grace to be everything He has called us to be.

There are plenty of verses in the Bible that remind us how God truly sees us and we can draw on them and declare them over ourselves whenever we begin to doubt our worth in God's eyes. Their truths will empower us to cling on to the truth that we *have* worth in God's eyes, despite our failings and the sense of unworthiness that so easily creeps in. Psalm 139 reminds us that we are, "*fearfully and wonderfully made.*" 1 Peter 2:9 calls us a "*chosen race, a royal priesthood.*" Isaiah 64:8 reminds us that we are the "*clay,*" and he is our "*potter,*" and that He is shaping us as He wants us to be.

In the imperfect world we live in, all of us will have grown up with a variety of influences, both positive and negative, that will have contributed to our self-image, and for many of us, our self-image will be fragile. Our upbringing, trauma we have faced, work situations, toxic comments and the knocks life brings can make us view ourselves as failures without a hope. It takes time and effort to retrain our brains to believe God's view of us – as precious, loved, purpose-filled and His – flaws, imperfections and all.

FOLLOW-UP IDEAS

1. READ

Read the whole of the passage: **Ephesians 2:1-10**

Are there any parts of the story that really strike you? Which and why?

2. LISTEN

Listen to the song *"You Say,"* by Lauren Daigle.

I love the idea the song expresses, that God counteracts our feelings of weakness and hopelessness with his words of love and truth.

Which lines speak to you?

3. THINK AND PRAY

As you pray, bring to mind times in your life when you have beaten yourself up for a thought, action or aspect of your character but God has helped you to see that he loves you, flaws and all. *Spend some time thanking God for those times today.*

Can you identify thought patterns that lead you to become stuck in a negative self-image? *Come to God today, and ask Him to fill your mind with His truths, to help you to see yourself as He sees you.*

REFLECTION 29

THE GOD WHO SEES THE WHOLE PICTURE WHEN WE CAN ONLY SEE A PART (PSALM 18:1-19)

Focus Scripture: Psalm 18:1-19

Focus verse: "He brought me out into a broad place; he delivered me, because he delighted in me," Psalm 18:19.

REFLECTION

Psalm 18 actually appears twice in the Bible: once in Psalms and once in 2 Samuel 22, at the point at which David wrote it, in response to the circumstances that were raging around him and the need to remind himself that God was bigger than all of it. It's a truth that we would all benefit from reminding ourselves of, to keep us anchored in the roughest of seas.

It is also a very personal one for me. I alluded, earlier, to having walked the difficult path of cancer with my sister and losing her, despite much prayer to the contrary. Psalm 18:19 was a verse I held onto, throughout her illness and after her death. It wasn't a magic wand that got me all my heart desired and there are no easy answers about why some are healed in such tough circumstances and others aren't. But this verse gave me a tiny, clinging, grip on a greater truth, that however difficult things were, God would somehow, some time, bring me through, to the *"broad,"* place my heart so desperately needed – rendered a *"spacious place,"* in the New International Version of the Bible. It was a much-needed hope, whilst I dwelt in the opposite kind of place, constricted and confined by the situation in which I found myself.

Other verses of Psalm 18, too, remind us to continually look to the One stronger and more powerful than ourselves, when circumstances threaten to overwhelm us. David gives us a whole vocabulary of strength, shelter and security in this Psalm, to help us fix our eyes on the God who can give us all of it: he calls God his, *"rock…fortress… deliverer…shield…horn of my salvation…stronghold…refuge…saviour,"* v2-3. Each one has such fortifying connotations, to give us hope, in our moments of weakness and difficulty, that we don't have to walk through them alone.

The hyperbolic language David uses illustrates to us that he wasn't just feeling a little bit off – he was at the end of his tether. He writes of *"cords of death,"* and *"torrents of perdition,"* v5, that are threatening to ensnare him and pull him under. He was facing invasion from his enemies and mutiny from within his household. The Philistines were relentless in their attacks. Sheba, son of Bikri, a Benjamite leader, was stirring up dissension towards David, and David's own son, Absalom had murdered his half-brother and was undermining David's rule.

• • •

David's poetic, hyperbolic words give voice to some of our feelings in our own challenging circumstances and give us permission to express them honestly to God too. But as with so many of his psalms, David doesn't stop at lament, but presses through into a declaration of trust and praise. He moves through recognition of God's cosmic power in verses 13-15, to a declaration of God's personal rescue and protection in his own life: *"He reached down from on high, he took me; he drew me out of mighty waters,"* v16, reminding himself that God is bigger, sees beyond the immediate and will deliver him.

So many of the other characters we have seen through these reflections temporarily lost sight of this truth – that God had a bigger plan for them than the individual moments they found themselves in. Elijah thought it was just him left, among God's prophets, and he was ready to give up and die. The widows in 1 and 2 Kings were sure that they had no more resources and no more hope. Joseph must have thought, more than once, that his life was over. The woman caught in adultery must have thought that the ring of accusers had brought her to her death. But all of these characters lived to tell a different story.

God's words to Israel (Isaiah 46) are just as encouraging to us, today, as they were to them then: *"Even to your old age I am he, even when you turn grey I will carry you. I have made, and I will bear; I will carry and will save,"* v4, continuing, in verse 10: *"for I am God, and there is no other; I am God, and there is no one like me, declaring the end from the beginning and from ancient times things not yet done, saying, 'My purpose shall stand, and I will fulfil my intention.'"* What a reminder that we can trust him with our lives and our futures, however our present is looking.

• • •

I've always loved the idea that God's view is of a vast panorama of our lives and of history, whilst we see only tiny snippets as we reach them. It has become an overused cliché but the point stands that God sees the end from the beginning, whilst we see only a part. We see the apparently interminable season we are in: He sees what is waiting on the other side and knows just how He is going to lead us gently through.

FOLLOW-UP IDEAS

1. READ

Read the whole of the passage: **Psalm 18:1-19**

Are there any parts of the story that really strike you? Which and why?

2. LISTEN

Listen to the song "Storyteller," by Morgan Harper Nichols.

I love the idea the song expresses, that God is writing our story and we can see His hand at work, as we look back over its pages.

Which lines speak to you?

3. THINK AND PRAY

As you pray, bring to mind times in your life when you have faced really tough circumstances but, looking back, you can see God's hand, guiding and strengthening you. *Spend some time thanking God for those times today.*

Do you need to be reminded, today, that God holds your yesterday, today and tomorrow in His hands and will give you the strength and hope you need to face all the challenges that come? *Come to God today, and ask Him to remind you that He is your rock, your stronghold and your deliverer.*

REFLECTION 30

THE GOD WHO WE GLIMPSE AND WILL ONE DAY FULLY SEE (1 CORINTHIANS 13:1-13, REVELATION 21:4-6)

Focus Scripture: 1 Corinthians 13:1-13

Revelation 21:4-6

Focus verses: "For now we see in a mirror, dimly, but then we will see face to face. Now I know only in part; then I will know fully, even as I have been fully known," 1 Corinthians 13:12

"He will wipe every tear from their eyes. Death will be no more; mourning and crying and pain will be no more, for the first things have passed away,' Revelation 21:4

REFLECTION

Congratulations on reaching the final reflection on this journey towards seeing God's heart for us and understanding that we are fully seen and known. I hope that the reflections have helped you to see old stories in the new light of the theme this book has explored.

. . .

As you have journeyed through and spent time reflecting, I'm sure there will have been days when the truths contained in the scriptures resonated with you, stirring your heart and giving you fresh hope that you are seen, understood, loved. There might have been other days when the truths explored didn't spark the hope and peace you were desperately seeking. In the broken world we live in, we will all have days like that. That's when it's so vital to have scriptural truths to hang onto when our weary souls are trying to sell us a different story to the one God is calling us to live.

I want to end the series of reflections with these two scriptures – one from 1 Corinthians 13 and one from Revelation 21, both of which explore different facets of the same idea: that we will never fully see and understand, in our mortal lives, everything that shapes and forms us, but that one day, standing in eternity, we will.

The passage from 1 Corinthians 13 comes towards the end of a letter from Paul to the church at Corinth. He had spent a year and a half among them, sharing the good news of Jesus and establishing a church, before leaving them to build it, whilst he continued his missionary work elsewhere. But reports of division and strife had come to him, so he writes to them, to help them iron out some of the issues they are facing and move forward with greater integrity and morality.

This passage about love, is extremely well-known and often read at weddings. However, the true context of it is a reminder that everything we do in all our interactions, not just our romantic ones, should be motivated by love – not power, status, popularity or looking "spiritual." I have heard more than one sermon where the preacher has suggested inserting our own name into the passage, instead of the word "love," to see how well we match up to this ideal.

It is verse 12 of this scripture that embodies the theme of being seen, known and loved so powerfully: **"For now we see in a mirror, dimly, but then we will see face to face. Now I know only in part; then I will know fully, even as I have been fully known," 1 Corinthians 13:12.** Paul acknowledges that, even our best efforts to know and understand the character and the love of God and how He views us, will only ever be like looking into a dim, cloudy, blurry mirror. But one day…one day we will see fully.

Yet, even though *we* cannot see fully or know fully while we are here, on earth, we are still fully seen and known by *God*. Although we don't see fully, He does. Although we can't understand all we go through, He can. The joy of our lives is to try, as haltingly and imperfectly as we can, to come to a place of knowing we are seen and we are loved by a God who sees it all. If we can love others, in the way the passage depicts, perhaps we might give them the gift of being seen in a way that might help point them to the God who sees them better than any human ever can. The whole set of reflections in this book has been an exploration of the joy that being known, seen and loved by God brings. I hope you have grasped these truths more deeply as you have journeyed through the reflections.

The verses from Revelation feel like a fitting conclusion to this reflection and to this book: in them, God promises an ultimate end, in eternity, to all crying, mourning and pain, as He himself wipes away all our tears and makes all things new (Revelation 21:4-5). God then announces Himself to be, *"the Alpha and the Omega, the beginning and the end,"* v6. This is the key. He is behind us and before us. He was there before the beginning of creation and is already there, at the end of time. He designated the day of our birth and knows when we will take our last breath.

He holds everything we have reflected on throughout this book and so much more in the palms of His hands – our delights and joys, our doubts and fears, our struggles and tears. And He sees it all – sees angles and facets we can only dream of. He calls us to surrender our limited perspectives back to Him, continually, trusting Him – El Roi, the God who sees, understands, rejoices and hurts with us - until, one final day when, at last, it will all make sense.

FOLLOW-UP IDEAS

1. READ

Read the whole of the passages: **1 Corinthians 13:1-13**
Revelation 21:4-6

Are there any parts of the story that really strike you? Which and why?

2. LISTEN

Listen to the song *"There Will Be A Day,"* by Jeremy Camp.

I love the scene the song depicts of, one day, seeing Jesus in heaven and having him personally wipe the tears from our eyes.

Which lines speak to you?

3. THINK AND PRAY

Are there times that come to you as you pray, when you have felt that sense of being fully known and understood? *Spend some time thanking God for fully seeing you, fully knowing you and completely loving you.*

What aspect of the *"God Who Sees You,"* are you still struggling with, now you've reached the end of this book? *Ask God to keep meeting you where you are and healing your hurts and disappointments. Ask Him to keep growing in you an unshakeable trust that He sees, understands and is walking with you.*

ACKNOWLEDGMENTS

Writing a book has been something of a dream for me for a long time, and one that wouldn't have come about without a great deal of support from some brilliant people.

Many thanks go to my family (my husband, Graham, and my sons, Ben and Samuel), who put up with me being permanently hidden behind a laptop for much of the last six months, and patiently listened to dinner-time readings of whatever I had written that day.

My writing community have been a vital support. I will always be grateful to the Association of Christian Writers for giving me the confidence and inspiration to write. Special thanks go to a wonderful group of ladies known as the *Incomperellas* (Deborah Jenkins, Fran Hill and Ruth Leigh) who cheer me on, daily, in writing and in life. Thanks too to my local ACW Group, Brecks, Fens and Pens, led by Jane Walters, for being a rock of support and encouragement.

Thank you to my church, the King's Centre, King's Lynn, for allowing me to experiment on them with my writing and especial thanks to my two Life Groups for praying for me and bolstering my courage when time and energy were failing.

Final thanks go to Amy Robinson of Kevin Mayhew, without whom this book would not have seen the light, and to my ever-patient and eagle-eyed editor John Cox, who tirelessly worked to help make this book the best it could be.

ABOUT THE AUTHOR

Georgie Tennant is a writer and English Teacher. She is a regular contributor to 'More Than Writers,' the blog for the Association of Christian Writers and is a contributor to the ACW-Published 'New Life: Reflections for Lent,' and 'Merry Christmas, Everyone.' She is a freelance writer for two local businesses and a regular provider of the 'Thought for the Week' for her local newspaper. This is her first devotional book.

All The Parts It Takes

Kate Mayor

ISBN:
978-1-916529-86-1 (Paperback)
978-1-916529-87-8 (ebook)

Cover design by Lynda Mangoro.

The Unbound Press
www.theunboundpress.com

For everyone who has had to rebuild from the inside out,
and who knows that the cracks are where the light begins.

1

Land acquisition

Ella wandered into the neon haze of the fairground, the lights needling her tired eyes with a joy she couldn't share. Her name badge – *Ella, Project Liaison* – sagged on her blouse, heavy as a question she no longer felt like answering.

Around her, laughter spilt too brightly. The kind of laughter that masked exhaustion, or silence. A whistle sliced through the lingering daylight, false-cheerful and urgent. Someone somewhere desperately needed these grown-ups to pretend they were having fun.

"Alright, team!" Carol from HR called out, her voice booming like an overzealous game show host. "We have done the hard work today – now it's time for some fun! Let's blow off some steam!"

Ella folded her arms, a human barricade against corporate enthusiasm. Around her, colleagues were already shuffling toward the dodgems; bright, plastic relics of every childhood they'd tragically outgrown. She stared at those gaudy little cars, flickering neon overhead and the relentless thump of Euro pop. Once, back when crashing into things yielded a delighted squeal, that might have felt thrilling. Now the promise of impact felt closer to a grim inevitability.

Her phone buzzed in her pocket. One long vibration. She didn't check it.

Someone – Pete from Comms – gave her a jovial nudge. "You in or what?" he asked, his grin stretched too wide. Ella mouthed the word,

"Yeah" before thought could catch up and tuck itself back under a polite excuse.

The scent of oil and candyfloss cloyed, turning her stomach. Her heels sank into the uneven tarmac as she trudged toward the ride, her chest a knot of something heavier than anticipation — an exhaustion that felt ancient, like a credit card balance she'd never quite paid off. Four hours of "team synergy," one trust-fall that ended with Karen from Accounts in tears, a motivational speaker hollering about unleashing her inner lion. Now, to cap the day — which was already running fifty minutes over time — pretend-fun rides. She wanted nothing more than to flop onto her sofa at home, hide under a blanket, and stare at the ceiling until her bones stopped hurting.

She clambered into one of the blinking cars, sliding against grease as she settled. Her fingers hovered over the wheel, uncertain as a child at the controls of something borrowed. The operator dropped the safety bar and the world jolted into chaotic spin.

Two colleagues barrelled into her with shrieks of delight. She gripped the wheel and tried to smile. The wheels spun uselessly, steering her nowhere. Around her faces lit with exaggerated joy, all neon and sugar as music looped like a taunt.

Her phone buzzed in her pocket — twice. She didn't need to look. Tom. His "check-ins" were audits: *What time are you home? Should I order takeaway, or do you have dinner organised?*

Her gut clenched. Dinner plans tumbled through her head — roast or pasta? Either way, the disappointment was waiting. Another collision jolted her spine and the taste of metal rose in her mouth.

The carnival clamour, the spasm of movement, the weight of being watched — it was all too much.

When the ride finally screeched to a halt, she slipped out, knees weak. Each breath felt rented. She stood just outside the gate as the others clustered together, comparing bruises and selfies as though all of this were a quaint anecdote, rather than her flesh in constant revolt. She let herself drift toward the edge of things; the popcorn stand, the carousel horses spinning slowly like they weren't quite sure why they were still moving.

Her phone rang again. This time she looked at the screen: Aunt June. The last person she wanted to speak to. She edged toward the railing that separated her from the electric misery and answered with brittle calm.

"Hello?"

There was a pause like an exhale in a cathedral. Then:

"Ella, love... I'm so sorry. Your Dad... he passed away this morning."

The announcement came with the weight of a verdict she hadn't prepared for. The wind tugged at her hair and, in the sudden quiet, the fairground's distant laughter felt miles away. She stared at the lattice of metal cars – half-empty now – blinking like wounded fireflies. Her father: dead. The words drifted above her, too hot to catch.

Every rote message crashed against her numbness:
You should feel something.
You should go home.
You should figure out dinner.

She didn't say goodbye. She just turned away and walked, weaving through food trucks and the last of the crowds, her eyes on the cracked tarmac as if it held all the answers. The fairground's carnival lights shrank behind her until it was just the cold hush of the car park and the wind pushing at her jacket, desperate to pull her away.

She climbed into the driver's seat and closed the door. The quiet almost knocked her sideways – no whistles, no music, no squeals. Her bag slipped off her shoulder, landing heavily in her lap. She sat, body rigid, hands frozen on the steering wheel. She felt as though her body were dust and a single breath might scatter it.

After a minute – maybe several – she pressed the start button. The engine roared to life and she drove on instinct, as if someone else pressed hands on the wheel. Her mind shut itself off, as each mile rolled beneath her.

At home, the lights were low. Shadows slid across the kitchen floor. Ella dropped her bag on the counter, ribs rattling with each breath, eyes fixed on the fridge door as if it might explain itself.

"Ella?" Tom's voice drifted from the living room – flat, distracted.

She stepped into the doorway.

"You're late," he said, still staring at his phone.

"My dad died." The words fell like a pebble into a well – barely a sound, no end in sight.

He didn't look up at first. Then: a blink, his phone lowered. "Wow. I'm sorry. Are you okay?"

He reached out, slid an arm across her shoulders like a reflex – automatic, practiced. She stayed rigid, tasting her own dryness. She should cry. She wanted to. Instead, silence roared.

"I didn't think you two were close," he said. Not unkind, just factual. As if measuring how upset she was allowed to be.

She blinked. "We weren't." But the grief was in her bones anyway – deep, cellular.

He nodded, as though that settled it. He stepped back. Too soon. Thumb already twitching back toward his phone.

"So... dinner?"

Her stomach dropped. "I... forgot to buy anything."

He sighed, irritated. She turned to the fridge, its hum suddenly intrusive. Tzatziki. A limp courgette. Half a bottle of wine.

She closed the door, rested her forehead against its coldness, and let the darkness catch her – an unstoppable, quiet certainty that in this dim kitchen, nothing felt familiar anymore. Everything else had just been a prelude. Now, she was alone with something final.

Her limbs felt too slow for the pace of life. It all suddenly seemed absurd: shopping, cooking, laughing with Carol on the dodgems, *any* of it. What did any of it mean? What did any of it matter now?

2

Site investigation

A second night of no sleep since the news of her father's passing. The darkness around Ella had taken on a kind of sentient quality; insistent, probing, as if it wanted to know exactly why she felt so unhinged. She lay beside Tom, listening to the metronome of his heavy breathing. He thinks it's comforting. She thinks it's a reminder of how separate they have always been: his steady chest rising, hers barely moving.

She slipped from their shared bed just before 3 a.m. and padded to the kitchen,, flicking on the light without shame. The bulb's harsh white glare felt fitting, like a spotlight on all the things she had ignored. She watched the kettle hiss, made tea she didn't drink. By 4 a.m., the sky had begun its slow coppery shift, and she felt at once too hot and too cold. The kind of ache that had nothing to do with temperature.

By the time Tom's alarm bled into the room at 6 a.m., Ella was already half-awake, curled in the liminal fog between pretending to sleep and refusing to feel. She didn't move, just lay still while her mind continued its looping audit: every conversation she'd ever had with her father, dissected and replayed.

He'd been warm, magnetic; the kind of man who turned strangers into disciples. "You'll love my dad," she'd told people. And they always had. Everyone did.

But under the night's hush, another truth whispered: Did anyone really know him? Had she?

She pictured him in a three-piece suit, smiling like a politician. No edges, no shadows. People praised his kindness, his enthusiasm, his unwavering presence. But why, then, had it been so hard to be his daughter? Why, in the seasons when she'd needed him most, had he remained just out of reach — a few-hour visit here, a polite call there? Disorientation sat heavy in her gut.

It was a two-hour drive to her father's house. With each mile, Ella felt her grip tighten on the wheel. A slow bracing. As though she was heading into weather. The road narrowed off the dual carriageway. Fields stretched wide and indifferent, fences cleaving them like healed wounds. She used to think these drives were long; now, it felt like not enough time.

The village crept up on her — the sign, the squat bungalows, then the modest rise of the main street. Two small supermarkets, a pharmacy, a bakery with a wonky awning. A church with a noticeboard still handwritten in careful, faded ink. The kind of village where news still travelled faster than cars, where someone would offer you a lift before you had a chance to call a cab. Small enough to know stories, big enough for yours to get a little lost if it needed to. It wasn't postcard pretty, but it held itself with quiet steadiness. There was space here — between buildings, between people. Her father had loved this place. He said it gave him room to think.

But Ella remembered that silence differently. It hadn't opened anything up, it had closed her in.

Ella slowed the car as she passed the green — a stretch of grass with a pair of swings and the same old wooden bench, still facing the school gates. Her old school was low-set and square-edged, its playground now ringed with a newer fence. She hadn't planned on this ache behind her ribs. A cluster of children darted across her view, laughing in the cold. One of them wore a bright red scarf, just like the one she'd had when she was seven. She blinked and the car veered slightly. The memory came, uninvited: her father tying it snug at her throat then immediately snapping at her for being late. She exhaled, sharp and shaky.

As she turned into the familiar lane, the trees rose up around her – tall, dense with early leaves, their shadows reaching across the road. Birds scattered ahead of the car in a sudden burst, startled by her return. Her stomach guttered, sharp and low.

Then the cul-de-sac appeared, quiet and crouched in the morning light, curving in on itself like a hand folding shut.

As she pulled up outside her father's house, the sky was flat as her mood, an unrelenting sheet of dull grey. The red brick façade of the house was mellowed by years of weather and a fine patina of moss along the mortar lines. The windows were dark, unblinking eyes that give nothing away. A low hedge – neatly trimmed, despite the house's sleepy air – marked the boundary between its small front garden and the neighbours. A narrow path of flagstones led to the porch, where an ancient mailbox still bore her grandmother's faded monogram.

She turned off the engine and sat for a moment, hands still on the wheel. *He's not here,* she reminded herself, and the truth of it felt distant and ungraspable.

Inside, the air smelled of stale aftershave and faint regret. It was quiet; too quiet. Not peaceful, just... hollow.

Ella stood in the hallway, eyes drawn instinctively to the spot by the door where they'd said he was found. A heart attack, they'd told her. Quick. Sudden. But she couldn't stop herself from wondering, had he been trying to reach the phone? Was he heading for the door, hoping to wave someone down, call for help? Or had it come on so fast that there hadn't even been a moment to decide? The uncertainty coiled in her chest, a slow ache. She crouched there, bag dropping to the floor and hand brushing the floorboards, as if she might feel some imprint of that final moment; some clue to what it had been like to leave the world alone.

She stayed there, knees folded awkwardly beneath her, the hallway dim even in the midday light. The silence wasn't oppressive, just dense, like it held stories too tender to speak aloud. Her back pressed against the wall, cool and familiar, and she let herself just be there without rushing to organise, to clean, to fix. The old runner rug scratched at her ankles. The scuffed skirting board caught the light where years of hoovering had chipped away the gloss.

She rested her head against the plaster, eyes tracing the place where his shoes used to sit neatly by the door. That simple, dependable rhythm of him: coat hung just so, keys in the tray, radio murmuring from the kitchen. All gone.

Reaching into her coat pocket, Ella found an old tissue, crumpled but dry. She held it in her lap like it might anchor her. But no tears came. Why could she not cry? Instead, she sat – quiet, listening – until the light shifted, and the house, as if gently exhaling, seemed to let her in.

When finally she stood and took slow steps across the hallway, each creak underfoot seemed to bring back a different year. She stood at the kitchen door but couldn't enter. It was as if the room was so crammed with memories, there was no space to stand. Behind it all, the steady drip of the kitchen tap marked time with an indifference that felt almost cruel.

She paused at the bottom of the stairs, eyes tracing the banister her father had polished every Saturday morning while she played in her room. The scent of old polish, faint and dry, clung to the wood and tugged her forward, carrying memory in its quiet insistence. Each step upward was a negotiation between curiosity and dread. At the top, she lingered in the doorway, taking in the muted light that pooled across the floor — her old bedroom exactly as she'd left it, yet somehow holding years in its stillness.

Her concert posters were yellow with age, the cracked lava lamp complete with orange ooze still on the dresser, and rows of swimming medals hung on the wall like tarnished promises. County competitions. National qualifiers. Gold, silver, bronze — all collected like evidence of something. Effort, maybe. Or value.

She remembered the way he used to stand at the end of the lane during training; arms folded, nodding as she sliced through the water. Driving her to morning sessions before school. Always punctual. Always silent.

And then, when she won — just for a moment — he'd smile. Clap her on the shoulder. "Knew you had it in you, El."

That was it. That was the warmth. Those few words. She'd waited for them like oxygen.

She lowered herself onto the bed, the medals behind her clinking once, sharp, hollow and almost mocking her. The grief came hard. Sudden. Cold. Not the kind that splits open into sobs, but something denser. It pressed against her sternum, huge and unmoving, as if her chest had become a locked room with no windows. She couldn't cry. Couldn't scream. Just sat there, gripping the duvet edge like it might tether her to something solid. The silence thick and watching. Heavy. Crawling. It felt like invasion. She wanted to scratch at her skin. She sat there in numbed silence for moments, or maybe hours.

"I don't know who I am without you," she whispered to the silence. But even as she said it, something cracked inside. It felt like she was standing on air. Because the 'you' she missed — the man she had always said was her rock — she couldn't seem to grasp. Her fingers curled into the duvet and she pressed her forehead to her knees.

"I just need… something solid," she said, voice breaking.

But the room gave her nothing. Just the echo of her own breath and the faint ticking of the hallway clock.

Her gaze drifted to the window, where afternoon light, muted and grey, pooled behind the curtains. She stood slowly, drawn forward, and pulled the fabric aside. The glass was cool beneath her palm.

Outside, the world continued as if nothing had ruptured. A child cycled past in a too-big helmet. A car rolled down the street, fog lights flickering briefly across the glass before vanishing. Everything was intact out there; predictable, cohesive. Inside, she felt like a page torn halfway from its spine.

She stepped back into the hall, an impulsive need to find a space to connect with her father. Lingering in the doorway to the living room, she felt him in its every fabric. It looked untouched, like time had paused the moment he left it. The worn leather armchair by the window — the one he always sat in — still held the faint impression of his body and the small table beside it still held his glasses case, closed. A cold mug of tea sat fossilised into the coaster.

She sat down on the opposite sofa, curling her knees beneath her and pulling the cardigan tighter around her shoulders. She imagined him seated in his chair as she asked him about his day, the latest football score, what was happening in the town.

It took her a while to realise what she was feeling.

There was grief, yes, woven through the fibres of her muscles, like a background frequency. But underneath it, or maybe alongside it, there was something else. Something she hadn't let herself name.

Relief.

It shocked her.

It felt disloyal.

But it was there, a quiet but undeniable exhale that had been waiting years to be breathed. She looked at the chair again and felt it more clearly now: the absence of him was... easier.

There was no longer a need to tiptoe around his moods. No need to anticipate the heaviness in the air before he even spoke. No need to become smaller just to keep him comfortable.

How long had she done that?

Made herself the buffer. The interpreter. The invisible caretaker of his emotional climate. She would watch his face at breakfast, noting the tightness of his jaw or the twitch in his brow, and adjust accordingly. She'd plan conversations days in advance, speak in a tone she'd rehearsed, make sure no one ever had to deal with his disapproval; *especially not him.*

And she thought that was love.

Her eyes pricked and she looked down at her hands. They felt like they'd been holding something too heavy for too long. A tear rolled down. Finally. It wasn't from sadness, but from exhaustion.

It was so much work. She hadn't even noticed it happening until now. She just knew that she never had the space to focus on herself until he was okay; until the mood in the room was steady, until his comfort was secured.

Keeping the balance. Keeping the peace. Keeping him happy — or at least not unhappy. And he never asked her to. But he never stopped her either.

She let her head fall back against the sofa. Her throat was tight and her shoulders were sore. But she could feel it, deep down, for the first time in her life: She didn't have to do it anymore. She didn't have to be the balm, the buffer, or the bridge.

The chair sat empty.

And now, with no one to calibrate around, there was nothing to tether her. The old reference points were gone. She was still. Free. But also adrift. They may not have been close by the end, but that didn't mean she hadn't carried him with her everywhere. Built stories out of scraps. Wished harder than she'd ever admit that he would turn into the father she needed. That something would come good in the end.

And now he was gone. And so was that possibility.

She needed air. Pulling the front door closed, the hollow thud echoed into the muted afternoon. The grey sky pressed down and the wind tugged at her hair, carrying the scent of damp earth. Her steps were unsteady; she was barely present — still floating somewhere between memory and numbness, when she saw him: the man next door, standing still in his garden as if part of the hedgerow itself. He was in his sixties maybe, with a knitted hat pulled down tight and mud-stained gloves on his hands. A spade leant against his leg like a third limb.

He didn't smile. Just looked at her with a stillness that made her stomach tense.

"You'll be Ella then?" He said, not quite a question.

She stopped mid-step, thrown by the casual knowing. "Yes," she replied slowly, the word coming out colder than intended.

He nodded like it confirmed something he already knew. "I wondered if you'd be back. Thought it might be a while. What's happening with the house? You thinking of living here?"

The questions came out in a tone that was both nosy and flat. No warmth, no real curiosity, just quiet, firm intrusion. Ella's body went rigid. Something in her recoiled at the way he stood there, like he belonged more than she did. She hated that he knew her name. Hated that she hadn't even asked his.

"I'm not sure yet," she said tightly, turning her eyes to the car as a not-so-subtle cue.

He didn't respond, just nodded again, once, and picked up his spade as if she'd just confirmed a long-held theory.

As she unlocked the car door, she felt his eyes still on her back. Watching. Judging. Or maybe just waiting. She wasn't sure which unnerved her more.

She drove, a little too fast, back home. Tom would be home from work soon.

The flat was warm when she stepped inside; too warm – stale air thick with central heating. Ella dropped her keys into the bowl by the door and stood for a moment, coat still on, scanning the quiet hallway like she was waiting for something to jump out at her.

She could hear the hum of the TV from the living room. Tom was home already. He would be there, half-watching, half-scrolling. She didn't want another conversation about how quiet she'd been the last couple of days, or if she'd remembered to pick up more oat milk. She just wanted things to feel normal.

Slipping off her coat she moved to the kitchen, opening cupboards with the same habitual rhythm she'd always had. Pasta. Tinned tomatoes. The half-used red onion from yesterday. Dinner didn't need to be interesting, it just needed to be easy. Something warm she could place in front of him like a peace offering.

As she chopped, her mind drifted uninvited to the funeral. Only four days away, June hadn't wasted a minute. Within hours of the news breaking, she'd booked the earliest possible slot at the crematorium and emailed everyone before Ella had even fully processed the word "dead". Her aunt's trademark efficiency — admired by the family for decades — made Ella feel both relieved and strangely displaced. All those decisions made for her, without her. It was easier not to have to think, and yet something about being cut out of the planning left her grief feeling unofficial. Like she was attending as a witness, not a daughter.

She boiled water and tossed in the pasta. The steam fogged her glasses.

She had two full weeks off work, a bereavement policy she hadn't read until now. Two whole weeks. At first, it had felt like a gift — space to breathe, to rest. But now, after just two days, the emptiness loomed large. It wasn't rest, it was absence. No one to answer to, no one needing anything from her during the day. Yet somehow she still felt wrung out.

Her husband's voice drifted from the living room. "You making dinner?"

"Yes," she called back, wiping her hands on a tea towel.

A pause. Then: "That's good. I'm starving."

She didn't answer. Just stirred the sauce, slow circles, anchoring herself to the motion.

She plated their dinner and carried it through to the table. He was already seated, head bowed over his phone, thumb scrolling through some distant feed.

"So... your aunt says the funeral's Thursday?" He asked, not looking up. "Do I need to take the day off work? Things are hectic. I could maybe come just for the service?"

Ella paused mid-step. Her breath caught somewhere between her ribs and her throat.

"I don't know if we were close," she said quietly. "But he was still my dad."

He glanced up at that, startled like he hadn't expected the weight of her words. "Yeah. Right. Of course. I'll see what I can arrange."

She nodded once, too sharply, and set the plates down. Steam curled upward, fogging the silence. She twirled a forkful, lifted it, chewed. The pasta was hot, bland. She couldn't taste it.

Across from her, Tom chuckled at something on his phone, a small snort of private amusement. The sound grated. She forced down another bite.

Grief didn't seem to make anything sacred. She swallowed. Felt her throat tightening, the old habit of shrinking kicking in. She forced herself to look at him. "He used to drive me to swim meets," she said quietly. "He was... proud then."

He nodded absently, already returning to his phone. Empathy measured out in tiny, interrupted sips – never quite enough. She kept eating, each bite heavy with things unsaid.

She'd married Tom almost three years ago. Promised things. Worn white. Let her father walk her down an aisle toward him. And here they were; two strangers divided by a table and a death, trying not to say too much.

And all the while, Aunt June's funeral spreadsheet hovered in her mind: guest list, eulogies, black attire, seating chart. Ella pushed it away, focusing instead on the warm plate in front of her and praying that, tonight at least, things could just be normal.

But the pasta still tasted like nothing.

3

Rubble

Ella arrived at St. Mark's 10 minutes early, just as Aunt June was making a final sweep of the guest list. June's heels clicked on the stone steps, each tap relentless, like a stopwatch chasing seconds. She wore black lace to the exact length her email had insisted upon, and clutched a clipboard that radiated self-importance.

"There you are," June said, surveying Ella with a quick, appraising nod. "Sit here, dear." She shepherded Ella into the front row with a half-turned flick of her hand, as if Ella's preference were a negligible footnote.

Inside, the church smelled of lilies and incense — a combination that felt designed to sanitise rather than soothe. Wooden pews stood packed with faces: neighbours nodding condolences like ritual, former colleagues blinking back watery eyes, and a handful of men in RAF fatigues straight from some half-remembered photograph. Ella felt the hush press in on her, the low murmur of whispered sympathies echoing like distant church bells.

Tom settled beside her, the sleeve of his jacket brushing hers like an afterthought. He didn't speak, just pulled out his phone and began tapping with the quiet urgency of someone placing a bet.

"I'll be quick," he murmured, eyes still on the screen. "Just need to send this before lunch."

Ella folded her hands in her lap. A small breath left her lips. It was too familiar, this quiet recalibration — shrinking around someone else's disconnection, tucking her grief into the corners so it wouldn't disturb the mood. He was here in the literal sense. But the weight of showing up — of really being with her in it — once again belonged to her alone.

The service began. The vicar spoke of duty, honour, and a life devoted to community. There was a recording of her father's voice — him introducing the film at a local film club. It sounded warm and steady, completely at odds with the rust inside her chest. She watched the room, felt their collective compassion wash towards her like a wave, but she had no way to catch it.

After the hymns and prayers, Aunt June took the microphone for the eulogy. Her voice was crisp, polished, rehearsed.

"Arthur Lawson was, above all, a man of connection. He never met a stranger. He believed that life was meant to be shared; the conversations, the jokes, the long evenings discussing everything from politics to plumbing. He supported our community with his time, his voice, and his steadfast confidence."

Ella listened, her chest tightening at each word. Connection. Confidence. Community. These virtues gleamed in every smile and nod, but to her they sounded like a perfectly tuned piano missing its low E string. She remembered instead the silence at the dinner table, the rigid set of his jaw when she announced she'd been accepted to university. She recalled tiptoeing around his moods — piecing together the alchemy of his approval like some frail science experiment.

When the service ended, mourners queued to drop roses on the polished oak casket. Ella remained seated, her hands folded in her lap. She watched as friend after friend stepped forward, voice hushed, offering condolences that felt rehearsed rather than heartfelt. They called him "steady," "dedicated," "dependable", none of which jibed with the trembling ten-year-old who'd flattened herself against the sofa whenever her father's voice had grown loud.

Outside, the wind carried the scent of damp earth. People clustered in small circles, offering stories of Arthur's generosity: how incredible he was to parent a small child all alone, and despite that he never missed a PTA meeting, how he always had time for a neighbour's plumbing emergency, how he once organised a Christmas choir in the village square.

A woman she barely knew approached, wearing a pale scarf and a sympathetic smile. "Your father was so chatty and warm," she said. "He always made time for everyone. He'd listen to your problems like they were his own."

Ella forced a nod and a murmured "Thank you." Inside, she felt a cold twist. Chatty? Warm? She'd been the one doing the listening, the one adjusting her speech tempo to match his. She'd been the one bending backward to earn a sliver of his approval.

Another mourner, an older man with a grey moustache, tipped his hat respectfully "Confident fellow, your dad. Always knew the best way to sort a problem at the plant. Never afraid to take the reins to get things done."

Ella inclined her head slowly and nodded in the man's direction. Fearless. Yes, her father had worn his confidence like armour. But an armour she remembered trembling under —his temper could flare so quickly if something wasn't done "properly."

Tom lowered his phone and slipped his arm around her waist. She accepted it without looking, grateful for the weight of his palm. He patted her back with the practiced awkwardness of someone reading from a rulebook: "I'm here," he seemed to say. But his eyes never quite met hers, and his smile trembled in a way that reminded her he had no real method for this.

Aunt June materialised behind them again, brisk as a surgeon. "They'll be taking him to the crematorium soon. I've arranged coffee back at the house. Do stay."

Ella exhaled. Of course there was more to do: more arrangements, more polite small talk about how "beloved" Arthur was, more logistics to navigate. She nodded, a knot already forming in her chest. She wanted to find a corner somewhere — perhaps under the yew in the churchyard — where her own truth could speak without interruption, even if it was only a tremulous whisper.

They arrived at Aunt June's just as the sun dipped behind neighbouring rooftops, slanting through the lace curtains like a final benediction. June's hallway was immaculate: polished oak floors, vases of white lilies, and framed quotations — "Home is where the heart is", "Family is everything," each one delivered with the gravitas of a creed.

June ushered them into the living room, where platters of canapés lay on a low table. There were sausage rolls; of course there were. Somewhere in the deep recesses of British grief protocol, sausage rolls were required alongside Battenberg, supermarket quiche, and something labelled vegetarian that no one touched. The mourners hovered in clusters, oscillating between grief and the stiff polish of public decorum.

"Ella, darling, how are you bearing up?" June began, but left no space for a response, as if reciting from a script she had perfected long ago, "Your father — what can I say? To have lost his wife so tragically, yet remain steadfast for his little girl… nothing short of heroic." She swept a hand toward a group of neighbours. "He never missed a meeting, a school event, a PTA call. Imagine that dedication." Nods and agreement murmured all around.

June righted a glass of rosé in Ella's hand. "You were so lucky," she proclaimed. "He adored you, you know. Crucified himself for you — bathed you, fed you, read bedtime stories every night. A single father who never missed a beat. And now you have Tom. Solid. Practical. Just like your father."

Ella's breath caught, shallow and thin. She took a sip she didn't want, the wine catching like static.

Tom, still tapping at his phone, glanced up for a moment. His eyes met hers briefly, then dropped again, thumb hovering over the screen as if uncertain what to do next. Ella felt needles prick at her sides, a contract of distraction between them. She turned toward the door, the need to breathe having finally outpaced the need to please.

Let June explain her absence. Let Tom look up, or not.

Standing at the edge of Aunt June's precise garden, her wine warm in her hand, she tried not to unravel.

"Ellaaa," came a voice from behind her, cheerfully out of place.

Leanne. Of course. "Christ, I've been looking for you. You disappeared during the sandwiches."

"I was hiding in the geraniums."

"Fair." Leanne gave a theatrical shiver. "God, death. So grim. I still can't believe it. I mean, your dad was just... you know. He *was*."

Ella nodded, because correcting her would have required energy she didn't have.

Leanne put a hand on her arm. "Seriously, though – if you need anything, call me, alright? I'll ignore work for you. Promise."

Ella gave a faint smile.

"But also–," Leanne's voice shifted, brightening like she was switching to a different radio station. "You are still coming to the hen do, yeah?"

Ella blinked.

"You have to come. It's going to be lush! That spa is heavenly. All the works – magnesium pools and even towels folded like swans. And I totally get if you don't want to do the whole thing, but honestly? You'll feel better. Chloe's organising, so you just turn up. No pressure. But you have to come."

Ella tried to picture herself in a white robe pretending to care about exfoliation while someone shouted about penis straws. She blinked. "I... don't know."

"No, no, no. Don't start cancelling life. Not on my watch."

There was something a bit aggressive in the cheeriness, but it wasn't unkind. Just Leanne's version of loyalty. Force-fed normalcy.

"I'll text you," she added, turning towards the house. "You're not getting out of it. Seriously. You need a laugh."

And then she was gone again, swallowed into the soft hum of bereaved small talk and over-brewed tea.

Ella exhaled, tasting the faint bitterness of obligation and absurdity. Grudgingly, she returned inside, only to be intercepted by June in the hall, tugging her toward the kitchen. June's voice dropped, drawing her toward a corner of the room as though they were conspirators in some clandestine whisper. "Ella, when will you finish clearing the house? It's best for both of us if we get it on the market soon, before things start falling apart."

She meant the house itself. But Ella felt her chest constrict as though June had spoken of her own collapse. The pressure coursed beneath her ribs, a familiar panic she couldn't quite name. Her father's house was suddenly just another asset to be pivoted, sold, converted into profit and split between the two of them, as decreed in her father's will. And June, brisk and final, had already decided the timeline.

"I... I'm working on it," Ella croaked, as if she had any idea what "working on it" meant.

June's eyebrows lifted. "I know you're grieving, love, but we mustn't let personal sentiment impede progress. The property market is fickle – homes like his seldom stay on the market long, but the longer it lingers, the more likely we are to lose value." June's pen tapped the clipboard. "Probate takes ten weeks; photos, brochure – two weeks; minor sprucing – four weeks. That means four weeks max for you to clear the place. Ready for my visit then?"

Ella's lungs tightened further. The breath she inhaled tasted of debris and obligation. She could hear the others' laughter echoing in the adjoining room, a jarring soundtrack to her private turmoil. *Why does this feel so wrong?* she thought, her vision blurring.

June misread the silence as resolve. "Excellent. I knew I could count on you."

Ella's heart thundered in her ears. She smiled weakly at June and moved past her back to the crowd of mostly strangers. June followed closely behind.

The stories of a doting father played on around her, each one a fairy tale she wasn't allowed to revise. The rhythm of her blood felt uneven. She placed her wine glass back on the lacquered table and exhaled so slowly it felt like a surrender, not of grief, but of herself. She needed the solitude of a veil that wasn't woven of expectations. She needed to breathe air that wasn't recapitulatory, praising what had been lost, while propelling her even further into obligations she hadn't chosen.

She remained at June's side, nodding in all the right places, but her thoughts drifted to her mother. Her chest seizing with a sudden desperate need: to find her mother's locket. It had always nestled at her mother's throat — a constant, golden promise — until the day she died. After that, her father vanished the locket somewhere in his study, and it was never seen again. If she could somehow lay her hands on that small circle of gold, perhaps she could anchor herself amid all this polished sorrow. Tomorrow, she would search.

Ella felt the room tilt, a slow spin that whisked her toward the door even before her feet moved. Aunt June hovered, before gripping her arm. "You must say goodbye to everyone," she instructed in that crisp tone that brooked no argument. "It's expected — you'll want to offer your thanks, your apologies for leaving early."

Ella's stomach had clenched into a steel trap. She lifted her hand in a shaky wave. "I'm… I'm just so overwhelmed," she whispered. "I need air."

June's lips pursed for a moment, as if weighing whether to scold now or later. Finally, she acquiesced. "Very well. But do make a circuit, at least the nearest few. It's the polite thing."

Ella nodded, her throat taut. She moved past June and towards a small cluster by the window — Mrs. Whittaker from the PTA, two of her father's parish friends. Each offered their condolences. Ella forced a vacant smile, her voice barely above a whisper: "Thank you. I appreciate you being here."

She shook hands with the older men, each handshake more perfunctory than the last and her skin prickling as if each palm squeezed out a fragment of what little composure she had left. She offered a brief word to Aunt June's friends, expecting to be led back into the full circle, but June's gaze lingered, calculating. One look at Ella's trembling shoulders, and she understood: letting Ella exit was safer than a spectacle. Image first, always.

Halfway across the room, she spotted Tom still tapping at his phone, eyes flitting between the screen and a line of new arrivals. He glanced up, brow furrowed, as though he sensed her silent plea.

Ella angled toward the door. A murmured "Sorry" drifted from her lips as she slipped past the last of the mourners. No one tried to stop her. She paused only long enough to let the cool evening air fan her cheeks. Then she exhaled, a soft sound of release and revolt.

4

Archaeological dig

Ella spent the first week after the funeral marooned on the sofa, exactly where she had once vowed she'd never return. A half empty bottle of red and takeaway dumplings at arm's reach. The cushions sagged beneath her as if conspiring to hold her there – horizontal, inert, and forgettable. The blinds stayed closed, the days leaking through in golden slashes across the carpet that came and went without permission.

It wasn't grief in the way people spoke of it — florid and poetic, full of catharsis. It was heavier than that. Static. A humid fog clinging to her skin, thickening beneath her ribs. Her sorrow didn't sob, it pooled. Quiet, relentless, filling her body until she could no longer feel where it ended and she began.

She didn't return to her father's house. She didn't go looking for the locket. She didn't even dress. Each day when Tom came home from work, she'd wordlessly migrate to the spare room, clutching her iPad like a shield. On the third night, he knocked. "I brought groceries," he said, the words careful, like he was tiptoeing across a minefield. She hadn't responded but he came in anyway.

"Ella?"

She'd muttered "Go away," into the pillow, and heard him sigh; an exhausted, paper-thin sound, like someone being forced to watch a scene he never asked for, convinced emotions were just noise best ignored.

He closed the door behind him with a quiet click. "Ella?" He set the groceries down as if arranging supplies for someone fragile. His voice was careful, rehearsed. "Can I ask you something? It's probably obvious, but... have you been thinking about hurting yourself?"

She heard the words and for a moment couldn't place them, like a stitch pulled from a seam. He held her gaze expectant, the way someone waits for the right answer to complete a checklist. "I read it's better to ask than not to," he added, as if the research might salve the dissonance.

She felt something harden inside her — part indignation, part shame. The question felt too big to be landed like that, too clinical for the hollow cavern she'd been moving through. She mouthed "No," small and flat, and clutched the iPad to her chest as if it could protect her from both the grief and the neatness of his concern. Tom nodded, relief briefly flickering across his face, box ticked.

His expressions made her ache; he'd meant concern, not distance. But the damage was done — her grief and his checkbox compassion had not met. Instead of feeling held, she felt observed, catalogued. It was the difference between being seen and being surveyed, and in that gap she folded smaller still.

She ached for human warmth; for the safety of arms that would hold her without expectation or judgment. But even as the longing rose in her chest, something inside her already knew: Tom wouldn't meet her there. The silence between them wasn't just absence, it was becoming a structure, putting down roots of its own. And she let it. Even kindness now felt like pressure, another shape she'd be expected to pour herself into.

Food tasted like cardboard. Even soy sauce, normally sharp and dependable, hit her stomach like a punishment. The wine numbed her brain just enough to dull the angles of thought, but left her body trembling with depletion. She moved only when absolutely necessary: tissue, wine, pizza slice, repeat.

What confused her was not the grief itself, but the force of it. They hadn't been close. Not for a long time. Their conversations were polite, hollow things — exchanges of weather and errands, nothing with roots. And yet she had always been the one who went to him. The one who travelled, made arrangements for birthdays, kept the door open. He never came to her home. Never asked what she needed. Never reached back. She'd held the thread between them long after he stopped noticing he was no longer holding the other end. So why was she the one dissolving daily now?

Outside, the world ticked on. Lawns mowed. Deliveries came. Children screamed at screens and dogs barked at nothing. And it all made her want to scream back. You people are carrying on, how dare you?

It was the quiet horror that maybe there was nothing underneath it all but more pain. The whole human project suddenly felt suspect. A factory line of yearning and disappointment. What was the point? You love people and they leave. You try to hold things together and they fall apart anyway. She curled deeper into the cushions, one hand against her chest like it could anchor her to the present.

On the fourth day of being holed up, curtains drawn and her world reduced to the sofa and single bed of the spare room, a hollow knock came on the bedroom door. Followed by Tom's voice. "Hey, Ella, mind if I bring someone in?"

She didn't want anyone, but Tom's tone carried the weight of desperation. He opened the door and ushered in Lynne Patterson, her best friend from University. She stood tall in gym gear; sleek leggings, a crisp zip-neck pullover, and water bottle in hand.

"Ella!" Lynne's face was all polished sympathy. She perched on the edge of the bed, knees together, posture immaculate. "I heard about your dad. I'm *so* sorry." She reached out open arms and Ella leaned forward to hug her. For a heartbeat, Ella nestled into the warmth, hot, sticky tears falling over her cheeks. She pressed her face into Lynne's shoulder, her whole body seeming to heave with grief.

Lynne patted her back awkwardly. "Aw, hey. You're going to be okay." She pulled back just enough to meet Ella's eyes. "Grief is horrible. But it's a normal part of life. Your dad had a good life. It's hard, I know, but he would hate to see you like this. You just have to wake up tomorrow and put one foot in front of the other."

Ella sniffed, and offered a tight nod, wiping her cheeks. "Right."

Lynne patted Ella's arm. "Look, grief is a process, right? You just have to keep moving forward. One step at a time. The experts say routine is key — fresh air, a workout, journaling. That kind of thing."

Ella felt her spine stiffen. "I — yeah."

Lynne set her water bottle on the bedside table, as though it contained all the answers. "You know what I do whenever things get rough? I schedule my week. I hit the gym at six every morning. I meal prep. Then I write three things I'm grateful for. Doesn't matter how I feel, I show up and the rest follows."

Ella's toes curled against the mattress, a small, urgent protest rising in her chest as Lynne went on to describe the angry man at the tube that morning and an office intervention for a woman who'd grown alarmingly thin. Lynne's voice bounced cheerfully around the room, full of colour and effort, as if she could stitch Ella back together with brightness alone. She laughed lightly, eyes bright with conviction. Ella smiled on cue.

"You didn't need to come," Ella murmured, glancing at the clock. "You should still be at work."

"I left early," Lynne said, tugging off her pullover. "Didn't feel right just going straight to the gym. Thought you might need some company."

Ella glanced at her, caught off guard. "That's... kind of you."

Lynne shrugged, brushing it off. "You'd do the same."

A small flicker of something moved in Ella then — not quite warmth, but the awareness of it. The quiet significance of someone rearranging their day not out of duty, but choice. She wanted to let herself feel held by it.

"Yes… thanks," she said, and meant it.

Lynne gave her a brisk smile and launched into a story about her latest 10k run, her voice quick and buoyant.

Ella mustered a smile. "That's impressive, Lynne."

"Oh, I was dying by kilometre six. But you've got to keep going, right?" Lynne said, tucking her feet beneath her. "It's the only way to stay sane."

Ella blinked at her, the words 'keep going' catching like grit. Each new anecdote – about running shoes, protein pancakes, someone's new boyfriend – landed like static in her chest. She couldn't find the right shape to receive it. It all felt slightly too loud, slightly too clean.

Ella stared at the pale carpet. The air in the room pressed in – too bright, too empty. Her tidy solutions: process, moving forward, routine, tinkled like broken promises.

"You know," Lynne added, "you should come to that yoga class I was telling you about. It's all about releasing grief through movement. Crying on the mat is basically encouraged."

Ella forced a smile. "I'll think about it."

Guilt pulsed at her temples. Lynne had made space, she was trying. And here Ella was, shrinking from it. What was wrong with her?

She shifted on the bed, tucking her feet tighter beneath her, needing smaller corners.

"I just…" she began, then trailed off, eyes fixed on the corner of the bedside table. "I think I need a bit more quiet today."

Lynne's face flickered. Hurt quickly masked.

"Of course," she said, standing. "I'll leave you to it."

Ella watched Lynne gather her gym bag, her polished brightness dimming at the edges. For a moment, their eyes met – Lynne searching for a familiar script to follow, Ella too tired to play her part. Still, the reflex kicked in. Ella straightened, feet shifting toward the floor, as if to walk her friend to the door. That was what good girls did. That was what she'd always done.

But the weight in her limbs said no. Even this small act — the motion of standing, of accompanying someone out — felt like a performance she couldn't summon. An apology bloomed under her skin, hot and restless, but it couldn't find its voice.

Lynne hesitated, then gave a tight smile and turned. The door clicked shut with a gentleness that somehow made it worse.

Ella exhaled, the sound half-sigh, half-surrender. She leaned against the wall, the stillness a balm and a blade. No more smiling, no more performing resilience. Just this: her breath, her ache, and the kind of quiet that held room for truth. Here, finally, no one asked her to be anything but broken.

She curled her toes into the bedsheets and let the silence stretch. And in that silence, her grief rose again — not louder, but deeper. And more hers.

She felt more alone than ever.

On the seventh morning, exactly one week since the funeral, her phone buzzed on the nightstand, sharp and insistent. She blinked into the blue glare of the screen.

Subject: *URGENT: Presentation Tomorrow Morning.*

Ella, I know you're technically still on leave, but Silverbell needs you. Meeting at 10 a.m. tomorrow. Please confirm ASAP.

The words barely registered at first — just shapes on a screen, corporate code breaking into the quiet ache of her cocoon. But slowly, meaning seeped in like cold water.

She hadn't showered in days. Her skin felt thin and stretched, her hair matted at the back where her head had pressed into the same sofa cushion day after day. The stale air smelled faintly of dumplings and her own detachment.

Her world had collapsed into rectangles: this screen, this bed, the light slicing through blinds. Her inbox belonged to another person; a version of Ella who had answers, who could lead teams, who smiled in meetings and said things like, "Let's circle back on that."

She stared at the email. Somewhere inside, something turned.

That evening, just as dusk pooled in the corners of the room and the air took on its familiar ache, a knock came sharp and uninvited. It seemed to echo inside her chest before it reached her ears.

Tom stood in the doorway, jeans slightly rumpled, thumb hooked into his pocket like he wasn't sure whether to come in or back away. "Gwen called," he said, voice flat. "They need you in tomorrow. Silverbell's yours. No one else can run the pitch."

Ella didn't answer. The weight of the words didn't land so much as slide past her. She stayed slumped in the tangle of blankets, her body shaped like a question mark with no answer.

"Tell her I'm..." Her voice was barely audible, a rasp swallowed by the pillow. "Tell her I'm very busy."

Tom's thumb hovered over the doorway frame for a moment, then he stepped in. "You have to go," he said, voice firm. His gaze flicked to her blankets, lingering a fraction too long, as if he half-wished he could hand her some comfort. "You can't risk losing this job. You can't just vanish."

His words held no malice, just that brittle certainty he always wore when something complicated threatened the stability he'd built. It wasn't about her grief, it was about the schedule. About normalcy. Ella felt the words land like a hand on her shoulder — one meant to steady, but instead pushed her back into a shape that didn't fit anymore.

She didn't argue. What was the point? He couldn't meet her where she was, not really. Not down here in the dim, where her grief had taken root like damp in a cellar. She didn't even blame him.

She sighed as she pushed herself up, a sound halfway between exasperation and surrender. She felt hollowed, as though someone had scooped her insides out and left only a shell. She pressed a hand to her ribcage, feeling each heartbeat drag her closer to collapse. She wanted to beg for another week of oblivion – just seven more days of numbness, but the cold reality was she'd already promised her father long ago that she'd keep his life's work alive, and "life's work" for Ella meant relentless professional competence.

So she moved, slowly, automatically, through the rituals of surface repair. A lukewarm shower that steamed up the mirror but didn't quite rinse the ache from her bones; jeans that hadn't seen daylight in a week;. a clean top pulled on like a costume.

The slide deck was already finished. Of course it was. She was always ready, always weeks ahead because life had taught her that being prepared was safer than falling apart. She skimmed the slides with rote attention, her brain tracing familiar paths while her chest stayed hollow.

Later, standing in front of the bathroom mirror, she blinked at the woman staring back. Her reflection looked like a version of herself rendered in half-light: bruised eyes, dry lips, hair coiled into a ragged knot.

She didn't flinch but she didn't look away, either. There was no rage, just a slow, spreading disappointment. How did I get here?

Not the grief – grief made sense – but the erasure.

She'd vanished into herself like smoke through floorboards, and no one had even noticed the moment it happened.

The next morning: Friday, 8 a.m.

Ella had imagined that stepping through the office doors might shock her system back into something recognisable. That the ritual of coffee machines, keyboards and clacking heels might jar her into momentum. But when the lobby doors slid open, all she felt was static.

Fluorescent lights hummed like they always had. The faint smell of burnt espresso and air freshener clung to the air. It was all too normal and that, somehow, felt grotesque.

She paused at the glass just before the entry sensors caught her movement. Her reflection stared back: drawn cheeks, lipstick barely convincing, posture upright only because she'd made it so.

She adjusted her jacket like armour.

Two weeks ago, her father's body had cooled on the floor. Her world had buckled. But the office hadn't paused — not for her, not for anyone. And now here she was, re-entering the bloodstream of a system that rewarded stamina over humanity. No time to break down. No space to bleed.

She inhaled sharply, stepped forward, and the doors opened.

Gwen intercepted her at reception like a heat-seeking missile, phone wedged between shoulder and ear, stilettos stabbing the floor with conviction.

"There you are — perfect." She said, not quite looking at Ella as she ended her call with a brisk, "I'll circle back." She turned fully then, smiling in that polished, practiced way that never quite reached her eyes. "Silverbell's been teetering since Wednesday. They want full ownership from us — strategy, execution, the whole deck live by noon. Oh, and they've added a 2 p.m. sit-down with their VP, so we'll need to finesse some slides."

Before Ella could respond, Gwen thrust a stack of folders into her arms — dense, weighty, freshly printed. The corners bit into her palms.

"I know you're... in the middle of things," Gwen added, voice lowering an octave to signal sympathy, "but honestly, you're the only one who can land this."

Her tone was sweetened with urgency. Her eyes were already scanning the hallway behind Ella, calculating time lost.

Ella managed a small nod, even as her arms trembled beneath the folders. "Of course," she said. The words came out like an echo from some obedient, pre-programmed part of herself. Grief didn't disqualify her from expectation. It simply had to be squeezed into the margins.

Gwen smiled again, approving, already pivoting towards the elevator. "You're a star. Let's circle in the boardroom just before ten. I'll loop you in with Freya."

Ella didn't move for a full breath. She felt like a wax figure of herself, holding the weight of the company's future in her hands while her insides sagged with everything she hadn't yet named. Gwen moved like someone whose nervous system had been permanently tuned to a higher frequency; always brisk, always five steps ahead of herself. Her heels clicked with purpose even when there was nowhere urgent to go. In meetings, she never sat back, always forward, pen in hand and body tilted like she was about to launch.

Ella remembered the first time she saw Gwen present at the annual conference — flawless navy dress, notes unnecessary, voice like a blade wrapped in velvet. The crowd had leaned in without even meaning to. It was hard not to admire her. Harder still to know what, exactly, lived underneath all that polish.

She had a habit of twirling her wedding ring when someone pushed back on her; just once, casually. And she spoke in soundbites so slick you didn't notice until later that she hadn't really answered your question.

Working under Gwen had always been an exercise in anticipatory tension: staying just useful enough to avoid scrutiny, but not so bold as to threaten the spotlight. It wasn't personal. It was velocity.

Gwen moved fast, and anything that couldn't keep up — doubt, grief, nuance — got left behind.

And now here she was again, handing Ella urgency like a hot plate, already spinning back toward the elevator with the rhythm of someone who assumed everyone was as tireless as she was.

Boardroom, 10 a.m.

The room felt airless, as if the walls had shrunk overnight. Every shuffle of paper, every clack of a pen, rang too loud, slicing through the thin veil of Ella's composure.

Nick from Strategy hovered by her shoulder. "Need anything?" He asked, voice low. Ella shook her head. She wanted to tell him how desperately she needed to vanish into oblivion. Instead, she cracked her knuckles and squared her shoulders. She knew the next two hours would define her sanity.

She lowered her coffee mug onto the polished surface and rubbed her temples as if trying to press clarity back into her brain. Her breath fogged slightly on the screen as she tapped to open her deck — charts, bullet points, colour-coded certainties that had nothing to do with death or aching or the smell of lilies in a church.

Across the table, clients arranged themselves like chess pieces; silent, poised, expectant. Gwen, stationed at the head, was already typing. Her colleague, Freya, offered a smile too wide to be comforting.

Ella swallowed and stood. Her voice, when it came, cracked slightly. "As forecasted, Silverbell's backend infrastructure currently supports 80,000 concurrent users — our proposed integration scales that to 150,000, with less than 1% downtime, even under peak load."

Click. Next slide. A funnel. A graph. More numbers than she could feel.

Each sentence felt like dragging herself across gravel. But she kept going, her mind split; half on the deck, half on the hollow in her chest where her father's voice had once lived. She spoke as she always had: cleanly, without fluff, drawing a straight line from insight to impact.

One of the Silverbell execs interrupted: "Can you speak to data sovereignty across your cloud integration? We've got compliance across three continents."

Ella blinked. Each bullet point was a tidal wave; she had rewritten this deck at midnight, her grief echoing in every lamp's glare. She'd fact-checked until her eyes were aquamarine with fatigue, rehearsed every contingency, every question the clients might lob. She closed her eyes for a second.

But something inside her sharpened.

"Yes," she said, evenly. "We've built in edge caching across all regions. GDPR and CCPA compliance are standard, and we've added 5% contingency to the budget for surprise audits."

Nick slid her a small nod. A signal. *You've got this.*

She clicked again. Another slide. More talking. Her voice grew steadier, as if it belonged to someone else entirely; someone who hadn't cried into a pillow the night before, who hadn't questioned the point of waking up.

When she finished, the room held a beat of silence — a quiet murmur of respect, not celebration.

The bald man near the centre nodded slowly. "That was comprehensive."

Not warm. Not enthusiastic. But enough.

Gwen stood, smoothing her skirt with the ease of a woman already moving on to the next war. "Excellent job, Ella. I'll tidy the visuals for stage two," she said, patting Ella's shoulder like a parent to a child after a piano recital. Already typing again.

The clients stood. Papers shuffled. Ella sat back down, staring at her own notes like they might turn to ash.

She had shown up. Poured herself into this room. And it had barely rippled the surface.

Ella sat for a moment, chest heaving, as if the world had stopped to watch her drown. Nick gathered his tablet, Freya rearranged her printouts; everything resumed its tidy orbit as though nothing monumental had just occurred.

Her throat went dry. She swallowed, tasted betrayal. She turned her gaze outward through the floor-to-ceiling windows: city traffic, rays of sunshine glinting off concrete. A bird wheeled high above a skyscraper.

Ella stepped out of the boardroom and into the corridor and veered toward the break room — deserted at this hour, just as she'd hoped. She sank into a swivel chair by the window and let her spine fold in on itself. The seat wheeled slightly, a hollow echo across the floor, like some ghost of her younger self gliding past — bright-eyed, sharp-suited, hopeful. She'd once thought these halls were stepping stones. Now they felt like corridors in a house she no longer lived in.

Her reflection stared back at her in the window hollowed cheeks, mascara clinging to lashes like soot and hair scraped into a knot she hadn't even remembered tying. Her blouse was crisp. Her voice had held. The pitch had landed. And none of it had reached her.

She rubbed her forehead, trying to scrub away the applause she'd never received.

The text from Tom buzzed into her hand: "*Hope it went well. Celebratory dinner at 7?*"

Celebration?

She let the phone slide back into her lap without replying.

She had poured herself into this performance — patched together poise from the broken glass of the past week — and all it had bought her was a nod and a meeting at two.

Was that it? Show up, hold your grief by the throat, deliver perfection, and still be invisible?

She leaned her forehead against the cool windowpane. Outside, the city surged forward; people darting between meetings, traffic snaking through lunch hour, conversations about performance metrics and promotions waiting at the curb. All of it moved on. And none of it had paused long enough to ask her what it had cost to keep pace.

Ella drew in a breath that trembled at the edges, and whispered, "I need out."

Not from the job. Not just yet.

But from the performance of being fine.

Just as Ella let her breath settle, the break room door creaked open.

Freya poked her head in, cheeks flushed, eyes expectant. "Ella? Lunch? There's a Thai place down the street. We should just have enough time. My treat."

Ella looked up, her thoughts still rippling from the undercurrent of everything she hadn't said in the boardroom — or the last seven days. She saw the hope in Freya's eyes: the invitation, the outreach. Maybe even a gesture of respect after a solid pitch.

But what Ella felt wasn't hunger. It was emptiness. A hollowness so full it crowded out anything as ordinary as pad thai or polite conversation.

She offered the softest shake of her head. "Thanks, Freya. I need to rest."

Freya blinked, caught off guard, then offered a quick, too-bright smile. "Sure, of course. Totally get it." She backed out, the door clicking closed behind her.

Silence again.

Ella closed her eyes and listened to the hum of the vending machine, the murmur of footsteps in the hallway, the life that kept spinning.

Two weeks ago, her father had died. And already the world had demanded productivity, precision, performance. She'd given it all. And in return, it had asked for more.

But here, now — alone in this echoing room with nothing but the sound of her own heartbeat — she felt the first flicker of refusal.

The decision to stop explaining herself to a world that only wanted the parts of her that produced, performed, perfected.

She rose from the chair slowly, as if stepping into her own body for the first time. She slipped out of the building, letting the cool afternoon air hit her face. Her chest too tight to speak. Her legs carried her forward on uneven pavements, each step a small reclaiming of space, of breath, of herself.

No meeting at two. Not today.

Let them call it unprofessional. Let them whisper.

This was her grief. And she was finally giving it permission to breathe.

5

Boundary lines

Wiping her face with the back of her hand, Ella moved across the car park, the dim light cloaking her pain. She climbed into the car like a survivor into a lifeboat. The engine offered its usual splutter of mechanical indifference.

It began just after the second roundabout. A tremor at first, then a surge. Her body shook out sobs from its depths; wracking sobs that seemed to rise from the floor of her being, like something ancient and unspoken had finally clawed its way loose. The kind of crying that empties you.

She pulled over, hands shaking on the wheel, breath hitching in shallow bursts. Part of her longed for arms around her, the steadiness of someone whispering, "I've got you". But the thought of it also made her flinch. She couldn't have borne it; not the softness, not the sympathy. It would have scalded. Like being touched in a place still raw and bleeding.

So she stayed there, alone, letting it rise and crest and crash through her, wave after wave. Grief for all of it – the almosts, the silences, the shape-shifting she'd done to make herself acceptable. And this time she didn't seal it up. She let it carve through her, unchecked. Let it ruin her posture, her breath, her dignity. It seemed the only honest response.

She drove home fast. Threw things into a bag with the grace of a getaway. Shoes, a hoodie, a charger. No plan. No one to ask.

Back in the car, GPS glowing, she typed in her father's postcode — that strange house she hadn't known what to do with. She didn't know what would happen there, only that she couldn't stay here inside the skin of her old life.

Her fingers shook as she turned the old brass key in the front door. She paused at the threshold, feeling the weight of years pressing in. The house, like her own heart, had been on pause for years, held in place by memory and dust. The walls, once bright with life, stood silent and cold: her father's fishing prints drained of colour, the lingering aroma of tobacco seeping from the skirting boards.

The study door loomed, once forbidden, now a silent challenge. Each step across the threshold felt like claiming space she'd long been denied.

Inside, the study was a cathedral of abandonment. Bookshelves sagged beneath leather-bound tomes, and her father's desk lay buried under a mountain of scattered papers and unopened envelopes as if he'd surrendered any claim to order once her mother was gone.

As a child, she'd only ever caught snatches of this room: the muted rustle of papers through a half-closed door, the soft click of a desk drawer, the glint of amber lamp light on leather-bound spines. It had felt like the inner sanctum of grown-up mysteries, a place reserved for men with important thoughts and heavy silences. She used to linger outside the door, imagining it filled with maps and secrets and ideas too complicated for children. She'd longed to be older; certain that one day, if she behaved just right, she might be invited in. But now, standing inside, all she could feel was the room's gravity — not of wisdom, but of grief. Every object seemed to sag with the weight of things unsaid, of pain that had quietly multiplied in shadow.

Her eyes landed on a small jewellery box, tucked beneath a stack of moth-eaten manuals — so unassuming, yet pulsing with possibility. She knelt, heart hammering in her ribs as she lifted the lid. The locket lay inside, its gold dulled by years of neglect but still warm to her touch, as though it carried a heartbeat of its own. She lifted it, pressing it against her chest, and memory flooded her senses: her mother swirling her round to dance in the dusky shadows with her, whispering: "This will be yours one day," as she fastened that very locket around her daughter's throat. In the wake of her mother's death, her father had spirited the locket — along with the solace it once promised — away in this forbidden room. Now, holding it again, Ella felt the full force of her longing: the primal human craving to touch something real, something that tethered her to a love that had slipped away.

Tears blurred her vision as she sank into her father's leather armchair, the locket settled against her collarbone. She let her thumb trace the engraved initials — M.L. — and watched the slanted afternoon sun illuminate the dust motes drifting in the air, each one a tiny witness to the fragile sweep of human life.

As her breath steadied, she noticed something wedged beneath the velvet lining of the jewellery box: a sliver of cream envelope, its edges curling upwards. She pried it free, heart jolting as she saw her name in her father's handwriting: *Ella.* Not scrawled or rushed, but written with care, the pen having pressed deeply into the paper as though to be sure it would last.

A breath of joy flickered through her, quick and bright. Something from him — for her. Not a will or a bank statement, not a duty or an errand. A letter. A private message meant for her alone. After all the silence, it felt like a hand reaching through time.

But the warmth didn't last. He had known she'd come here — known the locket mattered. And still, he'd locked it away. Like her grief was inconvenient. Like only he had earned the right to carry its weight. She clenched the envelope, torn between the aching proof that he had known her, and the quiet rage that he had let her suffer its absence all this time. She wasn't sure what hurt more: that he had left her something, or that he had hidden it first. A slow and steady tear slid down her cheek before she brushed it off with hostility at its presence.

It occurred to her then that this letter, this note, whatever it was, would either be another instruction; another list of what she should do, should feel, should be now that he was gone. Or worse, a plea for forgiveness she wasn't ready to offer. She sat still, afraid to open the envelope resting in her lap. Afraid that whatever lay inside might confirm what she feared most: that even in death, he couldn't quite reach her in the way she'd needed.

The stillness deepened around her, heavy and unmoving, like the kind that settles after a storm has taken everything down. Her eyes stayed fixed on nothing — a crack in the wall, the way the curtain lifted at the corner of the window — her mind emptied by the weight of too much feeling.

The letter was warm from her skin, but unopened. She wasn't ready. Not yet. With a slow breath, she slid it back beneath the velvet lining where she'd found it, pressing it down gently, as if returning a fragile thing to sleep. Then she stood, limbs leaden, and made her way to the living room.

She hovered for a long time in the doorway before stepping in. The room felt impossibly still. The side light was off, as it had been for days now, but she could still see the memory of her mother flicking it on every evening just as the light began to fade — never earlier, never later. The shade tilted slightly from where it had once been knocked by the dog's tail, and never quite straightened again.

The sofa yawned open to receive her, threadbare but familiar, and she let herself fall into it, curling around the ache without needing to explain it. Every object in the room seemed to hum with memory. Like background music you hadn't realised was playing. The bookshelf, full of spines she could recite from memory. The soft clink of the radiator — still on its heating programme — cooling down. The clock still ticking, faithfully, as if it hadn't noticed anything had changed. She wanted simply to lie there. To feel what it meant to be alone in a house that had once held her entire childhood; the comfort and the silence, the routines, the fear, the love.

The locket lay against her skin like a promise, a small heartbeat pulsing in tandem with her own. Her phone buzzed insistently on the coffee table. She unlocked the screen to see Tom's name lighting up: six missed calls and a string of texts:

"Ella, are you okay? We need you in the office." From Gwen. Followed by others from Tom: *"Where are you?" "Work just rang — you missed a meeting at 2 p.m.?"*

With a trembling thumb, she tapped out a single reply to Tom: *"I'm staying at Dad's tonight."*

The words felt heavier than she anticipated; on the other end came his response within seconds: *"Your Dad's? Why? You're supposed to be back for work. This isn't a holiday."*

Ella stared at the message, feeling the force of his confusion — he genuinely didn't understand why she needed this refuge. She opened a draft reply to her boss — something about "unforeseen circumstances" — but the words caught in her throat. Instead of sending, she watched the cursor blink before turning the phone off and sliding it face down on the table.

As the hunger inside her demanded tribute, she donned a thin coat and ventured out to Dawson's Corner, where the local shop still glowed under pale streetlamps that seemed to echo the quiet loneliness within her.

As she passed The Cormorant pub, a group of locals spilled onto the pavement, pints in hand. "Ella Lawson!" A burly man called, voice slurred with insistence, "Come join us — first round's on me."

But she gave a thin smile and shook her head, her voice a fragile whisper: "Maybe another time." Their laughter rose around her like a mist — warm, inviting, and yet utterly unreachable.

Inside the shop she collected bread, cheese, and a few tins of soup, catching her reflection in the freezer glass. Her hair hung loose and stringy, as though she carried the weight of her pain in every strand. The shopkeeper peered at her with genuine concern. "You okay, love? How are you holding up? Been ages since we saw you."

Ella offered a nod, her voice barely audible: "I'm fine," even as her chest threatened to cave in.

Back in the hush of her father's house, she prepared a simple supper with quiet reverence, letting herself eat without guilt. Returning to her position on the sofa, this time with a threadbare blanket from the dusty chaise longue in the corner, she curled her body into its recesses. The locket's cool chain pressed into her throat, memories flickering like fragile candlelight behind her closed eyelids — ghosts of all that once filled these rooms.

Sleep took her like a tide — slow at first, then all at once, pulling her under before she could resist. But her mind didn't quiet. It stirred instead, dredging the deep silt of memory, dragging her back.

She was eight again, barefoot on the stairs. Moonlight cut across the carpet. Something had woken her. Something felt wrong — off-balance, tipped. She didn't know what.

Then —

"Martha!" Her father's voice, sharp and furious. Not calling. Barking. Not frightened. Angry.

She flinched, then froze. Her fingers gripped the banister. The name echoed, ricocheting off the walls like something flung too hard.

A crash. Then a dragging sound.

Then silence.

Her body moved before her thoughts could catch up — down the stairs, one hand trailing the rail, the other pressed to her chest like it could hold something in. From behind the study door came a low sound, muffled and uneven. A sob? A cough?

She called out: "Mummy?" But it came out thin, almost swallowed by the dark.

Her small fists pounded on the study door. Behind it came the scrape of a chair, a muttered curse. She reached for the handle but didn't turn it.

She woke with a gasp, heart skittering, breath caught halfway between dream and memory. The locket she wore pressed hard into her palm. Her breath came too fast.

She swung her legs to the floor and padded barefoot through the hallway, trailing a hand along the cool wall. In the kitchen, she filled a glass with water she sipped at. She stood at the back door, fingers resting on the latch, staring out into the garden where shadows held the grass in their grip.

Her mother's face lingered. The sound of her father's voice — ragged, sharp — still echoed through the hollow spaces in her chest.

She had the sense that some part of her was still there — eight years old, barefoot, afraid — standing outside a locked door, waiting for someone to let her in.

Eventually, the pull of sleep found her again, softening the edge of things. She slipped back beneath the covers, heavy-limbed and raw, carrying the echoes of childhood fear and the pulse of the locket against her skin.

6

Loan approval

Morning slipped through the dusty curtains in pale threads, forgiving and soft. The dream clung to the edges of her mind, a bruise not yet visible but already aching. A cold shiver of apprehension curled in her stomach, as though some nameless blackness had followed her through sleep.

Yet, for the first time in weeks, something like purpose stirred inside her — fragile, but insistent. A truth was waiting to be claimed. This house held answers she could no longer ignore and, despite the dread of what she might uncover, she knew she would not leave until she faced it all. With a slow, deliberate breath, she rose from the sofa, locket warm against her chest, steeling herself to meet whatever truths waited in these silent rooms.

She began in the attic. The door creaked open with the same hesitant groan she felt in her chest. Dust lifted into the air as she climbed the narrow stairs, her hand trailing the railing worn smooth by decades. The air was dry and papery, dense with the scent of forgotten things.

She crossed the attic with care, stepping around boxes and warped furniture, and unlatched the small Velux window tucked beneath the slope of the roof. With a push, it swung open on stiff hinges, and she rose slowly until she was standing tall on the attic floor, her head poking out into the open air. A breeze lifted the hair from her face, cool and earthy, and she blinked into the light like something emerging from hibernation. The garden stretched below her, a patchwork of shadows and rustling trees. Birds flickered through the hedgerow. The village rooftops tilted and slouched in the distance, holding stories of their own.

For a moment, she stood there breathing it all in — fresh air, wide sky, the living world still turning. Then she laughed quietly to herself, imagining how it must look from the street below: a lone head sprouting from the roof tiles like some odd, watchful gargoyle. The absurdity of it made her smile. She let the moment settle, small and strange and perfect, before turning back to the chaos of the attic.

Boxes were stacked haphazardly, some bowed under the weight of years. She pulled one toward her, its label faded. Inside, wrapped in yellowing newspaper, was the wedding crockery — cream with a delicate blue rim. With a warm rush to her heart, she remembered the care with which her mother would handle it, always insisting it was "for special occasions," though she'd used it the Christmas before she died. That was the last time Ella had seen it. Her father must have packed it away afterwards, unable to bear the sight.

Nothing was ever given up. Things were shifted, hidden, buried under other things, but never let go. The boxes bore the weight of that as much as they bore the weight of years. A grief muted by time and careful packing, tucked away rather than confronted.

She moved to another box, lighter then the last and tucked beneath an old wool blanket. Photographs — loose, unlabelled. Her father, younger than she'd ever known him in life. Shirtless at the starting line of a local race, all sinew and fire, grinning into the sun. His face handsome, unlined. She held the image next to one from later — the drawn face, the slumped shoulders — from a birthday party after her mother's death. The difference cut sharply; more than years passing the loss was written across his frame. Her breath caught. She'd been so busy surviving her own grief, she hadn't seen how entirely it had reshaped him, too.

Up here, surrounded by what had once mattered and then been hidden, she felt how memory reshapes in silence — how forgetting becomes a form of survival.

She uncovered a small, battered tin box that rattled faintly in her hands. Inside were sepia-toned photographs: her mother in a white sundress, hair windblown as she leaned into her father's broad shoulder on a beach; another of them backstage at a local theatre, her mother's eyes alight and her father's grin luminous even under the dim stage lights. Ella studied each image as if she were deciphering an ancient script — examining the tilt of a head, the curve of a smile, the way their hands nearly touched. In those moments, she saw not just a bygone idyll, but proof of something universal: that people can conjure light deep enough to outshine their own shadows.

Beneath the tin box, a bundle of letters lay bound with a dusty pink ribbon. Ella unfolded the top page and read her mother's looping cursive:

"Dearest Arthur,

I never believed my life could change so completely the moment our hands brushed over that stack of papers in the county office. You gave me courage I didn't know I possessed. Every time I read your writing, I can hear your voice — steady, sure, a guide through my own fear..."

Her father's reply, scrawled in a spidery hand, spoke of admiration for her mother's tenacity and hope for their shared future. Each word shone with vulnerability and promise — and Ella ached to inhabit even a fragment of that closeness, even just for a breath.

She tried to summon memories of how it had really been between them — her mother and father — before her mother's death. But it was like grasping at light through water. Fleeting gestures. Half-heard tones. The impression of something just out of reach. Had there been affection? She remembered one holiday by the coast — chalky cliffs, salt in her hair — and they'd held hands briefly as they walked ahead of her. She'd been surprised by it then, the rare tenderness between them. And strangely, unsettled. As if their closeness somehow meant less love left over for her. Even as a child, she'd sensed the emotional scarcity that governed their home: too many needs, not enough tenderness to go around.

That single memory stood out like a shell among pebbles; small, intact, and inexplicably precious. She turned it over in her mind, trying to work out the precise moment when their radiant warmth had dimmed – when shared smiles turned to silence and comfort loosened its grip. But she could not find it. Instead, she felt a hollow ache at the realisation that affection between them had become as scarce as daylight in winter, replaced by murmured conversations behind closed doors and her father's hands falling to his sides whenever her mother drew near. Was this just what time did to people – wore down the softness until only the practical things remained? Or had something inside them cracked and never quite healed? She longed to ask them both, to sit across from them and ask not for stories but for truth. But truth, like love, was something she'd always had to piece together on her own.

Just as the silence settled back around her, her phone vibrated against the floorboards. Lynne's name glowed on the screen:

"Hey Ella — just checking in. How are you? Monday's your first day back? You'll smash it. Once back into the routine, it will all be OK. Fancy a latte later in the week?"

Ella watched the message hover in the blue light, Lynne's confident cheer folded into every line. That word – "routine" – hovered in the message, powerless against the grief she carried. She thumbed the screen, fingers pausing over the keypad before she let the phone slip back onto its side. Ella closed her eyes and let the quiet answers seep in instead.

7

Building design

The kettle clicked off with a sharp, officious pop. Ella stood barefoot on the cold kitchen tiles, hands wrapped around a mug she hadn't yet sipped from. Outside the window, the lawn was still touched with moonlight, although morning was beginning to uncurl over the fences and flowerbeds.

She'd watched hedgehogs the night before. Actual hedgehogs. Four of them. Snuffling about beneath the bird table like shy, spiky pilgrims. The moon had been swollen and ridiculous, casting a soft silver over the overgrown lawn, and she'd stood there, outside in striped pyjamas, arms wrapped around herself, not thinking anything in particular – just *being*. For the first time in months, maybe longer.

She'd felt... joy.

No audience. No Instagram filter. Just hedgehogs. Breathing. Present.

Now, she took her tea out to the back garden, still wrapped in her dressing gown, to paving slabs that were cool and uneven beneath her feet. Tilting her face toward the morning sun's first warm glance of the day, she let the heat settle lightly on her skin. Steam curled from her mug into the crisp air as she lowered herself onto the rickety outdoor chair, its frame creaking in protest. With her phone in hand, she tapped through the quiet. She needed to respond to Lynne, but still couldn't find the words. Instead, she ordered string lights, a pair of soft, weatherproof chairs – choosing orange over black because it felt brighter and bolder, like the colour of choosing joy – and a thick, inviting blanket. Next time the hedgehogs came, she wanted to be ready. Ready for warmth, for comfort, for more of this.

And then the car. She knew the sound before it turned onto the drive. His hybrid hum. Slightly smug. A sound like someone about to explain why you're wrong.

She sighed and walked down the side path toward the gate to meet the car, holding her tea like a peace offering.

Tom got out of the car with the confidence of someone arriving to do a favour.

"I thought I'd bring you home," he said, without preamble.

"No," Ella said.

He blinked. "Sorry?"

"I'm not coming back yet."

He stared at her, properly, like she was a maths equation missing a denominator. "You've made your point. You're upset. I get it. But let's just go. It's work tomorrow Ella and life moves on."

"I'm not making a point," she said, voice lower now. "I need time."

He shook his head. "Time for what? You've had days."

She held the mug tighter. "I'm asking for space, Tom. Not forever. Just a breath. Just one clear breath without having to explain it."

"This is mad," he said. "You're staying in your dad's house in your thirties like a teenager. You've gone full regression."

"Maybe I need to."

He scoffed. "You're being ridiculous."

And then he grabbed her arm.

Not violently. Not enough to bruise. But enough to shock. She froze, a current of disbelief racing beneath her skin, the sharp reminder that her body had a right to its own boundaries.

She flinched and tried to pull back. "Tom. *Don't.*"

"I'm not leaving you here," he said, voice low now. "You're not thinking straight. And you have work tomorrow. People depending on you."

She tried to twist free and dropped her tea. The mug clattered amongst the gravel.

And then –

"Everything okay, Ella?"

The voice came like a door slamming open, calm but heavy with intent.

They both turned.

Behind the low privet hedge stood her dad's next-door neighbour, gardening gloves on, a trowel in one hand. His eyes were steady on Tom.

Ella stepped back, brushing down her arm. "Morning. Er, yeah. All fine."

Tom had frozen. His hand dropped to his side.

Her neighbour didn't move. "Sure?"

Tom cleared his throat. "We were just talking."

The man gave him a long, considered look. "Well. She looks done talking."

There was a silence.

Tom exhaled, visibly recalibrating. "I'll go," he muttered. "This is clearly..."

He didn't finish, just shook his head and walked back to the car, the door closing with a muted thunk. The engine whirred, reversed, then faded into the sound of a leaf blower three gardens down.

Ella stared at the empty street.

"You alright?" Her neighbour said, not unkindly.

She turned, brushing her hair back from her face. "Yeah. Just... mornings."

He nodded. "Happens."

She looked at him then, properly, maybe for the first time in twenty years of knowing of his existence next door. His face was lined in a way she hadn't noticed before; not weathered, but grounded, like soil that had known many seasons. His hair was more salt than pepper now, his shoulders a little stooped, but he stood there steady and open, a kind of quiet presence that didn't ask anything of her.

It struck her how much she had missed over the years — not just about him, but about the world in general. How much had passed her by while she was racing to be useful, perfect, impressive. There was so much she hadn't seen because she'd been too busy planning her next steps.

"Thanks," she said.

He pulled off one glove with his teeth and scratched the back of his neck. "I didn't do anything."

She smiled then.

He nodded once. "Hedgehogs were back last night.

Ella smiled. "I saw them."

"Funny little things. Nothing urgent about them. Bit of a lesson there."

She laughed softly. "Yeah. There is."

He tipped an invisible hat and turned back to his flowerbed. "I'm David, by the way. Well. You know where I am."

8

Load bearing assessment

Ella hadn't set out to be dramatic.

She didn't even really believe in mental health days — not for herself, anyway. They were for people who cried in stairwells and posted vague emotional updates online. But this morning, she'd picked up her phone and called in sick before her brain had time to run the usual guilt script. No fever, no real symptoms, just a feeling she couldn't name. A bone-deep need for stillness.

That was new. Almost outlandish.

Each time she remembered she'd actually done it — as she pulled on clothes or made tea — it returned in a strange, fizzy wave. Like catching sight of yourself doing something bold in a dream. A small, secret smirk rose inside her, like a mischief she hadn't known she was capable of. Still, her body had spoken clearly. And for once, she'd listened.

The morning sun was already climbing as she walked the few streets to the café, not entirely sure what she was doing or what she needed. Habit carried her more than intention. A coffee, a walk, fresh air; maybe that would be enough.

The café door swung open to the hum of steam and conversation, the scent of espresso hugging her skin. Deep teal walls showed the ripple of old plaster. Mismatched tables — some polished, some scarred — each held a small vase of roadside wildflowers. Behind the counter, glass domes sheltered cake slices, and a chalkboard menu leaned lazily in one corner. An espresso machine hissed with effort as the morning sun slanted through the window, catching the rising steam like a quiet blessing.

Yesterday she'd come here by accident; really she'd just been trying to outrun the house, the altercation with Tom, the tightness in her chest. But the coffee had been good, and something about the warmth had steadied her. The barista — alarmingly symmetrical, as if airbrushed into existence — recognised her this time and handed over the cup with a knowing nod. She gave a polite one back.

She turned to leave — and then paused.

The group was there again. Five or six of them gathered at the long window table, mid-conversation, voices tumbling over one another. They weren't quiet people. That had been her first judgment: too loud, too open, too much.

Today, they waved.

"You should join us," said a man with wild, black hair and paint-smudged hands.

Her body angled toward the door, ready to go — but then her voice surprised her. "Just for a minute." The words felt foreign, like borrowing someone else's courage.

A chair scraped back. She sat, perching on the edge, alert as a cat near water. The man smiled warmly, then turned back to his conversation.

She sipped her coffee, eyes drifting, cheeks warm. Wondering how long she had to sit before it would be socially acceptable to escape.

Then the woman beside her turned.

"I'm Miranda," she said, her voice quiet and steady. She looked to be in her sixties, silver hair loose, face bare of makeup, presence radiant. She gave the impression of someone with time. The rarest currency.

"Ella," she replied. "I... saw you here yesterday. Same chair."

Miranda nodded. "It's got the best light. Ideal for people-watching."

"Oh. Are you writing a novel?" Ella asked, then immediately regretted it.

Miranda chuckled. "No. I just like people."

Ella gave an awkward half-laugh that somehow tried to say both '*me too*' and '*please don't talk to me*'.

"I saw you yesterday," Miranda said. "Early, like us. You looked like you were trying to solve something in your mind."

"That's probably true." Ella smiled weakly.

Silence stretched. The table buzzed around them, but Miranda didn't fill the space. She just sipped her tea.

Ella's mind scrambled for conversation – weather, books, work – but nothing landed. Irritation prickled. Why was she trying so hard? Why did it matter if this woman liked her?

Her old armour began to clink into place: distance, disinterest, a raised eyebrow of detachment.

Then Miranda asked, "Have you ever noticed how much effort it takes to keep holding things in?"

Ella blinked. "What do you mean?"

"The way we carry old stories in the body," Miranda said. "The mind keeps them alive, but the body–," she touched her chest, "The body remembers. Even when we think we're past it."

She paused. "I used to get this ache in my jaw, right here–," Tapping just below her ear, "every time I had to speak up for myself. I thought it was tension. But it started after years of being cut off mid-sentence. My body learned to brace."

She smiled, rueful. "Took a long time to let my jaw relax. To believe I had the right to finish a thought."

Ella let out a breath that wasn't quite a sigh. "Right," she said, too sharply. She looked away.

The statement had landed somewhere uncomfortable — half defensiveness, half recognition. Her body did feel like it was holding something. She rubbed her forearm insistently, without thinking.

"It's just coffee," she muttered. "I'm not usually... like this."

"Like what?"

"Awkward. Defensive. I don't know. I never do this kind of thing."

Miranda smiled, kind eyes steady. "Maybe there's a part of you that's ready to do things differently."

Minutes passed.

"You're staying at your father's house, right?" Miranda asked gently.

Ella nodded, surprised how easily people here knew things. In the city, no one noticed your absence. Here, it was... seen.

"Temporarily," she added, but it sounded hollow even to her.

Miranda raised an eyebrow. "That word's doing a lot of heavy lifting."

Ella laughed. "Well. I'm not really sure what I'm doing. I need to clear the place out for it to be sold. Then... back to the city, I guess."

"Family homes are funny," Miranda said. "You walk in and suddenly you're sixteen again. Even the way the tap drips can undo you."

Ella smirked. "At Dad's, it's the kitchen tap. Maddening."

They talked. Miranda, it turned out, had lived here "since before kombucha got gentrified." A retired therapist. Curious, not probing. At some point she mentioned, almost offhandedly, that a group of locals met here most mornings; nothing formal, just whoever felt like turning up around nine for coffee and gentle chat before the day pulled everyone into their separate lives.

"It keeps us stitched into each other," she said. "A soft way to start the day. No pressure. You'd be welcome, anytime."

Ella smiled, though something in her chest tightened. She couldn't remember the last time her day began anywhere but inside her own head.

She found herself laughing, confessing, saying more than she meant to; how it felt like her life had paused without her permission. Miranda didn't offer solutions. Just space.

An hour passed.

"I've got to go," Ella said, startled by the time.

"I'll walk with you," Miranda offered. "I'm not far from you."

They walked in silence. Warm sun, birdsong, the kind of stillness Ella hadn't let herself feel in years.

"Sometimes we think we're protecting ourselves by staying small," Miranda said. "But really, we're just repeating the same old patterns."

Ella looked at her. "Patterns like what?"

Miranda stopped at a crossing.

"Like believing you're alone. Or that ease has to be earned. Or that joy is suspicious."

Ella said nothing. But her ribs hurt in a way she couldn't explain.

Miranda added, "It shows up in the way we shrink. Or apologise. Even just for sitting in a chair."

"I didn't apologise."

“No… not out loud, at least.” Miranda smiled at her.

They reached Ella’s street. Miranda’s posture shifted, gently.

“You don’t have to fix anything,” she said. “Just notice how much of your life you spend trying to earn what you already are.”

The words hit something soft and unguarded.

“You don’t know me,” Ella snapped, too fast.

Miranda didn’t flinch. “I know. I’m not claiming to.”

“Then don’t talk to me like you do.” Ella bit out.

Miranda didn’t flinch, didn’t defend herself. She simply inclined her head, a small gesture of apology — or respect. Or both.

Ella turned away. She wasn’t even sure what she was angry about, only that her throat had tightened like a fist and her eyes were suddenly, stupidly full. She didn’t look back. She couldn’t. By the time she reached the door, tears had arrived hot and uninvited. She blinked hard, once, twice. Useless.

Ella stood for a moment in the doorway, her coat still on. Something in her chest was pulsing like a blister. She’d closed the door behind her as though escaping something on fire. Only, it wasn’t a blaze. It was just words.

“Notice how much of your life you spend trying to earn what you already are.”

She hated how easily the words came back. How perfectly it had lodged itself in her memory, like a parasite disguised as wisdom. Inside, the house was dim; curtains half-drawn, the kitchen neutral and emotionally vacant. Ella stood still.

She opened the fridge. Stared at nothing. Closed it again. She didn’t want food. She didn’t want wine. She didn’t even want distraction. She just wanted quiet. But not the kind that surrounds you; the kind that turns off the voice in your own skull. Somewhere behind her, the kitchen tap let out a fat, insolent drip. Then another. Each one landing like a taunt, a metronome for her unravelling.

She sank onto the sofa and let her head fall back. The silence in the house had a hum to it. Fridge. Pipes. Loneliness.

It wasn't that she wanted to cry. It wasn't that she was sad, precisely.

It was that she felt... exposed. Unzipped. Like someone had picked a lock without asking and was now rearranging the furniture inside her.

It was outrageous, really. The arrogance of it. That Miranda had seen her — Ella, self-sufficient, emotionally house-trained Ella — and spoken as if she had the right to diagnose.

Except.

Except she hadn't diagnosed anything. She hadn't patronised, or therapised, or pushed. She'd just... said what was true.

Ella's anger flared again, just for a second. But it was thinner now, brittle. She was tired of holding it up like a shield.

What had Miranda actually done? Asked a question. Made an observation. With calm eyes and turmeric tea and the kind of presence that made everything else feel performative.

Ella thought about the look Miranda had given her when she snapped. Not wounded or smug. Just... still. Like she understood the anger wasn't really hers to carry.

Ella pressed the heels of her hands into her eyes. Tears came again — this time, not as drama, but as pressure. Like unsent messages finally giving up.

She didn't sob — she wasn't going to be that kind of woman. But the tears slid out anyway, quietly, stubbornly, and she let them.

When it passed, Ella sat back, exhausted and breathing raggedly. A small pile of tissues on the coffee table bore witness to the fact that, apparently, she did sob now. At cafés. In living rooms. On perfectly ordinary Mondays.

"Fantastic," she muttered aloud, to no one.

There was a tension in her body she couldn't quite name. Like she'd been carrying an invisible bag for years and had just, for a moment, put it down. And her arms didn't quite know what to do without it.

Her phone buzzed again. Lynne's name glowed on the screen. Guilt flickered immediately, fast and familiar like muscle memory.

Ella's thumb hovered. She didn't feel ready to respond. She didn't feel ready for anything.

But even now, some old motor inside her started up — that low, rattling urge to fix it. To smooth the edges. To be the version of herself that people could slot back into their day.

She typed:

"Hey Lynne — sorry, yes, back at work next week instead. Would love to catch up then. Miss you! Xx"

Sent.

The message landed with a quiet chime. Something inside her dropped with it.

The phone slipped from her hand and thudded onto the carpet.

She leaned back and let out a long, slow breath. Her jaw hurt. Her eyes burned. Her body felt like it had been holding tension since forever. Like trying to swim in fog. Like carrying a room inside her that wouldn't open.

Over the next few days, the knot in her chest began to tighten into a running commentary. It arrived as small, sharp judgments that clipped at everything she did: the throat-clearing that seemed too loud in the quiet of a meeting – how annoying that must be to other people; the shoe laces she hadn't double-knotted that came undone on the pavement and made her stumble, and with it the private, infantile scold, *how stupid you are*; the back door she left unlocked for a minute while she chased down a new blind for her bedroom, and the little puncture of shame that buzzed in her ribs afterward as if she'd abandoned some basic competence.

She found herself snapping the plastic lid off a pen in the middle of a train journey – too much fiddling – and spent the next hour berating the motion as childish, ridiculous. In the quiet she would rewind the moment she'd raised her voice, playing variations of what she should have said instead, rehearsing better endings until her head ached. Every tiny slip became evidence: proof that she wasn't steady, proof that any softness would be seized upon and used as reason for people to walk away.

At night the catalogue of small failings lined the edges of her pillow like a litany. They felt absurd and enormous at the same time; petty as crumbs, but heavy enough to bruise. She caught herself thinking in footnotes – *if only I'd been neater, quieter, cleverer* – until even the breath felt tactical, an action to be judged rather than a respite.

9

Planning regulations

The spa smelled like eucalyptus and capitalism, a sort of humid cleanliness curated for the Instagram generation. There were towels that cost more than Ella's childhood duvet, too-white furniture, and a softly patronising woman in taupe linen who explained the magnesium pool like it was a portal to enlightenment.

Leanne was glowing. Of course she was — highlighter and hope. The sash that read 'Bride To Be' had been met with an eye-roll and then quietly embraced. Fifteen or so women — work friends, cousins, vague Pilates acquaintances — clumped into polite groups, talking loudly about eyeliner and renovations.

Ella had spent the morning submerged, literally and metaphorically, in the warm water, her thoughts stewing quietly while she smiled too much. Everything about the day had the sticky cheer of a badly planned surprise party. The women were nice enough but the energy was brittle, like a cracked plate still in use.

By dinner, they were at a coastal bistro that took itself far too seriously. The chef came out to explain the monkfish. No one cared; they cooed anyway.

Ella picked at her food. Her body was still loose from the spa, but her mind was a hair-trigger. Everything felt like a test of how well she could pretend to be having a normal day. The conversation — wedding favours, rose gold table runners, one woman's husband's IBS — was suffocating.

When the bill came, everyone split it with performative ease, except one cousin who insisted she hadn't touched the wine. A minor standoff ensued. Ella stared into her half-drunk glass and wondered if her silence had started to feel hostile. Probably. But if she spoke, she might say something inappropriate. Like how she wanted to scream into the leftover ice cream.

Later, they went to a club — someone's idea of reclaiming their youth. But they arrived too early. A few lone drinkers loitered beneath flickering lights.

The music was already loud. A heavy, thudding beat that seemed to demand something from her. Ella danced because everyone else did. Her calves ached. Her limbs dragged. But she moved, lifting her arms when others did, swaying more out of manners than momentum.

And just as the place began to warm, just as bodies started to move like they meant it – the night was over. The minibus, pre-booked in the name of cost and coordination, pulled up at 11:30pm. Punctual. Pleased with itself.

They filed out, the bassline following them down the street like a party they'd almost, but not quite, been part of. Ella couldn't tell if she was more relieved or disappointed.

Back at the house — a sprawling Airbnb with peeling wallpaper and an unsettling collection of Victorian dolls — the women peeled off in waves.

"So tired."

"Big drive tomorrow."

"Got to call my boyfriend."

Ella offered to help clear up, but no one seemed keen. The mood had shifted. The energy had frayed. The mess could wait. Everyone wanted to disappear into pyjamas and TikTok.

Within half an hour, the house was still, the kitchen smelling faintly of Prosecco and panic. Ella stood alone in the low light, holding a square of dark chocolate she didn't remember agreeing to.

Upstairs, her roommate was already in bed. Earlier, Ella had claimed the side nearest the door — an escape route, just in case. She'd dropped her bag by the bedside table and turned to face the true horror of the room: an antique pram beside the wardrobe, cradling a family of porcelain dolls in lace bonnets. All of them staring directly at the bed like tiny, judgmental sentries.

Leanne reappeared barefoot, face scrubbed clean and sash slung across a chair like it had outlived its expectation.

"God. That was grim," she said, flopping into a chair. "I mean, spa was lush. But the vibe? Dead."

Ella laughed, unexpectedly. "You're not supposed to say that. You're the bride."

"I know. Isn't that the worst part? It's my own hen do and I still feel like I was at someone else's party. Like I was playing myself, but the lines were all wrong."

Ella leaned against the counter. "I was worried you'd be offended. I've been completely crap."

"You've been real. That's more than I can say for most of them." Leanne poured herself a glass of leftover wine. "Sit. You're giving me anxiety just standing there like a haunted statue."

Ella sat slowly. Her body had been aching all day; not from the spa, but from containment. Something inside her had been pressing against her chest like a bird that needed out.

"I'm not doing great," she said. Flat and unplanned.

Leanne didn't flinch. Just tilted her head slightly.

"I'm really not okay," Ella said, eyes on the table. "I feel like I'm folding in on myself. Like if I let go of even one thing, the whole of me might collapse."

The words landed between them. Too true to take back.

She blinked. Flustered. “God, I’m sorry. What am I doing? This is your hen do. I shouldn’t be unloading–.”

“Stop apologising,” Leanne said gently, but with a quiet authority. “I want to know how you really are. No pretending today; I can’t take any more of that.”

Ella breathed then began slowly: “I went back to the flat,” she said, voice low. “Took everything I could carry and dumped it at my dad’s. Clothes, books, the mug I always used, even the weird little lamp from my bedside table.”

She paused. Her fingers toyed with the stem of her glass.

“I didn’t plan it. I just woke up one morning and knew I needed to go. Like if I thought about it for even a second, I wouldn’t be able to do it.”

Leanne looked at her for a long moment. “Are you… leaving Tom?”

Ella’s eyes drifted to the dark window. The night pressed in softly, like something listening.

“I don’t know,” she said. “I just know I couldn’t stay.”

She wrapped a strand of hair around her finger, and her voice dipped lower. “It was heavy, Leanne. The flat. His presence. Like I could feel the weight of everything I was still expected to hold. Nothing had moved. Not a dish. Not the mail. It was like I’d never left, and somehow that was worse than if it had all changed.”

Her throat clenched. “I had to move our wedding photo to get to my books.”

She let out a breath that wasn’t quite a laugh. “I couldn’t look at it. I just… turned it face-down.”

Leanne leaned back slightly, frowning – not with annoyance, but something closer to hurt. “Why didn’t you ask me to come with you?”

Ella blinked, caught off guard. "What?"

"When you went back to the flat. To move your things. Why didn't you call me? I would've helped."

Ella laughed, too quickly. "Oh God, no. That would've been ridiculous. You've got a wedding to plan. I was fine."

There it was again – her old voice, reflexive and brittle. Cut it off before it gets close; say you're fine before anyone can offer help you're not sure you deserve.

A beat passed. The silence after the words made her wince. She didn't take them back, but she felt the shape of them in her chest, like a locked door she'd slammed out of habit.

"Tom messaged me," Leanne said. "Asked me to talk to you. Said he's been trying to reach you."

Ella exhaled, a quiet breath that tightened on the way out. "Ignore him. Sorry he dragged you in."

Leanne gave a small shrug, not unkind. But it landed anyway; guilt pricked at her collarbone, an old reflex.

"I was scared," Ella admitted, her voice softening. "That if I told you all this, you wouldn't want to be friends anymore. That I'd be too much."

There it was. The real fear: that mess made her unlovable.

Leanne didn't respond right away. She wrapped her hands around her glass like she was grounding herself.

"I get that," she said finally. "More than you think. I used to think you were the strong one. The together one. I didn't want to be the one who brought you down."

She smiled then, small and crooked. "But if we're both hiding from each other... what kind of friendship is that?"

Ella looked up.

Leanne's eyes stayed on her, steady and unflinching. "I didn't become friends with you because you were easy. I became friends with you because you felt true. Big-hearted. Familiar in a way that made me feel less alone."

Ella sucked a breath in. The words landed too close, too gently. She looked away sharply, the glass in her hand suddenly fascinating. There it was again; the instinct to retreat, to shrink just enough so love wouldn't notice her.

A pause.

"I'm not going anywhere," Leanne added. "Even if it's messy. Especially then."

Ella nodded. Slowly. Less to Leanne than to herself.

"I don't really know how to do this," she said. "Let people stay. Let myself need them." Her voice wavered. "I think I've been lonely in ways I didn't even notice."

She hesitated. Then met Leanne's eyes. "So… thank you. For not backing away."

Leanne reached out for her hand. A quiet tether.

"Ells. Do you remember when we used to swim before school?"

Ella nodded. The memory hit like chlorine at the back of her throat.

"I used to bloody hate it," Leanne said. "But I kept showing up. Thought pushing through made me better. Stronger."

She tilted her head. "And I'd watch you. Always going further. Always holding your breath longer. And I wondered if you ever let yourself rest."

"I didn't," Ella said.

"Yeah." Leanne's voice softened. "Didn't think so."

They were quiet for a moment.

"This weekend..." Leanne continued, "I think I planned it to prove I'd done everything right. But I just felt flat. Like I was wearing the version of me that other people wanted to see."

Ella looked at her friend — really looked at her — and saw the brittle edge behind the bronze tan, the pressure behind the lashes. She swirled her glass, watching the wine catch the lamplight like something trying to dance.

"It's wild," she murmured. "How much judging I've been doing, without even realising. I used to think it was everyone else. Like the whole world was walking around ready to look down on me. But maybe... it was me. I was braced for judgment that wasn't coming."

"Like my neighbour," she added, a small, rueful smile tugging at her mouth. "I was so sure he was stiff, disapproving; the kind of man who trims his hedge too neatly and waves like it's a chore. But the other day he was really kind when it counted. No fanfare."

Leanne let out a dry laugh, low and knowing. "God, yeah. I think I judged all the time. Especially at swimming. I used to walk in and just... brace myself. Convinced everyone thought I wasn't pushing hard enough, or that I was soft, or lazy, or that I didn't belong. But the voice wasn't theirs. It was mine. And I'm so bloody tired of listening to it."

She looked at Ella, her smile more tired than teasing. "No wonder we're exhausted. We've been carrying around a whole courtroom."

They sat holding hands in the stillness. Then Leanne snorted.

"But seriously — what is with all the dolls in this house?"

Ella laughed, startled. "I had to turn three of them to the wall before I could change. Four of them in a pram. Judging me."

"Don't," Leanne groaned. "I swear one tried to whisper to me."

They dissolved into giggles — giddy, breathless, grateful for the absurdity. It was the kind of laughter that didn't erase what hurt, but wrapped a warm towel around it. And Ella felt it then; a tiny shift inside her ribcage, like a locked room airing out. It stunned her how good it felt to be witnessed without being analysed, fixed, or asked to perform strength she didn't have.

When the laughter settled, Leanne's gaze softened.

"I'm really glad you're here."

Then she stood and crossed to the counter, lifting an unopened bottle of red.

"No one's drinking this. Bloody shame."

She held it up. "One more? Or are we pretending to be sensible?"

Ella reached for the corkscrew, her fingers already moving before her brain caught up.

"God no," she said. "Sensible sounds exhausting."

As the cork popped free with a soft sigh, something loosened in her chest. They poured generously, the wine catching the glow of the under-cabinet lights.

Ella leaned back in her chair. But even as she smiled, her thumb grazed the inside of her palm, circling the skin the way she always did when she was anxious. She didn't notice she was doing it.

Still bracing. Still waiting.

10

Planning objections

Ella hadn't so much slept as endured a series of horizontal negotiations under a floral duvet controlled entirely by a woman named Tara. Tara, who had apparently been doing intermittent fasting and CrossFit for nine months and snored like a competitive lifter.

Her mouth tasted of red wine and righteous bonding. Her head felt like it had been lined with gravel.

She padded into the kitchen in borrowed socks and found Leanne already dressed, chewing a banana in that infuriatingly efficient way people with energy do in the morning.

"I made coffee," Leanne said, far too brightly.

Ella narrowed her eyes. "Thanks. Honestly, how are you like this in the morning? It's unnatural."

Leanne raised an eyebrow but didn't respond. Ella poured herself a cup, immediately spilling it all over the counter. Leanne handed her a cloth. Ella wiped up the mess, then took a cautious sip – grateful for the heat, for the ritual, for the way it braced her from the inside out.

Then came the knock.

Low. Uncertain. Like a decision being made mid-air.

Her stomach dropped with the kind of clarity only hangovers and intuition can provide.

When she opened the door, Tom was standing there. Canvas tote bag slung over one shoulder, visibly full of lemons and kale.

"Morning," he said, stepping forward like nothing was fractured. "You look—, " He paused, probably aiming for neutral. "Worn out."

"Wow. Thanks."

He glanced past her into the hallway. "Leanne said you were here. You've been ignoring my calls. I thought I'd come and take you home."

Because I've been living inside my own silent collapse, she didn't say.

"I thought Leanne was bringing me back," Ella replied, looking over her shoulder at Leanne, who was suddenly very invested in washing a mug.

"I just thought... you two should talk," Leanne said without turning around.

Ella nodded once. Tight. She understood the intention. Still wanted to shake her.

"Come on," Tom said, stepping back. "I've parked in that weird bit with the hedge maze, so I can't hang around."

She didn't want to go. But her body followed him anyway, dragging her suitcase like a reluctant child.

The drive was mostly silence. Not comfortable silence, but the kind that vibrated with unspoken indictments.

"You haven't been into work all week," Tom said eventually. "I called. No one knew anything."

"I called in sick."

"For a *week*?"

"I'm not going back. Not right now."

He blinked, head tilting. "Sorry, what?"

She pulled a folded slip of paper from her bag and placed it in the console between them.

"A doctor's note?"

"Three months."

"For what?"

"I don't know. Burnout. Grief. Life."

He stared ahead, blinking like he was trying to recalibrate her into someone familiar.

Once she'd called in sick the first time — with no real excuse — it had been surprisingly easy. One day blurred into another. And then she'd found herself in her GP's office, too tired to be convincing, too brittle to be vague. She'd opened her mouth to explain the heaviness, and burst into tears instead. Quiet ones. Relentless.

The doctor had responded with such careful kindness. She'd asked whether Ella ever felt like she didn't want to be here anymore.

Ella had looked down at her hands, surprised by how long it took her to respond.

No, she wasn't planning anything.

But if she didn't wake up one morning… she wasn't sure she'd fight her way back. She certainly couldn't remember the last time she had felt glad to be alive.

She'd been handed a three-month note without protest. Offered medication. She declined — reflex more than decision; some part of her still felt like needing help meant failure. She'd walked out with the slip in her pocket, feeling like she'd stepped off a moving walkway.

"You don't seem sick," Tom said eventually. "You seem…"

"Go on. Say it."

"Fine. You seem mental."

There it was.

Ella let out a sharp, humourless laugh. "The diagnosis. Thanks, Dr Tom."

He had the grace to wince. "You know I didn't mean it like that."

"I honestly don't. Because I don't think you've ever tried to understand me. You just expect me to keep going. Like a bloody fridge. Plug me in, expect cold air."

"Oh, come on. You're just being dramatic. You need to come home, have a proper meal. A shower. Reset."

"I *am* home. I'm going back to my dad's."

He swerved into a layby, turning to look at her like she'd announced she was joining a cult.

"That's not your life anymore."

"Exactly," she said. "That's your life. The one where I hold everything together so you don't have to notice what's missing."

"Jesus, Ella."

"You never asked what I needed. You just bought oat milk, booked the restaurants and called it intimacy."

Tom gripped the steering wheel tighter, jaw working. "So, what now? You're just staying at your dad's forever?"

She didn't answer immediately.

"I don't know," she said. "For now, yes. I need to be there. I need to feel what I'm feeling. I can't stay in that flat pretending I'm okay. Not when I can't breathe in it."

He scoffed. “So, I’m just supposed to wait while my wife figures out her feelings?”

“I’m not asking you to wait. I’m asking you to take me back to my dad’s. That’s it.”

For a moment he didn’t move. Then, with a breath like he was trying not to say something he’d regret, he started the engine again. He didn’t look at her. Just flicked the radio on, low and mindless, to something synthy and forgettable that filled the space between them. The rest of the journey passed in silence; the thick, unyielding kind that builds walls. Neither of them tried to breach it.

They pulled up outside her father’s house. The air was still. The roses next door overgrown and unapologetic.

“I think,” Ella said, unclipping her seatbelt, “we need a break.”

Tom stiffened. “What kind of break?”

“The kind where you stop calling me. And I figure out who I am when I’m not curating my feelings for your comfort.”

“Is this about your dad?”

She turned to face him fully. “It’s about everything.”

She got out before he could say anything else. Pulled her suitcase from the boot. Didn’t look back until she reached the front door.

Tom was still sitting there. One hand on the steering wheel, like he might steer his way back to how it was before. Staring at nothing. Like he still believed this was temporary.

But she knew better. Before was over.

Inside, the house was quiet. Not eerie quiet, just unbothered. Like it had been waiting.

Keys on the sideboard. Shoes tucked away, exactly where her father had always insisted they go. Bag slipping from her shoulder.

No need to think.

This was hers now. This stillness. This space. Familiar. Lived-in. Beginning to feel like home.

She went straight upstairs. No kitchen detour. No glass of water– because she 'should'.

The weekend still buzzed faintly in her bones; overlapping voices, synthetic bass, the hot press of obligation. And then Tom. The hum of his presence still clinging to her skin.

The stairs creaked. The landing narrowed. Her fingers curled around the familiar brass doorknob.

She hadn't moved into the big bedroom yet.

It was ready, technically. She'd cleared it. Aired it. Even bought curtains.

But stepping into that room still felt like trying on someone else's coat. Her parents had slept in that room. Too heavy. Too stitched with memory.

So instead: her old room. New bedding. Her own things. But wallpaper she chose age fifteen, a bed that still creaked in the same spot, and a window that still looked out over David's rusted greenhouse.

She sat on the edge of the bed. Didn't take off her earrings. Didn't cry.

Just pulled the duvet over her shoulders. Lay down to retreat.

Let the weight take her; not just tiredness, but surrender. Bone-deep. Necessary.

Let it come.

11

Planning consent

She sat cross-legged on the edge of her childhood bed, damp hair clinging to her neck, wrapped in the softest towel her father owned, still frayed at the edges.

What the actual fuck am I doing?

The thought wasn't new, but it landed with a thud today. More final. More raw.

Her body, though, remembered the day before in slow pulses: the hours she had drifted in and out of sleep, lying in bed after asking Tom for a break, letting the afternoon and evening pass without resistance. Each doze had been messy, fitful yet restorative, letting her muscles unclench, her mind slacken, her chest release its tight hold. Now she woke to a world that felt slightly unfamiliar, the edges of it softened, her nervous system quietly settling after the storm.

Like she'd stepped out of her own life and now couldn't find a way back in.

From the outside, she'd had everything: a decent husband, a two-bedroom flat with equity, reliable well-paid work, a life that moved in clean, predictable rhythms. It should have felt solid. It should have held.

So why had she so adamantly walked off the edge of this picture?

The towel slipped a little at her collarbone. She pulled it tighter, anchoring herself in the soft, frayed cotton.

Was she being stupid? Ungrateful? Self-sabotaging? Or just finally honest?

Throwing it all away for what: an emotional fog? An instinct she couldn't name?

Her chest tightened with the familiar pressure of needing to figure it out.

What was the plan here? She'd left, she was grieving, she was untethered. But to what end?

She thought about going back. About phoning Tom, about apologising — not because it felt right, but because it would end this feeling; the floating, the not-knowing.

But even as the thought rose, her body recoiled. There was no comfort in that path. Just the dull ache of repetition.

No clear answers, then. No master plan. Just this: one small moment, and then the next.

Maybe that was the only thing she could do: keep stepping forward. Not because she knew where she was going, but because standing still was worse. She exhaled slowly, the breath catching on something low in her ribs.

Okay then. She would stay. For now. She would try; give this strange, suspended life her best shot. And maybe — maybe — see what opened up from there.

But if she was staying, she'd have to start.

And that meant getting dressed.

She looked toward the heap of clothes on the chair; creased, mismatched, still holding the mood of earlier days. The idea of putting them back on felt like stepping into the wrong skin.

She stood and crossed to the mirror, towel clutched at her chest.

Her reflection met her quietly. Unmade. A little washed out. Her eyes softer around the edges than she remembered. Not bad. Just... blurred.

Without the daily drip-feed of other people's reactions – compliments, flirtations, micro-validations – how did anyone know how they looked anymore? What they looked like?

She tilted her head slightly. She didn't feel ugly. But she also didn't know how to recognise herself.

She hadn't worn much makeup since she left. The thought of it now – priming, smoothing, concealing – felt too performative. Too much like an old costume.

These are your best years, whispered one voice. *You should be making the most of them.*

But another voice, quieter and firmer, said: *Let it be. Let yourself be.*

She stood there for a long moment, toes curling on the old rug, then turned away.

The clothes she had were mostly work-smart blouses, tailored trousers, shoes that pinched if you wore them too long. The rest were city-weekend casual: trying too hard, too bold for this muted world of small villages and quiet kitchens.

Eventually, she pulled on a soft, slate-grey jumper she used to wear in winter with ankle boots that were perfect for a brisk walk to the tube. It didn't try too hard. It didn't say much at all.

She liked that. Neutral enough to pass.

She added jeans; one of the two pairs she'd been rotating since she arrived that were saggy at the knees, but familiar. She didn't bother with makeup. She ran her fingers through her hair, still damp, and tied it back in a loose knot.

Enough.

Downstairs, the house met her with its particular stillness: the quiet hum of the fridge, the faint tick of the hallway clock, and the weight of dust in corners she hadn't touched yet. It wasn't asking anything of her. But it also wasn't going to carry her.

If she was staying, she had to shape it. Bit by bit.

She couldn't wait around for clarity.

She began in the sitting room, circling the furniture slowly as if seeing it for the first time. Some pieces were beautiful, solid, but it was hard to know if she liked them or just recognised them. They were stitched into her childhood like wallpaper. Did she actually want the dark oak sideboard? The glass-fronted cabinet filled with figurines and plates? What did she like? The question felt almost impossible to answer. Was she allowed to not want them?

That felt like a bigger question. One she could come back to.

For now, she began with what was easy.

She started with the junk. The things no one would fight her on.

Old VHS tapes, a cracked lamp base, an unopened jigsaw with a faded lid. Drawers full of elastic bands, stubby pencils, expired batteries, stray buttons. It was as if the house had been holding its breath – every cupboard braced with objects kept just in case. For what?

Some decisions were easy. Others pulled at her strangely. The flannel pyjamas her dad used to wear every Christmas, even when it was too warm. A worn paperback with a soft spine and notes in the margins. And the photograph her father had blu-tacked up in the hallway, the only one of her and her mother on display. Ella, aged six, with arms looped around her mother's stiff neck, both smiling like it had been rehearsed.

Ella held it in her hands for a long moment, feeling the weight of the years, the absence, and the love that lingered. Then, gently, she placed it in a proper frame, choosing it's place herself. On a shelf bathed in morning light, it would breathe quietly, honoured, a witness to what had been and what she carried forward.

By lunchtime, tired but fuelled by some deep-rooted need to do, she'd filled eight bags for charity and six for the tip. She took a photo of the piles on her phone — not for Instagram, but just to prove to herself that something had moved. That she had.

The boot of the car sagged with the weight of donations. In the next town, she learned that charity shops now had limits — rules about what they'd take and when. She trailed from one to the next, parcelling out her bags like small acts of negotiation. A woman at the third shop offered her a smile when she saw the books.

"We're always short on good reads," she said, lifting one gently from the top of the bag. "These'll go quick."

Ella thanked her and left. It wasn't much, but the warmth of it settled.

By the time she pulled back into her father's drive, the sun was already easing lower in the sky. The house looked the same — still a little hunched, like it was waiting for something — but the air around it felt looser. Less suffocating.

She sat on the bottom step inside, body aching in that good, post-effort way. Without thinking too hard, she pulled up a browser tab on her phone and booked a skip for the following week. A small, practical decision, but it thrilled her more than it should have.

Not because she was sure. But because she wasn't, and she was doing it anyway.

She sat for a few minutes, soaking in the rare peace of that thought — until her phone buzzed.

June.

"Roast chicken tonight. Come over if you fancy. 6pm."

She stared at it, heart dropping a little.

She didn't want to go. The thought of talking, performing, even being in another person's home — especially June's — felt like slipping on a too-tight coat.

But June was family.

A thread to the past.

Something steady.

Ella typed a quick, *"Okay. See you then."* before she could talk herself out of it.

The drive to June's was short but heavy. Ella watched the low hills blur in the dusky light, her hands loose on the wheel. Some part of her was still back in the house among the half-emptied drawers, the open cupboards, the spaces where things used to sit. She hadn't wanted to leave it. But saying no felt like breaking something older than language.

The door opened before she reached the step.

June wore her usual apron — cream with faint blue stripes, too pristine to have seen much actual cooking — and her smile had the fixed quality of someone determined to be gracious.

"There you are," she said, stepping back. "I was about to text."

The house smelled of boiled vegetables and citrus air freshener. The table was already set for three. James, silent as ever, emerged from the living room where the news flickered muted on the TV.

"James, wine," June called, and he nodded like someone following stage directions.

The meal unfolded like a well-rehearsed routine: June orchestrating with clipped efficiency, James carving with practiced detachment, the food hot but oddly flavourless. The roast chicken glistened under too-bright lighting, the peas were aggressively buttered, and the potatoes held a softness that bordered on limp.

"You're slicing it too thin," June murmured, as James transferred meat to plates.

"It's fine," he said, without looking up.

June sniffed. "Well, it'll dry out before it hits the table."

Ella focused on her glass.

"So," June said, her voice rising in that way that meant she was shifting gears. "What have you been up to, dear?"

Ella placed her fork down carefully. "Actually, I went to Leanne's hen do. You remember Leanne, from school and swimming?"

June gave a vague smile.

"She's getting married soon. We've been really supporting each other lately. It's been… good."

June raised her eyebrows slightly as she patted her napkin onto her lap. "I hope she'll be doing it properly. All these weddings nowadays — dress down, alpacas and fireworks. You wonder if the couple even remember why they're there."

Ella smiled faintly, carefully. "I think it'll be a real reflection of the two of them. Simple, thoughtful. Just… true to who they are."

June gave a tight smile, slicing into her potatoes. "Hmm. Well. I've always thought weddings should be about tradition and commitment."

Ella's smile faltered. She reached for her glass.

June leaned back slightly. "I don't mean to sound critical. But I've long outgrown assigning emotional meaning to a bit of paper. It's just pageantry, really. A nice photo opportunity, and then… back to real life."

Ella's fork paused mid-air. There it was again: that strange knot in her chest. Not anger exactly, but something flatter. Worn. The familiar ache of trying to follow logic that bent in on itself. First weddings were sacred, then, they were meaningless. It wasn't about what June believed, it was about whatever let her hold the upper hand.

Ella didn't argue. She didn't have the energy. Instead, she took a sip of wine, slow and steady, and let the words pass over her like traffic noise. Nothing to fix. Nothing to follow. Just another maze of contradictions she no longer needed to get lost in.

June dabbed her mouth with her napkin and offered a smile that didn't quite meet her eyes. "Still, it'll be good for her, I'm sure. A wedding gives a girl something to focus on. A sense of direction."

She gave a small huff of laughter, like she was being playful, but her eyes were scanning Ella's face for something. Permission, maybe; or weakness.

Ella nodded faintly, her face neutral. She didn't bother responding. June's opinions were like weather fronts — best to let them pass.

James cleared his throat and asked if anyone wanted more potatoes, like a man offering a lifeline.

"How's the house clearing going?" June spoke over him, shifting tone as if to suggest she'd just offered something helpful.

Ella swallowed. "Pretty well. I've been staying there. Off work for a bit."

June paused mid-doling out more potatoes, though Ella hadn't wanted more. "Off work?"

"I've taken some time. Sick leave."

June blinked, as if she'd misheard. "Sick leave? But you're not ill."

Ella kept her tone neutral. "I needed to stop."

A silence passed.

June pushed a forkful of roast potatoes around her plate and fixed Ella with a cool glance. "Well," June said, clearly trying to recalibrate, "Don't leave it too long. You don't want people thinking you are not committed."

Ella's hand tightened around her fork. She glanced at James. He was cutting his carrots into uniform pieces, his face a studied blank.

June sipped her wine. "But I suppose at least you'll be able to clear everything out properly. That's what you want, isn't it? Clean rooms. Less painful."

Ella's mouth opened. Then closed again.

Ella nodded, though everything inside her itched at the word clean. That wasn't what she wanted at all. She wasn't looking for sterile simplicity. She was looking for something real.

June took another sip of wine and set the glass down a little too firmly, as if bracing herself. "And how about Tom," she said, with a sigh that somehow carried both sympathy and reprimand. "He must be utterly lost without you."

Ella didn't reply. Her fork was poised above her food, motionless.

"I mean, really, who's cooking for him? Has he been eating properly? Men fall to pieces when left alone, you know. Honestly, it's irresponsible to just walk out and leave him to it. He's your husband."

Ella blinked, once, slowly. The words landed hard, but not new.

June pressed on, warming to her own indignation. "Marriage is supposed to mean something. You don't get to just opt out when you're 'burnt out' or tired of real life. That's not how grown-ups behave. You stood up in front of everyone and made vows. Or was that just theatre too?"

Ella's throat burned. She took a sip of wine, let it cool her tongue before she spoke. She still said nothing.

"I just hope you're not going to throw away a good man because of some little identity crisis," June continued. "You get these women now, chasing 'self-discovery' like it's a holiday they forgot to book in their twenties. Honestly. It's not brave, Ella. It's selfish."

Ella stared at her plate, fingers locked together in her lap. There was a high, tight ringing in her ears. Her breathing stayed even, but inside, something churned — slow, deep and volcanic.

"And what happens next?" June added, now slicing her chicken with surgical precision. "You find yourself, and then what? Hope Tom's still sitting there waiting for you with a warm dinner and open arms? He'll only wait so long, you know. Decent men don't come along twice."

Ella nodded, faintly. Not in agreement, just in acknowledgment. Like a box being ticked.

Her silence wasn't compliance. It was a dam. And somewhere beneath it, the pressure was building.

And when June smiled like she'd made her point, Ella reached for her glass again and let the wine do its work; cooling the edges of everything she didn't want to feel.

June reached across, fingers brushing Ella's wrist. "Look, I don't mean to be hard. I just have to make sure you get proper guidance now your dad isn't around to give it. It's just, I know you, love. You get a bit... untethered. You always have. But you have to keep things under some control. Don't throw away something good just because you're feeling lost. This'll pass."

Ella said nothing. The room felt too warm now. Her skin prickled. The food on her plate blurred into shape and colour without meaning.

She sipped her wine slowly, letting the glass shield her.

The rest of the meal passed in a kind of echo. Words reached her, but none landed. June and James conversed in small, practiced exchanges. Ella nodded where it felt expected, her smile flickering on cue, but inside a low thrum began; a pulse of resistance she couldn't name yet, beating just beneath her ribs.

When she finally left, the drive home was darker than it had any right to be. Cloud cover smothered the stars and even the hedgerows felt closer, like the road was shrinking as she drove. The countryside blurred past in tunnels of headlight — trees, sheep, fence posts — all part of a landscape she couldn't seem to reach from the inside of her body.

Ella's hands gripped the wheel too tightly. Her jaw ached from being clenched. June's voice still rang through her like static, smug, scolding and certain.

'He must be lost without you.'

'Marriage is supposed to mean something.'

'Decent men don't come along twice.'

They looped through her brain like a bad jingle, ridiculous and infuriating and too sticky to shake. It wasn't just what June said. It was the tone. The unyielding confidence that Ella was doing life wrong. That she always had been.

A good woman doesn't leave her husband.

A good woman doesn't fall apart.

A good woman knows her place.

The bile of it crept up her throat. The familiar shame, the heavy loop of being wrong simply for feeling too much. For stepping out of the script. She turned the radio on and then off again. Even the music felt like too much; too orchestrated, too neat.

Ella's mind replayed the moment she'd asked Tom for a break, her voice trembling and heart swelling with needed relief. It stirred a hot, unsettled knot in her gut. Anger prickled at her spine, mingled with exhaustion; a raw ache of fear and being misunderstood.

Without planning to, she pulled onto a verge beside a field she vaguely remembered from childhood bike rides — just a dip of grass, a rusted gate, a few sheep barely visible in the dark. She left the engine running, hazards ticking in time with the thud in her chest.

And then she got out.

The air was damp, cool against her overheated skin. She crossed to the gate, grabbed the cold metal with both hands, and climbed up onto the bottom rail.

The night was huge around her. Bigger than the road. Bigger than June. Bigger than the invisible map of rules she'd been taught to follow since before she had language for dissent.

And from somewhere inside that vastness, from the very centre of the pressure building in her chest, Ella screamed.

Not a sound made for other people. Raw and ancient, and full of all the things she couldn't say at that dinner table — every accusation swallowed, every moment she'd made herself small. It tore through her throat like it had been waiting there since childhood.

The field didn't flinch. The sheep startled — one bleating nervously, another turning away.

The scream ended, echoing into nothing. Her breath came hard and shallow, her hands still gripping the rail. Her body trembled.

The sound of her scream left her raw and blinking as she climbed down off the gate. Suddenly, she became acutely aware of herself; small, alone, and absurdly human against the quiet countryside. A flush rose in her cheeks as she glanced around, heart ticking faster, half-expecting to find some witness to her unravelling — a dog walker, a farmer, anyone. But the fields remained still. Just sheep. Just her. Just sky.

And then, almost involuntarily, a laugh bubbled up.

It was short. Ridiculous, but real.

“I’m fine,” she muttered aloud to the night, to no one. “Perfectly normal behaviour.”

Her body was buzzing with the strange, unexpected relief of it, as she got back in the car. No one told her to quiet down or be reasonable or remember who she used to be.

The stillness around her had absorbed it all: her grief, her rage, her defiance, and handed her back a silence that felt earned.

She drove back with the windows down, hair whipping at her face, the cool air a kind of balm. The house greeted her in half-darkness. Still. Familiar. Hers.

She slipped around to the side, past the flowerbed and the broken gate latch, and sat down on the bench beneath the kitchen window. She tilted her head back. Above her, the sky remained closed — clouds refusing to part — but she didn’t mind. She didn’t need stars tonight.

She just needed this.

This quiet.

This bench.

This breath.

This moment that belonged only to her.

12

Contractor hire

The dream was so quiet it was almost silent. No fire, no blood, no cinematic screaming. Just the cold, tiled corridor of the hospital. The flicker of strip lighting. Her father's voice, clipped and sharp, telling the nurse not to use that tone with him. Her mother's eyes closed as they passed her bed.

When Ella woke, the light through the curtains was grey; the kind of light that made you feel like you'd already failed at the day.

Had there been an altercation at the hospital?

The facts, as she'd been told them, had never quite settled in her body. She'd been eight. Her mother had fallen, her father said, and had some 'confusion'. The word 'accident' had been dropped into conversation like an ashtray into a bin — quick, dismissive, final. When she tried to ask how it had happened, her father's mouth had flattened. "Don't start," he said. "Your mother's ill enough without your drama."

At the hospital, she was only allowed to see her once a day. Fifteen minutes. '*Your mother needs rest.*'

Her mother had reached for her hand with a strange, apologetic softness. "You alright, poppet?" she'd whispered, though her lips looked bruised, and her eyes were wrong. Then she came home. And over the week that followed, she got smaller. Quiet.

Then nothing.

A week later, she was dead.

The weight of it had settled into her then in ways no one acknowledged. The loss of the lightness in her life — the laughter, the small daily rituals, the feeling that someone's eyes truly saw her — vanished, and no one gave her permission to grieve. She learned quickly to shrink, to whisper her tears into pillows, to carry the dull ache like a secret companion.

Years passed in quiet coping. She folded the sorrow into herself, a soft, persistent pressure behind every smile, every polite word. It was there in the way she tucked herself into corners of rooms, in the careful way she held back questions, in the pauses where no one asked and she didn't volunteer. The grief became a shadow she learned to carry alone, always present but always unseen.

They never spoke of it again. Not once. Her father didn't even cry at the funeral, just stood at the edge of it all like someone supervising a fire drill.

Now, the house felt like it was pressing in against her skin. The rooms were thick with ghosts; not the haunting kind, but the memory kind. The kind that sat at the edge of chairs and under doorframes, reminding you what you never got to say.

She hadn't been back to the café since before the hen do. She'd avoided the bright chatter, the possibility of Miranda's calm eyes reading her too clearly. But today, she needed to get out of this house. Her body itched for movement, her legs tight with restless urgency. Her brain buzzed. She needed to move, just to prove she still could.

She dressed quickly, pulled her hair into something vaguely functional, and walked to the café.

Inside, the morning was already in full swing — mugs clinking, voices rising and falling in comfortable arcs. She ordered a flat white and scanned the room instinctively for absence: Miranda wasn't there. Relief and disappointment arrived together like awkward cousins.

There was one empty seat, near the daily coffee club and next to a man who appeared to be deep in conversation with a banana.

Ella hesitated. Then sat.

The man looked to be in his fifties — or possibly three hundred. Scruffy cardigan, tweed cap, the air of a retired children's entertainer who had never quite made peace with retirement.

"They tell me coffee is a conspiracy," he said, not looking at her.

Ella blinked.

"But," he added, "if I'm going to be controlled by a substance, it might as well taste like melted purpose."

And that, unexpectedly, made her laugh.

A proper, out-of-nowhere laugh. The kind that feels like it might dislodge something important, or sacred, or broken.

The man beamed. "See? You're not beyond hope."

They chatted. Or rather, he rambled in delighted nonsense and she nodded, kept laughing at all the wrong parts. His name was Trevor, he said, and he had three children, two dogs, and a llama in recovery.

Trevor was mid-sip when the door chimed and a tall woman swept in, tugging a twelve year old girl by the elbow. Trevor's eyebrows lifted.

"Emma! How are you?" he called.

The woman barely paused. "Fine, Trevor, thank you," she said briskly, hustling the girl toward the counter. To her daughter, in a loud whisper: "Tell me what you want, then be polite and say hello. You know how Mr Durrant likes to hear about your grades."

The girl's shoulders slumped. She hovered beside Trevor, eyes downcast, and offered the ghost of a smile.

Trevor leaned toward her, setting his cup down gently. "Hey, Sophie. Good to see you. How was football yesterday?"

Sophie glanced at her mother, then back at Trevor. "It was… fine."

"Did you score any goals?"

She gave a quick shrug. "One."

"That's brilliant," Trevor said, genuinely pleased. "You must be proud."

The girl glanced at her mother, who nodded once, and straightened. "Yes, Mr Durrant. I'm really proud."

"And school?"

"We're doing medieval castles," Sophie said, voice thin.

"Well. Who doesn't love a castle?" Trevor smiled.

When they moved to a table, the girl sank into the seat like she wanted the floor to swallow her whole. Her mother's voice floated over: "Don't fidget, darling."

Trevor gave Ella a rueful smile. "She's a sweetheart. But her mum has big plans."

Ella nodded, but her attention was elsewhere. She watched Sophie grip her hot chocolate like it might steady her, watched her mother beam her approval — her daughter performing exactly as instructed. Ella remembered how quickly that approval could vanish.

She remembered that grip. That posture. That weight.

The way you learn to rehearse yourself.

For a long moment, she just sat. Let the hum of the café carry on around her. Let the feeling settle in her chest. The barista called out Trevor's name and the moment broke. He returned with their drinks and a quiet smile.

"Everything okay?" he asked.

Ella nodded. "Yeah. Just… reminded me how careful I used to be. Around my dad. Like… I was always scanning the room before I even walked into it."

Trevor nodded like he knew. He didn't say anything wise or fixed. Just listened.

Then, lightly: "Hey, I'm throwing a birthday party for the smallest one. You should come. There'll be bouncy castles. And wine. Terrible combination. Spectacular in motion."

She was still laughing when Miranda appeared behind her, a warm surprise.

"Mind if I sit?" Miranda asked.

Ella turned, blinking. "Oh, sure."

Miranda sat, calm as ever. "I've been meaning to say, I hope I didn't overstep last time."

Ella looked down at her coffee, then up. "No. You didn't. I just wasn't ready to hear it. But I think… maybe I am now."

They spoke gently, the way people do when the edges between them have softened. Trevor excused himself to argue with the barista about biscuit hierarchy.

Eventually, the walk home began again, two women with slow steps and thoughtful silences. At the garden gate, Ella paused.

"Do you want to come in? For coffee?"

Miranda nodded. "I'd love to."

They sat at the kitchen table. The room had the stubborn charm of the 1970s; faux-wood cabinets with amber-toned handles, a tiled splashback in fading shades of rust and mustard, and a linoleum floor patterned in cheerful geometric swirls that had long since dulled with age. In the midst of all that retro character, a few modern appliances sat awkwardly like guests who hadn't quite dressed for the occasion: a sleek silver microwave perched on the counter beside a biscuit tin shaped like a cottage, and a freestanding dishwasher, too large for the alcove it occupied, was plugged in via a long extension cord that snaked inelegantly along the skirting board. Despite the mismatch, the room felt lived-in, layered, and unpretentious. Like it hadn't been designed, but simply accumulated.

Miranda eyed the mismatched cupboards with a smile. "So... this is where you grew up. How does it feel to be back?"

Ella smiled faintly, tracing the rim of her cup. "It's strange. Heavy. This house has seen it all. Birthday parties, family arguments, my first dodgy haircut, whole seasons of life. But there were secrets, too. Things unspoken that sort of lingered in the corners." She paused, glancing around. "Being back is stirring some of that up. But it's also... weirdly comforting. I love this house. It still feels like mine."

Miranda nodded, her eyes soft. "It's got good bones."

Ella laughed. "Good bones and terrible wallpaper. My dad never met a mustard tone he didn't love."

"Retro chic," Miranda grinned. "You're ahead of the curve."

Miranda stirred her tea. Ella looked out at the garden. A squirrel dashed across the fence like it had somewhere very important to be.

"I've always had this feeling," Ella said, eventually, "that life is... hard. Heavy. Like it's meant to be. Like if I'm not struggling, then I'm doing something wrong."

Miranda nodded, her eyes warm and unhurried. "Who told you that?"

Ella shook her head. "No one, I think. Or — everyone. It's in the air, isn't it? Suffering equals virtue, ease is laziness. And I've lived like that for so long I don't even know how to recognise the alternative."

"And if ease wasn't laziness? If it was alignment?"

Ella gave a short, incredulous laugh. "I wouldn't even know where to start."

Miranda tilted her head. "What would need to change in you, for things to be easy?"

Ella looked down at her hands, the skin dry from over-washing and the knuckles slightly raw.

"I think," she said slowly, "I'd need to believe I deserved ease. That I didn't need to earn it or justify it, that I could just... have it."

"And do you?"

The silence was long.

Miranda didn't fill it.

Eventually, Ella nodded, just a fraction. And a tiny part of her meant it.

They sat in the stillness for a while. Outside, a pigeon thudded down onto the fence like it had misjudged its own weight. Somewhere, a car alarm half-heartedly wheezed, then gave up.

Miranda tapped her teaspoon against her mug. "So," she said, lightly, "are you coming to the birthday party?"

Ella blinked. "The one with the bouncy castle and wine?"

"Trevor throws surprisingly good parties," Miranda said, straight-faced. "There was a magician last year who accidentally set fire to a card table. The kids loved it!"

Ella laughed. "I don't think I'm really in a birthday party mood."

Miranda shrugged, smiling. "Doesn't matter. Just come. Don't think of it as a party, think of it as... an experiment. You show up, you stand near cake, you leave if you hate it. What's the worst that could happen?"

Automatically, Ella's mind flipped through its usual catalogue of worst-case scenarios: awkward silences, misjudged jokes, a well-timed eye-roll from someone confirming her deepest fear — that she didn't quite belong. It was an old reflex, rehearsed and familiar. For so long, she'd lived as if preparing for an imaginary storm, bracing herself against disasters that never actually came. What a waste, she thought suddenly, of energy, of joy. Looking around now, she saw not judgment in these people but ease, generosity, and a softness she hadn't trusted before. The truth landed quietly: she had spent years expecting the world to hurt her and so she had kept herself guarded, brittle, apart. But possibly it wasn't the world that needed softening. Just possibly, it was her.

She gave a small nod. "Alright. Maybe."

Miranda reached into her coat pocket. "Here. I'll give you my number. We can walk together to the party, if you come. Or it's there if you just want to talk. About ease. Or hedgehogs. Or anything else."

They exchanged numbers. Miranda saved Ella under Ella — Cake Potential. Ella laughed. She didn't feel like cake potential, but maybe that was the point.

At the door, Miranda turned. "You're doing alright, you know. Better than you think."

Ella stood in the doorway, the scent of tea and second chances still clinging to the air.

13

Construction materials

Ella was brushing crumbs off the hem of her skirt when Miranda appeared at the gate, sunglasses skewed, with a chilled bottle of wine held aloft like a trophy.

"I come bearing sacrament," she grinned.

Ella raised the Tupperware of cookies in one hand and the awkwardly wrapped present in the other. "I brought sugar and capitalism."

They laughed, that quick laughter that lives just under the surface when you've recently begun to like someone you didn't expect to.

They turned and fell into step towards Trevor's house. Miranda shot her a sidelong look. "You'll understand this when we get there." She said, pointing at the wine.

Trevor's house, or rather his garden and the semi-wild field behind it, was a full-blown circus. Not in the pejorative sense but in the wonderful, mildly chaotic, everyone's-a-bit-feral sense.

There were children scaling trees like small monkeys, balloons tangled in their limbs. Adults lounged on picnic rugs, sipping rosé or dancing barefoot on the grass to the kind of music that hadn't seen a top 40 chart since 1998. Someone had set up a barbecue and was treating tofu skewers with the seriousness of a Michelin-starred chef.

Ella blinked at the sheer velocity of it. "This is a children's party?"

Miranda grinned, already halfway through screwing the wine bottle open. “This is a Trevor party. Children optional.”

Ella had kicked off her shoes within the first hour, the grass cool against her bare feet. By the second, she’d accepted a plate of paella – rich with saffron and those sweet, smoky chorizo bits – and laughed as a woman in glitter and Birkenstocks named Dalia pulled her into a clumsy swing step.

She stumbled, smiled, and stumbled again, Dalia’s voice warm in her ear: “Just let the rhythm drive you, babe.”

It was wonderful. Ludicrous. Joyous. Messy in the best way. She found herself talking to people she’d previously filed under not my kind, only to discover shared histories, absurd overlaps, and a general consensus that life was both too short and too long to take entirely seriously.

There was a moment, around dusk, when the kids collapsed into makeshift blanket forts under the fairy lights and the music shifted to karaoke. A battered speaker was rolled out, and someone – possibly high, definitely fearless – led with a caterwauling rendition of ‘Total Eclipse of the Heart’, off-key and all-in. Ella found herself clapping along, her heart lighter than it had been in months.

Miranda elbowed her gently. “We’re up next.”

“No, no. God, no.”

“Yes.”

“I have not sung in public since Year nine.”

“Well, you’re due,” said Una, appearing with a microphone in one hand and a glass of sangria in the other. “It’s so liberating!”

And somehow, without quite knowing how, Ella was sandwiched between Miranda and Una, belting out ‘Dancing Queen’ like it was an exorcism, a confession, and an act of communion all in one.

Her voice cracked and she missed half the words, but God, she laughed.

Not the careful kind of laughter. Not the 'I get the joke' laugh, the social smile, or the dry chuckle.

Big belly laughs; real ones, like her body had finally stopped resisting joy.

Later, cheeks pink, legs stretched out on a blanket, she watched as Trevor set off two small fireworks to a cheer of sticky-fingered children and slightly tipsy adults.

"I didn't think I'd have fun," she admitted softly to Miranda, who was curled beside her, wine glass dangling from loose fingers.

"So glad you did," Miranda replied. "And that you are learning to say yes."

Ella let that sit for a moment. The thrum of the music. The flicker of sparklers. Her own skin buzzing, with aliveness.

"Yeah," she said eventually. "Maybe I am."

Miranda clinked her glass against Ella's. "To saying yes. And to bouncy castles, bad karaoke, and birthday wine."

Ella laughed again — loose, loud, uncontained — and felt a flicker of surprise at herself. This wasn't the careful, polished version of her she recognised. And yet it felt utterly, wonderfully right.

***

The morning came with a dry mouth, a stiff neck, and the kind of psychological hangover Ella recognised instantly: *shame*. Not for anything particular she'd done wrong — no flashing, no karaoke mic drop, no drunken confessionals — but for the mere fact that she'd let go. Properly let go.

She winced at the memory of the karaoke mic in her hand, Miranda's arm slung around her shoulders, the full, mortifying reality of her voice rising to meet the chorus of 'Dancing Queen'. She caught herself wondering if she'd been too much, too loud, too visible.

That familiar instinct stirred: Pull it back, smooth it over, be palatable again.

"I can't believe I did that," she muttered into the pillow.

And then, after a pause: "God, it was fun."

She smiled, a little, just at the edges of her mouth. Caught herself trying to wriggle away from the joy of it, like the happiness might expire if she looked directly at it. That old instinct, again, to tidy the emotional mess before it stains anything. To apologise for exuberance.

Her phone pinged, cutting cleanly through her self-scrutiny.

Miranda: "*Sea swim in an hour. Me, Una, and a couple others. Coffee after. Hangover cure of champions. Come?*"

Ella stared at the screen like it had just delivered a dare.

Swimming. In the sea. With people who seemed largely impervious to embarrassment or hypothermia. The idea made her want to pull the duvet over her head and hermetically seal herself into safety.

She was halfway to typing "*Can't today, next time*" when something in her chest twitched.

That part of her that had danced barefoot on grass. That had howled into a microphone and laughed until her cheeks hurt. The part, maybe, that had been dormant a very long time.

She deleted the message. Rewrote: "*OK. See you soon. Do I need to bring anything?*"

***

The sea looked almost mythical in the early light — low mist clinging to its edges, sunlight slicing across the surface like brushed gold.

Miranda's battered Volvo was already parked up, a flask of something hot balanced on the bonnet.

"I have a spare towel if you need," she said, flinging it at Ella as they made their way down the sloped bank. "And just go for it. If you hesitate, you'll talk yourself out of it."

"Is this how people die of shock?" Ella asked, deadpan.

Miranda grinned. "That's the spirit."

The first toe into the water was worse than she'd imagined. A hard, shocking cold, like her skin had been turned inside out. Her body rejected it instantly. She gasped, teeth clenched and breath coming short and fast. The others were already ahead, swimming and whooping, one of them doing a synchronised-swimming style leg kick like they were auditioning for a 1950s pool revue.

"Jesus Christ," Ella muttered, forcing herself to wade deeper, inch by inch.

"You've got this!" Miranda shouted, already in up to her shoulders, slick and smiling like some kind of waterproof deity.

At waist depth, Ella nearly turned back. But something else kicked in; not pride, exactly, but the refusal to fold back into herself again. She plunged forward. It was like being baptised in discomfort – dragged through it, stripped bare. The cold knocked the breath out of her lungs. Her whole body rebelled, a violent cascade of sensation. But then… there it was: the other side.

Somewhere between the adrenaline, the shock, and the newness, a deep, chemical aliveness flooded her system. She could feel every cell singing. As if some layer had been peeled back, revealing a self underneath that could handle more than she'd ever allowed.

She laughed; loud, gasping laughter cutting through the morning air.

Later, wrapped in a towel, still damp and slightly shivering, she perched on the bonnet of Miranda's car with a cup of lukewarm coffee pressed into her palms.

"Bloody hell," she said. "I actually feel incredible."

Miranda nodded, legs crossed and hair half-frozen into gentle kinks. "It's the great reset button. Your brain can't hang on to misery when it's focused on not dying of cold."

Ella looked out over the water, now calm as if nothing remarkable had happened.

Slowly, she spoke out the unsteadiness in her gut. "I have to go back soon. To work. My doctor's note ends in six weeks and just the thought of my inbox makes me feel physically sick."

Miranda was quiet for a moment. Then: "You could. If it's what you want. Or you could ask yourself what you *actually* need. And then go from there."

Ella didn't answer right away.

"I keep thinking I should go back. That I must. That if I don't, I'm... failing."

"'Should' and 'must' are very rarely your soul talking," Miranda said, lightly. "They're just the language of old contracts you didn't sign consciously. It's okay to tear a few up."

Ella nodded slowly, letting the words filter through. *Old contracts I never signed.* She turned the words over in her mind. Felt them soften something. The water still hummed in her veins, like it had loosened something – her grip, maybe.

She smiled at Miranda, soft and wide and real.

"I'm so glad you messaged me this morning."

"I'm so glad you said yes."

She looked out over the water, the light breaking in slow, fractured lines across the surface. Her legs still prickled from cold. Her fingers curled tighter around the warm cup.

She didn't know what came next.

But for now, this was enough: her body awake, the morning quiet, the sound of her own breath not trying to outrun anything.

14

Dig

Ella stepped off the train into the city's pulse — a roar of traffic, the energy of people with places to be — and wound her way to the agreed glass-fronted café on the corner. Inside, every table was claimed by pinstriped suits bent over laptops, the low hum of stock-market tickers leaking in from open phones. A barista in a pristine apron moved with balletic precision, steaming milk into architect-level rosettas heels clicked on marble, coffee carts wheezed espresso shots, and the air was scented with polished timber and ambition. Ella settled into a small table by the window, her soft cardigan and jeans feeling incongruous amid the boardroom glamour. It was the world she'd left brushed up against the one she'd chosen, and in that sharp meeting, she felt herself contract and release all at once. She stared at her reflection in the window — pause-button hair, a cardigan too big, cheeks still hollow from sleepless nights — and wondered what Lynne would think. She'd been postponing this meet-up for days, ever since Lynne's last text:

"Come on, Ella — coffee tomorrow? I want to hear how it's all going."

Ella had drawn a breath, feeling the weight of every unsent message and swerved invite. Knowing that she couldn't hide any longer, she had decided to show up. She had tapped out "*Sure*" with a thumbs up and closed her phone, steeling herself to step back into the world she'd been avoiding.

"Hey, stranger," Lynne called, sliding her gym bag onto the floor, before drawing her cheek next to Ellas for a kiss. "You okay?"

Ella curled both hands around the warm mug. "I'm... here."

Lynne's brow drew up, eyes flicking over Ella's jeans and jumper before she spoke. "Just here? How's work going? You're not still off work?"

Ella nodded slowly. "A few more days." She didn't say weeks, or that her marriage was also on pause; that after all the striving and scaffolding and trying to hold everything up, she'd needed to step away from the very life she'd built, including Tom. Especially Tom.

Lynne sighed, reaching for her own cup. "Oh, Ella. Take the time you need I guess, but you can't hide forever. You are never going to feel ready until you get back out and into the swing of things."

Ella watched steam curl from Lynne's latte; simple comfort, but it felt alien. "I've been... enjoying quiet things," she said softly. "Gardening, relaxing, feeding hedgehogs–."

Lynne interrupted with a breezy wave. "Escape hobbies are fine. But you need purpose, routine, projects, Ella. You need... noise."

Ella swallowed. Noise. She remembered the hush of the fields, the birdsong under damp roses. "Lately it's the quiet that saves me," she whispered.

Lynne frowned, as if the word threatened her. She set down her cup. "All right, have the quiet sometimes. But life's moving. You'll get left behind."

Ella's chest tightened. She wanted to say, "No, you don't get it. Quiet is where I find myself again." But she had no words that would make herself be heard.

Lynne leaned back, checking her watch. "Look, I get you're grieving. I get it. But you have to start choosing to show up; job calls, client meetings. That's how you heal, too."

Ella nodded – slowly, politely – while her pulse drummed in her ears. She sipped her coffee, its bitterness anchoring her. Here, in Lynne's world, there was no space for the soft rebirth she was craving.

The clock ticked on as they chatted. Ella found herself catching sight of it every few minutes, surprised each glance at how little time had passed. As Lynne talked, Ella wondered if she'd ever find the words to convince her that sometimes, presence meant stillness and that healing could be an inside job, not a schedule to be filled.

Her body, however, was already speaking its own language. A tight knot had settled along the back of her neck, and a dull ache throbbed at her right side, subtle but insistent. It was as if every muscle, every sinew, was quietly pointing out the mismatch: the calm of the room against the tension she carried, the stillness outside against the storm inside.

Lynne stirred her oat milk flat white and asked lightly, "So… what have you been up to?"

It was an ordinary question, the kind that should've been easy. But Ella hesitated. The real answers — Trevor's party, Miranda's quiet jokes, the sea swims at dawn and the wild, laughing chats with Leanne — sat warm in her chest. They were delicate things still forming, like shells not yet hardened. Joys too new to be passed across a café table and held up to someone else's light.

She imagined trying to describe them. It would sound childish, or worse, indulgent. She could already feel the mismatch in Lynne's polite expression, the tilt of her head and the quiet concern behind it. Ella didn't want to explain why those moments mattered. She didn't want to have to defend them.

So, she gave a vague smile, said something about walking, reading and "taking it slow," and let the real stories stay unspoken. The clock ticked on as Lynne filled the space between them with news of work and old friends. Ella nodded, fingers curled around her mug, feeling suddenly full of words she didn't trust herself to say.

She set down her mug. "I'm glad we did this," she said, voice careful. "Thank you." She stood and fished her cardigan off the back of the chair.

Lynne looked surprised, offered a quick smile and looked down at her coffee, gulping to finish it. She slung her gym bag over one shoulder. They stepped toward the door together, paused for a brief hug in the café's threshold, and then drifted apart, each taking her own path. Ella watched Lynne's confident stride fade into the crowd and felt a rush of relief. I won't do that to myself again, she vowed, pressing her back against the glass.

Back at the house, she sank into the study chair and pulled her laptop onto the desk, the air heavy with lemon-polish and decades of settled dust. The room felt charged; every stack of unopened bills, every row of books with uncracked spines, every stubborn drawer that caught at her sleeve seemed to whisper of time paused. She squared her shoulders and began tackling the financial admin she'd postponed, each click and clack of the keyboard a small rebellion against the inertia that had held her so long.

When she went to hook up the printer, she discovered the cable was missing — proof, it seemed, that her father's vaunted 'filing system' was mostly Post-its scrawled with warnings and passive-aggressive folders labelled 'TAX — DON'T TOUCH'.

She was crouched by the old filing cabinet, rummaging through tangled leads and brittle instruction manuals, when her eyes caught sight of the jewellery box again. The letter. Her father's last words left to her. She stared at it for a moment and pulled it out again, thumb resting on the sealed flap. It pulsed with potential: revelation, regret, command. But she didn't want more pain, not today. Not when she was just beginning to feel a little solid underfoot. Opening it felt like stepping onto thin ice. What if it undid her, all over again? What if it pulled her back into the version of herself she'd been working so hard to step away from? She set it aside gently, aware — resentfully so — of how much power he still held over her, even now. Even from the grave.

Instead, she threw herself into the search with sudden, determined focus; unwinding each cable, laying them out in neat lines across the carpet like artefacts in a tiny museum of outdated technology. Printer cables, phone chargers, something that might have belonged to a long-dead camera. None of them what she needed. She exhaled sharply through her nose, the edge of frustration biting again, and tugged open the bottom drawer of the filing cabinet. It groaned in protest, stiff on its runners, revealing a chaotic jumble of mismatched folders and loose sheets. She reached in, still half-distracted by the physical task, until her fingers landed on something different.

It was a cardboard file marked 'MARTHA', like her mother had been a nuisance in paperwork form.

Inside was a chaotic archive of a life: birth and death certificates, funeral service leaflets, scrunched payslips whispering months of struggle, and envelopes stuffed with letters in her mother's graceful script. It was everything and nothing at once; a muddle of officialdom and intimacy, as though no one had known where to draw the line between what mattered and what didn't. It felt overwhelming and achingly familiar, like finding a half-finished jigsaw of her own history. Ella sifted through it hungrily, a strange urgency driving her, as if somewhere in the paper clutter was a thread she could follow back to something real, something lost. A crumpled note brought a flicker of memory: her mother in the garden, wiping sweat from her brow as she handed Ella a cup of elderflower cordial. Another leaflet — the church order of service — recalled the hush of gathered mourners, the sudden echo of her father's bare-knuckled grip on her hand. Driven by a strange urgency, she dug deeper until her fingers brushed something fragile beneath a stack of pastel Mother's Day cards; cards she had painstakingly decorated with glue and glitter as a child, longing for approval. She paused, breath catching, and drew out a pale slip of paper. Only then did she recognise what she was holding.

A hospital discharge note. Folded too many times, worn thin at the creases. One phrase was circled in biro — "internal trauma" — and it hit her like a punch, blunt and breathless.

DISCHARGE REASON: Patient removed against medical advice.

Family insistence. Patient agrees.

Injuries consistent with fall; Possible internal trauma. Monitor closely.

Advised inpatient care for minimum 2–4 days.

Husband signed waiver.

Ella slumped down on the floor without realising she was doing it. The silence in her chest collapsed. All the breath she'd been holding for years hissed out like a leak in a tyre.

He had taken her out of hospital against orders. Signed a waiver. And that was that.

Ella read the sentence again and again, her eyes snagging on the word waiver like it might unlock something if she stared long enough. The thought of her mother lying in a hospital bed, fragile and unwell, and her father — decisive and stubborn — walking in and saying, "We're going home now," made her stomach twist. Why would he do that? Had her mother begged to leave? Or had he insisted, certain he knew better than the doctors?

There was no note of hesitation in the documents, no sense of context. Just cold, medical language and a signature that looked far too calm for the weight it carried.

She tried to imagine the conversation: her father pacing beside a beige hospital curtain, arms folded tight, voice steady but firm. She could almost hear him saying it: "She'll rest better at home. We know how to take care of each other."

Ella's chest tightened. She didn't want to believe in villains, but there was something deeply uncomfortable about the silence that wrapped around this decision. It felt like standing at the edge of a dark pond, unable to tell how deep it went. She remembered that hospital bed, her mother's eyes and the way something in them had altered. The house afterward, filled with silence. Her father controlling her every visit into the room with her mother, hovering for every conversation. Her mother slowly receding into the folds of a pillow while he moved around the kitchen like a man making tea, not hiding something.

Now as she sat with the pieces of this information, there was a haze around it all; an ache of knowing something had gone terribly wrong, without quite allowing herself to assemble the pieces into one. She felt the shock of betrayal mingled with a dull nausea of shame, even though none of it truly belonged to her. She stood, legs trembling as if they'd forgotten how to work, her body jangling with the weight of unasked questions. And she'd never really asked — never dared. Because she knew better. Knew what it meant when a door slammed just a little too hard. Knew how language could be used as a scalpel or a rope. She understood that flipping that hidden switch in him could unleash a fury she had no way to weather.

Ella drifted into the garden without knowing how she got there, as if her body had struck out on its own. She sank into the new orange chair — bright against the drab of overgrown grass — and felt its woven back cradle her shoulders. The garden was just starting to waken; borders of lavender and rosemary huddled against the stone wall, a rosebush beginning to bud and a cluster of self-seeded foxgloves swaying in a hesitant breeze. The garden had once been immaculate — a testament to her father's countless hours of tending. Already the borders were a tangle of plants that might be weeds or, for all she knew, on the brink of bloom. It's slow unravelling had unsettled her at the beginning, each stray tendril a small stress. One she felt ill equipped to begin to tackle. But over the last weeks she had found herself beginning to welcome the wildness, sensing its freedom as something richer than perfection.

Above her, a blackbird launched into song, its clear notes trilling through the early evening air. Slowly, the melody threaded its way through the fog in her mind, tugging her attention back to the moment; the rough bark of her improvised side table under her fingertips, the faint scent of earth and herbs, the gentle tilt of the sky. With each sweet announcement, she felt a little more herself again, as though the world outside was knitting her scattered pieces back into place.

And still, the fact of it — the discharge note, the timing, the blunt proof that her father had made a decision that might have cost her mother her life — hovered in her chest like something both heavy and ungraspable. Her body didn't know whether to tense, collapse, or go numb. A part of her wanted to howl. Another part wanted to pretend she hadn't read it at all.

It was like the truth had entered her system but couldn't find a shelf to live on. Too big for rage, too old for shock, too real to disappear.

So, it just sat there, pulsing quietly beneath her ribs, waiting for her to catch up.

Her phone rang.

Leanne's name. She almost didn't answer.

"Hey?"

A choked breath on the other end. Then Leanne's voice, shredded and childlike. "I'm at the caravan. I just — I just needed to come out here. I didn't know who else to call. I'm sorry. I feel like everything's — wrong. I don't know what I want. I just feel so... lost."

Ella straightened. "It's okay. I'll come. Stay there, alright? I'll come now."

She ended the call and was halfway out the door when she remembered the car was still in the garage. Battery shot. Mechanic waiting on a part. For once, she didn't cry or rage. She just froze, muttering "Shitshitshitshit," under her breath.

She almost called a cab. But then she pictured the old bike, hanging like an artifact in the garage rafters.

Two minutes later, she was hauling it down, brushing off cobwebs. The tyres were soft, the chain crusted with neglect, but the pump still worked and there was enough oil to get things moving. Miracles came in unexpected forms.

She set off toward the coast road. The dying sun stretched its remaining glow over the hedgerows. The wind cut into her sleeves. Her legs were not the legs of her teenage self, but they moved. She moved.

And oh God, it felt like flying.

It wasn't the scenery or the salt air or even the faint gold of evening edging past the clouds. It was the feeling – unexpected and wild – that for once she didn't owe anyone anything. Not an apology. Or a performance. Not even an answer.

The caravan sat at the end of a lane with grass growing up the middle. She spotted Leanne curled on the wooden step, hoodie pulled over her knees, looking like someone trying to disappear into themselves.

Ella dropped the bike and ran to her, sat beside her. "Are you okay?"

Leanne didn't answer, just leaned in.

At first, Ella's mind flitted nervously, scanning for the right thing to say, a way to fill the quiet before it grew heavy. But she let her body soften into the stillness, realising that this silence wasn't laced with judgement or expectation. It asked nothing of her.

Leanne eventually muttered, "I hate this stupid place."

Ella smiled, without looking at her. "Yeah. It's awful. But the tea's usually decent."

Leanne let out a broken sound that might've been a laugh. "I feel like a kid. A really tired, melodramatic kid. Except now there's an engagement ring and everyone has a million expectations of me."

Ella hugged her knees. "You sound like you've been through the wringer. What's happening?"

Leanne ran a hand through her hair, eyes bright with fatigue. "I got home from work and told Anish I needed some time out. He was concerned, bless him. I told him it wasn't about him, I still wanted to marry him, that I just needed a few hours to sort myself out."

Ella leaned forward. "Well done – asking for time out. You've never done that before. What did he say?"

"He stared at me like I'd grown a second head," Leanne admitted with a rueful smile. "But then he nodded. Said, 'I trust you,' and sent me on my way."

After a long silence, Leanne murmured, her voice muffled, "I feel like I'm slipping back into old habits. Putting everyone first. Smiling, agreeing, doing the right thing — until I can't even hear myself anymore. I keep thinking the wedding will swallow me whole, and I'll wake up one day and realise I've disappeared again."

She gave a dry laugh. "Remember Mum's 60th?" Leanne said, her mouth twisting. "I baked two hundred cupcakes, organised every table, ran the whole show... and then spent the night trapped behind the cake stand, smiling like everything was fine. I wasn't fine. But instead of listening to that voice inside telling me to stop, I blocked it out and worked harder. That's what I always do. Swimming, family stuff, everything."

She sighed. "And now with the wedding... it's happening again. Last week Mum and Anish's mum nearly came to blows over the flower arrangements — flowers, Ella — and where was I? Sitting between them, nodding, smoothing it over like a referee at some ridiculous match. Afterwards I thought God, if I can't even hold the line over carnations versus roses, how am I supposed to hold on to myself in the middle of this whole circus?"

Leanne's voice cracked on the last word, and then there was only the distant sound of the sea dragging at the shore.

Ella felt the ache of recognition stir in her chest. She knew that helpless, swallowed feeling – the way a moment could slip from your hands until you weren't sure where you ended and everyone else's needs began.

She sat very still, letting the words hang sharp and unvarnished. She looked out toward the flat stretch of low tide, the horizon blurred like a watercolour left in the rain.

After a while she spoke, her voice quieter, as if not to disturb the rawness still in the air.

"You're not going to lose yourself. Just knowing you don't want to do that anymore is everything. You're already doing it differently. You're catching yourself before it happens." Ella glanced at her, a small smile tugging. "I wish I'd had your foresight at my own wedding."

Ella thought of her own vows. How carefully she'd crafted them. How she'd studied the shape of love like a blueprint and followed every line. Her marriage to Tom had been safe, steady, good on paper. He ticked all the boxes for her father, her aunt, the people she'd once believed mattered most; the kind of man everyone agreed was solid, respectable, the right choice. She'd convinced herself that was what happiness looked like: commitment, structure, a life with neat corners and predictable days.

But it had been built, in part, from fear. From a need for certainty after a childhood that had given her none. From the desperate hope that if she just did everything right, nothing would fall apart.

She had fallen in love with who Tom was. But she had stayed married to who she was afraid to be without him.

The ache of that realisation pressed deep into her ribs now. Watching Leanne, on the brink of her own forever and catching herself just in time, Ella felt something ancient stir. Longing. Grief. And, strangely, pride.

Leanne nudged her lightly. "It's funny. Because I used to look at you and think you had it all. The flat, the big-deal job, the husband who seemed so steady. I was jealous. I thought you'd cracked it."

Ella gave a short laugh, more breath than sound. "From the outside, maybe."

Leanne studied her, eyes flickering with something like disbelief. "So how did you do it then? With Tom. How did you find the strength to step away?"

Ella exhaled, eyes tracing the outline of the sea wall in the distance, already half-lost in the gathering blue of dusk. "I couldn't face it for a long time, ignored that quiet voice for years. I worked harder. I tried to fill the cracks with holidays, laughter, anything to distract myself. I kept telling myself I was the problem and I tried to plaster over the cracks because I couldn't bear to admit what was underneath. It pressed on me for so long. Until I couldn't keep pretending."

Her gaze dropped to her hands. "The thing is, I'd always believed I was someone who gave up too easily. Swimming especially. Like you, I hated every second. But I kept pushing until one day I just… stopped. And afterwards, I thought that meant I'd failed. That I was weak, flaky, someone who couldn't follow through. So, when I made a commitment later — my job, my marriage — I swore I wouldn't walk away. I'd prove I could stick, no matter what it cost."

Leanne was quiet, her face softened by the darkening light.

Ella drew a line in the damp with her fingertip, searching for words. "You're braver than you think. You don't need to be anyone's perfect version, Leanne. You just have to keep choosing you. Every day. That's the only way this works."

Leanne let out a shaky breath. "I'm trying. I really am."

"I know." Ella looked down at her hands, suddenly uneasy. The silence stretched, heavy but not uncomfortable.

"It's like —." She faltered, then started again. "I've never even been able to watch the swimming at the Olympics since. I'd tell people I wasn't interested, but really… I couldn't bear it. It pressed on something I couldn't look at."

She glanced at Leanne, half-apologetic, as if she wasn't sure if she'd said too much. "I think I was afraid I'd see myself in the people who kept going. That all that shame would be too much to bear."

Leanne was quiet for a moment, then said, "Or maybe it just hit too close to something you hadn't forgiven yourself for yet."

Ella looked up at that. She smiled faintly, the wind brushing her cheek like an exhale. "Maybe. Now, as I look back, I think that was the first time I really listened to myself. The first time I said no to something that didn't feel right. Even if I didn't have the language for it then."

Leanne let out a long breath and laid her head on Ella's shoulder. It was unexpected and oddly childlike, a surrender with no performance behind it. Ella put an arm around her instinctively.

For a moment, the world felt perfectly still, then somewhere a seagull screamed about chips or existential dread. Ella let herself smile, the absurdity somehow making the quiet feel lighter.

She thought about all the years she'd kept this friendship at arm's length. Thought Leanne was a bit much, a bit messy, a bit shallow. Right now, there was nothing superficial about it. Not in the way Leanne leaned into her without shame, or the way Ella held her without needing to fix a thing. Maybe this is how things change; in soft shoulders, quiet honesty, and finally giving yourself permission to feel it all.

As the sky deepened into night, Leanne stretched and yawned, her voice softening. "I think I'm going to stay in the caravan tonight. I'll text Anish to let him know." She glanced over at Ella. "You can stay too, if you want."

Ella hesitated, then asked gently, "Would you rather have some time alone? I don't mind heading back if you need space."

Leanne considered this for a moment, then nodded. "Yeah, probably would do me good. Thanks."

They rummaged through a drawer until they found some spare batteries, swapping them into Ella's bike lights. With a quiet smile, Ella swung her leg over the saddle and pushed off, the soft hum of the tyres on the gravel lane beneath her. Above, bats flitted through the cooling air, and a pair of rabbits scurried silently into the undergrowth. The peaceful night wrapped around her as she cycled slowly down the lanes, a small, steady light cutting through the dark.

15

Foundations

She awoke to a low rumble that shook the windowpanes – like distant thunder, but in her own front yard. Rubbing sleep from her eyes, she peered out to see a bright yellow skip, its sides emblazoned with 'Skips 'R' Us', sitting expectantly on the gravel verge. Her heart thudded. She had completely forgotten it was due today.

Pulling on slippers, she padded outside in her pyjama bottoms and a battered sweatshirt. The morning air was sharp, and the skip looked monstrous against the quiet brick façade; an open maw ready to swallow whatever she fed it. For a moment, she felt that old, familiar pressure: the weight of every decision, every memory, towering inside her as if the entire house depended on her next move. She had 3 days to fill it.

Then she remembered the creased discharge note, the whispered secrets of her father's choices. She'd let herself feel that fracture and, in doing so, she'd claimed the right to choose again. She wasn't entirely sure what she was throwing away. But she knew she didn't want to carry it anymore. The air in the house had become thick with memory, stale with things left unsaid. Maybe clearing space on the outside was the only way to make more space inside.

She exhaled, feeling something shift in her chest. The skip was a promise. She strode back inside, heart lighter, and began gathering the first pile of boxes; old photo albums, brittle manuals, the stack of half-finished journals she'd once used to bottle her tears. With each item she crammed into the skip, she felt the old energy thin, like smoke losing its sting. By midday, the front garden and pavement outside were lined with piles for charity and skip; empty wire shelving, bare picture frames, and the soft echo of space. And as she stepped back to survey the transformation, she realised she was no longer clearing a house, she was clearing herself.

She moved next into the sitting room, where sunlight flaunted over the sofa and walls. She looked hard at the sofa — once her mother's favourite reading spot — sat stark against the bare walls. Ella hauled out its faded cushions, stacking them on the drive, and swept the coffee table clean, uncovering coasters ringed with forgotten morning teas. She emptied bookshelves, sending novels and photo frames tumbling into neat piles by the skip. With each object she carried away, the room brightened, its emptiness humming with possibility rather than neglect.

Finally, she stood at the study door. She pressed her hand to the cool wood and closed her eyes, the memory of that discharge note still pulsing behind her ribs. How would she ever face the chaos inside? The mountains of paper, the secrets folded into file folders, the letter she hadn't dared open. The letter. Her breath fluttered. But this too was part of the clearing. She inhaled, squared her shoulders, and drew back the door — ready or not — to step into that final room of memory and loss.

She didn't pause. The moment the door opened, she moved with fierce clarity. Loose papers lifted into the air as she swept them into boxes marked 'SHRED', while manila folders landed in 'RECYCLE' without hesitation. Even the heavy file labelled 'MARTHA' went straight to the skip, for it wasn't the paper that she mourned. All except the discharge letter, which she pressed flat against the kitchen counter. Each time she put the kettle on and her eyes snagged on it, the jolt sent her tearing back into the house, clearing with a ferocity that left no corner untouched.

Every stapled report, every yellowed envelope, became fuel for her resolve. She moved like a woman possessed, her decisions swift and irrevocable: what once felt precious now felt like ballast. By the time the sun dipped low, the study's every surface gleamed bare and Ella stood at its centre; breathing deep, triumphant in her own merciless gentleness.

In the bottom drawer of the old dresser, wedged behind a stack of blank cassette tapes and a cracked photo frame, Ella found a cardboard box labelled 'SLIDES – FAMILY/PRE-'90' in her father's faded block capitals. The weight of it startled her. She sat cross-legged on the floor, the box resting in her lap like something fragile, half afraid to open it. But when she did, the familiar plastic cartridges made her inhale sharply: square, dusty, and marked with cryptic labels like 'Cornwall 1988' and 'New Year (snow) – Martha's camera'.

She remembered those evenings in the sitting room; her dad dimming the lights, the ancient slide projector humming like an insect as each image clicked into place on the living room wall. Her mother, always slightly impatient, fiddling with a wine glass. Ella, small and wide-eyed, loving the sense of being pulled into the past one image at a time.

That evening, long after the boxes had been stacked and the room cleared, she set up the old projector on the dining table. Its bulb still worked – just – casting a warm flicker onto the blank wall. She clicked through the slides slowly, methodically. There were blurry beach scenes, her mother's hair blown wild by the wind. Her dad crouched next to a young Ella, grinning behind aviator sunglasses. Her first pair of goggles. A snowman with no head.

One frame froze her in place: a photo of her, no older than five, on a pebbled shore, proudly offering a collection of rounded stones to the camera. The caption in her father's hand read: 'Ella's beach banquet – "chicken nuggets" made of pebbles'. She remembered that day: how she'd arranged the stones on a leaf, declaring it a feast for the Queen. How her mother had laughed and played along. She remembered the glee of it; how her tiny fingers had arranged the stones in a circle, the way she'd announced the flavours with breathless conviction. "These are roast chicken nuggets. These are pudding. These are extra." She'd believed in it so fully. The world had felt magical then, not because it was, but because she dared to name it so. That was the thing she'd forgotten – how unselfconscious her joy had once been.

Another slide showed a pre-school assembly, her younger self clutching a laminated certificate and beaming with gap-toothed pride. 'First Place — Nature Drawing Competition', the caption read. She hadn't thought of that in years; the rush of being seen, the thrill of being good at something just because it came from her.

But as she sat there, surrounded by images of what was, Ella felt no ache, just a clean, quiet affection. It was like looking at someone else's childhood — tender, but no longer needed to anchor her.

She didn't need the mess of half-recollections anymore, the bittersweet ache of trying to piece together who she'd been. The pictures had done their work. She had carried those moments long enough. Still, she kept a small envelope tucked to one side — just a few photographs and a handful of slides she couldn't part with. Not for what they showed, exactly, but for the feeling they stirred: fragments of light, glimpses of something soft and almost-known.

The next morning, she packed the rest of the slides neatly into their original box and carried them out to the skip. She hesitated. Her hand on the lid, that fluttering second where the mind tries to convince you to keep it all 'just in case.' But she caught herself. That was how the house got full in the first place; things held onto out of duty, not desire. And she didn't need these to remember anymore. One by one, she dropped the cartridges in, hearing them land with dull, final thuds. The projector she placed in a box marked 'CHARITY', slipping in a note that read: 'Still works. Needs a dust'.

Ella dusted her hands on her jeans, looked out across the garden, and felt something unfasten in her chest. No ghosts. No longing. Just space.

After the slide show the night before, she had moved out to sit on the step, knees hugged to her chest. It had become a kind of nightly ritual to sit in the garden before bed — the hush, the cool air lifting something heavy from her shoulders; the stars blinking quietly overhead, and the stillness that seemed to settle everything. Then, just as had happened a week before, the bramble at the far end of the garden rustled. Hedgehogs — two this time — had emerged with slow, deliberate steps, snuffling along the grass as if the space belonged to them. As ordinary as breathing, as magical as a fairytale. She'd watched them with the reverence one reserves for eclipses and kindness, and something in her chest had lifted.

They didn't care that she was there. Didn't flinch or run. Just came and snuffled around looking for food. Something about that – their lack of caution, their lack of need for anything from her – unravelled her a little. Maybe this was what it meant to be safe enough to show up as yourself. To be ordinary and welcome, without performance.

So it started, like most of Ella's better decisions lately, with a whim that tugged at her just enough to warrant attention. That morning, with a sudden and quiet sense of resolve, she'd typed 'what do hedgehogs eat' into her search bar, expecting something obscure and difficult. But there it was, plain as anything: meaty cat or dog food, non-fishy, non-gravy.

The village shop was quiet, save for the radio humming an early-2000s love song and the faint clink of restocking tins. Ella reached for the dog food with a small surge of self-consciousness, half-hoping nobody would—.

"Didn't know you'd got a dog, Ella." Rob, the owner, popped up behind the till like he'd been summoned by tin-sound alone.

"I haven't," she said, caught. "It's for the hedgehogs."

"The hedgehogs," he repeated, as though she'd said it was for an owl sanctuary she ran from the attic.

"They come out at night, just at the edge of the garden. I've been watching them." Her tone dared him to mock.

But Rob only nodded, slow and solemn. "They like the jelly kind. Less messy." Then he smiled, kind and a little shy. "Good on you."

That evening, she set it all up like she was laying out something holy. A low dish, tucked near the brambles but within view, a folded blanket on the step, a mug of tea cradled between her palms. No phone, no book, just her.

She'd expected to get fidgety. To rehearse emails or replay conversations or start a new internal war about her job. But instead, a silence. Not just around her, but inside. The kind she'd always thought was a lie people told themselves. But here it was: a moment with nothing pressing to say or do or fix.

She sat like that until the light began to fade and the garden settled into its blue-hour hush.

And then — the snuffling. The soft rustle of something small, wild and unbothered. Two hedgehogs, waddling out with the absolute confidence of things that have never questioned whether they're welcome.

They found the dish and tucked in, side by side, snouts deep in their feast. Ella didn't move, didn't breathe, almost. Her chest ached with the pleasure of it; not the cut-glass pain of nostalgia or sadness, but something rounder. Something gentle.

It was such a small thing. And yet it felt like joy. Actual joy, not the idea of it.

She stayed until the last hedgehog waddled back into the shadows, then stood and picked up the empty dish, heart warm. She padded inside, the faint smell of dog food on her hands, and laughed under her breath.

16

Damp proof course

The bricks were uneven, salvaged from behind the shed with cobwebs still stitched between them. Miranda arranged them with the quiet diligence of someone who had definitely built a firepit before. Ella, not so much. She kept shifting a brick and then shifting it back. The paving slab in the centre gave it all an air of ceremony, or of a makeshift altar which, she supposed, was exactly right.

In the kitchen, she stirred tea with more force than necessary. Leanne had texted half an hour ago — a cheery, rambling message about hiking shoes and self-help podcasts and her latest plan to delete Instagram for good. She ended with:

"What are you up to this weekend, queen of becoming? Tell me you're out there making wild, wise choices."

Ella had paused, fingers hovering over the keypad. Then typed back, before she could overthink it:

"We're having a small fire tonight in the garden — burning old stuff. Miranda's coming. It's kind of ceremonial. Want to come?"

And, almost immediately:

"Yes please. Sounds oddly perfect. I'll bring marshmallows and something cheap and fizzy."

That's when Ella's body had tightened, her mind turning traitor. What had she done? These were two entirely separate planets in her life: Miranda with her slow, compassionate incisiveness, and Leanne with her fizzing, all-caps emotional weather. Would she need to translate between them? Be the glue? Be nice?

She'd taken a breath — the kind Miranda always encouraged, the kind that moved past the lungs and into the gut — and told herself simply: "They're both lovely people. It's not your job to make everything seamless. Let it unfold."

As Ella stepped slowly outside, with eyes fixed on overfilled mugs of tea, she found Miranda crouched over a neatly built campfire frame, adjusting the kindling with quiet focus. Without looking up, Miranda called, "Hope it's okay, Trevor's coming too. His wife and kids are away this weekend, and he didn't fancy rattling around the house on his own. I told him to bring logs and marshmallows."

Ella paused for a beat, then smiled. She loved Trevor — his wild streak, his warmth. It would be good to have him there. Grounding and lightness, both.

As dusk settled, Ella set out four chipped mugs, a flask of hot chocolate, and a worn tartan blanket. This in-between hour — not fully day, not yet night — always struck her as a kind of exhale. The world loosened, edges blurred, and the light folded over everything like a shawl, asking nothing but rest. A time made for laying things down without explanation.

Ella sat back slowly, letting the sling chair take her weight. She didn't move, only watched as Miranda fussed at the hearth, nudging a log and adjusting kindling. The fire took its time to catch; paper curling inward like it was drawing breath, dry wood hissing softly, reluctant to let go of its stories. Then, all at once, it found its rhythm — a sudden whoosh of flame, a bright surge that turned kindling to gold. It roared into life, crackling with purpose, throwing warm light onto the brick wall behind it and casting long, unsteady shadows across the grass. At last Miranda settled beside her. They looked at each other and smiled, then turned their gaze to the flames.

When Leanne arrived, she bounded through the back gate like a retriever off-lead, holding up a paper bag. "The finest corner-shop Prosecco money can buy."

Miranda smiled with genuine delight, held out both arms for a hug. "You must be Leanne."

"Guilty," said Leanne. "Thanks for letting me crash your ritual. I've been dying to set something on fire — in a non-metaphorical way."

They got on. Of course they did. Not in the matching-jumpers, instant-soulmates way Ella had feared might be expected, but with the grace of two people who knew what it was to hold space for someone else's pain and let that be enough.

Moments later, Trevor appeared at the garden gate, a bulging sack of logs in one arm and two bags of marshmallows swinging from the other. "What a happy little scene," he grinned, letting the bags fall with a thud. He wrapped each of them in a warm, familiar hug before settling onto a broad stone between Miranda and Leanne, already radiating his usual mix of calm and mischief.

The four of them sat in a loose circle, the fire breathing warmth into the cool dusk. Flames licked and cracked, mugs of hot chocolate sent up soft curls of steam. No one spoke. Ella wrapped her fingers around the discharge note in her pocket, feeling its brittle edge as if it might cut her. She thought of throwing it on the fire without a word; letting the fire speak for her. But then, no. That wasn't how she wanted to live anymore.

"I found this in the study," she said slowly, voice catching in her throat, chin trembling. "It's something really important about my mother. I think it spells out some darkness I've always known deep down."

Silence. The flames licked towards her hand. She placed the paper into the fire. It flared like it had been waiting. They all watched as the paper twisted and curled, the fire consuming each word and the weight they carried, then ashes dropping softly into the pit below.

For a long while, none of them moved. The fire crackled and breathed, and the night seemed to hold itself still. The air felt heavy then slowly began to ease, as though it needed time to absorb what had been given to it. Each of them stayed quiet, offering Ella the space to feel the burn of release, to let the silence do its work.

“Right. My turn,” Leanne said, reaching into her bag. She pulled out a creased, sun-faded flyer for a weekend retreat — all extreme yoga, ice baths, and relentless punishing workouts. Across the top, in bold letters, it declared: ‘*No excuses. If you're not breaking, you're not trying*.’ She turned it over in her hands.

“I signed up for this in a moment of self-punishment—.” she admitted quietly. “I thought if I could just be tougher, harder, more disciplined, maybe then I'd finally feel enough.” She gave a small smile, then let the flyer slip into the flames, watching it curl and vanish.

But the next piece — a crumpled note scrawled with promises about being a better daughter, wife, and friend — was snatched by a mischievous gust, cartwheeling over the fire pit and twisting wildly like it had changed its mind.

“Oh no you don't!” Leanne shouted, leaping up and launching after it, narrowly missing a brick and almost losing a shoe. Miranda, Trevor and Ella sat frozen for a beat, and then exploded into laughter.

Leanne chased the paper across the lawn like a woman possessed, hair flying, swearing like a cartoon villain. “I am burning you, you patronising bastard list!”

When she finally caught it — pinning it with her body and elbowing it to the ground — she stood up, triumphant, her jeans grass stained. “Right. Let's try that again. WITH DIGNITY.”

Miranda was still laughing so hard she had to wipe her glasses. Ella and Trevor were doubled over, sides aching. It felt like the kind of laughter that scrubs you out from the inside; like some old, buried ache had been jostled loose and laughed out of the body.

They roasted marshmallows in the lull, faces lit orange, air fragrant with smoke and sugar. Leanne offered a sticky skewer to Trevor, who accepted it like communion.

Ella leaned back on her hands, the fire's warmth brushing her shins and its light flickering across the faces around her. She hadn't said much as she'd fed the discharge paper into the flames, but now a swell of feeling rose sharp and thick in her chest. There was so much she needed to say about what it had meant; about the weight of that letter, and the years wrapped inside it; about the ache of carrying a story no one had asked to hear. But for now, the words pressed tight against her ribs, too raw to release.

Trevor leaned forward, snagging his empty beer bottle and placing it down between them. "Spin the bottle?" he suggested with a crooked grin. "Truth, whoever it points to."

Leanne clapped. Miranda nudged the bottle with her toe. It spun once, twice — then slowed, wobbled, and pointed, inevitably, at Trevor. He gave a small, theatrical grimace, then cleared his throat, scratching the back of his neck like he might dig the words out.

"Alright... truth," he said. "My wife asked for a break a couple of weeks ago."

He paused, watching the fire gnaw quietly at the logs, as a breath shuddered its way out. "That's why she has taken the kids to her mums for the weekend. Said she needed some space. Which, I mean... fair enough, I guess. We've been together since uni. That's a long time to be anything without interruption. Maybe you get so good at being a couple that you forget how to be two separate people too."

He gave a short, brittle laugh. "Still, when someone says 'space', part of your brain hears 'ending,' no matter how nicely they say it. And I love her. That's the truth. She's home. And now I don't know if we're just tidying up around the cracks, or about to pull the whole place down. I'm scared, honestly. That she won't want to come back. That I already lost her while I was busy thinking we were fine."

He leaned forward, elbows on his knees. "She's been spending lots of time shut away in our spare bedroom. She's not ready to talk about why, and I'm trying to respect that," he said softly. "Just giving her the space she asked for. I hope that when she's ready, we'll be able to talk... I really do." He gave a small, grim smile, letting the words settle in the quiet around the fire.

"So, I'm trying not to collapse into panic. Trying to be gentle with myself. I've started sketching again," he added, almost shyly. "Used to do it all the time as a kid. Just... shapes and movement, a way to empty my head without drinking or scrolling. So, I'm doing more of that. Trying to meet whatever this is with something real. Build myself up, if nothing else."

For a moment, no one said anything. The silence of witness.

Miranda reached over, her hand resting lightly on Trevor's forearm. "It's hard," she said softly. "What you're going through, anyone would feel that. But you're addressing it with courage." Trevor gave her a small, grateful nod.

Leanne shifted on her blanket, pulling her knees into her chest. "It's scary to question things," she said quietly. "Most people just keep their heads down, year after year. But when you do ask the questions; when you let yourself see what's really there... even if it's messy, at least you're not sleepwalking through life."

Miranda, cross-legged, tilted her head. "Exactly," she said gently. "It doesn't make it easier. But noticing, questioning, standing back sometimes; that's how you give space for both of you to come back to each other, truer than before." She smiled. "And the sketches... I love that."

Ella had been listening so hard it almost hurt. Something about Trevor's honesty had brushed against a bruise she'd only just begun to name. Her glass of prosecco was still half full in her hand, but she wasn't drinking. She was watching the firelight paint amber into the curve of the glass, and thinking how quietly people changed; how tender and terrifying it was to be known and still in motion.

They sat there, legs stretched, shoulders bare, the sky turning lavender behind them — four people, grasping in their minds how their own versions of letting go could be a kind of staying.

Miranda flicked the bottle and watched it spin. It slowed with a small scrape against the wood, wobbling, then landed on her. She sighed with mock dread, then gave a crooked smile.

"Truth," she said. "Alright, let's do it."

She took a breath, her voice softening. "I'm scared to let someone in again."

The group quietened around her.

"I've done the work," she went on, hands folded in her lap. "Therapy, journaling, EMDR — you name it. I help other people through this kind of thing every day. And still, it feels sticky."

She glanced up briefly, then back down. "My last relationship wasn't dramatic, at least not from the outside. But it chipped away at me. Slowly. Quietly. I found myself walking on eggshells without even realising. I filtered myself to avoid his disapproval - what I wore, who I saw, what I wanted."

"I kept telling myself I was fine. That it wasn't abuse. That if I just got it 'right,' he'd soften. I still don't know why it took me so long to leave. That's the part that scares me."

She hesitated. "By the time I left, I didn't fully know what I liked anymore. Or if I could trust myself to make better choices next time. And that's the part that still stings. Because since then, I have learnt all the theory. I've said the words to clients a hundred times. But knowing it up here—," she tapped her temple, "And feeling it in here—," a small gesture to her chest, "Are two very different things."

She gave a wry little laugh, but there was no bitterness in it, just honesty. "Sometimes I feel silly for still carrying it. But I guess some things take longer to settle than we'd like."

Ella smiled gently towards her. "That doesn't sound silly at all. That sounds human."

Trevor looked at her, and something unguarded passed between them — a quiet, mutual recognition.

After a few minutes, Leanne leaned back on her elbows and said, "Alright, this game's officially getting too real. Someone spin before I start weeping into the houmous." And though Miranda's words still lingered, a soft laughter rippled through the group.

Leanne leaned in, gave the bottle a gentle spin. It came to rest on Ella. Ella's chest tightened, but the firelight seemed to steady her. She knew what she wanted to say.

"Truth," she said quietly, the firelight catching in her eyes. "The piece of paper I just burned; it was a hospital discharge letter. From just before my mother died."

She paused, drawing in a breath. "It was signed by my dad. I found it a few days ago. At first I didn't want to put the pieces together. I think part of me couldn't. But as we sit here now... I think I just did."

The group stayed still, the only sound the soft pop of the fire.

"I was told it was a fall. That she slipped. But I remember that night. I heard shouting. My father was angry. Crashing about in the study. Something in me knew then that it wasn't just an accident." Her voice faltered, but she kept going. "She was taken into hospital with possible internal bleeding. And yet, he got her sent home. I thought that maybe he didn't understand how serious it was. But how could he not? He was arguing with them. I think he was afraid. That if she stayed in hospital, she might talk. Say what really happened."

She swallowed. "That would have been like him. Keeping up appearances, whatever the cost. And maybe... maybe that cost was her life." Tears, hot and sharp, dropped over her cheeks.

Ella looked down at her hands, open in her lap. "She died at home a week later. And I think, deep down, I always knew something wasn't right. I just didn't let myself name it until now."

She breathed out a long exhale. "I wasn't allowed to ask. I wasn't told anything. Just ushered past things. Managed."

She felt the heat rising in her chest then, a slow, bitter burn that had nowhere to go. "I've carried this ache for years, like the truth was lodged somewhere in me I wasn't able to reach."

Her throat tightened. *All the things she never got. All the versions of her life that never happened. A mother teaching her how to braid hair. A warm body to curl into after nightmares. Someone to notice when she was hurting. Someone to choose* her.

"Coming back here, it's like the silence cracked open. And now I can finally feel what it cost me."

For a moment, the crackle of the fire was the only sound. Then Trevor reached over, cupping Ella's hand with his.

"I want to live differently," she said, quieter now. "No more secrecy. No more holding everything alone. I want to be someone who tells the truth. Even when it's messy."

Miranda gave a small nod. "Such freedom in that."

Leanne sniffed, wiping her eyes dramatically with the sleeve of her hoodie. "That's such a beautiful intention to hold after all of that."

Ella, cheeks wet and eyes glossy, gazed into the flickering firelight. She let her eyes move from face to face: Miranda, gently smiling as she stirred embers with a stick; Leanne, sniffing as her glazed eyes contemplated the fire; Trevor, relaxed and still, like someone who'd long since stopped pretending to be anyone but himself.

She thought, suddenly, of Tom. And Lynne. And Gwen from work. June. Her Dad. How tightly they clung to rules and structure, how they moved through life like there was only one correct way to do anything: the way it had always been done. She had lived like that too, for years. Mistaking discipline for safety, and consistency for love. But the people around this fire; they were different. They weren't afraid to shift, to question, to burn down what no longer served them. They didn't want her to stay the same, they wanted her to become more of herself – whatever that meant.

And just as the thought solidified, another memory slid in, unbidden: her father's hand reaching for brambles on a summer's day, her small fingers stained purple as they picked side by side. The wonder of never knowing if the next bush would be bare or overflowing, the thrill of sudden sweetness on her tongue. For a moment it glowed, rich and golden — a reminder of gentleness and of magic. Then the shame crept in, quiet and insidious: how dare she judge him when he had given her moments like that? The memory pressed down like a hand, urging her to stop assembling the truth, to fold the pain back into confusion. To stay loyal, even if it meant staying blind.

"Honestly," Leanne said, through a mouthful of marshmallow, "this might be the best night I've had since 2016. And that was only because someone mistook me for Gillian Anderson."

Miranda raised a toast with her mug of prosecco. "To truth, to fires, and to chasing your flying bullshit through a garden in the dark."

They clinked mugs, glasses, bottles together, and then, predictably, fell apart laughing all over again.

The laughter lodged in Ella's chest, bright and full, but underneath it a flicker remained: the sudden slip of blackberry juice on her tongue, the memory of her father's easy smile that day, how it wanted to rewrite everything she was only just beginning to face. A whisper urging her not to press too hard, not to rearrange what she thought she knew. She shook it off with the sound of her friends still laughing, but the unease stayed faint and unsettled, like smoke that wouldn't quite clear.

Back inside, after everyone had left, she double-checked the back door and was halfway up the stairs when her phone buzzed.

Una: "*Gathering at mine tomorrow? Lunch. Bring something to eat or share. Kids, chaos, dogs all welcome. Hope you can come xx*"

She laughed softly, thumbs tapping a quick "*Yes please!*" before switching off her phone. A warm sense of being wanted trailed after her as she climbed into bed. But even as she lay in the dark, that other memory hovered at the edges: sweet, sticky blackberries and a father she could almost believe had been safe. Almost.

17

Construction insurance

The next day brought sunshine with a little smugness to it – one of those first hot days of the year, when the air seems newly awake and everything carries the scent of green things stretching into the light.

Ella woke with the glow of last night's fire still in her, but also a strange heaviness, as though the laughter and truth-telling had settled somewhere deep in her bones and needed time to root. When Una's text pinged again that morning, reminding her about lunch, she hesitated, realising she wasn't sure she had the space in her chest for more people, more stories, so soon.

Still, she made the couscous salad, tucked a punnet of peaches into her bag, and told herself she could always slip away early.

When she arrived at Una and Martin's, the garden was already in full swing; kids shrieked from the trampoline, launching themselves into the air like popcorn, the scent of sweetcorn and halloumi curling in the air. She paused at the gate, watching for a moment. Everyone looked so easy together. She felt, unexpectedly, like a guest in a life she wasn't sure she could keep up with.

"Ella!" Miranda's voice carried over the clatter from the barbecue. She crossed the lawn in a few long strides and wrapped Ella in a slow, steady hug; one of those embraces that doesn't rush, that lets you settle into it.

"Better," Miranda murmured, reading her without needing to ask.

And it was. Not all the way, not yet, but enough to take a breath and step into the sunlight with the others.

The garden pulsed with life — shouts and music and the clink of ice in glasses. Adults and children slipped in and out of games and conversations without distinction; a teenager lobbed a football to a grown-up mid-sentence, younger kids amended the rules of a board game and were met with laughter and agreement. It felt... whole. As if everyone here was both held and holding.

A part of her felt the familiar pull to brighten her voice, throw in jokes, animate her face; the old performance that kept her safe and liked. But her bones ached with tiredness, and even lifting that mask felt beyond her. What she wanted was simply to sit among them, to breathe in their warmth without having to give anything back. And there was a bigger, steadier part of her now; one that knew she'd be welcomed here whether she was sparkling or silent.

As the sausages were crisping and wine was being topped up, Una attempted a handstand for the kids — nearly made it — and collapsed in laughter on the grass.

"Oh God," she wheezed, fanning herself. "I'm getting too old for that."

Trevor straightened up from the barbecue, eyebrows high. "I will not tolerate that kind of talk," he said. "No one's too old for anything in my presence. We're all only as old as we tell ourselves we are."

Una threw a carrot stick at him. "Says the man who just pulled his hamstring tying his shoe."

"Details," Trevor said with flick of his hand.

Someone unearthed a stack of board games from Una's living room. They were the slightly battered kind, with corners softened by years of wine nights and rainy holidays. Leanne grabbed Articulate! with the enthusiasm of a woman about to win something.

Ella took a seat at the edge of the table, content to watch. Leanne was already marshalling people into teams, eyes bright, hands clapping.

"Right, no excuses, people. I want sharp guesses and full effort."

The game began, laughter spilling across the garden as people stumbled over descriptions and mimed badly. A seven year old threw themselves into acting out 'tsunami,' sending the others into fits of guessing and shrieks of delight. A teenager high-fived Leanne after a particularly tricky round, and she high-fived back like they were old teammates.

Leanne's face flushed with determination, her voice growing sharper each round. When she snatched the buzzer out of Trevor's hand with mock ferocity, Ella leaned over and nudged her gently.

"Hey," she said, smiling, "you know it's okay not to win, right?"

Leanne blinked at her. Then something softened behind her eyes, and she let out a breath. "Yeah. Sorry. I just — forget sometimes."

"Easy to do," Ella said. "Especially with this lot."

Ella didn't join in, just listened. The shrieks of triumph, the groans of near misses. It was enough to let their joy lap over her without having to paddle herself.

When a toilet break was requested, a hush settled over the group — not awkward, just still. Plates were half-cleared, glasses refilled. Somewhere nearby, a blackbird called once and then fell silent.

Ella let her gaze move slowly around the table; Leanne idly tracing circles on her wine glass, Una stretching her legs out in front of her, Martin chuckling softly at something half-remembered.

This silence wasn't dangerous. It didn't ask anything of her. It was the kind that welcomed you in without ceremony; the kind that said: you're okay here, even if you don't say a word.

And then, like something rising through the floorboards, it brought with it an older quiet.

A kitchen. The cold press of the chair beneath her thighs. Her father at the stove. The smell of scorched toast: her father angrily scraping the black bits off before tossing the excoriated remainder on Ella's plate. That tight, invisible tension hanging in the air like smoke before a fire.

"Are you just going to sit there in pitiful silence?" He'd snapped, his voice splintering the quiet.

She hadn't realised, until now, how much she'd learned in that moment. That silence was not neutral, that silence was a threat to be defused. That her safety depended on quick words, careful smiles, filling the pause with questions, knowing what someone needed before they even asked.

And yet here she was, years away from that kitchen memory, with people who didn't need managing. No one rushed to fill the gap. No one bristled or reached for a distraction. They just... let it be. The glass in her hand sat lighter.

The back door whooshed open and Trevor reappeared, hands raised in mock triumph. "Fear not, my bladder is emptied and my brain is rebooted."

He took his place back at the table. "Right, final round. Let's finish this properly."

The game picked up again, voices tripping over clues, a child squealing with delight at a wild guess that somehow landed exactly right. Ella stayed in her seat, smiling at the chaos, tossing in a quiet "That's it!" or "You've got it!" when she felt like it, but letting the rest wash over her.

When the buzzer finally sounded and Leanne announced her team the victors with a pose worthy of an Olympic podium, Trevor stood and stretched. "Alright," he said, a new spark in his eyes. "I've got something for you lot. A different game. Quotes. Famous lines from speeches. Guess who said it, and bonus points for the year."

Groans, laughter, mock protests.

"You'll love it," he said, already unfolding a crumpled piece of paper.

"And yes, I made it myself. You're welcome."

He cleared his throat. "We are not makers of history. We are made by history."

Voices called out guesses: Churchill, Obama.

Trevor shook his head. "Nope. Martin Luther King Jr., 1963. Before the March on Washington. Little philosophical gem before the big one."

Ella let the words settle in her. "We are made by history." She thought of the firepit last night, the things they'd burned, the truths they'd shared. How much of herself had been shaped before she'd even realised it.

Another quote: "Women's rights are human rights."

Leanne shot her hand up. "Hillary Clinton. Beijing, 1995."

Trevor raised his hands in mock surrender. "Give the woman a prize."

Martin whistled low. "That line shook the world, didn't it?"

"It was at the UN's Fourth World Conference on Women," Leanne added. "People were furious she said it."

Trevor scanned the list. "Alright, here's one for you: There is no such thing as society. There are individual men and women and there are families."

Groans all around.

"Thatcher," Una said flatly.

"Ding ding," Trevor confirmed. "1987."

Ella felt the familiar sting of words used to shrink the world instead of expand it. She thought of the garden around her now; adults and children together, laughter spilling without boundary. A small, quiet proof that society existed after all.

Trevor cleared his throat, took on a theatrical gravitas, and delivered the line: "I am no bird; and no net ensnares me: I am a free human being with an independent will."

Ella smiled faintly. Some lines didn't lose their power, no matter how old.

"Charlotte Brontë," Una said.

Martin nodded. "Jane Eyre. 1847. Radical then. Still radical now."

"And before any of you start groaning, yes — fiction counts. Don't argue with the quizmaster." Trevor glanced around, gauging the mood. He squared his shoulders again, this time leaning forward slightly.

"The arc of the moral universe is long, but it bends toward justice."

"Wasn't that MLK, again?" Ella said quietly, surprising herself with the certainty in her voice.

Trevor grinned. "Yes — and he was quoting Theodore Parker, an abolitionist preacher. King just made it famous."

The group nodded, the mood both thoughtful and light. Someone murmured, "Would be nice if it bent a bit faster."

Miranda leaned forward. "I've got one. Tell me, what is it you plan to do with your one wild and precious life?"

Ella didn't even need to think. "Mary Oliver. *The Summer Day*."

Miranda gave a little bow. "Beautiful. And — correct."

Ella found herself smiling again — at the game, the warmth, the easy respect in the group. She noticed, just for a second, how she'd spoken without running it through the old safety checks. No rehearsal, just the truth in her mouth, landing in the open.

Trevor waved the paper dramatically. "Game over. Nothing left but glory and burned sausages."

The afternoon had taken on a soft glow, not just from the fading daylight, but something quieter; a kind of ease. They chatted until the wine ran out, laughter laced with quiet thinking.

By the time the stars began to prick the sky, Ella felt her shoulders loosen. The day had asked nothing more of her than to be there; no constant words, no filling space that didn't need filling. Just being part of the whole, exactly as she was.

Later, once home, she flipped off the kitchen light and stepped into her own garden. The hedgehogs were already snuffling at the saucer of food she'd left earlier, tiny feet rustling in the grass. She stayed there a long time, hands tucked into her pockets, breathing in the unhurried quiet.

18

Substructure walls

Ella was going alone to the wedding and was mildly astonished at how significant that felt. Her own car, her own route, her own mood — undiluted. No Tom at the passenger seat fiddling with the sat-nav, no quiet bracing for how much of the day she'd need to manage for them both. She had mascara in her handbag and a spare pair of tights in case anyone laddered theirs, but she wasn't in the rescue business today. She was simply showing up. A woman in a navy dress with decent arms, who had not only survived the past couple of months but, against all logic, felt more herself in their wake.

That morning, just as she'd zipped up her dress, the skip had finally been collected. Despite the severe "have your skip ready in 3 days for pick-up. There will be no leeway" warning, it had sat on the driveway for over a week, groaning with the remnants of a life that wasn't hers: pieces of wardrobe that still smelled faintly of her father's aftershave, brittle curtains yellowed with time, old kettles and toasters kept in the attic just in case.

She stood at the kitchen window and watched the lorry winch it up. The whole metal box shuddered, then rose, carrying away the weight. The sound of it rattling into place was sharper than she expected; she felt it in her ribs.

The road twisted gently toward the coast and she remembered, with a strange fondness, the last time she'd been to Leanne's family caravan. Leanne's sobbing, raw and unsure. For Leanne, that night had been a hinge for something; the first time she'd said the things she usually locked away. The first time she'd not tried to sugarcoat. A new rhythm had begun there, quiet and radical.

The caravan, when she arrived, looked oddly glamorous in the morning light. Maybe it was the context: the swish of satin inside, the clink of glass already echoing across the deck. Leanne flung open the door and practically launched herself at Ella, pulling her into a hug so fierce Ella lost her footing.

"You're luminous," Ella said, holding her at arm's length.

Leanne smirked. "I cancelled the florals. The posh cake too. Also, the bouquets. And heels — we're all in flats."

She beamed. She did glow, actually; not in that beatific, bridal-magazine way but with something deeper and more settled. Like a woman who had thrown off a costume that pinched in all the wrong places.

Inside, there was a healthy level of chaos: curling wands like weapons of glamour warfare, champagne bottles sweating in the heat. Someone burnt their finger on the straighteners. Nipple tape was improvised with Sellotape from the kitchen drawer.

"You know," Ella said, accepting a fizzing glass from someone with one eyebrow meticulously pencilled and the other as-yet-undone, "this actually feels like fun. No pre-wedding stress here."

"It *is* fun," Leanne said. "I decided it had to be. Or what's the point?"

When it was time to leave, they piled into Leanne's dad's battered estate car like teenagers off to a sleepover, legs tangled and laughter bouncing between them like a hot potato.

The barn was strung with white drapes and lights. Sheep peered through the fence like curious guests. The vows were funny, heartfelt, and a little botched in places. The music cut out once. The rings were almost dropped. It was perfect.

Later, with champagne sweating in flutes and lemon drizzle cake leaving a trail of crumbs across the tablecloths, Leanne's new husband stood to speak.

Ella felt her chest tighten, unprepared for the way this scene took her back.

Her own wedding day: the heavy heat trapped under her dress, the fizz of adrenaline that kept slipping into something tighter. The speeches rolled out like a script she was supposed to believe in — all these words about love, connection, a shared future — but they seemed aimed at a woman she didn't quite recognise. A version of herself who was more certain, more accommodating, more willing to laugh at the jokes that landed wrong.

She remembered the strange dissonance of it; smiling as her throat closed a little, swallowing hard so it wouldn't show. Feeling the pressure of every gaze in the room, as if turning away, even for a second, would be a betrayal. At one point during Tom's speech her mind had floated off somewhere quieter, where she could breathe, before she caught herself and reeled it back in, fixing her attention on Tom; young, nervous, and wanting to please. She'd searched his face for an anchor and found him performing too; she had wondered, just for a moment, if they were already doing it for everyone else.

Now she sat in a wooden chair with the breeze drifting through, watching Leanne beam at Anish, no trace of any act between them. She felt the contrast like a bruise pressed twice.

"So," Anish said, "turns out, when you're about to marry someone, they sometimes go through a radical six-week identity unravelling that terrifies and delights you in equal measure. You think you're marrying one woman, and then, just before the wedding, she decides to fully become herself. Which is alarming and amazing, and apparently involves cancelling the floral arrangements."

Laughter rippled.

"But truth is," he went on. "I loved Leanne before. Of course. But this version? This brave, honest, no-bullshit Leanne? I didn't know it was possible, but I love her more. For showing up exactly as she is."

Ella felt something catch in her throat. She looked at Leanne, who had one hand at her mouth and the other pressed flat to her chest, as if anchoring herself.

And somewhere — somewhere quiet and steady inside her — Ella knew. She didn't want a life that asked her to hold her breath anymore. She didn't want a relationship where her vulnerability was something to conceal, or her mess something to apologise for.

She wanted what Leanne and Anish had just claimed in public, in flat shoes, without apology.

As dusk settled over the field like an exhale, the fairy lights strung through the hedgerow flickered on. A low thrum of Nina Simone curled out from the barn, carrying the scent of trampled grass and spilled wine. People were barefoot, refilling bowls of crisps, and hugging with unselfconscious affection.

Ella found herself still, unusually so. She was in her body in a way she hadn't quite experienced before; not floating above things, scanning for exits or emotional snares, but present. Legs warm from dancing, skin salt-slick from laughter and a slow-building happiness she didn't have to interrogate. She took a bite of chocolate cake — rich and unpretentious, a world away from the usual wedding cake — and chewed it slowly, deliberately, as if rehearsing what it meant to be alive.

Ella moved to one of the long wooden tables outside, the grain rough beneath her palms. Warm glass lanterns glowed along the centre, drawing small moths that thudded softly against the glass.

A woman from the next table shifted closer, wine glass in hand, eyes bright with curiosity. "You here on your own?" She asked.

Ella hesitated, then chose honesty. "I am. I'm married… but I think we might split."

The woman's expression shifted— not pity exactly, but a knowing tilt of the head. "Ah. Well, maybe it won't come to that. Nothing's perfect, love. Maybe you can stick with it. Find a way through."

Ella smiled faintly, unsure if it was politeness or muscle memory.

"I mean," the woman went on, warming to the point, "you can spend your life chasing some fantasy, or you can pick someone decent enough and make it work. My Roger snores like a pig and never remembers the bin, but we muddle along. That's the real secret. You learn to tolerate the flaws."

Ella let the words settle, noticing how they pressed in two directions at once — part of her wanting to shrink into them, to accept the comfort of resignation; another part rising, sharp and clear, saying no.

She thought of her wedding day again; the closed throat, the floating mind, and knew she couldn't go back to living in that half-self. For a second, uninvited, she pictured Tom. Not a whole scene, just him at a kitchen table somewhere, head bent over his phone, the familiar crease in his brow. The thought gave her a small, inner lurch, like a missed step on a staircase. She swallowed it down, bringing herself back to this barn, these faces, this air that didn't tighten in her lungs.

"Maybe," she said softly, "the secret is finding someone who doesn't require you to shrink at all."

The woman gave a small shrug, as if the thought was too big to bother with, and turned her attention back to her table.

Her words still rang in Ella's ears as she stepped back into the barn; that brisk, matter-of-fact certainty that "perfect doesn't exist" and "you just need someone you can put up with." It had lodged somewhere under her ribs, an uncomfortable splinter.

She didn't go back to the table. Instead, she hovered near the open doorway, letting the warm night air soothe the heat that had risen in her face. Laughter spilled from the dance floor, the music lifting and falling like a tide she wasn't quite ready to wade into.

Her chest still felt tight. Not in panic exactly, but in that old way she knew too well: the body tensing as it worked to keep its expression pleasant, to smooth over the part that wanted to say, "That's not my truth."

The music swelled into something faster, the rhythm pulling clusters of people onto the makeshift dance floor. Leanne spun in flat sandals, skirt flaring, Anish steadying her with both hands and laughing as though they'd invented the word.

For a second, Ella felt the tug to join, to step into the noise and movement, to be seen. But her body whispered for stillness and she stayed planted at the edges. Her phone buzzed quietly in her bag. A message from Lynne.

"Hey stranger. You've been quiet. How are things? Fancy a catch-up soon?"

Ella held the phone for a moment, feeling into possible responses. Gone were the days of rushing to reply, shapeshifting into warmth even when she didn't feel it. She took a breath, letting the question settle, noticing the gentle resistance in her chest — not unkind, just honest. Then she typed,

"Hey, thanks for checking in. I've been doing my best to stay out of the city and keep things quiet for a while. Trying to build something slower, outside the noise. So, I won't be in town anytime soon. Hope all's well with you."

She hit send, and set the phone back in her bag, feeling something settle — a small, necessary boundary laid with care.

After a while, she wove her way through tables sticky with spilt prosecco, smiling as she passed strangers mid-conversation to find a seat on the edge of things. She felt no pressure to be anything but exactly what she was in that moment: slightly tired, newly honest, cracked open and oddly whole.

A woman Ella vaguely recognised, from the next table leaned toward her, half-twisting in her seat, wine glass sloshing slightly in her hand.

"It's Ella, isn't it? From Leanne's birthday last year?"

Ella blinked, then smiled. "Yes. Hi."

"I remember you telling us about your job," the woman said, eyebrows lifting as if waiting for an update. "Still in the same place?"

Ella hesitated, just long enough that the silence answered for her. "I've actually taken some time off," she said carefully. "Just... stepping back for a bit. Trying to work out what I actually want to do with my life."

The woman's face softened, her wine-flush shifting into something more sincere. "Oh, that's *so* sensible," she said, tapping her glass against the table for emphasis. "If you don't question it, you wake up at 56 realising you've given your life to something you never even wanted. I've been saying for years I should retrain, but—." She shrugged, "Life gallops on."

Ella's stomach tugged, not unkindly. "You still could," she said. "There's time."

The woman gave a small, surprised laugh. "Maybe. Maybe you're right." Then, softer, "Good for you, though. Not many people actually do it."

They sipped in silence, and Ella felt the words settle into her bones like heat after cold. Someone had seen the choice, not the failure. She had said something real and it had landed without recoil, without eye-rolling or thin smiles or dismissive shrugs.

Leanne spotted her from across the room and made her way over, weaving between guests. She looked flushed, strands of hair sticking to her temples, eyes bright from hours of talking and dancing.

"You okay?" She asked, resting a hand briefly on Ella's arm, as she plonked down into the chair next to her.

Ella nodded. "Yeah," she said quietly. "Just... done peopling for tonight."

Leanne's mouth curved into a knowing smile. "I get that. There's a lot of love in here, but it's a lot."

"It is," Ella admitted. She glanced around the room — the swirl of dresses, the noise, the clink of glasses — and then back to Leanne. "You did an amazing thing today. Really."

"Go get some sleep, gorgeous. I'll see you in the morning." Leanne squeezed her hand, the gesture warm and steady, an unspoken permission to slip away without guilt.

Ella made her way out, the cool air wrapping around her like a shawl. The short walk to the hotel felt longer than it was, the quiet pressing in after so much light and sound. By the time she reached her room, the fatigue had settled deep in her bones — not a bad exhaustion, but the kind that comes from holding yourself open for hours.

She kicked off her shoes, unzipped her dress, and let it pool at her feet. The bed waited so she slid beneath the crisp covers, still wearing the remnants of the night on her skin; makeup, sweat, the faint smell of champagne. For a moment she stared at the ceiling, the room unfamiliar in the dark.

And that was when it landed: not the thought, but the truth of it, the thing her body had known long before her mouth said the words.

She couldn't go back to Tom.

Not just for now.

Not just "until she felt better."

It was done.

The realisation didn't feel clean or triumphant. It was a dull, heavy thud somewhere in her ribs, like grief remembering it had more work to do.

She let out a slow breath, one hand resting flat on her stomach as if to quiet something restless inside her.

There would be fallout. Conversations. Explanations. But not tonight.

Tonight, there was only the ache of choosing herself, and the unfamiliar space that choice left behind.

19

Roof beams

Ella, Una and Miranda walked the coastal path in a steady rhythm, the horizon spilling wide beside them. Una, who always wore dangly earrings (even in the sea), had outdone herself today with bright pink fuchsias which swung and clinked softly with every step.

Miranda walked with the kind of ease Ella envied; posture relaxed, pace steady, and eyes scanning the hedgerows as if she had time for every detail. Ella was still carrying a faint hum of tiredness from the wedding. Not the kind of tired you fix with sleep, but the deeper kind that comes from holding so many new feelings in a single day. Now, walking between these two women, she felt quieter – like she'd slipped into a pocket of observation.

The sky was staining into golds and apricots above the high hedgerows. The path wound inwards now along the old trail just outside the village, where the air smelled of warm earth and cow parsley. A breeze lifted their hair, cooling their faces.

"Feels like the kind of light that should come with a string quartet," Una said, tipping her head back.

"Or a big realisation," Ella said, half-smiling.

Miranda chuckled. "I think I've had enough of those lately."

They came to a low wooden stile and sat for a while, the last rays of sun catching on Ella's knuckles and Miranda's cheekbones.

“I don’t think I’ve ever asked,” Ella said, “but what made you want to be a therapist?”

Miranda tilted her head, surprised, then thoughtful.

“I always wanted to understand people, not just to help them, but because I needed to make sense of my own world. Even as a kid, I’d watch my parents argue — my dad going silent, my mum getting louder — and I’d wonder why it all felt so unsafe. When I started training as a therapist, I thought it was for other people, but it became clear early on that I was healing myself too. Every tool I learned, every new way of seeing, felt like a door opening for both me and my clients.”

Miranda paused. “My old admin job drained me. This… this gave me back parts of myself I didn’t even know I’d lost. And I think that’s what made me stick with it, even when the money was uncertain or the hours were long. Because it wasn’t just about making a living, it was about making a life I could actually bear to live.”

“So, you just left your old job?” Una asked.

“I went part-time at first. Then I took the full leap — left the steady paycheque, the pension, the idea of certainty. Left the relationship I was in, too. Terrifying.”

“But you did it anyway?” Ella asked quietly.

“I did. And just after that, I stumbled on a new therapy centre on the other side of town. Total chance. I never go that way, but one day I got off the bus early and saw the sign. The owner walked past right then and asked if I was interested. Low rent, sunny rooms, high windows… I stepped inside and just knew it was right.”

Ella felt a flicker of something — envy, maybe — but under it, a tug of longing. She couldn’t think of a time she’d acted from that kind of knowing. Most of her biggest choices had been made because they seemed sensible, or because someone else needed her to.

“And clients?” Una asked. “Weren’t you worried no one would come?”

"Oh, constantly," Miranda laughed. "But then... they did. And they kept coming. I think when you're doing something that you truly feel passionate about, people can feel it. Doors open."

They sat in silence for a beat. Then Una, flicking moss from the stile, said, "OK. If you could change one thing about your life tomorrow, what would it be?"

Ella didn't plan an answer, but the words arrived before she could stop them.

"I'd stop waiting for permission to be me."

Her own voice startled her. The other two women didn't flinch, just nodded silently, as if she'd said something entirely reasonable. The knot in Ella's chest loosened a little.

They began walking again, the estuary opening beside them, the light now buttery and low.

Miranda picked up her story again. "A couple of years ago, something shifted. I started dreading the client sessions – not because of the people, but because I'd gone flat inside them. I was helping, but I wasn't growing. So, I cut back. Now I see maybe five clients a week, and I run retreats every few months. Always near water. It's deep work. And it fills me up."

Ella imagined it: people gathered in a circle, the hush of a shared morning, the feeling of being invited to bring all of yourself.

"That sounds terrifying," she admitted.

"Oh, it was," Miranda said. "Every time I launch one, I think, 'who am I to do this?' But the truth is, you don't have to be perfect. You just have to hold the space."

They walked on, wild fennel and cow parsley brushing their legs, birds wheeling overhead.

Una was quiet for a moment, then said, "And such an important space to hold I think. I went to a talk last week at the community hall about folklore. The speaker was saying how, for centuries, women passed down knowledge through stories. Not written down, not official, just spoken. Around fires and in kitchens, while shelling peas or braiding hair. The stories weren't just entertainment, they were maps. Ways of living: how to grieve, how to love, how to survive men and winters and war. Whole wisdom lineages."

She nudged a wild stem with her boot. "I was just thinking retreats are a modern version of that. Women gathering, to share, to heal, to remember. To pass the wisdom on."

Ella felt something warm move through her: A recognition.

"I'd like to try a retreat some time," she said eventually.

Miranda turned, warm and steady. "Then come to the next one, help out. If you like it, maybe the one after that, you can help me run it."

"Really?" Ella asked.

"Ella," Miranda said, slowing to look at her, "you'd be perfect. People already feel safe with you. This is just a natural next step."

Ella didn't answer immediately. She watched the grass flow in the breeze, the idea slotting into place in her chest like a pebble in the right hollow.

They walked a few paces in silence, giving space to the openings.

"I've never taken a leap because it just felt right. It's always had to make sense on paper. But, I want to live like that," Ella said, trailing her fingers over the long grass. "Even if it scares me."

"You already are," Miranda smiled. "Look at your last few months. Even hedgehog catering counts."

Miranda looked out to the horizon. "When you make a decision from that quiet knowing, the world organises around it. Not instantly, and not always the way you think. But the real shift is that you start trusting yourself."

Una groaned theatrically. “Does it organise laundry? Because mine is currently ready to stage a coup.”

“Mine’s become a housemate,” Ella said.

“And what does it want?” Miranda asked, deadpan.

“Snacks. And never to be folded again.”

Laughter unspooled between them, out into the long grass, catching on the breeze like kites.

It settled them, somehow; that mix of honesty and silliness like skipping stones across deeper waters. They leaned into one another as they resumed walking, the space between them warm with shared ease.

***

Once home, Ella stepped into the garden just as the first shadows were swallowing the edges of the lawn. The fairy lights she’d strung up weeks ago winked on in the hedge, a soft constellation she could reach out and touch.

She sat at the little table with her notebook and a pen, the evening warm enough to linger. She drew a line down the middle of the page and, at the top of the left-hand column, wrote in slow, deliberate letters:

What Dad Gave Me:

- Manners
- A firm handshake
- Stubborn work ethic
- Dry humour that could cut tension at a dinner table

She wrote each one without judgement, pausing between them to see if another surfaced. After ten, nothing else came. She shifted to the right column and wrote:

What Dad Took From Me:

- Made me feel like a burden
- Withheld comfort when I needed it
- Taught me to silence my needs
- Left me believing love was conditional
- Clipped my wings with his anger
- Denied me the truth about Mum

The words came faster than she expected, her pen trembling toward the end. Her throat tightened. Tears fell, unbidden onto the paper, smudging ink into tear-streaked shapes.

She realised with a thunderbolt of clarity that beneath every one of those losses was a single, aching truth: she had always longed to be held. She pressed the heels of her hands into her eyes, letting the weight of that admission settle, unhurried.

When she opened her eyes, with a steadier hand, she flipped the sheet over and drew three new columns:

What I've Given Myself

What I've Learned

What I Deserve

This time the lists carried more light:

- Moved across the country on a whisper of hope
- Allowed myself to sit with silence

- Chosen friendship over obligation
- Walked away when fear said stay
- Made space for joy, rest, and play

By the time she finished, the air had cooled. She folded the page as if it were something fragile and slipped it between the covers of her notebook.

Her mind drifted briefly to Miranda's offer, the idea beginning to stretch its limbs. A retreat, the circle of people, the possibility of work that felt alive in her heart. It scared her in a way that felt good, like standing at the edge of a diving board with the sun on her back. She wasn't ready to leap tonight. But there was the flicker of something open within her which she wanted to keep moving towards.

She sat for a long time in the hush, the night pressing softly against the windows of the world. Her mind drifted to the place in the study, where her father's letter lay like a weight she'd learned to skirt around. She'd thought that tonight might be the night; that mapping it all out, laying it bare in ink, would be enough to make her brave. But the thought of unfolding it made her stomach clench. Not yet, she thought. Understanding wasn't the same as readiness. Some things needed more time; some things had to be circled a while, like a shy animal in a clearing.

20

Roof tiles

The kitchen smelled faintly of toast, slightly burned, even though she hadn't made any. The house had developed this strange habit of conjuring memories through its walls: a phantom scent, a flicker of her mother's dressing gown in the corner of her eye, the creak of the stair as though someone had just gone up ahead of her. She'd stopped trying to dismiss these things, They were part of the atmosphere now. Like weather, like grief, they seemed to say 'You belong here'.

Ella was still in her pyjamas — an old t-shirt of Tom's, soft from years of washing — when her phone pinged. June. Short message. Clinical tone. *"I'll pop by in 20 minutes to see how the house is coming along. Shouldn't take long."*

Ella's stomach dropped. She scanned the room: unopened mail fanned across the counter, dishes in the sink calcifying into their own little art installation, a tottering pile of muddy shoes by the radiator. Upstairs wasn't better. Her bedroom looked like someone had moved in without unpacking, which was true.

For a moment, panic rose; the old instinct to tidy her existence into something presentable before the inspection. But she didn't move. She stood at the counter, gripping the edge, and breathed. *You don't have to be perfect to be worthy. You don't have to be ready to be seen.*

The bell rang at the 22-minute mark, precise as always. June stepped in, cardigan draped like a cape, her gaze flicking over the hallway without softening.
"Oh," she said, pausing just long enough to make it sting. "It's... still

quite chaotic, isn't it?"

Ella just nodded. No defence. No apology.

"I thought you might've started sorting," June went on, that faux-helpful tone smoothing over the jab. "We'll need a plan, really. A schedule. Boxes, piles, maybe a skip. I can draw something up."

Ella didn't answer.

June sat — reluctantly — at the kitchen table, smoothing her trousers over her knees. "It must be overwhelming. It's a whole lifetime in here. And everything... it must all mean something to you."

"It does," Ella said. "More now than before."

June looked at her, wary.

Ella's voice was quiet but unwavering. "I'm not going to sell the house. I'm going to stay. I'll buy out your share."

The words came before she'd even decided to speak them; a clean, unhesitating truth that startled her as much as it did June. It felt like her body had spoken first, her chest loosening as if some inner lock had clicked open, her feet suddenly heavier on the kitchen tiles, as if they'd claimed the ground. She hadn't sat down with spreadsheets or calculators. But the moment she said it, her body recognised it as something already chosen.

The silence stretched, almost pleasant in its weight.

June blinked. "Sorry?"

"I'll work it out. I've started working a few things out actually."

June blinked, then stared. "Wait — you and Tom would live here? With your jobs in the city?" Her tone sharpened. The name hit with a faint jolt; not pain, but surprise. She realised she hadn't thought about him for days.

"I'm talking about me," Ella said, keeping her tone level.

June's mouth opened, closed, then opened again. "Ella… you can't just—."

"I can," she said gently but firmly. "I want to live here."

June frowned, eyes narrowing, and reached for her handbag as though it contained some document or law that would make the idea impossible. The beginnings of protest still hovered on her lips.

"On your own?"

"Yes."

"This place is full of ghosts, Ella."

"Maybe," she said, holding her gaze. "But they're mine."

She felt the words settle through her like a stone into deep water; solid, irreversible.

Something unreadable flickered in June's expression — disapproval, confusion, the quiet disorientation of watching someone you'd had pegged for years slip out of an old, familiar mould.

Then her expression shifted; a tight smile, but with something sharp behind it. "Well, I'll need the money quickly. I'm building an extension."

"An extension?"

"Yes," June said, almost breezily. "We simply need the extra space."

A flicker of astonishment passed through Ella mixed with a sour twist of hurt. Here was June, urgent about the money not because she needed it to survive, but to add an unnecessary room to an already ample home. For status. While Ella was piecing together a future from scraps, June was framing out a vanity project.

She walked June to the door without fuss. June gave a vague wave and disappeared down the path, her shoes clicking efficiently away.

When the gate clinked shut, Ella stayed there, one hand braced against the doorframe. Her body still hummed with the aftershock of what she'd said; not just the words, but the solid, irreversible weight of them. She hadn't planned to decide today, hadn't even consciously allowed herself to picture buying the house. And yet here it was, the decision lodged in her chest as something she'd been carrying for months without knowing it.

She hadn't asked permission. She hadn't panicked. She had spoken what she wanted and the sky hadn't fallen in. Her heart was beating harder, but the ground felt steadier under her feet. The house seemed to exhale – walls softening, floorboards settling – as if it, too, had been waiting for her to claim it.

The maths was loose at best: some savings, some old redundancy money, and somewhere in the background, the flat with Tom – the thought of which she pushed away before it could gather weight. And she was still technically on leave from work. Unpaid, soon enough; three more weeks unless she returned. Which she would have to. She would have to.

She closed her eyes, letting her breath find its rhythm. She didn't move for a while. Just stood in the kitchen, the cool tile under her bare feet. She could feel the thud of her pulse in her palms. It was absurd, really; deciding to take on a whole house in a worn t-shirt and socks with holes in the heels. She didn't even own matching cutlery. But something in her muscles already knew how to hold this, even if her brain was still scrambling. Maybe she couldn't hold it all gracefully. Maybe not all at once. But perhaps there was a way – some new configuration that didn't require her to be seamless.

The thought of holding it all – work, the house, the fragile self she was coaxing into daylight – pressed against her chest. Her heart seemed fuller and sorer at the same time.

The kettle clicked off. She didn't remember turning it on.

She poured the tea and looked out to the hedge. Tiny yellow blooms had opened since yesterday, still half-folded as if unsure. They didn't wait for perfect weather, they just started.

"One thing at a time," she murmured, letting the words settle into her shoulders, her spine.
Then, smiling faintly, "...and all of it."

21

Construction security cameras

Ella was playing tag in Trevor's backyard with his three children: Connor, ten and all elbows and knees; Milo, six, a blur of scraped shins and bravado; and Isla, three, toddling after them in joyous zigzags.

She'd offered to watch them so Trevor and his wife could take a tentative step toward mending things — a quiet lunch, just the two of them. The early summer sun gilded the grass, every blade a tiny torch.

She dropped into the grass with exaggerated defeat. "I surrender," she announced.

Connor hovered. "Can I watch TV?"

Ella blinked up at him, momentarily blank. She had no idea what the screen-time policy was here — was it Montessori? Screens after dinner only? Something Scandinavian and wholesome? "Sure," she said, then added, "Just half an hour," the phrase slipping out like a borrowed piece of adulthood.

Milo practised wheelies. Isla chased butterflies. Ella felt a simple, steady joy bloom in her chest as she watched them — bright sparks of life, unguarded and free. For a moment, she let herself sink into the warm grass, half-closed eyes taking in the blur of motion and laughter. Something in her chest softened.

Earlier that morning she'd stopped at the community noticeboard and seen a flyer: *Introduction to Massage — for connection and fun.* The words had lit something in her like a struck match. She'd torn off a paper tab before she could talk herself out of it and, two hours later she was on the phone to Fran, the soft-voiced organiser. She'd signed up by the end of the call, bemused and oddly thrilled. She didn't want to be a masseuse — at least, she didn't think so — but the thought of learning with her hands, of doing something entirely for curiosity and touch, had felt right.

Then a scream: high, jagged, wrong.

Ella shot upright. Milo was by the greenhouse, arm and handlebar through a broken pane. His face blank with shock.

Panic ripped through her. She scrambled forward, nearly tripping over a tangle of hoses. "Milo!" She gasped, sliding onto her knees. She reached for his arm only to recoil, her fingers slick with his blood. Tears stung her eyes as she fumbled for something clean, knocking over a pot of soil in her haste. Her pulse roared in her ears.

His wide, frightened eyes found hers. "Aaaggghh… mmmmm," he whimpered.

Her mind scrambled. She pressed the corner of her T-shirt against the wound, but it soaked through almost instantly. Guilt slammed into her chest: *Why wasn't I paying attention? I should have been watching.* She glanced at the other two, frozen by the patio door, and felt the weight of responsibility crush her chest.

"Milo, stay still. Stay still, sweetheart," she murmured, but her voice trembled.

She dialled emergency services, the words tumbling and clumsy.

"I… I'm sorry Milo," she choked out, heart racing. She dropped her head, wishing she could undo the moment. Sweat beaded her forehead.

She grabbed her sweater and pressed it over Milo's arm, murmuring assurances she didn't quite believe. Every heartbeat echoed like a drum as they waited for the ambulance. Connor appeared at her side, eyes wide in shock, his fear a fresh wave that nearly knocked her off balance. Her own tears blended with Milo's blood on her shirt, hot and sticky.

Dizzying relief soaked Ella, as the ambulance siren swept the garden. The paramedics moved with calm efficiency, their voices distant and reassuring. In no time at all, they had Milo onto a stretcher, moving with practiced ease as they packed his arm in a splint and covered him with a foil blanket. One of them — a woman with calm, steady eyes — looked up at Ella and asked, "Is there someone who can stay with the other children?"

Ella shook her head. "I… I don't know who."

"OK. Don't worry – Milo will be just fine." the paramedic said gently. "You follow behind us to A&E. They'll tell you where to find us."

Ella swallowed, panic crashing in around her. She fumbled her phone and dialled Trevor. "I'm so sorry," she managed, voice trembling. "Milo's cut his arm. It's bad. Lots of blood. He's just going in the ambulance to hospital. I — I'll meet you there with Connor and Isla." Trevor's voice came through the crackle of the line, tight with worry and fear.

She hung up and turned to the children. "Come on," she said, striving for steadiness. "We have to go too."

She hastily shepherded Connor into the rear seat of her car, before lifting Isla into the back. Shit, no car seat. She bit back guilt and breath. I should have asked for the car seat just in case. I should have stayed with Milo. I should have been watching. She strapped Isla's little body into the adult seatbelt, praying that nothing more could go wrong.

The drive blurred; red lights, brake lamps, Connor's endless questions, Isla's shocked silence. Her knuckles whitened on the wheel. *I've ruined everything. They'll never forgive me.*

At A&E, she stammered Milo's name at the reception desk, her voice catching. The receptionist pointed to the vinyl chairs.

Ella led the kids into the waiting area, heart pounding with every echo of the sliding doors. She sank onto a chair, pulling Isla onto her lap while Connor sat rigid beside her. The minutes stretched thin and tense.

Trevor and Sara arrived minutes later, faces drained. "Where is he?" Trevor demanded.

"They're treating him now," Ella said, the words crumbling into apology. "I'm so sorry. I should've—."

Trevor's gaze flickered to her once, searching. Ella braced for blame. Instead, he and Sara rushed to the receptionist, raking off for details. Isla ran to her mother. Connor followed.

Ella stepped back, suddenly surplus to the scene. An interloper in this family crisis she had created, certain that she was the last person they'd want beside them now. She stood quietly. "I'll... wait at home," she murmured, unheard.

Outside, the breeze was sharp and unforgiving. She longed for reassurance. She gripped the steering wheel so tightly her knuckles ached, the taut silence in the car echoing her own guilt and shame.

22

Windows

She woke with her cheek pressed into the sofa's armrest, the morning light slanted across her face like an unwelcome spotlight. Her body felt leaden, every muscle steeped in yesterday's residue of fear, guilt, exhaustion. She blinked up at the ceiling, as if it might offer some clue about what to do next.

She reached for her phone, fingers stiff. Trevor's message, sent the night before, glowed in warm, steady text:

> *"Milo's fine. They patched him up, he's asking for lots of kisses. Thanks for everything."*

Ella stared at the words. *He's fine. Thanks.* It felt like a small promise that she hadn't completely ruined everything. A cautious hope fluttered in her chest, fragile as a moth's wing. She noticed the relief arriving in layers; first in her stomach, then in her chest, finally in her shoulders, which dropped an involuntary half inch.

Dragging herself upright, she shuffled to the bathroom. She stepped straight under the shower, the water cold before the warmth came through. She shot out an exhale. Letting the spray wash her hair, she scrubbed her face until her fingertips tingled. Chose clothes without really seeing them — soft jeans and an old sweater, something that wouldn't judge her. In the mirror, her eyes looked hollow but determined.

Back in the living room, she settled on the edge of the sofa and let the silence gather around her. Her old panic whispered that this text would seal her fate: Do you know how I always mess up? But another, quieter voice said: You have to try.

Her thumb hovered over the phone. She drew a breath, the kind that clears the cobwebs. Then she typed:

> *"I'm so glad to hear Milo's OK. How are you all this morning? I'm sorry again for the chaos yesterday — and thank you for trusting me with the kids."*

She hit send before she could second-guess herself. The message whooshed off into the ether, and she felt the soft stir of possibility in the spaces she'd thought were broken.

Seconds later:

> *"Come for breakfast at ours — 9am? I'd really like to say I'm sorry in person."*

Her first instinct was to refuse – to give him space, to give herself more time to feel the consequences she was sure she deserved. A lifetime of believing she had to earn her way back into people's good graces pressed hard against her ribs. *You don't get welcomed back this easily. You're supposed to pay first.*

But there was no anger in his words. No hesitation. Just an open door she didn't quite know how to walk through.

Old Ella would have hidden.

Today's Ella — exhausted, unsure, but trying — barely managed to type:

> *"Okay. 9am."*

And even as she sent it, she half-expected the invitation to be withdrawn.

By 9., the Durrants' garden was bathed in soft morning light. Trevor stood at a small bistro table draped in linen, pancakes steaming, coffee scent curling through the air.

"Ella," he said, voice low but warm. "I'm so sorry you had to deal with that yesterday. You were amazing with Milo. Thank you."

The praise sat awkwardly in her chest, like wearing someone else's coat, but she let it stay.

"I was so worried you wouldn't speak to me again," she admitted.

"God, no. Kids have accidents all the time," Trevor said. "We're just grateful for you."

Before she could respond, he opened his arms and pulled her into a huge hug, pressing her into the warmth of his chest. She felt the steady rhythm of his heartbeat. He brushed a loose strand of hair from her face. Ella's throat tightened, the kindness in his eyes was more than she'd dared hope for.

Milo appeared then, wobbling on bare feet, sleeve rolled high to display his tidy stitches. He beamed, thrusting out his arm. "Look!" he crowed, the morning sun catching the stitches into a brief sparkle.

Trevor's relief was palpable. He wrapped an arm around Milo's shoulders. "Thank goodness," he murmured. "And no nerve damage. He'll heal perfectly."

They took their seats beneath a climbing rose whose pale pink blooms shivered in the light breeze. Birds darted through their song. Trevor poured Ella a cup of coffee – dark and rich, with just a hint of cardamom, from a grinder he'd picked up on impulse. The aroma curled around her senses, steadying her.

As they tucked into pancakes, he leaned forward, lowering his voice. "Sara and I… yesterday really helped. It feels like we are getting somewhere. And then, the hospital – it reminded us what matters. We talked for hours last night. It brought us closer." He gave her a small, hopeful fingers crossed. "So thank you for giving us that space."

Ella's eyes welled. She traced the rim of her mug, tasting the quiet strength in his words. The children's laughter rose again; Isla chasing

Connor around the table, Milo practicing gentle hops on one foot.

In that unfolding morning, Ella felt the tight knot of guilt and fear unravel just enough for gratitude to slip in. The simple act of breakfast – shared, forgiving, and real – felt like a small miracle.

The drive home felt buoyant, as though the morning's warmth had seeped through the car windows and settled in her bones. She stepped out of the car and let the sun catch her face, breathing deeply as she surveyed the overgrown hedge that had been taunting her for weeks. The branches were wild, jutting out over the pavement and tangling together like unruly thoughts, but today it looked less like a chore and more like a canvas. She fetched shears from the shed. With each snip, she shaped the greenery back into form; the hedge resisting her in a satisfyingly tactile way. Each snip of the shears brought a small pile of clipped green to the ground, the scent of it fresh and earthy.

Ella had never understood the appeal of gardening before, had always seen it as something other people grew into, like an interest in golf or jazz. But there was something about this particular task; about shaping something wild without forcing it into unnatural order, that felt deeply right. She was sweaty, slightly scratched, and oddly content.

She didn't hear him at first. The hedge had muffled the sound of the gate opening, but then: "Looking good."

It was David. Gardening gloves again, but this time slung into his pocket.

"Oh, hi," she said, lowering the shears and brushing a strand of hair off her face. "I'm getting there. Turns out it's actually sort of... enjoyable?"

He nodded. "There's something about doing stuff with your hands. Clears the head." He paused, shading his eyes against the sun. "By the way, how are you settling in here? Wasn't sure if you would be staying around."

Ella paused in mid-snip. "It's... coming together," she said, her voice lighter than she expected. "Still finding my feet."

He smiled, picking up a stray branch. "Well, if there's anything you need help with in the house, or the garden, I'm pretty handy. Just say the word."

Ella opened her mouth to give the usual automatic no, the polite deflection she'd perfected over the years. But then she paused. The breakfast hug, the way the garden smelled, the fact she'd survived yesterday... her shoulders a little lighter than they'd been in a long time. And maybe it would be nice to let someone help her. To not always be the one holding it all up.

She smiled, a little sheepish. "Well, actually. There's a dripping tap in the kitchen that's been driving me slowly mad."

He laughed. "Let me take a look."

Inside, he crouched under the sink while she fetched him a cup of tea, feeling half-awkward, half-grateful. A few moments of rattling, the odd metallic clang, and he emerged.

"Washer's gone. Easy fix. I need to head to the hardware store anyway — I can pick one up." He paused. "Want to come?"

Her instinct was to say no. She had dirt on her face, didn't know if she wanted company, and had planned to get back to her hedge in solitude. But then something tugged; the same quiet impulse that had led her to sign up to the massage course or buy dog food without a dog.

"Sure," she said. "Why not?"

The shop was a cavern of quiet possibility. Not the sterile kind of big-box DIY place, but one of those old-fashioned, slightly chaotic local stores where everything smells like metal and paint, and there's a real person behind the till.

As he searched for the washer, she wandered.

She ran her fingers along curtain rods and handled ceramic drawer knobs like they were jewellery. In the paint aisle, she stopped.

The colour leapt at her before she even understood why: a warm yellow — sun-drenched, a little golden, but soft too. The name on the tin was *Dandelion Milk*, which sounded both ridiculous and perfect.

She didn't overthink it. Just grabbed the tin, two brushes, a roller and a tray. Bought a drop cloth too, which felt deeply grown-up.

Back at the house, he fixed the tap in less than ten minutes — the drip silenced with one swift twist. She clapped like a child, and he laughed.

Ella leaned against the counter, watching him with a mix of amusement and gratitude. "You've just given me the gift of uninterrupted sleep. Thank you."

He chuckled, folding the tea towel neatly and setting it down. "Well, I'm just next door. Seriously, if anything else crops up, don't hesitate."

At the door, he paused, one hand on the frame. "It's nice," he added, softer now, "to feel useful."

She met his eyes and nodded. "It is."

When he left, she didn't sit down. She shoved furniture to the middle of the sitting room, threw open windows, and changed into an old T-shirt.

She painted until well after the sun went down. Music played low from the speaker on her phone, and her whole body buzzed with the rhythm of movement, of progress, of making something new. The walls glowed richer with every stroke, the yellow wrapping the room in a soft kind of joy.

She stood there a long moment — barefoot, paint-splattered, arms aching with effort — taking it in. The room had shifted on its axis: lived-in, warm, hers. It wasn't flawless; there were streaks of yellow where they shouldn't be and the roller had left clouds of paint on the floorboards. But it was certainly joyful, alive; a room that didn't apologise for its brightness. The walls looked happy. She realised, with a jolt, so did she.

23

Floor joists

The café was too bright. Not just the white walls and Scandi chairs and the one enormous skylight that made everything look clinically hopeful, but the whole show of it. Tom's choice.

Ella stirred her tea — peppermint, trying to be gentle with herself. The hum of conversation blurred until the door swung open and there he was: crisp blue coat, scarf knotted with Monocle-reader precision, that careful half-smile of someone arriving for a negotiation rather than a reunion.

She watched him approach, and something in her chest softened — not the ache of longing or regret, but a quieter warmth, like the fondness you might feel for a younger cousin who'd once needed your help tying their shoelaces. Tom, with all his earnestness and good intentions, his curated playlists and loyalty like clockwork. There had been love once. Maybe there still was, in the way you can love someone while knowing you're no longer meant to walk the same road.

"Ella," he said warmly, kissing her cheek. She let him.

They sat. He ordered a flat white. The silence was civilised but porous before he said, "You look... good."

"I'm sleeping again."

A smile flickered. "That's good to hear."

He leaned in, elbows on the pine table. "I've been thinking. About us. About everything. And, I know it's been hard, but I thought we were solid enough to make it through. I really believe in our forever." His voice cracked a little, the kind of vulnerability he rarely let slip.

A toddler was loudly negotiating for a second cinnamon bun. The barista called out "matcha for Matt" like it was a line from a sitcom.

Her throat tightened. "You gave me something solid, Tom. Something I could lean on when I didn't know how to stand. I'll always be grateful for that."

Just then, a man hovered awkwardly at Tom's shoulder, clutching two coffees and eyeing the sliver of space behind his chair. There was no way through, but Tom sat planted, gaze locked on Ella, oblivious to the bottleneck he was causing. The stranger shifted from foot to foot, lips pursed in polite frustration, until Ella leaned forward with a small, weary smile. "Tom, maybe edge in a bit? Let him through." Tom scraped his chair forward without looking round, his expression vacant, offering neither apology nor acknowledgment, just a mechanical adjustment before settling back into place.

His eyes searched hers. "Then, what needs to change for us to work? Tell me, and I'll do it. We could try something different. I could come to your dad's house at weekends, keep our place in the city during the week. Just… don't throw us away without trying."

The offer landed between them with the burden of its reasonableness. She felt herself tip sideways inside; part of her thinking maybe that would work. Maybe she owed him that. Maybe it would be easier to try than to stand by what she'd come here to say.

But underneath that swirl there was a quieter, steadier knowing: she didn't want to negotiate her life into something almost-right. She didn't want to spend her energy patching a structure that she knew could no longer fit her shape.

Her voice was softer now. "It's not about you not trying. It's about me needing to live in a way that feels like me. Even if every compromise sounds reasonable… I know, deep down, that I'd still be shrinking."

He looked at her for a long moment, his jaw tight but his eyes damp.

"I think," she said carefully, "we've always wanted such different things. And we didn't know it at first. Or we ignored it. Because we liked the shape we made together."

He looked at her, mouth twitching slightly, eyes somewhere between wounded and trying to understand. "So, that's it then?"

Ella took a breath. Not a defensive one, or the inhale that prefaces a retort, but something deeper. A full breath, like she'd practised in the woods or in bed after dreaming too much.

She hesitated. There was a kindness in her that wanted to soften the blow. But she knew better now. Knew what it cost to sugarcoat the truth until it rotted.

She nodded. "Yes. It's the kindest thing I can do for both of us."

He stared into his coffee like it had betrayed him. She almost reached out, but stopped herself.

"There's something else," she said, steadying her voice. "I want to sell the flat."

His head snapped up. "Sell it?"

"Yes. It's the only way I can keep the house."

"You mean your dad's house? Buying it?"

She nodded.

A faint, incredulous laugh escaped him. "I don't understand, Ella. That's our place. I thought the house was temporary until… well, until we were ready to start our life properly again."

She felt the wobble in her chest; the one that comes when someone names the future you once wanted, even though it's no longer yours. "I thought so too. But being there… it feels like the first place I've been able to breathe in years. I can't walk away from that now."

His voice was calm but sharpened at the edges. "You're really choosing a crumbling old house over me?"

She winced. "It's not that simple."

"Feels simple from here," he muttered, then ran a hand over his face. The fight went out of him almost as quickly as it had come. "I just. I thought we'd be together always. You were my future, Ella."

She swallowed hard, the weight of his words pressing in. There was a temptation to fold, to say maybe, to buy herself time. But she could feel it; the exhaustion that would follow, the quiet erosion of herself.

"I know," she said, her voice catching. "And I'll always be grateful for what we had. But I need to live my life in a way that actually fits me now. Even if it means letting go of what we planned."

His face flickered — shock first, then something more calculating, as though he were already weighing what this shift might mean for him. "Right. Well, I hope you know what you're doing."

"I do," she said quietly, though she knew that 'knowing' was less about certainty and more about trust.

When she stood, he didn't follow. The café spun on around them: orders called, babies howled, strangers laughed at the brightness of being alive.

Outside, the wind was sharp and bracing — unusual for June. Her hands felt oddly light, as if she'd set something down she'd been carrying for years, and yet there was a tremor running through her. She stood there for a beat, letting the cold kiss her bare neck. The wind shifted slightly, lifting the hem of her top. And, like a thread tugged loose from somewhere deep inside, she heard it: her mother's voice, not loud or ghostly, but quiet and familiar, the way it had sounded when Ella was small and shaky and trying to be brave.

You know when it's time.

That was all. A quiet thought, or maybe a memory, rising like mist.

It had been years since she'd heard her mother's voice like this, not since those first months after her mother died, when it had risen often, comforting and insistent. Ella let it settle in her chest now, warm and steady. She closed her eyes for a moment, wanting to hold onto it – this feeling of her mother close, of being guided without being pushed. She smiled, small and real, and tried to let the moment take root inside her.

Her phone buzzed as she reached the car.

Leanne: "*How did it go?*"

Ella smiled faintly, thumbs poised over the screen.

"It actually went quite well. He took it without a fight. Feeling all sorts but mainly relief."

A beat, then another message came through:

"Definitely the right decision then. See you soon. I think there's something important we need to do."

Before she'd met Tom that morning, she and Leanne had sat on the caravan steps with mugs of coffee, the wind pulling at their hair and the sea air sharp with salt. Leanne had been gentle but thorough, asking questions that left no easy escape.

"Is there any part of you that thinks you might regret this?"

Ella had shaken her head.

"Anything worth salvaging?"

She'd searched for the flicker of a yes, but found only the steady quiet she'd been carrying for weeks. They'd talked about how Tom might try to bargain, how he might offer to bend the shape of their life together. Leanne had reminded her that the real challenge was whether she could hold on to her own clarity when his feelings inevitably muddied the air.

But clarity was a clean, abstract thing when it lived in the quiet;

when her only company was the wind off the sea and someone who wanted her to find the truest answer, not the most convenient one. In the café, faced with the heat of Tom's hope, it had been different. His voice, his familiar hands wrapped around a coffee cup, the slight tremor in his jaw — all of it pulled at old loyalties like loose threads. Saying no in theory was one thing; saying it to a man who'd been her anchor for years was something else entirely.

Tom's face lingered in her mind: the way his voice had caught when he'd said you were my future, the hopeful tilt in his shoulders when he'd suggested spending weekends at the house to "see if it worked".

It was reasonable. Gentle, even. The kind of request you couldn't fault without feeling mean. She could imagine people she knew — colleagues, old friends — saying, "Why not give it a try? You owe it to yourselves."

She pushed her head back against the head rest. That was the trap, wasn't it? Reasonableness. You could get tangled in it for years, trying to honour it, until you woke up one morning unable to find your own outline in the mirror.

The truth — the one her body had known long before her mind caught up — was that she didn't want to spend more precious weekends managing herself into a shape to fit. She wanted to be in the house on her own terms, to keep building whatever had started quietly growing in her since she moved back.

The temptation to say yes had flared in the café but in the space of the drive, it loosened. She could see now that saying yes would be the beginning of a slow retreat from herself. And she'd promised herself, even if only silently, that she wouldn't go back to that.

But as the miles slipped by, clarity gave way to a heavier current, slow and insistent. Her father would have been horrified. A commitment was sacred, weathered through good and bad, never abandoned. The thought of his disapproval pricked at her, sharp and familiar, and, for a moment, she felt the weight of it press down.

By the time she turned into Leanne's lane, her eyes stung and her throat felt tight, though she couldn't have said exactly why. The decision — to end things fully, to sell the flat, to keep her home as her own — rested somewhere deep inside her, not yet a calm certainty but a steady, quiet weight she could feel even through the tears.

The caravan door was already propped open. Leanne stepped out and pulled her into a long, quiet hug. At first Ella held herself stiffly, breath catching against the weight of all that had been gathering in her chest. Then the dam gave way. The tears came hot and sudden, her face pressed into Leanne's shoulder, her body slackening as if it had been waiting for this moment of surrender. Grief — old and shapeless, carrying her father's shadow, Tom's expectations and her own unspoken fears — slid through her in waves. And in the circle of her friend's arms, she let it move, let it empty, let herself simply be held.

"You okay?" Leanne murmured, once Ella's breathing had steadied.

Ella nodded into her shoulder. "Yeah. It was… what it needed to be."

Leanne eased back, searching her face for any cracks. Then, with a small, tentative smile: "Then, I think there's something we should do."

Inside, the table was crowded with food: sourdough, olives, grilled vegetables, torn mozzarella, a bowl of strawberries sitting like punctuation. A bottle of wine was already open. But in the corner, the small TV glowed with a paused frame: the Olympic rings. Swimming coverage about to start.

Ella raised an eyebrow at the screen, half-laughing, half-touched — really?! But beneath it was a warm flicker of gratitude. Trust Leanne to know that forward motion, to keep stepping into things that once felt impossible, was exactly what she needed right now.

They didn't say anything more. Just poured themselves wine and sat side by side in the shaded caravan while the world outside blew around in high winds. Leanne pressed play.

For the next hour, they watched every length, every turn, every breath. Sometimes they gasped at the form. Once, Leanne muttered "elbows" under her breath and they both dissolved into laughter. But mostly, they watched in reverent silence, as if bearing witness to something long abandoned but not forgotten.

When the final medal ceremony ended, they stood and hugged, wine glasses in hand. They didn't need to say it out loud; what it meant to sit and watch, to not look away. To reclaim something once tangled in shame and pressure and half-swallowed grief.

Ella murmured, "Thanks for making me do that."

The wind rattled the caravan, but inside, everything felt still.

Leanne glanced sideways, her eyes soft. "Thanks for joining me." They clinked their glasses gently.

24

Underfloor heating

The swim had been cold enough to sting, the kind that made her lungs expand in surprise. Now, wrapped in towels on the wind-ruffled sand, they sat in a loose semi-circle, steam curling from enamel mugs as Trevor doled out hot chocolate with a covert splash of brandy. The laughter was loud enough to send the gulls wheeling further down the shore.

Ella blew across the surface of her mug, watching the steam curl. "God, I am totally converted to this cold swimming thing!" She declared, cradling the warmth of the mug against her ribs.

Leanne snorted. "I'm with you. This — this is pure magic. Raw, wild, honest; a far cry from our schoolday swims, eh?"

Una took a sip, then wrinkled her nose. "Brandy in hot chocolate? Trevor, you're a genius — or a psychopath. Jury's still out."

Miranda stretched her legs into the sand, lifting her cup toward the horizon. "It's perfect. Cold water, warm hearts, boozy beverages."

Trevor flopped down beside them, sand sticking to his swim robe. "Who needs therapy when you've got brandy and friends?"

Their laughter merged with the hiss of the waves. For a moment, the world was just that: wind, salt, the ache of muscles used well. That quiet joy again, found in something as simple as being cold, wet, and vividly alive.

Trevor broke the quiet. "Remember when we first met you, Ella? All tense and guarded, like you'd built a moat." He reached out to put his hand on her shoulder.

Una laughed. "I thought you'd never let anyone in."

Leanne raised her mug in mock salute. "And now look at you. Dawn swims, brandy for breakfast."

Miranda's eyes glinted. "You've done more than let us in. You've opened the whole estate."

Ella swallowed, chest warm. "I'm still scared sometimes. I don't always know if I'm making the right decisions. But... you've helped me understand what trust feels like. I'm so grateful for you all."

Each of them reached towards her; a hand on her knee, a shoulder leaned against hers, a soft "we've got you," murmured from somewhere behind her. It wasn't dramatic. Just presence. Safe, ordinary, steadying. The kind of quiet care she still wasn't used to receiving without having to earn it.

And then, life being what it was, the reality of her situation tapped back in. Ella remembered back to just a few hours ago. The estate agent had called to say the flat was now on the market. The crisp enthusiasm of someone who'd already moved on to the next commission. "We will have this flat sold in no time at all," she'd said. "Great bones, great light. A few viewings booked in already." It had all happened so fast. Tom – kind but distant in their conversations – already receding into a separate timeline.

She had hung up the call and moved through the rooms with the tentative steps of someone mapping a new country. Coffee made. Left cooling. Laundry half-folded, then abandoned on the sofa arm. Opened the laptop. Refreshed the inbox. Again. And again. No news coming. No news expected. She stood in the doorway of the bedroom, then the kitchen, then the hall. Couldn't settle. Couldn't land. Every space felt a little unfamiliar, like she'd returned to a house she used to know. She oscillated between the thrill of building a life from her own blueprint and then – fifteen minutes later, feeling like a fantasist. The nagging thought that maybe she was just playing house. She missed someone saying yes, that's right, the mirror of approval. But the swim had rinsed some of the noise out of her. Her pulse felt slower now, her skin still tingling from the salt and the cold.

Leanne gave a little nod, her gaze steady. "Three days ago, you let go of something huge, and you did it without flinching."

Miranda tipped her mug toward her. "Big, brave choices don't always feel good right away. Sometimes they just feel true."

Trevor's hand found hers for a quick squeeze. "And for what it's worth, we think you're doing brilliantly."

The walk back from the beach left salt drying on her skin, the cold settling into a steadier warmth low in her chest. With each step, the choice she'd been gripping onto felt less like effort and more like something that had already taken root — quiet, stubborn, undeniable.

She drifted a little ahead, letting the others' voices wash over her. Their chatter rose and fell like the tide until Leanne proclaimed pancakes the "undisputed king of breakfasts." Laughter broke out, mock-arguments about toppings flying back and forth. By the time they reached her street, Ella found herself smiling, turning to invite them all over the next morning to put their pancake theories to the test.

***

The next morning dawned bright and full of potential. Ella opened the door in a pair of soft joggers and a ponytail, her kitchen already humming with the scent of butter and batter. Leanne arrived first, waving a jar of chocolate spread in one hand and a bunch of overripe bananas in the other like she was holding a trophy. Miranda followed moments later, serene as ever, with a paper bag of strawberries and a chilled tub of crème fraîche.

"Hope you're ready to have your minds changed," Miranda said, placing her offerings on the table.

"Please," Ella scoffed playfully, flipping a pancake with theatrical flair. "Lemon and sugar walked so the rest of you could run."

As the kitchen filled with the warm, slightly chaotic energy of toppings and friendly sabotage, Ella grinned and wiped her hands on a tea towel. "Before we eat," she said, "there's something I want to show you."

Ella glanced at the living room door, feeling a small pulse in her chest. She wanted to share the thing she didn't quite known how to explain, even to herself.

She led them through, and stopped in front of the fireplace.

Above it, the painting glowed. A wild tangle of hedgerow plants — foxgloves, brambles, dandelions gone to seed — danced across the canvas, lit by a low silver moon in a velvet-blue sky. The longer you looked, the more there was; moths mid-flight, a snail's glinting trail, ivy curling through moonlit nettles. Wild, intricate, and impossibly alive.

"I saw it in a shop window two weeks ago," she said, her voice quieter now. "And I couldn't stop thinking about it. It feels like a marker. For now. For this. For choosing for myself, even when I'm not entirely sure what comes next." She smiled, a little breathless. "I bought it yesterday after our swim. Most expensive thing I've ever bought that wasn't a car."

"Ella," Miranda breathed. "It's stunning."

Leanne stepped closer, her gaze caught in the weave of the brambles. "It's exactly you." Then she glanced sideways, eyes softening. "And... buying something like this, so soon after telling Tom? That's bold, Ella. Brave. That's clarity. Like you're saying out loud that this is your life now."

For a moment, Ella felt the old flicker of doubt — had she gone too far, spent too much, claimed this shift too soon? But it passed. She folded her arms, with the quiet pride of someone who had planted a flag in her own life.

Back in the kitchen, the pancakes were slightly more chaotic than elegant — some burnt edges, some too thick — but it didn't matter.

They took turns constructing stacks, each defending their topping like it was a national treasure. Leanne insisted banana and chocolate was the "ultimate indulgence-meets-health-food combo," while Miranda's case for strawberries and crème fraîche was rooted in "balance, elegance, and bite." Ella rolled her eyes at both of them and continued to douse her own creation in citrus and sugar, unapologetically old-school.

Eventually they migrated to the table, plates loaded, laughter light. The morning sun poured through the open back door, catching on the syrup and glinting in their mugs of coffee.

Miranda leaned back in her chair, stretching. "So, Mrs Leanne Young. How's married life treating you?"

Leanne smiled into her fork. "Honestly? Lovely. Not in the big grand way people always expect you to say. Just… consistently lovely. It's like this quiet foundation beneath me. It changes everything."

Ella felt a subtle lurch in her chest. Not envy, exactly, but something wistful. The sweetness of being seen like that, folded into someone else's life with intention.

She looked down at her pancake, the sugar glistening. "That sounds… really beautiful."

The knock came mid-second pancake assembly. David stood there with a fistful of leafy greens, damp from the soil.

"Morning," he said, cheerfully. "Was just out pulling up the last of the wild onion before it bolts. Thought you might like some?"

Ella blinked. "Um. Wild onion?"

Behind her, Leanne and Miranda were already leaning in, grinning. "Ooh, you would love wild onion soup," Miranda declared. "It's like summer in a bowl."

Ella laughed, taking the bunch. "I have no idea what I'm doing with this."

"That's the beauty; you don't need to," David said, shrugging. "Just chop it up and throw it in a pan."

"Actually," Ella said, warming to the ridiculousness of the moment, "Come in. We're in the middle of a very serious pancake tasting panel and there's a spare seat."

David hesitated, a bit startled, then smiled. "Well… if you're sure."

Ella handed him a plate while Miranda gestured grandly to the array of toppings.

"You may choose only one," she said, mock-serious. "Crème fraîche and strawberries, chocolate and banana, or the purist's choice: lemon and sugar."

David blinked, looking genuinely overwhelmed. "That's… more variety than I've ever seen on a pancake."

"Choose wisely," Leanne said, tapping her fork against her plate.

He eventually opted for strawberries and crème fraîche after declaring that banana was "a risk this early in the day", and they all burst into laughter.

By the time he left, David had promised to drop off a wild onion soup recipe ("no pressure, just if you want it"), and Miranda was halfway through a story about a disastrous vegan pancake experience involving a wasp, a wind chime, and a rogue blender.

Ella stood in the doorway waving him off, the taste of lemon still on her lips and laughter in the kitchen behind her.

The rest of the morning passed in soft conversation and clattering forks, the plates eventually empty but the sense of connection full and warming. And all the while, hanging quietly above them, the hedgerow moon watched on.

25

Floorboards

Miranda's house was the kind of place that made you breathe differently. Light filtered in through old sash windows, softened by linen curtains that moved just enough to let you know there was a breeze. Shelves lined with books and small, deliberate objects; a stone bowl of conkers, postcards pinned with brass clips, a pottery vase like a shrug of the shoulder. Everything spoke, but nothing shouted.

Ella stepped inside the back door, holding her breath in that way she did when entering other people's well-tended lives. She had brought cake, still warm and carried in both hands. Ella realised she was holding her breath, suddenly uncertain whether this conversation would leave her more exposed or more equipped.

Miranda's voice called through from the next room: "Come on in, kettle's just boiled. Grab a seat in the sitting room."

The sitting room was scattered with comfortable chairs, none of them matching but all of them inviting. A woven throw trailed over one armrest, and on the windowsill, a small lamp pooled amber light onto a notebook already open. Ella took it all in as she moved quietly to the edge of the room, heart thudding with something she hadn't yet named.

She took a comfy looking seat by the window, letting the sound of Miranda making tea hum around her.

"I bought oat milk. Is that right?" Miranda called from the kitchen.

"Oh, yes, thanks. You didn't need to. I go rogue with cows' milk every now and again. But thank you"

Miranda appeared in the doorway, tray in hands, balancing two mugs of tea and a card propped between the sugar bowl and a mismatched jug of milk. Flowers wrapped in brown paper were held under the tray. She nudged the door open with her hip, grinning as she came through.

"For you," she said, passing the flowers to Ella, while setting the tray down with gentle ceremony and handing Ella the card.

Ella raised an eyebrow, already smiling. She opened the envelope and unfolded the card — a deep blue watercolour sky with a tiny figure mid-leap between two cliffs. Inside, Miranda's handwriting slanted neatly across the card.

You are going to walk into that place like the absolute star you are. You will be brilliant, not because you pretend to be okay, but because you know now that you don't have to be perfect to be powerful. I hope it's kind to you in there — but if it's not, I hope you remember that you can leave. Sending all the love and boldness. — M x

Ella stared at it for a moment, then let out a breath that trembled just slightly at the edges. "This is... beautiful."

Miranda sipped her tea and shrugged, casual as ever. "You don't need a pep talk. Just a reminder. You're stronger than that building, no matter what happens in it."

"And these, my favourites of all. How did you know?" She said, touching the sunflowers gently, their golden faces just beginning to unfurl.

"I don't usually... ask," Ella said after a beat, fingers wrapped tightly around her mug. "For help, I mean."

Miranda nodded, easing herself into the other chair. "I know. I was pleasantly surprised when you did."

Ella stared into the tea, then glanced up, sudden heat prickling the back of her neck. "It feels... exposing. Like I'm admitting I'm not sorted, not ready, not enough."

Miranda's eyes softened, no judgment in them. "Needing help doesn't make you less. It just means you've stopped pretending you can carry everything on your own."

Ella swallowed hard. She felt the trembling edge of something. Not fear; it felt like the lowering of long-held armour, one strap at a time.

Ella smiled faintly, grateful for feeling known. "I've only just stopped flinching every time someone says the word 'return.' As if I'm boarding a plane back to some land where I used to be functional."

Miranda nodded slowly. "So, you definitely are?"

"What? Functional?" Ella blew a sharp breath from her nose. "Debatable."

"No! Returning," Miranda laughed, "Just checking all options are being considered here. Choosing something you want, something that makes sense. You don't *have* to do anything."

Ella leaned back in her chair, the wood of it stiff against her shoulder blades. "I am going to go back, yeah. But because it's a bridge. Because I need money and I'm not entirely delusional."

"Those are very polite ways of saying 'I'm compromising.'" Miranda raised her eyebrows, sipping her coffee. "But that's okay. We all do. But if you know it's a compromise, then that gives you a kind of edge. You're not pretending it's something it's not."

Ella nodded her head, slowly. "I need to talk through the return-to-work interview," Ella said finally. "I've been rehearsing it in my head, and I keep veering into either full-blown corporate warrior or small apologetic child."

Miranda smiled with quiet empathy. "Then let's find the version that's neither."

Miranda tucked her legs underneath her and reached for the notebook on the arm of the chair. "Alright," she said, playful now. "Let's pretend. I'll be the terrifying HR person with a clipboard and zero emotional range."

Ella groaned and buried her face in her hands. "God. I already want to leave."

"Too bad. You've arrived. Let's get started." Miranda flipped an imaginary page. Her voice dropped into crisp, bureaucratic tones. "'Ella. Good of you to come in. We'd love to hear how you're preparing to reintegrate into the demands of your role.'"

Ella peeked through her fingers. "Are you serious? That's your opening line?"

Miranda smirked. "'We also want to understand your recent growth mindset outcomes, and how they align with cross-functional delivery goals.'"

Ella laughed; a short, startled bark of sound. "You're killing me."

"No, no, stay with me," Miranda said, straightening imaginary glasses. "'Would you describe yourself as robustly engaged with your own resilience architecture?'"

That did it. Ella burst out laughing, clutching the mug against her ribs so it wouldn't spill. "Resilience architecture! That's not a thing!"

"It is now," Miranda said, grinning. "Right. Your turn. Be serious. What would you actually say?"

Ella caught her breath, eyes still wet from laughing. "Okay. Let me try."

She sat up straighter, planted both feet on the floor. Her tone shifted – still light, but grounded. "I'd say... I'm returning with clarity about what enables me to do good work. I'm thoughtful, measured, and I've become much more aware of how I manage my time and energy. I want to contribute meaningfully, but not at the cost of my health."

Miranda raised an approving eyebrow. "Ooh. That was actually good."

"Was it?" Ella flushed, surprised.

"It was clear. Confident. Not defensive. You sounded like someone who knows herself."

"I'm trying," Ella said. "I want to show up as the real me this time."

Miranda softened, closing the notebook. "Then let's keep practising until we can get that into a shape that is passable in their world too. No more shapeshifting. Just you."

Ella's voice dropped. "I'm scared I'll get sucked back in. The deadlines, the praise, the constant treadmill of being indispensable: I was really good at being needed."

Miranda nodded again, that same serene, impossible calm she always seemed to carry like a shawl. "Of course. That's the trap. You build your life around the proof of your usefulness, but the cost is yourself. And worse: the wrong kind of commitment twists everything else around it. Your energy doesn't stay obedient. If you pour it into a life that doesn't fit, it leaks. You start losing joy in the places where you used to find it. Even rest feels suspicious."

Ella looked down at her coffee and traced a finger over the rim. "So what do I do? Just quit and start a candle-making business?"

Miranda laughed — a sudden, bright sound. "Only if you want to be broke *and* smell like lavender forever." They laughed, and for a moment the weight of trying to fit expansive things into a box eased.

"I think," Miranda went on more gently, "you keep walking the bridge. You keep saying no to what drains you and yes to what stirs you. But most importantly, you keep noticing. You already know how it feels when your energy is aligned. That kind of clarity doesn't lie."

Ella stirred her tea for something to do with her hands.

Miranda paused for a moment, then added, "You know the offer still stands for you to help out with the retreats. It might not be a perfect fit, but it's certainly more aligned than spreadsheets and client decks. You can try it, see what you think."

Ella looked up, something soft flickering behind her eyes. "I do want to. But I would have no idea what I was doing."

Miranda smiled. "None of us know what we're doing at first, that's not the point. The point is how it feels. Start there, and the rest has a way of unfolding."

She exhaled slowly. "I've been thinking," she said, almost more to herself than to Miranda. "About how much time I've spent in work and life just... being functional. I want whatever I do next to feel meaningful."

Miranda nodded, her gaze warm. "Then that's your compass. Even if you don't know the map yet."

Ella smiled faintly, like she was hearing a language she once spoke and only just now recognised. They sat for a while in silence. Outside, the breeze sent petals skimming like small, purposeful messengers.

"What happens when you start choosing from that place of meaning and the things that bring you joy?" Ella asked, her voice lower now, confessional.

Miranda smiled warmly. "Things start moving. It's not always neat. Often, everything unravels at first – jobs shift, people leave, the stories you told yourself about who you are start to dissolve. But you know this already; then something else happens."

Ella waited, watching her.

"Life begins to co-conspire with you. The right conversations appear. The next step shows up without you having to thrash your way toward it. It's like the universe exhales and you finally get to stop bracing."

Ella blinked. That last part lodged itself somewhere in her gut.

"So, all I have to do," she said carefully, "is follow what feels... light?"

"Not *easy*," Miranda corrected. "Aligned. There's a difference. Easy is skipping the conversation. Aligned is having the hard talk because not having it costs you more. Easy is going back to the job, the husband, the version of you that doesn't ruffle feathers. Aligned is knowing when to let something end, even if it terrifies you."

Ella looked out the window. A child passed by on a scooter, shrieking with delight. She felt something open in her chest — small, but definite.

"You're not behind, you know," Miranda added, more gently. "You're just on the first page of a better chapter."

Ella looked back at her and exhaled. "I don't know where it's all going yet. I don't really understand what's happened to me these last few months."

"You're not supposed to," Miranda said. "That's the beauty of it. You're not building a career anymore. You're building a life."

Ella leaned back, the chair creaking a little as she settled. As the pool of sunshine across the floor began to diminish, Ella realised how deeply held she felt. For once, she wasn't figuring it all out alone.

"You're going to do just fine," Miranda said.

Ella nodded slowly. "Yeah. I think I might."

Later, Miranda had walked her to the door. "Oh — and here," she added, reaching for a cloth tote bag resting on the console table by the coats. "Thought you might find these helpful."

Inside was a stack of old home magazines, their pages thumbed but lovingly kept. Some glossy and aspirational, others quiet and earthy, full of beautiful finds and rooms lit by lamplight.

"I had them delivered for a while after I moved," Miranda said with a soft smile. "Full of great ideas, inspiration."

Ella took the bag, her heart big at the thought of flicking through them later with a cup of tea and a pen. Dreaming in soft-focus about colours and corners. The kind of life that could be built when you didn't have to ask permission.

"Thank you," she said, the words full.

Miranda just squeezed her arm and opened the door. "By the way, Leanne and I were talking... we thought we'd treat you to something after your first week back at work. Spa day, train trip, I don't know, whatever you fancy. You pick."

Ella blinked, caught off guard by the gesture's simplicity. And its precision.

"I... that's really kind," she said, her voice thinner than she meant it to be. "You don't need to—."

"We know," Miranda said, smiling. "We want to. It's a big week for you."

Ella stood for a beat, coat in hand, the door open behind her but not quite ready to step through.

"Thank you," she said. "I'll think about what I'd like."

What she meant was: *I can't believe you see me so clearly.*

What she meant was: *"You understand how much this is costing me."*

What she meant was: *"Thank you for helping me hold the weight."*

And then she walked out into the afternoon, steadier than when she'd arrived.

The walk home was slow. She took the long way — past the bakery, the crooked post box, and the cottage with the purple shutters — letting Miranda's words move through her like music. She noticed the small things: the scent of warm bread trailing from an open door, the clack of bicycle spokes, the poppies leaning over a garden wall.

And then, passing the old iron gate of the park, she remembered the letter.

It had been sitting in the desk drawer so long it had become an object, not a message.

But today… today she felt ready to open it. Not because she expected comfort, but because she could bear whatever it held.

At home, she set the tote on the counter, hung up her coat, and went straight to the drawer.

The letter was lighter than she remembered.

She carried it to the kitchen table, sat down, and let her fingers rest on the envelope like she was holding a bird.

She didn't sit tall, she didn't brace, she simply let her body curl around it, like an animal instinctively softening against impact.

His handwriting was smaller than she remembered. Neater and almost careful, as though he'd known how little space there was left for misunderstanding.

Ella–

I don't know what good this letter will do. I don't even know if you'll read it. But I want to try, because I think you deserve something — anything — that feels closer to truth than what I gave you.

I failed you.

She stopped. Exhaled.

That sentence alone cracked something clean in her.

No justification, no clever redirection. Just the flat weight of those words, unapologetic in their sorrow. She kept reading.

Not in the way people mean when they talk about absent fathers or harsh words, although I know there was some of that too. I failed you in my refusal to see you clearly. In turning away every time you needed me to turn towards you. I wasn't what you needed — God, I knew that. I think I knew it the moment you came home from school crying because someone called you strange, and instead of asking you why it hurt, I told you to toughen up.

The truth is, you reminded me of everything I lost. Of your mother. Of the things I did and didn't say. Of the ways I let her down. You reminded me of love, and joy, and softness, and I had decided somewhere along the way that I wasn't allowed those things anymore.

I see now how much I mistook control for care. I kept us busy, didn't I? Tasks, routines, swimming, tidiness — everything ordered, timed, contained. It was the only way I knew to hold the grief back. If I let even a corner of it in, I was afraid the whole thing would come crashing through and take me with it. And you... you were all the things I couldn't bear to feel. Bright. Unruly. Feeling everything. I didn't know how to meet that. So I tried to shut it down. In you. In me. I kept the days neat and the emotions locked out of sight. That wasn't love, not the way you needed it. I see now what a cruelty that was. And I am so sorry for that.

I wanted to say that none of it was your fault. That you were never too much or too difficult or too strange. You were radiant. And I couldn't bear to be near it.

I'm sorry I couldn't tell you this in person. I'm sorry that shame and fear won. I hope you keep choosing the things that make you feel alive, even if I never could. That would be enough for me. That would be more than I deserve.

I love you. I just didn't know how to show it.

Dad

When she finished, the silence was thick. Her body still trembling, her chest tight, a ball lodged in her throat. Tears spill without warning, warm and unstoppable.

She left the letter open on the table, as if folding it might somehow diminish its truth. It sat there, humming silently. A presence. A wound. A mercy.

First came the urge to forgive.

He said sorry.

He saw me.

Her mind scrambled to rewrite the story, to dress the years in softer fabric. Maybe it hadn't been so bad. Maybe love had been there all along, just hidden.

She thought of being eleven, standing by the pool after winning her race, shivering and clutching the medal, him already halfway to the car. The guilt she had felt for him having given up his time for her.

Of sitting in silence across from him at breakfast, tracing patterns in her cereal while he read the paper, the air thick with everything unsaid.

Then — fury.

Where had this clarity been when she was fifteen, hollow-eyed from school?

When she'd sat across from him, begging without words for him to look up?

It was easy to be noble when you were gone. The dead always got the last word.

She paced. Fast, sharp bursts across the kitchen.

Half wanted to throw the letter out.

Half wanted to frame it.

The cards of her emotions scattered on the floor: grief, resentment, longing, a small and bitter triumph.

She wasn't crazy. She hadn't imagined it. His silence had been violence.

And under it all, something gentler.

A tenderness. Not yet for him, but for the girl who had grown up in that silence and still found ways to laugh.

For the woman who now stood barefoot in her own kitchen, crying not because she was broken, but because something inside her had finally been acknowledged.

She took the letter outside.

The garden was hushed except for the small, determined sounds of life — bees working the lavender, a butterfly lifting and settling on the fence, the breeze combing gently through the tall grasses.

Late-afternoon light spilled across the lawn, warm and angled, touching everything as though it might coax it into bloom.

She sat in the grass, the earth cool beneath her, and let the air steady her breathing. The letter was folded now, but still in her hand.

She felt emptied. Rewired. A little more established.

26

Insulation

The office hadn't changed; same sterile white walls with motivational quotes in Helvetica, same potted plants trying too hard to look natural in their concrete planters. Even the receptionist's clipped nod was identical — recognition dulled by corporate indifference.

Ella walked through it all as someone returning to a place she plotted to escape. Her heels found a dull, steady rhythm on the grey carpet tiles. People glanced up from their screens, some blinking in performative surprise, others avoiding her altogether, a couple of smiles. No one said her name.

Gwen was already standing when she arrived, one hand resting on the back of her chair like she'd been waiting for a photo op. Her smile was wide but hollow. She gestured towards the seat opposite.

"Ella. You look great," she said, the compliment landing with the weight of a formality. "We've all missed you."

Ella nodded once and sat. The silence stretched, not uncomfortable for her, but enough to make Gwen shift her weight.

"So," Gwen began, "I wanted us to have a proper chat about how you come back in. No pressure. It's all about your wellbeing, obviously. We want this to work for you—– starting Monday."

Ella didn't respond right away. She adjusted the sleeve of her coat and looked out the window, where the city moved on, indifferent to her pause.

"I'll start with working from home three days a week," she said. "And if it works, I'd like to continue that."

Gwen nodded, too quickly. "Of course. Phased return. We can absolutely do that. There are some big accounts we've kept warm for you — things you'll want to get your teeth into, I imagine. Good for you, that sense of… structure. Normality."

"And I'll need an assistant."

Gwen's eyebrows flicked up. "An assistant?"

"I've been holding an entire team's worth of work for a long time," Ella said, even and calm. "If I'm coming back, it has to be sustainable. Or it's a no."

There it was: her voice. Steady, unshaken. The old conditioning still stirred in the background — *don't ask for too much, don't make a fuss* — but it sounded like static from another room.

Gwen laughed, quick and sharp. "Well, I mean, we're all stretched. Budgets, resourcing. But we can… look at support."

"No," Ella said, her voice firmer. "It's not a request. It's a requirement."

Something flickered in Gwen's face. The smile softened into something closer to curiosity. "You've changed."

"I had to."

Gwen opened her mouth to speak and then decided otherwise. They sat in a long, cool silence. Gwen fiddled with her wedding ring, eyes narrowing just enough to register calculation. Ella could almost hear the unspoken line running under Gwen's expression: "*You're not going to be easy anymore, are you?*"

Gwen already working out how long she could keep Ella before she found something better. Something saner.

And she would. Not yet but soon. She could feel it, like Spring underfoot. This wasn't where she would stay, but it would be the stepping stone. The necessary middle.

"I'll email over a revised scope for my role," Ella said, standing, buttoning her blazer. "You'll have it by the end of the day."

Gwen stood too, slower. "It's good to have you back," she said, but it sounded like "I'm watching you."

Ella didn't bother with a platitude in return. She walked out through the sea of screens, past the hum of work on autopilot. People tracked her like a chess piece they hadn't quite identified. She didn't glance back.

By the time she reached the lift, her spine felt taller, her breath deeper. There was power in walking into a place and knowing it no longer owned you. She didn't belong here anymore. But she could survive it — just long enough to launch herself somewhere else.

As the lift descended, her mind flickered to Tom's words from weeks ago: *"This is not a holiday, you know."* The line burrowed in; a quiet echo against the small, assertive requests she'd just made — working from home, support, permissions she wouldn't previously have dared to ask for. Things that would make her life lighter, easier, give her more time for what mattered to her. The thought rose with a sliver of unease: did she deserve these small concessions? Was she asking for too much?

She let the feeling slide past like a shadow, not giving it power. It felt like having new skin; tender in places, but strong. A year ago, she'd have twisted herself into knots trying to prove her worth, to be liked, to be safe. Now she'd asked for what she needed, stated her terms, and the floor remained steady beneath her feet. Not everyone would like this version of her. The one who took up space. The one who could say no and mean it. But if it didn't work here, it would work somewhere else.

By the time she got home, the day's heat was softening. The garden path still held the warmth and the air smelled faintly of cut grass from somewhere down the lane.

She paused at her porch, one hand on the wooden post, and sat on the little wooden seat under its cover. This place wasn't grand, but it was hers. Out here, there were no clipped smiles to decode, no invisible lines to stay within. Just the sound of bees working the blooms and the slow, easy drift of clouds toward evening.

It struck her then: the clean difference between holding your ground because you're braced for a fight, and holding it because you know you belong.

She leaned back, bare feet on the opposite seat, the air cooling against her skin. Whatever came next, she wasn't anchored by anyone's approval anymore. She was anchored by herself. And, more than ever, she was home.

27

Staircase

They arrived early, before the music began, and found the air inside the village hall alive with chatter and possibility. Bunting hung like constellations from the beams, and a chalkboard by the door promised: *'Barn Dance Tonight! All welcome. No rhythm required.'*

Ella stood with a glass of wine, laughing as everyone inspected Una's cowboy boots.

"Purely aesthetic," Una declared. "Structurally useless for actual dancing."

Miranda was deep in conversation with Trevor about folk bands. Leanne had already flung her coat onto a chair and was stretching like she'd entered some competitive warm-up.

Ella looked around and felt that swell in her chest again. These people knew her. Not the version she used to sculpt for safety. The real her — the cracked, soft, loud-quiet, stubborn-hearted woman she was still getting to know; and they loved her because of it.

There was no script anymore. No managing, no posturing. Just a flow of being with others who let her be; who she could hold and be held by. The weightlessness of that filled her like a second breath.

The band struck up — fiddle, guitar, drum — and they were off. Leaping, stomping, spinning, arms flailing, and laughter rolling like a tide against the walls. Ella collided with Trevor, who spun away in a theatrical flourish. She caught Miranda in a do-si-do and they dissolved into helpless giggles, both forgetting the next step.

They danced for hours; wild, ridiculous, and joyful. It was the kind of night that would stay stitched into the fabric of her memory because of the way it made her feel: utterly alive.

At one point she saw Trevor and his wife, Sara, arms looped loosely, foreheads tipped together in a soft moment that somehow held steady against the swirl of bodies. A new ease between them. Their kids tore through the village hall like joyous animals, sticky with cider and cake, their laughter rising above the fiddle and stomp of boots on floorboards.

At the makeshift bar, Miranda leaned toward a silver-haired man in a rolled linen shirt, laughing; not the brittle kind Ella remembered from past parties, but something looser, lighter.

Between dances they gathered at a table, cheeks flushed, hair sticking to foreheads. Anish brought over a round of drinks.

"So, Ella," Leanne began, "serious question. Now that you're single and fancy-free, ideal partner: Go."

"Oh God." Ella leaned back, mock-horrified. "We're doing this?"

"Essential conversation," Miranda said, grinning.

"Alright," Ella said, pretending to think. "Someone kind. And funny. Thoughtful. Likes food. Can drive a manual car. Oh, and tall. Like, proper tall. I want to feel like I have to stand on tiptoes to kiss him."

"Here we go," Leanne teased. "She's ordering from a catalogue."

"Fine," Ella laughed. "Emotionally intelligent, good at back rubs, and owns at least one jumper that smells like fresh laundry and woods."

"You forgot: stormy-ocean eyes and a tragic past," Miranda added, sending the table into howls.

Una's voice was quieter when she spoke. "I thought I'd know too. But it wasn't a list. It was just… a click. Like I could finally exhale." She rested a hand on Martin's sleeve. He met her eyes like there was no one else in the room.

There was a pause, gentle and thoughtful.

"Yeah," Miranda added. "I'm thinking it will be more like chemistry than criteria. Something you can't put in a list."

Ella didn't argue. She felt a small lurch inside. It felt something like readiness.

"OK. The list is out! I am open," she said simply, throwing open her arms. "To however it happens."

Later, as the music slowed and the last of the dancers began to peel away toward coats and leftover cake, Ella slipped outside into the cool hush of the evening. The stars were out, scattered wide and blinking, and her skin hummed from the heat of the hall and the press of bodies and laughter.

Her phone buzzed in her pocket. It was a message from Gwen. "Just wanted to say we've arranged for you to have an assistant when you're back – should take a bit of the pressure off. We're looking forward to seeing you Monday."

Ella read it twice, then once more, her lips curling into a slow, surprised smile. She had asked for help. Said it out loud. Held her boundary strong. Something that would have once felt outrageous – selfish, even. And they'd just said yes; no battle, no negotiation, just a clean, unfussy yes.

The sheer strangeness of it warmed her more than the wine had. She slipped the phone back into her pocket and let herself feel it fully: the unfamiliar, exquisite lightness of being backed, not just tolerated. That she could set terms and not be discarded.

Ella turned back to the dancers, cheeks flushed, feet sore, and heart unaccountably full. So much had shifted. Not all at once and not cleanly, but enough to believe that maybe love could remake itself. That maybe she could too.

As they walked back through the sleepy streets, still high on the magic of the night, they sang half-remembered lyrics and made up the rest. The stars hung low, listening.

At home, she peeled off her shoes, made tea, and stepped into the back garden wrapped in her oldest blanket. Two hedgehogs were already there, eating in small, decisive bites. She watched them, breathing in the cool night air. Monday hovered; not as a threat, but as a tide she could swim with.

If it didn't work, she would adjust. She wouldn't ignore the signs again.

She sat there a long time, listening. Not just to the rustle of hedgehogs or the echoes of music still dancing in her blood, but to the quiet voice inside; the one she had finally made space for.

The possibilities stretched out before her, not like a path to follow, but like a dance floor — open, expansive, waiting for her next wild, beautiful step.

28

Front door

She arrived in the lobby 11 minutes early, jacket buttoned, takeaway coffee cooling between her palms.

Her phone buzzed softly in her pocket — the estate agent. Two offers had come in that morning; solid ones. One from a cash buyer, no chain, and £20,000 over the asking price. It felt surreal, how simple it had been in the end. No protracted negotiations, no last-minute setbacks. Just a clean shift forward, as if the universe had quietly agreed: this chapter is done.

She stared at the message for a moment, half-expecting a catch, then slipped the phone back into her coat. The lift pinged. She breathed in, straightened her spine. Maybe things didn't have to be hard. Maybe sometimes, the path cleared when you were finally ready to walk it.

Upstairs, the office unfolded like a draft. Exposed ducts, a forest of desks — identical, unanchored — and the constant churn of conversation without direction. No one looked up when she entered, or if they did, they blinked and returned to their screens with such disinterest it felt like theatre; a curated nonchalance.

The brashness wasn't loud, not in the auditory sense — it was attitudinal. The way people dressed (performatively effortless), the speed at which they walked (too fast to mean anything), the overlapping jargon flung across the room like competing radio channels. It was a place addicted to appearing busy.

She walked through it without hurry. Her flat shoes made no sound. When someone brushed her elbow, she didn't apologise.

At her desk — unclaimed until yesterday, now with her name spelled correctly — she wrote the date in her notebook. That was her ritual: a beginning, even in places that didn't deserve one.

Gwen passed at speed, already talking into her phone. "Ella, coffee at 11," she called over her shoulder. "Just a quick catch-up, so you can hit the ground running."

The words were smooth, clean, slightly caffeinated. Corporate choreography.

She nodded, just once, and Gwen was gone. Already absorbed by whatever came next.

In the silence that followed, she felt it begin. The microscopic recalibrations. Her system shifting — heart picking up half a notch, breath stretching thinner. Muscles not exactly tensing, but listening. A readiness forming in the blood. Like a tide pulled forward; not quite anxiety, but something ancestral. A signal.

She'd have to draw up energy. Not theatrics, not performance, but a certain precision of presence. Brightness in the eyes. A quickness in speech. Something readable, attuned, and alive to the rhythm of this place that ran too hot, too fast.

And she could do it. Of course she could, that was never the question. The cost, though, was real. Not visible, not billable. But real. She closed her notebook, then opened it again.

Wrote, 11 a.m. — Gwen (coffee). Then underlined it, lightly. She would show up. Not as someone else, but slightly edited; slightly leaned forward. Enough to signal fluency. Enough to buy herself the space she'd need, later, to lean back.

They met in the corner of the café space on the second floor, a pseudo-informal zone with warm lighting and hard chairs. The coffee was free but tasted transactional; burnt at the edges, and in orange plastic cups, like everyone had somewhere more important to be.

Gwen arrived with her own drink already in hand and a tempo that suggested she was doing this between real things.

“So,” she said, lowering herself into the chair opposite, “how is it to be back?”

There was a beat — just enough room for a breath, maybe the first syllable of an answer — and then:

“I’m sure it’s a lot. Everything’s moving fast, obviously. But you’ll catch the rhythm. We’ve switched over to Stackstream since you were last in, you’ll get your head around it.”

She waved a hand vaguely as she continued — Q4 Retention, Ops pivot, “light touch” — waving at the words like furniture in a room she didn’t plan to stay in.

“Oh. Your assistant, Chloe. She’s shared with CapDev, so you’ll have her two and a half days a week.”

The sentence was tossed out lightly, but Ella felt it ± the small split in the seal. Her ‘requirement’ turned into a convenience. The quiet recalibration of her terms without her permission.

She nodded once, more reflex than consent. It was too early to fight. And maybe that was the dangerous part — not the concession itself, but the ease of swallowing it.

“Good to have you on board,” Gwen said, already standing. And then she was gone.

She watched Gwen walk away, clipped strides, already shifting to the next demand. She exhaled once, carefully, and lifted her cup. Still warm. Still awful.

Back at her desk, she opened Stackstream. It greeted her with too many panels. Columns nested inside columns. Color-coded tags with no key. Tasks flowing sideways, upward, in every direction at once.

The interface felt like trying to read a map where every street had changed names overnight.

Khalil, the guy across from her, leaned over when she asked. "Red means late. Grey means it's late but no one says so." He offered a smile, then the earbuds went back in. Connection closed.

She moved onto the emails. It was a task she'd dreaded; had been circling all morning like something rancid in the fridge. And now there was no excuse left.

She opened her inbox. Four thousand, six hundred and thirteen unread.

She stared at the number for a full breath. It wasn't shock, it was something quieter, older: recognition. This was the tax of stepping away; the digital sediment of everyone else continuing without her.

There were subject lines from people who'd moved on, people she didn't know, acronyms that had changed meaning, threads she had once been at the centre of and now couldn't even decipher. She scrolled without clicking. Names blurred. Priorities dissolved. It was all too much and not enough.

By 12:59 she was in her jacket and heading for the river. She didn't tell anyone.

Down the stairwell, out past the clustering smokers, the standing lunchers with their branded salads, through the gates, toward the river.

And there it was: wide, low. Carrying off scraps of leaf and city dust.

Around her, the city kept on. Joggers. A couple arguing gently in French. Colleagues comparing meal deals. A woman crying discreetly while holding a bag from Boots.

It was all there. A parallel world, unmanaged and unmeasured.

Ella didn't check her phone, didn't rehearse anything. Just sat.

Eventually, she reached for her phone. A message from Tom:

"The cash buyer's keen. I can move ahead with them today if you're happy?"

She stared at it for a moment, then typed back: *"Yes. Go for it."* Then put the phone face-down beside her. No second thoughts.

She let herself have it: the full hour. Returned at 2 minutes past the hour. No one had noticed she'd been gone. Or if they had, they'd filed it under 'Not Urgent'.

The office hadn't moved much. A low buzz, occasional bursts of stifled laughter from behind screens. The smell of microwaved spinach and printer toner. Someone had emailed round a shared playlist that no one acknowledged.

She sat down. Began shaping scraps of information into something usable. Not brilliance. Just enough to pass through the system. Her fingers moved steadily. A kind of muscle memory took over, one that didn't need belief, only fluency.

In the background, Stackstream blinked and reshuffled itself like a bored magician. She ignored it.

At one point, Khalil asked if she'd seen a note about the Layer 3 tag. She hadn't, but said she'd find it. He nodded, satisfied, and turned away. It wasn't personal; none of this was.

At 4:47, someone cracked a flat joke about pivot fatigue.

At 4:55, Gwen walked past briskly, phone to ear, nodding at no one.

At 5:03, Ella saved her document, closed her laptop, and stood.

She put on her jacket slowly, precisely. She didn't make eye contact, but she didn't avoid it either.

She felt it then: eyes lifting, the quiet shift in collective air pressure.

This was not the done thing. Leaving at five minutes past five. Not after your first day. Not without a sentence about "just heading out" or "working from home later." Not without a signal that you understood how things worked here.

But she didn't say anything. She walked to the lift, pressed the button, and waited.

It arrived too brightly. She stepped in, alone.

As the doors closed and the lift began its slow descent, a memory rose without warning. A holiday years ago, in a tall apartment block by the sea. She and her dad riding the lift down to the beach each morning, towels draped around their necks. He had been loose, even playful, there. Sunglasses crooked, making bad jokes about the lift being powered by sand, laughing in a way that felt rare, and precious.

The image landed sharp and sweet, and with it a twinge of guilt. Almost as if her body was tugging at her sleeve: *See? The system can hold good things too. Don't push so hard against it. Don't risk stepping out of line.* The warmth of that memory blurred with the unease of the present, unsettling her chest. She gripped her bag tighter, wondering why standing up for herself — simply leaving on time — felt like betrayal.

29

Expenditure assessment

The forest smelt of pine, damp earth, and the kind of silence that still holds sound in it: birdsong, the faint snap of ropes, the far-off clang of carabiners slotting home.

They arrived just after 10, with coffees half-drunk and yawns still stretching their faces. Ella had booked it two days ago, telling them only that she'd thought of the thing she wanted to do. Nothing fancy, nothing luxurious. Now, standing beneath a canopy of tall, watchful trees, the others followed her gaze upwards to a zigzag of cables forty feet above.

"Mate," Trevor said, hands on hips, squinting. "I thought we were going somewhere relaxing. Like a garden centre, or brunch."

"Welcome to my version of brunch," Ella said, grinning and holding up her harness.

Miranda's eyebrow went up as a man in fluorescent orange passed with a coil of rope. Una was already tightening her helmet strap, eyes bright. "God, I've always wanted to do this."

Ella smiled. "I used to drive past this place all the time," she said, stepping into her harness. "Always thought, 'God, that looks terrifying'. And then I'd keep driving." She glanced up at the ropes, swaying in the breeze. "Figured it was time to actually stop."

She paused as she tightened the waist belt. "I don't want to keep avoiding the things that scare me. I've done enough of that. This is about... trying. Seeing what happens when I stop moving away."

Miranda looked over at her, something soft flickering behind her eyes. "So, you're choosing fear?"

Ella looked up toward the trees, the ropes swinging in the breeze, the wooden platforms like little sentry posts in the canopy. "I'm choosing not to be ruled by it," she said.

They clipped in, one by one, gloves secured, nerves showing in different ways; Leanne cracking jokes, Trevor whistling tunelessly, Miranda double-checking her gear like a pro. Ella stepped up to the base of the first ladder, her heart thudding not with dread, but anticipation.

"I might scream," she said over her shoulder.

"We expect nothing less," said Leanne, already reaching for the video on her phone.

And then Ella started to climb — one foot and then the next — the trees swallowing her slowly, the ground falling away like the version of herself who thought this was impossible.

The platform wobbled slightly beneath her boots.

Ella had made it to the top, limbs shaky but intact, heart thumping against her ribs like it wanted to renegotiate the terms of their agreement. The trees were taller up here, more present. The branches no longer background but immediate — green, rustling and close enough to touch. Below, oh my God, way below, the forest floor was a patchwork of shadow and noise: shouts of encouragement, laughter, the occasional clatter of someone fumbling a carabiner.

She was clipped in. Safe. That's what the instructor had said.

Still, the first crossing — a series of narrow wooden slats suspended by ropes — swayed in the breeze like something from a survival show. Ella exhaled slowly, fingers tightening around the safety line. Her throat felt dry. Her legs were already bargaining. Her pulse thundered; a wild thing fighting to escape.

"This is horrible!" she yelled down, laughing.

"That's the point!" Trevor bellowed. "Now scream about it!"

So she did. The sound came out sharp with nerves, then broke open into something else entirely: a shout pulled through with exhilaration.

Behind her, Miranda called up gently, "You've got this. One step at a time."

And that's what it was. One step. Then another. Her breath shallow but steady. The wooden slats creaked and dipped beneath her weight. The whole thing felt absurd: dangling in a harness above a small forest, choosing fear on a Saturday. But something underneath the absurdity burned bright.

Halfway across, she let out a laugh; wild and sudden and real.

By the time they reached the final section – the zip wire high over the river – her muscles ached and her palms were sweating, but her grin was fixed in place.

"You sure you want to go first?" the instructor asked, checking her harness.

She nodded. "I'm totally ready."

He clipped her in, stepped back.

"You'll pick up speed halfway," he said. "Lean into it. Let yourself go."

She stood at the edge of the platform, staring out at the trees, the sweep of river catching sunlight below like a silver ribbon. Her breath caught.

And then she jumped. The drop yanked her stomach into her throat, wind tearing at her sleeves, and then the line caught, turned the fall into flight. The trees blurred, the river flashed silver below, and she threw her arms wide, screaming pure joy into the canopy.

She landed breathless; hair wild, heart hammering with the kind of triumph that doesn't need an audience.

Una zipped in behind her, whooping. "You looked like bloody Superwoman!"

Ella's cheeks hurt from smiling. She unhooked her harness and stood for a moment just watching the others fly in; Leanne shrieking, Miranda laughing, Trevor flailing dramatically like he was being attacked by bees.

Once they had found their land legs again, they headed to a café. It was one of those half-rustic, half-industrial places with exposed brick and potted ferns and a menu that featured words like "heritage" and "labneh." They pushed two tables together and collapsed into chairs, still smelling faintly of bark and adventure. They ordered like people who had earned every bite.

"I still can't believe you screamed 'I'm free!' on the rope bridge," Leanne said, tears of laughter on her cheeks.

Trevor shook his head. "I swear you made a squirrel fall out of a tree."

Una scrolled through videos — Leanne's awkward launch, Miranda's graceful glide, Trevor's flailing limbs — each replay making them howl again. Then Ella's turn: arms flung wide, head tipped back, mouth open in a scream that cracked into laughter halfway across the trees.

She barely recognised herself. Not the shape of her body or the tilt of her head, but the looseness in her; the unarmoured joy.

"Holy hell," she murmured. "I did that."

Miranda tapped her glass to Ella's. "Yes. You did."

Plates arrived in colourful waves; pancakes with berries, halloumi with charred tomatoes, eggs in pools of turmeric oil. The table became a riot of talking over each other, passing things without asking, snorting into napkins.

Ella leaned back, mimosa in hand, watching her friends through the soft haze of contentment. These people had seen her scream, swear, shake, soar — and here they still were, laughing beside her.

She'd spent years moving past things that scared her. Today, she'd stopped. Stepped in. Jumped. Her legs buzzed, her palms were damp, her heartbeat was loud in her ears — and she was *inside* all of it, not watching from a safe distance.

30

Sewerage connection

Her alarm went at 6:10. Not the soft kind that gave you time to unfurl; the insistent buzz that jerked her out of sleep before her body was ready. By 6:50 she was at the station, clutching coffee in a paper cup, shuffling with the others toward the same carriage they always seemed to choose. Three months in and her morning routine had been shaved down to its bare edges: efficient, repeatable, and slowly starving the part of her that used to imagine alternatives.

The train was full of phones, headphones, and faces already set to neutral. She found a seat, slid into it. A man beside her folded his newspaper like origami, elbow grazing her sleeve. Her own reflection wavered in the glass: eyes shadowed, shoulders rounded forward. She tapped a message to herself in her notes app — something about looking up other jobs — and shut the phone again, too tired to type more.

Three years, she thought, just three years. Long enough to clear the mortgage. Then she could think about something else.

By 8:30 she was at her desk. Gwen was already circling the office, a bundle of hair and heels and manic speed, holding a paper cup in one hand and typing on her phone with the other. "Morning, Ella," Gwen said without slowing, voice pitched high like caffeine itself. She moved on before Ella could answer.

Ella opened her calendar. Two meetings later that week had been changed to in-person. Her work-from-home days shrinking right before her eyes. *Great if you could join us in the room, we'll need to workshop this.* She closed the email. Reopened it 30 seconds later.

The office had the usual stale brightness: humming air-con, carpet the colour of surrender. Someone left a pastry box by the printer. She ignored it, circled back twenty minutes later, took one without thinking.

The first meeting: an hour of nodding, bullet points, slide deck. The second: Gwen driving the team through quarterly targets, voice sharp, quick, unstoppable. Ella's leg bounced under the table, her chest buzzing with that old hum. She remembered how she'd once lived inside that hum, mistaking it for energy. Now it felt like erosion.

Three years. Keep the job. Pay it down. Then, freedom.

Lunch never quite happened. A ping at 12:25, another at 1:00, and by the time she looked up it was nearly 2. She ate a sandwich at her desk, crumbs on the keyboard. Told herself she'd go outside tomorrow.

She saw her friends less. Once a week now, maybe, on a Saturday. A dinner with Miranda, Leanne, Trevor, Una. Laughter, wine, the quick intimacy she missed, but rationed like medicine. And yet, even within that small rhythm, she noticed how much they worked to keep her close. They met her off the train for an impromptu drink at the pub, squeezed visits in around her schedule, left voice notes and little video messages to tell her how much they missed her. She loved it, truly; felt a warmth she hadn't let herself feel in months, but there was also a quiet pressure threaded through it. Sometimes she wanted nothing more than to hide, fold herself up, disappear inside her own small space. The closeness, the care, the insistence that she be part of their world was both a balm and a weight.

She'd started meeting Lynne on Thursdays. Old friend, kind enough, someone she'd once kept at arm's length for reasons she could no longer defend. They'd sit in a city café, order soup, talk about nothing urgent. It was easier, somehow, than admitting she missed the others daily.

By four, her eyes ached. She pressed fingers to the bridge of her nose, clicked into another meeting – faces tiled on a screen, everyone talking over each other. She thought again about always taking the stairs that she'd once promised herself. Now she stood on the escalator, carried up with the rest, without moving.

At 6:30 she left the office, light already dimming outside. Back on the train, wedged into a seat by the window, she opened a mortgage calculator, ran numbers again: what if she overpaid by a hundred each month, what if she cut spend at weekends, or put in more hours to get the bonus?

The carriage swayed, the stations dragging past. Her jaw tightened. The train felt like a wall; an obstacle that consumed hours morning and evening, eating into time she could have spent breathing, stretching, doing anything that felt alive. It was a silent tax on her days, costing her energy and patience, costing her presence. If it weren't for that, and for the fact she had made some crazy decision to live so far out, she could leave this job sooner.

Why was she doing this?

Why fight for a mortgage on a house she didn't really need? Why spend hours on trains when she'd once lived in the city, everything close? Why keep pushing down the thrum of disappointment in her chest each day, pressing it flatter and flatter until it stopped trying to surface?

She stared at her reflection. Around her, the carriage swayed. People scrolled, dozed, leaned on elbows.

Maybe she had made all the wrong decisions. The leaving, the returning, the buying, the planning. Maybe she should have just stayed where she was, with Tom, the focus on the job, no detour into "possibility". It would have been easier. Numb, maybe, but easier. She closed her eyes.

When she opened them again, the darkness outside had turned the glass into a mirror. Her own face looked back at her, pale in the carriage light, hair flattened from the day. She blinked, and for a moment saw two versions of herself layered on top of each other: the one who endured, who calculated, who obeyed the grind; and the other — the woman from three months ago — waking in her own house to bird calls, bare feet on kitchen tiles, shoulders open, breathing slow — who wanted to chase something luminous.

The split was so sharp she almost flinched. The two versions pulled at her in opposite directions: the woman who'd chosen the house and the mornings and the friendships, and the one who knew how to survive here, inside fluorescent hours and trains that never gave back the time they took.

When the train slowed into her stop, she opened her eyes again. Her reflection blurred in the motion. She gathered her bag, stood, stepped off. Neither version of herself felt more real than the other.

Back home by eight. Country air, yes, but her body only wanted the sofa. She dropped her bag, lay down, closed her eyes.

She turned out the light at 10:30, already calculating the next day's train. For a moment she wondered what it would feel like to erase the three months she'd had off. Easier, maybe, less cruel to live without comparison, pretend she'd never known better.

Three years, she told herself again. Just three years. Then sleep took her.

***

Saturday evening she went to Leanne's. The house already smelled of garlic and wine when she arrived, coats piled in the hallway, music low in the kitchen. Trevor handed her a glass almost before she'd shut the door.

It was easy, slipping into their rhythm again — the fast jokes, the half-overlapping stories. She found herself laughing more than she had all week, and it was almost physical, the way her shoulders dropped.

Halfway through the meal, Miranda leaned across the table.

"The retreat," she said. "Two months away. You're still good to come?"

Ella nodded before she thought. "Of course."

But the word landed awkwardly in her own chest.

She remembered the first time Miranda had mentioned it, months ago, when her days were still slow and wide. She'd felt a spark then; real excitement, a sense of stepping further into the life she was building. Now the thought of it came wrapped in logistics: taking the Friday off work, arranging cover, losing the weekend to something that wasn't rest. Even imagining it made her tired.

Still, she smiled, because they were all looking at her. "I can't wait," she said, and clinked glasses with Una.

The laughter picked up again. Plates were cleared, more wine poured.

But sitting there, watching her friends, she felt the split again. One part of her was here in the light and warmth of this kitchen – alive, almost herself. And the other part was already on Monday's train, eyes on the mortgage calculator, telling herself three years, three years, three years.

She stayed until late, not because she wasn't tired, but because leaving meant stepping back into the other version of herself. When she finally pulled on her coat and kissed them goodbye, she paused at the door. She felt the line of tasks stretching ahead – each one a little domino she had to tip before she could return to this quiet, loving energy.

31

Electrical wiring

She woke slowly. The air was thick with heating, heavy and slightly stale, pressing in around her. Her body felt stuffy, mismatched, like the wrong size for the life it carried.

It was her birthday.

She hadn't told anyone. Not because she didn't trust them — she did, deeply – but because old reflexes die slow. Partly, it was that she didn't know how she would feel come the weekend. Sometimes the thought of anything social felt exhausting, too much, a weight she couldn't carry. Other times, the desire to be seen, to have someone mark the day for her, was sharp and aching. But asking for it herself felt like asking for love.

And partly, it was habit. She had learned to manage her birthdays for herself. Her mother had made them matter, right up until she couldn't. After that, they faded – acknowledged only in passing by her father, whose gestures were more about duty than celebration. By the time she could make her own choices, she had chosen small: a book, a walk, a gift to herself without fanfare. Once, a massage; another time a train ride to a place she didn't stay long enough to remember.

Today, she planned the same. Tea in the good mug. A new pair of pyjamas she had spent ages choosing, delivered yesterday. Possibly the bakery, possibly not. Leanne had remembered and said she would drop in for a birthday cuppa late morning.

She reached one arm across the duvet now, fingertips grazing the smooth edge of the bedside table. She didn't need to get up yet. The morning was hers.

At eight thirty, she eased her bare feet onto the soft carpet, toes sinking into the fibres. A quiet luxury compared with the bare wood floors of her childhood room.

She slept in the master bedroom now, the one her parents used to sleep in. It had taken time. She hadn't rushed it. But one quiet Saturday, a few days after the house had been signed over to her, she'd found herself painting the walls a pale, chalky pink – warm and soft. She chose a bedframe made of bamboo, low with soft corners that didn't demand anything of the room. A wardrobe to match. Now, it felt like hers. Entirely.

She owned the whole house now, yes; but more than that, she occupied it. Every corner. Every drawer. Her books stacked on windowsills. Her towels folded the way she liked. She could feel it: walls that remembered her, rooms that bore her shape, the new sofa she'd chosen without compromise, the pictures, now hung.

She stood in front of her wardrobe, fingers grazing the familiar fabrics. At the back hung a dress she'd been saving; nothing fancy, just a comfortable favourite she loved but had been too careful to wear. She'd worried it might get worn out, or stained, or somehow lose its quiet magic if she pulled it out too often. But today felt different. Enough waiting, she thought. Gently, she slipped it off the hanger, and put it on. She smiled at her reflection.

Standing by the open back door, coffee in hand, she watched the small garden in its loose morning arrangement.

At some point, she opened a book. Drifted sideways into it. Answered a message from Miranda about something irrelevant. Thought about buying her favourite oat biscuits as a treat later.

She'd just gone to the kitchen to make toast when the knock came.

Not the doorbell. The back door, softly twice.

She turned.

Leanne. Smiling like she was up to something.

Behind her: Miranda, Trevor, and Una, all grinning like conspirators.

"Happy birthday," Leanne said, holding up a takeaway bag and a bottle of wine like they were evidence.

Miranda wrapped her in a tight, warm hug. "Did you think we didn't know?"

Una stepped forward, arms already outstretched, a bright bunch of flowers in one hand. "Happy birthday, fabulous friend."

Trevor followed, giving her an air kiss, as he juggled three cake boxes with theatrical exaggeration and muttering something about choice paralysis.

Trailing behind them were Isla and Milo — Isla clutching a glittery homemade card, and Milo charging ahead with his usual comic intensity. "I helped bake the cake!" he announced proudly.

Ella crouched to their level with a grin and high-fived them both. "A dream team," she said. She gently touched Milo's arm. "That's looking like a proper adventurer's scar now."

He beamed, clearly pleased. "It doesn't even hurt anymore!"

"Good," Ella said, her chest warm. She stood again, catching Leanne's eye, who gave her a smile.

They moved through her house like it was theirs too; coats on hooks, cushions rearranged, someone put on a playlist.

Ella blinked, and not from surprise. From something older. From the knowledge that this, this exact feeling, had never happened on this day before. She stood still for a beat. Just enough time to register the soft, bright hum behind her ribs.

Then came the gifts. Not presented all at once — just eased out of bags, shared in gestures that didn't need explaining.

Trevor and Una handed her a long, narrow box wrapped in brown paper. Inside was a planting voucher and a note:

For the south wall — an apple tree. Something steady and sweet, to root you here. One day, you'll eat from it and remember this beginning.

She smiled, already picturing it, a thrill in her heart. Spring blossoms, small fruit, the satisfaction of pulling sweetness from a branch with her own hand.

Miranda passed her a folded square of card, inside which was a single ticket to a festival she'd once vaguely mentioned wanting to try, if she ever got brave enough. "We will camp," Miranda said. "Or at least try. I've already bought glitter and antihistamines."

And from Leanne, a slim, flat parcel. Wood, engraved. A house name plaque.

'Rise Cottage'

She ran her thumb slowly over the letters, tracing them like a memory. They'd joked about the name once, sitting around the table weeks ago — how the place was rising back up, how she was too. A passing comment, thrown out with laughter and wine, but somehow it had stuck.

She said nothing for a long moment. Then, softly, her voice catching:

"Thank you. Thank you all so much"

Not just for the things. For making her feel she mattered. For seeing her. For marking the day in a way that was real.

Later, they gathered around the coffee table, eating with their fingers, conversation looping and laughter catching. Miranda's stories trailed off in giggles, Trevor topped up glasses while telling them jokes, and Una's laugh set them all off again.

And at one point, Leanne put a hand on her knee, looked at her —

really looked — and said, "Happy birthday, my lovely friend," like it wasn't just a day but a small, private coronation.

Ella didn't know what to say. Didn't need to.

She was here. In her home. With her people.

Love. Joy. Peace. They weren't luxuries. They were the new form of resistance. The new architecture for a life well lived.

32

Joinery

Tuesday 6:30 p.m., city air damp, Ella walked to the library with her coat buttoned tight. Miranda had asked her to lead a short meditation at the retreat. Five weeks away. Enough time, but still she wanted to prepare.

She found the 'Alternative' section tucked into the back corner. Two small tables lined the wall. One was already taken so she slid into the other, spread her notebook, and stacked three titles in front of her: *Breath Practices for Beginners*, *Guided Visualisation*, and *The Quiet Body*.

She opened one at random. Words on breathing. Words she already knew. Her pen hovered over the page but didn't move.

The silence pressed in around her, thick as water. She wanted it, and yet it made her ache.

A shadow crossed the book.

"Mind if I sit here?"

She looked up. A man, mid-thirties maybe. Grey jumper, laptop tucked under one arm, a stack of photocopies under the other. He gestured vaguely at the shelves. "It's by the journals I want."

There were at least four other empty tables in the room.

Her jaw tightened. "There are... others." She cast her arm around the room indicating space elsewhere.

He nodded once. “But this one’s closest.” He set his things down before she could answer.

The scrape of the chair across the carpet jarred.

She bent over her book, pretending to read. The words blurred.

He unpacked in silence: laptop, papers, then a notebook swollen with clippings and folded pages. He opened it carefully, as if it mattered, and began to write.

She felt irritation rising in her chest, sharp and disproportionate. What was it to her if someone else sat here? Still, it prickled. She wanted the quiet back. She wanted the silence; except when it arrived, it only reminded her of the gap inside her, the dull weight she’d been carrying since she went back to work.

Her pen tapped against the paper. The silence between them thickened, no longer neutral.

She turned a page, too loudly.

He glanced up then, briefly, and gave the smallest nod, as if to say he’d noticed her frustration but wasn’t moving.

She looked away. Her cheeks burned with a mix of annoyance and something harder to name.

Beside her, the faint scratch of his pen faltered. He shook it, tried again, then pressed harder, scrawling useless marks in the margin. The repeated drag and scratch set her teeth on edge, each failed attempt raising her pulse.

Finally, he huffed a quiet laugh under his breath at the pen’s stubbornness, and turned slightly in her direction.

“Mind if I borrow one of yours?” he asked, nodding toward the neat line of spares she always kept by her pad.

The request — so casual, as if it cost her nothing — only tightened the knot in her chest.

Without looking at him, she plucked one from the row and held it out. He took it from her fingers, the brush of contact fleeting but electric, too much for such a nothing moment. She pulled her hand back quickly, eyes fixed on the page in front of her as if the words there mattered more than the small ripple in her chest.

"Thanks," he said simply, already bending back over his notes.

She nodded, though he couldn't see it, willing her face to stay neutral. The irritation lingered, but threaded through it was the unsettling awareness of how easily he'd crossed the invisible line she guarded so carefully.

Then he sneezed; a loud, unexpected burst that made her flinch. She blinked, startled, and inwardly cringed – no one sneezed like that. It was sharp and insistent. She found herself irritated in a way that felt almost ridiculous, as if her body was rebelling against him in micro-bursts of judgment.

At 7:45, a voice came over the tannoy: the library would close in 15 minutes.

Ella blinked down at the open book. She hadn't taken in a word. Three chapters skimmed, nothing absorbed. Just sentences sliding off the surface of her brain. She shut it with more force than she meant to.

Across from her, her pen still scratched in his hand. He didn't look up.

She stood and stacked the books together. Cleared her throat – sharper than intended – and when he still didn't glance up, said, almost casually, "The pen, please."

She held out her hand, palm open across the table.

He paused, finally lifting his eyes to hers, and for a heartbeat it was as if the room went still around them. Then, wordless, he set the pen in her hand. His fingers brushed against her skin as he let go – fleeting, accidental, but enough to spark that same restless flicker in her chest.

The pen lay warm against her palm, heavier than it should. She tightened her grip on it, not trusting her expression, unsure if she'd just won back some tiny sliver of control or given something else away entirely.

As she zipped the pen into her bag, her eyes caught on his notebook. Pages swollen, ink smudged, newspaper clippings folded and taped in. Each line written in the same compact hand, as if the act of gathering and preserving mattered as much as whatever it was for. She looked away quickly, annoyed at herself for noticing.

She took the books to a self-service screen, didn't feel like talking to anyone. Scanned her library card and books, and hauled them into her bag. The weight of them dragged at her shoulder immediately. Lugging them across town, onto the train, back out into the dark. It all felt hard.

"Closing," the librarian called again.

By the time she stepped outside, the air was damp and the streetlights shone slick on the pavement. She shifted the strap of her bag higher on her shoulder, wishing she'd just left the books there, wishing she could leave everything there.

33

Drainpipes

By 10 o'clock, Ella could already feel the vibration in her chest. The meeting room was too bright, air thick with the scent of coffee and the faint tang of Gwen's perfume. Gwen stood at the front, hair tied high, her voice pitched to urgency as if the entire quarter's survival hinged on this single hour.

"How can we sharpen the delivery? New angles, fresh language. Ideas?" Gwen's eyes swept the room, sharp and expectant.

Ella sat with her hands folded, silently repeating: *not me, not me, just keep quiet this time*. She'd promised herself she would conserve energy today, no extra commitments. She had work enough already.

But Gwen's gaze lingered a beat too long. The hum in Ella's chest turned to heat in her throat. Before she could stop herself, she leaned forward. "We could restructure the deck — start with case studies instead of numbers. If I put together a mock-up, it might—."

She heard the words spilling, too fast, offering more than she meant to. By the time Gwen smiled and clapped once — "Perfect, Ella. If you could draft something by Monday, that'd be great," — it was too late to pull back.

Nods around the table. Someone typing the action into the minutes.

Ella sat back, pulse hammering. She wanted to swallow the words back down. *Why did I do that?* She could feel the old pattern: step in, be useful, over-deliver, then regret it as soon as it landed. Her chest buzzed harder now, a nervous fizz she knew wouldn't ease all day.

At noon, she met Lynne at a café down the street. One of those chain places with glass counters of cling-wrapped sandwiches and metal chairs too cold against the legs. They found a table by the window, traffic roaring past outside.

Ella rolled her shoulders once, then again. The tightness was back: right side of her neck, down through the shoulder blade, as if something inside her had been clenched for days. She pressed her thumb into the knot, hoping it would ease. It didn't. She blamed sleep. Or the lack of it. She didn't have energy for a deeper reason.

Lynne smiled easily, already unwrapping her sandwich. "Love our Thursday meet ups," she smiled. Her voice carried the warmth of old familiarity, but also something heavier; nostalgia, almost need.

Ella matched her smile, unwrapped her own. She tried to click back into it — the easy chatter, the comfort of old friends. But she felt strained, performing. Her stomach tight, chest still buzzing from the morning.

Lynne talked about colleagues, mutual acquaintances, the small dramas of everyday life. Somewhere in the stream she mentioned bumping into Frances the week before. "She's on six figures now, can you believe? Says it's exhausting, but worth it. Honestly, I think I'll be there next year if I can finally get my boss to see reason about a raise." She gave a little laugh, half proud, half weary.

Ella nodded at the right times, pushed half her sandwich around on the napkin.

Then Lynne leaned in, lowering her voice as if confiding. "Oh, and I heard Tom's seeing someone. Just started. She's younger. Looks nice."

The words landed like a stone dropped into still water.

Ella froze. A flash of heat shot through her chest, her jaw stiffening. She tried to smile, but it felt brittle. "Oh. Right."

Lynne took another bite, kept talking, oblivious. "Apparently they met through friends. Seems early days, but you never know..."

Ella barely heard the rest. Inside, a storm rose sharp and confusing. Did she regret leaving? Did she want him back? Or was this grief for something else — the life she'd once had, the version of herself that had belonged somewhere, with someone? The unfairness of him moving on while she felt stuck in circles?

She checked her phone, though there was no notification. Anything to break eye contact. "Sorry, I've got to head back early. Deadline."

Lynne blinked. "Already?"

"Yeah, sorry." She forced a smile, pushed back her chair, gathered her things.

On the pavement, she inhaled hard, like she'd been underwater. Cold air stung her lungs. She walked fast, no destination, just needing the movement. Tom, seeing someone. The words looped, jagged. Each step felt unsteady, as if the ground itself had shifted.

Eventually, practicality edged back in. She had the whole afternoon to get through. She needed caffeine.

She ducked into the café near the office. Warm air, a hiss of steaming milk, the smell of roasted beans. The queue was short, two people ahead of her. At the counter, a man was talking to the owner, leaning slightly forward, holding a stack of papers.

Soft voice. Familiar. From the library.

"...Just a few flyers," he was saying. "It's a fundraiser — small venue, nothing fancy. Proceeds go toward research for my brother's condition. We've done it before, good turnout."

The owner nodded, took the flyers, and began tacking one up near the till. He handed over another stack with quiet persistence. Not pushy exactly — steady, deliberate.

Then he turned, scanning the queue, and his eyes landed on her. Recognition flickered. “Hi. From the library, right?”

Ella stiffened. “Yes.”

He stepped closer, holding out a flyer. Bold lettering, a date, a grainy photo of a band onstage. “Would you mind putting one of these up at your office? Even one flyer helps.”

She took it automatically, her fingers brushing the thin paper. “I’ll see what I can do.”

“Appreciate it.” His tone was calm, almost matter-of-fact.

She glanced at him, the way he stood — easy, grounded, unhurried in a way that felt alien next to the constant buzz in her own chest. But she dismissed it just as quickly; pushy, she thought. Probably living some eternal-student lifestyle, playing gigs, chasing causes, no mortgage deadlines strangling him at night.

Her order was called. She grabbed the cup, stuffed the flyer into her bag, and walked out without another word, already rehearsing how she’d survive the long stretch of the afternoon.

Back at her desk, the office whirred in its afternoon hum. Phones ringing, keyboards clattering, heels clicking past in urgent bursts. Ella sat, coffee cooling by her elbow, the flyer crumpled in her bag beside her laptop.

She should have been working on the deck she’d volunteered for. Instead, she opened the same slide three times, changed one word, changed it back. Her chest hummed with static.

Tom. Seeing someone. The words kept circling, jagged and insistent. She tried to reason with herself — she didn’t want him. She’d left. She’d chosen differently. But still the image burned: Tom with someone younger, someone fresh. The unfairness of it. The sting of being replaced.

She reached into her bag for her phone and her fingers brushed the paper of the flyer. She pulled it out, smoothed it flat against the desk. A photo of a band mid-song, faces blurred with motion, bold text announcing a night she'd never go to.

Her eyes caught on the smaller print: "All proceeds in aid of research for rare skin conditions."

His voice echoed faintly, "*my brother's condition*". The way he'd said it; steady, no drama, no apology. Just fact.

She shoved the flyer back into her bag, irritated with herself for thinking about it at all.

Across the floor Gwen's laugh rose, sharp and bright, before vanishing into another room. Ella glanced at her blank slide deck, at the coffee cooling, at the inbox filling faster than she could empty it.

She exhaled slowly, turned back to her screen and began typing again, her chest still buzzing with all the things she hadn't chosen.

34

Plumbing

Saturday mornings were different. The air felt expansive as she rounded the corner towards the community centre. Already she could feel the weight of the office, which pressed down on her like a lid, sliding from her shoulders; the clipped instructions, the endless emails, the pressure to be 'stepping up'. All of that could be parked for the next three hours.

She stepped through the doors, slipped off her shoes, and the rhythm shifted again. A ripple of warmth moved through her as familiar faces turned towards her. Hugs, easy chatter, small smiles the low buzz of people glad to be here. The tutor, Fran, calm and measured, moved through the room with an ease that Ella found contagious.

She carried a cushion into the circle on the floor, tucking her legs beneath her as they settled together.

They went round one by one, sharing anything that felt important. When it came to her turn, Ella let her smile widen.

"I look forward to this all week," she said simply. "It's such a relief to walk in here. And massage..." she glanced around the circle, catching a few nods, "it's changing me. My mind, my body – everything feels different. I'm really grateful for all of you."

There was a murmur of agreement, small smiles from the others.

She hadn't planned for it to be more than the introduction course, but when it finished she had just... carried on. Enrolled in the diploma without overthinking, without weighing pros and cons. It had felt like something she wanted to keep doing, and that had been enough.

The first part of the morning was a deep dive into anatomy – muscles and fascia mapped out on diagrams, terms that once felt impenetrable now beginning to take shape in her mind. She liked the precision of it, the way her hands could begin to connect what she learned on paper with what she felt under skin.

When the theory gave way to practice, Fran looked around the group. "Massage isn't about fixing," she reminded them. "It's about listening. About making space."

Ella let those words settle. They felt like a rebellion against her week: no urgency, no endless proving. Just listening. Just being.

They opened and locked massage tables into position, adjusted sheets, rolled shoulders loose. Ella's partner today was Grace, a woman a little older than her with laugh-lines that deepened every time she grinned. Grace stretched out on the table and Ella warmed oil between her palms, the simple ritual already slowing her heartbeat.

They moved into practice. Today it was shoulders and upper back, a new technique demonstrated by Fran before they paired off. Ella placed her hands over Grace's back, feeling the warmth build.

At first, she tried to recall Fran's demonstration – the angles, the strokes, the pace. But gradually her body seemed to know what to do. Her palms found rhythm, her fingertips sensed the give of tissue, her breath synced with Grace's. The noise of the week fell away. The world thinned to presence, to the slow rhythm of her hands, the rise and fall of breath beneath them. Flow carried her, simple and true.

Grace exhaled, a soft sound of release. "That's incredible," she murmured.

The words barely registered. Ella felt herself dissolving into the flow, as if the work was happening through her rather than from her. Time unspooled. By the time the tutor called them to switch, Ella's body felt both lighter and more rooted, like she had landed back inside herself after weeks of drifting.

When Grace's turn came, Ella lay on the table, skin tingling with leftover energy from her own work. She let the pressure come and go, but part of her still replayed the sense of alignment she'd just touched: wild and free, but anchoring too, as though she'd tapped into something unshakable.

At the end of class, they gathered in a loose circle. The tutor asked for reflections. Grace spoke first, still flushed. "I don't know what Ella's got in her hands, but it's special. Honestly, it felt like she'd been doing this for years."

There was a murmur of agreement, a few heads turning her way. One of the men added, "Yeah. Magic hands. You can't teach that."

Heat rushed to her cheeks, a mix of pride and disbelief. For weeks she had been hollowed out at her desk, invisible. Here, she was seen.

As people began packing away, Ella pulled a sheet of paper from her notebook. Her voice trembled slightly, but she pushed through. "Why don't we swap numbers? Start a group chat? We could arrange practice sessions, share notes?"

There was instant enthusiasm. Pens clicked, numbers scribbled. The paper passed from hand to hand until it returned to her, filled with names.

By the time they finished, the energy in the room was easy and unhurried. From the second week, they had begun going together to the café for lunch. They pushed little tables together, ordered sandwiches and mugs of tea. Conversation meandered – favourite films, travel stories, bits of family life.

Ella sat among them, the noise of laughter and overlapping voices wrapping around her, grateful for this pocket of aliveness in the middle of everything.

35

Ceilings

The rain had been falling since morning, steady, fine and unrelenting. By her lunch break, the streets shone slick and grey, puddles gathering at every crossing. Ella hurried to the library with her umbrella angled low, tote bag heavy with books already a week overdue. Fines mounting on titles she hadn't even cracked open.

Inside, the air was warm, damp wool and paper. She dropped the stack at the returns desk, then carried her laptop to the same back corner as before. The table was empty. She slid into the chair, set her bag down, opened a fresh document.

She had one hour of focused time to finalise the meditation she would lead at the weekend. A circle, some breathing, something simple; just ten minutes. She wanted to write it out now, draft the words. But as she stared at the blinking cursor, her chest hummed again, the same high buzz that had been building for weeks. She no longer felt calm enough even to fake it. The thought of telling others how to breathe felt absurd.

Rain ticked against the high windows. The room settled into silence.

The door opened. She looked up.

Him. Grey jumper (did he not own any other clothes?), damp at the shoulders, a folder tucked under his arm.

He caught her eye, lifted his hand in a small gesture of hello. No words, just that. Then he sat opposite her, pulling out his thick, battered notebook, the one swollen with clippings and folded pages.

She stopped typing. For a moment, she simply sat, feeling his presence opposite her. Not intrusive this time. Just... calm. An odd steadiness, like a weight on the table between them.

Against her own instinct, she asked: “What are you researching?”

He looked up, surprised, then smiled faintly. “Different things. Mostly treatments, case studies. My brother’s condition isn’t well understood. So, I keep digging.” He tapped the notebook. “Sometimes there’s something useful. Sometimes not.”

She nodded, not sure what to say. The rain drummed harder against the glass.

He hesitated, then: “I’m Alex.”

She looked at him cautiously, before replying. “Ella.”

“Will you come to the fundraiser night?” he asked.

She blinked. “The gig?”

“Yeah. It’s on Wednesday. Small place, good atmosphere. Worth it for the music, even if you don’t care about the cause.”

She let out a soft, humourless laugh. “I’ll probably be working late. And I have plans.”

“Fair enough.” He didn’t push. Just bent back to his notebook, pen moving in that compact hand.

Ella looked at her screen. The cursor blinked, waiting. She tried to type again, but her eyes kept flicking back to the notebook, to the quiet way he kept going.

Her chest still buzzed. But for the first time in weeks, she noticed another layer beneath it: a quieter rhythm, steady, almost like breathing.

At ten to one, she closed her laptop. The page was still mostly blank, a few false starts scattered like debris. She stuffed it into her bag, stood, and pushed her chair back too quickly – the legs scraping across the floor.

Alex didn't look up. Just kept writing, as if the outside world couldn't touch the steady arc of his pen.

She hesitated, wanted to say something more, but found no words that didn't feel clumsy. So, she gave a small nod he likely didn't see, and walked away.

The rain had thickened. She opened her umbrella, merged into the stream of bodies hurrying back to offices, heels splashing, coats dark with water. The city's rhythm roared around her; buses grinding gears, horns sharp, people clipped and fast.

Her chest buzzed again with the familiar hum of urgency. But somewhere underneath, faint and almost out of reach, she could still feel the echo of the library's hush. The quiet of the table. The calm that wasn't hers, but which had been near enough to touch.

She gripped her bag tighter, lengthened her stride. The office tower rose ahead, glass slick with rain, swallowing her reflection whole as she reached the door.

36

Plastering

By the time Ella clicked send on the last email, the office was almost empty. Screens dark, chairs pushed in, only the faint hum of the air-conditioning left. Gwen had left an hour earlier, breezing out with her usual half-wave, but Ella had been told — directly, firmly — that the client needed the draft *tonight*.

Eight o'clock. Her eyes ached, shoulders pulled tight as if someone were cinching invisible straps across her back. That familiar knot at the base of her neck throbbed. She closed her laptop with a flat snap and slid it into her bag. As she yanked the zip, something resisted; a corner of paper caught, slipped free, and fluttered to the floor: the flyer.

She stared at it, creased and bent. *Fundraiser. Live music. Wednesday 7 p.m.*

The gig was tonight. Her first instinct was to shove it back. But something in her recoiled from the thought of heading straight home — train, pyjamas, collapse — the loop she'd been caught in for weeks. She didn't want her life reduced to office and sleep.

Almost before she decided, she was on the tube, then walking streets she didn't know well, following directions from her phone.

The venue was small; low stage, wooden beams, the smell of beer and damp coats. People pressed close, faces lit by soft orange bulbs. The music was already rolling when she pushed through.

Folk.

Not her style. She liked grit, bass, noise that rattled bones. This was fiddles and soft guitars, harmonies winding like thread. She almost turned around. But the crowd was swaying, bodies loose, people clapping in time. The room itself seemed to breathe.

She bought a drink, stood at the back. Watched.

At first, she resisted; stiff, arms folded, telling herself it wasn't her thing. But the longer she stood, the more the resistance ebbed. The music was simple, yes, but full of care. Lyrics she couldn't quite catch but felt anyway. A warmth moved through her, loosening something she hadn't known was clenched.

And there he was: Alex. On stage, guitar in hand, head bent, voice low but sure. Not charismatic in the glossy way of frontmen. Steady, unshowy. The crowd seemed to anchor around him.

She found herself watching him more than she meant to. *Not my type,* she told herself. Too calm, too earnest. She liked edge, spark, sharpness. Still, her gaze lingered.

By the time she finished her first drink, the band was winding toward the end. She ordered another, half-hoping the night would stretch.

Alex thanked the crowd, announced the last song. People groaned, cheered louder. Ella stayed, swaying slightly now, not ready to leave. As the music stopped and people began to file out, she took a seat at the bar. She picked up a bar mat and set it on its edge, turning it over and over in her hand.

Alex and his bandmates appeared beside her, hair damp with sweat, guitar case now leaning against the wall. He ordered a water then turned and caught her eye.

"You came," he said, with a half-smile that was more observation than surprise.

"Barely," she admitted. "I only got here halfway through. Work kept me."

He nodded. "That figures. You look like someone who gets pulled into staying late."

She frowned, defensive. "What's that supposed to mean?"

He lifted his shoulders. "Just, when we met in the library, you had that... over-clocked look. Like your head was racing two speeds faster than your body."

She huffed a small laugh, though her chest tightened. "Nice. Thanks."

"I didn't mean it as an insult." His tone was even, not apologetic. "Just an observation."

She picked up her drink, turning the glass in her hands like it might distract from the strangeness of him standing next to her.

Alex leaned an elbow on the bar, casual. "So — what did you make of it?"

She raised an eyebrow. "The gig?"

He nodded.

"Honestly?" She let out a breath. "Not really my thing. I'm more... rock, I guess. Loud, messy. That was..." She gestured vaguely toward the stage. "Pretty."

He smiled, not offended. "Fair enough. Folk isn't for everyone. But you stayed."

"Because I didn't feel like going straight home to collapse into bed. That's about it."

"Still counts." He took a sip of water, unbothered.

Ella studied him, curious despite herself. "So, you do this a lot? Play these nights?"

"Here and there. Whenever we can. Some charity gigs, some just for the music. It keeps me balanced."

"Balanced?" she asked, a note of scepticism in her voice.

He shrugged. "Work, family, all of it; it can get heavy. Playing lightens the load. Reminds me there's more than the grind."

She shifted, uncomfortable at the implication. "Well. Some of us don't get much choice about the grind."

He met her eyes steadily, not backing off, but not pushing either. "True. But sometimes we forget we still have choices."

She looked away, stung. Took a sip of her drink, then said briskly, "And your brother? You said... the research?"

"Yeah," he said simply. "He's had a rare condition since childhood. Lots of skin reactions, constant testing, treatments that don't always work. This—," he gestured at the flyers stacked near the till, "Is one way of helping. Not everything, but something."

Ella softened despite herself. "That's... good of you."

"It's just family," he said, as if that explained everything.

They stood in silence for a moment, the bar clinking around them.

She surprised herself by asking, "So what do you do when you're not... fixing the world?"

He gave a quick laugh. "Hardly fixing the world. Day job's boring, honestly. Admin stuff, mostly from home. This—," he tapped the bar lightly, meaning the band, the cause, the night. "This is what I actually look forward to."

She met his eyes then, for longer than she intended. And when she looked down again, she found herself smiling despite herself. He nodded like he understood too much.

The crowd had thinned to clusters, people pulling on coats and voices carrying toward the door. On stage, cables were being coiled, cases snapped shut.

Ella glanced at the time. She should go. She shifted her bag higher on her shoulder.

Alex drained his water, set the glass down, then turned back to her. His tone was almost offhand, as if he were asking nothing at all.

"Fancy a walk one lunchtime? Nothing dramatic. Just to clear the head."

Her instinct leapt in first. "I don't really take lunches." Too quick, too sharp.

He smiled, not put off. "That figures."

"I mean—." She started, then stopped. There was no explanation that didn't sound like excuse.

"Fair enough," he said easily, shrugging it off. "Another time, maybe."

He bent to pick up his guitar case. She finished her drink, suddenly unsure what to do with her hands.

When she finally slipped out into the cool night air, her chest still carried the buzz of the office, but threaded through it now was something else; a lighter hum leftover from the music, the conversation, his steady gaze. She pulled her coat tighter and walked fast toward the station, whispering to herself, almost like a ward: "Not my type. Definitely not my type."

37

Porch

The sea appeared before she expected it – a sudden stretch of silver through the car window, flecked with white, shifting under a pewter sky. On sight, her body relaxed.

She parked on the gravel drive, hands tight on the wheel for a moment longer than needed. It was Friday evening and she was already tired after cramming work in to leave at 4 p.m., to be here. Part of her still wondered why she'd said yes to this.

The house stood square and pale, with huge windows that caught the last of the light. Through the glass she could already see women moving inside — laughter spilling faintly, a glimpse of colourful scarves, mugs clutched in hands.

Her instinct was to retreat; to invent a reason to drive home. Instead, she breathed once, deeply, and got out of the car.

Miranda was at the door before she could knock, her energy brisk and warm, arms already open. "You made it," she said, pulling her in, her voice rich with certainty, like there had never been a chance she wouldn't.

Inside, the space was large and glowing; a long wooden table scattered with notebooks and bowls of fruit, the sea framed in the windows like another guest. Women moved easily around one another, laughter bubbling and introductions flowing.

Ella felt herself fold in, shoulders lowering and voice steadier than she expected when she spoke her name. They set intentions for the weekend, each one a quiet thread of hope laid into the circle. “To finally trust my gut,” one woman said, drawing nods. “To stop apologising for everything,” said another. When it came to Ella, she surprised herself by saying aloud: “To stop feeling split down the middle. To live in one piece.”

There were murmurs of recognition. A woman next to her reached out, squeezed her hand briefly.

By the time they cooked together, chopping vegetables shoulder to shoulder with laughter sparking in the air, Ella was no longer weary. She was awake, alive and threaded into something she hadn’t known she needed.

***

Morning came pale and cool, gulls rising above the water. Ella sat before the circle of women with their eyes closed, her palms damp, her breath shallow. She had written notes, doubted them, scrapped them, rewritten. But once she began speaking – guiding them into breath, into stillness, into noticing – her body knew. Her voice found a rhythm. The room fell quiet, soft, receptive.

When she opened her eyes again, she saw faces loosened and shoulders lower. Someone gave a small smile of thanks. After a pause, a whisper, “That was beautiful. I feel like I can breathe again.” Her own chest felt wide, clear.

Afterwards, Miranda offered a sound bath, bowls resonating through the wooden floor, vibrations threading through bone and skin. Then a walk along the coast, the air sharp and salted, until someone dared them into the sea. Shrieks, splashes, bodies emerging pink and alive.

Later, wrapped in blankets, mugs steaming in their hands, someone mentioned their shoulders aching from desk work. Ella found herself offering a massage, the techniques from her course flowing naturally through her hands. Soon others were asking, and she moved from chair to chair, laughing with them; feeling useful in a way that lit her whole body. The feedback was immediate, delighted: "You've got magic hands," one woman said. Another: "Do you *do* this?"

By Saturday night, Ella's skin felt almost porous with connection.

In the small annex where she and Miranda slept, the air smelled faintly of damp wood and lavender soap. They lay in their twin beds, lamps low and voices hushed.

Miranda turned slightly, eyes soft in the lamplight. "So… what do you think of the retreat so far?"

Ella drew a slow breath, feeling the lingering warmth of the day settle into her chest. "It's perfect… and you are such a beautiful host." She beamed with warmth at her friend. "I didn't realise how much I needed this," she admitted, voice low but steady. "It's like I've been carrying all this weight and didn't know it, I can actually feel it shift."

Miranda smiled, a quiet glow in her eyes. "And your meditation this morning… it was wonderful, Ella. So grounded, so present. You really held the space for everyone."

Ella's cheeks warmed. "Thank you. I just tried to stay out of the way of whatever was coming through."

"And your massages," Miranda added, her tone full of genuine admiration, "The way you move with people, the care you give – it's really something. You've got a natural flow, Ella. People are responding to it in a way that's really special."

Ella felt a small, steady thrill run through her chest.

She turned onto her side, before sitting up again. "Someone asked me out," she said into the quiet.

Miranda snorted softly. "Of course they did. Who?"

"Just a man I met… at the library. Then at a gig." She hesitated. "He's kind. Calm. But, no. Definitely not my type. I just… I think maybe we could be friends."

"Friends," Miranda echoed, with that knowing lilt.

Ella pulled the blanket up to her chin. "Yes. That's all I want. I don't need anything more. Not now."

Miranda made a small sound — not agreement exactly, not disbelief either. Just a sound that held space. Then she reached over, squeezed Ella's hand once across the gap between the beds.

And for the first time in weeks, Ella fell asleep with her chest quiet.

***

Sunday morning began in laughter. Not polite giggles, but wild, messy, tears-down-cheeks laughter, led by Miranda who had them rolling on the floor, clutching their bellies, and gasping for breath. The absurdity was the point: letting go through silliness, through laughter that refused to be contained.

From there, music swelled. Someone dimmed the lights, someone else shook a tambourine, and the room tipped into dance. At first, Ella felt self-conscious, shuffling a little, her limbs uncertain. But soon the beat caught her, and she was moving without thought, spinning, hair loose, arms wide. Around her, women stamped, twirled, swayed with abandon. The sea glinted through the windows, mirroring their energy. Her body felt unbound.

Later, flushed and glowing, after a breathwork session, they collapsed into a circle. Miranda passed a basket of small cards and pens. "One last thing," she said. "Write a note for each person here. Just a few words. What you see in them. What you want them to carry home."

Silence settled over the circle, broken only by the soft drag of pens on paper. Ella paused at first, unsure where to begin; but the moment she wrote the first name, something in her opened.

There was no distance between them now. No polite small talk. Just the strange, steady sense that she had known these women for far longer than a few days — as if some part of her had always been waiting to meet them.

As she wrote, gratitude rose like warmth in her chest. She wanted to keep them all. To hold onto this rare, effortless belonging. The words poured out; flashes of admiration, quiet recognitions she hadn't expected to notice in strangers.

When the cards were gathered, sorted, and redistributed, she found a neat bundle in her lap with her name on the top. One by one, she unfolded them.

'You radiate warmth when you forget to try.'

'Your voice is steady and calm. It carries.'

'There's a fire in you. You have the means to realise your dreams.'

Her throat tightened. They weren't vague kindnesses, they saw her: pieces of herself she'd half-believed lost.

Ella felt weightless, as if the air itself had become lighter over the two days. Her shoulders hung loose, her cheeks ached from smiling. The goodbyes were long and reluctant. She moved from hug to hug, each one warm and unhurried; words of thanks were murmured and phone numbers tapped into phones with real intent to keep in contact. One by one, the women drifted down the gravel drive until the house was quiet.

The sea glittered outside, restless but calm. She stood by the window for a long moment, imprinting the scene into her chest. Miranda was radiant, shepherding bags to cars, laughing loudly, promising follow-ups. Someone pressed a book into Ella's hands — "for the train on Monday. I hope you enjoy it" — and she nearly cried at the softness of the gesture.

Ella and Miranda stayed behind to tidy. They stacked mugs, folded blankets, straightened cushions, the sea still glittering through the windows.

"That was... wonderful," Miranda said at last, rinsing a bowl. "More than I'd hoped for."

Ella leaned on the counter, her cards still in her hand. "I loved it. I didn't want it to end."

Miranda dried her hands, turned. "So, don't just be a guest next time. Run the next one with me."

Ella blinked. Her mind scrambled. Part of her wanted to nod immediately, to leap at the chance, but another part froze; a small, stubborn voice whispering she wasn't enough. She wasn't experienced enough, wasn't worthy of guiding others in something so meaningful.

"I... I don't know if I can." She admitted finally, her voice a mixture of wonder and hesitation.

Miranda's smile was gentle, unwavering. "Exactly why you should. You have the heart for it, Ella, that's what matters. The rest you'll learn along the way."

Ella swallowed, the tightness in her throat softening slightly. The feeling of possibility stretched out before her, bright and trembling – but real. "I'd like that," she murmured, almost to herself, and then looked up at Miranda. "Really, I would."

"Then that's settled. I want to make them longer – five days. We could do so much more." Miranda excited, almost tripping over her words, "You'd be incredible. The meditation, the massages – you lit up. You could lead whole parts of it."

Ella's chest flared with warmth. "I'd love that," she said before she could filter it. The idea glowed.

But the glow snagged almost instantly. "I just... don't know how I'd manage. Time off. Work. Planning. I can barely..." She trailed off, meaning the commute, the emails, the fatigue.

Miranda's voice was gentle. "It doesn't have to be solved tonight. Just

— don't dismiss it out of habit."

Ella nodded. She thought of what she'd said in the circle: I want to stop feeling split down the middle. To live in one piece.

Now here was a clear pull. And the other pull, heavy, inevitable, waiting in the morning. She didn't yet know how to make either work without tearing something.

Later, driving away, the sea shrank in her rear-view mirror. The cards sat on the passenger seat, words still radiating from the paper, edges fluttering in the breeze from the open window. The glow of the weekend clung to her skin, to her ribs.

It wasn't until she was alone, pulling onto the narrow road away from the coast, that the silence hit. The women's laughter no longer wrapped around her. No sound but the engine, the faint rush of wind.

And then the looming of tomorrow. Gwen's clipped voice. Emails. Meetings. The hard glass tower. The tight air. Her chest caved slightly.

She drove on, the weight of two directions pulling at her chest, the sea shrinking in her mirror.

38

Alarm system

By Thursday, the glow had thinned to a faint trace. The office air felt too sharp, too fast. She sat at her desk, fingers hovering above the keyboard, the spreadsheet in front of her pulsing with lines of figures she couldn't quite absorb.

Instead of typing, she found herself opening a browser.

Typed: '*Alex folk band The Embers.*'

A cascade of posts appeared: grainy photos of him on stage, his bandmates mid-song, an awkwardly cropped flyer, links to donation pages, a thread about money raised for rare illness research. She scrolled.

Some of it impressed her: the amounts, the evident commitment. Some posts made her cringe: earnest hashtags, badly written appeals, a kind of scrappy amateur energy that felt far from her polished office world.

What am I doing? She thought, closing the tab too late. The act itself left a residue.

She switched to another tab, quick, impulsive. Booked the third-level massage course. The confirmation email pinged into her inbox almost instantly. Her chest flickered; excitement, guilt, relief all layered in one.

Back to the spreadsheet. Try again.

Her phone buzzed. Miranda.

> *"Any plans for Christmas? Come to mine if not. Just me and you. You'd be welcome."*

Ella stared at the screen, thumb hovering. The idea glowed, tempting, a small smile tugging at her chest. Yet another part of her longed only to sink into silence, to curl on the sofa with no words demanded, no brightness to step into. Some days stillness felt like the only balm, even if it brushed up against loneliness.

She typed back something noncommittal. "*Will think about it. Thank you. See you in a few hours xx"* Then slipped the phone face down on the desk and stared at the monitor until her eyes stung.

Tonight was the post-retreat integration session. She'd blocked her calendar, told herself she'd leave the office early to make it across town.

At 6:15 p.m., she was still at her desk. Gwen had dropped another "urgent" into her inbox at 5:40. By the time she'd cleared it, the idea of crossing the city was impossible. She logged on instead, laptop propped awkwardly in a breakout room, camera flickering.

At first, nothing, just a frozen icon, her face pixelated in the corner. Then, finally, the grid of faces appeared. Familiar smiles. Bright scarves. Hands waving. She felt her chest lift.

But no sound. Just mouths moving. The women laughing, eyes shining, and silence on her end.

"Can you hear me?" she said into the void. Nothing.

She tried again. Adjusted settings. Restarted. Still nothing.

For 10 whole minutes she wrestled with it; their voices must be there somewhere. She slammed the trackpad, muttered curses, tried again. Still nothing. The laughter of women she'd hugged just days ago was out there, filling a room she couldn't reach. Finally, she typed into the chat: 'Can't get sound. So sorry. Missing you. Have a beautiful evening xx.'

A couple of thumbs-up emojis popped back, hearts in reply. They were kind. But she couldn't bear it. She shut the lid too hard, the screen snapping dark.

Her body jolted with the sudden absence. Then came the outburst, her fist hitting the table once, sharp. "For fuck's sake!" The words tore out loud, raw and hot.

She pushed her chair back, stood, paced the room in tight circles, breath jagged. Angry at work. Angry at herself. Angry at the way her life narrowed back so quickly, as if the weekend had been only a dream.

Instead, she pressed her palms to her face, muffling another ragged sound, and let herself sink over the table.

Alone. Again.

***

By Saturday she was back at Leanne's kitchen table, a mug of tea in front of her, crumbs from a shared cake still on the plate. Trevor had his laptop open like a conspirator, Una leaning over his shoulder, Miranda perched with her glass of wine, eyes gleaming with mischief.

"We're doing it," Trevor announced. "No arguments."

Ella groaned, pulling her jumper sleeves over her hands. "I can't, dating apps are..."

"Necessary evil," Miranda cut in. "And you need some fun."

Una squeezed her hand. "We'll help. That way you don't end up sounding like you're writing your CV."

Leanne grinned, pulling the laptop closer. "Okay, pictures first. Which ones do you have?"

They bickered good-naturedly over photos; dismissing anything too polished, rejecting the ones she'd half-hoped might pass, laughing at Trevor's attempts to find her "sultry angle." At last they agreed on three: one from the retreat (someone had caught her mid-laugh); one of her on a coastal walk, hair wild; and one simple, close, soft.

Then came the words.

"What do you love?" Miranda asked, pen poised.

Ella hesitated. "I don't know. Walking. Cooking sometimes. Reading. Massage, now, I guess."

Trevor typed as he spoke aloud: Loves books, outdoors, new adventures. Learning massage. Has a proper laugh, occasionally snorts when wine is involved.

"Delete that last bit!" Ella yelped.

By the time the profile was live, her cheeks hurt from smiling. For a moment she let herself enjoy the ridiculous solidarity of it – all of them crowded around, teasing, typing, egging her on.

That night at home, she had messages waiting. Bland greetings, the odd cheesy opener, one or two more thoughtful. She found herself replying to a man named David; professional-looking photo, friendly smile.

Two nights later, she met him at a bar near the station.

He was exactly as pictured: neat, well-dressed, with that relaxed smile that put her at ease. He told her stories about work travel, about his marathon training, about a friend's wedding disaster involving a runaway dog. He was funny, animated. She laughed more than once.

She told him bits about herself; snippets of her hometown, her time off, the massage course. He nodded along, chimed in with another anecdote of his own.

The food was decent. The wine helped. She caught herself thinking, *This is fine. This is good. He's nice.*

But as the evening stretched, something began to itch. She realised he hadn't asked her a single question, not one. Not why she'd been off work, or what she loved about books, or what the massage training meant to her. She was an audience, not a participant.

Walking back to the Tube together, his stories spilling over the pavement, she turned it over in her mind. He ticked boxes: kind eyes, stable job, easy humour. *Am I being too picky?* She thought. *What if this is what's out there and I'm dismissing it?* A sharper thought followed close behind, one she barely let herself name: *What if I'm someone who doesn't know how to follow through at all?*

But beneath the surface evaluation, something deeper sat stubborn: This is not enough. She wanted more than boxes ticked. More than pleasant chatter.

She wanted to feel met. Seen.

At the barrier, he gave her a polite hug. Promised to be in touch. She smiled, thanked him, went down the escalator alone.

39

Driveway

It was raining again at lunchtime and Ella told herself she was only ducking into the library to keep dry. But her feet seemed to know otherwise, carrying her past the automatic doors, the familiar hush pressing in.

And there he was. Same table, same posture; a bit hunched, but easy. Alex, with his scattered notes and an open laptop, pen tucked behind his ear.

She hesitated. She could leave. She could drift into another aisle. Instead, she heard her own voice: "Hi."

His head lifted. That immediate smile. "Hey. Good to see you." He pushed a chair out with his foot, casual. "Have a seat."

Something about the way he did it, like she belonged there, softened her enough to take the seat.

She went to find books, came back with two on massage and put them down in front of her, almost defiantly. "I've started a course," she said. "Third level now."

"Massage?" His eyes lit up. "That's brilliant. How are you finding it?"

And he waited, actually waited. She found herself talking about techniques, about feedback she'd had, about how people at the retreat melted under her hands. He listened, nodding, leaning in slightly as though this mattered.

When he spoke, it was to share. "I'm actually working on a festival," he said, tapping his pen against the table. "Bit mad. I know a lot of bands, been to loads over the years. Thought, why not pull it together myself? But it's… big. I'm a bit in over my head."

He pulled a folded map from his notebook, spread it between them. Lines and shaded blocks, arrows marking entrances. "The problem right now is the campers. How to get them in without clogging up the main gates. Look, this track here—."

She bent over the page, unexpectedly absorbed. His enthusiasm was messy but real, spilling over as he described morning yoga sessions, sound baths, meditation tents, afternoons of music, stalls, food.

"Oh, hey. Would you…" He hesitated, eyes flicking to hers, "Maybe want a stall? Doing massage?"

She felt herself spark. A flare of warmth in her chest. "Actually, yes, I'd love that." And before she could stop herself: "I know someone who could lead a meditation too if you need that. She's incredible. Miranda."

"Perfect." He grinned, scribbled her name in the corner of the map like it was already happening.

Then: "What's your number? Just so I can confirm details once things are final."

For a heartbeat, she hesitated. The tiniest prickle of caution; she barely knew him, and a part of her wondered if she was handing herself into a scam. But the warmth in his eyes steadied her. She gave it anyway, the digits tumbling from her lips with a strange mix of nerves and trust. For a moment, she was caught by the possibility, the strange joy of being asked, of being useful in the right way.

Then her phone buzzed; a reminder to head back. She stood, slipping the books into her bag.

"Listen," he said, almost too lightly, "if lunch hours don't work for you, how about a drink after work sometime?"

Her stomach dropped. Heat rising, fast. Of course. That's what this was. Not about massage, not about the festival. He'd only asked because he wanted something else.

She forced a polite smile, half turning away. "I'll... think about it."

Walking back into the rain, books heavy in her bag, she felt the familiar twist; hope tipping into irritation, possibility soured into suspicion. She wanted to believe she was being asked for her ideas. For once.

But wasn't it always about something else?

Rain needled sideways. Ella tucked her chin into her coat and walked fast, phone cold against her ear.

Miranda picked up on the second ring. "Hey, you. Survived Monday part two?"

"I just came from the library," Ella said, breath fogging. "He was there."

A beat. "Alex?"

"Yes. Same table, like he's part of the furniture." She stepped around a puddle, failed, felt the cold soak her sock. "He... asked me if I'd do massage at a festival he's organising."

"A festival?" Miranda sounded delighted. "That's very you."

"It's probably not even real," Ella said too quickly. "He had a map and everything, but it could be... I don't know. A doodle, a fantasy. People talk."

"What did the map look like?"

"Like a map," Ella snapped, then softened. "Entrances, arrows, scribbles. Morning yoga, sound baths, meditation. Then music and stalls. The kind of thing that would make me stupidly happy if it existed."

"So... why are we trying to prove it doesn't?"

Ella stopped at the crossing, watched the traffic nose past in shining lines. "Because the second I lit up, he asked me for a drink after work. And now I can't tell if the massage thing was just... tactic."

Miranda hummed. "Or maybe he's a human man who liked your ideas and wants a drink."

"Don't be reasonable," Ella muttered, stepping off the curb. "I'm busy catastrophising."

"Did you say yes?"

"I said I'd think about it." She paused. "I don't want to be a hook for someone's hobby. I want to be... asked for real."

"Did he ask you for your ideas? Did he listen?"

Ella pictured the map between them, his pen tapping, the way he waited when she talked about the course. "Yes," she admitted. "Annoyingly, yes."

"Then hold both truths," Miranda said. "You were seen for your work and he fancies you. That's not a crime."

"It complicates things."

"It's life," Miranda said lightly. "Also, a stall means you could practice. That spark in your voice? I could hear it from here. If the festival is real, you should do it. And I'll lead the meditation. Obviously."

Ella felt the small tug in her chest again, traitorous and warm. "I hate how much I want that."

"I love how much you want that."

They walked each other's silence for a few steps; the rain, the distant siren, the clatter of someone's umbrella flipping inside out.

“Text me the details when you have them,” Miranda added. “Or, if it’s a grand delusion, we’ll start our own festival in a field.”

Ella laughed, surprised by the sound. “Fine. But only if there’s a massage tent.”

“Non-negotiable.”

“I’m nearly at the office,” Ella said, the glass tower rearing up, rain slicking its sides. The buzz in her chest began its familiar climb. “I’ll… try not to Google him again at my desk.”

Miranda smiled through the line. “Or do. And then email your notice.”

“Too soon,” Ella said, and ended the call before she could entertain this line of conversation. She slipped the phone into her pocket, wiped rain from her brow with the back of her wrist, and pushed through the revolving door into the bright, humming air.

40

Garden path

The restaurant wasn't fancy: brick walls, wooden tables, candles in jars that dripped uneven wax down the sides. Ella had suggested somewhere neutral, not her usual places, and not his. It was halfway between their train stops, which seemed important.

In the days since they'd exchanged numbers, messages had gone back and forth. Quick notes about the festival site, ideas for stalls, a photo he'd sent of the field under a bright sky. Then, casually, he'd added: *"I'd love to chat more about this sometime. Maybe grab a bite after work one day?"*

She'd stared at the screen for a moment, weighing it. The thought of stepping into something unknown prickled, but she'd typed back: "*Why not. Just as friends.*" He'd replied with a thumbs-up and a smile.

He was already there when she arrived, jacket slung over the back of the chair, a pint half-drunk in front of him. He stood as she shrugged her coat off; easy smile, no fanfare.

"Good choice," he said, gesturing at the table like it had been waiting for them all week.

They ordered food neither of them pretended to care much about, though Alex made a point of quizzing the waiter about the dessert menu.

When the plates came, they ate at first in the ordinary way, conversation circling work, weather, trains. But then something shifted; a pause, a lean closer, an ease.

He told her about the people he kept around him. “Life’s too short for average,” he said, tearing bread with his fingers. “I’ve got this motto: eat cake every day. Not literally, though sometimes literally. Just... don’t settle. If the choice is between good and mediocre, why on earth would you pick mediocre?”

Ella tilted her head, watching him. “That’s... almost charming. Almost smug.”

He grinned. “Smug cake is still cake.”

And then they were off. She found herself talking about the importance of the right people, how the wrong kind can dull you, make you small. He nodded fiercely. “Yes. That. People who live half-asleep; it rubs off. I can’t do it.”

She thought of the office, the humming glass box. How she shrank there.

He asked questions, waited for answers. She surprised herself with how much she said. About Miranda. About the retreat. About silence, and how it was both terrifying and necessary. She didn’t feel like she was trying to impress. Just... sharing.

When the plates were cleared, he leaned back, arms folded. “So, Cake every day. What’s yours?”

She blinked. “My cake?”

“Yeah. What you won’t compromise on. The thing that makes life worth it.”

The question sat between them, heavy and kind. She sipped her drink, felt the warmth bloom low in her chest.

“I think...” She paused, choosing carefully. “It’s about feeling alive. Work; that’s numbness, and right now I can’t see a way around it. But because of that, I need to make sure I fill the rest with things that wake me up. Friendships, swimming in the sea, massage, nights like this. If it doesn’t spark something, I don’t want it.” She hesitated, voice lower. "And maybe one day I'll find a way to make it more than the edges. I'll build a life where it's the centre."

When she looked up, Alex's gaze was steady on hers, the faintest crease between his brows, as if he'd caught the yearning tucked beneath her words. But he didn't press, just lifted his glass.

"To not being numb."

Her mouth tipped into a smile as their glasses met, but inside, the words lodged deeper; not a toast, but a quiet vow. They clinked, the sound small but definite.

She felt the possibility of something — not romance, not yet, maybe not ever — but the spark of being in company that lifted rather than pressed her down.

The waiter cleared the last of the plates, left them with their drinks and a plate of shared cake — Alex's insistence, of course.

The door swung open and two men breezed in, eyes searching the room for a free table. Alex's face lit up. "Oi! Dan, Rob!" he called, waving them over.

They grinned, weaving between tables. "Typical to find you in the pub," one of them teased.

"Always reliable," Alex shot back, standing to clasp their shoulders in quick hugs. He turned to Ella, his hand resting lightly on her chair. "This is Ella. Ella, these two reprobates are Dan and Rob. Old friends; bandmates, once upon a time."

"Still the talented one," Dan said, jerking a thumb at Alex.

"Still the late one," Rob added, and they all laughed.

"Sit down, join us. Have some cake," Alex said, pulling out a couple of spare chairs without hesitation.

Conversation darted easily — old stories about missed trains, a tale about a disastrous pub quiz where they'd bet a round of drinks and lost spectacularly. Ella found herself laughing, caught in the gentle rhythm of it, surprised at how naturally she was drawn in. She realised it wasn't just the jokes or the stories; it was the way Alex wove her into the circle, like she'd always been there.

After half an hour, Dan checked his watch. "We'd better head – curtain's up soon. See you Thursday, mate?"

"Wouldn't miss it," Alex said, clasping his hand.

They waved their goodbyes and were gone, leaving behind a faint wake of laughter and something lighter in the air. The table seemed smaller now, quieter, as if the evening had folded itself back around just the two of them.

Alex shifted his chair a little closer, easy and unhurried, as they leaned in over the last of the cake. Candlelight caught the curve of his cheek, warm against the shadows. His knee brushed hers — casual at first, then less so when it didn't move away.

Ella felt the spark in the contact, a hum that lingered. Her body noticed him; the warmth, the nearness, the way he seemed to carry a quiet anticipation just beneath his skin.

They were still laughing over something ridiculous — Miranda's plan to bring antihistamines to a festival — when he tipped his chin toward her, elbow on the table, voice dropping low.

"You know, I really like talking to you."

She held his gaze, steady. The flicker in his eyes made it obvious what he meant. Chemistry buzzed between them, a live wire.

And yet inside, a quiet certainty: *I don't want this to be more.*

She smiled, soft but firm. "I like it too. But just to be clear — for me, this is friendship. I'm not looking for anything else."

Something flickered across his face — surprise, maybe disappointment — but then he nodded, quick recovery, lifting his glass as if in toast. "Friends then. I'll take it."

She let out a breath she hadn't realised she was holding, grateful for his grace.

But inside, she felt the mix: How good it was to sit with someone who got her, who cared about the same things, who asked and waited for answers. How alive she felt in conversation, lit in a way she rarely did in the city. And how clear she was that he could never be more than this. Even with the spark, even with the brush of knees and the candlelight heat, she didn't fancy him.

It was a relief, almost. To enjoy the closeness, the ease, without tumbling into the hunger that used to eat her alive.

They stepped out into the night, cold breeze soft against their coats. Alex opened the door for her, shoulder brushing hers as they stepped onto the pavement. The night had that after-dinner hush — traffic muted, city softer. Alex walked beside her, their shoulders almost touching. She could feel his presence; warm, willing and open.

And she thought, this is what I've been longing for: more friends who see me.

For a few steps, they walked close, her arm catching his as they dodged a puddle. The warmth of him lingered, too near, and she felt the charge again.

She hated it.

Why did he have to go and ruin everything? She'd loved the conversation; the spark of ideas, the rare sense of being seen without performance. But now it felt tainted, threaded with an expectation she didn't want to meet.

Why couldn't he just let it be what it was: two people connecting, without the tilt into something more?

They reached the station, said their goodnights. He hugged her lightly — friendly, but not quite neutral — and she managed a smile before turning toward her platform.

On the train, pressed against the window, she let her thoughts spool.

She didn't fancy him. Chemistry was one thing; her body responding to closeness, the accident of candlelight. But attraction was different, and she knew herself enough now not to blur the lines.

So, friendship, she thought. If he could hold to that, if he didn't push.

And if he did? She'd walk away.

Because she wasn't going to bite her tongue again, not for anyone.

She remembered how it used to be with Tom. The early days, when she'd brushed off her own hesitations. When the first red flags felt more like tiny flickers, easily ignored. How she'd told herself to push past them, to be grateful someone wanted her.

Back then, she had bitten her tongue so often it had almost become reflex. Let him fill the space, let him decide the pace. And later, the biting wasn't just silence, it was swallowing whole parts of herself.

She'd lived years inside that ruin.

Tonight was different. The spark with Alex had been real – the rare joy of feeling seen, of ideas bouncing bright and easy. And still, the tilt into wanting more had soured it. But she'd caught it as it happened. Named it. Drawn the line.

That was new.

41

Tiling

Ella had tidied the kitchen twice before he arrived, fussed with cushions, then scolded herself for fussing at all.

When the knock came at the door, she felt the oddest flutter; anticipation dressed as irritation.

Alex turned up in his usual way: no flourish, a smile that reached his eyes. He paused just inside, eyes taking in the sitting room.

"This is lovely," he said simply, trailing his fingers along the edge of the shelves of her books and favourite items. "Feels… lived in. Warm."

She gave a small laugh, half deflecting. "It's just a sitting room."

"Yeah, but it all feels like you."

Ella shifted, uncomfortable at being so clearly seen. "It's coming together."

He smiled, softer. "I like it."

He wandered across the room and stopped in front of her new painting on the wall. For a moment he just looked, head tilted slightly, the silence thick with attention.

"This is beautiful," he said at last, voice low, almost reverent.

Ella moved to stand beside him, following his gaze. "I bought it the week I decided to do things differently," she said quietly. "When I'd finally chosen the house, and chosen myself, and stopped waiting for someone else to give me permission."

Her fingers brushed her forearm, not nervously this time, almost reverently.

"It felt like the first thing I'd ever owned that wasn't tied to someone else's version of me. No shared taste, no compromise, no 'will this fit the life I'm supposed to have?' Just... something I wanted. A marker."

She exhaled, a small shake of disbelief in the breath.

His eyes stayed on the painting for a long beat, then shifted to hers. "You chose well," he said simply, and she felt the words land in more ways than one.

She busied herself pulling on her coat, boots waiting by the back step – one of three pairs now scattered in different corners of the house. Some in the old shoe rack out of habit, some left by the front door, one pair kicked off wherever she'd happened to stop. Just lived-in, allowed. Her father's strict shoe rack rule now a distant memory.

"Shall we?"

And then they were outside, boots crunching through the damp grass, hedgerows whispering on either side. The fields opened out gradually, the land dipping and rolling towards the hint of sea. The air smelled faintly of salt, though they were still a good mile inland. They walked easily for a while, shoulders brushing now and then, silence that wasn't awkward. Ella broke it first.

"So, tell me about the festival. Really. How did this all start?"

He glanced at her, then back at the path. "Honestly? I've always loved them. The mix of it; music, sure, but also everything else. Strangers camping side by side, sharing food. Kids running half-wild. People lying on the grass at two in the morning listening to a band they'll never remember the name of. It's like... a temporary city where everyone belongs. People come alive. They dance with people they'd never meet otherwise. It's a kind of magic; a community that only lasts a weekend, but for those days it feels like the best possible version of the world."

Ella nodded slowly, watching the outline of the coast inch closer. She could picture it; his version of belonging, of connection, pulsing through tents and fields. Part of her thrilled at it. Part of her envied how simply he could claim it.

"So… how do you manage it?" she asked lightly. "Financially, I mean. Festivals can't be cheap."

He didn't flinch. "They're not. But… I get a stipend from my family. Enough to live on, cover the basics. They've got money. So I'm not scraping by. I can take risks, try things."

Something in her tightened.

She kept her eyes forward, but the cold ran through her chest. Of course. That's how. The ease, the freedom – it was cushioned by something she'd never had.

"I know it's a privilege," he said quickly, maybe catching her shift. "Believe me, I do. And I'm investing and hoping I can build something through this festival so that I can stop relying on it."

Her mouth twisted. "It's just… different, isn't it? You get to dream. You can make mistakes. There's always a net."

"And you didn't."

"No." Her voice came out blunt. She pulled her coat tighter. "I've never had the luxury of free-fall. Every choice I've made has felt like survival. Mortgages, bills. One wrong step and it all collapses."

He didn't argue. Somehow that made it worse.

They walked in silence, gulls looping overhead. She could feel him beside her, warm, steady, and, infuriatingly, she wanted to lean into that steadiness even as she resented it. A part of her wished he'd reach over and hold her hand.

"I've always hated money." She said finally. "It's always been pain. Limitation. What it cost me to make money."

Alex watched the horizon, his voice gentle. "So, money's always been punishment. Not possibility."

"Yes."

He glanced at her then, eyes clear. "But don't you see? You hate it, but you still let it rule you."

The words hit hard.

"That's not fair. I've had to—."

"Maybe. But you just told me: the house, the job, every decision you've made. You call it chains, but you still hand it the keys."

Her chest flared with anger; but underneath, something uncomfortably close to recognition.

They reached the rise, sea spread wide and grey beneath them. Wind tugged at her scarf.

Alex pointed toward a scatter of gulls, circling. "Look at them: seemingly chaos, and somehow they never crash."

She followed his gaze. The birds wheeled and darted, wings overlapping, white against grey. For a moment, she let the sight steady her.

"They just... trust," she said, surprised at her own words.

He gave her a sideways glance, a small smile. "Exactly. Trust there's space for them. Trust they won't fall."

She hated that the metaphor landed. That it made sense. That it showed her what she didn't want to admit: money wasn't the enemy. It was her relationship to it that had carved so much fear into her choices.

Something in her chest eased. The sharpness of their earlier exchange thinned, gave way to a quieter current. They talked more easily then; about music she'd loved in her twenties, about a neighbour's dog that had taken to barking at her kitchen window. She laughed, brittle but real, when he told a story about nearly burning down his flat with a frittata. The air eased. Their steps found rhythm again.

Still, inside, the pebble remained: What would I need to change so money stops ruling my decisions?

She could feel his arm brush hers now and then, heat flickering up her skin. Part of her wanted to slip closer, another part called that weakness; a dangerous softness.

He wasn't her type, not even close. And yet the chemistry threaded between them; undeniable, unwanted, a current she both resented and craved.

As they turned back towards the village, gulls still looping overhead, she tried to breathe into both truths at once:

The joy of being seen, and the fury of the divide between them.

The spark, and the certainty it could never be more.

By the time they reached the cottage again, a quiet had settled over them. Charged, like something waiting to be named.

At the back door, she reached for the handle. He lingered just behind her, his presence warm in the cooling air.

"Thanks for today," he said. "It was... good."

She turned, met his eyes, and the pause stretched. He leaned in slightly; not a kiss, but close enough that she felt the pull of it, the question hovering.

Then he stepped forward and wrapped his arms around her. Not the brisk squeeze of friends but something longer, slower. She felt herself soften against him for half a beat before pulling her spine straighter, resisting the drift into his warmth.

Her heart jolted, her skin alive with the contradiction of it. She wanted, and she hated that she wanted.

When he let her go, she laughed lightly, deflecting. "You could come in… for a tea, if you like."

But even as she said it, her body betrayed the truth – her hand tightening on the doorframe, her shoulders angled towards the house as though ready to retreat, her tone too casual.

He caught it, of course he did. His smile was easy, but his eyes searching. "Not tonight. Another time."

Relief flooded her chest. She nodded, stepping back into the doorway. "Yes. Another time."

He gave her one last look, something unreadable in it, then turned down the lane, boots scuffing against the gravel.

Ella closed the door gently behind her, leaning against it for a moment. The hug still lingered in her skin, an echo she didn't want to concede she missed already.

She breathed out, long and shaky. Alone was what she needed. Alone was safe.

Still, the question throbbed inside her:

Why did part of me want him to come in, when I know I don't want him at all?

The hug lingered longer in her body than she wanted to admit. For the next few days, she felt it like an imprint; not just on her skin but somewhere deeper, unsettling.

They began messaging regularly, at first light, ordinary things – a photo of the sea, a joke about a bad sandwich, a song recommendation. Then longer exchanges: voice notes, late-night phone calls where she curled under her duvet, phone warm against her ear.

Sometimes she found herself slipping, sending pictures not because she wanted to, but because she thought they showed her in the right light; a meal plated neatly, a view she imagined he'd approve of. She could feel the old pull of performing, of curating herself for someone else, and even when she noticed it, she couldn't quite make her fingers stop.

It was ridiculous, she told herself, they weren't together. And yet she found herself looking forward to his name lighting her screen, to the small ping that pulled her out of work, to the easy flow of his voice in the evenings.

If she squinted, it looked exactly like a relationship. She hated that thought. She loved it too.

One evening, his voice sounded more ragged than usual. "It's the entrances," he muttered. "Security wants barriers in some key places, but if I put them in, everyone's going to bottleneck. It'll be chaos."

She frowned, half-smiling at his intensity. "Send it to me and I'll take a look."

There was the sound of paper shuffling, his phone taking a shot. A minute later, her phone pinged with a photo of the map, arrows thick and urgent.

"See? Nightmare," he said.

She leaned over the image on her screen, tracing the routes with her finger. "Not if you split the campers. One path for the early arrivals, another for late check-ins. Stagger it."

There was silence, then a low laugh. "That... actually makes sense. Better than what I had."

"Of course it does," she said, grinning in spite of herself. "Just call me festival consultant."

"Then you'd better come and see it. The site; help me figure it out properly."

She hesitated, the words catching in her chest.

"Just the site," he added, voice softer now. "I'd like you to see it. You'll get why I care so much."

Ella stared at the map glowing on her phone, her own reflection faint in the glass.

"All right," she heard herself say. "I'll come."

42

Landscaping

The lane narrowed before opening into the field. A wide, wet sprawl of grass bordered by hedges and the faint shimmer of sea beyond.

Alex was already there, leaning on his van, a notebook tucked under his arm. His grin was immediate and unguarded.

"You came."

"Of course I came," she said, as she stepped out of the car, though part of her still wasn't sure why.

"Thanks," he said, pushing himself off his van. "I'm very grateful for another pair of eyes."

They walked side by side into the open space, their boots leaving soft tracks.

"So," Alex said, waving the notebook. "Picture this: entrance here, stalls lining this side, stage on the rise at the far end. People spread out with blankets, kids running around, food vans at the edge."

Ella squinted, trying to imagine the empty field alive. "If the healing area is near the food, no one will relax. You need it further back. Away from the bass and the chip fat."

He paused, then laughed. "You're right. Of course you're right." He scribbled, shifting his plan. "Okay, healing area here. Hammocks in the trees."

"And you'll need a water station," she added, pointing to a corner. "People will be half-dead by noon if you don't."

"Perfect." He jotted that too. "See? I told you I needed you."

They carried on like that; him sketching, her correcting, both of them laughing as their ideas stacked on each other. The map began to fill, arrows and circles crisscrossing, the whole thing alive with possibility.

She found herself animated, waving her arms as words tumbling out faster than she could filter them. And he matched her, excited but grounded; scribbling down everything like it mattered.

They stopped at a patch of grass marked out for the children's section, Alex shading in a square with his pencil as he talked through puppet shows, painting stations, storytelling circles. She listened, but underneath the pictures he painted rose a hollow ache; a deep well of longing she didn't dare touch. A childhood where laughter wasn't barbed, where weekends weren't heavy with silence or sharp with anger. She wanted to step into the scene he described and stay there forever. But she said nothing, he wouldn't understand.

Alex glanced up then, catching her quiet. "Feels good, doesn't it?" His voice softened. "Like we're making space for the kind of things we wish we'd had."

Her throat caught. He couldn't know how close he was to the centre of it, but somehow, he did. She managed a nod, eyes stinging, and he went back to sketching as though nothing had shifted; except everything had. She let the ache sink down, choosing instead to ride the spark of their ideas, tossing out half-jokes and wild suggestions until they were laughing again, momentum carrying them forward.

By the time they reached the far hedgerow, wind lifting their hair, she was flushed with the kind of energy she thought she'd lost.

"Thank you," he said suddenly, folding the map. His voice was quieter now, almost reverent. "I haven't felt this... clear in months."

Without thinking, she hugged him. He folded into it easily, warm and solid. She felt a deep thrum in her chest — not desire, but care, like a string tied between them; a tether.

"Anytime," she said softly, stepping back.

The week that followed surprised her.

It wasn't just the festival logistics, though there were plenty of those. Messages pinged through her days: half-baked ideas, stupid memes, questions about incense, sketches of stall layouts photographed on the back of receipts. Evenings ended at the bar, papers and notebooks spread between them, empty glasses pushed aside.

And somewhere in the middle of it all, she realised it felt like her project too, not his alone. The maps, the schedules, the wild what-ifs scrawled on napkins: they were building something together. Equal partners in something that suddenly felt huge, bigger than either of them.

But the festival wasn't the only thing they talked about.

One night, with two pints between them and a bowl of chips gone limp and cold, his voice shifted. Lower. Slower.

"My brother," he began, almost cautiously.

Ella looked up, giving him her full attention.

He told her about the endless appointments, the doctors who said different things, the revolving door of treatments all through his childhood. About how his parents had lived in a constant state of fear, their lives circling around his brother's health. About the toll it took; the way birthdays, holidays, even simple meals tilted always toward one child, leaving him with the scraps.

"I don't blame them," he said quickly. "How could I? But... when you're a kid, you notice the gaps. What isn't there."

His fingers tightened around his glass. "By the time I was fifteen, I had rituals. Washing my hands until they bled, checking locks over and over. I don't even know if I thought it would stop anything bad from happening. It was more... a way to hold everything in. To make sure I didn't spill over, didn't take up more space than I should. If I could keep myself under control, maybe everything else would hold together too."

He gave a short laugh that didn't quite land. "It didn't, of course. And it nearly swallowed me. OCD, they called it. I clawed my way out in my twenties, but the fear of it coming back—." He broke off, shook his head. "It never fully goes."

Ella sat very still, every muscle alert. He wasn't asking for sympathy, he was handing her something raw and unpolished.

And for a moment she felt it: how much he carried, how much he had always carried.

Another night, it was her turn. She found herself telling him more than she had told anyone — not Miranda, not even Leanne. The truth about her father: the quiet manipulation, the small cruelties, the way she had built stories to survive. How Tom's silences had felt like echoes of those early years, stretching into a marriage that slowly starved her of oxygen.

She talked about the sick leave, the unravelling, about Rise Cottage, her father's letter. About painting the walls herself, about standing barefoot in the kitchen and feeling, for the first time, that it was hers.

She half-expected him to interrupt; to deflect with humour, but he didn't. He just listened, eyes steady, nodding occasionally as if every word mattered.

For those nights, she believed it too.

By the third time at the bar, scribbled paper stacked high between them, the conversation shifted again.

"Ella."

His voice was different this time. He wasn't smiling.

Her chest tightened. She knew before he said it.

"We're good together." He gestured at the mess of papers, the scrawled maps, then at the empty space between them. "Not just this, not just the festival. Us. Why wouldn't we make this... better? Why wouldn't we try?"

Her breath caught. The room seemed louder suddenly: the clatter of glasses, laughter from the bar. Her own heartbeat in her ears.

She thought of the past week; the flood of messages, the laughter that made her belly ache, the way she'd caught herself looking forward to his voice. The maps spread between them like blueprints of a shared dream. It felt like a partnership.

And still, deep in her chest, the answer was clear.

She shook her head, gentle but firm. "No. I don't feel that way about you."

Something flickered across his face — hurt — then a quick recovery. "Really? After all this? I thought..." He stopped himself, forced a smile that didn't reach his eyes. Shook his head slowly, breathing out a sigh. "Okay. Friends, then."

She felt irritation rise alongside the ache. Why did he have to push? Why assume that because there was chemistry, because she wanted his company, she must want him? Why risk ruining what was good?

They stacked the papers in silence. Outside, under the streetlamps, he hugged her longer than felt neutral. She held herself stiff, caught between the urge to soften into it and the need to pull away.

"Friends," she said again, her voice quiet but steady.

"Friends," he echoed, but there was a shadow behind it.

His footsteps retreated down the street, leaving her breath clouding in the night air, the echo of his arms still around her.

The next morning, her inbox pinged.

Ella,

I can't do this anymore. I thought I could, but it's too painful being this close and not more. I'm really sorry, but I need to step back. Please, no more contact. I wish you well. Truly.

She read it once. Twice. By the third time her hands were trembling.

The festival, the hugs, the laughter over chips, the sharing of wounds; it all collapsed into the white space around his words.

Her office hummed on around her, but she sat frozen, screen glaring.

Reeling.

43

Internal doors

Christmas had come differently this year.

No strained phone calls with Tom, no half-hearted truce over a turkey she never enjoyed. Instead Miranda's cottage, low-lit and easy, the fire soft in the grate.

The day unfolded in slow rhythms. They walked after breakfast, boots crunching frost, the hedgerows bare and etched against the pale sky. Back at the house, they opened crackers at the table, paper crowns crooked on their heads, both of them snorting with laughter at the worst kind of jokes.

For lunch they ignored turkey, ignored sprouts, ignored everything they were "supposed" to eat. Instead, they filled the table with what they loved most. Miranda chose duck pancakes, messy and delicious, the sauce staining their fingers; Ella's choice was wild mushroom risotto, earthy and rich; and for pudding, lemon meringue pie, tall and glossy, because neither of them could resist it. It wasn't tradition, it was indulgence; a feast stitched together from favourite things.

Later, they stretched out on the sofa, a film running low in the background, the weight of food making them quiet and content.

It was easy, warm. A kind of Christmas she hadn't known could exist.

And yet, as dusk folded itself over the fields, Ella felt the other presence; the space Alex had left.

Three weeks since the email. Three weeks since she'd felt the sharp crack of something closing. Since then, she'd thrown herself at everything else: the massage course, work, nights with her friends. Busy, always busy.

But Christmas left room.

She missed him. Not just him, but the energy between them; the way ideas had spun into air, the messy joy of building something together. She missed the messages, the pings, the scribbled maps on napkins, the way he listened like her words carried weight.

She tried to push it down; reminded herself of the pushiness, the assumption, the hug that lingered too long. But memory didn't obey logic. It carried its own rhythm, surfacing when she least wanted it.

Miranda handed her another slice of pie, cheerful and unbothered, and Ella smiled, grateful.

By five o'clock, the streets were already dark, fairy lights flickering in windows as Ella and Miranda wandered arm in arm towards Una's. The air had that bite that made cheeks glow.

Una's house was already buzzing. The hallway was a jumble of coats and half-unwrapped toys; from the living room came the shrieks of children showing off their new treasures. Milo was racing a remote-control car in dizzying circles, while Isla insisted everyone admire her improbable number of unicorn accessories.

"Come in, come in!" Una called from the kitchen, cheeks flushed, a glass of prosecco in one hand. Leanne and Anish were perched on the sofa, balancing plates of crisps and olives. Martin was opening another bottle, making a pantomime fuss of the cork, while his youngest tried to feed the dog mince pies.

It was easy at first. Ella slipped into the noise, took a glass from Leanne, laughed when Sara rolled her eyes at Trevor's exaggerated story about accidentally using custard powder in a béchamel. The table was scattered with plates of whatever people had fancied: bowls of crisps, wedges of cheese, sausage rolls gone slightly cold. Everyone had eaten too much already, but they kept picking anyway.

She managed. For a while.

But somewhere between Martin's deadpan retelling of his Christmas morning Lego disaster and the relentless unicorn parade, Ella felt it: the hollow.

It wasn't that she didn't love them all. She did. But their laughter seemed to skim just above her, like she couldn't quite catch it. Beneath the warmth and the chatter, another thread pulled hard: Alex.

She thought of the spark in his eyes when an idea caught. The way he scribbled furiously in his notebooks, pages already littered with arrows and crossings-out. The ease of their late-night talks and how her stories had spilled out unfiltered in a way they never had before.

What was Alex doing right now? Sitting with his family in some big, rambling house she pictured without ever having seen. His parents bustling in a kitchen full of noise, his brother nearby, laughter rising and falling? Or was he alone somewhere, feet up, a half-finished notebook on the table, music drifting in from the next room? Did he miss her?

Or had he met someone else — someone easier, someone who hadn't said no?

The questions pressed against her, sharp with a kind of longing she didn't want to admit.

The thought landed urgently: *I wish he was here.*

Her chest squeezed tighter. The next thought shocked her more: *I want to kiss him.*

Her glass stilled halfway to her lips. Heat crept up her throat. What the hell?

Miranda, sharp as ever, caught it. "You've gone quiet. What's happening in there?"

Ella blinked, set the glass down too quickly. "I… I don't know. I keep thinking about Alex."

Trevor gave a low whistle. "The folk-band boy?"

She winced. "Yes. Him. And it's ridiculous, because I don't want him. I know I don't. But sitting here, watching all of you, I suddenly wish he was with us. And I…" her voice dipped, cheeks hot, "I actually wanted to kiss him."

The room stilled for a beat, laughter thinning. Leanne tilted her head, curious.

Trevor arched an eyebrow. "Kissable, then? That sounds like progress."

Ella groaned, burying her face in her hands. "Or desperation. Do I actually want him, or do I just not want to be alone? Why have my feelings shifted like this? A week ago, I was clear. Certain. And now—." she gestured vaguely, hands fluttering, "Now I feel like I'm betraying myself."

The kids crashed through again, showing off another round of presents, their noise briefly filling the silence.

When they'd gone, Miranda reached over, steady hand on Ella's. "You're not betraying yourself, love. You're feeling. And feelings don't line up neatly. They blur, they contradict. That's human."

Ella stared at the table; the half-eaten sausage rolls, the crumbs in the lamplight. Her chest was a storm of longing and regret, clarity and ache, loneliness pressing at the edges.

She whispered, almost to herself: "I wish I could just know."

Miranda squeezed her hand tighter. "You do know. You just also wish it were easier."

Ella gave a small, shaky laugh, blinking hard against the sudden sting in her eyes. "Yes. Exactly that."

Someone cracked another joke, the kids shrieked from upstairs, and the room swelled with laughter again. Ella joined in, even smiled.

But the hollow didn't move. It stayed there — the space where Alex should have been.

When she returned home that night, the cottage quiet and still, she sat with that truth of missing him. Not in the frantic way she had once missed Tom; not with hunger or panic. But with something steadier, sadder.

She curled on the sofa, the glow of fairy lights reflecting in the window, and whispered it aloud into the empty room.

"I miss you."

The words dissolved into the air, unanswered.

***

Ella woke with a dry mouth and a head heavy with wine. For a moment she lay still, letting the blurred warmth of Miranda's laughter echo through her memory, the clatter of cutlery, Trevor's teasing.

Then the ache pressed in. Not a hangover, but Alex.

She rolled onto her back, staring at the ceiling. I want to kiss him. The thought was as clear as it had been last night, only sharper now for having survived sleep.

"No," she said aloud to the empty room. "It'll pass."

But it didn't. Through coffee, through toast, through the shuffle of shower and hairdryer, the ache held. By mid-morning, she gave herself a bargain. If it's still there in two hours, I'll message him.

The clock ticked, household chores were completed, but the tug didn't shift. If anything, it grew.

At noon, heart hammering, she stared at her phone for a long time before beginning to type. Three weeks of silence, three weeks of biting down the urge to reach for him and today, on Boxing Day, she couldn't hold it anymore.

Her thumbs hovered, deleting, retyping, until finally she let it sit:

"I've been thinking. I don't want to lose what we had. I know you said it's too hard to stay just friends... so if you're open, I want to give a relationship a go. Can we meet and chat?"

She read it twice. Her stomach flipped. Then she pressed send.

The reply came fast, like he'd been waiting.

"Yes. Tell me where."

They met outside a small bar she'd barely noticed before, all wood and dim windows. But she noticed him walking toward her in jeans and a jacket, hair ruffled by the wind, shoulders slightly hunched as though he wasn't sure she'd actually come.

Something leapt in her chest she couldn't contain.

"Hi," she managed.

And then he was pulling her in. She thought it would be careful, tentative — a testing of ground after all those weeks. But the hug broke and he kissed her. Straight away.

For a split second she froze. His lips were warm, his hand steady at her back, and her mind spun in two directions at once:

This is too much, too fast.

God, I've wanted this.

She kissed him back.

And in the same moment, her mind faulted it: too much tongue, the angle awkward. She noticed it all even as heat surged low in her belly, surprising and insistent.

When they pulled apart, he grinned at her like she'd given him oxygen.

Inside the bar, the night slipped easily into drinks and talk, laughter and more kisses, his hand brushing hers like it was the most natural thing in the world.

And yet beneath it all, a whisper threaded through her: What will Lynne think? June? Even Tom? Gwen and work colleagues? She could picture their faces, their silent judgments.

A folk-band dreamer. A man with messy hair, scribbled maps and no steady ground.

Terrible choice, they would say.

She tilted her head toward him, kissed him again anyway.

Because in that moment, with his smile close and the calm in her chest opening like a door she hadn't realised was shut, she didn't care.

44

Wood burner

The first weeks with Alex unfurled gently, almost against Ella's will.

Sometimes his touch felt suffocating, too constant, too certain of its welcome. And yet she found herself laughing harder with him than with anyone else. She loved his quickness; the way his mind leapt, how he always spotted the overlooked details — a bird call, the exact shade of a leaf in evening light. His company filled a space she hadn't realised was so cavernous.

He was calm in a way she didn't recognise, like time bent differently for him. At his flat, he'd move slowly, unhurried, setting music playing, making tea, telling a story with his hand absently tracing circles against hers. She leaned into it, found herself laughing more easily than she expected, relaxing against his shoulder on the sofa as though she'd belonged there all along.

And yet, even in the warmth, the voice ran underneath. *Look at his shoes. His T-shirt. You don't really fancy him. Not your type. Weak.* She hated the voice, hated how it slipped in and ruined moments. So, she kissed him harder, curled closer into his chest, trying to silence it with touch.

At her place, it was much the same: him sprawled on the sofa, legs tucked under, telling her about some old camping trip, the memory of it lighting his face. She loved it — the steadiness, the way he looked right at her when she laughed. But she couldn't stop noticing how different they were, how he could sink into time while she always seemed to be stealing it, cramming him into corners of her week between work and commuting, between the house and her course.

He never complained. He simply arrived when she did, calm, attentive, affectionate.

One night, they pulled the festival papers across her kitchen table again, candles flickering between the notebooks, wine half-finished in their glasses. For a moment it was like before: the thrill of building something together, their ideas sparking across the paper, their laughter punctuating the scribbles.

But then he pulled a page gently back toward him.
"Ella, I love your ideas. I do. But this part—," he tapped the sketched layout. "I need to keep hold of. Otherwise, it slips away from me."

The words stung, sharper than she wanted to admit. She felt the rejection coil in her chest: hadn't she helped shape this, made it partly hers?

But as she looked at him, saw the way his hand steadied on the map, she knew. It wasn't hers to lead. She was part of it, yes, but it lived in him first.

She exhaled, forced a smile. "Okay. I'll step back."

The quiet after lingered. She poured more wine, the candle sputtered, and she wondered why it was so hard to let go of something she hadn't meant to claim in the first place.

Later, she boarded the train home from his flat, the city lights slipping past the window as the carriage rocked gently forward. She rested her forehead against the cold glass and thought of time again; how his life seemed to stretch, expansive and unhurried, while hers felt like a calendar she could never quite fit herself into. He had hours to dream, to walk at dusk, to sit and listen. She had snatched evenings, weary lunch breaks, exhausted weekends.

The contrast unsettled her.

She knew what it felt like to live slowly. She'd had those months — mornings that stretched without alarm clocks, afternoons that belonged to nothing but a walk, an unhurried meal, silence. She knew the softness it created in her chest, the way her body sighed open when there was no demand pressing down.

But for her, that time had always felt borrowed; fragile like a bubble that could burst at any moment. For him, it was normal,. the way he lived. The way he moved through the world as if time were elastic, as if there would always be enough.

Part of her burned with irritation at this: what did he know of deadlines, of mortgages, of waking up tired and still pushing on?

And layered over this was another voice entirely, reckless and familiar. She was already planning. Already imagining him in the countryside, walking the fields with her, planting himself into her world. Hoping he'd want it too.

It was absurd, she knew. Here she was, not even certain this was right, while a part of her was ten steps ahead, sketching a future neither of them had asked for yet.

She closed her eyes as the train rumbled on, scarf tucked tight against her.

Every time his hand found hers, every time he kissed her with that steady tenderness, she felt it: the possibility of rest, of letting go of the constant chase. But was that softness an invitation or a trap? Would leaning into him mean losing her edge, her fight, the careful structures she'd built to keep herself afloat?

She exhaled, watching her reflection ghost back at her in the dark glass, exhausted with the to-ing and fro-ing of her mind.

***

Miranda's kitchen was already alive when Ella arrived. Candles flickered on the counter, wine glasses half-full, music humming in the background. Trevor was stirring something at the stove with his usual flourish, Una leaned against the doorframe with a bowl of olives, Leanne was perched on a stool, already flushed with laughter.

Ella stepped in first, Alex just behind her. "Everyone, this is Alex," she said, her voice pitched brighter than she felt.

He offered his easy grin, a casual wave. "Thanks for having me."

And just like that, he was folded in. He poured himself a glass when Trevor shoved the bottle his way, asked Una about her kids, complimented Leanne's earrings, made Miranda laugh with some story about the disastrous early gigs of his band.

Within half an hour, they adored him. Trevor clapped him on the back like they'd known each other years. Leanne leaned into Ella's shoulder, stage-whispering, "He's refreshing, not like the usual men we meet." Miranda's smile was sly, approving, her eyes glittering as if she'd known Ella was underestimating him all along. Even Una, usually more reserved with newcomers, lit up when Alex asked about her garden, comparing notes on tomato plants and compost.

Ella sat at the edge of it, wine in hand, watching. Relief loosened her ribs — they liked him, they really liked him. He was charming, engaged, present in a way that made the room buzz brighter.

And yet.

The more they accepted him, the tighter her chest grew. Their praise, their warmth, their laughter wrapping around him; it should have felt like a victory. Instead, it left her unsettled, almost claustrophobic. Something darker stirred: an urge to push him away before he settled too deeply in.

At dinner, his hand slid onto her thigh under the table. A simple gesture, affectionate, grounding. She flinched — tiny, involuntary — then forced a smile when he glanced at her.

Later, as coats were shrugged on and goodnights exchanged, Miranda caught Ella's eye with a grin that said more than words. "Good one," she mouthed, as if Alex were a prize Ella should be proud to show off.

Ella smiled back, but the knot in her stomach only tightened.

That night, he stayed over.

They slipped into bed with the same ease the evening had carried; coats dropped by the door, wine still soft in their veins, the faint smell of incense clinging to their clothes.

Alex pulled her close, kissed her forehead. "Your friends are brilliant," he said quietly. "Warm, funny. I felt like I'd known them for years."

Ella smiled into the dark. "They loved you," she admitted. "Leanne told me you were 'refreshing.'"

He laughed softly, the sound rumbling through his chest beneath her cheek. "Refreshing? I'll take that." He kissed her again, slower this time. "Mostly I just liked seeing you with them. You lit up."

She curled into him, and felt the warm steadiness of his body under hers. There was something disarming about how natural it felt. His arm curved around her shoulders, his breath slow and unhurried, as though he'd been holding her like this for years.

Their intimacy unfolded gently, almost unexpectedly. Kisses deepening, touches that grew warmer, the simple delight of skin on skin. When at last they lay tangled together, limbs loose, the sheets kicked down to their waists, she thought how lovely it felt just to be naked beside him. The weight of his thigh against hers, the rise and fall of his breathing, the quiet afterwards that wasn't awkward but full.

And at the same time, a flicker; sharp and uninvited. A part of her, unwanted as it was, comparing the curve of his stomach, the line of his back, to Tom's. A ghost-trace of another body, another life.

She hated it the moment it arrived. Hated that it intruded here, of all places. She pushed the thought aside, pressed her face closer into Alex's shoulder, tried to lose herself again in the warmth of his skin, the ease of his presence.

He kissed the top of her head without comment, as though sensing the shift but not needing to name it. His hand rested at the small of her back, steady and sure, until finally her breath matched his. In the darkness, Ella let herself soften again.

In the morning, sunlight streamed pale across her bedroom, soft against the curtains. For a while it was quiet. Alex shifted beside her, arm heavy across her waist, breath slow and even. She lay still, listening, letting herself rest in the warmth of him.

When his eyes blinked open, he smiled, kissed her temple lazily. "Morning."

She smiled back. "Morning."

He looked at her then, properly, his gaze steady and unguarded. There was so much in it: care, affection, a warmth that felt like it might undo her. She had to glance away, unable to bear the weight of it. But after a breath, she let her eyes return to his, and in that beat something passed between them, quiet and certain, as if the world had stilled around just the two of them.

She rested her head on his chest and they lay like that for a little while, silence that felt companionable; her fingers tracing idle patterns on his arm, his hand brushing her hair back. She thought, *I could get used to this.*

Then his phone buzzed on the nightstand. Once, then again, insistent.

He groaned, rolled over to grab it. "Sorry. Just a sec."

Ella sighed but stayed quiet, though irritation coiled in her chest. It was their morning. Did the world really need to intrude right now?

He sat on the edge of the bed, phone pressed to his ear. "What? No, double? You gave me an approximation. Now the final's twice that because of the new plans? You can't just—." His voice climbed, sharp, then dropped low as he tried to argue.

She pulled the duvet higher, watching the muscles in his back go taut, his shoulders hunched, every line of him braced.

When he hung up, he pressed both hands hard against his face. His voice was raw. “Security costs have doubled. This could sink the whole thing. I don’t know how the hell I’m going to pull it off.”

Something in Ella snapped at that; the I, not we, as if she hadn’t been there night after night, sketching, thinking it through with him. Her irritation surged, hot and uncontained.

“Maybe you should’ve thought it through more carefully.”

He spun on her like she’d slapped him. His eyes blazed. “Are you kidding me?” His voice cracked with fury. “Do you have any idea what I’ve been holding together? Any idea how much I’ve already fixed? I’m killing myself trying to make this work and you—,” His hand cut the air between them. “You sit there and sneer about planning?”

She jerked upright, heat flooding her face. “I wasn’t sneering! I was—.”

“You were. Don’t deny it. You think I’m some useless dreamer who can’t hack it.” His voice was louder now, raw, every word laced with hurt. “You’ve thought it from the start.”

Her own anger flared, matching his. “And you think shouting makes you right? You think you’re the only one under pressure? Try living my life for a week, Alex. Constant work pressure, mortgage stress, commutes, deadlines. I don’t get to gamble everything on a field and a map. I can’t afford it!”

They were both on their feet now, breath sharp, words colliding and spilling, the tenderness of the morning obliterated.

For a long moment, neither spoke. His jaw was clenched so tight she could see the muscle jump. Then he pulled on his clothes, grabbed his jacket from the chair, muttered something under his breath she couldn’t catch, and stormed out. The slam of the front door ricocheted through the house.

Ella stood where she was, chest heaving, the air still vibrating with his anger. Her hands shook faintly at her sides.

How dare he? The thoughts came fast, hot. She'd been trying to help, to name what was right in front of him. And he'd turned it into an attack.

She sat down heavily on the edge of the bed, breath jagged. *Good*, she thought, bitter. *Better to know now. To see how quickly his temper flared, how sharp it could cut.* She'd lived with that kind of fury as a child; the slamming doors, the unpredictability, the way it made the air feel unsafe. She would not live inside it again.

Her shoulders rose, then dropped as she forced out a long, slow breath. The silence pressed in, but it wasn't entirely hostile. Just... space. Wide and raw.

She lay back against the pillows, staring up at the ceiling. For a long while, she let herself just be there — her heartbeat slowing, the edges of her anger softening — though the ache beneath remained.

Eventually, her thoughts circled. Would he calm down? Would he message? Would he realise how far he'd gone and apologise?

Maybe. Maybe not.

But she knew one thing with clarity: she wouldn't be the one to reach out. Not this time. He had crossed a line, and she would not chase after him. If he wanted to repair what had snapped between them, he would have to step forward first.

45

Garden fence

The tennis balls bounced wildly off rackets, walls, fences; anywhere but the neat rectangle of the court. Ella doubled over laughing, her breath clouding in the cold February air.

"I told you," she panted, straightening with her racket limp at her side. "I'm useless."

Leanne was already jogging to the far corner to retrieve the ball, grinning. "No, no. We're brilliant. We've invented a new sport. Extreme fetch-tennis."

"Catchy."

They played on, rallies lasting only three, maybe four shots before one of them lunged too far or missed entirely. Every time, the ball skittered away and one of them had to chase it, slipping on the frosty edge of the court. Neither cared. They laughed, shouted, teased each other. Ella felt her blood moving, the cold in her fingers replaced by warmth, her body shaking off the static that had clung to her these last weeks.

Still, Alex crept in. He had been creeping in every day.

Two weeks had passed since he'd stormed out and Ella had been on a rollercoaster since. Rage, grief, indifference, longing – they'd all taken turns. One afternoon she'd typed his name into Google, fingers almost trembling, and found it: the festival website still selling tickets, a fresh video of him on YouTube, animated and confident as he introduced the line-up, even articles in the local press about the event's growth.

He had sorted it. The security problem hadn't stopped him. She realised with a sting how little credit she'd given him, how quickly she'd assumed collapse. That knowledge bobbed in her mind now, rising between serves even as she tried to stay present with Leanne.

After half an hour they gave up, laughing at their hopelessness, and sat down shoulder to shoulder on the cold wooden bench at the side of the court. Ella tugged her coat tight around her while Leanne unscrewed the lid of a flask. Steam drifted into the chill air.

"Tea," Leanne announced, pouring into two small cups. "The real post-match essential."

They cupped the warmth in their hands, cheeks pink from cold and effort. For a while they just sipped, breath misting.

"So. What's on your mind? You've seemed... distracted."

Ella let out a shaky laugh. "That obvious?"

"Yep." Leanne gave her a sideways look, gentle but insistent. "And don't bother dodging. I saw you and Alex at Miranda's that night; the way he looked at you, the way you lit up. I've never seen you like that. And now? It's like you've got a cloud hovering."

A slow pressure gathered beneath Ella's ribs. She hadn't told her friends about their argument, hoping it would smooth itself out, as if silence could undo it. Part of her felt ashamed; that after finally bringing him into her circle, she'd let them see a version of her that was already breaking apart. She wanted to seem steadier than that. More stable.

She stared into the steam rising from her cup. "We had a fight. A big one."

Leanne frowned. "About what?"

Ella let out a hard breath. "He was stressed, I made a sharp comment, and... he exploded. Proper anger. Slammed the door on his way out. It blindsided me. And I just thought no. Absolutely not. I've had enough of that in my life. I swore I'd never let it in again."

Her voice wavered. "So, I told myself, if he wants to fix this, he has to reach out. He has to apologise. I can't smooth it over, not when it comes to anger like that."

"Has he?"

Ella shook her head. "Nothing. No word."

Leanne was quiet for a beat. Then: "Were you scared of him?"

Ella's lips pressed together. "Not... not in that way. Not like when my dad—." She stopped, throat tightening. Raised voices, doors slamming, the sick thrum of walking on eggshells. "It wasn't that. It just... hit the same place; the noise, the suddenness."

"And Alex himself? Do you think he's like your dad?"

Ella closed her eyes, replaying Alex's face: the softness of his smile, the way he leaned in when she spoke, how gently he'd told her about his brother. Not cruel, not volatile, just... hurt, triggered.

"No," she said at last. "He's not like my dad. He is kind, he is soft. But he did get angry and I hated it. I don't want to excuse that."

"You don't have to." Leanne's hand brushed hers, steady, grounding. "But maybe the anger wasn't the whole story. Maybe it's more about what it woke up in you."

Ella sat with that, chest tight. The chain-link fence behind them rattled in the wind.

After a while, she whispered, "I was mean too. I jabbed at him when he was already under pressure. If I want him to own his part, I have to own mine as well."

Leanne gave a small, certain smile. "That sounds fair."

Ella managed a laugh, brittle but real. "I hate how reasonable you are."

They sat in silence a little longer, the cold seeping into their legs, the steam thinning from the flask. Ella's mind still whirled, but there was a shift too; the realisation that she could stand firm *and* reach out without betraying herself.

Ella was washing dishes the next morning when her phone buzzed on the counter. A group message from Miranda lit up the screen:

"Trevor's in a bad way. If anyone can come to mine just now, please do. He needs support."

Ella dried her hands quickly, heart tightening. One by one, the others replied – apologies, kids. No one else could make it until later.

She grabbed her coat.

When Miranda opened the door twenty minutes later, she folded Ella into a hug so tight it made Ella's breath hitch. Miranda's voice was low against her ear.

"It's Sara. Cancer."

The words sank slow, heavy. Ella pulled back, searching Miranda's face, but there was no softening there.

Inside, Trevor sat on the sofa, elbows braced on his knees, his face buried in his hands. The sight of him – usually all brightness and quips – undone like this jolted Ella.

She crossed the room quietly, lowered herself onto the sofa beside him. For a moment she just sat, their shoulders almost touching, before she reached across and took his hand. His fingers tightened around hers, desperate, and then let go, pulling back into himself. She eased back, giving him space.

When he finally spoke, his voice was hoarse, breaking. "She didn't tell me. For months, she carried this and said nothing. And then when she finally spoke a few months back," he lifted his head, eyes red, face twisted with anguish, "it wasn't to tell me she was ill and having treatment. It was to say she needed space; that she was questioning everything."

Ella's heart dropped.

Trevor let out a strangled laugh, half-choke, half-cry. "Can you imagine? She was in the spare room, saying she needed space to think about us, and I believed her. But it wasn't that at all. She was recovering from the treatment. And I… I thought she was pushing me away, rejecting me. And all the time." His voice cracked. "All the time, it was this."

His eyes lifted, red-rimmed, bewildered. "Two days ago, first thing I hear about any of this, she tells me she's had the all-clear. The *all-clear*. Do you get what that means? I wasn't even there for her when she needed me most. She decided I wasn't part of it. She decided she didn't need me."

Miranda crouched on his other side, hand steady on his back. "She didn't want you to look at her differently. Didn't want to become 'the ill one' in your eyes."

"But she *is* ill!" Trevor's hands cut through the air. "And I should've been the first to know. I'm her husband. We promised – we said we'd carry it all together. And instead, she makes me feel like I'm already out of the picture. Like I don't get to stand beside her in this."

Ella's stomach clenched.

"I thought I was fixing our marriage," Trevor went on, his words tumbling now, raw. "I thought I was the problem. I went into a spiral; looking at myself, at us, trying to figure out what I'd done wrong, how to put it right. She let me believe our marriage was crumbling instead of telling me the truth."

He drew in a shaky breath. "And the thing is… she asked me not to tell anyone. Said she didn't want you to know. But I told her I had to or I'd go mad holding it in. And the look she gave me," his voice faltered, grief slicing through, "like I was already betraying her. Like just needing to speak it made me disloyal."

His shoulders heaved, breath tearing ragged from his chest. His hands twisted in his lap. "And I can't even tell her how angry I am, how shut out I feel. Because she's still recovering, and I want to be kind. I want to protect her after all she's been through. So instead, I bite my tongue, sit on my hands, and swallow it down. But inside..." He shook his head. "Inside it's tearing me apart."

His words cracked on the last syllable. His face crumpled, nose running, tears spilling fast. Miranda wrapped both arms around him, steady. He looked utterly adrift.

Trevor's voice broke again, softer now, reverent. "And yet, I'm proud of her too. She went back to the doctors three times before anyone took her seriously. Three times. They brushed her off, said it was nothing, and she kept pushing until they listened. Such strength. And self-trust. And I see it, I do. But it makes the rest even harder to swallow. Because she fought them... and she shut me out."

He shook his head hard. "And then the kids. She doesn't want them to know, thinks it's not helpful. So, I'm meant to walk around smiling, carrying this huge thing inside me, pretending, lying. I hate it. This isn't how a family should work. I don't believe in shielding them from life like this. But I can't say that. I have to honour her wishes. So I sit there with all this anger, all this fear, all this grief boiling inside me, and the only thing I'm allowed to show her is compassion."

He sat back suddenly, wiping at his face with the back of his hand. "I don't know how to forgive all this. I don't even know if I can. Because it wasn't just hiding the illness. It was shutting me out. And now..." His voice dropped, flat with exhaustion. "Now I wonder what else I don't know. What else she's decided not to share."

The silence held. Ella stayed still, her own chest aching.

She reached toward him again, her hand hovering before it found his forearm. "God. I am *so* sorry, Trev."

Her voice was quiet, useless maybe, but it was all she had. The room felt small, still with the weight of what couldn't be solved. Ella sat back, hands resting against her knees now, letting the stillness arrange itself.

When Trevor finally quieted, his face blotched red, the room felt heavy, like even the air didn't want to move. Miranda kept her hand on his back, quiet, just staying steady beside him.

Ella sat still, her whole body taut. The rawness of his pain wasn't abstract; she felt it inside her, tight across her chest, knotted in her stomach. She wanted to reach in and take some of it from him, to ease the jagged edges, but there was no way.

She realised she was holding her breath. Slowly, carefully, she let it out.

Trevor's words looped in her head. Each sentence pressed into her ribs like stones. The thought of him pacing their kitchen, second-guessing every look, every silence, believing their marriage itself was under threat, while all the time it was something else entirely; the unfairness of it winded her.

It wasn't just betrayal, it was loneliness. That enforced exile from the truth. And sitting beside him, Ella could feel how deeply that isolation cut.

She reached out again, laid her hand over his. This time he let it rest there, his thumb trembling faintly against her fingers.

"I wish I had the right words," she whispered. "But I don't. I just… I see how much this hurts."

Trevor's breath shuddered, uneven, and for a long while that was all there was. The three of them sat in the muted room, grief and silence folding around them like another layer of fabric.

Later, walking home through the freezing dark, she still felt it like a band across her chest. The sharp unfairness of his exclusion. The way love can twist when the truth is withheld.

Her mind flicked, unbidden, to Alex. To the slammed door, the silence that had stretched for weeks since. She'd told herself she was right to wait, right to hold the line until he came to her. But now, with Trevor's pain still burning through her, she felt the echo. The cost of being shut out. The way it corrodes trust even in the strongest bonds.

She dug her hands deep into her coat pockets, her breath clouding in the early afternoon.

Maybe what mattered wasn't who reached out first. Maybe what mattered was refusing to let silence do the damage.

46

Name plaque

Ella left the office at five on the dot, the winter sky already dimming into blue grey. She'd half-expected Gwen to stop her with a last-minute "urgent" email, but for once, she made it out clean. On the train into the city that morning she had drafted the message three times before settling on something simple:

"Can we talk? I'd like to see you."

His reply came within minutes. *"Come over after work if that suits?"*

By the time she stood outside his flat, a converted terrace with peeling paint around the doorframe, her chest felt tight with nerves. But when he opened the door, his smile was cautious, hopeful.

"Hi."

"Hi." She stepped in, the warmth of the flat closing around her, faintly scented with sage or incense.

They sat opposite each other at the small kitchen table, mugs of tea untouched between them. The silence pressed for a moment until Ella let out a breath.

"I'm sorry," she said simply, "for what I said. It came out sharp, and I know it landed badly. You were stressed, and I made it worse."

Alex rubbed his palms together, staring down at them. "I shouldn't have shouted. Or walked out like that. Sorry. I hate that you saw me like that."

Her lips tugged into a wry smile. "I've seen worse. But it scared me. Took me back."

He looked up then, brows knitting. She nodded slowly. "My dad. Anger was… the air we breathed. When you slammed the door, even though I knew it wasn't the same, my body just… reacted."

Something softened in his face. "I get that. And it's not who I want to be. It's just…" He trailed off, searching for words. "I've always felt like I wasn't good enough. My parents, they piled all their expectations on me because Ben couldn't begin to meet them. Every grade, every choice, every screw-up, it all mattered twice as much. By the time I was a teenager, I had this voice in my head telling me I'd never measure up. The OCD didn't help. Obsessing over stupid rituals, because," he exhaled. Let his head drop back, and then brought his gaze back to her eyes. "They gave me something solid, that I could count on, in a mess of uncertainty and pressure."

Ella's chest ached. "That sounds exhausting."

"It was. Still is, sometimes. When you said I hadn't thought things through with the festival, it hit that raw nerve. Like you were confirming what I already fear: that I'm just a dreamer, not capable. And I snapped."

Her hand hovered above the table before she finally let it fall over his, a pulse of warmth. "I don't think you are just a dreamer. You are doing it – creating something amazing."

Her fingers tightened lightly around his. "But Alex… can I say something?"

He glanced at her, wary but open.

"Maybe it's time you stopped making yourself come second. With your brother, with everything. I see how much you carry, how often your needs get pushed aside so you can be the good one, the steady one. But you matter too. You don't always have to fix him."

He exhaled slowly, his gaze dropping to where their hands touched. A shadow crossed his face, not resistance so much as recognition.

"I know," he said quietly. "It's just hard to shake the habit."

"Maybe the festival is your chance," she offered. "To choose yourself. To put your energy where it lights you up, not just where it's expected."

His took her hand in his. Her fingers lingered there, and then she drew in a shaky breath. "And… I need to tell you something else. Sometimes I feel myself pulling back. Or wanting to find fault in you before you can hurt me. It's like this old instinct that flares up; if I criticise first, if I keep a bit of distance, then maybe I'll stay safe." She looked down, ashamed. "But I don't want that to run the show anymore. Not with you."

Alex's hand tightened over hers. He didn't speak, just let the words settle between them. Then he exhaled.

"I get it," he said quietly. "Maybe more than you think. I've done the same in my own way; holding back parts of me, hiding what I really need, because I thought asking would be too much. That it'd drive people away." His thumb brushed the side of her hand, tentative, steady. "I don't want that to run the show either."

She glanced up, surprised by the softness in his eyes. Nothing demanding or defensive. Just open.

"I can't promise I won't screw up," he went on. "But I'll talk if I feel myself clamming up, and if you feel yourself pulling back, tell me. Don't do it alone."

She nodded, a small breath of relief easing her shoulders. Something in her chest loosened at the thought of a space where her fear could sit alongside his steadiness.

Her throat caught. She rose halfway from her chair, the movement small, uncertain, before he stood too, closing the space. His arms went around her with a kind of gentleness that undid her, careful and steady until she pressed into him, forehead against his shoulder, tears hot in her eyes.

"I don't want to do it alone," she whispered into the fabric of his shirt.

"You don't have to," he murmured, his chin resting lightly on her hair.

For a long moment they stayed like that, the weight of words giving way to breath and warmth, the silence finally soft instead of heavy.

Alex's voice came low, almost muffled against her hair. "I was so nervous about tonight. About whether it would work. Because..." He drew a shaky breath. "Because I like you. More than I know how to say."

She stilled, her cheek pressed to his shoulder.

"I tried to write, you know. A couple of times. Long messages, trying to explain. But I'd just stare at the words and think, no, she's furious, she won't want to hear it. She won't be interested in me, now." His arms tightened briefly around her, like he needed to check she was still there.

When they drew apart, there was no rush, no need to fill the air. Alex brushed his sleeve across his eyes and gave a small, crooked smile.

"Tea's gone cold," he said.

Ella let out a laugh that was half a sob.

"Come on." He squeezed her hand, guiding her toward the kettle. "Let's try again."

They moved around the kitchen together, a little awkward at first, then settling into a rhythm. She tipped the cold tea down the sink while he filled the kettle again, their movements brushing close but not quite touching. When the water boiled, he carried the mugs through to the living room and set them on the table. A small plate of biscuits followed, placed carefully between them, his smile subdued but warm.

Soon they were curled on the sofa, legs tucked beneath them, steaming cups in hand. The lamplight threw a quiet glow across the room. No big speeches now, no confessions. Just the sound of rain against the window and the faint creak of the house settling around them.

Ella leaned her shoulder against his, the contact light but steady. He reached across and covered her knee with his palm. And for the first time since the fight, she felt her body let go, in small, quiet increments.

After that, the air between them loosened. He moved toward the oven, wiping his hands on a tea towel. "I made something earlier," he said, almost offhand, though his voice carried a careful weight. "Chicken and leek pie. Thought it might be good for you. Proper food after a day at the office."

Ella blinked, the words catching somewhere between her chest and throat. The pie sat waiting on the counter, while he pre-heated the oven. It was the kind of meal someone made when they wanted to take care, when they'd thought ahead, when they'd pictured you sitting at their table.

Her fingers tightened around her mug. She couldn't meet his eyes. Too much tenderness in the gesture, too much of what she hadn't known she craved. "That's... nice," she murmured, gaze fixed on the steam rising from her tea.

Later, Alex cut into the pie with deliberate ease, as if not to crowd her with the fact of it. The sound of pastry breaking filled the quiet, a small domestic crackle that felt strangely intimate.

Ella stayed by the counter, raw under the weight of his care. She wanted to thank him, to let him see what it meant. But all she managed was another sip of tea, eyes low, as if gratitude itself might split her open.

Over second helpings of delicious pie, they talked about the festival. His face lit as he told her tickets were selling fast – better than he'd dared hope – and about the slot he'd been given on local radio. "I was bricking it," he admitted with a grin. "But it worked. Sales spiked after. And I've managed to restructure things so security won't bleed us dry. Found a smaller firm who are actually a much better fit."

She smiled at his energy, the relief visible in his whole body. "Sounds like it's really happening."

"It is," he said, pride flickering through his grin. "It actually is."

She twirled her fork slowly, then said, "I wish you could've seen Trevor last week. He's... he's not himself. Sara's been ill, really ill. She had cancer. And she didn't tell him until after the all-clear. He's heartbroken. Not just because she was sick, although obviously there is pain in that too, but because she shut him out. He's reeling."

Alex's expression sobered. "That's brutal. For both of them."

"I don't quite know how to help him. I just sat there with him and Miranda while he unravelled. It felt like the only thing I could do."

"That probably meant more than you think," Alex said gently. "Sometimes just not being alone with it... is everything."

Ella nodded, eyes stinging unexpectedly. She pushed a forkful of pie around her plate, grateful for the hum of warmth between them.

After dinner, Alex cleared the plates, then glanced back at her. "Will you stay?"

She met his eyes, felt the weight of the question, and nodded once.

He poured a glass of wine, set it gently in her hands and then seemed to change his mind. He took it from her and placed it on the side, crossed the small space between them, and folded her into his arms.

Steady, quiet, lingering; the kind of hug that asked nothing but gave everything. Ella let herself lean in and simply be held.

And then, as if some hidden wire between them sparked at once, the stillness fractured. She pulled back just enough to meet his eyes, and what she saw there — heat, care, unspoken need — undid her. Their mouths found each other, tentative for half a breath before giving way to something fiercer.

The kiss deepened quickly, hunger rushing in where hesitation had been. His hands cupped her face, then tangled in her hair; hers slid over his shoulders, drawing him closer, needing no space between them. Every brush of lips and teeth carried urgency, a fast, breathless desire, as though they'd both been waiting too long.

47

Snagging

The pub was bustling by the time Ella and Alex arrived, laughter bouncing off low beams, plates of roast potatoes and Yorkshire puddings weaving through the crowd. At the long oak table, Una beamed under the glow of a birthday badge pinned proudly to her dress. The children clambered on and off laps, giggling, weaving between chairs, scattering crayons and half-finished drawings across the table.

Sara sat bright as ever, her laugh cutting clear across the hubbub, eyes shining as if nothing in the world was amiss. Trevor, though, looked worn thin; his shirt collar a little crumpled, eyes shadowed, and a heaviness around his jaw. But he was playing the part. He slapped Alex on the back, grinned across at Miranda, even coaxed Milo into showing off a magic trick with a bread roll. But when he lifted his pint, Ella caught the faint tremor in his hand.

Alex slipped into the seat beside Anish and within minutes, the two of them were deep in conversation about music and travel. Ella sat back, letting their voices blur with the hum of the pub, and realised she wasn't bracing herself the way she once would have. No tight coil of nerves about how he came across, no inner critic whispering what others might be thinking. Just the quiet warmth of watching him, his shoulders loose, his laugh quick, curiosity drawing Anish out.

It had been this way for weeks now — easier. The constant tug-of-war inside her had stilled, at least a little. She thought of last Tuesday when he'd cooked for them in her kitchen; the two of them leaning against the counter, eating prawns straight from the pan. His hand brushing hers as naturally as breathing. Later, they'd sat in the garden in shared stillness and awe, watching the first hedgehog of the year shuffle out from the shrubs. Or the Sunday morning when they'd walked the lanes near her cottage, his scarf wrapped haphazardly around his neck, and he'd tucked her hair back with such tenderness she'd had to look away, the ache of it catching her off guard.

Midway through the meal, Trevor gathered up glasses for a refill. Ella rose too. "I'll give you a hand."

At the bar, the noise softened to a manageable hum, the rugby on TV drawing most of the background cheers. Trevor leaned against the counter, shoulders rounding inwards. Ella watched his profile for a moment, the flicker of exhaustion etched there.

"I've been thinking of you," she said gently. "A lot."

His jaw tightened, then loosened. He kept his eyes on the taps. "I feel like I'm splitting in two," he admitted, voice low. "There's the version they all see today: me laughing, playing the dad, making it all look easy. And then there's the one that wakes at 3 a.m., staring at the ceiling, wondering how the hell to keep going."

Her chest ached. "That sounds unbearable."

He gave a short, humourless laugh. "Yeah. But what choice do I have? I keep going. For her. For the kids. What else is there?"

The bartender slid their drinks over, and Trevor pulled himself upright, shoulders squaring, mask sliding back into place. "Right," he said briskly. "Birthday pints."

Back at the table, conversation swirled around them. Ella stole glances at Trevor as he smiled, his hand steady again, his voice bright. She carried the crack in his armour like a stone in her pocket.

Later, when the puddings arrived, Una's came with a sparkler fizzing cheerfully from its crown. Everyone whooped, clapped, called for a speech.

Una stood a little, grinning, and began; a few words about friendship, laughter, how much she loved them all. Ella leaned back, soaking in the glow of the moment. Then her gaze slid sideways.

Trevor, head bowed slightly, napkin in hand. A single tear traced down his cheek before he wiped it away quickly, unnoticed by anyone else.

48

Appliances

It was Thursday, and Ella's mind felt like it had been running on two tracks all week — neither of them the one she was meant to be on. She'd sat through meetings, written lists, answered emails, but her thoughts kept slipping sideways: into small, bright flashes of Alex, or into the heavier, unfinished space where Trevor's sadness still lived.

She kept seeing that moment at Una's birthday lunch: the quick tear he'd wiped away before anyone else had noticed, the way it had lodged in her chest afterwards. He was coming over to her house tonight with Miranda. He'd asked for it, said he needed to talk. She hoped he'd found some way to be steadier.

And then there was Alex — the memory of him so gentle it almost embarrassed her — the way he listened, laughed, made the room feel softer. Those tiny daydreams drifted in, never staying long, always within reach.

Now she sat in the glass-walled conference room, two chairs from the end, notebook open but empty. Around her, pens moved, laptops clicked, the low hum of office focus. Gwen was speaking — sharp, precise — and Ella tried to anchor herself in the sound of it. But her mind flickered again, tugged by things that weren't happening here.

Then Gwen said something that didn't just pull her back, it landed in her chest like cold water, shutting down the drift instantly.

The most important deadline for her key client. *That* Friday. The day the festival opened. The day she had already booked off, written in her calendar with a bright circle and a secret thrill. The Friday she would be helping get everything set up, perfecting her massage stall and standing beside Alex, as people trickled in and the whole thing came alive.

Her pen moved almost automatically: Friday 21st May. She circled it. Once. Twice. Harder, until the nib threatened to tear through the paper.

Gwen went on, detailing timelines, dependencies, contingencies. Then, with the finality of a gavel, she added: "And to be absolutely clear, all annual leave in the two weeks leading up to the deadline is cancelled. Non-negotiable."

A heat rushed through Ella's body, sharp as panic. Cancelled. Her carefully carved-out days: the Friday before, and the Monday for celebration after. Now, in a handful of words, Gwen had slammed a door.

Don't spiral. She sat straighter, forced herself to breathe. *Just get your head down. It'll be fine. You'll figure it out. Something will shift, something always does.* She imagined divine intervention, some miracle untangling of schedules that meant she could be everywhere she needed to be. She clung to that thought like a rope.

But the other thoughts crept in anyway. Her stomach clenched as her mind played both films at once:

Staying. Sitting at her desk on that Friday night, the office a tomb of blue-white light. Everyone exhausted. Gwen's cool gaze passing over her with approval, her colleagues muttering about how reliable Ella was. And in her pocket, a message to Alex she hadn't wanted to send: *"I can't come. Work has me."*

She shook her head slightly, to dislodge the thought. Pressed harder with her pen.

But then, leaving. Shutting her laptop, walking out into the spring dusk, heading for the train while the office buzzed behind her. The looks, the whispers, Gwen's outrage and possible dismissal; at the very least a ledger entry against her name.

Her breath shortened. The two paths blurred, crashing into one another until her vision went grainy.

"Ella?"

Her head jerked up. Silence stretched across the table. Gwen's gaze cut like glass.

"I asked whether you can cover the vendor approvals," Gwen said. No anger, just a flicker of disappointment. Somehow worse.

"Yes," Ella blurted, too quickly. "I can handle it."

Gwen's eyes lingered a fraction longer before sliding away. She clicked to the next slide, already done with her.

Ella bent her head, scribbling meaningless lines across the page. Her heart still thundered, her body caught between two futures. One red circle on two calendars.

And she couldn't yet see how she could survive both.

The meeting finally wound down. Chairs scraped, laptops clicked shut, and voices rose in low chatter as people began to file out. Ella gathered her notebook slowly, hoping to disappear into the shuffle.

But Gwen was suddenly there, blocking her path. Pristine and unreadable with eyes sharp as glass.

"Ella."

She froze. "Yes?"

Gwen's gaze held steady, level, without a flicker of warmth. "Where were you in that meeting? You looked like you'd drifted for half of it."

Ella opened her mouth, then shut it again. Heat prickled at the back of her neck.

"You're a big part of this project," Gwen continued, tone flat, clinical. "I need your full attention. Whatever is getting in the way of your focus here needs to be sorted. Immediately."

No anger. No softness either, just that matter-of-fact efficiency that cut deeper than either would have. Gwen waited only a moment, as if expecting a promise carved in stone, before adding, "Can I count on you?"

Ella's throat was tight. She nodded. "Yes. Of course."

"Good." Gwen gave the faintest of nods, already turning away, the conversation dismissed, closed.

Ella stood for a moment, notebook clutched to her chest, pulse thudding. On the outside she looked compliant, recommitted. But inside she felt smaller; cornered as though Gwen had glimpsed all the chaos she was trying so hard to bury.

And the truth hit her harder than ever: one way or another, the 21st was coming. And no matter what face she put on for Gwen, she could not keep both worlds from colliding.

By the time Ella closed her laptop that evening, her body hummed with a low, nervous ache. The red circle around Friday 21st burned in her mind like an alarm that wouldn't stop ringing. She packed her bag slowly, dragging herself through the motions, reminding herself: *Trevor's coming tonight. Miranda too. Just get home. Breathe. Cook.*

***

Ella's kitchen was warm with the smell of garlic and roasted vegetables, candles glowing in the centre of the table. She'd kept it simple: pasta and bread, bowls of salad; comfort food. When the knock came, Miranda was first through the door, pressing a bottle of wine into Ella's hand. Trevor followed, shoulders hunched and eyes ringed like he hadn't slept in weeks.

They ate at first in easy rhythm, Miranda sharing about a woman who had fallen asleep mid-yoga, her voice tender as she spoke of the sheer exhaustion people carried. Ella poured wine, Trevor listened with half a smile. He nodded at the right moments, but his eyes were far away, and his shoulders never really dropped.

When the plates were mostly cleared, Trevor pushed his aside. The fork clattered against the dish, sharp and abrupt.

"I can't..." His voice cracked; he rubbed his face, tried again. "I can't keep doing this."

Miranda stilled, glass in hand. Ella felt a weight settling across her ribs.

"Every day," Trevor said, eyes on the table, "I lie. To myself. To the kids. To her. I can't say how I feel. I can't ask if she's okay. It's like... pretending is the rule. And I'm dying inside."

His hands trembled slightly against the wood. "I want to nurture her, to take care of her; but that's not allowed. I'm supposed to ignore it; smile, carry on, make sure the kids see nothing wrong. And what does that teach them? That honesty is dangerous? That pain must be hidden?"

He leaned forward, head low, voice tight. "And I'm tense all the time; worried I'll say the wrong thing; filtering myself. I can't even laugh or joke the way I used to, live in the moment. I'm trapped inside my head, not here." He pressed his fist to his chest.

Ella's chest was a coil of tension and her stomach clenched. She felt the tremor of his exhaustion through her own spine, like two systems connected.

"And if I speak up," he continued, "I'll look self-absorbed. Maybe I'm the bad guy. Maybe I don't deserve... to have needs."

Miranda's hand landed on his, firm. "Trevor, enough. You do have needs and they are real. Naming them isn't selfish, it's survival. This is you staying alive in your own skin. Not disappearing. Not vanishing."

Trevor blinked, swallowed hard, shaking slightly. "I… I want honesty. I want to say: 'This is breaking me.' And hope she can hear it. That I can still be… present. Not just a housekeeper or a shadow."

He sat back, fists unclenching slightly; voice raw, ragged. "I want the kids to see it's okay to grieve, to feel, to still be strong. Not to hide behind rules that hollow you out. I want us to face it. As a family. Fully."

Ella shifted in her chair, leaning closer, heart thudding. Her hands itched to hold him steady, her chest felt like it might burst with the ache of wanting to protect and understand all at once.

Miranda's voice sharpened, slicing through the heaviness. "Then speak it, Trevor. Don't wait for permission, don't measure it. You're allowed to be here, fully. You're allowed to ask for what you need."

Trevor let out a long, shaky breath, as if letting go of something too heavy to hold. He rubbed both hands hard over his face, then rested them on the table, trembling but still.

"If I keep following her wishes," he said finally, voice low and raw, "I'll lose myself. Completely. And then… what's the point? Nothing would be real."

He sat back hard, exhaled and shook his head, stared at his knuckles whitening. "I've been trying to work it out," he whispered, "what I need. How to even say it. And I think… the only way I survive is by saying all of it. Every single piece."

Miranda's grip on his hand tightened briefly. "It's terrifying. But you've already started: you've named it. That is the only way you'll survive. That is the only way you'll be present for them and for yourself. Now, speak it; claim it. Don't flinch."

Trevor's eyes glistened. He nodded, a slow, shaky gesture of willingness, almost disbelief. Ella's heart pressed upward, a mirrored pulse of awe and fear.

The room settled into a quiet rhythm. The tick of the clock, the faint hum of the fridge, and the shallow draw of their breaths holding the rawness together.

When they finally left, Ella stood at the sink, hands braced on the counter. Plates stacked, candles guttering low. Her body hummed with the aftershock of his truth. *I can't keep doing this. I'll lose myself.* The echo of him pressed against her own looming decision: to live by hollow rules, or to risk claiming herself, fully.

The silence was unbearable.

She dried her hands quickly and pulled out her phone. Pressed Alex's name before she could talk herself out of it.

It rang once, twice.

"Ella?" His voice warm, surprised at the hour. "Everything okay?"

Her breath left in a rush. Just hearing him, the steadiness underneath, loosened something in her chest. "I... yeah. I just wanted to hear your voice."

A pause, and then softer, certain: "I'm glad you called."

She sank onto the sofa, tucking her knees under her, eyes closing like she could lean into the sound of him. "The dinner with Trevor and Miranda, it was... a lot. I can't explain it yet, just heavy."

"Poor Trevor," Alex said, his voice low with care. "Well, I'm here whenever you need."

She let the quiet stretch between them. Not empty, but full — a tether she could hold; something steadier than her own thoughts.

Her voice came out small, but steady. "I really care about you."

His exhale hummed down the line, long and sure. "I really care about you too," he murmured. "More than I've known how to say."

Ella pressed her cheek into the cushion, eyes still closed. The warmth of his voice sank through her like a blanket laid across her ribs. She didn't say it aloud, maybe couldn't, but what pulsed underneath was clear: *Please still be here when the rest of it falls away.*

49

Final inspection

Ella woke with a jolt at 3:04 a.m., heart beating fast though no dream lingered to explain it. The room was dark, the silence of the countryside thick, pressing. She rolled onto her back and stared at the faint outline of the ceiling, waiting for sleep to pull her down again. It didn't.

Instead, her mind began to move. Trevor's words drifted back, raw at her kitchen table only hours earlier: "*If I keep living like this, I lose myself.*" She had felt the burden of it then. She felt it still, lodged like a stone in her chest.

Her gaze flicked to the clock again: 3:08. In less than five hours she would be standing under the glass roof of the office lobby, badge pressed against the reader, stepping into another day she didn't believe in. Another day where she would trade herself away in increments: a missed lunch, an email answered late at night, a smile plastered on when her body wanted to scream no.

It hadn't happened all at once, of course. It was the slow creep. The small compromises that built into something larger: putting up with last minute requests because you said yes to the last one, shortening lunch breaks until they disappeared altogether, nodding through Gwen's clipped instructions even when they pressed against her ribs like iron. Piece by piece, she had let the job bend her away from herself.

But now there was something else. Another life forming in the cracks she'd once ignored. The festival – alive, messy, improbable – but real. The hours she and Alex had spent sketching maps and batting around ideas until they were laughing, exhilarated, and lit up in a way she hadn't felt in years. His steadiness, his listening, the way he looked at her as if what she said shifted the whole shape of things. With him she felt seen, not for her role or her output, but for herself.

It wasn't only him. It was the circle of friends by the sea, who had held her and mirrored her. It was the way her own hands had learned to heal, to coax release from other bodies and feel something rise in return. It was the sudden ease of sitting with her friends and not twisting herself into what they expected. The pulse of this life was colour not grayscale.

She had been letting those things hover at the edges, like dreams too delicate to name. But lying here, in the thick quiet of 3 a.m., she knew she could no longer pretend.

At the collision of safety and pleasure, she would no longer choose safety. She had done that for too long: clinging to the job, the house, the pay cheque, believing they kept her whole when, in truth, they hollowed her out.

She was ready to turn her full attention toward joy. Not as a luxury, not as something stolen in scraps around the edges, but as the centre. To stop treating it like air — fleeting, invisible — and give it the weight of water; something that could carry her, hold her when the ground felt uncertain. The bargain she had struck with herself, to endure the job so long as it paid down the mortgage, had cost her more than money; It had been draining the marrow of her days. She didn't know how the numbers would add up now, how she'd keep the roof steady over her head. But she knew this: to stay would be to hollow herself out completely, to lose the possibility of so much more. And so, she chose. Even in the unknowing, she chose.

Her fingers shook as she opened the laptop, but her chest felt steady. The resignation letter formed quickly, almost faster than she could type. Just truth. Gratitude, and then the line she had thought she would never dare to write: that she would not be there for the 21st, that she was done. Each sentence was a loosening, each word a returning.

Halfway through, a thought cut in sharp and practical: You only have six weeks of savings. That's it. The fear flared, hot and familiar, but she breathed through it and the deeper current pressed on, urging her to keep going.

When the letter was finished, she sat back and exhaled. Her eyes drifted to the calendar pinned above her desk. She pulled out her phone, opened the HR app, and scrolled through the days of leave she still had left. She began counting, lips moving silently.

One, two, three...

When she reached the end, she froze.

Taking the annual leave she was owed would carry her exactly to the Wednesday before the festival.

A shiver ran through her. It felt like a sign. A quiet affirmation from somewhere beyond her own reasoning: *you are in alignment.*

Ella closed her eyes, let the breath ease out of her, and whispered into the stillness, "Okay."

When she pressed save, she sat back, hands trembling faintly. But they didn't shake with fear. They shook with release, the way a body does when it finally drops a weight it wasn't built to carry.

The clock read 3:56. She slid back under the covers, body still humming, eyes wide open. She didn't expect sleep, she didn't need it; the decision had been made.

***

Ella sat at her desk with the letter open in her hand. Her heart drummed against her ribs, but her body felt steady. She rose, walked the quiet corridor to Gwen's office, and knocked.

"Come in," Gwen's voice called, cool and precise.

Ella stepped inside. Gwen looked up from her screen, expression unchanging, the same glassy calm she wore for everything.

"I've come to hand in my notice," Ella said, placing the letter on her desk. Her voice surprised her; clear, unwavering, carrying more authority than she expected.

Gwen's eyes flicked to the paper, then back to Ella. No shock, no pause. "I see." She skimmed it quickly, then said, flat as policy, "In that case, you won't be able to take your annual leave. You'll be paid it out instead."

The words landed heavy. Instinct tugged at her immediately — the familiar urge to nod, to fold, to accept the rule. It was how she had survived here: by erasing her edges and fitting herself into the machine. A flicker of panic pressed at her ribs. *What if she's right? What if I can't fight this?*

Her throat tightened. For a moment she hovered, teetering.

Then something bristled inside her. Small but sharp, rising through the fear. She straightened, lifted her chin.

"No. That's not a possibility."

Gwen's brow twitched, the faintest crack in the mask. Her gaze sharpened, cold, weighing the new steel in Ella's voice.

Ella pressed on before she could shrink back. "I'll take the leave I'm owed. You'll need to replace me on the project. I won't be here past the end of the leave I am owed."

The silence stretched. Gwen studied her, eyes scanning for weakness, for the old compliance. Ella's pulse roared, but she held her gaze. She did not flinch.

Finally, Gwen gave the smallest nod. "Very well. I'll make the arrangements." She set the letter aside as though it were nothing more than another item on her desk.

Ella walked out, hands trembling, but beneath the shaking was something else: a fierce, liberating lightness. As if she'd not only snapped a chain, but reclaimed the ground beneath her feet.

Ella found him waiting in the café, back to the window, scanning the doorway. The second he saw her, he stood, his whole face breaking open into a smile.

She hugged him before she could think, then slid into the seat opposite, her pulse still racing from the morning. "I did it," she said, breathless. Then, stronger: "I handed in my notice."

For a moment he just stared at her. Then he laughed, a bright, uncontained sound that made the people at the next table turn. He leaned across, caught her hands in his, squeezing them so tightly she could feel the beat of his pulse.

"Ella! You did it." His grin was boyish, alive, his eyes lit from within. "God, I'm so proud of you." He pressed her knuckles to his lips, then against his chest. "We should celebrate. Champagne. Fireworks. A whole bloody parade."

She laughed too, the sound spilling out before she could stop it, her joy rising to meet his. For a few moments they simply sat there in the glow of it, the café around them fading, their excitement sparking off one another.

But when the laughter softened, a hush came over them. His smile gentled. He didn't let go of her hands.

"I'm so glad you've done this," he said, voice lower now. "You don't know what it means."

Her throat caught. "It was so hard, Alex. When Gwen said I couldn't take my leave, that it would have to be paid out instead… every part of me wanted to just nod, to go quiet. I nearly folded." Her voice cracked, but she pushed on. "And if I had, if I'd given in one more time, I think I would've lost myself completely. I can't do that anymore. I want to live in flow, not behind someone else's rules. But God, it's terrifying. What if it all falls apart? What if I can't make it work?"

Alex squeezed her hands, steady. "Then it falls apart," he said softly. "And you'll still be you. That's what matters. The best bits of life are messy, Ella. That's where it's real, not in the neat little boxes you've been cramming yourself into."

Her breath trembled out of her, a tear sliding free. She let it. "It means everything to me that I stood my ground today. That I didn't betray myself. I chose what I actually want, not what keeps me safe."

He leaned closer, his gaze warm, unwavering. "And look where it brought you," he murmured. "Here. With me. With your whole self intact."

Her laugh cracked through the tears, shaky but real. "I don't even know how I'm going to make money now."

He smiled, his thumb brushing over her knuckles. "We'll figure it out. Together."

50

Decor

Ella had never felt this kind of ease with him before. The current between them had always been strong, even in the early days, but now there was no shadow of her job tugging her attention away. She wasn't split in two anymore.

They spent evenings watching films at his flat or walking the lanes near her house, their hands brushing until one of them finally closed the gap. They cooked together; simple meals that kept turning into long conversations, laughter spilling through the kitchen. Sometimes they'd abandon the recipe entirely, improvising with whatever they had, arguing mock-seriously over whether his chilli habit was a personality flaw.

They met his friends for pub quizzes, and hers for swims in the sea, daring one another to stay in for "just ten more seconds" as the cold ripped through them, exhilaration curling up their limbs. There were inside jokes now, small looks across tables, moments where one word was enough to send them both grinning. And when they talked about the festival, Ella felt herself leaning forward instead of holding back.

One evening, Alex set his fork down and leaned back in his chair. "There's something I'd love your advice on."

Ella looked up, curious. "Go on."

"It's this guy," Alex said, rubbing the back of his neck. "Local businessman. At first, he offered to help with the festival; gave a bit of sponsorship, which was great. But now... every time we meet as organisers, he takes over. Talks about things that don't matter or, worse, things that go against what I want this festival to be. It feels like he only cares about what's in it for him. Not the ethos, or the community."

Ella's brow furrowed. "So, what are you thinking?"

"I think I need to meet him one-to-one," Alex said slowly. "Lay it out; the values, the aims, what's not up for compromise. And if he can't accept that – if he wants to keep steering it his way ± then I'll have to shut down those conversations. And he'll be free to walk away."

Ella reached across the table, touched his hand. "That sounds clear. Strong. It's your vision, the integrity of it matters. If he's not on board with that, better to know now than have it unravel later."

Alex gave a small smile, relief flickering across his face. "Yeah. You're right. I needed to hear it out loud."

Another night, as they sat outside in the late spring air, Alex turned to her. "You feel different," he said quietly, tucking a strand of hair behind her ear.

"How do you mean?"

"Like you're fully here. Before, I always felt you were half in and half out. Even with me." He kissed her hand. "But now, you're all the way here. And it's incredible."

The words landed inside her with a warmth that spread right through her chest. She felt it too: present. Breathing with all of her being for the first time.

Later, as they sat hoping for hedgehogs, Alex checked his emails. "Guess what?" Alex's grin was unstoppable. "The Sunset Riders said yes. They'll headline the second stage!"

Before she could respond, he was already spinning around the garden, arms flung wide, laughter bubbling from him. He kicked off a little improvised dance, light on his feet, ridiculous and contagious, and Ella couldn't help but laugh, letting the joy of the moment lift her fully.

One weekend, five weeks before the festival, Ella woke to the weight of Alex's arm draped over her, his breath warm against her shoulder. The blind let in pale light, soft stripes across the sheets. She lay still for a moment, listening to the quiet, then turned to face him.

"Hello," he mumbled, voice gravelly with sleep.

She smiled, brushing her fingers through his hair. "Hello."

There was no hurry in him, none of the weekday rushing she lived with. Just the steady calm of someone entirely at ease in his own body. They stayed like that for a while, trading warmth, until he eventually swung out of bed to put the kettle on. He returned with two chipped mugs, and slid back under the duvet.

Tea steamed between them. She tucked her toes against his leg, and they sipped in silence that didn't need filling.

When his mug was empty, he set it down with a grin. "Festival's finally under control. I think. Which means..." He paused for dramatic effect. "We've got the whole day. I want to show you something."

She arched an eyebrow. "Something good?"

"Something I think you'll love. We'll cycle there. I've got an old bike in the shed – bit dodgy, but it'll do."

Out in the courtyard, she watched as he crouched over the bike, sleeves shoved up, pumping air into the tyres. He tested the brakes, gave the handlebars a firm tug, then lowered the seat as far as it would go.

She climbed on, wobbling, and found her feet just brushing the ground. "Still too high."

He grinned. "You'll manage. Just don't stop pedalling."

She swatted at him but laughed anyway, the sound carrying as she pushed off down the path.

The old railway line stretched wide, trees arching above, leaves budding on branches scribbling across the sky. The rhythm of pedalling steadied her. Alex rode easily beside her, pointing out a robin on a fence post, the faint haze of buds opening on hedges.

After twenty minutes, he waved her into a café tucked beside the path. The bell on the door jingled, and the smell of fresh bread and coffee washed over them. The woman behind the counter had paint smudged across her overalls and a bright scarf looped three times around her neck.

"Out for the first ride of spring sunshine?" she asked, eyes dancing between them.

"Something like that," Alex said, glancing at Ella with a smile.

The woman poured their coffees and leaned closer. "You look like a couple ready for adventure."

Ella flushed, laughing it off, but her chest felt warm all the same.

They sat outside, fingers wrapped around hot mugs, watching a dog tug its owner down the path. Alex told a story about his first festival job — carrying crates of beer for an entire afternoon before realising he wasn't even working for the right stall. She laughed so hard her stomach hurt, wiping tears from her eyes.

Back on their bikes, they rode another ten minutes until the city thickened around them. Alex chained the bikes to a railing, then led her through a narrow passage between two buildings.

The space opened suddenly into a hidden park. Ella stopped dead.

Murals climbed the walls: swirls of colour, lines of poetry, sketches of wings and flowers. Quotes looped in bright painted plaques: *Trust the leap. Beauty lives in the cracks. Nothing real can be broken.* Trees and shrubs softened the brick edges, and benches curved into sheltered corners. It was a pocket of stillness in the heart of the city.

"Alex..." She breathed. "It's... incredible."

His grin was small but proud. "Thought you might like it."

They wandered slowly, pausing at the walls, tracing words with their fingers, smiling at a spray-painted sketch of a fox peering out from under ivy. She crouched to look at crocuses pushing up through the grass, pale purple petals catching the light.

They found a quiet spot beneath a tree, where he unfurled a paper-wrapped parcel of sandwiches, a wedge of cheese, and a bottle of wine.

"You're brilliant," she said, laughing.

They ate in companionable silence, sipping wine from plastic cups. The air was soft, and for once she felt no weight pressing her forward, no nagging thought of what she should be doing instead.

Her phone buzzed against her leg. She pulled it out, thumb hovering when she saw Trevor's name.

"Had the talk. Went as well as could be expected. She's away to think about it. I'm relieved, but also wrung out. Thank you for listening the other night. It helped me get there."

Ella read it twice, her chest big with tenderness. She typed back quickly, *"I'm proud of you. Rest if you can. Thinking of you."* Then slipped the phone away.

Alex noticed her softened expression but didn't pry. He just reached over, brushing her hand with his, anchoring her back to the moment.

She exhaled slowly. "Work's been so strange this week. They've taken me off the big project, so I just... sit there. Pretend to be busy. But honestly?" She smiled faintly. "It's been the most peaceful week I've had in that office. Like I don't belong to it anymore."

He nodded. "Your body's already left. Paperwork just has to catch up."

She laughed, and the truth of it settled low and warm in her belly. At first she had felt guilty for having nothing to do while her colleagues stressed around her. Then, slowly, she had felt free.

They drifted into talk of what came next. "Massage," she said quickly, almost before he finished asking. "I want to do it properly. Turn the study into a treatment room, maybe. Light the fire in winter, decorate it with flowers in the summer, make it feel really homely."

His face lit up. "Yes. That. And I can help — set up a website, get some photos done. You don't need to go big, just enough to let people find you. I can see it already."

The way he said it, as though it was already real, loosened something in her. She let the idea have real weight.

She laughed again, this time with a mixture of nerves and giddy possibility. "It's crazy. But it feels... possible."

"It *is* possible. More than possible," Alex said, gripping her hand, steady and sure. "This is the life you chose by handing in your notice. No more folding down."

They clinked their cups together. Around them the park hummed with quiet life, spring in full rise, and Ella thought: *this is what beginning again feels like.*

51

Keys

Saturday morning sunlight streamed through the back windows, catching the edges of the flyers Ella had left on the kitchen table. She had been fussing since breakfast — straightening cushions, adjusting the flowers in the vase, pacing between the kettle and the hallway. She hadn't wanted him to see it until it was ready. And now it was.

The past few weeks had been intense; Alex buried in festival planning, juggling permits, schedules, and endless calls, leaving little time for them beyond snatched coffees, brief walks, and stolen moments over text. Yet somehow, those moments had felt more real, more anchored than months of uninterrupted hours. Despite the lack of idle chatter or long evenings together, their connection had deepened, threaded with a new trust and understanding.

Ella had taken the time to pour herself into her own projects; transforming the study into a serene space, creating a logo, perfecting systems to manage client appointments.

The knock came, steady and familiar. She opened the door to Alex, his hair ruffled from the wind, smile easy.

"Hi," he said, leaning down to kiss her.

She hesitated, then tugged gently at his sleeve. "Before we go... there's something I want to show you."

He raised a brow, curious, but followed her down the hall. She paused at the closed door at the end, heart skipping, then pushed it open.

Light streamed through the window, soft and generous, falling across the massage table draped in fresh linen. The pale driftwood walls seemed to glow in it, grounding the space in quiet warmth. A rug she had agonised over softened the floor, its muted pattern pulling the room together. Towels sat neatly rolled in a wicker basket, oils lined up in glass bottles that caught the light. From the ceiling, trailing plants spilled gently from macramé hangers, their green a living softness against the white. Candles stood ready on layered shelves and, on the windowsill, a vase of wildflowers brought a burst of colour, as if the meadow had been invited in. The air itself seemed to breathe calm — lavender lingering, subtle and steady.

Alex stepped in slowly, as though crossing a threshold. His gaze moved over the room — the careful details, the sense of calm woven into the corners — before settling on her.

“Ella…” His voice was quiet. “It’s perfect.”

She swallowed hard. “I wanted it to feel like… stepping out of the world. Just for a while.”

“It does.” He brushed his hand along the edge of the table, then noticed the flyers on the desk. He picked one up, turning it over. “These have come out so well. You’ve really done it.”

She gave a nervous laugh. “And already two clients booked in! They emailed last night. I had to squeeze them in tomorrow around work. But it’s coming together.”

He crossed the room and caught her hands in his. His palms were warm, steady. “You should be proud. Every piece of this room is you.”

Her chest ached, full and fragile. For a moment she let herself imagine the weeks ahead; the quiet mornings, the soft voices of clients arriving, the rhythm of this space becoming part of her.

She squeezed his hands back. “Thank you. I didn’t want you to see it until it was finished.”

His smile deepened. “I’m honoured you showed me first.”

The warmth lingered between them, wrapping itself into the day.

"Come on," she said reluctantly, "or we'll be late."

The pub garden was busy when they arrived, the low sun glinting off half-drunk pints and children weaving between tables. Miranda and Trevor were already there, waving them over.

Trevor looked lighter than he had in weeks, though his eyes still carried shadows. Sara was approaching things more openly now, he explained once they were settled with drinks; they had told the kids together this week. Some things had shifted, others were still delicate, and they were working out a way forward. The weight was still heavy, but shared now, not hidden.

"There were many tears," Trevor admitted, his voice rough but steady. "But I feel like I can breathe again. Like I can actually support her rather than standing by. It's... different now. The trust will take time to rebuild." He shook his head slowly, looking down at his hands. "Hopefully we can both keep listening, paying attention, following what feels right. Step by step."

Ella reached across, squeezed his hand. He squeezed back.

The four of them laughed over lunch, voices lifting easily. Miranda teased Trevor about his terrible taste in wine, Alex cracked a story about gently trying to convince the manager of the children's area at his festival that five-minute gaps between activities would be too intense, and they laughed imagining stressed children rushing from one activity to another. Ella found herself watching them all with a strange, grateful fullness.

Alex's phone buzzed on the table. He silenced it. The second time it rang, he glanced at the screen, apologetic.

"Sorry, I've going to have to go once I've finished this drink," he said. "A few last teething issues before next weekend. Security wristbands, stall placements..." He shook his head with a grin. "It never ends."

Trevor leaned back in his chair, smiling at him with open admiration. "Honestly, Alex, it's incredible what you are pulling off. I can't wait to see it all."

"Me neither," Miranda added. "It's exactly what people need right now."

Trevor paused, then chuckled. "Actually, on a more practical note... I need a sleeping bag. Anyone got one spare? The kids have pinched all ours for their den in the loft." Ella laughed, promising to dig one out.

When Alex slipped away — hugging them all quickly — Ella watched him go with a mix of pride and a faint ache at the constant tug of the festival. His energy left a kind of brightness behind though, like he'd carried his spark into the garden.

Trevor tipped his glass toward Ella, half a smile tugging at his tired face.

"He's a good one," he said simply. "Really good. You can see how much he cares about you — it's written all over him. I'm bloody delighted you found each other."

The sudden rising of warmth caught her off guard. She ducked her head, brushing a fingertip around the rim of her glass, but her chest swelled at the gentleness in Trevor's voice.

Miranda, eyes twinkling, reached into her bag and pulled out her diary, thumbing to the back pages.

"Ooh," she said, grinning, "I've been meaning to tell you, I've set the dates for the next three retreats. And you," she jabbed her pen lightly in Ella's direction, "are officially on the flyer this time. Co-host."

Ella's heart lifted, a different kind of thrill rushing through her as she imagined her name on the flyer. "Three?"

"Three," Miranda confirmed, scribbling them down on a napkin and sliding it across the table. "Mid-summer, September and one in November. All booked, all waiting. You'll lead meditations, provide massages. We can see if we want any guest facilitators for variety. Each one five days, we go way deeper, more space for the women to expand. I can't do it without you."

Ella traced the dates with her eyes, a fizz of excitement sparking beneath her skin. For a moment, she felt the tug of both worlds again: the one she was stepping out of, all deadlines and glass offices, and this new one forming around her: retreats, the therapy room, Alex. Life was building in ways she hadn't dared to hope for.

52

Home

Morning seeped into the van in a wash of pale light as the alarm woke them. She shifted against the mattress, surrounded by the warmth of sleep and Alex. He stirred beside her, hair tousled, eyes still soft with dreaming, and when he smiled, something deep in her chest answered quietly back.

For the past two days they'd worked alongside the others, watching the field transform from an empty sweep of grass into something breathing. Cables trailed like roots, stalls stood half-formed, and the hum of generators blended with bursts of laughter and the metallic clatter of tools. There was a rhythm to it now; a kind of shared heartbeat gathering strength.

The best part had been the mornings: sliding open the van door and stepping straight onto cool grass, the earth solid beneath her feet. She'd padded around barefoot most of the time, hair unbrushed, face free of make-up, coffee in hand. Everyone on site seemed to move in the same gentle rhythm, calling greetings, sharing tools, swapping food. There was a quiet power in it; building something together from nothing, watching shape and colour emerge across the fields.

She'd spent hours lifting, tying, painting, carrying – her body aching in that good, honest way that made her feel alive. And each evening, she and Alex would wander the site as the light turned gold, pointing out new additions: a freshly strung banner, a finished archway, fairy lights winding up a stall.

Now, it was Friday; by afternoon, people would start arriving, spilling out of cars with armfuls of tents and excitement.

Within five minutes, Alex dressed, kissed her forehead goodbye and was out into the cool dawn air, walking the layout, checking deliveries, coordinating schedules. Ella lay, eyes closed for a while, listening to the slowly waking festival grounds, the promise of the weekend stretching out around her.

Two hours later, showered and wandering through the grounds, she smiled at the final pieces being set into place. By ten she had her stall set; massage table draped in crisp linen, bottles of oil gleaming in neat rows, a vase of wildflowers at the edge, and a hand-painted sign fluttered gently in the breeze that read: 'Rest. Restore. Release.'

Everything felt improbably smooth. She looked around the grounds – bunting strung between poles, food vans ready, the main stage looming at the far end, and speakers being tested in bursts of static. Best of all, the weather was glorious; the sun shone brightly and the forecast promised clear skies all weekend.

Miranda arrived just before midday, striding across the field with mats rolled under one arm, eyes bright. "Healing tent looks beautiful" she said, pressing a quick kiss to Ella's cheek. "I'm on at four. You ready?"

Ella nodded, heart swelling. Ready didn't even cover it.

By two, the gates were open and people streamed in. The buzz rose instantly: tents staked, sleeping bags unfurled, children tumbling through grass. Alex was everywhere, striding from sound booth to entrance to stalls, clipboard under his arm, stopping by to kiss her hair as he passed. Each time he did her whole body lit, as if she'd been plugged into his joy.

By late afternoon Una and Martin arrived with their kids, Trevor's family following soon after, and Leanne and Anish trailing behind with armfuls of camping gear. They set their tents in a circle, chairs in the middle like a makeshift hearth. Laughter already spilled from it as if they'd been camped for days.

She gave a couple of massages before dusk — the kind that left the recipients soft-eyed and grateful, then packed down for the night and joined the others. They danced at the main stage as twilight bled in, the bass thudding through their bones. Later they spilled into the silent disco, headsets glowing, arms raised under the stars.

Ella couldn't remember when she'd last felt her heart so loose, so free.

Saturday dawned with Alex awake before the alarm, joy written across him so vividly it was almost childlike. He kissed her quick, hair sticking up, and skipped off towards the stage crew, leaving her laughing at his back.

She breakfasted in the circle with her friends; Trevor and Sara's children still buzzing as they showed off glitter tattoos, Una passing round fresh coffee in enamel mugs. The kids were already tugging each other towards the children's area, where a cluster of wooden balance games had been set up beside a circle of small drums. Later, they'd add logs to fires under careful watch, skewering marshmallows on long sticks, the air sweet with sugar and smoke.

With a bright, easy smile, Ella opened her stall and was quickly swept into the current of the day; one person after another, each body a new story beneath her hands. Strangers exhaled and softened, shoulders unwinding, faces loosening. There was the older man who spoke about the festivals of the seventies, about how they'd always made him feel vividly alive. The young woman with wide, uncertain eyes who whispered she'd never let anyone touch her shoulders before — and how she felt lighter now. Others booked again for the next day, or tucked flyers carefully into their bags, promising to come for regular sessions. Every thank you landed somewhere deep in her chest, quiet and solid, as if each one anchored her a little more firmly in herself.

At midday, she closed up for Miranda's breathwork session, lying back in the healing tent as her friend's voice guided the room into stillness, then release. The air seemed charged when she opened her eyes, bodies unfastened, faces glowing. As they embraced afterwards,

Miranda's smile said it all.

Later, Ella wandered into the ecstatic dance, barefoot on cool ground, music thrumming until her body moved without thought. Sweat dampened her skin, but she felt uncaged, almost giddy. Afterwards, she and Miranda met outside in the late light.

"I've just had the most amazing chat with the woman who runs that," Miranda said, eyes shining. "She's been leading ecstatic dance for years. Maybe one for our retreat?"

Ella laughed, wiping her forehead with her sleeve. "Yes. Absolutely yes."

She spotted Alex crossing the field, radio in hand, and caught a stolen cuppa with him. His hand rested briefly over hers on the mug, warmth passing between them, before another call tugged him away.

In the afternoon Lynne appeared, smart shirt still catching city dust, her smile warm but bemused. "I haven't seen you in forever," she said, scanning the stall with raised brows. "So, this is you now?"

Ella grinned, unbothered. "This is me."

"And Alex? Do I get to meet him?" Lynne glanced around, curious.

At that moment Ella spotted him striding past in the distance. She called his name, waved him over. He jogged across, cheeks flushed with work.

"This is Lynne," Ella said.

She caught it then; the flicker in Lynne's face, a disturbance she might once have shrunk under. Not now. Not today. She simply slipped her hand into Alex's, lifted her chin, and smiled.

Lynne laughed, shaking her head. "I thought it would be all mud and wellies. But it's... civilised. Fun."

Ella just laughed.

That night was immense. Firelight throwing wild shadows across faces, the pulse of drums and fiddles, bodies leaning into one another, laughter rising like smoke. Ella danced until her legs ached, drank wine from a shared bottle, hugged everyone who came close. Her heart beat wild and free, no coil, no weight.

Sunday blurred in a haze of warmth and work: more massages, more stolen moments, more dancing. The evening wound gentler, people drifting sooner to bed and the fire burning lower.

By Monday morning the field was already a scatter of folded tents and cars edging out. There was a brief snarl at the gates — a tide of vehicles stuck — which Alex ran to steady, directing with raised arms, steady, calm, and impressive. Within minutes the flow eased.

When it was done, he came back, collapsed beside her on the grass. The two of them lay flat, sky stretching blue above, her hand finding his.

They were bone-tired, bodies sore, but freer than she had ever known.

Later, at the pub, she stood, glass in hand, as the small group of organisers gathered around one long table. A few of Alex's friends had come too, their cheers adding warmth and noise to the celebration. Alex flushed pink beside her, eyes lowered as if embarrassed by the attention.

"To Alex. He pulled off something extraordinary," Ella said, her voice clear, steady. "And I couldn't be prouder. This is only the start; I can't wait for next year."

The room roared with applause, glasses clinked, and Alex lifted his head, eyes shining. Smiling shyly, he raised his glass, voice steady but brimming with gratitude. "I couldn't have done this without all of you. Every hand, every smile, every moment — it's made this the success that it was. Thank you. And thank you, Ella, for being the heart of it with me."

A local councillor came over to shake his hand warmly, praising the energy and care that had gone into every detail. Volunteers and participants murmured congratulations, sharing little stories of moments they'd loved over the weekend: the children dancing in the sun, the conga that wove between dancers picking people up along the way, the quiet magic of a shared sound bath.

Ella sat, sliding her hand into his under the table, watching him. He spoke, animated and passionate, about the work behind the festival – the long hours, the challenges, the joy – and she felt admiration bloom all over again for the man who had built this from nothing but vision and care.

This, she thought. This is the life she had chosen.

Acknowledgements

This book exists thanks to the many people who believed in it before it was real — especially those who contributed towards the funding of it. Your trust and generosity built the bridge that carried these pages into the world.

To all the teachers, healers, friends, and fellow travellers who have, in countless ways, helped me find my way back to myself — thank you. Your presence, wisdom, and courage live quietly between every line.

And to Jamie and Sofia — my greatest teachers in love, patience, and truth. You remind me every day what it means to keep becoming.

About the Author

Kate Mayor is a writer with a background in therapeutic work. This is her first novel — a story born from the long work of coming home to herself. She is now exploring what it means to live fully aligned, on and off the page.

Hey unbound one!

I hope you enjoyed this magical book brought to you by The Unbound Press.

At The Unbound Press we believe that when women write freely from the fullest expression of who they are, it can't help but activate a feeling of deep connection and transformation in others. When we come together, we become more and we're changing the world, one book at a time!

This book has been carefully crafted by both the author and publisher with the intention of inspiring you to move ever more deeply into who you truly are.

We hope that this book helps you to connect with your Unbound Self and that you feel called to pass it on to others who want to live a more fully expressed life.

With much love,

Nicola Humber

Founder of The Unbound Press
www.theunboundpress.com

Printed in Dunstable, United Kingdom

79662347R00218